L'ARMÉE FRANÇAISE

L'ARMÉE FRANÇAISE

An Illustrated History of the French Army
1790 – 1885

by
EDOUARD DETAILLE

Text by
JULES RICHARD

Translation by
MAUREEN CARLSON REINERTSEN

Translated from the 1885 – 1889 edition of L'Armée Française by Boussod, Valadon and Company at Asnières-sur-Seine.

WAXTEL & HASENAUER

NEW YORK

This edition published in 1992 by
WAXTEL & HASENAUER
with the Quantum Printing Company
437 West 16th Street, 4th fl.
New York, NY 10011

L'Armée Française—An Illustrated History of the French Army, 1790 – 1885 was previously published under the title *L'Armée Française—Types et Uniformes*, by Boussod, Valadon and Company at Asniéres-sur-Seine, 1885 – 1889. The original drawings were composed and executed from 1883 – 1888.

The text of this English version of *L'Armée Française* is based on a translation by Maureen Carlson Reinertsen. A glossary of foreign retentions and military ranks has been included.

Library of Congress Cataloging-in-Publication Data

Detaille, Édouard.
    L'Armée Française—An Illustrated History of the French Army,
    1790 – 1885
    Translation of L'Armée Française—Types et Uniformes.
    1. France, Army—History—19th Century. 2. Uniforms, Military—
History. I. Detaille, Richard, joint author. II. Title
355.35
Library of Congress Catalogue Card Number 92-60331
ISBN 0-9632558-0-0

10   9   8   7   6   5   4   3   2   1

This book was printed and bound in the United States of America

VOLUME I

GENERALS - GENERAL STAFF - SCHOOLS

TEXT

Summary: State of the army in 1789 - List of Generals in 1790 - École de Mars - General Staffs under the Republic and the Empire - General staff of the army of Sambre-et-Meuse - General staff of the Grand Armée at the Battle of Austerlitz - Military schools - Polytechnic schools of Fontainebleau, Saint-Cyr and Saint-Germain - General staff under the Restoration, Louis-Philippe, and the Republic of 1848 - General staff of the expeditionary force to Rome - General staffs under the Second Empire - List of the Marshals of France - General staffs of the Army of the East, the expeditionary forces to the Baltic, China and Mexico - the Army of Italy - the School of War (l'École de guerre) and commissioned officers ....Pages 3 to 22

ILLUSTRATIONS

HISTORY OF THE INFANTRY

TEXT

Summary: INFANTRY OF THE LINE - Before the Revolution - 1789 - National Guard and old troops - Army of the Eastern Pyrenees - Armies of the Republic - First demi-brigades - New demi-brigades - The Army of Italy - Consulate and Empire - The regiments -Foreign corps - Regiments of the line and of light infantry created under the Empire - Campaign of 1805 - Régiments de marche and provisional regiments - The Grande Armée of 1812 - reorganization of the infantry in 1813 - French and foreigners - Campaign of 1814 - First Restoration - Remaking the regiments - The One Hundred Days - Infantry of the Army of the North - Second Restoration - Departmental legions -Their composition - Reestablishment of the regiments - Composition of the Army of Spain - Successive modifications to the infantry - Composition of the expeditionary army to Algiers - The July Government - Disbanding the Royal Guard and the Swiss Corps - Modification of the regiments - Composition of the Army of the North in 1832 - Conquest and occupation of Algeria - Transformation of the uniform - Republic of 1848 - The Army of the Alps (1848) - Composition of the expeditionary corps to the Mediterranean (June 1849) - Second Empire - Crimean War (1854) - Infantry regiments which took part in the Crimean War - Campaign of Italy (1859) - Composition of the Army of Italy - Brigading of the infantry - Campaigns of Syria (1860), of China (1858-1861), of Cochin-China (1858-1863), of Mexico (1861-1867) -Occupation corps of the Pontifical States (1849-1870) - The Chassepot rifle - Composition of the Army of the Rhine (1870) - Régiments de marche - Government of the national defense - General statistics of forces ready to serve in 1870-1871 - Organizations of the Paris - Organization of the provinces - The garde mobile - Members of the national militia - The volunteer corps - The Commune of Paris (1871) - Formation of twenty provisional regiments - New organization of the infantry - Table giving dates of formation and the origins of the 144 infantry regiments - Modifications in dress - Tunisia - Tonkin ....Pages 23 to 74

CHASSEURS A PIED - Origins - Tirailleurs of Africa - The ten battalions of 1840 - Sidi-Brahim - Chasseurs à pied in Africa and at Rome - The twenty battalions of 1853 - Chasseurs à pied in Italy, at Bomarsund, in the Crimea, in Italy, in Syria, in China, in Mexico - The thirty-three batallions de marche of 1870-1871. Final organization at thirty battalions - L'esprit de corps ...... Pages 75 to 84

ILLUSTRATIONS

HISTORY OF THE CAVALRY

TEXT

Summary: State of the cavalry in 1789 - Distribution of 1791 - The cavalry from 1791 to 1803, creation of the regiments, transformations, mergers - Foreign regiments - Cavalry in the armies in 1793 - Modification of the light cavalry - Armies of Sambre-et-Meuse, of Italy, of Egypt - The Consulate - Marengo - The 14,000 cavaliers of the Army of the Rhine - Organization of 1803 - Uniforms - New regiments created under the Empire - Provisional regiments as numerous as permanent regiments - Deprivation of the cavalry - Colonels of the light cavalry - Cavalry in the armies: 1805, 1812, and 1813 - Creation of the Lancers - Dragoons under the Empire - Their colonels - Lancers under the Empire - First Restoration - Reorganization of the cavalry - The One Hundred Days - Efforts of the Emperor to renew a cavalry - Regiments during the campaign of Belgium (1815) - Second Restoration - Remaking of the Cavalry - New regimental formation; new uniforms - Regiments of the Army of Spain (1823) - New reformation of the cavalry - Difficulties in maintaining the cavalry in a suitable manner - Expedition of Morocco - Taking of Algiers - Accession of Louis-Philippe - Reorganization of the Lancers - New regimental formation - Regiments of the Army of the North (1832) - Influence of memories and of men from the Empire - Changes in uniforms - Advances in firearms modify cavalry tactics - Light cavalry regiments in Algeria - Creation of new regiments in 1840 - The Republic of 1848 - Cavalry of the Army of the Alps - Second Empire - The Imperial Guard - Secondary role of the cavalry in the campaigns of the Second Empire - Regiments which took part in these campaigns - Campaign of 1870-1871 - Regiments used by the Army of the Rhine - Régiments de marche - Their redistribution to the armies of the provinces - Their merger with old regiments - Cavalry during the civil war - Origins and dates of formation of the 70 regiments forming the cavalry in 1873 - New Uniforms - Conclusion ..... Pages 85 to 170

ILLUSTRATIONS

COLOR ILLUSTRATIONS

VOLUME II

HISTORY OF THE TROOPS OF THE ARMY OF AFRICA

TEXT

Summary: The special Army of Africa - The Zouaves - Origin of this corps - The Zoudaouas - First Formation - The second siege of Constantine (1837) - The first flag (1841) - The Zouaves formed into regiments (1842) - List of field officers of the old regiment - The Zouaves formed into three regiments (1852) - List of the colonels of the three first Zouave regiments - The Zouaves in the Crimea (1854) - Customs of the Zouaves - The Theater of the Zouaves - Program of performances - The Zouaves in Italy (1859) - The eagle of the 1st Regiment decorated with the cross of the Legion Honor - The eagle of the 3rd Regiment decorated with the gold Medal of Merit of Sardinia - King Victor-Emmanuel and the Zouaves - The Zouaves in Mexico - The eagle of the 3rd Regiment decorated with the cross of the Legion of Honor - The Zouaves during the campaign of 1870 - The 4th Regiment - The Régiments de Marche - The Zouaves of the Imperial Guard. The Algerian Tirailleurs. The Koulouglis of 1836 - First formation (1841) - The Turcos in the Crimea - The three battalions become three regiments (1856) - The Turcos in Italy - The Turcos in Senegal (1860-1861) - The Turcos during the campaign of 1870 - Formation of a 4th Regiment - List of field officers of the Tirailleur regiments - The eagle of the 3rd Regiment decorated with the cross of the Legion of Honor (1863). The Interpreters. First organization (1830) - Interpreter gendarmes (1831) - Creation of the permanent corps (1845). The Foreign Legion. First formation (March 21, 1831) - The Foreign Legion given to Spain (1835) - New formation (1837) - Constantine - Zaatcha - Crimea - The second Foreign Legion - General mustering out (May 21, 1856) - Formation of two foreign regiments (1856) - The 2nd Regiment in Italy (1859) - New organizations (October 14, 1859; December 14, 1861) - The foreign regiment in Mexico (1863) - Camaron - The foreign regiment during the campaign of France and in the Army of Versailles - Actual status - Tuyen-Quan (1886). The Light Infantry of Africa. Creation of two battalions (June 13, 1832) - The Zephyrs - The siege of Constantine - Mazagran - The 3rd Battalion (1833) - The volunteers of la Charte - The companies of discipline. The Chasseurs d'Afrique. The expedition of Algiers - Chasseurs, carabiniers and chasseurs lanciers of Africa - Algerian chasseurs - Chasseurs d'Afrique (1831) - List of colonels of the four regiments - The unusual combat of Captain Morris and of the chief of the Merdes tribe (1833) - The Chasseurs d'Afrique in the Crimea, Italy, Mexico. - The charge of Sedan - The death of General Margueritte - The Chasseurs d'Afrique at Tonkin. The Spahis. Spahi regulars (1834) - The uniform (1841) - Regimental organization (1845) - The colonels of the Spahi regiments - The Algerian Scouts (1870)- The 4th Regiment .... Pages 189 to 232

ILLUSTRATIONS

HISTORY OF THE ARTILLERY

TEXT

Summary. State of the artillery in 1789 - Progress which stamps the artillery with the war system of the Revolution - Mounted batteries - The artillery in the armies of the Republic - Organization of the artillery train - The artillery under the Empire - The Imperial Guard - Effectives and cadres - The artillery generals and colonels of the Empire - Reorganization of 1814 - The One Hundred Days - The Emperor's organization of the territorial defense - State of the companies, officers and effectives of the artillery in the Army of the North (June 1815) - Returning the artillery to the status of 1814 - The artillery of the Army of Spain - The artillery of the Army of Morocco - Reorganization of 1829: new materiel; merger of the artillery and the train companies; creation of the battery - Tactical unity - Campaign of Belgium and siege of Anvers - Successive organizations of new regiments - Expedition of Rome - Reorganization of February 17, 1854 - Transformation of the materiel - Situation of the artillery in the Army of the East on September 8, 1855 - Campaign of Italy - Composition of the artillery in the Army of Italy - Disposition of the artillery in the Army of the Rhine - Considerable efforts of the artillery administration in Paris and in the provinces to create new batteries - State of the artillery in the various corps of the armies of Paris, the Loire, the North and the East - Reorganization after the war to 38 regiments of pontoniers - Note on the history of the pontoniers - The artillery at Tonkin . . . . Pages 233 to 258

ILLUSTRATIONS

HISTORY OF THE ENGINEERS

TEXT

Summary. History of the Engineer troops before 1814 - The six companies of miners existing at the time of the Revolution, turned into the artillery - Organization of Carnot; creation of twelve battalions of sappers - Committee of fortifications - Aeronauts - The Engineers in the armies under the Republic and under the Empire - Mustering out of 1814, organization of three regiments - The Engineers in the Army of the North (1815) - Permanent organization of the service under the Restoration Administrations, Schools - Spanish campaign and Greek campaign - Algerian expedition - General staffs and troops attached to the expedition - Campaign of Anvers - General staffs and troops attached to the Army of the North - The Engineers service in Algeria; its role in the colony - The siege of Rome: General of Division Vaillant - The siege of Sebastopol - Height of glory of the Engineer Corps - Report on the troops and on the general staff of the service at the beginning and the end of the siege; Generals Niel, Bizot, Frossard; Lieutenant Colonel Guerin - The assault - Influence of the service on the future of the French army - Campaign of Italy - Campaign of Mexico, siege of Puebla - The Engineers in the colonies - Campaign of 1870-1871 - The Engineers in the Army of the Rhine; general staffs and troops - The Engineers, absorbed by the armies, insufficient in some areas - The siege of Paris - General Chabaud-Latour and General Tripier - The Engineers in the provincial armies - The Engineers in the Army of the North - Reorganization of the service into four regiments of five battalions. The Engineers at Tonkin ....Pages 259 to 280

ILLUSTRATIONS

HISTORY OF THE GENDARMERIE

TEXT

Summary. Gendarmerie. Abolition of the constabulary and the mounted police; creation of the national gendarmerie - The twenty-eight divisions of 1791-1804; creation of the permanent general inspection of the gendarmerie - The legions are successively expanded to the figure of thirty-four following the conquests - Influence of the gendarmerie - The elite legion of gendarmerie; its history; its service and its function in campaigns - The gendarmerie of Spain (1809); its formation, its exploits - The Restoration - Reform of the gendarmerie; twenty-four legions - Revolution of 1830; major modifications in the personnel of the gendarmerie - Creation of provisional corps in the West - Creation of the 25th Legion - The regiment of gendarmerie of the Imperial Guard; it is formed with the gendarmerie mobile - Crimean expedition - Interior services - Mustering out - The gendarmerie under the Empire - Campaign of 1870 - The provisional regiments - The mobilization of the gendarmerie - Various reorganizations since peace. Troops of Paris. The police in Paris - The Guard of Paris before July 14, 1789 - The paid National Guard, the gendarmerie, the legion of police - The Guard of Paris - Its campaigns - Malet Conspiracy - Mustering out - Imperial gendarmerie - Royal gendarmerie - The Revolution of 1830 - Formation of the Municipal Guard - Its role under the July Monarchy - The riots - February Revolution 1848 - Order through disorder - The rioters act as the police - The Montagnards - Foot garde mobile - Mounted garde mobile - Reaction - Organization of the Republican Guard - Guard of Paris, its music - 1870 - Two legions in Paris - Reform of 1886 - The firemen - Their history - Transformation of the corps .... Pages 281 to 306

ILLUSTRATIONS

HISTORY OF THE ADMINISTRATION

TEXT

Summary. The military administration under the Ancien Régime - The law of September 20, 1791 - The Terror - The Committee of Public Safety - The requisition - Organization of the Year III (1792) - Bonaparte and the Ordonnateurs - Civilian courage - The expedition of Egypt - Bonaparte the administrator - How the army was administered and how accounts were settled under the Empire - Dress - Provisions - Hospitals - Administrative troops before 1815 - Elimination of the Review Inspection and the War Commissariat - Creation of the administrative affairs service of intendance (1817) - Organization of 1822 - The Spanish War - Administrative inability of the Duke of Bellune - The Duke of Angoulême and Ouvrard - The role of chief intendant of an army - Expedition of Algiers - Admirable preparation - Fresh bread twenty-four hours after landing - The costs of the expedition paid by the conquest - The chief intendant Denniée and his assistants - The campaign of Anvers - Unusual proceedings - Algeria - The Crimean campaign - Mortality during the campaign - French rule starves the soldier - Typhus is the disease of hunger - Administrative personnel in the Crimea - Administrative personnel in the Army of Italy - The French navy in its relations with the military administration - Administrative sections and troops - The campaign of 1870 - Budgetary and political preparation flaws - Administrative personnel of the armies of the Rhine, Paris, and the provinces - In Paris, Subintendant Poirrier saves the army and the populace - The role of the Parliament - The role of the demagogue - Controllers of the army administration - State of the administrative forces - What the command in the administration should be .... Pages 307 to 328

ILLUSTRATIONS

HISTORY OF THE NAVAL TROOPS

TEXT

Summary. The Naval Marines - State and recruitment of the colonial troops under the Ancien Régime - Creation of six regiments for the building service (June 14, 1792) - The naval demi-brigades - The expedition of Santo Domingo - The ravages of yellow fever - Similarity established by Napoleon between the home service and the colonial service - History of the naval artillery regiments - Their fine conduct in 1813 - The marines of the Guard - Histories of garrisons in the colonies - Legions, infantry regiments, colonial battalions - The July government creates two then three naval infantry regiments - Good administration of these troops; its good spirit - Campaigns and expeditions - Creation of the 4th Regiment, Crimean campaign - Expeditions in the Baltics - The campaign of 1859 in the Adriatic - The campaign of China, of CochinChina - The naval infantry in Mexico - Campaign of 1870-1871 - The naval infantry division at Bazeilles - The naval infantry sends four battalions to Paris and eight to the provincial armies - It distinguishes itself in all encounters - The Laurent Battalion at Vierzon - History of the increases and the subsequent improvements of the service - The Tonkin War; naval infantry losses in this campaign - History of the naval artillery regiment - Its rights and duties - List of the generals of division and the colonels of the naval infantry and the naval artillery - Native troops - The golden branch ....Pages 329 to 349

ILLUSTRATIONS

ACKNOWLEDGMENTS

        In addition to the acknowledgments given under a particular illustration the publishers would like to mention the following individuals and institutions, whose contributions toward this work have been a great help.

        Roberta Wiener for editing and advice during the preparation of this book. Historian James R. Arnold, for the foreword to this book. Barbara Collier for assistance in French translations. Fay Perotta for graphics support.

        We gratefully acknowledge the assistance given by the museums and collections. We would like to thank Mark Murray, Assistant Vice President, 19th Century European Paintings, Sotheby's, New York. Margaret Kelly, Curator of Forbes Galleries, New York. Helen Campbell, Photographic services of the Art Gallery of New South Wales, Sydney. The Musée de L'Armée, Service Photographique, Paris.

        Above all we wish to thank Maureen Carlson Reinertsen without whose superb translation effort none of what follows would have been possible.

                                                                                David Waxtel
                                                                                Richard Hasenauer

TRANSLATOR's PREFACE

This translation of the late 19th century French book, *L'Armée Française,* offers data and insights into the history of the French army from 1789 to 1885. A thoughtful and well-researched text by Jules Richard accompanies fine drawings by the French artist Édouard Detaille. This combination of writing and artwork warrants the attention of European and military history buffs alike.

Unfortunately, the intricate linguistics and the florid style of the 1889 version would daunt all but the most dedicated of readers. By employing "free translation," I have tried to preserve the spirit and tone of the original French text. Such an approach not only tames the inevitable Victorian hyperbole but also provides a more accessible work for today's reading public.

I have observed some basic rules in my translation. French words, titles, ranks, proper names and terms which are typically anglicized generally appear in their English forms. Words, phrases, and some proper names which prove difficult or impossible to render into English remain in the original French. Original errors and questionable spellings have been corrected when obvious but retained when obscure or uncertain.

French Revolutionary dates are often difficult to equate with the Julian calendar. In accordance with one accepted system, I have established Year I as 1792, and so forth. Unfortunately, this choice sometimes results in conflicts with the dates given in the original text. Richard seems to have moved freely between two accepted methods of dating for this period in French history.

Military titles and ranks often proved misleading when translated directly. Moreover, a rank or title was often subject to multiple changes, depending on the period of history. For example, "brigadier" could mean brigade commander, as in "brigadier Lannes" of Napoleon I's 1798 Egyptian campaign. It could also designate a lower rank as in "la trompette brigadier" or corporal trumpeter. Terms such as the rank of "mestre de camp" or "les ailes de hanneton" (may-fly wings) on a uniform prove more elusive. At times, I found no suitable English equivalent. Extensive footnoting to describe such terms was not possible, given the scope of this translation. However, a glossary of French to English terms is provided as an Appendix.

Since my overall aim was to translate with minimal editing, a few oddities reflecting the author's goals, viewpoints, and bias remain. One of the most striking of these is a penchant for enumerating the names of seemingly all officers involved in a given corps or a battle. Perhaps this technique anticipated modern marketing, with potential sales revenues corresponding to the number of individuals cited.

Rlchard tended to casually allude to social, polltical and military aspects of his day. He sometimes used popular plays, politicians, and lesser conflicts of the period to illustrate a more significant event or character. These references may be lost on a twentieth century audience.

The author mirrored the growing Republican egalitarianism of late 19th century France in venting his frustrations. These focused on "parliamentarianism", the press, and the military authorities of the 1880's. No doubt his words echoed the thoughts of many of his contemporaries. He also berated some of the reforms, and plans for the future of the French Army while bemoaning the antimilitarism of the general populace. Thus, he revealed his own personal biases. These tended toward royalist and imperialist deference, as evidenced in this sympathetic description of Napoleon III's attempts at military reform in the 1860's, from page 152. "The Emperor, full of good intentions, very open, very desirous of doing the right thing, was unfortunately under the influence of persons for whom a military career was only a means to a political end."

L'Armée Française presents a comprehensive and ambitious look at an influential segment of 19th century French history and society. Many parallels may be drawn between its reflections on a changing *fin de siècle* world and current global events and their effects on military power. I am pleased to be able to contribute some insights from the past through the publication of this book.

I would like to acknowledge those who helped and supported me in this effort and without whom this translation would not have been possible. Dr. Marie-Michelle Mamie spent precious hours helping untangle the grammar and idioms of the Second Empire. Madame Janine N. Gros, Madame Anna Rykart, and Dr. Christoph De Weck each contributed their time, knowledge and multi-lingual talents on the spur of the moment. And finally, my husband, Ralph Roy Reinertsen, provided indefatigable assistance with tables and lists, identification of obscure historical references and terms, and his continuous enthusiasm for and encouragement of my efforts in this endeavor.

Maureen Carlson Reinertsen
Basel, Switzerland
March 1992

FOREWORD

The years 1790 to 1885, the time period covered by *L'Armée Française*, begin with France's rise to Continental domination under Napoleon I and end with her trying to recover after an abject surrender to expansionist Prussia.

Napoleon Bonaparte forged a war machine of surpassing quality. He harnessed French revolutionary fervor to create an army that dominated Europe between the years 1796 and 1812. Employing brilliant man management—"men are led by baubles," he once said—he inspired French soldiers to amazing feats of valor. His imperial ambitions ultimately fell afoul of the nationalist spirit which the French Revolution had awakened throughout much of continental Europe. Prussia, in particular, rose from defeat to join an allied coalition that slowly drove Napoleon I back first to Paris, and then to exile.

After his fall, French politicians and military men alike tried to recreate the military machine that had performed so well during the Napoleonic era. But it was never to be the same. French soldiers fought in the Crimea, engaged in colonial wars of expansion in North Africa and Indochina, and participated in the struggle for Italian independence. Led by officers much less able than Napoleon I and his marshals, these Frenchmen triumphed, but without the overwhelming domination of their predecessors. Battlefield success masked underlying weakness. Then came the war against Prussia in 1870.

On the eve of that war Napoleon III, nephew of Napoleon I, believed the French army invincible. In battle after battle the common French soldier supported his belief by exhibiting valor worthy of those who had marched with Napoleon I. However, French leadership proved unequal to the demands of modern warfare. Pitted against Prussian professionalism exemplified by Helmuth von Moltke, the legions of Napoleon III suffered debilitating battlefield setbacks and defeat. In 1871 France accepted humiliating surrender terms that ordained Prussia the paramount European power.

This then was the milieu in which Edouard Detaille painted his pictures and Jules Richard wrote his text illustrating and describing the evolution of the French army. Richard had military experience as a member of the French National Guard in 1848. Detaille had seen combat in the war against Prussia as a member of the 8th Battalion of the Parisian Guard Mobiles. Separately they had derived certain lessons from their military experience, and jointly they thirsted for revenge against Prussia. Their motive in collaborating on a book devoted to the French Army was to sustain French military spirit during a trying period. Thus, we read French defeats described as valiant combats against overwhelming odds and thus we see military exploits rendered in a heroic style.

The reader can distill much of value from *L'Armée Française*. However, one must be alert to how the author's nationalism and prejudices—which foreshadow the ignominious Dreyfus Affair of 1894—influence his writing. Similarly, recognize that the artist seeks to inspire the youth of France to fight once more by emphasizing war's heroic dimension. Yet the author also presents hard facts about the evolution of the French military over a period of acute interest, and here also are scenes illustrated by Detaille, one of the renowned masters of military art. Detaille's evocative pictures of the Napoleonic era reflect great historic realism while capturing the spirit of the Napoleonic legend. The French government censored his Franco-Prussian War work to eliminate any defeatist scenes. Instead we see action scenes such as "The Defense of Champigny". Here is the quintessential Detaille: a realistic depiction of urgent preparation for desperate combat intended to remind the French public of what they must do the next time France confronts Prussia. Even with the passage of time, such scenes cannot fail to stir the spirit.

James R. Arnold
Bluemont, Virginia
April 20, 1992

L'ARMÉE FRANÇAISE

1ᴱᴿ VOLUME

EDOUARD DETAILLE

General staff of a general-in-chief (1796).

GENERALS – GENERAL STAFF – SCHOOLS

(1789 – 1884)

Student of the Ecole de Mars (1794).

n 1789, upon the outbreak of the Revolution, the army of the King contained 172,384 officers and soldiers and 1,183 generals, including 15 marshals. This averaged out to one general officer for every 170 men. Given these figures, it is understandable that one of the principal concerns of the first parliamentary assembly was the reorganization of the army.

The army was in good condition - we will have occasion to repeat this *ad infinitum* - well dressed and well disciplined. Yet incredible abuses took place within its ranks under the shadow of royal authority. These abuses had to be addressed every time there was a question of violating the rules, rules which were ignored even while enforcing them. From the moment the good life was abolished, other abuses were born, thrived proliferated and were not about to be eliminated. Never before had greater excesses been witnessed than during this period. Consequently, for the first time, the National Assembly set limits on the number of general officers and decided that, in the future, there would be no more than 4 generals-in-chief, 30 generals of division, and 60 generals of brigade (August 18, 1790). A few days later, the Assembly announced its appointments to these positions which received 40,000 francs, 20,000 francs and 10,000 francs, according to their respective ranks.

These figures are rather odd if one examines them together with the payroll, the general officers, and the actual troop strengths.

Our military establishment today comprises 100 generals of division and 200 generals of brigade. Above and beyond this should be included in the roster 3 marshals of France and a number of generals of division who were supported beyond retirement age because, as commanders-in-chief, they had faced the enemy. According to the payroll, a corps commander of the army receives 30,384 francs; a general of division 19,566 francs; and a general of brigade 15,948 francs. If the case arose, a special agreement would establish the payment arrangements for a commander serving as chief of the army. However, the tables scrupulously anticipate pay supplements granted to general officers on special missions. Our standing army is approximately 515,000 men in times of peace and could be expanded to 1,200,000 men in times of war simply by

mobilizing the men in our military institutions. Thus one could say that there is only one general officer for every 1,666 men in normal times. It should be noted, however, that one general officer is not sufficient for 4,000 men in times of war. It is likely that the body of officers of the general staff would be enlarged and reinforced under these circumstances.

The National Assembly attempted to limit the number of auxiliary officers attached to the command at the same time it established the number of general officers. The quotas for determining these limits were set into law on October 5, 1790 as follows: 30 adjutant generals, including 17 colonels, and 13 lieutenant colonels were to command the general staff of 30 generals of division.

List of Generals in 1790.

Commanders-in-chief —Marshals de Mailly, de Rochambeau, de Bouillé.

Generals of Division (Lieutenants-Généraux)—de Vaubecourt, de Ray, de Chamborant, de Grandpré, de Falkenhain, de Gelb, de Belmont, Lukner, Coincy, de Durfort, de Jumilhac, Fumel, Verteuil, Toustain de Viré, Crussol d'Amboise, Drunmont de Melfort, La Roque, d'Affry, Alexandre de Sparre, Esparbès, de la Morlière, Chabriant.

Generals of Brigade (Maréchaux-de-camp)—Boistel d'Elbeck, La Marck, La Noue, Sarlaboust, de Plantade, d'Heymann, de Klinglin, d'Hoffelize, de Frimont, de Franc, de Pagnat, de Wimfen, de Wittinghoff, de Choisy, de Kellermann, Toulongeon, Kellerman, de la Salle, Ferrières, Custine, Moyeux, du Muy, d'Albignac, de Montesquiou Fezensac, Cholet, Gontaut, Chilleau, d'Aumont, Dumouriez, d'Harambure, Cely, Canclaux, La Valette, Thumery, Liancourt, Casteja, Chaluss, LaFayette, d'Affry, Noue, Rostaing, Crillon the elder, d'Hallot, Marce, d'Harville, Bercheny, Bouthellier, Biron, Rossi, Behague, Sombreuil, Duportail.

This list includes only the general officers chosen by the king, to which many other names would be added later.

Guide, general staff (1800).

This was the situation of the general staff operating under the Revolution and the Empire. Many of these officers emigrated; some continued to serve the Revolution. Many of them lost their heads to the guillotine; others survived the Revolution and served the Empire. That glorious Marshal Kellermann, Duke of Valmy, and the courageous and honorable Canclaux are examples in this latter category.

Among the many generals who were forced into inactivity during the Revolution, a number rejoined the service from 1791 to 1792. However, they were still denied full participation. The others, for the most part, joined the princes at Coblentz or went to England or Russia where they were well received.

Ecole de Mars (School of War). Under the Reign of Terror, the Convention created the School of War, as much to impress the revolutionary demagogues as to attempt to inflame the nation's youth.

On the Sablons plain, 3,203 young men were hastily organized, and a very rudimentary encampment was set up along with a huge amphitheater. The only students of the School of War who would later leave any imprint on the annals of history were: General Manhès, former viceroy of the Calabres; General Berge who headed the school at Metz; Lemarrois, the future emperor's aide-de-camp; Doctor Fouquier; and the military intendant Fromentin from Saint Charles. It can only be concluded that recruitment for this school was as laughable as its uniform was theatrical and its administration badly managed.

At first the school was headed by General Berteche then by Chanez after the 27th of July.

Its existence was ephemeral. The tens, hundreds and thousands of cannoneers, piquiers, fusiliers, and cavaliers who comprised the body of the school were never sufficiently clothed nor adequately armed. They merely played a role in the public celebrations and in revolutionary demonstrations, then were mustered out on October 23, 1791 after 6 months of continual unruliness.

The school uniform was designed by David and its rules were written by Carnot, Robespierre, Lebas, and Peyssard. In the minds of its founders, it was predominantly a political institution. They had envisioned an enlisted force to support the Jacobin club, a force which was to be ready at a moment's notice and capable of swinging the balance of opinion to the Jacobin side. However, the School of War fell short of their expectations. On the 27th of July, the school rallied to the cause of the Convention and against the Mountain and the Commune. It rendered significant service only on the 31st of August when the powder works at Grenelle blew up. Its distaste for arms was notorious. Shouting with enthusiasm: "Back to our homes!" the students received permission to return to them as quickly as possible, parting ways once and for all.

Peoples' representative to the armies (1793).

General of division and adjutants of the general staff (1799).

REPUBLIC AND EMPIRE

The staff, excessively cut back in terms of commanding generals and adjutant officers as decreed in August 1790, was soon overwhelmed. Events moved rapidly with an increase in the officer corps matching the pace.

As of 1791, the 94 general officers proved inadequate. On the 4th of June, sixteen new generals were commissioned of whom twelve were *maréchaux-de-camp*. In September, twelve more were commissioned including 2 *lieutenants-généraux*. Finally, in January 1792, the staff grew to 142 through the addition of 8 new *lieutenants-généraux* and 12 *maréchaux-de-camp* for a total of 48 *lieutenants-généraux* and 94 *maréchaux-de-camp*. This proportion of one general of division for every two generals of brigade would henceforth invariably serve as the rule by which the legal and organic composition of the general staff would be established.

Moreover, between 1792 and 1797, neither laws nor proportions were observed anymore. The *lieutenants-généraux* and the *maréchaux-de-camp* had now taken names more logical and appropriate to their functions: generals of division and generals of brigade, although the Convention had reserved the right for naming them to itself. They were appointed by all the powers and sometimes even nominated themselves. Besides the sixty uncouth representatives of the people regularly sent by the Convention to the eleven armies of the Republic (some of whom showed both a certain talent and a fervent patriotism) were mixed together the *clubs*, the *gardes nationales*, and the municipalities. The Santerres, the Pache, the Rossignol, the Westermann, the Ronsin, the Hanriot, the Doppet and the Léchelle, forerunners of the famous *perceurs* of 1871 were sad examples of what an ignorant populace could produce when overwhelmed by fear. There is nothing new under the sun. This Léchelle mentioned

above was the inventor of a plan which consisted of "marching majestically and *en masse* toward the enemy." Naturally, the Saint John the Baptist of this outrageous sortie would remain in the rear, even as he sent others to the front. Fortunately these rogues were in the minority. Courageous people have always been numerous in France.

Description of the regulation general staff of a French army in 1796 can be served by listing the troops comprising the legendary and celebrated Army of Sambre-et-Meuse:

General-in-chief: JOURDAN
Chief of staff: Ernouf, General of Division
Adjutants:
Attached to the General-in-chief: Ducheyron, Daultanne, Espagne
Attached to the chief of staff: Rochefort, Coulange
Commander of artillery: Bollemont, General of Division
Second in command: Debelle, General of Brigade
Commander of engineers: Léry, Colonel
Commander of the left wing: Kleber, General of Division
Aides-de-camp: Buquet and Mutelet

ADVANCE GUARD	4th DIVISION	6th DIVISION
General of Division Lefebvre	General of Division Grenier	General of Division Championnet
Generals of Brigade Dhaulpoult, Leval, Richepanse, Soult	Generals of Brigade Dalesme, Olivier	Generals of Brigade Damas, Legrand, Klein
Adjutants: Cayla, Mortier	*Adjutants:* Saligny, Cacatte	*Adjutants:* Daclon, Barbier, Balmont
2nd DIVISION	5th DIVISION	CAVALRY RESERVE
General of Division Collaud	General of Division Bernadotte	General of Division Bonnaud
Generals of Brigade Jacopin, Lorge, Bastoul, Ney	Generals of Brigade Barbou, Simon	Generals of Brigade Oswald, Palmerol
Adjutants: Malerot, Ormancey	*Adjutants:* Sarrazin, Mireur	*Adjutant:* Radet

The 1st Division, composed of the brigades of Hardy and Daurier, was detached in front of Mayence and Cassel.
The 3rd, Poncet's, was in front of Ehrenbreitstein and the reserve infantry, commanded by General of Division Bonnard, was at Frankfurt.

As one can see, there is no great difference between the composition of the general staff of Jourdan's army and that of the First Army of the East assembled in April 1854. The considerable number of adjutant generals who were included (19) leads us to the topic of the officers of the general staff. Naturally, given this number of generals, the number of the adjutants who assisted them grew enormously. When Aubry was charged with organizing the *cadres supérieurs* under the reform of 1795, he discovered a surprising number of generals of division and of generals of brigade but an even greater number of adjutant generals and commanders. By law only 30 were authorized, yet there were 366, that is, 336 beyond the permissible number.

On the rolls there remained nothing — or almost nothing of the 1790 organization with respect to generals as well as to officers of the general staff.

In 1795, Posseld, a German historian who was a professor at Karlsruhe, published in his *Annales Européennes* the following statistics on French generals who had played a role up to this point: 24 dead on the battlefield or assassinated; 16 dead from natural causes or suicide; 57 shot or guillotined; 21 prisoners; 24 emigrants; 278 arrested or cashiered; 230 employed. The proportion must have been the same amongst adjutant generals because the general staff was almost always affected by the lot of its leaders.

General staff of the Emperor (1804-1815).

Students of the Special Cavalry Military School (l'École spéciale militaire cavalerie) (1885).

Students of the Special Infantry Military School (l'École spéciale militaire infanterie) (1885).

However, a new generation had surmounted these circumstances. From amongst the non-commissioned officers of the *Ancienne Armée* and the middle class youth who had joined the army for love of their country, 20 men of genius, 100 men both devoted and courageous, rose from the ranks and led their comrades to victory.

Aubry treated these men of good intentions with disdain. His work, tinged with bias and inaccuracies, is suspect however. It was after all this same Aubry who, in his great wisdom, declared General Bonaparte to be incapable of serving in the artillery.

The general staff was always overburdened. Many officers of the general staff were required to assist the generals of the Republic. Splitting up the corps, the creation of the new light artillery, and frequent use of the bayonet forced the generals to try harder to express their thoughts, to explain their wishes on the field of battle. A general was valued no more or less than his lieutenants and his aides-de-camp. The famous Army of the East of 1798, the Army of Egypt, recruited and filled out with care, included all together only 56 battalions and 40 squadrons. But Berthier had already been Bonaparte's chief of the general staff. The hero of Italy, he had as generals of division: Dammartin, Caffarelli, Desaix, Regnier, Morand, Kléber, Bon, and Dumas; as brigade commanders: Belliard, Friand, Damas, Verdier, Lannes, Lanusse, Vial, Mercier, Rampon, Murat, Leclercq, Dumas, Dupuis and Zayonseck. Everyone was renowned in the Army of Egypt; the aides-de-camp of the general-in-chief were named Marmont, La Valette, Croisier, Louis Bonaparte, Sulkowski, Duroc, Colbert, Eugène Beauharnais, and Junot. Those who were not killed — sword in hand — in Africa, such as Croisier and Sulkowski, became generals, marshals, dukes, princes and even king. Desaix had Rapp and Savary as aides de camp. Both would later join the First Consul's general staff after Marengo.

Students of the cavalry school of St. Germain (1806).

The general staff was organized by a decree issued in September 1799 on the following basis: 110 adjutant-generals (colonels or lieutenant-colonels), 6 colonels as aides-de-camp, 30 majors as aides-de-camp, and 484 adjutant captains or lieutenants. By 1801, this staff of 550 officers had more than doubled; in 1806 it was tripled; in 1813 it was greater than 2,000. The high command wanted the largest general staff ever, filled with the most celebrated or noble names and resplendent in their flamboyant, variegated colors. Thus, the officers of the general staff paraded, wearing the most amazing hussars' jackets and pelisses of expensive fur. They stood out against their general's simple uniform which had remained in its blue and gold form since the beginning of the century.

GENERAL STAFF OF THE ARMY AT THE BATTLE OF AUSTERLITZ

December 2, 1805

Aides-de-camp of the Emperor: Generals Junot, Caffarelli, Lauriston, Savary, Lemarrois, Rapp, Mouton, Bertrand, Lebrun, Reille.
Officiers d'ordonnance of the Emperor: Castille, Eugéne de Montesquiou, Amédée de Turenne, Falkouwski, Deponthon, Lamarche, Scherr, Bongard, Berthemy, Maulnois, Parrain.

5th CORPS (Left)	CAVALRY (Center)	1st CORPS (Center)	4th CORPS (Right)	3rd CORPS (Right flank)
Marshal LANNES *Chief of staff:* General of Brigade Compans *Commander of artillery:* General Foucher *Commander of engineers:* Colonel Kirgener *Inpecter of reviews:* Buhot *Ordonnateur:* Wast	His Royal Highness, Prince MURAT *Chief of staff:* General of Division Belliard LIGHT DIVISION - Kellermann Generals of Brigade: Picard, Van Marizi, Milhaud, Treilhard	Marshal BERNADOTTE *Chief of staff:* General of Division Berthier *Commander of artillery:* General Eblé *Commander of engineers:* Colonel Morio *Inspector of reviews:* Lalance *Ordonnateur:* Michaux	Marshal SOULT *Chief of staff:* General of Division Saligny *Commander of artillery:* General Pernetty *Commander of engineers:* Colonel Poitevin *Inspector of reviews:* Lambert *Ordonnateur:* Arcambal	Marshal DAVOUT *Chief of staff:* General of Brigade Daultanne *Commander of artillery:* General Sorbier *Commander of engineers:* Colonel Andréossy *Inspector of reviews:* Laigle *Ordonnateur:* Chambun
1st DIVISION - General Suchet Generals of Brigade: Becker, Valhubert, Claparède Adjutant commander Allain	DRAGOONS: 1st DIVISION - General Beaumont Generals of Brigade: Boyer, Scalfort Adjutant commander Devaux	1st DIVISION - Rivaux Generals of Brigade: Dumoulin, Pacthod Adjutant commander Chaudron- Rousseau	1st DIVISION - Vandamme Generals of Brigade: Schiner, Ferey, Candras Adjutant commander Dubois	1st DIVISION - Friant Generals of Brigade: Kester, Luchet, Heudelet Adjutant commander Marés
2nd DIVISION - General Caffarelli Generals of Brigade: Demont, Eppler Adjutant commander Coehorn	2nd DIVISION - General Walther Generals of Brigade: Roger, Boussard Adjutant commander Lacroix	2nd DIVISION - Drouet-d'Erlon Generals of Brigade: Frére, Werlé Adjutant commander Luthier	2nd DIVISION - Saint-Hilaire Generals of Brigade: Morand, Thièbault, Waré Adjutant commander Binot	CAVALRY DIVISION - Bourcier Generals of Brigade: Laplanche, Sahuc Adjutant commander Drouhot
	HEAVY CAVALRY – General of Brigade d'Hautpoul General of Brigade Saint-Sulpice Adjutant commander Fontaine		3rd DIVISION - Legrand Generals of Brigade: Merle, Féry, Lavasseur Adjutant commander Cosson	
	DIVISION NANSOUTY Generals of Brigade: Piston, Lahoussaye, Saint-Germain Adjutant commander Pelissard		CAVALRY BRIGADE– Margaron	

The Revolution passed on to Bonaparte only a single military school: the polytechnic school. He soon saw the need to create new schools for the preparation of a new crop of general staff officers and generals.

Napoleon was more pragmatic and serious than the idealists of the Convention when he organized his schools at Fontainebleau, Saint-Cyr and Saint-Germain. He knew well that he would ruffle feathers amongst the seasoned veterans of the Pyramids and Marengo if he commissioned youngsters who hadn't been baptized under fire. At the same time he kept in mind that he himself had imbibed the solid principles of the art of war as well as the highest military code of honor at the military school of Champ-de-Mars.

There is the story of Berthier who, wishing to obtain for a colonel a promotion to general, repeated over and over again to the Emperor: "He can taste the powder! He can taste the powder!"

"Of course," replied Napoleon, " but it would be better if he tasted sweat."

In fact, what was lacking in a general of the Republic and of the Empire was neither valor nor experience on the battlefield. It was more often training and almost always education.

After having founded a military academy at Saint-Cyr for children of his officers killed on the field of honor, he created the school of Fontainebleau on January 28, 1803. This school was relocated to Saint-Cyr on June 15, 1808. In the same year, the academy was transferred to La Flèche, and on March 14, 1809 he founded the school of Saint-Germain.

What the polytechnic school — his goose with the golden eggs — supplied him as material for the special services, Saint-Cyr was able to provide for the infantry and Saint-Germain for the cavalry.

As might be imagined, the students of these two latter schools would monopolize the entire officers' ranks. Between 1804 and 1807, Fontainebleau had supplied 1,200 officers to the army from the 1,348 students admitted. Between 1807 and 1815, Saint-Cyr supplied 3,357 officers from its 5,042 students. This difference in numbers between admissions and commissions revolves around the petty officers taken out of Saint-Cyr for emergencies.

The school of Saint-Germain ultimately provided a total of 315 officers to the cavalry out of 558 students admitted.

It should be noted that graduates of Saint-Cyr often went directly into the light cavalry or the dragoons.

Napoleon was not mistaken when he sought to establish a good means of recruiting general officers for the future. In fact, of the students graduated from Fontainebleau and from Saint-Cyr during this same period, there were: 1 marshal of France, 55 generals of division and 94 generals of brigade. From the graduates of Saint-Germain there were: 1 marshal, 3 generals of division, and 3 generals of brigade.

It should be added that the school of Saint-Cyr competed with the polytechnic school in its recruitment of artillery officers until 1815. In this regard, Saint-Cyr can take pride in having produced the following names: Marshal Pélissier; Generals of Division Bonet, de Bressoles, Perrodon, Buisson d'Armandy, and Larchey; and Generals of Brigade Tournier and Barbier.

Throughout the Empire, the number of generals and officers of the general staff was limited only by the needs of the moment. Thus, in 1810, the imperial almanac recorded the names of 153 generals of division and 298 generals of brigade, all employed and active. Beyond this there were three lieutenants to His Majesty, the King of Spain, the King of the Two Sicilies, and the Viceroy of Italy, twelve Marshals of the Empire, and 4 senators with the title of Marshal. Three years later in 1813, there were 168 generals of division and 379 generals of brigade, while the figure for high-ranking officials had grown in proportion.

Even by adding the generals on leave of absence or in disgrace, we do not approach the 1,198 general officers of the old regime.

One hundred forty-six foreigners were registered on the lists of the general staff. Not only did they command foreign troops in the service of France but they also became French by annexation. Such was the case of the immortal Masséna. France was not always so fortunate; the open-armed welcome she offered to newcomers produced more than one

Officer assigned to the army general staff (1804-1815).

Jomini. The Emperor only understood this at the end of 1813, but it was too late. Treason had wiped out his efforts.

The campaign of 1812 and the intensified reverses in Spain had reduced the Empire to a haphazard military situation. Napoleon's colleagues were themselves in despair. They began to tire of the struggle whose fatal outcome inevitably became the ruin of their marvelous good fortune, a fortune they owed to their general. The glorious campaign of 1813 demonstrates that Napoleon was still obeyed, but not unquestioningly. However, in 1814 it was a war of patriotism and of heroism; there were left only the faithful, the veterans, the people who loved Napoleon more than life. Now, one hundred men were really worth a thousand. The generals took saber in hand as if they were sub-lieutenants. Napoleon even aimed a gun at Montereau. It was not the throne and the Empire that had to be saved. With France it was the honor of the general himself. It was also the great conquest of the Revolution of 1789 which was personified in the glory and the name of the victor of Marengo and of Jena.

The tricolor flag was the shroud in which one had to be buried. Otherwise everything one had done had to be renounced. Like Soult, former coporal of the Picardy regiment in 1790, all of these dukes, all of these kings, all of the military counts thought that they would not be granted permission to wear the white cockade on their old uniforms. If some showed themselves so pliable afterwards, it was that they would have preferred anything, even the Republic. Napoleon himself was afraid, but it was after all the Revolution. He was intoxicated by deceptive dreams of his dynastic glory. And yet everyone would have been willing to die for France and for him!

There were never any reliable rules for determining how to advance in the military under the Empire. Napoleon was moved largely by caprice in rapidly advancing one of his favorites to the highest rank. If he named Bessières Marshal of France in 1804 despite the fact that the latter had not yet served as commander-in-chief, it was only that he wanted to honor the imperial guard through this example. Bessières was one of the most veteran soldiers of the Imperial Guard and was, in a way, the most striking of its personalities. Although Napoleon made some young men from Faubourg Saint-Germain major-generals in only eight years, he did not spare them on the field of battle and made them pay dearly for their stars. Moreover, he came to power following a regime — the Republican regime — under which the political whims of the assemblies always took precedence over the army's laws of merit and of seniority.

Regardless of how the first Emperor showed partiality, it was not by using generals who had not supported him when the Consulate was succeeded by the Empire. The lengthy banishment of Lecourbe for the glory of the Emperor is an unfortunate example.

Napoleon's enlightened and well considered favoritism was a natural transition from the whims that were exercised by the former monarchy and the Convention to the system of absolute law. He bequeathed to France a phalanx of men, still young if exhausted by war who, served their country well until the end.

Students of the Polytechnic School (1814).

Polytechnic School and School of Saint-Cyr.

On February 4, 1814 the polytechnic school, that wonderful offspring of the Convention which Napoleon had so generously endowed, shed a good deal of blood in defense of the great soldier before the throne. It was remembered that Napoleon had written on its flag: "For Art and for Country." Its students fought on alone until the end of the battle.

Six students were made prisoners; two drummers were killed. One officer and 19 students were wounded: Lieutenant Rostan and the students Deroys, Liger, François, Leclerc, Garserie, Lenfant, Daudelin, Castaignède, Villeneuve, Gournaud, Salomon, Petit, Bonneton, de Cullion, Dupuy, Hourau, Reydellet, Moultzon and Menjaud.

The School of Saint-Cyr could not play as brilliant a role in the campaign of 1814. Here is what a historian tells us on this topic:

"In 1814, General Meunier replaced General Bellavène. The School of Saint-Cyr was located far from the capital during these events which changed the face of the nation. The students heard the noise of the battle on March 30th and wanted to take part in it. They were refused, but that very night, they received orders to escort the Empress to safety and to take their own cannons with them to which requisitioned horses had been hitched. This sad expedition did not last long. The twelve hundred young men arrived at Blois with their artillery. Then, sent back to Orleans, they returned by stages to Saint-Cyr."

RESTORATION

The First Restoration proved to be relatively easy for those who had served the Republic and the Empire. Less inspired, the Second Restoration did not understand that, when it spilled respected blood which had been spared by enemy bullets, it exposed itself to harsh reprisals.

The year 1815 was a sad one in terms of glory. Real generals were forced into hiding to avoid the fate of Ney and of Labédoyère. Meanwhile, a crowd of *voltiguers* from the period of Louis the 16th, heros of the army of Conde who were jokingly called *"rentrants à la Bouillotte,"* (homebodies) lounged along boulevard de Gand. They wore a part-military/part-bourgeois dress which Louis the 18th also wore for his great ceremonies, no doubt to justify them.

Were they really generals? It seemed possible to believe at first. However, it soon became necessary to put an end to this development which was going to give defeated France more generals than the Emperor himself had ever named in all of his victories.

On July 22, 1818, a royal decree intervened in the situation by fixing the number of generals of division at 130 and that of the generals of brigade at 230. Of this number, 80 of the former and 160 of the latter were allocated to the active staff; the rest were put in reserve. Many officers of the Empire were thus reinstated to the staff and some even returned in favor. At the time of the Spanish campaign, one could not do without them.

The main contribution of the Restoration was the creation of a school and of an exclusive corps of the general staff. The honor of creating this dual institution goes to Marshal Gouvion-Saint-Cyr. The institution amply provided for the needs of the French army during the campaigns in Spain, Africa, Anvers, the Crimea and Italy.

The comedy of generals who dominated the stage at the beginning of the Restoration had authorized an orgy in the general staff. To command the Department of Corsica, General Bruslart formed his own general staff consisting of a temporary head provisional colonel, two assistants (a colonel and a lieutenant colonel), two majors and two captains plus two captains serving as aides-de-camp. Marshal Gouvion-Saint-Cyr organized the newly established staff in the following manner in 1817: 30 colonels, 30 lieutenant-colonels, 90 majors, 270 captains, and 125 lieutenants. In the future, no one could belong to this corps without having graduated from Saint-Cyr or having been recruited from: the polytechnic school, amongst the young nobles, or from amongst the second lieutenants of the army.

Inspector General and officers of the Corps Royal, general staff (Second Restoration).

General staff of the princes of the Army of Africa (1840).

LOUIS-PHILIPPE I

The July Revolution, while restoring the tricolor flag to the army , led to the exclusion of all the legitimist officers. In the same way, the Restoration of 1815 had led to the exclusion of many officers of the First Empire. These two reactions, following one upon another over a very short interval, were born of two governments which had both claimed to be conservative. Responsible citizens reacted with great outrage. It is understandable that in a country where a political revolution happens periodically, say every fifteen or sixteen years, it is necessary to put the army above and beyond revolutionary currents.

It was therefore deemed necessary to reaffirm military awareness by allowing an officer to claim and maintain his proper rank. From this point on, the general officers were no longer at the mercy of arbitrariness or of political developments. Upon reaching a specific age (62 years old for a general of brigade, 65 for a general of division) they had to move from active staff (*cadre d'activité*) into the reserves. The active staff itself was limited. The decree of November 15, 1830 fixed it temporarily at 150 generals of division and 250 generals of brigade, until casualities reduced it by 100 positions in each of the two categories. Ultimately, the law of August 4, 1839 restored the staff to 80 generals of division and 160 generals of brigade. These figures had only been modified temporarily until the actual reorganization took place (March 13, 1876).

Although it did not want a war, the constitutional monarchy of 1830 made a great show of possessing an army which it could present with honor before distinguished visitors to Paris. The slow and patient conquest of Algeria periodically provided the army with self esteem and at the same time was of service as a military school for princes as well as an outlet for passionate ambitions. Meanwhile, it was the period of handsome regiments, of dashing uniforms, and of established maneuvers. The old divisions of the Empire used up the last of their energies in these noble games which should not be looked down upon too much, especially today.

The Army of Africa fared well. It produced the two most illustrious men of war that France had put forward since 1815: Bugeaud and Pélissier. In addition, the leaders of this army — Saint-Arnaud, Canrobert, Bosquet, and MacMahon — who had played a considerable role in the wars of the Orient and of Italy, acquired the soldier's blind courage without which no command is possible. Less fortunate than these were Lamoricière, Bedeau, and Changarnier whose careers were cut short just as they were on the verge of winning the Marshal's baton. This is proof positive that the military man must distance himself from political battles. Unfortunately we have not yet seen in France a revolution that respects services rendered to one's country, regardless of political affiliation.

Under Louis-Philippe, much was done for the schools. The school of Saint-Cyr, reestablished by the Bourbons in 1818, was of great importance in recruiting officers. It became a breeding ground from which sprang the vast majority of generals and of intendants. From its annual publication of 1883, one sees that 63 generals of division out of 98 and 131 generals of brigade out of 200 were graduated from this brilliant school. In conjunction with the cavalry school of Saumur and the school of application for the general staff, Saint-Cyr provided the army with as many officers as it needed until the unfortunate campaign of 1870.

Non-commissioned officer cadets of the School of Saumur (1840).

Officer of the Corps Royal, general staff and students of the Special Military School (l'École spéciale militaire) (1835).

The polytechnic school remained the goose with the golden eggs in terms of supplying the special services. Most of our generals who did not graduate from Saint-Cyr came from this school. Unfortunately the school had to provide the majority of its elite students to the most important public offices. Its spirit was affected to a certain extent by this concentration. The very popular uniform of the polytechnic school was for the most part worn by a budding engineer who felt slighted if his military service number relegated him to the infantry or the corps of engineers. The polytechnic school was therefore not actually a military school but rather a mixed institution. It should be added that, perhaps due to this lack of militarism, a spirit of independence was nourished there. This sometimes proved fatal in terms of discipline but was also the source of the school's superior scientific achievements. If the polytechnicians had all become second lieutenants, many would probably have neglected their studies, seeing no point in them vis-a-vis their future careers.

In any case, the graduates of the polytechnic school who joined the army improved upon their military studies as well as their scientific ones at the school of application for the special forces. This school is today located at Fontainebleau.

Over the past thirty-five years, the curricula at these different schools were not substantially modified. Nor were the admissions requirements. Despite changing tastes and the current craze for assimilating the customs, the institutions and even the uniforms of the armies that we have fought, Saint-Cyr and the polytechnic school remain blissfully untouched.

Parisians appreciate the students of these schools for two very different reasons. Residents of the capital love to see the First Battalion of France perform maneuvers in the grand reviews. They also recognize that the polytechnicians are always amongst the first to man the barricades when it is a question of defending their country.

From 1828 until 1830, the school of Saint-Cyr accepted approximately 1,800 students; from 1830 to 1848 approximately 3,600. This gives a total of 5,400. Almost all graduated as commissioned officers. The mass resignations that followed the Revolution of 1830, the discharges, and the special resignations did not exceed between 150 and 175 in total. Initially 150 students were graduated, a number that was raised to 300 in 1840. In 1841, there were even two graduations, the first occurring in April. The second, resulting from the annual examination, involved fewer numbers.

In addition to Saint-Cyr, there was the military academy of La Flèche. This institution long served as a preparatory school for Saint-Cyr. A given number of openings at the special military school were reserved for students of La Flèche. Almost all were given to sons of officers. The other openings were awarded on the basis of competition. This method of enrollment had its good points. It helped perpetrate pride of duty and a certain hungering for glory within military families. However, the procedure was abandoned after the July Revolution. Our customs are becoming more and more democratic. Now rigorous examinations are the sole means of determining admissions. The unfortunate but hardworking candidate with a low grade

must persevere. In this respect, privates and non-commissioned officers are allowed to apply to Saint-Cyr up until twenty-five years of age. This rule has been adopted at the polytechnic school as well.

The school of Saumur produced captain instructors, second lieutenants, and non-commissioned officers of the cavalry. It also trained trumpeters and provided instruction for young blacksmiths.

Under the First Empire and even under the Restoration, the number of military personnel teaching at the various schools was limited. Under Louis-Philippe, however, their numbers grew considerably.

THE REPUBLIC OF 1848

Although the February Revolution respected the general organization of the army, it severely affected the general staff. Complaints were not in order, however, since the Africans rallied to the army. Except for a few generals attached to the King's household, some deputies, and peers of the former majority, the army received favorable support.

A decree of April 11, 1848, which was signed by Arago for want of a general willing to sacrifice his comrades, did away with the group of reserve officers of the general staff in or near retirement *(cadre de resérve)*. Further, it forced into retirement generals who had taken part in the revolt. It also reduced the active staff to 65 generals of division and 130 generals of brigade through the decree of May 6. These last appointments were reinstituted in February.

At the same time, the general staff was fixed at 25 colonels, 25 lieutenant-colonels, 90 majors, 280 captains, and 100 lieutenants.

War was feared, or rather the semblance of fearing war was desired, so the guidelines were set for the general staff. Lamartine, however, demonstrated his pacifist intentions from day one. Eight squadrons were ordered up but only three were formed, and that number was soon reduced to two. It brought back memories of the First Republic. Each general-in-chief had a company of foot and horse guides dressed generally either as chasseurs or as hussars. The most well-known were those famous guides of General Bonaparte who remain legendary even in our own times. They formed

---

GENERAL STAFF OF EXPEDITIONARY FORCE TO ROME
May 22, 1849

Commander in chief: General of Division OUDINOT DE REGGIO
Aide-de-camp: Major Espivent de la Villeboisnet
Officiers d'ordannance: Faber, Artillery Captain; Oudinot, Cavalry Captain
Chief of Staff: Colonel Le Barbier de Tinan
Assistant chief of staff: Major Montesquiou Fezensac
Assistants: Captains Poulle, Castelnau, Osmont
Commander of artillery: General of Brigade Thiry
Director of the park: Lieutenant-Colonel Larchey
Chief of staff: Major Soleille
Commander of engineers: General of Division Vaillant
Chief of staff: Colonel Niel
Administration: Paris, chief intendant

1st DIVISION	2nd DIVISION	3rd DIVISION
General Regnaud de Saint-Jean-d'Angély	General Rostolan	General Guesswiller
1st Brigade, General Molliére	1st Brigade, General Charles Levaillant	1st Brigade, General Jean Levaillant
2nd Brigade (Cavalry), General Morris	2nd Brigade, General Chadeysson	2nd Brigade, General Sauvan

---

the nucleus of the Imperial Guard's regiment of guides, having already served in the Consular Guard. The guides of 1848 formed a fine cavalry which, despite its unprepossessing uniform — trousers and chasseur's jacket in navy blue and epaulettes, trouser stripe, aiguillettes and shako in amaranth (purplish red) — always cut a fine figure. After 1851, they assumed the uniform of the old guides which was further embellished with the creation of the regiment.

The general staff was given a new opportunity to distinguish itself with the reunion of the Army of the Alps first under General Oudinot, then Marshal Bugeaud, and with the dispatch to Rome of two divisions under General Oudinot. Since 1815, the French army had appeared successively in Spain, Greece, Italy (at Ancona), and in Belgium. But all the campaigns it undertook were constrained from the start by a limited objective. The expedition of Rome could lead to serious complications. From the army's point of view, this expedition was a welcome development. With Napoleon's arrival on the scene, the military was eagerly looking forward to a series of wars more important than the campaigns of Africa.

SECOND EMPIRE

The events of December 2nd, rapidly followed by the restoration of the Empire, allowed the general staff to right the wrongs imposed against it by the legislators in February 1848.

The reserve staff was reinstated. The general officers who had been forcibly retired were reintroduced either into the reserve staff or into the active staff, according to their ages. This resulted in a total of 80 generals of division and 160 generals of brigade.

Due to the absolute and unassailable order which the Restoration had introduced in budget accountability, the army's general staff no longer enjoyed the fantastic flexibility it witnessed in the great days of the Republic and the Empire. The command of the territorial divisions and of Algeria had to be supplied from the 240 general

Cavalier, squadron of guides (1852).

General of division holding a review (1858).

officers. With this same group of officers, the general staffs of 25 infantry divisions, 14 cavalry divisions, and 3 divisions of the Imperial Guard had also to be mobilized. Moreover, they had to provide the special services with superior commanders.

The general staff, comprised of 35 colonels, 35 lieutenant-colonels, 110 majors, 300 captains, and 100 lieutenants no longer offered inexhaustible resources.

In examining the tables of the active general staffs under the Second Empire, one begins to realize the difficulties facing the imperial government when it had to organize the Army of the East and that of Italy.

In 1859 the entire army was formed into divisions. Besides the 18 divisions of infantry and of cavalry in the Army of Italy, the armies of Paris, the East and Lyon accounted for 22 divisions.

Too much was staked on the ability of the French armies to pull themselves together on the spur of the moment. Europe was not organized into divisions and brigades as it is today. For every war, there was a certain amount of preparation time. When we describe the infantry and the cavalry further on, we will address the slow pace which allowed the troops to gather and thereby the general staffs, who together took Sebastopol, and the much speedier operation involving the formation of the Army of Italy.

There were 62 Marshals of France, a title which was reestablished in 1804. They are listed as follows:

Name	Year of birth	Year of promotion	Death	Name	Year of birth	Year of promotion	Death
BERTHIER	1753	1804	Mysteriously in 1815 at Bamberg	DE BOURMONT	1773	1830	Struck off the list in 1830; died at Bourmont in 1846
MONCEY	1754	-	At Paris in 1842				
MASSÉNA	1758	-	At Paris in 1817	GÉRARD	1773	-	At Paris in 1855
MURAT	1771	-	King in 1806; by firing squad at Pizzo in 1815	CLAUZEL	1772	1831	At Secourrieu in 1842
				COUNT LOBAU	1770	-	At Paris in 1838
JOURDAN	1762	-	At Paris in 1833	DE GROUCHY	1766	-	Restored in 1831; died at Saint-Etienne in 1847
AUGEREAU	1757	-	At la Houssaye in 1815				
BERNADOTTE	1764	-	King in 1818; died in Stockholm in 1844	VALÉE	1773	1837	At Paris in 1846
BRUNE	1763	-	Assassinated in Avignon in 1815	SÉBASTIANI	1772	1840	At Paris in 1851
MORTIER	1768	-	Killed by Fieschi at Paris in 1835	DROUET D'ERLON	1765	1841	At Paris in 1844
LANNES	1769	-	Killed in 1809 near the Island of Lobau	BUGEAUD	1784	1843	Of cholera at Paris in 1849
SOULT	1769	-	At Saint-Amand-la-Bastide, 1851	REILLE	1775	1847	At Paris in 1860
NEY	1769	-	By firing squad at Paris in 1815	DODE DE LA BRUNERIE	1775	-	At Paris in 1851
DAVOUT	1770	-	At Paris in 1823	JÉROME BONAPARTE	1784	1850	At Paris in 1860
KELLERMANN	1735	-	At Paris in 1820	HARISPE	1768	1851	At Bigorre in 1855
BESSIÈRES	1768	-	Killed at Lutzen in 1813	EXELMANS	1775	-	At Paris in 1853
PERIGNON	1754	-	At Paris in 1818	VAILLANT	1790	-	At Paris in 1872
LEFEBVRE	1755	-	At Paris in 1820	LEROY SAINT-ARNAUD	1801	1852	Of cholera on board the *Berthollet* in 1854
SÉRURIER	1742	-	At Paris in 1819				
MACDONALD	1765	1809	At Courcelles in 1840	MAGNAN	1791	-	At Paris in 1865
MARMONT	1774	-	Struck off the list in 1830; died at Venice in 1852	DE CASTELLANE	1788	-	At Lyon in 1862
				BARAGUEY D'HILLIERS	1795	1854	At Lyon in 1879
OUDINOT	1767	-	At Paris in 1847	PÉLISSIER	1794	1855	At Algers in 1864
SUCHET	1770	1811	At Saint-Joseph in 1826	RANDON	1795	1856	At Geneva in 1871
GOUVION-SAINT-CYR	1764	1812	At Hyères in 1830	CANROBERT	1809	-	"(Sic - died 1895)
PONIATOWSKI	1762	1813	Drowned in the Elster in 1813	BOSQUET	1810	-	In 1861
DE GROUCHY	1766	1815	Not recognized by the Restoration	MAC-MAHON	1808	1859	"(Sic - died 1893)
DUC DE COIGNY	1737	1816	At Paris in 1821	NIEL	1802	-	At Paris in 1869
CLARKE	1765	-	At Neuviller in 1818	REGNAUD DE ST-JEAN D'ANGÉLY	1794	-	At Nice in 1870
DE BEURNONVILLE	1752	-	At Paris in 1821				
DE VIOMÉNIL	1734	-	At Paris in 1827	D'ORNANO	1784	1861	At Paris in 1863
DE LAURISTON	1768	1823	At Paris in 1828	FOREY	1804	1863	At Paris in 1871
MOLITOR	1770	-	At Paris in 1849	BAZAINE	1811	1864	Condemned to death in 1873; pardoned
PRINCE DE HOHENLOHE	1765	1827	At Paris in 1829				
MAISON	1771	1820	At Paris in 1840	LEBOEUF	1809	1870	"(Sic - died 1888)

ARMY OF THE EAST
September 8, 1855

Commander in chief: PÉLISSIER, General of Division

Aides-de-camp: De Waubert de Genlis, Lt. Colonel; Reille, Lt. Colonel; Cassaigne, Lt. Colonel; Duval, Captain
Officiers d'ordonnance: Pélissier, Lt. Colonel of the naval artillery; Dupont, Captain of the 97th;
De Montauban, Lieutenant of the 2nd Chasseurs d'Afrique

GENERAL STAFF
Chief of staff: De Martimprey, General of Division
Assistant chief of staff: Jarras, Colonel
Attached to the general staff: Renson, Lt. Colonel; Lallemand, Major; De Beaumont, Major; Hartung, Major; Lourde, Captain;
Schmitz, Captain; De la Hitte, Captain; De Bouillé, Captain; D'Orléans, Captain; Rolin, Captain
Chief of the topographical staff: Desaint, Colonel
Attached to the topographical staff: Beaudoin, Major; Berthaut, Major; Valette , Captain; Mircher , Captain; Davenet, Captain; Saget,
Captain; Perrotin , Captain
Commander of army headquarters: Chaulan, Captain of the 26th
Attache to the English army : De Suleau de Malroy, Lieutenant Colonel
Attache to the Sardinian Army: De Talleyrand-Périgord, Duke of Dino, Captain
Commander of artillery: Thiry, General of Division
Director of the park: Mazure, General of Brigade
Commander of engineers: Niel, General of Division
Intendant general: Blanchot
Provost marshal general: Damiguet de Vernon, Colonel of the Gendarmerie
Chief medical officer: Scrive
Head chaplain: L'abbè Parabère

1st CORPS
De Salles, General of Division

Aide-de-camp: Boudet, Captain
Officier d'ordonnance: Duhamel Grandprey, Captain of the 79th
Chief of staff: Rivet, General of Brigade
Assistants: Manèque, Major; De la Sougeole, Captain;
Campenon, Captain; De Beurnonville, Captain; Petit, Captain
Field officer of the trenches: Raoult, Lt. Colonel
Assistants: Faure, Major; Tordeux, Lieutenant; Durdilly,
Captain of the 1st Chasseurs d'Afrique;
De Ligneville, Lieutenant of the 14th;
Diquemare, Lieutenant of the 1st Hussars
Commander of artillery: Leboeuf, General of Brigade
Commander of engineers: Delesme, General of Brigade

1st DIVISION
D'Autemarre, General of Division
Aide-de-camp : Loverdo
Officier d'ordonnance :
Rouet, Lieutenant of the 3rd
General staff: Colson, Major;
Gallot, Captain; Taffin, Captain
1st Brigade, General Niol
2nd Brigade, General Breton

2nd DIVISION
Levaillant, General of Division
Officiers d'ordonnance:
Pitié, Lieutenant of the 21st;
Labbe, Second Lieutenant of the 98th
General staff:
Letellier-Valazé, Lt. Colonel;
Hubert-Castex, Captain;
Witz, Captain
1st Brigade, General Trochu
2nd Brigade, General Couston

3rd DIVISION
Paté, General of Division
Aide-de-camp: Gaillard, Captain
General staff: Borel de Breitzer, Colonel;
Wengel, Major;
Jumel and Pagès, Captains
1st Brigade, General Beuret
2nd Brigade, General Bazaine

4th DIVISION
General of Division, Bouat
Aide-de-camp: Clemeur, Captain
Officier d'ordonnance:
Lefèvre, Lieutenant of the 18th
General staff: De Puibusque, Colonel;
Fourchault, d'Ornant and Lucas, Captains
1st Brigade, General Lefebvre
2nd Brigade, General Duprat de la Roquette

CAVALRY DIVISION
Morris, General of Division
Aides-de-camp: Folloppe and Gervais, Captains
Officiers d'ordonnance: Thornton, Captain of cavalry
Bonaparte, Lieutenant of the 7th Dragoons
General staff: Pajol, Colonel; Hecquard, Major, de Montigny, Captain
1st Brigade, General Cassaignolles
2nd Brigade, General Feray

2nd CORPS
Bosquet, General of Division

Aides-de-camp: Balland, Major; Fay, Captain
Officiers d'ordonnance: De Dampierre, Captain of the 1st Spahis;
Thomas, Captain of the 1st Chasseurs d'Afrique;
Bochér, Captain of the 5th Chasseur Battalion
Chief of staff: De Cissey, General of Brigade
Assistants: Henry, Major; Lefebvre de Rumfort, Major;
Clappier, Captain; De Jouffrey D'Abbans, Captain; Wachter, Captain
Field officer of the trenches: Besson, Lieutenant Colonel
Surgeon-lieutenant: Dantin, Captain
Surgeon-lieutenant: Minot, Captain of the 100th
Surgeon-lieutenant: Brocard, Lieutenant of the 80th
Commander of artillery: Beuret, General of Brigade
Commander of engineers: Frossard, General of Brigade

1st DIVISION
Mac-Mahon, General of Division
Aide-de-camp: Borel, Captain
Officier d'ordonnance:
D'Harcourt, Second Lieutenant of the
18th Chasseurs
General staff: Lebrun, Colonel;
Broye, Bresson and Beau, Captains
1st Brigade, —
2nd Brigade, General Vinoy

2nd DIVISION
Camou, General of Division
Aide-de-camp:
Grangez du Rouet, Captain
Officier d'ordonnance:
Monassot, Captain
General staff: De Bar, Major;
Leroy and Samuel, Captains
1st Brigade, General de Wimpffen
2nd Brigade, General Vergé

3rd DIVISION
Espinasse, General of Division
Officier d'ordonnance:
Mocquard, Second Lieutenant
of the 7th Dragoons
General staff:
Dupin and Mancel, Majors;
Regnier and Becque, Captains
1st Brigade, General Manèque
2nd Brigade, General Tournemine

4th DIVISION
Dulac, General of Division
Aide-de-camp: De Carrières, Captain
General staff:
Magnau, Lieutenant Colonel
Gruizard, Warnet and—
Fouque, Captains
1st Brigade, General Saint-Pol
2nd Brigade, General Bisson

5th DIVISION
De la Motterouge, General of Division
Aide-de-camp: De Laboissière, Captain
Officer d'ordonnance : De Ménorval, Lieutenant of the 82nd
General staff:
Delaville, Lieutenant Colonel
Royer, Conigliano and Loizillon, Captains
1st Brigade, General Bourbaki
2nd Brigade, —

CAVALRY DIVISION
d'Allonville, General of Division
Aide-de-camp: Marigues, Captain
Officier d'ordonnance: De la Jaille, Captain of the 5th Hussars
General staff: Joinville, Lieutenant Colonel;
Gondallier de Tugny, Major; Lespinas, Captain
1st Brigade, General Walsin-Esterhazy
2nd Brigade, General Coste de Champeron

continued next page

General staff of a general of division (1884).

General staff officer (1852-1870), campaign dress.

ARMY OF THE EAST *continued*

RESERVE CORPS
Provisional commander: Herbillon, General of Division

Aide-de-camp: De Sachy de Fourdrinoy, Captain
Officier d'ordonnance: Herbillon, Lieutenant of the 62nd
Chief of staff: De Vaudrimet-Davout
Assistants: Chautan de Vercly, Lieutenant Colonel; Sumpt, Devanlay and Gilly, Captains
Commander of artillery: Soleille, General of Brigade
Commander of engineers: De Béville, General of Brigade

IMPERIAL GUARD	1st DIVISION	2nd DIVISION
Mellinet, General of Division	Herbillon, General of Division	d'Aurelles de Paladines, General of Division
Officier d'ordonnance: Commandants Lacroix and de Keeffer	*General staff:* De Villers, Colonel; Martenot de Cordoux, Lesieur and Farcy	*Aide-de-camp:* Carnet, Captain
General staff: Loverdo, Colonel; De Beurmann, Andrieux and Déaddé, Captains	1st Brigade, Sencier	*Officier d'ordonnance:* Des Barbieux, Lieutenant of the 30th,
1st Brigade, General de Failly	2nd Brigade, Cler	*General staff:* Dieu, Colonel; Morel, Major; Granthil, de Mecquenem, Captains
2nd Brigade, de Pontevès		1st Brigade, de Montenard
		2nd Brigade, de Marolles

Cavalry Brigade, General de Forton
Infantry Brigade (unattached), General Sol

EXPEDITIONARY FORCE TO MEXICO
July, 1864

Commander in chief: BAZAINE, General of Division

Aides-de-camp: Willette, Major, and Blanchot, Captain
Chief of the office: Boyer, Colonel
Assistant: Vosseur, Captain
Chief of staff: Manéque, Colonel
Assistant: Loysel, Major
Adjutants: Warnei, Roussel, Garcin, Bidot, Mieulot, Lahalle, Captains
Officers at the disposition of the general in chief: Bousquet, Lieutenant Colonel; Vanson, Magnan, Truchy, Furst, Captains
Probationary officers: Niox and Thomas, Captains; Cremer, Simon, Babin, de la Tuollays, Ligniéres, Tisseyre, de Montfort, de Vaudrimey-Davoust, Lieutenants
Commander of artillery: Courtois Roussel d'Hurbal, General of Division
Chief of staff: De Lajaille, Lieutenant Colonel
Commander of engineers: Vialla, General of Brigade
Chief of staff: Doutrelaine, Colonel
Chief of administrative services: Wolf, military intendant; Friant, assistant intendant

1st DIVISION	2nd DIVISION
Castagny, General of Division	Douay (Félix), General of Division
Chief of staff: Lewal, Colonel	*Aides-de-camp:* Davenet and Seygland, Majors
Adjutants: Billot, Major; de Fayet, Guillot and Darras, Captains	Osmont, Colonel, *chief of staff*
1st Brigade, General de Bertier	*Adjutants:* Loizillon, Sennell and Noiret, Captains
Aide-de-camp: de Rancy, Captain	1st Brigade, General Baron Neigre
2nd Brigade, General Baron Aymard	*Aide-de-camp:* Deville-Chabrol, Captain
Reserve, General Baron de Maussion	2nd Brigade, General Brincourt
Aide-de-camp: Doé de Maindreville, Captain	*Aide-de-camp:* Tordeux, Captain
	3rd Brigade, General Lheriller
	Aide-de-camp: Bourcart, Captain

Cavalry Brigade, General de Lascours
Anti-guerilla commander: Dupin, Colonel of the general staff

Officer of the general staff corps (1852-1870).

EXPEDITIONARY FORCE TO THE BALTIC
August 1854

Commander in chief:
BARAGUEY D'HILLIERS, General of Division

Aides-de-camp: Captains Melin and Foy
Chief of staff: de Gouyon de Saint-Loyal, Colonel
Granthil and de Jouffroy, Captains
Commander of engineers: Niel, General of Division
Commander of artillery: de Rochebouet, Lieutenant Colonel
1st Brigade, General d'Hugues
2nd Brigade, General Grezy

EXPEDITIONARY FORCE TO CHINA

Commander in chief: COUSIN MONTAUBAN, General of Division

Aides-de-camp: Deschiens, Major and de Bouillé, Captain
Officiers d'ordonnance: De Pine, Lieutenant; Cousin de Montauban, Captain of cavalry
Chief of staff: Schmitz, Lieutenant Colonel
Adjutants: Campenon, Major; de Cools, Chanoine, Captains; Dabry, Captain of infantry
Chief of topographic service: Dupin, Lieutenant Colonel
Adjutant: Foerster, Captain
Commander of artillery: De Bentzmann, Colonel
Chief of staff: Schneegans, Major
Commander of engineers: Dupré-Derouléde, Lieutenant colonel
Chief of administrative services: Dubut, military intendant - first class
Religious service: l'abbé Trégraro
Provost marshal: Janisset, Captain
Adjutant: Faure, Lieutenant
1st Brigade, Jamin, General of Brigade, *second in command of the expedition*
Aide-de-camp: Laveuve, Captain
2nd Brigade, Collineau, General of Brigade
Aide-de-camp: d'Hendecourt, Captain

ARMY OF ITALY
April 30, 1859

Commander in chief: HIS MAJESTY THE EMPEROR

IMPERIAL HEADQUARTERS

Aides-de-camp:
Count Roguet, General of Division
De Cotte, General of Division
Count de Montebello, General of Brigade
Yvelin de Béville, General of Brigade
Prince of Moscow, General of Brigade
Fleury, Colonel
De Waubert de Genlis, Colonel
Marquis de Toulongeon, Colonel
Count Lepic, Colonel
Count Reille, Lieutenant Colonel
Favé, Lieutenant Colonel

Officiers d'ordonnance:
Count d'Andlau, Captain
Klein de Kleinenberg, Captain
Viscount Friant, Captain
De Tascher de la Pagerie, Captain
De la Tour-d'Auvergne-Laoragais, Captain
Eynard de Clermont-Tonnerre, Captain
Darguesse, Captain
Viscount Champagny de Cadore, Captain
Prince Joachim Murat, Lieutenant
Baron de Bourgoing, equerry
Davilliers, equerry
Baron N. Clary, equerry
Medical service: Conneau, Baron Larrey
Chaplain: Abbot Laine
Secretaries: Robert, Maitre des requetes; Lemarié, auditor

GENERAL HEADQUARTERS
Army chief of staff: Marshal Vaillant
Chief of staff: Martimprey, General of Division
Assistant chiefs of staff: Baret and Rouvray, Generals of Brigade
Commander of the general headquarters: Rose, General of Brigade
Commander of artillery: Leboeuf, General of Brigade
Commander of engineers: Frossard, General of Brigade
Intendant general: Paris de Bollardière
Provost marshal general: Damiguet de Vernon, Colonel of Gendarmerie
Baggage master general: Dalche de la Rive des Planels, Lieutenant Colonel of
Gendarmerie

IMPERIAL GUARD
Regnaud de Saint-Jean-d'Angèly, General of Division

Chief of staff: Raoult, Colonel
Commander of artillery: General Sevelinge

1st DIVISION
Mellinet, General of Division
Chief of staff: de Tanlay, Colonel
1st Brigade, General Cler
2nd Brigade, General de Wimpffen

2nd DIVISION
Camou, General of Division
Chief of staff: Colonel Besson
1st Brigade, General Manèque
2nd Brigade, General Decaen

CAVALRY
Morris, General of Division
Chief of staff: Colonel Pajol
1st Brigade, General Marion
2nd Brigade, General de Champeron
3rd Brigade, General de Cassaignoles

1st CORPS
Marshal Baraguey d'Hillars

Chief of staff: Foltz, General of Brigade
Commander of artillery: Forgeot, General of Brigade
Commander of engineers: Bouteillier, General of Brigade

1st DIVISION
Forey, General of Division
de la Tour-d'Auvergne, Colonel
1st Brigade, General Beuret
2nd Brigade, General Blanchard

2nd DIVISION
De Ladmirault, General of Division
Hecquard, Lieutenant Colonel
1st Brigade, General Niol
2nd Brigade, General De Nègrier

3rd DIVISION
Bazaine, General of Division
Letellier-Valazé, Lieutenant Colonel
1st Brigade, General Goze
2nd Brigade, General Dumont

CAVALRY
Desvaux, General of Division
Dupont, Lieutenant Colonel
1st Brigade, General Genestel de Planhol
2nd Brigade, General de Forton

2nd CORPS
Mac-Mahon, General of Division

Chief of staff: General Lebrun
Commander of artillery: General Auger
Commander of engineers: Lebaron, Colonel

1st DIVISION
De la Motterouge, General of Division
de Laveaucoupet, Colonel
1st Brigade, General Lefebvre
2nd Brigade, General Polhés

2nd DIVISION
Espinasse, General of Division
Poulle, Colonel
1st Brigade, General Gault
2nd Brigade, General de Castagny

CAVALRY
Gandin de Villaine, General of Brigade

3rd CORPS
Marshal Canrobert

Chief of staff: de Senneville, Colonel
Commander of artillery: General Courtois Roussel d'Hurbal
Commander of engineers: Chauchard, General of Brigade

1st DIVISION
Renault, General of Division
Anselme, Colonel
1st Brigade, General Picard
2nd Brigade, General Jannin

2nd DIVISION
Trochu, General of Division
de Place, Colonel
1st Brigade, General Bataille
2nd Brigade, General Collmeau

3rd DIVISION
Bourbaki, General of Division
Marlenot de Cordoux, Lieutenant Colonel
1st Brigade, General Vergé
2nd Brigade, General Ducrot

CAVALRY
Piortonneaux, General of Division
de Gaujal, Lieutenant Colonel
1st Brigade, General de Clerambault
2nd Brigade, General Dalmas de la Pérouse

4th CORPS
Niel, General of Division

Chief of staff: General Espivent de la Villeboisnet
Commander of artillery: General of Brigade Soleille
Commander of engineers: Jourjon, Colonel

1st DIVISION
Vinoy, General of Division
Osmont, Colonel
1st Brigade, General de Martimprey
2nd Brigade, General de la Charrière

2nd DIVISION
De Failly, General of Division
de Rosières, Colonel
1st Brigade, General O. Farrell
2nd Brigade, General Saurin

3rd DIVISION
De Luzy Pelissac, General of Division
Pissis, Colonel
1st Brigade, General Douay
2nd Brigade, General Lenoble

CAVALRY
Cavalry Brigade, General Richepanse

5th CORPS
His Highness Prince Napoleon

Chief of staff: de Beaufort d'Haulpoul, General of Brigade
Commander of artillery: General de Fiereck
Commander of engineers: General de Coffiniéres

1st DIVISION
d' Autemarre, General of Division
de Suleau de Malroy, Colonel
1st Brigade, General Neigre
2nd Brigade, General Correard

2nd DIVISION
Chrich, General of Division
Regnard, Colonel
1st Brigade, General Grandchamp
2nd Brigade, General Canvin du Bourguet

CAVALRY
Cavalry Brigade, General de Lapeyrouse

As can be seen in the preceding tables, each general has his aide-de-camp or his orderly. Depending on his position, he might have many more. The Minister of War has as many as ten or twelve. A commander-in-chief of the army often avails himself of even more. He generally chooses them from the troops under his command, but this method is not set in stone.

Generals commanding a number of units possess a general staff directed by a chief of general staff in addition to these officers at hand whom they employ as they see fit. The chief of staff is charged with expediting the military business of the division, of the army corps, or of the army.

A general staff of a division consists of a chief field officer and two assisting captains.

A general staff of an army corps consists of a brigade general or a full colonel, a lieutenant-colonel or major, and three or four adjutants.

An army composed of a number of corps acting together possesses a large general staff. This staff is always directed by a general of division. It also includes many assisting field officers as well as an unlimited number of captains.

When there is a general-in-chief commanding many armies, the chief of the general staff takes the title of chief of staff.

Officers, general staff (1870-1871).

The perfect prototype for the chief of staff was Marshal Berthier, the right hand man of Napoleon. Berthier was not present at Waterloo, having mysteriously died at Bamberg. Soult replaced him. Despite his enormous talents, the Duke of Dalmatia was not up to the detailed work of the general staff. Poor execution of orders must be included amongst the many reasons for the defeat of Napoleon in this battle. A good chief of general staff is indeed a rare bird, a marvel of marvels in the military hierarchy. General de Martimprey exhibited great expertise in his functions at Sebastopol. Marshal Leboeuf, however, was not prepared through any special training when in 1870 he was employed in this position.

Marked ability of officers, strength of numbers, and reliability of soldiers together do not an army make. What matters more is the heightened awareness of its leaders and the influence it buys with their men. We have seen that in 1870-1871 many of the highest ranking leaders of the French army lacked character. The public belief was that they were equally wanting in training and that they were badly supported by their subordinates, the officers of the general staff.

All citizens, all classes should have borne equal responsibility for this war, entered into in an untimely manner and deplorably conducted from its beginning until the moment of peace. Unfortunately, this was not to be the case. The imprudent Prime Minister who declared war believes himself justified in claiming that he thought the Ministry of War was ready. The Minister of War complains that his orders were not executed. The generals-in-chief maintain that they did not have sufficent means at hand. The soldiers claim that they have been betrayed, and the people imagine that a mere sergeant could have taken care of everything.

Better to have kept still after defeat and worked in silence. Unfortunately we do not know how to keep our mouths shut!

The courtyard at the Polytechnic School (1884).

The army works hard. Public opinion is satisfied with the elimination of the corps of the general staff, its replacement by commissioned officers belonging to all the arms of the service, and by the inauguration of an institute of higher learning for war where these officers are educated. Yet up to this very moment, there are no appreciable results despite these efforts.

Twelve years of peace have left nearly unknown to us those who were the best officers from past battles. It was almost impossible to distinguish oneself in combat with the generals of 1870 and 1871. A new generation of leaders was required; it is on the horizon.

The war of 1870 forced the dispatch of seven eighths of the superior officers of the army to the Army of Metz and to that of Sedan. When the capitulation of Sedan and the immobilization of the Army of Metz required improvisation of a new corps, an unanticipated promotion to the rank of general was bestowed upon officers who had not expected such good fortune. They proved themselves more or less worthy, but none was exceptional. The tales of 1870 and of 1871 will prove to our children that there are always immense resources within France. Yet they will also uphold our belief that victory is not a matter of improvisation. In generously pouring out their own blood for their country, the generals of the last two armies of the Empire are absolved of their faults and weaknesses. The pseudo-leaders at Tours and Bordeaux proved to be less generous with their lives than the Abel Douays, the Raoults, the Maires, the Colsons, the Doens, the Decaens, the Marguerittes, the Legrands, the Morands, the Marguenats, the Tilliards, the Girards and the many others whose names are now forgotten. In Paris, the Renaults, the Guilhems, the Blaises, the La Charrières knew equally well how to die for their vanquished country. Scorn for death, hot-headed courage or simple recklessness are not the qualities that make a good general, nor do they impress the people. It is imperative that scientific training and education that promotes character are added to the equation.

Above all, the nation and the army has sinned through lack of character before, during and after the fatal war.

The school of war must produce intelligent men and, most importantly, men of character. This is crucial.

This military school of higher learning is the guiding light of our miltary renaissance. It has taken as its motto: "Science above all and might beneath it." ("*La science en haut et le nombre en bas.*") If with its 2,600,000 man army (including the territorial army) France finally has generals who know, make use of, and inspire it, then she will not regret the passing of those elite soldiers who are no longer with us. Despite what anyone says, the final vestiges of these elite appeared in the glorious but very ill-fated Army of Metz, so valiant and so badly led.

God would wish it for the honor of our country!

Officer's accessories.

The Marshal's baton

HISTORY OF THE INFANTRY
Infantry of the Line

◆

*Grenadier, infantry of the line
(1789).*

inking our army's present and past history is a glorious tale which is embroidered on its flag in golden letters. Although a drastic period of mass dismissals ended in 1815, the story of the brave deeds of the regiments of the First Empire — those offspring of the demi-brigades of the Republic which mixed veterans with volunteers — belongs to today's regiments, the descendants of those famous regiments of the Empire.

The French infantry is actually composed as follows: 144 regiments with 4 battalions of 4 companies each plus 2 depot companies; 30 battalions of chasseurs à pied (ight infantry), each having 5 companies with one being a depot company; and, finally, the special corps in our African colony and 4 regiments attached to the Ministry of the Navy and of the Colonies.

We will begin by recounting the history of the troops of the line, or regular troops, from 1789 on. Following this is a section on the chasseur à pied battalions which date from 1840. This leaves for the end a discussion of the special troops of the Army of Africa and of the naval infantry who should, in all fairness, be dealt with separately.

It is beyond the scope of this work to provide a detailed history of each infantry regiment from 1789 to the present. Such a study would cover the history of the entire world. There isn't a country which has not been visited by our infantrymen who are hardworking, courageous under fire, hardened against fatigue —consequently they are formidable.

It was assumed that, despite the mergers, changes, and reductions, a regimental number always shielded the same corps and bound it to a continuous heritage of indestructible glory. This assumption is reinforced by the fact that the names of: Jemmapes, Hohenlinden, Zurich, Marengo, Austerlitz, and Wagram were written beside those of Anvers, Isly, Sebastopol, Solferino, Palikao and Puebla on the regimental flags. We have respected this chronology of names since it gave rise to the religion of the flag. This religion can bring victory to our side on the day of a battle when all other faith is lacking.

The French infantry epitomized and reaffirmed all the qualities of the army. It is in itself an army , capable of everything, ready for anything, good at everything. Has it not provided support to all the armed services — to the artillery, to the corps

of engineers, to the administration —with generosity and aplomb in many a campaign? On distant expeditions, it has bravely commandeered local horses and become a mounted infantry. It had cannons under the First Republic and under the First Empire. It constructed the forts of Paris and surrounded Sebastopol with heavy fortifications. When it is not fighting, it constructs roads, builds cities, and digs canals.

The infantry has been said to be the queen of any battle. It can also be said that the French foot soldier is a citizen of the world because he is at ease anywhere. Nothing surprises him, nothing worries him: neither the pyramids of Egypt nor the porcelain forts of China; not the magnificence of the Kremlin nor the moving sands of Algeria. Under that grey coat beats the heart of a true citizen and of a real worker. He never forgets his faith, his home, or his family. No matter where he finds himself, he considers himself to be a representative of the French way of life. He lives abroad, anxiously awaiting the day or the circumstances that will return him to his tools or to his plow, to marry and establish a line of brave sons, good Frenchmen, loyal servants of the country.

Regimental soldier, colonel general and National Guards of Paris (1789).

BEFORE THE REVOLUTION

When the Revolution broke out in 1789, the infantry comprised 104 regiments of the line of which 79 were French and 23 foreign, plus 12 battalions of chasseurs à pied, 7 colonial regiments, one naval regiment and the provincial troops.

All these regiments had 2 battalions except le Roi, No. 28 which had 4. A battalion included 4 companies of fusiliers, plus one of grenadiers in the first battalion and one of chasseurs in the second. With an effective strength of approximately 120 men per company, including staff, there was a total of 1,200 men. The regimental staff did not differ appreciably from the active general staff. All the regiments had a music section, a drum major, and a squad of sappers. The French regiments wore white uniforms, the Swiss and the Irish a madder (wine, from Madeira) colored one, and the other foreign regiments a deep blue uniform. The royal regiments had royal blue lapel facings, cuff facings and collars. Those of the princes' regiments were scarlet. The others, separated by group, were distinguished by sky blue, matte black, iron grey , rose, jonquil yellow, crimson, silver grey, golden rose (aurore) and dark green. The chasseurs à pied wore a green uniform with lining, facing, and collar of a distinctive color. The provincial troops were in white with royal blue collars. The uniform was similar, in terms of cut and design, to that adopted by the regiments in 1793. It was worn without major modification until 1803.

In order to account for the 104 regiments listed above, the infantry's system must be used. Thus, Regiment No. 64 was assigned to the Royal Artillery (itself divided into 8 regiments) and Regiment No. 97 was assigned to the provincial troops.

Infantry of the line (1789).

These two regiments were composed of 13 royal regiments, 14 provincial regiments, and 78 garrison battalions, all recruited by lottery in the parishes. In wartime, the provincial troops took the place of the permanent regiments in the garrisons. When required, as in the Thirty Years' War, they also provided contingents to campaign armies. On the other hand, permanent regiments were recruited through solicitation. A foot soldier cost the King 100 pounds accounted for as follows: 30 to the new recruit the moment he signed on; 36 for a billet note to which he had access upon arrival at the corps; 24 to cover expenses for food and lodging; and finally, 10 to the recruiter. The solicited recruit signed a contract for eight years. At the end of his first term, he could re-enlist every two years at the rate of 25 pounds for each two year term. After 24 years of service, he was paid 20 pounds a year.

Advancement for solicited recruits was normally limited to the sergeant's stripes after which there was retirement or the Invalides. Despite the barriers separating commissioned from non-commissioned officers, a solicited recruit, from the quai de la Ferraille for example, could become colonel or even general. However, this was rare. The position of flagbearer and of second lieutenant of the grenadiers was specifically reserved for the solicited recruit.

A complete and accurate table describing the foot troops at the collapse of the Ancien Regime results from adding to the above lists and details: a corps of French Guards comprising 6 battalions and one of Swiss Guards with 4 battalions.

1789

Amidst the early turbulence which followed the reunion of the Estates-General, these well-disciplined troops at first displayed a military spirit of unity far exceeding that exhibited in national politics. It conducted itself in an orderly enough manner. However, with the seizing of the Bastille by 800 men of the French Guard Regiment and the revolt at Nancy of the King's Regiment and the Swiss of Chateauvieux, it was soon evident that privileged troops were not often the most faithful. It also demonstrated that the aristocratic make-up of the army was doomed. Thus, within months, the revolutionary spirit took a gigantic step forward.

From now on, each regiment had its committee director who maintained contact with the new municipalities. The regiments of Condé, La Courrone, and Royal-Vaisseaux opened an era of military insurrection. Lorraine-infantry, Artois, Bresse, and Hesse-Darmstadt followed their example. Poitou threw its lieutenant-colonel into prison. Noailles refused to replace Languedoc (which had left its garrison without orders) at Montauban. Royal-Champagne insulted its officers and threatened them with rifles. Beauce and Normandy composed an address promoting federation of all the regiments of the army and charged the city of Paris with serving as their intermediary. Bassigny ousted its colonel, de Suffren. A decree dismissed him but it was impossible to execute this decree. Non-commissioned officers and soldiers everywhere clamored for dividing up the regiments' funds and kicking out the officers of noble blood. The army was no longer in a position to defend the country. It was at this juncture that Danton chose to fire up his patriotism at the tribune of the Constituent Assembly. Desertion commenced in the ranks. It can be noted on October 1, 1790 that the effective strength was reduced by 30,000 men. This may be attributed to the fact that solicitation of recruits was about to be abolished, given that commitments were gratuitous. At the end of 1790, the general effective strength of the army was no more than 156,000 men of whom 116,399 were with the infantry.

An ordinance from January 1, 1791 abolished aristocratic appointments within the regiments. Following thereafter on March 4th, the Constituent Assembly completed the ruin of the old army by disbanding the provincial troops and the lottery through which they were recruited. From this point forth, the army had no tradition, no recruitment and no reserves.

Indeed the army was ready for a patriotic awakening. However, the endangered country had to appeal to these souls already scarred by lack of discipline and the worst of passions, worked up even moreso by revolutionary rantings and ravings and by the deplorable examples of the municipalities.

NATIONAL GUARD AND OLD TROOPS

While the Revolution proceeded methodically and with care to destroy the old army, a major movement was taking shape in the country.

In the aftermath of July 14, 1789, Parisians felt the need to organize themselves under the command of LaFayette. They had already hastily armed themselves and joined in the singular spectacle of 800 French Guards and 93 Swiss of the Salis-Samade forcing 82 invalids to surrender. The invalids had already participated in the rioting; the Swiss had been abandoned by the military authorities. Immediately, the National Guard of Paris was formed and incorporated — under the name of paid companies — from the French Guards which were in fact disbanded on July 31st. These companies allowed the National Guard of Paris to immediately assume a creditable appearance.

Officer, infantry of the line (1789).

White uniforms and blue uniforms (1792).

Following the example of the capital, each provincial city was determined to have its own battalion.

Military history for the years 1791, 1792, and 1793 has been written with more passion than accuracy. Some have touted the volunteers of 1791 and 1792. Others have claimed that without the white coats (the old regiments), the blue coats (volunteers to the National Guard) would have been continuously battered.

The truth lies somewhere between these two positions. An effort will be made to try to present it clearly.

On the one hand, the standing army had been morally and militarily weakened by the Revolution. However, when facing the enemy, it regained much of its strength. On the other hand, the National Guard was full of spirit as it contained only volunteers and fought for liberty, but it worsened after the massive levy and the requisition. After two years of administrative experimentation and military defeats, the first demi-brigades emerged from a merger of the two elements: the National Guard and the army. Thus it may be asserted that the armies of the Revolution owed their soundness to time, experience and hard work. It was only beginning in 1794 that France had an army which, though not absolutely homogenous, was molded to its military needs. In the end, a soldier of the levy was indistinguishable from an old white coat, at least amongst those who actually fought.

When France launched a glorious challenge to the European Coalition in April 1792, the National Guard and the regular troops had not yet established relations amongst themselves. Moreover, the former group recruited whereas the latter did not. The National Guard had pulled together a reasonably good officer corps from the disbanded provincial troops whereas the old regiments had lost almost all of their officers. A great fuss has been made about some admirable non-commissioned officers who became generals. Certainly there were extraordinary and meritorious cases such as that of Soult. He was a corporal in the Picardie regiment in 1788, becoming Marshal in 1804.

However, the legend is exaggerated and should be confined to a few exceptional examples. The old infantry included at most 5,000 non-commissioned officers. The Republic required 20,000 officers to command its foot soldiers. The young men of the bourgeoisie who had been selected through the requisitions provided the majority of these officers. The rest were selected from those amongst the illiterate soldiers who fought well, were healthy and aggressive, and who served as the foundation of the regiments until the end of the Empire. These soldiers rarely acheived a rank higher than captain.

The effective strength of the standing army was supposed to be 205,000 men on June 26, 1792. It was only 178,000 despite great efforts to attain the larger number. Below is the effective strength of the 4 actual armies:

> Army of the North, Commander Luckner, counting 25,049 men of troops of the line;
> Army of the Center, Commander LaFayette, totalling 25,227;
> Army of the Rhine, Commander Lamorlière, totalling 20,943;
> Army of Midi, Commander Montesquieu, totalling 23,380.

As best as possible, battalions of volunteers or of the National Guard took their places beside these old troops. Once the war commenced, the National Guard, the volunteers, the men on requisition, and those of the levée en masse or mass levy were merged as soon as they arrived at their designated postings. The gathering of 170 battalions of the National Guard had been decreed on July 21, 1791. This number was expanded to 200 by another decree of March 5, 1793. The first battalions were supposed to have 524 men, including the staff. The second decree directed the 200 battalions to each have 800 men; this gave a total of 160,000 foot soldiers, supplementing the standing army on campaign. In June 1792, 168 of these battalions already had to be divided up amongst the four armies as follows:

> Army of the North, 44 - Army of the Rhine, 32 - Army of the Center, 58 - Army of Midi, 50.

Their effective strength was poor, their clothing wretched, and their discipline very elementary. Although the battalions from the provinces were most often noted for their submissiveness, the Parisians threatened to hang their generals. No doubt this came in response to the advice given them by Marat in *l'Ami du Peuple*. A battalion of the Lombard region in Dumouriez'

Infantry of the line—Bugler, campaign dress (1885).

Infantry of the line, full dress (1885).

Grenadier, infantry of the line (1794).

army, which had a reputation for unruliness, was among the others, and without orders, it fell back on Châlons on its own authority. A few days after the French victory at Valmy, this same battalion fled before a squadron of Prussian hussars, shouting that they were being butchered. Twenty-five men had their heads shaven and were driven out of the camp, disgraced.

This poor showing caused the old corps to regain their spirit as they tried to distinguish themselves from the National Guard.

The Assembly which was established in the Convention on September 21, 1792 welcomed the fruits of its labor: the old army, which wanted to obey, no longer had effective strength; the new army, which wished to argue, was the largest.

On August 23, 1793, the mass levy was finally decreed.

If this operation had been rigorously adhered to, it may have saved the Republic from its own excesses. However, despite the eloquence of the decree, every thief and every schemer seemed to move into the loosely run Revolutionary administration. They continued to walk and to bloody the streets of the capital and the major cities under the name of the Revolutionary Army, protected by the leaders of the Reign of Terror. Thus, this great measure for the protection of the general public designed to produce 1,500,000 men resulted in only 400,000 ... and not even that many.

The decree said that young men would go into combat. Married men would forge weapons and transport supplies. Women would make tents and uniforms and would serve in the hospitals. Children would tear up old linens for bandages. The elderly would be carried through public places to inflame the hearts of the warriors. National houses would be converted into barracks and public places into workshops. Basement floors would be washed with a solution to remove the saltpeter. Saddle horses would be requisitioned to fill out the cavalry corps. Draught horses, excepting those used for farming, would pull cannon and munitions.

On February 21, 1793, six months earlier, it had been decided in principle to merge the old corps with the new, the standing army with the National Guard and the volunteers. This never occurred due to the serious concerns of the moment.

As the generals had their hands full with the enemy, they resisted this change with all their might. They believed the veterans would lose their good qualities upon contact with the volunteers. Conversely, the members of the Convention feared the volunteers would all too quickly be shaped by the exercise of discipline. Although officers of the nobility had been driven out by decree and wearing the white uniform had been prohibited, the old troops still raised fear in the hearts of the men of the Revolution.

Persecuted, hunted, not wishing to emmigrate, many gentlemen and officers hid themselves in the lowest ranks of the miltary hierarchy. They accepted service to the country in obscurity rather than fighting under a foreign flag. On the regimental rosters appear borrowed or altered names which disguise the secret patriotism of a group of brave men. A captain of the line named Senaux, reduced to this level by proscription, was taken into a demi-brigade as a non-commissioned officer. He later became the drum major of the 1st regiment of Grenadiers of the Imperial Guard and there acquired a deserved reputation for bravery and military style.

The report on the state of an army of 1793 will give a clear idea of the internal organization of all the armies of the Republic in this year and of the proportion of troops of the line and of volunteer corps which were represented.

ARMY OF THE EASTERN PYRENEES
September 1, 1793

Regiments of the Line—7th, 61st, 70th, 1st battalion of the 53rd, 1st battalion of the 79th; a battalion of combined grenadiers, 1st battalion of light infantry

Battalions of volunteers—3rd and 4th battalions of the Ariège; 4th, 5th, 6th, 7th and 9th of the Aube; 3rd of the Paris; 1st and 2nd of the Béziers; 2nd and 8th of the Upper Garonne; 2nd of the High Alps; 1st, 2nd, 3rd, 4th and 6th of the Maritime coast; 1st of Gers; 1st and 2nd battalions of the Chasseurs of Lot; 1st of Mont Blanc; 2nd and 4th of Gard; 1st and 2nd of Tarn; 3rd of Montpellier; 2nd and 4th of the Eastern Pyrenees; 1st and 2nd of the High Pyrenees.

Corps francs—Miquelets; Conscripts of Saint-Gaudens; Legion of Corbières; 1st battalion of the Chasseurs flanquers

---

On April 15, 1794, a little after the merger of the old and the new armies actually took place, a state official reported to the Convention on the total effective strength of the eleven armies which the Republic was maintaining (right).

The effective strengths of the corps used by the Army of the Center whose principal headquarters were in Paris, should be added to this figure of 794,334 men. Military depots and corps in training should also be added. Therefore, the Republic officially had 850 to 900 thousand men in active service. In fact, a more truthful count is obtained by subtracting a good quarter from the total.

Designation	Infantry	Cavalry	Artillery	Total
Army of the North	212,063	24,257	9,502	245,282
Army of the Ardennes	27,190	8,168	2,272	37,630
Army of the Moselle	82,267	16,562	4,494	103,323
Army of the Rhine	82,711	10,932	4,747	98,390
Army of the Alps	36,616	2,877	3,509	43,042
Army of Italy	58,292	550	1,780	60,622
Army of the Eastern Pyrenees	64,919	2,758	2,831	70,508
Army of the Western Pyrenees	46,217	2,110	2,455	50,782
Army of the West	16,576	1,936	4,007	22,519
Army of the Brest Coast	30,538	625	3,216	34,379
Army of the Cherbourg Coast	25,244	321	1,828	27,388
			Total	**794,334**

The soldiers of the Republic, poorly paid and badly fed, remained loyal only to their flag. They were very often influenced by revolutionary passions against the generals who were condemned to death on the slightest suspicion by the tribunals. Fighting on all fronts against the European Coalition, they had yet to fight the civil war in the Vendée. Although they could not foresee an end to their efforts, they were not discouraged. A decree of the Convention saying that they were worthy of their homeland was enough to satisfy their ambition.

This year was perhaps the one in which the French soldier's devotion was the most pure and selfless. It was the year of the combat of the ship *Vengeur*. It was also the year when Bonaparte began to worry the civilian powers. He had become general after the taking of Toulon in December 1793. The man who would so profoundly affect French military spirit was appointed by the Convention in 1794 only to be arrested and imprisoned in the fort at Antibes a few months later.

23rd demi-brigade (1796).

THE FIRST DEMI-BRIGADES

To escape the chaos just described, it was decided that the merger of the old corps with the new ones would be done in the following manner. Each regiment of the line, from first to last in the order of their numbers, would form the nucleus of two new corps. The first battalion would become a regiment with an uneven number and the second battalion a consecutive, even-numbered regiment. Two or three battalions of volunteers were attached to them. Those which came from the regiments of the line were called full brigades (*brigades de bataille*). Those forming with a light battalion took the name of light brigades (*brigades légères*).

Through a series of further changes, the infantry regiments still existing numbered 111. In addition there were 21 light battalions, 6 light legions of 2 battalions, and a fixed quantity of others not given numbers.

More than 800 battalions of volunteers were counted. In addition, there were requisitioned battalions and battalions formed from the mass levy. They all had different internal set-ups which became confused when they joined together. There were also the corps raised by men of enthusiasm or with special influence. These people found themselves of a rank more or less important, according to the number of men they had assembled under their command. A good number of these military travesties are born and die almost immediately. History attempts rather unsuccessfully to condemn them. They do however,

have their useful side since they mollify the wild and excessive elements of society. Even when they perform only a mediocre service, they do manage to whip up enthusiasm. What's wrong, for example, with a legion of the Midi or of Americans that is founded by and of foreigners, happy to tread the land of liberty? The citizen Saint-Georges who commanded such a legion proved to be a good servant of the Republic and of France as were also Commander Hercule and General Dumas. The Basque chasseurs, the Corsican chasseurs, the Miquelets of the Eastern Pyrenees and twenty other corps who operated all over had no other roots than these.

For various reasons arising from the disorder, a great number of demi-brigades were not organized. Remaining empty were the numbers 7, 8, 11, 15, 18, 30, 32, 37, 57, 58, 62, 63, 64, 77, 78, 81, 82, 88, 96, 98, 106, 115, 119, 120, 124, 125, 126, 133, 135, 136, 137, 151, 153, 155, 156, 158, 160, 167, 168, 187, 188, 189, 190, 191, 192, 195, 198, 210 and 212 of the line; and numbers 17, 24, 25, 26, 27, 28 and 31 of the light.

On the contrary, 15 brigades of the line were provisionally numbered 1 to 15; 24 others carried special names; plus the 200, 201, and 202 demi-brigades *bis* were formed successively from diverse elements.

In the light infantry, there was a 4th *bis*, a 14th *bis*, a 15th *bis*, a 16th *bis*, a 17th *bis*, an 18th *bis*, a 19th *bis*, a 20th *bis*, a 20th *ter*, and a 21st *bis*. (Note: *bis* and *ter* are equivalent to *a* and *b*, as in 20a, 20b)

The new demi-brigades also all had to be formed of three battalions of nine companies, one being of grenadiers and eight of fusiliers, along with a battery of six four-pound cannon.

This artillery division has a long and often interrupted history which will now be recounted so as to ensure it is told.

The law of May 7, 1794 (18th of Floréal, Year III) stripped the infantry battalions of one of every two cannon. Invariably this meant that each battalion would no longer march with more than one cannon instead of an entire battery section. Under these conditions, the cannon were no longer very useful to the infantry. The decree of May 2, 1802 (12th of Floréal, Year XI) did away with the cannon entirely.

The infantry, meanwhile, was sorry to see them go. On May 15, 1809, the Emperor ordered that two cannon of the 3 or 5 pound type taken from the Austrians would be attached to each regiment of Davout's, Masséna's and Oudinot's corps. These cannon were provided with 150 to 200 rounds. They were hitched up and tended by drivers and cannoneers assigned to the regiments and were protected at all costs by the ensigns. Usually the best officers and soldiers fought for the honor of belonging to a regimental artillery company. By 1812, however, these companies had disappeared.

With the creation of departmental legions in 1816, the idea of an artillery regiment was raised once again but was as quickly abandoned.

Demi-brigades de bataille, or full battle demi-brigades wore a double-breasted coat which had red facings and a white lining, a white waistcoat, and white pants with full leggings. The coat, waistcoat and pants of the light regiments was blue with white piping. These uniforms were very quickly worn out, perhaps moreso from misfortune than from victory. Anything and everything was employed to clothe a soldier: the flag, requisition canvas, and often even items made from captured enemy belongings.

The ragged condition of the Army of the Republic was such that on September 14, 1794 (28th of Floréal, Year III), the Convention decided to grant officers a complete new uniform and monthly compensation worth 8 pounds in silver — not in *assignats* (Republican notes) !!! In actuality, generally only the uniform materialized; even that was incomplete. The head of

Light infantry (1797).

the general staff of this well-known army remarked on July 15, 1796: "In two months, the Army of Sambre-et-Meuse was decreased by 6,000 men through desertion into the countryside, the result of deprivation of the troops and of lack of punishment for desertion."

Meanwhile, the Convention had disappeared. The Directorate succeeded it, a power undoubtedly less bold but equally devoid of any administrative standards. The organization of the early regiments had not yet been completed. Some volunteer and National Guard corps had been eliminated by the decree of February 21, 1793. A number of demi-brigades had not yet been formed while others had disappeared. Confusion rose to such a level that no one could make any order from the chaos. However, at the beginning of 1796, 238 existing demi-brigades were recognizable which could be classified as follows:

165 demi-brigades formed in 1793-1794 (151 full and 14 light);

73 demi-brigades formed later including 37 auxiliary (17 full and 20 light) and 36 provisional (15 full and 21 light, unnumbered).

In addition to these, a number of departmental battalions and various non-classified corps managed to maintain their independence. It is for this reason that the 1st Battalion of Nyons, the 10th Battalion of l'Ain, the 1st of Maine-et-Loire, the 8th Battalion of Saône-et-Loire, and the 5th Battalion of l'Herault are cited in the army which campaigned in Italy in 1796. This was the situation as of April 10, consequently, after the decree mentioned above. These battalions were reduced to three hundred men and even less. The auxiliary companies were sometimes attached to the demi-brigades or were independent. The tirailleur (skirmishers) battalions appeared among the auxiliary companies also and were evidence of the substantial irregularities in military affairs of the time. The remarkable notebooks of Captain Coignet, published by Lorédan-Larchey, show that, even in 1799, the auxiliary departmental battalions were still preparing batches of raw recruits for entry into a demi-brigade.

Meanwhile, on January 8, 1795 (18th of Nivôse, Year IV), the Directorate had reduced the number of full battle brigades (*brigades de bataille*) to 100 and the light demi-brigades (*legères*) to 30. Yet only ten days later, the number of demi-brigades of the line retained amounted to 110, due to another decree. It will be seen that increased order was exerted over this second formation. Without it, the complete differentiation which resulted after 1815 and again after 1871 could not have been achieved. The territorial estates-major exercised only nominal authority and the civil servants — who controlled everything — were short on aptitude.

The goal of this reorganization was to form defined cadres and to completely eliminate payment to all corps whose existence was not legally recognized.

Thus, there was no reason to do away with one or another of the military units such as the demi-brigades. Moreover, the numbering method was out of order and had even been duplicated. There was a more important reason for not disrupting

Army of Sambre-et-Meuse (1795).

the army, however. It had been decided that the new demi-brigades would be formed in each of the seven armies, in place and by a lottery. They would use whatever men were available to them and the specially numbered troops would also be drawn by chance in each of the armies, according to the following order (below):

Although this time the merger was organized by the army, in place, it did not happen immediately in the first three armies. It was almost completed within a year in the second three armies. For the Army of the Interior, however, the process dragged on until 1799.

Evidently, this reorganization proved useful in terms of discipline. The rules for promotion began to be established and followed. However, distribution of provisions and of clothing was no smoother than before. General Bonaparte's proclamation (March 1796) to the Army of Italy, where he had just taken command, offers proof of the problems involved.

"Soldiers!," he said, "you are naked, badly fed. We owe you so much, but we have nothing to give you. Your patience and the courage which you show are admirable, but these bring you no glory. I come to lead you into the most fertile plains of the world. You will have in your power wealthy lands, great cities. And there you will have riches, honor and glory. Soldiers of Italy! Do you lack courage?"

> **Army of the North** —12 demi-brigades of the line and 2 light (numbers 1, 8, 15, 22, 29, 36, 42, 48, 54, 60, 66, 72nd of the line; 1st and 8th light).
>
> **Army of the Sambre-et-Meuse** —21 demi-brigades of the line and 5 light (numbers 2, 9, 16, 23, 30, 37, 43, 49, 55, 61, 67, 73, 78, 83, 86, 92, 96, 99, 102, 105, 108th of the line: numbers 2, 9, 15, 20, 25th light).
>
> **Army of the Rhine and Moselle** —21 demi-brigades of the line and 5 light (numbers 3, 10, 17, 24, 31, 38, 44, 50, 56, 62, 68, 74, 79, 84, 89, 93, 97, 100, 103, 106 and 109th of the line; numbers 3, 10, 16, 21, 26th light).
>
> **Army of Italy** —14 demi-brigades of the line and 6 light (numbers 4, 11, 18, 25, 32, 39, 45, 51, 57, 63, 69, 75, 80, 85th of the line; numbers 4, 11, 17, 22, 27, 29th light).
>
> **Army of the Alps** —5 demi-brigades of the line and 4 light (numbers 5, 12, 19, 26, 33rd of the line; numbers 5, 12, 18 and 23rd light).
>
> **Army of the Ocean Coasts** —16 demi-brigades of the line and 6 light (numbers 6, 13, 20, 27, 34, 40, 46, 52, 58, 64, 70, 76, 81, 86, 90, 94th of the line; numbers 6, 13, 19, 24, 28, 30th light).
>
> **Army of the Interior** —21 demi-brigades of the line and 2 light (numbers 7, 14, 21, 28, 35, 41, 47, 53, 59, 65, 71, 77, 82, 87, 91, 95, 98, 101, 104, 107 and 110th of the line; 7 and 14th light).

In fact, this Army of Italy lacked everything as was also the case with the Army of Sambre-et-Meuse. There was no jealousy. Misery was equal in all the armies, but discontent mounted higher in the Army of Italy than anywhere. Counter-revolution was smoldering within its ranks as was evidenced by demonstrations as well as by royalist songs. Conspicuous within its ranks was a company of the *Dauphin*, a type of military club organized in the image of the *Clichiens* of Paris.

Bonaparte and the victory he brought with him changed everything in a matter of fifteen days. On April 11th, he beat the Austrians at Montenotte and again on the 14th at Millesimo. His men took cities and magazines from the enemy, resupplied, and re-outfitted. They decked themselves out and there were no questions of politics or of counter-revolution.

Unfortunately, few generals could equal Bonaparte in seeing things from the soldier's point of view from the start. The Directorate was very harsh when it came to money, as taxation wasn't faring well in France. It often required the generals- in-chief to put pressure on the local citizenry on whom they and their armies depended. They were supposed to wring significant payments from the defeated populace and send it on to Paris. It's all well and good to fight without pay for the glory of France and the triumph of the Republic. However, to fight to send money to the Directorate and the Directors and, on top of all that, to be deprived of everything went beyond the patriotism of many a soldier. This same Army of Italy, so devoted to Bonaparte in 1796, revolted against Masséna in Rome in 1798 and against Gouvion-Saint-Cyr in 1799 at Genoa. These revolts were always caused by the poor pay, lack of supplies, and the tributes raised in foreign countries in the name and for the profit of the Directors. The generals-in-chief often shared in the spoils. The scandalous fortunes they amassed from 1796 to 1811 came solely from plundering and pillage. The revolts were promptly quieted, especially the second one. However, they aptly characterized the standard, physical state of the army.

Toward its end, the Directorate (law of the 19th of Fructidor, Year VI or September 6, 1797) established a conscription which required all young men from 21 to 25 years of age to join the military service. However, it called only those whom the country needed. This was the point of departure, the origins of the system for regular recruitment which Napoleon the First would

In Italy (1796).

Army of Italy (1796).

abuse and which the Restoration would promise to abolish. It is a system which, despite its egalitarian tyranny, remains the safeguard of the country, its honor, and its best law when administered wisely.

The competent organization of provisions dates from the time of General Bonaparte. It was the cause of his immediate military popularity. At the time of his departure for Egypt, it was an honor amongst officers to be admitted into his army. One never knew exactly where he was headed; he was going with Bonaparte and that was good enough. Defeat would come later, implacable and terrible, however, disillusionment would not follow in its footsteps. The Egyptian veterans who returned to France after the evacuation quickly pardoned their old general for their sufferings which had conferred upon them eternal glory.

The 6th, 7th, 17th, 19th, 61st, 68th, and 79th demi-brigades and the 2nd and 21st light demi-brigades who had all distinguished themselves before on the fields of battle of the Republic were joined with the glorious 2nd, 5th, 18th, 32nd, 69th, 75th, and 85th demi-brigades and the 4th and 22nd light demi-brigades who had participated in the first campaign of Italy with Bonaparte.

CONSULATE AND EMPIRE

◆

This is the culminating point of the French infantry's history. France will probably never again see the likes of those magnificent divisions formed at the camp of Boulogne. They maneuvered "as one man" equally as well on the field of battle as in the Tuileries court. Although the formation of the Imperial Guard, the wars, and the far-flung expeditions (Santo-Domingo) had already stripped the ranks of many brave men, the regiments of the camp of Boulogne were almost all elite regiments. They all carried a victorious battle name under their regimental numbers and never proved an embarrassment to Napoleon when he awarded them an eagle. "In the future be as you were on such a day!" he said, and that was enough to kindle their spirits. The spirit of the army would change under the influence and the will of the great captain. In the future, the soldiers would not march to the call of the country. Rather they would seek favor in the eyes of the master when they went into combat. The Roman phrase: "Such a corps well serves the country," would be succeeded by these words which electrified an entire army when they were spoken by the Emperor: "Soldiers, I am pleased with you!"

An order of the First Consul dating from the 1st of Vendemiaire, Year XII (September 24, 1803) did away with the name of demi-brigade and established that of the regiment. This was valid for both the infantry of the line and for the light infantry. In addition, it fixed the number of regiments of the line at 90 (19 with 4 battalions and 71 with 3) and the number of regiments of light infantry at 27 (3 with 4 battalions and 24 with 3).

The 90 regiments of infantry, numbered from 1 to 112, and of light infantry regiments, from 1 to 31, left vacant the numbers of the demi-brigades which had not formed, were disbanded or were previously destroyed. The numbers retained corresponded to those of the demi-brigades from which they were composed and which took in the cadres and the effectives of the last numbers which had disappeared.

Numbers remaining vacant in 1803: Line Infantry - 31, 38, 41, 49, 71, 73, 74, 77, 78, 80, 83, 87, 89, 90, 91, 97, 98, 99, 104, 107, 109, and 110. Light infantry - 11, 19, 26, 29, 30.

One notices amongst these numbers those of 71, 74, 77, 89, 98, 107, and 110 of the line infantry, and of the 11th and 19th light infantry. These regiments, who were almost destroyed at Santo Domingo, saw their miserable remnants made prisoner at Morlaix just as they were to return to France.

These organizations had been developed through much trial and error. Napoleon wanted to bring the army up to a standard which he so brillantly described in the *Memorial of Saint-Helene* but which he never achieved. He himself had violated this standard in order to satisfy his generals' and

Infantry of the line. End of a day's march. Grand maneuvers (1885).

Infantry of the line, office of sergeant-major (1885).

republican soldiers' eccentric or fleeting tastes for the corps. Hadn't he organized the camel regiment in Egypt, a regiment composed of foot soldiers but classifed as a gendarmerie or police force? Typical of these short-lived organizations was the reserve volunteer legion created in Dijon by order of the consuls on the 17th of Nivôse, Year VIII (January 6, 1799). It comprised two battalions of infantry dressed as for the line and two squadrons of hussars in light yellow pelisses, thus called "the Canaries." It participated in the campaign of the Army of the Grisons and was disbanded in Year X (1801). It was commanded by Colonel Labarbée and was recruited from amongst the young well-to-do. Also noteworthy were the foot hussars, two battalions created by decree on the 13th of Floréal, Year XII (May 2, 1803). They wore pants and jackets of wolf grey with collar; cuff facings and braids of madder (madeira); blue waistcoat; leather shoe gaiters; and the trappings of a foot soldier. They were never engaged outside the reserve army.

Under the Republic as under the Consulate, France welcomed foreign troops. Early on, royal foreign regiments were considered as French regiments. Next the foreigners were called patriots and revolutionaries from the French ranks. The Italian Legion, the Polish Legion, etc., dated from the earliest days of the Republic.

At first the French service did not seem to gain much benefit from these auxiliary troops. The Greek Legion and the Copt Legion were organized in Egypt. In September 1801, after being decimated, they had to follow the remnants of the French army brought back to France. The 3rd Helvetic demi-brigade, the German battalions, the 1st Piemontese Legion, and the 113th and the 114th demi-brigades of the line, which were entirely Polish, added to the list of corps lost in the disgraceful expedition of Santo Domingo. However, this did not stop the annexation of troops from conquered countries.

If the history of the military organization under the Republic is difficult to write, that of the imperial armies is hardly less so. No archivist of the Ministry of War has been tempted by this admirable but arduous task. Moreover, no knowledgeable eye has been permitted to view certain documents which belong to the people of this country but which an incomprehensible and proud bureaucracy and military has confiscated until now. In order to shed a bit of light on this subject, one needs first to clearly establish the chronology of the organization of regular regiments. This should be done in numerical order subsequent to the decree of 1803 and prior to 1815.

From 1803 to 1808, the Imperial Army was magnificent. It was at the camp of Boulogne that Napoleon's greatest military idea was executed. This was an idea that the Prussians borrowed from him: the organization of the Grande Armée in corps, divisions and brigades, complete with general staffs and their equipment, always ready to march.

The Emperor created companies of voltigeurs. He also assembled that admirable division of grenadiers at Boulogne. The grenadiers performed wonders under Oudinot and rendered even the Guard jealous.

The victories from 1805 to 1810 were both easy and decisive. France had the best army which had ever existed in Europe up until that time, an army which would be swallowed up in Russia in the campaign of 1812 and which it will no longer be

REGIMENTS CREATED UNDER THE EMPIRE

Date of creation	Number	Elements entered into the formation
LINE REGIMENTS		
May 29, 1806	113th	Foot troops of the Grand Duchy of Tuscany.
July 7, 1808	114th	1st Provisional Regiment of the Army of Spain.
"	115th	3rd Provisional Regiment of the Army of Spain.
"	116th	5th Provisional Regiment of the Army of Spain.
"	117th	9th Provisional Regiment of the Army of Spain.
"	118th	11th Provisional Regiment of the Army of Spain.
"	119th	13th Provisional Regiment of the Army of Spain.
"	120th	17th Provisional Regiment of the Army of Spain.
January 1, 1809	121st	3rd, 4th and 5th Reserve Legions.
"	122nd	1st and 2nd Reserve Legions.
September 1810	123rd	2nd Dutch Regiment and the 2nd battalion of the 6th Dutch Regiment.
"	124th	3rd Dutch Regiment and the 1st battalion of the 7th Dutch Regiment.
"	125th	4th Dutch Regiment and the 2nd battalion of the 7th Dutch Regiment.
"	126th	5th Dutch Regiment and the 1st battalion of the 8th Dutch Regiment.
February 3, 1811	127th	Troops of the Hanovarian Legion.
"	128th	Troops of the Hanovarian Legion.
"	129th	Troops of the Hanovarian Legion.
March 3, 1811	130th	1st, 3rd and 6th auxiliary battalions of the Army of Spain.
"	131st	Walcheren Regiment, created in 1810.
"	132nd	Regiment l'Île-de-Ré, created in 1810.
"	133rd	2nd Mediterranean Regiment, created in 1810.
January 6, 1813	134th	1st Regiment of the Guard de Paris.
January 12, 1813	135th to 156th	Each with 4 cohorts of the National Guard.
LIGHT REGIMENTS		
March 29, 1808	32nd	Foot troops of the Grand Duchy of Tuscany.
September 1808	33rd	Provisional troops of the Army of Spain; dissolved in 1809; reformed in 1810 with Dutch troops.
March 9, 1811	34th	2nd, 4th, 5th and 7th auxiliary battalions of the Army of Spain.
March 9, 1812	35th	1st Mediterranean Regiment, created in 1811.
March 9, 1812	36th	Regiment Belle-Isle, created in 1810.
February 7, 1812	37th	Detachments taken from the lowest departmental companies.
REGIMENTS OF THE LINE AND LIGHT CREATED UNDER VACANT NUMBERS		
December 9, 1813	104th	Line Battalions of the 52nd, 67th and 101st.
January 1, 1814	107th	Line Battalions of the 6th, 10th, 20th and 102nd.
January 1, 1811	11th Light	Diverse elements.
January 1, 1814	19th Light	Diverse elements.
January 1, 1812	20th Light	Diverse elements.

Carabinier, light infantry (1806).

Drummer, infantry of the line (1806).

Infantry of the line (1806).

possible to reorganize on the same footing. The standardization of the uniform also dates back to 1804. For a while, the Emperor thought about returning to the white uniform of the infantry (1806). His concern was not born of caprice but was closely tied to the projected modification of the flags and the adoption of the Emperor's green livery for the drummers and the trumpeters. As the fortune-blessed General of the Republic, the Soldier of Arcole, the Hero of the Pyramids, did he want to erase from the minds of the people and the army the revolutionary memory of the demi-brigades? This well may have been, but it should also be pointed out that of all the colors, white was the least easily soiled and the one which least affected the wool of the uniform.

In any event, blue prevailed (1807). The shako, which was at first reserved for the voltigeurs, was given to the companies of the center, then to those of the grenadiers. The *capote* or greatcoat was used in general by the entire army.

Napoleon maintained theories regarding the uniform which are useful to examine. He maintained that the height of the plume at 200 meters modified the appearance of a soldier and could briefly lead the enemy shot astray. He believed in the influence of handsome uniforms on the national consciousness. He also believed, although no one would admit to it today, in giving a stylish uniform to people who otherwise could not have worn one and who were truly destined to wear it for a long time.

Little by little, as soon as new organizations developed, Napoleon was forced by necessity to return to these ideas. Even in the Guard, the uniform became simpler. The waistcoat disappeared from the line. The neckline changed from V-line to round, the coattails decreased in width and length, and breeches and high leggings were replaced by pants. But the *capote*, that ample greatcoat buttoned on the right under which one could wear a jacket, became the best liked article of clothing amongst recruits and veterans alike.

At the very end would come the moment when *capotes* were not available to give to the soldiers. We will see the Bretons at Fère-Champenoise, barely enlisted and led by the police of their villages, being killed in their peasant garb for lack of uniforms. Already in Egypt and later in Portugal, French soldiers had to make uniforms from local materials, lacking cloth from their own country. There was a decree by Kléber regulating use of light pink cloth, jonquil yellow and light green. In Portugal, the entire infantry received pants in chestnut-colored cloth. As for the rest, the French on the whole made use of arms and equipment which they took from the enemy during the ten years of continual warfare.

Returning to the soldiers of the Grande Armée, it will quickly be shown how the magnificent military structure was petered away in less than seven years between 1805 and 1812. Napoleon patiently brought it back under the Consulate and during the first year of the Empire. The numbers of the regiments who fought at Austerlitz are listed below.

The Emperor, wishing to dispose of the reserves previously organized, envisioned the creation of five legions for border defense (decree of March 20). Anxiety over being prepared with military resources showed through in every line of the decree. These five legions were formed at Lille, Metz, Rennes, Versailles and Grenoble. At first each had 6 battalions of 8 companies with 160 men, then a company of 120 men served by 8 cannon. These battalions were endlessly repeated. Thus, there was a permanent force of 39,000 men taken in the remainder of the classes already named, and of 40 cannon. The organization of this group was given to Generals Colaud, Sainte-Suzanne, Demont, Laboissière and Valence.

The uniform was that of the infantry so that when the troops were incorporated into the regiment later, it was at no extra cost.

Number	Colonel	Killed	Wounded
3rd Line	Schobert	56	376
4th Line	Bigarré	18	193
8th Line	Autié	—	2
14th Line	Mazas	22	209
17th Line	Couroux	25	75
18th Line	Ravier	30	102
28th Line	Edighoffen	9	75
30th Line	Walter	23	338
33rd Line	Saint Remond	17	300
34th Line	Dumoutier	19	178
36th Line	Houdart-Lamotte	30	373
40th Line	Legendre	24	255
43rd Line	Viviès	41	421
45th Line	Barrié	1	8
46th Line	Latrille	20	288
48th Line	Barbenégre	17	125
51st Line	Bonnet	15	49
54th Line	Philippon	—	1

Number	Colonel	Killed	Wounded
55th Line	Ledru	44	306
57th Line	Rey	6	75
61st Line	Nicolas	9	22
64th Line	Nérin	15	73
75th Line	Lhuillier	15	82
88th Line	Curial	46	122
94th Line	Razout	11	101
95th Line	Pecheux	2	27
103rd Line	Higonnet	148	316
113th Line	Gay	10	121
13th Light	Castex	25	141
15th Light	Desailly	31	142
17th Light	Vedel	9	30
24th Light	Pourailly	126	364
26th Light	Pouget	54	262
27th Light	Chanotet	4	57
Corsican Chasseurs	Ornano	—	57
Pô Tirailleurs	Hulot	29	154

Sapper, infantry of the line (1806).

When the first three battalions of each legion were formed, General Dupont led them into Spain where most were made prisoners at Baylen. They were immediately replaced in Spain by the latter battalions.

Little by little, the Emperor grew used to these precautionary efforts. Moreover, his correspondence shows that in 1806, he had already ordered more legions with much less publicity.

By now all regiments of the infantry of the line or light infantry had been uniformly rounded out at four battalions. The fourth battalions, which were drawn from the depot, were most often used to form provisional regiments. However, in Marshal Davout's corps in March 1809, all the fourth battalions from its three divisions formed a new unit of three brigades, each with 2 provisional regiments. These would reinforce the corps' total effective strength.

When the fourth battalions proved insufficient, fifths were created.

It is fairly interesting to understand how Napoleon resupplied his regiments with men during a campaign. When one or more battles weakened the *battalions de guerre* (full war battalions), they were replaced by one or two which remained with the army. Meanwhile, the cadres of officers and non-commissioned officers of the others were sent to the depot. They returned soon thereafter as a full battle complement to reassume their places in active service. Then it was the other battalions' turn to go to France for a period of recuperation. This occurred up until the campaign of 1812 when the procedure was changed. *Régiments de marche* were formed from detachments drawn from the depots. Once they got to the army, these *régiments de marche* — which were quite different from the provisional regiments — turned over the soldiers they had brought with them to the regiments to which they had been assigned. The underlying principle of this system was that the detachments had to always be battle-ready and formed in divisions once they passed the border.

Despite his clear, decisive genius, the Emperor was often mistaken about the value of these troops. They were improvised from the dregs, the lowest levels of the classes previously called by conscription, or from amnestied deserters. He also thought he could conceal from the rest of Europe the actual state of his army through his irregular numbering system as well as through the creation of new corps. With regard to the former, the administration was not so constrained as it is today by inflexible rules. Napoleon added a sixth and even a seventh battalion after the fifth battalion. The same numbered regiment appeared in the events taking place in both Spain and in Russia. Meanwhile a battalion was detached to Upper Italy or to Holland.

Infantry of the line, company of grenadiers (1812).

There are not yet enough documents available to clearly establish the statistical chronology of the minor formations of the Empire. There is one, however, which we have only been able to trace in the correspondance of the Emperor (October 7, 1809) and which is particularly striking. At Schoenbrunn, the Emperor gave Clarke the order to form a *régiment de marche e* with the depots of the 34th, 114th, 115th, 116th, 117th, 118th, 119th, and 120th of the line. "This regiment," he said," will remain together at Bayonne until it is well outfitted, well disciplined

Infantry of the line (1813).

and at a strength of 4,000 men." Note that these depots, with the exception of the first - the 34th - belonged exclusively to the regiments formed in 1808 from legions sent to Spain. What kind of substance, what esprit de corps could such troops have had?

One need look no further than this superficial organization to discover the reason for the enormous consumption of men by the Empire from 1808 until 1813.

The Senate voted for an army of 1,716,000 men from which a tenth at least must be subtracted as deserters. In fact, desertion was so prevalent that at the Ministry of War, the Division of Military Justice took the title of the Division of Military Justice and of Desertion under the direction of Tabarie, inspector of reviews.

The Empire never had more than a million French in active service. Since it never regularly discharged a soldier, the figures of men enrolled vis-a-vis men actually in hand need to be adjusted. The difference is largely due to the manner in which those fine regiments which had gained so much glory from 1806 to 1811 fell apart in 1812.

In his interesting *Military Memoirs*, the Duke of Fezensac counted the losses of the 4th Regiment of the line during the campaign of Russia. This regiment had crossed the Rhine with 2,150 men and took in thereafter 850 more. Two hundred of them returned to France and 100 remained behind as prisoners. Losses: 2,700 men. Of 109 officers who left with the regiment or who were promoted during the campaign, 40 died, 20 remained behind as prisoners. and 49 returned, of whom 35 were wounded. The 18th Regiment, commanded by Pelleport, fared even more badly. Of 4,000 men, barely 300 returned and 81 officers were killed, lost or imprisoned. The 4th and 18th Regiments formed Joubert's brigade.

Let's multiply this loss by the number of regiments, since all were pretty much equally affected. We then arrive at the secret of the Empire. Of six hundred thousand men utilized by the Grande Armee, many were too young to join the Russian campaign.

It is obvious that the brave men who brought back to France the eagles of the 4th and 18th Regiments of the line had participated in the Battle of Austerlitz and were soldiers capable of withstanding anything.

In the *History of the 82nd Regiment of the Line* (formerly the 7th Light Regiment or legère), it can be seen that the remains of the 1st Corps, assembled at Thorn in December 1812, were composed of 996 officers and of 2,362 non-commissioned officers and soldiers. Of these, 729 officers and 1,807 soldiers were in fighting condition. Eight months before, this magnificent corps consisted of 5 divisions and was commanded by the Marshal, Prince of Eckmuhl. For division commanders it had Morand, Friant, Gudin, Dessaix, Compans and Girardin and included within its ranks 83,108 men.

The list to the right gives the regiments of the French infantry which suffered enormous losses in 1812.

The 5th, 6th, 7th, 8th, and 10th Corps, commanded by Prince Poniatowski, Marshal Gouvion-Saint-Cyr, General Reynier, the Duke of Abrantes and the Duke of Tarente, composing the 7th Division, General Grandjean; 16th Division, General Zaionsheck; 17th Division, General Dembrowski; 18th Division, General Kaminiecki; 19th Division, General Deroy; 20th Division, General de Wrede; 21st Division, General Lecocq; 22nd Division, General Funck; 23rd Division, General Tharreau; 24th Division, General d'Ochs; 27th Division, General d'Yorck, being solely composed of foreign troops.

Thus, fifty regiments of French infantry were almost annihilated in less than eight months. On January 15, 1813, the Russian government admitted to having burned 243,712 corpses and 123,362 horses at the beginning of the retreat from Russia (*Gazette de Vienne* from November 21, 1813). The state of effective strength

Colonel, infantry of the line (1812).

1st CORPS Prince of Eckmuhl	1st Division -	Morand: 13th Light; 17th and 30th Line
	2nd Division -	Friant: 15th Light; 33rd and 48th Line
	3rd Division -	Gudin: 7th Light; 12th, 21st and 127th Line
	4th Division -	Dessaix: 33rd Light; 85th and 108th Line
	5th Division -	Compans: 25th, 57th, 61st and 111th Line
2nd CORPS Duke of Reggio	6th Division -	Legrand: 26th Light; 56th, 19th and 128th Line
	8th Division -	Verdier: 11th Light; 2nd, 37th and 124th Line
	9th Division -	Merle: 123rd Line
3rd CORPS Duke of Elchingen	10th Division -	Ledru: 24th Light; 46th, 72nd and 129th Line
	11th Division -	Razout: 4th, 18th and 93rd Line
	25th Division -	Marchand: (Foreigners)
4th CORPS Prince Eugene	13th Division -	Delzons: 8th Light; 84th, 92nd and 106th Line
	14th Division -	Broussier: 18th Light; 9th, 35th and 53rd Line
	15th Division -	Pino: (Foreigners)
9th CORPS Duke of Belluno	12th Division -	Partonneaux: Regiments formed with battalions of the 10th and 29th Light, 36, 44, 51, 55, 125 and 126th Line
	26th Division -	Daendels: Foreigners
	28th Division -	Girard: Foreigners
11th CORPS Duke of Castiglione	30th Division -	Hendelet: Regiments formed with battalions of the 2nd, 4th, 6th, 8th, 16th, 17th, 18th, 21st, 28th Light; 14th and 28th Line
	31st Division -	Lagrange: 27th Light; 63rd Line
	32nd Division -	Durutte: French regiments Rhé, de Walcheren, Belle-Isle and Mediterranean.
	34th Division -	Morand: 3rd and 29th Line

Grenadiers of the Polish legions (1812).

at the departure of the army on March 1, 1812 was cited as being 680,000 men, drawing rations and 176,850 horses.

Therefore, reconstruction of the infantry after the Russian campaign was not a simple matter. Despite some theories, one cannot just strike the earth and expect legions, armed and ready for battle, to spring forth. Napoleon's correspondence bears witness to the difficulties which he had to surmount. The cadres, especially those of the officers, were low in manpower. Masses of young recruits whose numbers were called before they were of age now had to be trained. There was a shortage of weapons, equipment, and clothing which could not be assembled on the spur of the moment. Without a doubt, Napoleon placed too much confidence in his good luck. His great military patriotism didn't matter. He wanted to return victory to France. If he did not obtain it clearly or decisively through sacrifice, he at least delayed the invasion of the country by one year. The entire continent of Europe would have to join together in order to triumph over him. The glory that this union won did not diminish that of our brave if green soldiers fighting against all the veterans of the great powers, against their enemies of twenty years and against their former friends. Treason and desertion was experienced in the numerous foreign troops and consequently in our own ranks.

Napoleon used everything he had. He made a regiment of the line out of a regiment of the *garde municipale de Paris* (Municipal Guard of Paris) which had been compromised in Malet's conspiracy. From the troops of the original *garde nationale* (National Guard) assembled in 1812, he formed 22 regiments. He moved the four artillery regiments of the Navy into the infantry divisions. Finally, despite numerous desertions as mentioned above, he called upon a great number of foreigners to fight under the French flag.

The gathering of the Grande Armée of 1813 has been compared incorrectly in two well-known books to the activity of 1792 and 1793. In fact, these two great events had nothing to do with each other. At the beginning of the Revolution, France was overflowing with illusions and especially with blood despite the many examples of cowardice or of indifference. With equal abandon, she lavished blood on the field of battle, in riots, and on the scaffolding of the guillotine. It was a time of major mistakes in the name of patriotism and of heroic dedication. In 1813, on the other hand, France was exhausted. She gave Napoleon what little strength she had left without conviction and even with defiance. For his part, Napoleon, the great manipulator of men, no longer distinguished between French and foreign soldiers. The regiments were now no more than pawns for him. He played them all with equal cold-bloodedness. At any rate, weren't these foreigners whom he had exploited through the right of winner-takes-all also his subjects? Why would even not they love him? Hadn't he been for a long time the master and the idol of the French whom he had enslaved with his laws?

The following table gives the statistical condition of the Grande Armée of 1813 in terms of nationalities and kinds of regiments.

FRENCH

Regiments of 6 battalions—One: 2nd Marine.
Regiments of 5 battalions—Two: 13th Line; 1st Marine.
Regiments of 4 battalions—Twenty-nine: 3, 12, 17, 18, 19, 21, 23, 25, 30, 33, 37, 48, 51, 56, 57, 61, 72, 85, 108, 111, 112, 113th Line; 7, 13, 15, 22, 24, 26, 37th Light.
Regiments of 3 battalions—Thirty-four: 2, 4, 6, 14, 46, 93, 100, 101, 131, 132, 135, 136, 138, 139, 140, 141, 142, 144, 145, 146, 147, 148, 149, 150, 151, 152, 153, 154, 155, 156, 157th Line; 11th Light; 3rd and 4th Marine.
Regiments of 2 battalions—Thirty-two: 7, 10, 15, 36, 44, 45, 50, 51, 52, 55, 64, 67, 70, 76, 96, 103, 105, 121, 133, 134th Line; 3, 8, 9, 18, 23, 27, 29, 32, 33, 35 and 36th Light.
Detached battalions—Seven: 42nd, 60th and 2 battalions of the 65th Line; 1st, 6th and 29th Light.
Regiments and provisional demi-brigades with or without numbers—Thirty formed with 2 battalions and three with three battalions detached from regiments of the line or light.
This gives a total of 374 French battalions.

FOREIGNERS

Polish—7 regiments of infantry of 2 battalions(the 1, 2, 8, 12, 14, 15 and 16th). - 14 battalions.
Danish—Battalion of the Schleswig Chasseurs—Regiment of Tirailleurs of Holstein, 2 battalions—Regiment of the Queen, 1 battalion—Regiment of Oldenberg, 4 battalions—Regiments de Fionie, 1 battalion—Regiment of Holstein, 2 battalions—Regiment of Schleswig, 2 battalions—13 battalions.
Baden—1st and 3rd Regiments of 2 battalions—4 battalions.
Bavarian—2 battalions of light infantry(the 3, 4, 5, 7, 8, 9, 10 and 15th battalions of line infantry). - 10 battalions.
Hessian—Hessian Guard—Guard Fusiliers—2nd Infantry Regiment—4 battalions.
Ilalians—1, 2, 6, 7th Regiments of the Line of 2 battalions; 2nd Light of 2 battalions, 5th Line of 4 battalions; 1st Light of 3 battalions—17 battalions.
Neapolitan—Elite Regiment, 1st Battalion—4th Light, 2 battalions—3 battalions.
Wurtemberger—3 line regiments of 2 battalions; 2 battalions of light infantry—8 battalions.
Spanish—Regiment Joseph Napoleon—1 battalion.
Saxon—1 battalion of the Guard Grenadiers; 2 battalions of combined grenadiers; 17 infantry battalions—20 battalions.
Westphalian—Guard Fusiliers, 2 battalions and 2 battalions of the 4th and 8th Light Regiments—4 battalions.
This gives a total of 99 foreign battalions.

This huge army, for the most part taken from the cavalry and even moreso from the artillery, did not include more than 360,000 men. The Emperor saw that the number and quality of his foot soldiers was considerably reduced. The majority of those available were recruits recently enlisted, so he wanted to reassure them with cannon. He asked his arsenals to fully arm the artillery batteries; he never had enough of them. We will see later how his contemporaries judged the efforts he made for the Campaign of 1813 when the artillery was involved. It is obvious that throughout this year a decisive victory was not won and that the day after each battle the French were forced to withdraw. These negative results may be attributed as much to the vast expanse of the front of operations as to the troops' lack of soundness. The decline of the French infantry was at the same time the decline of French glory.

To the foreign troops listed on the previous page should be added 11,500 men of the same type who remained in cantonments in either French or Spanish Midi.

A decree on November 25, 1813 mustered out all these foreign troops but it was much too late. Thus, an unusual event was witnessed: the corps which one day were considered comparable to the French troops in terms of honors and privileges were the next day disarmed and held prisoners of war. Weapons were in great demand; therefore, wouldn't it be better to entrust those they could get their hands on to the French?

List of troops mustered out: 1st Foreign Regiment (Prussian), the Regiment of Issembourg, the Regiment of Illyria, the Croatian regiments, the Regiment Joseph-Napoleon, the Spanish Royal Guard, the Royal Foreigners (royalétranger), the Regiment of Castille, the Portugese troops, Westphalians, those of Baden, of Wurzburg, of Frankfurt and of Nassau.

For some time, conscription had filled our regiments with anti-French recruits. As long as Fortune smiled upon Napoleon, the citizens of the annexed departments submitted to military service. But as soon as the first reversals pointed to the day of reckoning and then Napoleon's fall, not only did the allied troops commit treason but also the regiments in which orders to join the service had introduced too many men from annexed regions.

Thus, in 1814, the French army found itself oddly reduced in size. Nonetheless, the soldiers who did appear in the ranks fought like heros. After a few weeks, the army once again became France as it was comprised of only the brave French and some Poles who remained faithful to the great man in bad times as well as in good. This admirable campaign of 1814 wherein the Emperor recaptured the genius and energy of his youth could not however be victorious. A handful of heros faced all of Europe to whom they themselves had taught the art of fighting and conquering over the past twenty years. All the social classes were mixed as though in a crucible in this great army. Soon it will be no more than a glorious memory, but this memory will never die.

The French nation could renounce in an instant the benefits from the first, great revolution. However, she will never forget that under the Republican colors, under the imperial eagle, deserving men of courage and intelligence were raised to the highest levels of society. Simple soldiers became marshals and kings. Even the Emperor, that great Emperor, began as nothing more than a low ranking officer. Democracy is maintained when access to the highest ranks is available to all. There will be those who try to prevent this. However, it will be reestablished, willingly or unwillingly, on the day the French soldier, who has become an equal citizen by right and by glory, must again face the enemy.

Infantry of the line, review (1814).

FIRST RESTORATION AND THE ONE HUNDRED DAYS

Upon their return to France, the Bourbons were not initially hostile toward the Imperial Army. In a very gentlemanly and French manner, the princes exhibited great respect for the famous leaders who had guided them on the battlefield of Europe. Even the new tradition of regiments was, in part, respected. Only the cadres were reduced to proportions more in keeping with the peaceful state which was underway. The number of regiments of infantry of the line was set at 90 while that of the light regiments was 15. The regiments were numbered from 1 to 90 and from 1 to 15 in the two armies, keeping to their traditional order and filling in the missing numbers. The regiments which had been mustered out provided the staffs and the soldiers to those retained.

At the end of the Empire, Numbers 31, 38, 41, 49, 68, 71, 73, 74, 77, 78, 80, 83, 87, 89, 90, 91, 97, 98, 99, 109, and 110 of the infantry of the line were vacant. Therefore, to complete the 90 regiments of the First Restoration, one had to go as far as number 111. The disbanded regiments numbering 112 to 156 were turned into the remaining corps as were the entire Young Guard. The first ten regiments of infantry of the line received the names of le Roi (the King), la Reine (the Queen), le Dauphin (the heir apparent), Monsieur (relative of the King), Angoulême, Berri, Orleans, Conde, Bourbon, and Colonel-Général.

Since no number was missing in the first fifteen regiments of light infantry of the 1st Empire, their order did not need to be modified. Numbers 16 and 37 were assigned to the fifteen others. The first seven took the names of: le Roi (the King), la Reine (the Queen), le Dauphin (the heir apparent), le Monsieur (a relative of the King), Angoulême, Berri, and the Colonel-Général.

This reorganization came to an end when the Emperor landed, having come from the island of Elba. On the 30th of April the regiments again took their former numbers as well as the tricolored cockade, as was established in a decree of the same date. Nothing new was created in the line. However, in the lists of 1815, some light infantry regiments appear which had been withdrawn in 1814. They probably belonged to armies which had been belatedly repatriated, such as that of Hamburg, and which the Emperor used since he found what remained of them more or less prepared.

The soldiers on leave were called up again, the *garde nationale* was mobilized. As in 1792, normal and compulsory retirees showed a great deal of enthusiasm. Those historians who are least favorable to Napoleon estimate that 25,000 men of this type returned to active service. In all the regiments, a 3rd, 4th and 5th battalion was formed. The First Restoration kept only two for the most part and an effective strength of 900 men of whom 600 were barely fit for battle. Officers on half-pay found suitable employment within these battalions. Enthusiasm ran wild. The old popular hate against the old regime rose again, making anything possible. The sight of the beloved tricolor inspired everyone. In his memoirs, Rapp reveals that young girls in Alsace vowed never to marry anyone except the French who had defended the borders. Napoleon had once again become General Bonaparte in the eyes of the people. However, ten years of power had erased any confidence the Emperor might have had in the poeple. The campaign was conducted in an imperial rather than a revolutionary manner which was a serious mistake. Nonetheless, great, generous and intelligent efforts were made.

On June 1, 1815, 570,000 men were present. On March 1st, there had been 145,000. Napoleon hoped to have 750,000 men by the end of June and 900,000 at the end of July. They would be supplied by means of a levy and a series of summons to the

service. This was an impossible dream for the Emperor and one which even a selfless champion of French liberty would not have been able to realize in the face of the Coalition of the foreign armies.

That great patriotic illusion which seized the majority of the French left thoughtful people completely cold. Some of those who remained unconvinced were even to be found in the army and on the Emperor's general staff. Napoleon felt that all orders given for the massing of the various armies and observation corps along the borders had to be kept secret. He left no visible trace of the orders of march nor of the composition of the army for his last campaign. No historian up to the present has been able to give a complete description of the status of the Army of Waterloo because no complete official document has survived the great defeat. With the help of Colonel Perrier, director of the war depot, a document reconstructed by Captain Sergent can be offered which outlines the situation on June 1, 1815 (right).

The Army of the Alps, commanded by Suchet, Duke of Albufera, was comprised of 15,000 men of whom approximately half belonged to the National Guard. The 14th Regiment of infantry of the line, under the command of the future marshal Bugeaud, was part of this regiment. The 14th inflicted great losses on the Piemontese and Austrian soldiers at Conflans, Moutiers, and l'Hôpital (June 15th, 22nd, and 28th, 1815). The Army of the West (General-in-chief Lamarque, 16,600 men) retained the third battalions of many regiments from the 3rd and 4th Corps of the Grande Armée. They were to assemble after the pacification of the Vendée.

SITUATION ON JUNE 1, 1815	
Troops of the line and the Imperial Guard ready to enter the campaign	214,000
200 battalions of the elite garde national mobilisée	112,000
Regiments of sailors	30,000
Naval gunners	8,000
Coast guards	6,000
Veterans	10,000
Old soldiers for garrisons	32,000
National gendarmarie	12,000
Troops in depots or marching to join their corps	146,000
Total	570,000

The fifth corps of the Grande Armée, under the command of the courageous Rapp, was detached to Strasbourg under the name of the Army of the Rhine. It was composed of the 15th and 16th Divisions of infantry and counted 22,000 men at the beginning of the hostilities. Lecourbe, established at Belfort, defended the remains of Switzerland and the Franche-Comté with 4,000 men and was expecting 20 elite battalions from the National Guard. Brune defended the Mediterranean coast, Decaen the Eastern Pyrenees, and Clausel organized an army in the Gironde.

Meanwhile, Europeans under a new coalition were unaware of the force which was driving France. They truly believed the Emperor to be at bay in the Tuileries, caught between the liberal parliamentarians and the Bourbon conspiracy. Suddenly, renegades informed them that the French army, with the Soldier of Arcole and of Montereau, the Conqueror of Austerlitz and of Jena at its head, had crossed the northern border.

ARMY OF THE NORTH (1815) - Commander in Chief: THE EMPEROR; Chief of Staff: Marshal SOULT				
Army Corps	Divisions and Lieutenant Generals	Numbers of Men	Generals of Brigade	Regiments and Colonels
1st CORPS Lieutenant General DROUET-D'ERLON Chief of Staff: General of Brigade Delcambre Commander of artillery: General of Brigade Dessales Commander of engineers: General of Brigade Garbé	1st - Alix	4,000	Bourgeois Quiot	54th Line, Col. Charlet; 55th Line, Col. Morin; 28th Line, Col. Saint-Hilaire; 105th Line, Col Genty.
	2nd - Donzelot	5,132	Schmitt Aulard	13th Light, Col Gougeon; 17th Light, Col. Guenuel; 19th Light, Col. Trapet; 51st Line, Col. Baron Rignon.
	3rd - Marcognet	3,900	D'Arsonvalle Noguès	21st Line, Col. Carré; 46th Line, Col. Dupré; 25th Line, Col. Degrométrie; 45th Line, Col. Chapuset.
	4th - Durutte	3,853	Pégot Brue	8th Line, Col. Ruelle; 29th Line, Col Gousselot; 85th Line, Col. Garnier; 95th Line, Col. Masson.
2nd CORPS Lieutenant General REILLE Chief of Staff: Lieutenant General Pamphile-Lacroix Commander of artillery: General of Brigade Pelletier Commander of engineers: General of Brigade de Richemont	5th - Bachelu	4,103	Husson Campy	3rd Line, Col. Vautrin; 61st Line, Col. Rouge; 72nd Line, Col. Thibault; 108th Line, Col. Higonnet.
	6th - Prince Jerome	7,819	Bauduin Soye	1st Light, Col. Cubières; 2nd Light, Col. Maigron; 1st Line, Col. Cornebise; 2nd Line, Col. Trippe.
	7th - Girard	3,925	De Villiers Piat	11th Light, Col. Sebastiani; 82nd Line, Col. Matis; 12th Light, Col. Mouttet; 4th Line, Col. Faullain.
	9th - Foy	4,788	Gauthier Jamin	92nd Line, Col. Tissot; 93rd Line, Col. Massot; 100th Line, Col. Braun; 4th Light, Col. Peyris.
3rd CORPS Lieutenant General VANDAMME Chief of Staff: General of Brigade Revest Commander of artillery: General of Brigade Duguereau Commander of engineers: General of Brigade Nempde	8th - Lefol	4,541	Billard Corsin	15th Light, Col. Brice; 23rd Line, Col. Vernier; 37th Line, Col. Menu; 64th Line, Col. Dubalen.
	10th - Habert	5,024	Gingoult Dupeyroux	34th Line, Col. Mouton; 88th Line, Col, Baillon; 22nd Line, Col. Fantin-Desodoards; 70th Line, Col. Terrier; 2nd Foreign Regiment (Swiss), Col. Réal de la Chapelle.
	11th - Berthezène	5,565	Dufour Lagarde	12th Line, Col. Beaudinot; 56th Line, Col. Delaye; 33rd Line, Col. Maire; 86th Line, Col. Bussière.
4th CORPS Lieutenant General GÉRARD Chief of Staff: General of Brigade Saint-Remy Commander of artillery: General of Brigade Baltus Commander of engineers: General of Brigade Valazé	12th - Pécheux	4,719	Rome Schaeffer	30th Line, Col. Ramand; 96th Line, Col. Delarue; 63rd Line, Col. Laurède; 6th Light, Col. Ferra;.
	13th - Vichery	4,145	La Capitaine Desprez	59th Line, Col. Laurain; 76th Line, Major Coudamy; 48th Line, Col. Péraldy; 69th Line, Col. Gaillard.
	14th - Bourmont, then Hulot	4,237	Hulot Toussaint	9th Light, Col. Baume; 111th Line, Col. Sausset; 44th Line, Col. Paolini; 50th Line, Col. Lavigne.
6th CORPS Lieutenant General MOUTON, Count of Lobau Chief of Staff: General of Brigade Durrieu Commander of artillery: Lieutenant General Noury Commander of engineers: General of Brigade Sabatier	19th - Simmer	3,953	Bellair Jamin	5th Line, Col. Rousselle; 11th Line, Col. Ollivet; 27th Line, Col. Gaudin; 84th Line, Col. Chevalier.
	20th - Jannin	2,202	Bony Tromelin	5th Light, Col. Curnier; 10th Line, Col. Roussel; 47th Line, Col. Dauléon (detached to the Vendée); 107th Line, Col. Drouot.
	21st - Teste	2,418	Laffitte Penne	8th Light, Col. Ricard; 40th Line, Col. Weller; 65th Line, Col. Boussard; 75th Line, Col. Mativet.

Infantry of the line, campaign of Belgium (1815).

SECOND RESTORATION

During the fifteen days preceding the One Hundred Days, King Louis XVIIIth was sorely disillusioned. The French army had not forgotten its old general. The miraculous reappearance of the tricolor as well as the great name of Napoleon were responsible for the ease with which soldiers had deserted the royal cause. To punish them, the King resolved that from then on, no reminder of the Republic or of the Empire would be allowed to survive. This ban extended to the organization, the uniform and the numbering system of the army.

The decree of August 3, 1815 created one legion of infantry per department. These legions had to be uniformly composed in the following manner:

1. 3 battalions including one of chasseurs. The battalions had eight companies. In the battalions of the line, there was a company of grenadiers and one of voltigeurs; in the battalions of chasseurs, there were no elite companies. Each company had 3 officers, a sergeant-major, a quartermaster, 4 sergeants, 8 corporals, 52 grenadiers, fusiliers or voltigeurs and 2 drummers. Companies of chasseurs were composed in the same manner but with only 28 chasseurs.

2. 2 depot companies, each one with half a cadre.

3. 1 company of horse guides: a lieutenant, a second lieutenant, a sergeant-major, 2 sergeants, a quarter-master, 4 corporals, 36 scouts, and 2 trumpeters. The Morbihan Legion actually only had its cavaliers and its artillerymen.

4. 1 company of artillery: a captain, a lieutenant, a sergeant-major, 4 sergeants, a quarter-master, 4 corporals, 4 artificers, 2 workers, 8 first class cannoneers, 20 second class cannoneers, and 2 drummers.

The general staff included a colonel, a lieutenant-colonel, 3 majors, a major or field officer in charge of administration, 4 battalion adjutants, an officer in charge of accounts and records *(capitaine-tresorier,)* a captain in charge of materiel *(capitaine d'habillement)*, a paymaster *(officier payeur)*, a color bearer, a surgeon-major, and 3 assistant surgeons for a total of 18.

In total there were 97 officers and 1,604 men in the ranks.

Battalions of the line were dressed in white with white breeches and high leggings. Light battalions had green coats and long pants of the same color. The shako was of felt with a fleur-de-lys on the plate. The lapels, collars, coat facings, cuff facings, and piping all had distinctive colors.

These legions were formed of men coming from the same department with the exception of the officers. They took the alphabetical order of the department in which they were organized at the principal town. The

Mounted chasseurs and scouts of the departmental legions (1816).

Corsican legion was at first classified separately and without a number. However, when the department of Mont-Blanc was lost from French territory, its legion's number, No. 54, was given to the Corsicans.

From the start, these unnecessary complications produced poor results. Since the departments were unequal in population, they either didn't contribute men at all, or doubled the regulation number of draftees. As of February 19, 1819, a new order intervened which distributed the 258 battalions of infantry of the line and of light infantry amongst the departments as follows:

8 departments at 2 legions with 3 battalions	48
3 departments at 1 legion with 4 battalions	12
48 departments at 1 legion with 3 battalions	144
27 departments at 1 legion with 2 battalions	54
Total : 94 legions	258 battalions

Departmental legions (1816).

The 3 legions (Morbihan, Lower Rhine, Somme) with 4 battalions had their fourth battalions composed of chasseurs a pied; 10 legions with 3 battalions (Ariège, High Alps, Low Alps, Creuse, Corsica, Eastern Pyrenees, High Vienne, Jura, Vosges) and the 27 with 2 battalions were solely composed of chasseurs a pied. This gives a proportion of 88 battalions of chasseurs versus 170 of the line. From this point on, the battalions of light infantry were of the same strength as those of the line and had likewise 2 elite companies.

Of course there were no more depot cadres nor companies of guides or of cannoneers.

A foreign legion called de Hohenlohe had also been organized along with 6 Swiss regiments of which 2 belonged to the Royal Guard.

The recruitment law called the "Law of Gouvion-Saint-Cyr," which revived the suddenly halted conscription under

Infantry of the line (1824).

Infantry of the line. Captain, battalion adjutant (1885).

Infantry of the line. Musician (1885).

another name, put an end to regional recruitment. Regimental numbering was once again required.

The decree of October 22, 1820 reestablished recruitment. It also noted at first that the decrees of August 3, 1815 and of February 17, 1819 had never had their full effect since certain legions never had more than one battalion. The new decree established that henceforth there would be 80 regiments: 60 of the line and 20 light. The first 40 regiments of the line were at 3 battalions. The last 20 and the 20 light had only two. The regiments all had, by regulation, a small general staff, a music section, a non-military company of workmen, instructors, etc. They had 88 officers and 1,942 non-commissioned officers and soldiers when at 3 battalions but only 62 officers and 1,297 men in the ranks when there were just 2 battalions.

The transformation was made by numbering the legions according to their alphabetical order. The component elements of the fourteen legions which had to disappear would fill in the gaps of the weaker legions during the reorganization.

Thus we finally arrive at the true birth of today's regiments, at least for those numbered from 1 to 60 and from 76 to 95. From here on, changes will no longer have to be noted. However, it will be seen that, after each internal political revolution, after each European upset, the number of French regiments rose successively from 80 to 84, to 100 and finally to 144. The number of battalions varied from 2 to 4 while that of the companies was reduced from 8 to 6 per battalion and finally to 4. The regiment remained the same, however, sustaining the modificatons which tactics and politics inflicted upon it. The uniform was also changed, returning to blue for the jacket which itself went from short to long again. This gave way to the tunic, returned to the jacket only to return once again to the tunic. The red pants and white gaiters of the *chaussés-menus* would symbolize through dress the typical French infantryman. In Europe, one would say *les pantalons rouges* or "the red pants" to characterize the tireless French marching units. Armaments would be revolutionized twice. Individualism would arise, even within the community of the army. The glory of France's foot soldiers never paled. Their epic tale will now be told.

Although just heavily reorganized, the French infantry had to prove its worth in Spain.

Today there is no doubt about the effort it must have taken to assemble this army of one hundred thousand men who brought with them only one cannon per thousand men. At the opening of the Congress of Verona the preceding October, the official figure for the general effective strength of the French army was 241,000 men, including officers. To complicate matters, neither the army nor the people were in sympathy with the Spanish War. Nonetheless, this war must have resulted in a reconciliation on the battlefield between officers of the old and the new armies.

In the adjacent table, it may be noticed that all the regiments of the line called up to contribute to the formation of the First Army of Spain belonged to the list of the first 40 which only had three battalions. The light regiments had to leave cadres of four companies at the depot even though they only had two battalions.

On February 2, 1823 at the beginning of the campaign, a royal decree had created the 61st, 62nd, 63rd, and 64th Regiments of the line.

The expedition of Morocco, much less popular than the Spanish War, was carried out by a division of three brigades under the command of General of Division Marquis Maison and the generals of brigade Tiburce Sébastiani, Higonnet and Schneider. The 9 regiments of the line designated were: the 8th (Colonel de Salperwick), the 16th (Colonel de Borgarelli d'Ison), the 27th (Colonel Despans de Cubières), the 29th (Colonel Delachau), the 35th (Colonel Bullière), the 42nd (Colonel de la Serre), the 46th (Colonel de Mylius), the 56th (Colonel Fos), and the 58th (Colonel Dupont de Quesnay). Three amongst them — the 27th, 29th, and 35th — had already participated in the Spanish War.

In 1823, mixed brigades composed of cavalry and of light infantry were established. For the campaign of Algiers

---

INFANTRY REGIMENTS WHICH COMPOSED THE FIRST ARMY OF SPAIN

1st CORPS - Marshal OUDINOT, DUKE OF REGGIO
Chief of staff: General Grundler
3 divisions of infantry and one of dragoons. The first brigade of each infantry division contained one regiment of light infantry and two of cavalry.

1st DIVISION - General d' Autichamp
1st Brigade, General Valin: 9th Light, Col. Nicolas
2nd Brigade, General St-Hilaire: 23rd Line, Col. de Labesse; 28th Line, Col. de la Béraudière
3rd Brigade, General Berthier: 37th Line, Col. Tissot; 38th Line, Col. de Cherisey

2nd DIVISION - General Bourke
1st Brigade, General Larochejacquelin: 7th Light, Col. Lambot
2nd Brigade, General d'Albignac: 15th Line, Col. de Rascar; 22nd Line, Col. Monchoisy
3rd Brigade, General Marquerie: 30th Line, Col. de Landevoisin; 35th Line, Col. de Laurétan

3rd DIVISION - General Obert
1st Brigade, General Vitré: 2nd Light, Col. Duke of Crillon
2nd Brigade, General Toussaint: 20th Line, Col. de Montcalm; 27th Line, Col. O'Neill
3rd Brigade, General Millet: 34th Line, Col. de Farincourt; 36th Line, Baron de Mauren

Effectives: 27,485 men, 5,879 horses, 24 cannon.

2nd CORPS - Count MOLITOR
Chief of staff: General Borelli
2 divisions of infantry containing 20 battalions of infantry. The first brigade of each infantry division contained one regiment of light infantry and two of cavalry.

4th DIVISION - General Loverdo
1st Brigade, General Pottier: 4th Light, Col. Buchet
2nd Brigade, General Corsin: 1st Line, Col. de Saporta; 11th Line, Col. de Houdetot
3rd Brigade, General Ordonneau: 10th Line, Col. Salleyx; 20th Line, Col Delachau

5th DIVISION.- General Pamphile Lacroix
1st Brigade, General Saint-Chamans: 8th Light, Col. Levavasseur
2nd Brigade, General d'Arbault-Joucques: 4th Line, Col. d'Hautpoul; 13th Line, Col. Foulon de Doué
3rd Brigade, General Pelleport: 24th Line, Col. Verdier; 39th Line, Col. de Bois-David

Effectives: 20,312 men, 4,984 horses, 12 cannon.

3rd CORPS- Prince DE HOHENLOHE
Chief of staff: General Meynadier
2 divisions of infantry containing 16 battalions of infantry and a division of dragoons, plus one division of Spanish refugees.

6th DIVISION - General de Couchy
1st Brigade, General Jeannin: 9th Light, Col. O'Mahony, 6th Line, Col. Coloumb-d'Arcine
2nd Brigade, General Quinsonnas: 9th Line, Col. Bremont; 14th Line, Col. de la Forest d'Armaillé

7th DIVISION - General Canuel
1st Brigade, General Goujeon: 21st Line, Col. Birard de Gontefrey; 25th Line,–
2nd Brigade, General Schoeffer: 5th Light, Col. Rapatel; 17th Line, Col. d'Aubusson de la Feuillade

Effectives: 16,476 men, 2,700 horses, 12 cannon.

4th CORPS- Marshal MONCEY
Chief of staff: General Desprez
3 divisions of infantry containing 22 battalions of infantry. The 1st Brigade of the 1st Division was mixed as were those of the first two corps and the 2nd Division had just one brigade of infantry as the second contained only cavalry.

8th DIVISION - General Curial
1st Brigade, General Vence: 6th Light, Col. Hurel
2nd Brigade, General Vasserot: 26th Line, Col. de Cadudal; 32nd Line, Col. Dutertre
3rd Brigade, General Picot: 7th Line, Col. d'Arlanges; 18th Line, Col de FitzJames

9th DIVISION - General de Damas
1st Brigade, General Maringoué 1st Light, Col. Revel; 5th Line, Col. Broussier

10th DIVISION - General Donnadieu
1st Brigade: 12th Light, Col. Lapoterie; 2nd Line, Col. Vigo-Roussillon
2nd Brigade: 3rd Line, Col. Fantin Desodoards; 13th Line, Col. de Choiseul

Effectives: 21,099 men, 4,376 horses, 24 cannon.

RESERVE CORPS - General BORDESOULLE
Chief of staff: General Bourbon-Busset
One division of infantry of the Guard, one of Guard cavalry, one of cuirassiers, Garde du corps, etc.
Effectives: 9,690 men, 3,470 horses, 7 cannon.

(1830), *regiments de marche* were formed from light infantry, each comprising 2 detached battalions. The Restoration thus has to its credit three campaigns and the creation of 84 infantry regiments.

COMPOSITION OF THE ALGIERS EXPEDITIONARY ARMY

Commanding general: Lieutenant General Count DE BOURMONT
Chief of staff: Lieutenant General Desprez
Assistant: General of brigade Tholozé

1st DIVISION Lieutenant General Baron Berthézène	2nd DIVISION Lieutenant General Count Loverdo	3rd DIVISION General of brigade Duke d'Escars	RESERVE DIVISION Lt. General Vicount de Montesquiou Fézensac (Stayed at Toulon, Marseille, and Aix)
1st Brigade, Poret de Morvan 3rd Line, Colonel Roussel 2nd Light, Colonel Bosquillon de Frescheville 4th Light, Colonel Bosquillon de Frescheville	1st Brigade, Count de Daurémont 6th Line, Colonel Nouail de La Villegille 49th Line, Colonel Magnan	1st Brigade, Viscount Bertier de Sauvigny 1st Light, Colonel Marquis de Neuchéze 9th Light, Colonel Marquis de Neuchéze 35th Line, Colonel Rullière	1st Brigade, Count de Rochechouart 18th Line, Colonel de Fitz James 60th Line, Colonel Lamarre
2nd Brigade, Baron Achard 14th Line, Colonel de La Forest d'Armaillé 37th Line, Colonel Baron Feuchères	2nd Brigade, Monck d'Uzer 15th Line, Colonel Mangin 48th Line, Colonel Leridant	2nd Brigade, Baron Hurel 17th Line, Colonel Duprat 33rd Line, Colonel Ocher de Beaupré	2nd Brigade, Count d'Arbaud Joucques 40th Line, Colonel de Roquefeuil 56th Line, Colonel Baron Hoche de la Condamine
3rd Brigade, Baron Clouet 2nd Line, Colonel Horric de la Motte 28th Line, Colonel Mounier	3rd Brigade, Colomb d'Arcine 21st Line, Colonel Birard de Goutefray 20th Line, Colonel Delachau	3rd Brigade, De Montlivault 23rd Line, Colonel Count de Montboissier 34th Line, Colonel Count de Roucy	3rd Brigade, Baron Desmichels 4th Line, Colonel Bellangé 36th Line, Colonel Paty

Effectives: 30,782 infantry, 534 cavalry, 2,327 artillerists, 1,310 engineers and administrative personnel. Total: 37,507 men.

THE JULY GOVERNMENT

Although the July Government had staked its reputation on avoiding any conflict with Europe, this administration obviously did the most to return the army to an imperial status. Moreover, it enacted a law on promotion and a law on the status of officers. These admirable instruments allowed it to recruit a magnificent officers' corps which was both quite unified and well instructed. To satisfy the legal sector of the country — meaning the deputies — this government had to support the system of substitution and all the abuses it entailed. Although it was able to carry out the siege of Anvers and to wage war in Algeria, the army which it bequeathed to the following government had no reserves. Later, the law of recruitment had to be completely revamped in order to conquer the Russians and the Austrians. Nonetheless, the army was superb from 1830 to 1848, particularly the infantry whose training and well-being were constantly in the minds and actions of the ministers of war of the period.

The first military measure taken by the July Government (August 11 and 17, 1830) was to muster out the Guard and the Swiss regiments. The 65th and the 66th Regiments of the line were created to make use of the soldiers and the general staffs coming from the Guard. On January 5, 1831, the disbanded Legion of Hohenlohe became the 21st Light Regiment. On May 4th of the same year, the 67th Regiment was formed in Africa with Parisian volunteers from the regiment of *la Charte*. Considerable activity in voluntary resignations amongst the higher ranking legitimist officers led to great changes in the general spirit of the army. The colonels and the commanders promoted in 1815 (whom the Restoration had kept idle by refusing to recognize their ranks) took up the sword again. They were no strangers to the re-establishment of military spirit in the ranks of the French army. This spirit had been worked up by diametrically opposed ideas under the influence of the Restoration's religious politics. Thus, the chaplains of the regiments were removed and no one dared dispute this measure when it was remembered how these same chaplains had been selected with so little care. Wasn't *Abbé Chatel* after all a military chaplain in the Royal Guard?

Europe, meanwhile, had not cast an indulgent eye upon Louis-Philippe when he ascended the throne. Not only was the Revolution rectified in his person, but also the order of succession to the throne was broken with a single blow. Like Napoleon, Louis-Philippe represented the Revolution crowned, "the best of the Republics," as LaFayette said. France had to be ready for any eventuality. All the regiments of the line and light regiments were expanded to 3 battalions of 8 companies. Soon fourths were organized in all regiments of infantry of the line which were put on a war footing. This lasted until 1834. This expansion also permitted all the lesser-ranking officers of the Empire, who had been removed in reaction to the events of 1815, to re-enter active service.

Infantry of the line,
company of grenadiers, company of voltigeurs, center company (1835).

Light infantry (1832).

Commander in chief: Marshal GÉRARD
Chief of staff: Lieutenant General Saint-Cyr Nugues
Commander of artillery: Lieutenant General Neigre
Commander of engineers: Lieutenant General Haxo

ADVANCE GUARD
His Royal Highness the Duke of Orleans
4th Light, Colonel Lecourt, called Fontgarnière
and two regiments of light cavalry.

1st DIVISION	3rd DIVISION
Lieutenant General Tiburce Sébastiani	Lieutenant General Jamin
1st Brigade, General of brigade Harlet	1st Brigade, General of brigade Zoeptel
11th Light, Colonel d'Aussaguet de Laborde	9th Light, Colonel d'Hennaut de Bertaucourt
5th Line, Colonel Gréard	18th Line, Colonel de Nettancourt
2nd Brigade, General of brigade Rumigny	2nd Brigade, General of brigade Georges
8th Line, Colonel Maingarnaud	52nd Line, Colonel Carel
19th Line	58th Line
2nd DIVISION	4th DIVISION
Lieutenant General Baron Achard	Lieutenant General Fabre
1st Brigade, General of brigade Castellane	1st Brigade, General of brigade Rapatel
8th Light, Colonel Bourkoltz	7th Line, Colonel Tardieu de St-Aubanel
12th Line, Colonel Boarini	25th Line, Colonel de Boyer
2nd Brigade, General of brigade Voirol	2nd Brigade, General of brigade d' Hémicourt
22nd Line, Colonel Levasseur	61st Line, Colonel Berner
93rd Line, Colonel Guillabert	65th Line, Colonel Arnaud

The events which arose in the Netherlands necessitated the army's entry into Belgium (1832).

A fifth division, organized under the command of General Schramm, did not cross the border.

Among the seventeen regiments with 3 battalions — thirteen of the line and four light — which were called upon to besiege Anvers, only one made the trip to Algiers: the 15th Regiment of the line.

The old generals of division of the Empire who had retaken control of high level military affairs brought with them the tradition of tightly organized regiments. From this point on until 1873, the use of well-knit regiments would more or less be the rule. In 1873, however, the system of immediately available reserves would be inaugurated.

There were two companies of grenadiers and one of voltigeurs of the 65th Regiment who had the honor of taking the lunette of St. Laurent. In the same year, the 66th Regiment's 1st and 2nd battalions seized the citadel of Ancona (December 25, 1832). Meanwhile, the 3rd and 4th battalions of this same regiment were sent to reinforce the Army of Africa.

The 65th and the 66th Regiments were formed from the old soldiers of the former Guard. Within two years of their founding, they served as an example of the best military values through their actions in Belgium and in Africa.

The foremost and greatest task of the infantry under Louis-Philippe was the conquest of Algeria. All the King's sons served consecutively in this land which at present belongs to France. Every rock there is colored by the blood of French soldiers. Each Algerian plain serves as a burial ground for a number of brave Frenchmen. Algeria indeed served as a good training ground where the troops learned patience and dedication. However, it has often been said that the generals and officers made a poor showing there, having forgotten the rules and traditions of large-scale warfare.

There is no question of marching quickly in Africa where everything has to be carried along. One has to march for a long time in order to wear down and exhaust the enemy's force.

France was not always victorious on African soil. There were critical moments where she had to maintain as many as 85,000 men in Algeria. As noted above, a special section of this book will be dedicated to the Algerian troops, as they are rightfully called. However, their own glory cannot overshadow that of the infantry of the regiments of the line and the light infantry who made possible the conquest of Algeria and the consolidation of French power in North Africa. Almost all of the old regiments spent time in Algeria. During the first years of the conquest, the regiment of the line was the foundation of the Army of Africa. With the outburst of the February Revolution, 57 regiments out of 100 had already been on campaign in Africa. All were formed previous to the decree of November 7, 1840. This decree had expanded the number of regiments to 100 through the creation of new ones as follows: the 68th, 69th, 70th, 71st, 72nd, 73rd, 74th, 75th of the line and the 22nd, 23rd, 24th, and 25th light.

Infantry of the line. African dress (1837).

LIST OF THE REGIMENTS WHICH CAMPAIGNED IN AFRICA BEFORE 1848

1st Line 1837 to 1842. Colonels: Locqueneux, Deuvaux, de Lusset, Paté	26th - 1837-44. De la Voirie, Loyré d'Arbouville, Froidefond-Desfarges	59th - 1833-36. Petit d'Hautrive
2nd - 1842 to 1848. Vidal de Lausun, de Buttafoco	28th - 1830-32. Mounier	61st - 1837-46. Monpez, Josse, Herbillon
3rd - 1830. Roussel	29th - 1830-31. Delachau	62nd - 1836-42. Levesques, Lafontaine, D'Alphonse
4th - 1831 to 1834. Courtôt	30th - 1830-31. Ocher de Beaupré, d'Arlanges	63rd - 1835-39. Hecquet
5th - 1845 to 1850. Roche, de Monet	31st - 1840-48. Amat, Chivaud, Régeau	64th - 1841-48. Picouleau
6th - 1830. Nouail de la Villegille, Boullé	32nd - 1842-48. Cavaignac (Ant. Stan.), Le Flô	66th - 1832-36. (2nd battalion without a colonel)
8th - 1847-52. Jamin, Chalon	33rd - 1840-48. Comman, Camou, Bouat	67th - 1831-34. (Organized in Algiers). Friol
9th - 1847-52. De MacMahon, Regnault, de Tournemine	34th - 1830-31. De Roucy, Hurault de Sorbée	1st Light 1830. D'Eu de Marson, Baraguay d'Hilliers
11th - 1835-39. Levéque de Vilmorin	35th - 1830-31. Rullière	2nd - 1830. Bosquillon de Frescheville
12th - 1837-39. Roux	36th - 1841-48. Lafeuille, de Géraudon, Levaillant (Jean)	1835-40. Menne, Changarnier
1848-1854. Daulomieu-Beauchamp	37th - 1830-31. De Feuchères, de Contreglise	3rd - 1839-47. Champion, Chambry, Gachot
13th - 1834-36. De Koenigsegg	38th - 1845-50. Bergounhe, de Barral, de Grandchamp	4th - 1830. De Pineton de Chambrun
14th - 1839-31. De la Forest d'Armaillé	41st - 1839-47. Evrard, Roguet, de Mac-Mahon	6th - 1841-48. Thiéry, Renault, O'Keeffe
15th - 1830-32. Mangin	43rd - 1845-51. Cornille, Loreton-Dumontet	8th - 1847-52. De Cambray, Etienney
16th - 1845-50. Van Heddeghem, Bosquet, Jollivet	44th - 1844-49. Faivre	9th - 1830. De Neuchèze
17th - 1830-31. Dupra, Vielbans	47th - 1835-39. Combes, de Beaufort	10th - 1831-36. Marthe
20th - 1830-32. Horric de la Motte, Marion	48th - 1830. Léridant	12th - 1845-51. Pourailly, Maissiat
21st - 1830-31. Birard de Goutefray, Lefol	1837-44. Rambaud, Leblond, Regnault	13th - 1840-48. De la Torre, Molliére
22nd - 1839-46. Levasseur, Lebreton	49th - 1830. Magnan	15th - 1840-46. Tempoure, Chadeysson
23rd - 1830-41. De Montboissier, Beaufort de Canillac	51st - 1845-50. Siméon, Claparède.	17th - 1835-41. Corbin, Bedeau
1836-41. Gueswiller, de Macors	53rd - 1840-48. De Schmidt, Leroy de Saint-Arnaud	19th - 1842-48. De Latour du Pin, de Chasseloup-Laubat
24th - 1836-42. De Reissenbach, Duvivier, Gentil (Duke d'Aumale, Lieutenant Colonel)	55th - 1832-34. Chadabet	
	58th - 1839-47. Mocquery, Allemand de Illens, Blangini	

Some of these regiments made a reputation for themselves under the command of colonels whose names have rightfully remained celebrated. These colonels have since been raised to the highest ranks of the military hierarchy.

Regimental administration was firmly established under Louis-Philippe. The dress of the soldiers and all their equipment were always complete and well-maintained, with an eye for good quality. General Hecquet worked hard on this question of a soldier's uniform, equipment, headgear and footgear. Although the ultimate answer has not yet been found, he made a name for himself in the history of the army administration. He fought hard over this uniform for which he even designed a model. It bore great resemblance to the uniform of the French Guards in its voluminous coattails and its *ailes de hanneton* (mayfly wings). The tunic, of which Enfantin spoke highly and after whom it was named, prevailed over the jacket. This was in large part due to the officers returning from Africa where almost no one would wear the jacket.

Civilian styles had a great influence over military styles. Regardless of the rules, civilian designs were introduced with disastrous effects in military wear. The setting of jacket sleeveholes and the fashion, called *de Peking,* of letting the pants fall over the shoes were two such influences. The Ministry of War tried to outlaw them in vain despite its energetic efforts and its authority. In our opinion, the tunic only became the uniform of the entire army because at the same time, the redingote, of English origin, had become the national dress of France. It replaced the clothing which was previously worn in public by the bourgeousie and artisans as well as by the nobility. If the dolman jacket became king, it was thanks to the *jaquette.* This latter was copied not only in its shortened and tightened form but also in the rather practical placement of breast pockets. In fact, the tunic would be an excellent component of military garb. It could be the best, from the soldier's point of view, if worn open over a uniform vest and if the weight of the saber-bayonet and of the cartridge box didn't fall on the hips while digging into the stomach. This would be, however, the uniform from before the Revolution: "Nothing is new under the sun."

As for headgear, this is an unusual topic which has not yet been addressed.

The Restoration made use of the shako dating from the last days of the Empire without a murmur of complaint. It was only modified by replacing the eagle plaque with a *fleurs de lys* plaque. The July Government at first did away with all political emblems. Next it tried to lighten the weight of the traditional *boisseau* or shako. After many experiments, it adopted a tapered shako, covered with woolen fabric. This was a compromise between the old shako and the kepi, an African invention, which will be discussed later. This new shako first had a white stripe, then a red or yellow one. For a while it even had a competitor in the form of the famous Roman helmet made of leather which was tried by the 45th Regiment of the line. This was worn at the same time as the early tapered shakos.

The standard model finally adopted pretty much resembled the shako with leather stripes which has been recently replaced by the kepi. The only difference was that it had a plaque with a crowned cock which the Republic removed and which the Empire replaced with an eagle.

Recently there has been an attempt to make the kepi the sole headgear for the entire army. It is a simple police cap. It is also the former cap of the cavalry stable to which a visor has been added. The actual headgear used in Africa was either a high kepi without any form or a small shako (*schako-casquette*), good-looking in wool fabric, very low, tapered at the front of the head whence it takes its form, very light, with a number and a cockade attached with a band. The cavalry even added a small pompom to it in the shape of an olive. Since the corps made these hats themselves, there were various shapes according to the tastes of the colonels or of the commanders of the province. Some regiments wore it covered with waxed canvas. Others covered the top with a white coating to reflect the sun's rays.

The wine or madder-colored pants which the Restoration had begun to test as of 1829 became a required component of the uniform throughout the army in 1831. They were worn either wide or narrow, according to the tastes of the colonel, until 1845. At this time its appearance was strictly controlled and it was tightened. In 1839 the leather gaiter replaced the cloth model.

Captain of the infantry of the line, African dress (1837).

Drummer, light infantry (1845).

The lifestyle in Africa led to great abuses in the officers' dress. Some colonels permitted the tunic to be worn with a pleated skirt or with two rows of buttons. Some even pushed the limits by allowing a spencer jacket covered with frogs. The simple cape of white flannel striped in silk was also quite stylish. In Paris, I have seen with my own eyes an officer of the line of the Army of Africa strolling along. He was decked out in a green cape lined with white and accented in gold. He topped it all off with a magnificent red fez with blue fringe which was as large as a drum major's busby. Inordinately wide pants twisted around his legs and fell in cascading folds onto his boots of which only the toes could be seen. A very large cane — the "matrack" — completed this amazing outfit which epitomized the best of African chic. Add hair in the Lamoriciere style, a fashion which the famous Marshal Canrobert would never give up. You will then have a good idea of the most outlandish, the most overdressed officer who came to rest from his tiring journeys on the steps of Tortoni, after having been on expeditions in 1843 from Oran to Constantine.

When the Duke of Aumale returned from Africa with the 17th Light Regiment, he showed the Parisians his men in march dress. They wore the turned-up greatcoat, pants in white gaiters, a cartridge box of cloth at the stomach and the African kepi. Some days later, these transformed soldiers paraded with a platoon of sappers topped by busbys with yellow bags, while the officers wore red and white waistbelts of goatskin, a present from their young colonel. It was supurb but it wasn't regulation. Marshal Soult, guardian of the regulations, dispensed with all these whimsical embellishments, nice as they were. In 1845, the tunic was regularized and was used throughout the army.

More of a revolution than the tunic was the adoption of the percussion musket (1842 to 1845), an early improvement which presaged greater ones to come. The musket Napoleon had used to conquer Europe was finished. The entire military already realized the importance of this new weapon which was going to conquer the field of battle through its ability to shoot in all kinds of weather, even in rain and snow.

With the elimination of misfires in combat, tirailleurs now possessed limitless self-assurance and unquestionable value. The superiority of the cavalry was almost completely neutralized. The infantry could now compare itself favorably against the artillery in terms of its value on the battlefield. This situation would continue until the day the artillery developed a cannon which would outmode hand-to-hand combat and the men involved in such actions. Under these conditions, the army participated in the Revolution of 1848 which it neither impeded nor supported. Rather the army acted as an indifferent spectator. The spirit of opposition and of division was introduced into the ranks of the main part of the general staff. This was due to parliamentarism which destroyed that old discipline of the French army, re-established after 1830 along with the traditions of the First Empire. Discipline was weakened as much by the atmosphere of political indecision as by the blow of military defeats.

REPUBLIC OF 1848
PRESIDENCY OF PRINCE LOUIS-NAPOLEON

The February Revolution brought as much harm as good to the army. A few regiments were disarmed in Paris but they were soon reorganized, only to remember this humiliation. The lesson was well learned and examples of apparent weakness would only appear twenty years later. Even then, they would be unusual and could be attributed to greater national weaknesses.

Although it was reasonable to fear European complications, the Republic showed itself to be prudent and hardly provocative. It created nothing new in the military. It was content for the moment to fill out the infantry battalions with eight companies, a number which had fallen to seven in the last years of Louis-Philippe's reign. It was also in 1848 that infantrymen blackened their leather belts and straps. An army, called the Army of the Alps, was assembled in the southeast but it was not sent outside the border.

This army, originally composed of three divisions of infantry and one of cavalry, had at first been placed under the command of General of Division Oudinot. After the election of December 10, it was turned over to the command of the great Marshal Bugeaud. At right is a description of its initial organization.

1st DIVISION
Commander: General of division Bedeau, *at Grenoble*
1st Brigade, General Gueswiller: 4th Battalion of Chasseurs; 13th and 22nd Light Infantry Regiments
2nd Brigade, General Salleix: 15th, 66th and 68th Line Regiments

2nd DIVISION
Commander: General of division Baraguay-d'Hilliers, *at Lyon*
1st Brigade, General Talandier: 3rd, 15th and 20th Light Infantry Regiments
2nd Brigade, General Buhot: 7th, 22nd and 49th Line Regiments

3rd DIVISION
Commander: General of division Magnan, *at Mâcon*
1st Brigade, General Guillabert: 2nd Battalion of Chasseurs; 16th and 25th Light Infantry Regiments
2nd Brigade, General Renault: 17th, 50th and 67th Line Regiments

Infantry of the line (1848).

Its formation was seen as a major and particularly admirable military feat. The belief that 45,000 men could be brought together had been lost. Thus, when Lieutenant-Colonel Charras supervised the formation of the Army of the Alps in his role as Under-Secretary of State for War, he immediately acquired a reputation as an expert at organization. It is true that the Army of Africa was diminished a little by this move, however, it seemed to have been given some respite by the subjection of Abd-el-Kader. Nonetheless, the assembly of the Army of the Alps brought honor to its instigators. Today it would still be considered something special, particularly with respect to the new conditions imposed by contemporary warfare. All the great modern military systems have been established with a view to general mobilization, excluding the organization of small armies. This system is evident in Tonkin.

If the February Revolution hardly required an increase in the number of infantry regiments, the misery which it augmented rather than relieved obliged the governing body of 1848 to form twenty-five battalions of the *garde nationale mobile.* These battalions were composed of men from the working class who were quickly transformed into soldiers through pride of carrying a rifle and wearing a uniform. Thanks to their instructors who all belonged to the the active army, this short-lived troop left behind a good reputation. Generals Duvivier, Damesme and Bréha were especially responsible for their training. These men were killed when they threw themselves upon the enemies of society. The *garde national mobile* of 1848 have been cited in this history of the regular infantry in order to commemorate them.

Due to the politics of General Cavaignac, the protection of Pope Pius IX and of the Papal States was handed down to Prince Louis Napoleon. A small expeditionary army under the command of General of Brigade Mollière, had embarked but then landed again in November 1848. The expedition was finally commenced in March 1849. Its goal was to stop the Kings of Naples and of Spain and the Emperor of Austria from taking over the Roman States and from pledging allegiance to these States under the pretext of destroying the Mazinien Republic. The Prince President Louis Napoleon sent General Oudinot to Civita-Vecchia at the head of the expeditionary force. His army, at first comprising only a small infantry division, was later expanded to three powerful divisions.

MEDITERRANEAN EXPEDITIONARY FORCE (JUNE 1849)

Commander in chief: General of division OUDINOT DE REGGIO
Chief of staff: Colonel Le Barbier de Tinan
Commander of artillery: General of division Thiry
Commander of engineers: General of division Vaillant

1st DIVISION General Regnaud de Saint-Jean-d'Angély	2nd DIVISION General de Rostolan	3rd DIVISION General Gueswiller
1st Brigade, General Mollière 1st Battalion of the Chassuers a pied. 17th Line, Colonel Sonnet 20th Line, Colonel Marulaz 33rd Line, Colonel Bouat	1st Brigade, General Ch. Levaillant 2nd Battalion of the Chassuers à pied. 32nd Line, Colonel Bosc 36th Line, Colonel Blanchard 66th Line, Colonel Chenaux	1st Brigade, General J. Levaillant 16th Light, Colonel Marchesan 25th Light, Colonel Ripert 50th Line, Colonel Leconte
2nd Brigade, General Morris Cavalry	2nd Brigade, General de Chaduysson 22nd Light, Lieutenant Colonel Espinasse 53rd Line, Colonel d'Autemarre 68th Line, Colonel de Leyritz	2nd Brigade, General Sauvan 13th Light, Colonel de Lamarre 13th Line, Colonel de Comps

---

SECOND EMPIRE

◆

The Empire at first made no changes in the organization of the infantry. However, it immediately set about increasing the military's visibility in the eyes of the public. The *galette* worn on the shoulder by fusiliers and chasseurs was replaced with an epaulette fringed at first in blue then in green. This modification did not reduce any of the prestige of the elite companies although it increased that of the center companies.

The creation of the military medal was intended exclusively to ornament the chests of soldiers and non-commissioned officers as well as those of the generals-in-chief. It also proved to be very useful. It provided more marks of distinction for the Legion of Honor. Many excellent compatriots who were previously neglected could henceforth be recompensed with the orange ribbon edged in green which brought to mind the Iron Crown.

From 1852 to 1855, the 100 regiments, now expanded to 24 companies, were to supply the entire cadre with six new battalions of Zouaves, 120 companies of chasseurs à pied and 4 regiments of infantry from the Imperial Guard. After some preparation, they appeared to be represented in good order in the Army of the East.

France's military intervention in the conflict arising in the Crimea was at first limited to sending an army corps of 40 to 45 thousand men. Marshal Leroy Saint-Arnaud, then Minister of War, was given lead command and ordered the early preparations. The best African troops were selected for the first shipment. However, when they were instructed to support

some regiments of the interior, it was immediately obvious how empty of meaning the recruitment law of 1831 was. Despite their twenty-four companies, the regiments of France designated to produce sixteen companies at 150 men each not only had to empty the eight companies they had left in France but also had to ask for eight hundred men from the regiments who were not on active duty. The response was enthusiastic. A number of sergeants and sergeant-majors took a drop in rank in order to participate in the campaign. Nonetheless, the law of 1831 on recruitment had to be modified by the so-called law of exoneration in order to keep old soldiers in active service.

Moreover, after the taking of Sebastopol, the 20th, 39th, 50th and 97th Regiments of the line were recalled to France. (The triumphal welcome accorded them in Paris is still well remembered.) They were replaced in their divisions by the 64th, Colonel d'Esgrigny; the 11th, Colonel Gelly de Moncla; the 31st, Colonel de Maudhuy; and the 35th, Colonel Metman.

In addition, a 12th division of infantry composed of the 69th, Colonel Domon; the 81st, Colonel Sutton de Clonard; the 33rd, Colonel de Fayet de Chabanne; and the 44th Regiment of the line, Colonel Pierson left the camp of Helfaut to reinforce the Army of the Crimea. A brigade formed of the 1st, Colonel O'Farrell and the 84th Regiment of the line, Colonel Piétrequin occupied Constantinople. The Sol brigade reformed with the 94th, Colonel Ollivier, returned from France, and the 4th regiment of naval infantry settled in at Kertch and at Kamiesch. Thus, 50 infantry regiments out of 100 went to the Army of the East, without requiring formations other than a 101st and a 102nd Regiment. These regiments were each composed of 24 companies taken from the 48 regiments of France and were not replaced. With the signing of peace, they quite simply returned to their respective regiments. An attempt was made to assemble a foreign legion on the eastern border made up entirely of Swiss, but it was unsuccessful. General Ochsenbein, who claimed he could put together an elite brigade in a matter of days, was only able to gather 500 or 600 men. Finally, to complete the list, there was a short-lived attempt to form a division of reunited grenadiers and voltigeurs at the camp of Boulogne (April 1855).

Infantry of the line, Army of the East (1854-1855).

Infantry of the line, Army of the East (1854-1855).

LIST OF REGIMENTS SENT TO THE CRIMEA IN ORDER OF DEPARTURE

Departed in April 1854
1st DIVISION - General CANROBERT
7th Line; Colonels de Pequeult de Lavarande, Decaen, de Maussion
20th Line; Colonels de Failly, Orianne
27th Line; Colonels Vergé, Adam, Neigre

2nd DIVISION - General BOSQUET
50th Line ; Colonels Traüers, Granchette, Nicolas-Nicolas
7th Light; Colonels Janin, de Castagny
6th Line; Colonels de Gardarens de Boisse, Goze, Granchette

3rd DIVISION - Prince NAPOLEON
20th Light; Colonel Danner
22nd Light; Colonels Sol, Paulze d'Ivoy

4th DIVISION - General FOREY
19th Line; Colonels Desmarets, Guignard
26th Line; Colonels Niol, de Sorbiers
39th Line; Colonels Beuret, Comignan
74th Line; Colonels Breton, Guyot de Lespart

Departed in June 1854
5th DIVISION - General LEVAILLANT
21st Line; Colonel Lefèvre
42nd Line; Colonels Le Sergeant, d'Hendecourt, de Montaudon, de Bras de Fer
5th Light; Colonel Laterrade
46th Line; Colonel Gault

Departed in October 1854
6th DIVISION - General PATÉ
28th Line; Colonel Lartigue
98th Line; Colonel Conseil Dumesnil

Departed in December 1854
DIVISION DE SALLES
18th Line; Colonel Dantin
79th Line; Colonel Grenier
14th Line; Colonel de Négrier
43rd Line; Colonel Broutta

DIVISION DULAC
57th Line; Colonels Dupuis, Huc
85th Line; Colonels Javel, Veron called Bellecourt
10th Line; Colonel de la Serre
61st Line; Colonel de Taxis

Departed in January 1855
DIVISION BRUNET
86th Line; Colonel de Bertier
100th Line; Colonel Mathieu
49th Line; Colonels de Kerguern, de Mallet
91st Line; Colonels Picard, Meric de Bellefond

Departed in April 1855
DIVISION HERBILLON
47th Line; Colonel Lemaire
52nd Line; Colonels de Lostange, de Capriol de Pechassaut
62nd Line; Colonel de Perusse
73rd Line; Colonel Dubois

DIVISION D'AURELLE DE PALADINES
9th Line; Colonel Bessiéres
32nd Line; Colonel Cavaroz
15th Line; Colonel Guérin
96th Line; Colonel de Malherbe.

Departed in May 1855
BRIGADE SOL
30th Line; Colonel Roubé
35th Line; Colonel Dumont

Infantry of the line (1856).

The regiments destined for the Army of the East first left with two battalions of 8 companies. It became obvious that this formation put too many forces in the depot and deprived the full war battalions of the help of two elite companies from the 3rd battalion. In May 1855, all the infantry regiments were divided into 4 battalions. The first three, called full war battalions, had two elite companies. The 4th, called the depot battalion, was commanded by the major and had no elite companies. The 40 regiments then in the Crimea received at the same time the elite companies from the depot who arrived with the staff of the former 3rd battalion. These troops, along with the 5th and 6th of the first two, constituted the new 3rd battalions. This reinforcement with 12,000 grenadiers and voltigeurs had its price at the moment of assault.

With the uniform use of the infantry rifle during the campaign (December 12, 1854) the light regiments all came to look like the regiments of the line. The exceptions were the collar, the facings, and the piping on their tunics. The light regiments took the name of the regiments of the line and the numbers from 75 to 100 in the general list of the service.

In July 1855, a division of infantry was attached to an expedition which was sent to the Baltics. The following regiments took part in it: 3rd Regiment of the line, Colonel Ducrot; 48th Regiment of the line, Colonel Vidal de Lauzun; 51st Regiment of the line, Colonel Perrin Jonquières; and 77th Regiment of the line, Colonel Suau. After the taking of Bomarsund, they returned to France.

In 1859, three years after the glorious and fruitful Peace of Paris, France had to take up arms once again.

It took more than eighteen months to assemble the army which took Sebastopol. There was a lesson in this. In 1859, it took only four months to prepare for the Italian War. The infantry regiments of the line which were called to take part initially numbered 49. Due to the law of exoneration, the old soldiers kept in active service by means of substantial benefits supplied these regiments as well as the corps *hors ligne* or out of quarters and the Guard with a good nucleus of troops and a solid foundation. In this war, one had to act rapidly while fearing that the German Confederation would create a diversion on the Rhine in favor of in Austria. Thus, the entire army was formed into divisions. The infantry of the line which was not in Italy at the time reinforced the 2 regiments (101st and 102nd) as in 1854 by supplying: three divisions to Lyon under the command of Marshal de Castellane; four to the East commanded by Marshal Pelissier; four for the Army of Paris and of the North which were under the direction of Marshal Magnan, plus seven regiments to Africa and two to guard Rome. This effort to form the entire army as well as the cavalry into divisions was unfortunately abandoned after the war. If it had been firmly adopted, perhaps a portion of the 1870 disasters could have been avoided.

INFANTRY REGIMENTS OF THE FIVE CORPS IN THE ARMY OF ITALY		
Army Corps	**Division and its origins**	**Regimental numbers and names of Colonels**
1st CORPS BARAGUEY-D'HILLIERS	1st Division, from Paris 2nd Division, from Paris 3rd Division, formed in Toulon (decision of April 9)	74th, Col. Guyot de Lespart; 84th, Col. Cambriels; 91st, *Col. Meric de Bellefond*; 98th, Col. Dumesnil 15th, Col. Guérin; 21st, Col. de Fontanges de Couzan; 61st, Col. de Taxis; 100th, Col. Mathieu 33rd, Col. Bordas; 34th, Col. Micheler; 37th, Col. Susbielle; 78th, Col. Levassor-Sorval
2nd CORPS MAC-MAHON	1st Division, from Africa 2nd Division, from Africa	45th, Col. Manuelle; 65th, *Col. Drouhot*, then Menessier; 70th, *Col. Douay*, then Eudes de Boistertre 71st, Col. Duportal-Dugoasmeur; 72nd, Col. Castex
3rd CORPS CANROBERT	1st Division, from Africa 2nd Division, from Lyon 3rd Division, formed in the Durance Valley (March 20)	23rd, Col. Auzouy; 90th, Col. Charlier; 56th, Col. Doens; 41st, Col. de Bourjade. 43rd, *Col. Broutta*; 44th, Col. Pierson; 64th, Col. de Jouenne d'Esgrigny; 88th, Col. Sanglé-Ferrière 11th, Col. Gelly de Moncla; 14th, Col. Duplessis; 46th, Col. Blaise; 59th, Col. Hardy de la Largère
4th CORPS NIEL	1st Division, from Lyon 2nd Division, from Lyon 3rd Division, (formed April 9)	30th, *Col. Lacroix*; 49th, Col. de Mallet; 6th, Col. Dupin de Saint-André; 8th, Col. Courson de la Villeneuve, then de Waubert de Senlis 52nd, Col. Capriol de Péchassaut; 73rd, Col. O'Malley; 85th, Col. Véron called Bellecourt; 86th, Col. Bertier 2nd, Col. Lévy; 53rd, *Col. Capin*; 55th, *Col. de Maleville*; 76th, Col. Béchon de Caussade
5th CORPS PRINCE NAPOLEON	1st Division, from Africa 2nd Division, from Paris	75th, Col. de Lestellet; 89th, Col. Pelletier de Montmarie; 93rd, Col. Pissonnet de Bellefond; 99th, Col. Gondalier de Tugny 18th, Col. d'Anterroches; 26th, Col. de Sorbiers; 20th, Col. Chardon de Chaumont; 88th, Col. Bequet de Sonnay

At the beginning of the Italian War, Lyon and Paris permanently maintained six divisions with their own integral existences in addition to the Guard. In 1857, another division was sent by General Renault to make an expedition into the great Kabylie. Thus to obtain the thirteen divisions of the Army of Italy, only six new ones had to be created. As of May, Renault's Division returned to France and set itself up at the camp of Sathonay, next to the three divisions of the Army of Lyon. At the same time, a new division was formed on the Durance. Then, nine infantry regiments with special colonial troops arrived from Africa. They converged with the three assembled divisions for a total of eleven. Two other divisions were organized on April 9th with troops taken from the Midi garrisons. In this way, the five corps of the army were formed.

The infantry of the line only lost the following: 7 colonels whose names are in italics in the above list; 7 lieutenant-colonels: Menessier of the 70th (just promoted to colonel of the 65th), Hémard of the 61st, Campagnon of the 2nd, Bigot of the 85th, Ducoin of the 37th, Neuchèze of the 8th, and Vallet of the 94th. Seventeen majors: Duhamel of the 43rd, Lacretelle of the 84th, Duchet of the 98th, Bertrand of the 70th, Boulet of the 73rd, Delord of the 85th, Mariotti of the 90th, Angevin of the 61st, Hébert of the 53rd, Kléber of the 15th, Groüt de Saint-Paer of the 15th, Guillaume of the 61st, Mennessier of the 12th, Nicolas of the 55th, Tiersonnier of the 55th, Noël of the 74th, and Rolland of the 6th, without counting the senior officers belonging to the Guard, the Zouaves and to the Algerian Tirailleurs who perished at Magenta, at Melegnano and at Solferino. This short campaign was called the "campaign of the soldiers," because on both sides, the generals-in-chief were particularly struck by the simplicity of their maneuvers. It has been said maliciously that the French general staff made as many errors as the Austrian general staff. It would be more accurate to say that the Austrian army was astonished by the French soldiers' spirit and that the French had only to march forward to beat them. France was facing troops comparable to its own in terms of training, arms, and recruitment but without prestige or a military past. By contrast, four fifths of the regiments in the Army of Italy arriving from Africa had been in the Crimean campaign. It was by far the best group of troops which France had put together between the years 1813 and 1870. The army of 1823 in Spain had been good but very slow, and they did not have a difficult objective. The Crimean Army experienced much trial and error as well as a number of efforts which were no longer replicable in 1859. Europe was struck by the relative resilience of French military means. Prussia, which had already been watching, resolved to arm all its foot soldiers with needle guns.

In the final days of the campaign, one of the three divisions from the Army of Lyon was called upon to cover the passes of the Alps. It was formed from the 19th, 22nd, 27th and 50th Regiments of the line. In addition, the 68th Regiment of the Geraudon Division also came from Lyon to take up its place in Cremona, Pavia, Genoa, Novare, etc. Finally on June 27th, a small corps formed of naval troops, chasseurs à pied and three battalions of infantry (one from the 3rd and two from the 9th) were sent to the Adriatic to support the operations of the fleet.

Peace having been made, an occupation corps was left in Lombardy under the command of Marshal Vaillant. It was composed of the Bazaine, Bourbaki, de Failly, d'Autemarre, d'Erville and Uhlrich Divisions.

With the return of the occupation corps to France, this excellent organization of infantry into 26 active divisions, including the Guard but excluding Algeria and Rome, found itself dismantled for good. In addition, although there were only a few withdrawals of corps, no reforms were introduced into the army. Meanwhile, a few days before the triumphal return of the Army of Italy into Paris the Emperor was with the corps at Saint-Cloud, who were deliberating the defects of the French military organization. He drew attention to the fact that he himself could pinpoint these problems, having seen them firsthand. Although they were capable of accepting combat from the Austrians or the Russians on a limited and defined field of operations, the French army was incapable of simultaneously sustaining the struggle on the Rhine and on the Adige. The Emperor did not want to call upon the means which a sovereign uses solely for the defense of his own territory.

Amongst these means was the mass levy. This resource was insufficient yet all-powerful, as will be seen further on. It is resorted to by nations which do not have their eligible manpower formed into regiments in an easily mobilized reserve.

As of 1789, the term *garde nationale* (National Guard) had been misused. Despite memories of the first Revolution, the National Guard had been counted on paper as a reserve likely to be used, especially under Louis-Philippe. Three revolutions over a period of forty years demonstrated that the Guard was really a troop belonging only to civil war. It was equally as dangerous for order as for liberty whether it attacked or defended the established power.

France's easy success had dazzled too many people; reform was not well received in the country. It took defeat to open eyes.

The French army did not rest long. The expeditions to China (1860), to Syria (1860), to Mexico, and the faction which was mounted at the doors of the Vatican gave occasion to send troops abroad.

Among the troops which made the expedition to China were the 101st, Colonel Pouget, and the 102nd, Colonel O'Malley.

Infantry of the line (1859).

The rifle of the Crimea and of Italy.

These regiments were formed during the Italian campaign. For the expedition to China, their companies were expanded to 180 men and they were also appointed an additional second lieutenant.

The troops which made the expedition to Syria under the command of the courageous and worthy General Beauford d'Hautpoul were drawn from the Army of Africa and from the camp of Châlons. The numbers of the infantry regiments designated were: the 5th and 13th of the line.

Since the name of the camp of Châlons appears here, it will be touched on immediately prior to discussing the expedition to Mexico and before returning to the occupation of Rome.

Under the Restoration and Louis-Philippe, the camps served as much to establish regular relations between the reigning princes of the dynasty and the army as to train the troops. The camps always proved very useful but none so much so as the camp of Châlons. Every autumn, three infantry divisions and one of cavalry went there for three months to experience unadulterated military life. They came outfitted with all their equipment and operated on a quasi-war footing. Of course, moralists could blame the whims of the Big and the Little Mourmelon and the rain of extravagant and untimely favors which poured down from general headquarters. To the present day, however, no better system has been devised. Grand maneuvers, which are accounted for and justified solely by the short-term call to the reservists, does not and cannot give infantry regiments the solid training that they would get from extended, permanent contact with the romance of war and the realities of life in the open.

The camp of Châlons had the advantage of momentarily expanding the number of infantry divisions ready to march to eleven, including the Guard. This was the situation at the start of the War of 1870. It should be remembered that on August 6, 1870, the 26,000 men of the camp of Chalons engaged in combat with the 5th, 13th, 14th, and 16th German divisions at Spickeren-Forbach. The French inflicted upon the Germans a loss of 49 officers and 794 troops killed, 174 officers and 3,482 troops wounded and 372 unaccounted for. In total, 4,871 men were put out of action. If Castagny's and Metman's divisions had marched to the sound of the guns this same day, they would have arrived in time to confirm victory for the French 2nd Corps commanded by General Frossard, private tutor to the Imperial Prince. The 2nd Corps itself had 4,078 men disabled.

The homogeneity of a troop unit and the confidence which the men gain in finding themselves habitually together was acquired especially in training camps, the best schools of war.

The campaign of Mexico raised an opportunity for the infantry of the line to prove its courage and its aptitude. They marched beside the Zouaves and the chasseurs a pied who never surpassed them in terms of dedication. They began the campaign with few troops as do all distant expeditions wherein governments can neither visualize nor limit the scope of operations. In 1866, the infantry of the line employed enough people that serious difficulties arose when it was believed that France would intervene between Austria and Prussia. At first comprised of a brigade, then of a division and finally of two divisions and a brigade in reserve, the expeditionary corps of Mexico had six infantry regiments in its ranks as follows:

From February 1862 to December 1864: the 99th Regiment of the line, commanded in succession by Colonels l'Herillier then de Saint-Hilaire; *From August 1862 to March 1867:* the 51st, Colonel Garnier; the 95th, Colonels Jolivet then Camas; the 62nd, Colonel Aymard; *From September 1862 to March 1867:* the 81st, Colonel de la Canorgue then de Potier; Finally, *from February 1863 to March 1867:* the 7th Regiment of the line, Colonel Giraud.

After the Crimean campaign, the principle generally adopted was that, from this time on, the regiments would march with 3 full battalions at 6 companies of which 2 were elite companies. They would leave the 5th and 6th of the three battalions at the depots under the command of the major. This procedure was followed for the Italian campaign, but the number of companies was decreased. Infantry regiments of the line were sent to Mexico with two battalions at 7 companies. The chasseurs battalions only had six companies while the Zouave battalions had eight of them.

Head of a column of a regiment, line infantry (1858).

Headgear of the infantry (1805-1887).

Under the disastrous ministrations of Marshal Randon, disorder reigned throughout the army. This was a period of rapid disorganization for the French army in which any memory of its constant success was also laid to rest.

As noted above, the occupation of the Pontifical States employed only two infantry regiments throughout the Italian War. After the transfer of Lombardy to King Victor-Emmanuel and his take-over of the duchies, the conquest of the kingdon of Naples and even of the Pontifical States was essential to Italian politics. All the opposing parties came together in this effort with admirable patriotism. At the same time, the French Emperor — who had dictated the Peace of Villafranca — had to at least respect the person of the Pope, his ally and his protege. The occupation corps was thus increased in terms of its strength and expanded to two infantry divisions (7th, 19th, 29th, 51st, 59th, 62nd, 69th, and 71st Regiments of the line). It was reduced to one division by the successive departures of the 51st, 62nd, and 7th for Mexico. Finally, at the time of the Convention of

Infantry of the line (1865).

September 15th, the Italian government was committed to respect and to make Rome respected, and the Roman states were evacuated. This did not last for long however. Less than four years later in October 1867, two divisions under the command of General de Failly (1st, 19th, 29th, 35th, 42nd, 59th, 80th, and 87th Regiments of the line) protected Rome from Garibaldi's attempts and from the bands which Victor-Emmanuel declared himself incapable of checking.

When the War of 1870 took France by surprise, its infantry counted 100 regiments at 24 companies, in addition to the Imperial Guard, the chasseurs a pied, and the African troops. The companies eliminated by Marshal Randon had been re-established by Marshal Niel. The 101st and the 102nd had been mustered out after the China campaign. Consequently only a 103rd which was formed after the annexation of Savoy passed into French service along with the Sardinian military. The disbanded elite companies permitted their best shots to join other companies. The Chassepot, superior to the German rifle, had replaced the percussion rifle.

France was no longer confronting an ordinary military power. Instead it was facing a Germany unified by the ambitious genius of Bismarck and disciplined by the studied patience of von Moltke. It is now known that, after long consideration by the Emperor and Archduke Albert, Marshal Niel's plan was modified at the last moment for illogical and somewhat dangerous reasons. A notable one was the decision to give more independence to each army corps commander.

Marshal Niel, who had presided over the reformation of the French army, had at his disposal neither the latitude nor the money to resolve all the problems. The law of 1868, which modified the conditions of military service and instituted the *garde nationale mobile*, was hardly useful. An official document dating from 1869 which, in view of the coming elections must have been written by Rouher, contains this phrase: "When the new law has been fully implemented, that is to say in 1877, France will have 750,000 men in the active army and 570,000 *gardes nationaux mobiles*. This statement does not indicate immediate, war-like intentions. Even the government had given Europe proof of peace by decreasing the figure of the annual quota at the request of Thiers.

In the end, France was surprised by the election of a Hohenzollern prince to the Spanish throne and the possibility of war. While inexperienced ministers struggled with riots, Marshal Leboeuf, a most valiant soldier but an administrative novice, was embroiled in the most serious of parliamentary difficulties. All the same, it was enough that if the questioning of Cochery did not take place then war would be avoided and put on hold. The question of Luxembourg happened in much the same way.

The Army of the Rhine was at first composed of seven army corps in addition to the Imperial Guard. The entire French infantry were included in these corps, minus ten infantry regiments of the line, the regiment of the Legion, and the three African light infantry battalions for a total of 96 regiments and 20 battalions of chasseurs a pied. Since 1813, France had not united such a formidable standing army in terms of numbers of men and of regiments. From a stance of parliamentary peace, it had to instantly move to a full-fledged war footing without preparation or a transition period. Because of limited organization, political practices, and new recruitment, France was defeated before having fired a shot. That was the opinion of the perceptive but it was not the opinion of those in the administration.

Infantry of the line (1870).

The list below shows the distribution of the 90 line infantry regiments.

FIRST CORPS
Marshal MAC-MAHON, then DUCROT.

In addition to the 4 battalions of chasseurs and the 6 regiments of Africa (Zouaves and Turcos) this fine corps contained 10 picked infantry regiments: those of the first division from Strasbourg and Belfort; those of the second from Langres, Neuf-Brisach and Colmar; those of the third from Marseille; and those of the fourth from Montpelier.

1st DIVISION, General Ducrot, then Wolff

1st Brigade, General Moreno
18th, Col. Bréger
96th, Col. de Franchessin, then Bluem

2nd Brigade
General de Postis du Houlbec, then Wolff
45th, Col. Bertrand

2nd DIVISION, General Douay (Abel)

1st Brigade, General Pelletier de Montmarie
50th, Col. Ardouin
74th, Col. Theuvez

2nd Brigade, General Pellé
78th, Col. de Carrey de Bellemare

3rd DIVISION, General Raoult

1st Brigade, General L'Herillier
36th, Col. Krien, killed, then Beaudoin

2nd Brigade, General Lefebvre
48th, Col. Rogier

4th DIVISION, General Lartigue

1st Brigade, General Fraboulet de Kerleadec
56th, Col. Mena

2nd Brigade, General Lacretelle
87th, Col. Blot, then Rollet

SECOND CORPS
General FROSSARD
Formed of 3 divisions from the camp of Châlons.

1st DIVISION, General Vergé

1st Brigade, General Letellier-Valazé
32nd, Col. Merle
55th, Col. de Waldener Freundstein

2nd Brigade, General Clinchant
76th, Col. Brice
77th, Col. Février

2nd DIVISION, General Bataille

1st Brigade, General Pouget
8th, Col. Haca
23rd, Col. Rolland

2nd Brigade, General Fauvart-Bastoul
66th, Col. Ameller
67th, Col. Mangin, then Thibaudin

3rd DIVISION, General de Leveaucoupet

1st Brigade, General Doens
2nd, Col. Saint-Hillier, then Voynant
63rd, Col. Zeutz, then Griset

2nd Brigade, General Micheler
24th, Col. Darguesse
40th, Col. Vittot, then Nitot

THIRD CORPS
Marshal BAZAINE, then General DECAEN, then Marshal LEBOEUF
The first 3 divisions belonged to the Army of Paris; the 4th had been formed at Metz and Nancy.

1st DIVISION, General Montaudon

1st Brigade, General Aymard
51st, Col. Delebecque
62nd, Col. Dauphin

2nd Brigade, General Clinchant
81st, Col. Colavier d'Albici
95th, Col. Davout d'Auerstaedt

2nd DIVISION, General Castagny

1st Brigade, General Nayral
19th, Col. De Launay, then Duez
41st, Col. Saussier

2nd Brigade, General Duplessy
69th, Col. Le Tourneur
90th, Col. Roussel de Courcy, then Vilmette

3rd DIVISION, General Metman

1st Brigade, General Pottier
7th, Col. Cottret
20th, Col. Lalanne

2nd Brigade, General Arnaudeau
59th, Col. Duez
71st, Col. d'Audebard de Ferussac

4th DIVISION, General Decaen

1st Brigade, General Bauer
44th, Col. Fournier, then Thoumini de la Haule
60th, Col. Boissié

2nd Brigade, General Sanglé-Ferrière
80th, Col. Janin
85th, Col. Le Breton, then Plauchut

FOURTH CORPS
General LADMIRAULT
All of the regiments of this corps belonged to the garrisons of the East and the North. The first division was at Sedan, Mézières, Nancy and Thionville. The second at Amiens, Béthune, Calais and Dunkirk. The third at Soissons, Arras, Condè and Valenciennes. They only had to draw closer to each other.

1st DIVISION, General de Cissy

1st Brigade, General Brayer
1st, Col. Frémont
6th, Col. Labarthe

2nd Brigade, General de Golberg
57th, Col. Giraud, then Verjus
73rd, Col. Supervielle, then Charmes

2nd DIVISION, General Rose, then Grenier

1st Brigade, General Bellecourt
13th, Col. Lion
43rd, Col. de Viville

2nd Brigade, General Pradier
64th, Col. Lèger
98th, Col. Lechesne

3rd DIVISION, General de Lorencez

1st Brigade, General Pajol
15th, Col. Fraboulet de Kerleadec, then Deroja
33rd, Col. Bounetou

2nd Brigade, General Berger
54th, Col. Caillot, then Grébus
65th, Col. Sée

FIFTH CORPS
General DE FAILLY, then WIMPFEN
This corps included in infantry the Army of Lyon which had been taken away from General Cousin-Montauban's command to be entrusted to an aide of the Emperor.

1st DIVISION, General Goze

1st Brigade, General Grenier
11th, Col. de Behagle
46th, Col. Pichou

2nd Brigade, General Nicolas
61st, Col. Dumoulin
86th, Col. Berthe

2nd DIVISION, General de Labadie d'Aydren

1st Brigade, General Lapasset
49th, Col. Ponsard
84th, Col. Benoit, then Nicot

2nd Brigade, General de Maussion
88th, Col. Courty
97th, Col. Copmartin

3rd DIVISION, General Guyot de Lespart

1st Brigade, General Abbatucci
17th, Col. Weissenburger
27th, Col. Barolet

2nd Brigade, General de Fontange de Couzan
30th, Col. Wirbel
68th, Col. Paturel

SIXTH CORPS
Marshal CANROBERT
Formed from scattered regiments from the North, West, Center and Midi.

1st DIVISION, General Texier

1st Brigade, General Pechot
4th, Col. Vincendon
10th, Col. Ardant du Picq,
then Mercier de Sainte-Croix

2nd Brigade, General Le Roy de Days
12th, Col. Lebrun
100th, Col. Grémion, then de Brem

2nd DIVISION, General Bisson

1st Brigade, General Noël
3rd, Col. Roux, then Lombardeau
14th, Col. Louvent

2nd Brigade, General Maurice
20th, Col. Louveau de la Guigueraye
31st, Col. Sautereau

3rd DIVISION, General Lafont de Villiers

1st Brigade, General Becquet de Sounay
75th, Col. Gibon, then Pean,
then Hochstetter
91st, Col. Daguerre

2nd Brigade, General Colin
93rd, Col. Ganzin
94th, Col. de Geslin

4th DIVISION, General Levassor-Sorval

1st Brigade, General Marguenat
25th, Col. Gibon, then Morin
26th, Col. Hanrion

2nd Brigade, General de Chanaleilles
28th, Col. Lamothe
70th, Col. Henrion Berthier

SEVENTH CORPS
General DOUAY (Abel)
As badly divided as the 6th Corps, it was waiting for its troops from all parts of the territory.

1st DIVISION, General Conseil Dumesnil

1st Brigade, General Nicolai
3rd, Col. Champion
21st, Col. Morand

2nd Brigade, General Maire
47th, Col. de Gramont
99th, Col. Chagrin Saint-Hilaire, then Gouzil

2nd DIVISION, General Liebert

1st Brigade, General Guiomar
5th, Col. Boyer
37th, Col. de Formy de la Blanchetée

2nd Brigade, General de la Bastide
53rd, Col. Japy
89th, Col. Munier

3rd DIVISION, -

1st Brigade, General Bordas
52nd, Col. Aveline
72nd, Col. Bartel

2nd Brigade, -
82nd, Col. Guys, died
83rd, Col. Seatelli

Infantry of the line. Barracks (1885).

Infantry of the line. Inspection in the rooms (1885).

This vast organization used up nine tenths of the active battalions. Only the 35th and the 42nd Regiments of the line were in reserve at the garrison in Rome. The 16th, 38th, and 92nd were in Algeria, and the 22nd, 34th, 58th, and 79th were in Midi. This last group, which had been intended for the formation of an observation division in the Pyrenees, later became the 1st Division of the 12th Corps.

Upon his departure for the army, Marshal Leboeuf's position in the Ministry of War was taken over by an acting replacement as was typically done following first defeats. General Cousin-Montauban, judged too old for battle, took charge of affairs as of July 6th. His indefatigable genius would immediately provide France with troops. There was no lack of men for this truly popular war. Voluntary enlistment ran high and reservists returned quickly. Some regimental histories claim that they had 2,000 men in their depots at the end of August. It was only a matter of organization, precision, and methodology. General Dejean, in the meantime, was full of good intentions, but he was not all too familiar with the mechanism of an administration stamped by a routine predating the new law of recruitment. In matters of mobilization, this administration still followed the procedures of 1859 by which the Army of Italy received its reserves on the eve of the armistice. All the energetic and intelligent officers aspired only to glory on the field of battle. The generals directing the Ministry of War had to be replaced with civilians. They were worn to a frazzle but could prove amazing in their patriotic vigor, as did the Count of Palikao.

Infantry of the line, on reconnaissance (1870).

The massing of 244,828 men on the border within twenty days (on August 2, 1870) was a masterful display of speed when compared to the Crimean and the Italian campaigns. Unfortunately it was insufficient in the face of the million German soldiers which Thiers had publicly claimed were a figment of the imagination! Even before the shocking reversals at Spickeren, Reichshoffen and Wissenbourg had demonstrated our inferiority, the creation of new depot cadres was ordered as well as the formation of fourth battalions in all the regiments. The First Corps had been shaken as much by the poor instructions given for its retreat as by the defeat at Reichshoffen. When they had to be reorganized early on, the 12th, 13th, and 14th Corps were created from whatever was available, General Montauban culled the required troops from the fourth battalions which he formed into *régiments de marche.* In the eyes of the Minister, the 12th Corps, at first assigned to General Trochu then to General Lebrun, had to form a veritable independent army. It had to serve as a reserve for General MacMahon's army. It proved to be excessive in its first strength. Four infantry divisions were added to the Parisian *garde mobile* which itself had seven regiments. One of the new four was a naval regiment, one a *régiment de marche e,* and two were regiments of the line. Two divisions of cavalry and considerable artillery completed this group. General Trochu's nomination to the government of Paris derailed this organization. The Parisian *mobiles* returned to the capital. The first two *régiments de marche* were placed in the 1st Army Corps which had become the Ducrot Corps. Number 1 (4th battalions of the 1st, 6th, and 7th of the line) went to the 2nd division and Number 3 (40th, 62nd, and 64th) into the Fourth.

The 12th Corps (Division General Lebrun) remained permanently formed: 1st of Granchamp's division composed of regiments from the Pyrenees division; 2nd from a division of two brigades, the first composed of what was remaining of Frouard's 14th, 20th, and 30th of Bisson's Division of the 6th Corps which was retired to Châlons, and one brigade of *régiments de marche* (2nd régiment de marche e, 8th, 14th, and 33rd - 4th régiment de marche e, 65th, 91st, and 94th); 3rd from a fine division of naval infantry.

The 13th Corps (Division General Vinoy) also had three divisions commanded by Generals d'Exea, de Maudhuy and Blanchard and composed of the 35th (Colonel de la Mariouse, then Fournes) and the 42nd (Colonel Avril de Lenclos, then Comte) coming from Rome and ten *régiments de marche* as follows:

1st Division - 5th de marche (2,9 and 11), 6th de marche (12, 15 and 19), 7th de marche (20, 23 and 25), 8th de marche (29,41, and 43);

2nd Division -9th de marche (51, 54, and 59), 10th de marche (69, 70 and 71), 11th de marche (75, 81, and 86), 12th de marche (90, 93, and 95);

3rd Division - (1st brigade) 13th de marche (28, 32, and 49), 14th de marche (55, 67, and 100).

Finally, the 14th Corps (Division General Renault), also had 3 divisions formed of 12 régiments de marche.

1st Division - 15th de marche (10, 14, and 26), 16th de marche (35, 38, and 39), 17th de marche (42, 46, and 68), 18th de marche (82, 88, and 97);

2nd Division -19th de marche (16, 27, and 58), 20th de marche (73, 83, and 87), 21st de marche (5, 37, and 36), 22nd de marche (72, 76, and 99);

3rd Division - 23rd de marche (3, 13, and 21), 24th de marche (30, 31, and 34), 25th de marche (47, 48, and 61). 26th de marche (66, 69, and 98).

As one can see, the formations improvised by General Cousin-Montauban provided seven good infantry divisions to which were added almost one quarter of the national forces. On the eve of September 4th, this distinguished military man sent orders to assemble a 15th Corps and outlined plans for a 16th. The 27th *régiment de marche e* was thus created with the 28th following soon thereafter. The four infantry regiments of the line remaining in Africa — four *régiments de marche* of Zouaves and of Tirailleurs — were called to France along with the Foreign Legion. This latter could easily be expanded to 2 regiments.

This gave only a total of 14 regiments, but the number of soldiers forming fourth battalions in the depots was around 1,500 to 2,000. It was therefore conceivable that, with the two hundred new companies created in the infantry, a dozen strong, new regiments could still be organized. The governing body of September 4th found in this last group the resources which would be joined with 91 regiments of *garde mobile*. Beyond this output of men lay the unknown.

Of the Imperial Guard, the 2nd, 3rd, 4th, and 6th Corps were holed up in Metz. The 1st, 5th, 7th, and 12th Corps had been made prisoners at Sedan. The 13th Corps were in a race with the Prussians for Paris. The 14th Corps gathered in the capital and in the provinces. While waiting for superior troops from Africa, they organized those in the country.

From Sedan to Paris, the enemy thus met no obstacles and marched freely.

Simple logic would have dictated that neither the government nor the only two army corps which could hold the country should have been left in the capital. However, with the Empire still in power, politics dominated the marching orders of the armies. Even after the Empire's fall, politics still dominated the course of the war. Paris was enclosed by a Prussian circle within which were trapped the only standing army and the government. Thus when the capital fell, France inevitably fell with it.

Joinville-le-Pont (November 20, 1870).

GOVERNMENT OF THE NATIONAL DEFENSE

Under the First Republic, the mass levy was to have produced 1,500,000 men but resulted in only 400,000. The same results in a different guise were reproduced under the Third Republic.

The dying Empire and the rising Republic had decreed this mass levy in which they called all eligible citizens less than 40 years old into active service. However, as in 1793, many young men who should have joined the army or the *mobile* stayed permanently in the National Guard. This was due to corps from various origins. Many eligible men who were supposed to return to their regiments slipped away. It can truly be said that no rules were obeyed; everyone followed his own conscience. There were even some who hid themselves in their offices and others who simply set off for Belgium or England. The innumerable men who joined the national defense have never been precisely counted.

An effort will be made here to extract truth from the hopeless chaos of *régiments de marche* (provisional regiments), *garde mobile* and legions of *mobilises* (militias), *corps francs* (volunteers), and the *garde nationale mobilisée* or *sedentaire* in which everyone found a position according to his tastes and capacities.

As noted above, the Army of the Rhine contained 244,828 men on August 2, 1870.

The Army of the Rhine and the Army of Chalons counted between them 300,000 at the end of August. If those made prisoner and those killed in the first battles are added to this round figure, the number of soldiers of the regular army can be set at 350,000. It was this army which the Empire set against the German armies and which disappeared after the capitulations at Sedan, Strasbourg, and Metz as well in lesser places in the North and the East.

In his excellent work, General Vinoy gave the figure of Paris' defenders on the day of its capitulation as follows:

National Guard (armed men)	183,000
Troops of the line (all weapon types)	129,720
Navy (transport, infantry, artillery)	14,031
Gardes nationales mobiles (of Paris and the provinces)	105,391
Total	**432,142**

The status of available armies in the provinces at the moment of peace expands their effective strength to:

Men present in the various armies	275,000
Algeria, camps, depots, etc.	354,000
Men from the class of 1871 already called	132,000
Total	**761,000**

Regiment de marche (1870-1871).

If one adds the figures for dead, prisoners and the regiments which had taken refuge in Switzerland to the total assembled, which came to 1,543,142 men, it can be said that the War of 1870-1871 affected all together the lives of 1,650,000 Frenchmen.

The Germans never had more than 936,915 men in France. They claim to have successively brought in 1,146,355. However, given losses on the field of battle, the ill, and the marches and counter-marches along the border, one can reconcile these two different figures.

France's one and one-half million men had never been encouraged, armed or disciplined nor even regularly counted. In order to reconstruct this number of troops, the figures given by General Chanzy must be assumed, supported by his opinion that the war could be continued. This opinion was only natural since he was General-in-Chief.

Of what value were these 761,000 men who as a whole displayed a pride which was more patriotic than practical? Within a few weeks, 132,000 were called up and 354,000 were either in Algeria which was in revolt, or in the camps where the civilian commissioners in particular taught the art of never being prepared to go to the front.

It was not that France did not make noble and energetic efforts, be it in the provinces or in Paris. However, the trade of the soldier is at least as difficult to learn as that of a lawyer, and besides, it requires more training. The best troops had been made prisoner at Sedan and at Metz. Paris retained sixty-six fourth battalions of infantry of the line and twenty-two provisional regiments of *gardes mobiles* in addition to the six formed by its own citizenry. The government of Tours demonstrated great powers of organization. It was rightfully given considerable recognition in the eyes of the public. However, this power was badly used and poorly directed. Gambetta put too much emphasis on quantity and not enough on quality. At Bordeaux as at Tours, it was too often believed that an order given was an order executed, that a gathering of men was in itself a force, and that the art of war thrived on improvisation and sudden shocks. On the other hand, in Paris, where the appearance

The Chassepot rifle and the Dreyse rifle (August 6,

of governmental bureaucracy was propagated, everything proceeded with slowness to the same effect. Though more solid at first glance, this actually produced the same results.

Organizations of Paris. With its own funds Paris organized seven regiments of line infantry, the 28th de marche with the depots of the seven Imperial Guard regiments and the 34th to the 39th de marche with the following components: (The *régiments de marche* of Paris took the numbers 105 to 126, 128 and 134 to 139 on November 30, 1870.) The organization of the six last ones is very unusual:

September 27, 1870

34th de marche 1st battalion, companies of the 5th, 11th, 16th and 19th Line. 2nd battalion, companies of the 20th, 24th, 25th and 33rd. 3rd battalion, companies of the 41st, 43rd, 46th and 54th.

35th de marche 1st battalion, companies of the 55th, 64th, 65th and 68th. 2nd battalion, companies of the 69th, 73rd, 75th and 83rd. 3rd battalion, companies of the 87th, 91st, 93rd, 97th and 99th.

September 28, 1870

36th de marche 16 companies of new cadres.

October 2, 1870

37th de marche 1st battalion, 6 companies of the 7th, 15th and 18th chassuers à pied. 2nd battalion, 6 companies of new cadres. 3rd battalion, companies of the 38th, 66th, 82nd, 86th and 100th.

October 19, 1870

38th de marche 1st battalion, companies of the 4th, 7th, 26th, 32nd, 56th and 62nd. 2nd battalion, companies of the 71st, 72nd, 81st, 90th, 95th and 35th. 3rd battalion, companies of the 61st, 77th, 23rd, 99th, 9th and one new cadre.

October 18, 1870

39th de marche 1st battalion, companies of the 12th, 14th, 21st, 67th, 98th and 97th. 2nd battalion, companies of the 36th, 48th, 94th, 47th, 88th and 76th. 3rd battalion, companies of the 3rd, 22nd, 42nd, 52nd, 89th and one new cadre.

It should be noted that these 66 cadres of companies corresponded to the 66 fourth battalions which contributed to the composition of the *régiments de marche* of the 13th and 14th Corps. It was through taking men from the *régiments de marche* of the first formation that the six new ones were organized.

The regiments of the Army of Paris were maintained in a very respectable manner through volunteer enlistments, the calling up of old soldiers, and the call to the class of 1871. All these regiments in the second series of one hundred took numbers corresponding to their provisional numbers. At the time of the capitulation, their total effective was 2,035 officers and 78,058 men. Their strengths, however, were unequal. The 139th which was the strongest counted 3,340 men in its ranks whereas the weakest, the 122nd, only counted 1,447.

Montbeliard (January 1871).

Organization of the Provinces. Before the Prussians encircled Paris, the capital had regularly supplied the armies of the provinces with the 29th, 30th, 31st, 32nd, and 33rd *régiment de marche*. The fourth battalions thus found themselves depleted. Note that some which were under siege could not rejoin the *régiments de marche* to which they had been assigned. For example there were: the fourth battalions of the 18th and the 96th which participated in the defense of Strasbourg, that of the 45th which distinguished itself at Belfort, and that of the 63rd which was trapped at Phalsbourg.

After the 33rd *régiment de marche*, the provincial delegation formed 59 other *regiments de marche* which took the numbers from 34 to 92. They were distributed in the corps of the army as follows along with those already created.

15th Corps: 30th and 34th. 16th Corps: 31st, 33, 36, 37, 38, 39, 40, and 62nd. 17th Corps: 41st, 43, 45, 46, 48, 51, and 64th (1st battalions). 18th Corps: 42nd, 44, 49, 52, and 53rd. 19th Corps: 55th, 65 (2nd battalion), 65, 66, 70, and 71st. 20th Corps: 50th. 21st Corps: 56th, 58th, and 59th. 22nd Corps: 67th, 68, 69, 72, and 73rd. 24th Corps: 60th, 61, and 63rd. 25th Corps: 74th, 75, 77, 78, and 79th. 26th Corps: 80th, 81, 82, 85, 86, and 87th. Reserve brigade of the 1st Army: 29th. Cremer's Division: 32nd, 47th, and 57th. Loisel's Division (at le Havre): 76th, 88th, and 89th. At Lille: 83rd and 84.th At Bordeaux and at the camp of Saint-Medard: 90th, 91st, and 92nd. The 35th was at Belfort, the 54th at Bitche.

Chasseurs à pied. Bugler, full dress (1885).

Chasseurs à pied. Sergeant-major, campaign dress (1885).

It should not be forgotten that an infantry *régiment de marche* was formed from the remains of the 1st Corps which sought refuge at Strasbourg after the Battle of Woerth. It took no number but was engaged in service. It had five battalions and was placed under the command of Lieutenant-Colonel Rollet of the 47th. It apparently included in its ranks some intact elements, notably an entire battalion of the 21st of the line and many companies of the 74th and 78th. As for the rest, a number of hamlets and villages in Alsace received the fugitives from Woerth. It seems that after this battle, the army of Marshal MacMahon was shattered as it felt the powerlessness of its efforts on that epic day. Many of its regiments did not have time to reform and presented themselves at Sedan in the worst condition.

The *régiments de marche* of the provincial armies were formed consecutively and should not be too harshly judged. Some of them performed courageous marches, but many were ready too late. There had been no time to make a cohesive force from the often very different components which made up a regiment. From that moment on, contact between the officers and the soldiers was non-existent. Moreover, the weapons and the uniforms were so faulty!

Below is a description of how they were generally organized.

Each depot of the old regiment, having filled out a battalion to the best of its abilities, assigned it to a specific village where three battalions of the same type were placed under the command of a lieutenant-colonel.

There was a crying need for cadres of non-commissioned officers whereas the cadre of officers was overflowing. Everyone would accept the officer's epaulette, but no one wanted to be a sergeant. All the officers who had resigned re-enlisted. All the candidates at Saint-Cyr were named second lieutenants. Some willing young men thus slipped into the ranks of the army. This created a rather diverse officers corps but one always full of eagerness and especially of illusions. If there had been a year of preparation as with the First Republic, these improvisations would have turned out well in the end. After all, didn't the volunteers of 1791 and 1792 become good soldiers in 1794?

Officers who escaped from enemy prisons also performed great deeds. These men should be treated with respect. They can be divided into three very distinct categories.

The first, which is fairly numerous, is comprised of the officers who, in the general disorder and through their own daring, managed to escape at the moment of a capitulation rather than fall into enemy hands.

The second group is less common than might be imagined. (*The Monitor of Seine-et-Oise*, the official Prussian newspaper, cites only 112 names associated with this category.) It consists of officers of all military service branches loosely interned on condition that they respond daily to the roll-call but who escaped from this requirement.

Finally, the third group, even more rare still, includes the officers who refused to take on any engagement and who escaped from the fortresses where the enemy kept them.

As for the officers who signed the *revers*, this meant they consented to sign a promise not to rejoin the service for the duration of the war in order to regain their freedom. One should pity them for having leaders who allowed such a clause to be included in the capitulation agreements.

Before addressing the operation of mustering out the Army of 1870-1871, some words should be said about the *régiments de la mobile*, the *garde nationale mobilisée*, and the *corps francs*.

Through a series of organizations, the *régiments de la mobile* reached 104 in number.

Three were sent to Algeria; the 9th (Allier), the 21st (Creuse) and the 43rd (Bouches-du-Rhône). They served well there and were only repatriated some time after the peace.

These corps were often of high caliber as their soldiers were generally energetic, intelligent and resolute. They could be faulted a bit for their officers' corps which in the beginning lacked military training. However, little by little they developed and by the end of the campaign, many of the

Gardes mobiles of the provinces. Bugler (1871).

provisional regiments (*garde mobile*) were better than some *régiments de marche* (line). Some unusual circumstances appeared. In the provinces, the *mobile* was used in the same manner as the line. In Paris, however, the line was much more productive than the *mobile*. This was because, in Paris, Generals Trochu and Ducrot, the great leaders of its defense, only believed in *les pantalons rouges*. In the provinces, however, under the influence of Gambetta, the generals treated all the troops in the same way.

The *garde nationale mobilisée* was poorly used in Paris. In the provinces, it was used unevenly and often not at all. Clearly better advantage could have been taken of the situation.

In Paris, the *garde national mobilisee* was slowly organized and was only ready for Buzenval where it did what it could and should do. It was generally commanded by inexperienced officers more concerned with their bearing than with the supervision of their men. It had resolution but lacked tenacity. It marched bravely under fire but could not sustain this for very long. It reflected fairly accurately the manner in which it was led.

In the provinces, on the other hand, the *garde national mobilisée* sometimes proved itself worthy. When it was actually mobilized and taken far from its native soil, it was truly militarized.

As for the *corps francs*, their numbers were excessive. Although there were some which never performed any worthwhile

service, others were useful auxiliaries for the army.

When peace was finally concluded, the first act of Thiers, who had been elected chief of the executive power, was to dissolve everything that was not to be included in the standard reorganization of the permanent army.

This mustering out affected two very distinct elements: the men and the corps.

All the men (officers and soldiers) who had been called into active service just for the duration of the war had to return to their homes.

All the corps of *mobiles*, of the *gardes nationales mobilisées* and of the *francs-tireurs* (guerillas or partisans) were disbanded.

It was an inevitable move. The only difficulties experienced had to do with the German occupation of a major portion of the territory.

As for the regular army, it found itself confronting a tough problem. Very few of the old corps had been able to escape from the unfortunate necessity of capitulating. A considerable number of new corps already had deserved the right of recognition from the country.

There were 98 *régiments de marche* for just the infantry of the line:

27	formed before September 4th of which 4 had been imprisoned by the enemy;
7	formed at Paris;
64	formed in the provinces.

Total   98

General of division and staff officers (1884).

In addition, the 3 regiments of grenadiers and the 4 of voltigeurs of the former Guard, henceforth disbanded, had 105 regiments which had to be merged with the one hundred old regiments of the line.

Any difficulties in deciding how to do this were cut short by the new government which required the following mergers as of February 1871. All *régiments de marche* would be assigned to the old regiments corresponding to their numbers. Also, the old regiments numbered 93 to 100 would take in: the 37th régiment de marche (from Paris), the 1st Grenadiers, the 38th régiment de marche (from Paris), the former 2nd Voltigeurs, the 39th régiment de marche (from Paris), and the former 3rd Grenadiers.

The 3rd and 4th Voltigeurs were to be merged into the old 83rd and 84th of the line.

In addition, 4 new regiments (101 to 104) were to be formed from the remains of the *régiments de marche* — Numbers 34, 35, and 36, numbers duplicating those formed in the provinces. However, this decision was never executed and, except for the 35th which became the 135th, these regiments disappeared. Their remnants were actually merged into the 34th, 35th, and 36th regiments of the line and *régiments de marche*.

The events of March 18th surprised the government which was in the middle of reorganizaton. Everything which had not been mustered out at this point was retained. The primary objective was to face the internal enemy who had just compounded the great disaster of the German invasion.

The regiments 31, 32, 36, 38, 39, 41, 46, 67, 68, 69, 76, 88, and 89 de marche which had been called to Paris before March 18th were joined at Versailles by the regiments 26, 31, 37, 45, 48, 51, 55, 58, 64, 65, 70, 71, 74, 82, 85, and 87 de marche. This amounted to 29 regiments. Given new uniforms, strengthened, and energetically commanded, these troops quickly shaped up and assumed a very strong military character.

In addition, the 109th, 110th, 113th, 114th, 119th, and 135th of Paris, which had not been mustered out, were retained.

Next Thiers decided that, as quickly as the officers and soldiers returned from enemy prisons, they would be formed into 30 provisional regiments numbered from 1 to 30.

This was an inspired idea. France was faced with the incredible revolt of Paris and the war in Algeria. The Commune also showed its teeth in many of the larger provincial cities. Things had to move quickly and especially with no disorganization in the ranks of the *régiments de march* which were developing more cohesion with every passing day. The provisional officers who had been retained in the ranks by means of a war department memorandum would be frightened to see their legal

replacements arriving. In fact, by staying in the ranks they gained new titles, and the creation of new corps allowed them to hope that their efforts would be rewarded. General Le Flô, then Minister of War, presided over the formation of the new regiments which were called provisional regiments. In this case, he showed a method, a talent and sound judgement which ranks him among the best of military administrators. It can only be regretted that he was left shut up in Paris during the war. The memorandum which he wrote on this occasion was a model which could still be used when the French army needs a makeshift elite military body. When the Imperial Guard was originally organized, no one showed such a flair and confidence although France ruled its own territory then and there were only four regiments.

On March 27, 1871, General Le Flô ordered Generals Clinchant and Ducrot to go to Lille and to Cherbourg, respectively, and to organize there companies formed as much as possible of officers and soldiers belonging to the same regiments, all of whom were returning from enemy prisons. When they had six companies, they should create a battalion. When they had three battalions, a colonel and a general staff would be assigned and an offical report would confirm the permanent formation.

The memorandum was issued on March 27th. On April 7th and 8th, the first four provisionals were already prepared to leave for Versailles.

The newly uniformed men, supplied with their equipment and ninety cartridges, were identified by a madder-colored crescent of fabric attached to the number that they wore on their kepis and by the collar of their greatcoats. Twenty regiments (Nos. 1 to 19 and 21) were rapidly formed in this manner. They soon took their places alongside the *régiments de marche* to defend Algeria and the public order of Paris threatened by a horde of ungodly and unpatriotic louts.

Naturally, the prescribed merger in the aftermath of peace suffered from ill timing. The previously commanded formation of the 101st, 102nd, 103rd, and 104th regiments was countermanded. Then, as quickly as people were available, the remains of the old regiments which had not been included in the formation of the provisional regiments joined up with the *régiments de marche.* At the end of 1871, France possessed one hundred and twenty-six regiments of infantry as follows:

Special Military School, review (1884).

One hundred old regiments of the old formation of which the first 92 had received general staffs, the soldiers of the former Guard, and soldiers of the *régiments de marche*. All had three battalions of eight companies;

Six *régiments de marche* which had become the 109th, 110th, 113th, 114th, 119th, and 135th of the line who came from the defense of Paris. They had three battalions of six companies;

Finally, twenty provisional regiments also with three battalions of six companies.

On April 10, 1872 these three organizations were made into one. The regiments were numbered amongst them, the old ones at the head of the list with the provisional and the former *régiments de marche* following the order which will be given later. In the process of this painful reorganization, a parliamentary commission tried to revise the titles so freely granted during the campaign. However, this was done with a truly regrettable partiality. In taking upon themselves a job which logically was the responsibility of a committee composed of the generals-in-chief, Parliament assumed a heavy burden. The results provided a very poor historical precedent. The legislature should never perform the tasks of the executive, especially for the army. The army was affected by and would feel the effects of the Commission for the Revision of Ranks during the next ten years.

France, however, was producing a new military organization. She had been beaten — heavily beaten — because she had had little regard for what was happening on the other side of the Rhine. In having not wished to understand what the armed nation was she had lost two provinces, her international prestige and domestic peace. In 1873, France decided therefore to do once again what she had done after the Italian campaign in 1860.

The country submitted to mandatory service in-person, mitigated by the protective institutions of laws and civil needs displayed by an enlightened nation. It finally adopted the system of immediate mobilization supported by the general staffs, the permanent cadres, and the effective strengths of peacetime. In this system, the reserves were the first to be called up. It was more or less the Prussian system revised according to French ideas and customs. Service for five years which was adopted at the end of the Empire was now modified. At the end of active service, the citizen still had to remain in the reserve service until thirty years of age, or until forty in the territories. Thiers obstinately persisted in envisioning the continuation and evolution of replacement in the form of a voluntary one-year service term. This one year stint was at first too generously lavished upon the bourgeoisie, then reduced, but it was too miserly in the reduction. True progress was made in the system of mobilization. Advances were also made with the creation of 18 permanent army corps, each including two divisions of infantry at two brigades which each had two regiments — all together 144 regiments. It thus became necessary to create eighteen regiments. To do this, the seven old regiments called upon to form an army corps each detached three companies and formed regiments with three battalions of seven companies. The law of the cadres would standardize all these differences in the constitutions of regiments. It instituted 144 regiments of infantry at four battalions with four companies each plus two depot companies.

Practice march (1884).

Having arrived at the end of this study on the modern history of the infantry of the French army, a pause for brief reflection is in order.

Progress has touched the entire army. The result is that soldiers remain in active service for only some forty months. For this reason the French regiments no longer exhibit the same spirit or the same appearance as in the past. Through wear and tear, the value of the new institutions are recognized. Time and events will judge our organization. For the moment, we will just focus on its practical aspects. A regiment and, by consequence, the entire army should be able to move from a peaceful mode to a war footing in a few days. Some say in four days; others say six. Every infantry regiment fields on average 5,590 men including the reserve and its men on leave. With this effective strength, it must first assemble three battalions of one thousand men, called full war battalions. Companies have 250 men, 4 officers of which one is in reserve, 9 non-commissioned

officers, and 16 corporals. Immediately thereafter, they must form a fourth battalion of the same strength called the fortress bataillon which includes civilians. This battalion is assigned either to guard fortified towns or to increase the number of army corps with the *régiments de marche.* Finally, fifth battalions are to be formed from the depot cadres using available reserve officers. These battalions must be ready to reinforce the full regiment if need be.

In addition, there are as many territorial infantry regiments as there are regiments of the line. There is actually even one more of the former type.

ORIGINS AND DATE OF FORMATION OF THE 144 REGIMENTS COMPOSING THE INFANTRY OF THE LINE

1st Line	Formed, in 1820, from the Ain Legion.
2nd -	Formed from the Aisne Legion.
3rd -	Formed from the Allier and the Nievre Legions.
4th -	Formed from the Aube and the Deux-Sévres Legions.
5th -	Formed from the Averyon and the Drome Legions.
6th -	Formed from the Bouches-du-Rhône Legion.
7th -	Formed from the Calvados Legion.
8th -	Formed from the Cantal and the Vendée Legions.
9th -	Formed from the Cher and the Indre Legions.
10th -	Formed from the Corréze and the Lozére Legions.
11th -	Formed from the Côte d'Or Legion.
12th -	Formed from the 1st Côte-du-Nord Legion.
13th -	Formed from the Dordogne Legion.
14th -	Formed from the Eure Legion.
15th -	Formed from the Finistére Legion.
16th -	Formed from the Gard Legion.
17th -	Formed from the Haute-Garonne Legion.
18th -	Formed from the Gers and the Landes Legions.
19th -	Formed from the 1st Gironde Legion.
20th -	Formed from the Herault Legion.
21st -	Formed from the 1st Ille-et-Vilaine Legion.
22nd -	Formed from the Isére Legion.
23rd -	Formed fro the Loire-Inferieure Legion.
24th -	Formed from the Maine-et-Loire Legion.
25th -	Formed from the 1st Manche Legion.
26th -	Formed from the Morbihan Legion.
27th -	Formed from the Moselle Legion.
28th -	Formed from the 1st North Legion.
29th -	Formed from the 2nd North Legion.
30th -	Formed from the Oise Legion.
31st -	Formed from the Orne Legion.
32nd -	Formed from the 1st Pas-de-Calais Legion.
33rd -	Formed from the Puy-de-Dome Legion.
34th -	Formed from the Bas-Rhin Legion.
35th -	Formed from the Haut-Rhin Legion.
36th -	Formed from the Saone-et-Loire Legion.
37th -	Formed from the Sarthe Legion.
38th -	Formed from the Seine-et-Oise Legion.
39th -	Formed from the 1st Seine-Inférieure Legion.
40th -	Formed from the Somme Legion.
41st -	Formed from the Aude and the 2nd Ille-et-Vilaine Legions.
42nd -	Formed from the Charente Legion.
43rd -	Formed from the Charente-Inferieure and the 2nd Manche Legions.
44th -	Formed from the Doubs and the 2nd Pas-de-Calais Legions.
45th -	Formed from the Eure-et-Loir Legion.
46th -	Formed from the Indre-et-Loire Legion.
47th -	Formed from the Loir-et-Cher and the 2nd Seine Legions.
48th -	Formed from the Loiret Legion.
49th -	Formed from the Lot and the 2nd Gironde Legions.
50th -	Formed from the Lot-et-Garonne and the 2nd Seine-Inferieure Legions.
51st -	Formed from the Marne Legion.
52nd -	Formed from the Meurthe Legion.
53rd -	Formed from the Meuse Legion.
54th -	Formed from the Rhone Legion.
55th -	Formed from the 1st Seine Legion.
56th -	Formed from the Seine-et-Marne Legion.
57th -	Formed from the Tarn Legion.
58th -	Formed from the Tarn-et-Garonne Legion.
59th -	Formed from the Vienne and the 2nd Côtes-du-Nord Legions.
60th -	Formed from the Yonne Legion.
61st -	Formed from various detachments by the ordinance of February 2,1823 at the start of the Spanish war.
62nd -	"
63rd -	"
64th -	"
65th -	Created by the ordinance of August 17, 1830 with the remnants of the Royal Guard.
66th -	"
67th -	Formed in Algiers by the ordinance of May 4, 1831 with Parisian volunteers from the Regiment of la Charte.
68th -	Formed by the ordinance of September 29, 1840 from various detachments at the moment when European complications were feared.
69th -	"
70th -	"
71st -	"
72nd -	"
73rd -	"
74th -	"
75th -	"
76th -	Formed under the name of the 1st Light Infantry in 1820 from the Ardennes Legion. Became the 76th in 1854.
77th -	Formed as the 2nd Light in 1820 from the Basses-Alpes Legion. 77th in 1854.
78th -	Formed as the 3rd Light in 1820 from the Hautes-Alpes Legion. 78th in 1854.
79th -	Formed as the 4th Light in 1820 from the Ardéeche Legion. 79th in 1854.
80th -	Formed as the 5th Light in 1820 from the Ariége Legion. 80th in 1854.
81st -	Formed as the 6th Light in 1820 from the Creuse Legion. 81st in 1854.
82nd -	Formed as the 7th Light in 1820 from the Haute-Loir Legion. 82nd in 1854.
83rd -	Formed as the 8th Light in 1820 from the Loire Legion. 83rd in 1854.
84th -	Formed as the 9th Light in 1820 from the Haute-Loire Legion. 84th in 1854.
85th -	Formed as the 10th Light in 1820 from the Corsican Legion. 85th in 1854.
86th -	Formed as the 11th Light in 1820 from the Haute-Marne Legion. 86th in 1854.
87th -	Formed as the 12th Light in 1820 from the Mayenne Legion. 87th in 1854.
88th -	Formed as the 13th Light in 1820 from the Basses-Pyrénées Legion. 88th in 1854.
89th -	Formed as the 14th Light in 1820 from the Hautes-Pyrénées Legion. 89th in 1854.
90th -	Formed as the 15th Light in 1820 from the Pyrénées-Orientales Legion. 90th in 1854.
91st -	Formed as the 16th Light in 1820 from the Haute-Saone Legion. 91st in 1854.
92nd -	Formed as the 17th Light in 1820 from the Var Legion. 92nd in 1854.
93rd -	Formed as the 18th Light in 1820 from the Vaucluse Legion. 93rd in 1854.
94th -	Formed as the 19th Light in 1820 from the Haute-Vienne Legion. 94th in 1854.
95th -	Formed as the 20th Light in 1820 from the Vosges Legion. 95th in 1854.
96th -	Formed as the 21st Light by the ordinance of January 5, 1831 from the Hohenlohe Legion. 96th in 1854.
97th -	Created as the 22nd Light by the ordinance of September 29, 1840. 97th in 1854.
98th -	Created as the 23rd Light by the ordinance of September 29, 1840. 98th in 1854.
99th -	Created as the 24th Light by the ordinance of September 29, 1840. 99th in 1854.
100th -	Created as the 25th Light by the ordinance of September 29, 1840. 100th in 1854.
101st	Created as the 1st Provisional (circular of March 27, 1871). 101st on April 4, 1872.
102nd -	Created as the 2nd Provisional (circular of March 27, 1871). 102nd on April 4, 1872.
103rd -	Created as the 3rd Provisional (circular of March 27, 1871). 103rd on April 4, 1872.
104th -	Created as the 4th Provisional (circular of March 27, 1871). 104th on April 4, 1872.
105th -	Created as the 5th Provisional (circular of March 27, 1871). 105th on April 4, 1872.
106th -	Created as the 6th Provisional (circular of March 27, 1871). 106th on April 4, 1872.
107th -	Created as the 7th Provisional (circular of March 27, 1871). 107th on April 4, 1872.
108th -	Created as the 8th Provisional (circular of March 27, 1871). 108th on April 4, 1872.
109th -	Created in August 1870 as the 9th de marche with the fourth battalions of the 51st, 54th and 59th Line. Became the 109th on November 1, 1870.
110th -	Created in August 1870 as the 10th de marche with the fourth battalions of the 69th, 70th and 71st Line. Became the 110th on November 1, 1870.
111th -	Created as the 11th Provisional (circular of March 27, 1871). 111th on April 4, 1872.
112th -	Created as the 12th Provisional (circular of March 27, 1871). 112th on April 4, 1872.
113th -	Created in August 1870 as the 13th de marche with the fourth battalions of the 28th, 32nd and 49th Line. Became the 113th on November 1, 1870.
114th -	Created in August 1870 as the 14th de marche with the fourth battalions of the 55th, 67th and 100th Line. Became the 114th on November 1, 1870.
115th -	Created as the 15th Provisional (circular of March 27, 1871). 115th on April 4, 1872.
116th -	Created as the 16th Provisional (circular of March 27, 1871). 116th on April 4, 1872.
117th -	Created as the 17th Provisional (circular of March 27, 1871). 117th on April 4, 1872.
118th -	Created as the 18th Provisional (circular of March 27, 1871). 118th on April 4, 1872.
119th -	Created in August 1870 as the 19th de marche with the fourth battalions of the 15th, 27th and 58th Line. Became the 118th (sic) on November 1, 1870.
120th -	Created as the 35th de marche on September 27, 1870, became the 135th on November 1, 1870 and the 120th on April 4, 1872.
121st -	Created as the 21st Provisional (circular of March 27, 1871). 121st on April 4, 1872.
122nd -	Created as the 9th Provisional (circular of March 27, 1871). 122nd on April 4, 1872.
123rd -	Created as the 10th Provisional (circular of March 27, 1871). 123rd on April 4, 1872.
124th -	Created as the 13th Provisional (circular of March 27, 1871). 124th on April 4, 1872.
125th -	Created as the 14th Provisional (circular of March 27, 1871). 125th on April 4, 1872.
126th -	Created as the 19th Provisional (circular of March 27, 1871). 126th on April 4, 1872.
127th -	Created September 29, 1873 with companies drawn from the 1st, 8th, 33rd, 43rd, 73rd, 84th and 110th Line.
128th -	Created September 29, 1873 with companies drawn from the 45th, 51st, 54th, 67th, 72nd, 87th and 120th Line.
129th -	Created September 29, 1873 with companies drawn from the 5th, 24th, 28th, 36th, 39th, 74th and 119th Line.
130th -	Created September 29, 1873 with companies drawn from the 101st, 102nd, 103rd, 104th, 115th, 117th and124th Line.
131st -	Created September 29, 1873 with companies drawn from the 31st, 46th, 76th, 82nd, 85th, 89th and 113th Line.
132nd -	Created September 29, 1873 with companies drawn from the 26th, 37th, 69th, 79th, 91st, 94th and 106th Line.
133rd -	Created September 29, 1873 with companies drawn from the 21st, 23rd, 35th, 42nd, 44th, 60th and 109th Line.
134th -	Created September 29, 1873 with companies drawn from the 4th, 10th, 13th, 27th, 29th, 56th and 95th Line.
135th -	Created September 29, 1873 with companies drawn from the 32nd, 66th, 68th, 77th, 90th, 114th and 125th Line.
136th -	Created September 29, 1873 with companies drawn from the 2nd, 25th, 41st, 47th, 48th, 70th and 71st Line.
137th -	Created September 29, 1873 with companies drawn from the 19th, 62nd, 64th, 65th, 93rd, 116th and 118th Line.
138th -	Created September 29, 1873 with companies drawn from the 14th, 50th, 63rd, 78th, 80th, 107th and 108th Line.
139th -	Created September 29, 1873 with companies drawn from the 16th, 38th, 86th, 92nd, 98th, 105th and 121st Line.
140th -	Created September 29, 1873 with companies drawn from the 22nd, 30th, 52nd, 75th, 96th, 97th and 99th Line.
141st -	Created September 29, 1873 with companies drawn from the 3rd, 40th, 55th, 58th, 61st, 111th and 112th Line.
142nd -	Created September 29, 1873 with companies drawn from the 12th, 15th, 17th, 81st, 88th, 100th and 122nd Line.
143rd -	Created September 29, 1873 with companies drawn from the 7th, 9th, 11th, 29th, 39th, 88th and 126th Line.
144th -	Created September 29, 1873 with companies drawn from the 6th, 18th, 34th, 49th, 53rd, 57th and 123rd Line.

These are fine regiments commanded by retired officers or those who have resigned. They are composed of men aged from 30 to 35 years old who have all spent time in active service. If the nation was called upon to take up its past position in a European conflict, there is no doubt that these regiments would respond as well as did the *mobiles* of 1870 — and they would be ready faster.

Modifications in Dress. Under the Empire in 1859, the tunic with its single row of buttons was replaced by a small jacket with a circular skirt. This was fine and had already been tried by the chasseurs of the Guard. However, it was never required to be worn by officers as the wearer needed to have a trim waist and good legs. The inconveniences of this uniform were quickly perceived. Thus, the tunic and long pants came back although the tunic now had two rows of buttons.

The current practice of adopting a specially designed jacket for officers has provided the military outfitters with endless problems. It is not at all typical of the French to dress their leaders differently than their soldiers.

On the other hand, it can be said that, over the past forty years, the battle uniform has always been in the same colors just as the French flag has always been the same colors. This uniform consists of red pants, gaiters, the grey greatcoat, and the red kepi. It provides a standard form of dress which allows the men to be at ease in many a difficult situation. It was worn in Africa, at Anvers, at Rome, in the Crimea, at Bomarsund, in Italy, in China, and in Mexico. Today, while awaiting development of an improved version, it has appeared in Tunisia and in Tonkin.

A reinforcement brigade, commanded by General Maurand, was composed of the 30th Battalion of Chasseurs and of the 20th, 38th, and 92nd Regiments of the line.

All these regiments were formed of 2 battalions with 4 companies of 150 men. The disorganization that occurred when they were sent to Tunisia resulted in so many complaints that they were brought back as quickly as possible. They were replaced by the fourth battalions. Fourth battalions were also detailed to Africa and the Tonkin. The *régiment de marche* supplied by the infantry of the line for the latter expedition was composed of 3 fourth battalions of the 23rd, 111th, and 143rd Regiments of the line.

Despite all the improvements in the past twelve years, the French infantry is still the subject of continual, bitter debate. France is always in a state of military revolution which worries the officers and disrupts the nation's confidence in its army. In the interests of France, it is high time that the military institutions enter into a period of calm. Only stability can promote progress and give the regiments that self-confidence which was the secret of France's superiority and victories in the past.

TUNISIAN EXPEDITIONARY CORPS
Commander in chief: General of division FORGEMOL DE BOSTQUÉNARD *Chief of staff:* Colonel Polignac

LEFT COLUMN General of brigade Logerot	RIGHT COLUMN General of division Delebecque
1st Brigade, General Logerot 2nd Algerian Tirailleurs 82nd Infantry Regiment, one battalion of the 1st Zouaves	1st Brigade, General Vincendon 7th Battalion of Chasseurs 40th, 96th and 141st Infantry Regiments
2nd Brigade, General de Brem 27th Battalion of Chasseurs 27th and 142nd Line	2nd Brigade, General Galland 20th Battalion of Chasseurs 18th, 22nd and 52nd Infantry Regiments
	3rd Brigade, General Caillot 2nd and 3rd Zouaves Regiments de marche (1st and 3rd Algerian Tirailleurs)

The flag of the First Battalion of France (1885).

Trophies of chasseur à pied batallions.

Chasseurs à Pied

The chasseurs à pied began as a small battalion formed first by General Grosbon and thereafter by subsequent commanders. Early on it bore the title of Tirailleurs of Africa. It was first seen in action in 1839 in the expedition of *Portes-de-Fer*.

Organized temporarily on a trial basis by a royal decree of November 14, 1838, it was permanently established by the decree of September 16, 1839 at 6 companies with an effective strength of 824 men. It was based at Vincennes where it had already completed its first formation. Its weapons were very advanced for the times and its dress somewhat unusual. The sunburned complexion of some of the veterans from the Army of Africa were visible in its ranks. Parisians were immensely taken with the quick pace of its marching, and they held the chasseurs in high esteem. Immediately its soldiers were christened with the name "chasseurs of Vincennes," a name which they kept despite their dispersal and a number of decrees. For a long time, the populace also called them "les vitriers" (glaziers). This was due to their habit of slinging their canvas sacks over their carbines at rest-stops during a march, just as itinerant glaziers carried their glazing sacks over their rules.

Marshal Soult said in presenting the first battalion to the King: "I would like not one but thirty battalions such as this in the French army." The Marshal's wish has been granted today. However, the chasseurs battalions have an organization exactly the same as that of a battalion of the line. Given, the colors of their uniform have been retained and with them the soundness and resilience of their esprit de corps.

In 1839, they were armed with Minie carbines which terrified the Arabs. When these Arabs saw horsemen placed at what was thought to be a safe distance fall from the shots of these carbines, they believed themselves confronted by demons. They gave the African Tirailleurs of Africa the name "lascars negros" (black foot soldiers), which was added to their already long list of nicknames. At the battle of Col, the adjutant Pistouley of the first battalion, since made Colonel, had amazed the Duke of Orléans with his precision shooting. This is perhaps one of the reasons which persuaded the royal prince to enlarge their organization. He had the consent of Marshal Soult who dominated everything concerning military affairs. Thus, he was easily able to create new corps like the ones formed by Grosbon. They were commanded by the future general Ladmirault.

A decree of August 28, 1840 ordered the creation of ten battalions of chasseurs à pied , each at eight companies, including one of carabiniers armed with special carbines. This company was disbanded in the month of March 1849. King Louis-Philippe wanted to commemorate the part played by the royal prince in the creation of this group. On August 18, 1842 after the death of his oldest son, he decided that the chasseurs would bear the title "Chasseurs d'Orléans." Naturally, the Revolution of 1848 restored their name to chasseurs à pied which they have retained ever since.

On November 1, 1840 under the noble direction of the Duke of Orléans, inspector general of the new corps, they proceeded ahead with their formation and training which was rapidly carried out. The Duke of Aumale and General of Brigade de Rostolan had been added to the group at this time. As one might imagine, given the princely names of the patrons of the new troops, nothing was spared in rendering them magnificent. The best officers, non-commissioned officers and soldiers to be found were sent to the camp of Saint-Omer. Never in military history had such a splendid group of officers and young soldiers been seen. They were

Tirailleurs of Africa (1839).

enthusiastic and ready to enter into a campaign. It was like a young Royal Guard which the princes had carefully formed from the elite members of the French infantry. However, promotion was slower for the lieutenants and the second lieutenants than in the rest of the army. Despite this disadvantage which was soon recognized, the first numbers of the School of Saint-Cyr continued for a long time to choose the chasseurs à pied battalions upon leaving the infantry. The names of the first ten battalion leaders who commanded them show the care taken in choosing them at this time:

Chasseurs of Orléans marching by (May 4, 1841).

1st battalion, Ladmirault	6th battalion, Forey
2nd battalion, Faivre	7th battalion, Répond
3rd battalion, Camou	8th battalion, Ulrich
4th battalion, de Bousingen	9th battalion, Clèrc
5th battalion, Mellinet	10th battalion, de MacMahon

Two of these distinguished leaders became Marshals of France. The battalion adjutant Canrobert from the 6th battalion had the same good luck. To be named a major of the chasseurs à pied was for a long time, as it still is today, a kind of coupon for the rank of general. It would be used in the future, and the promise of a generalship would almost always be honored under normal circumstances.

In April 1841, the chasseurs already served Europe as models for a type of elite troop. However, with the vanishing fears of a European war, they were considered for use in Africa.

They were first summoned to Paris so that knowledgeable persons could admire them and learn the new maneuvers which later would become standard for the entire French army. With the exception of a few companies of the 1st Battalion which were with the Army of Africa, they all camped in the plain of Saint-Ouen. There they demonstrated their shooting skills to good effect. On May 4th, the king reviewed them and put them into active service. Probably only a few Parisians remember this military event. Already favorably impressed by these hearty and well chosen soldiers, the populace was enormously thrilled when they saw these 8,000 men. The soldiers were dressed in dark colors, wore black plumes in their shakos and were preceded by a lively and loud fanfare. They moved down the boulevards at a jogging trot and plunged into the Cour de Carrousel without hesitation, with no reduction in speed, and with no disorder, just like a long serpent.

As of the following day, the ten new battalions received orders to return to the garrisons to which they had been assigned. These garrisons were in cities having artillery target ranges where they could practice their shooting. The full war companies of the 3rd, 5th, 6th, and 8th left for Algeria. The 2nd stayed in Vincennes with the company flag.

Upon their arrival in Africa, the chasseurs à pied were the pride of the entire army: the 6th Battalion in the combats of the Oued-Sada (1842); the 9th in the expedition of Flittas where it lost its commander, Clèrc; the 8th at Djemaa-Ghazouat where almost the entire force was overcome as it rallied around the commander Froment-Coste. This action is written on the unusual flag of the chasseurs à pied under the words "Sidi-Brahim."

This last event was one of the greatest armed actions of the Army of Africa but also one of its greatest losses.

All the chasseurs battalions — the old as well as the new, those from 1840 and those from 1853 — consider the combat at Djemaa-Ghazouat as their supreme moment of glory. Although they were later to engrave their numbers on all the battlefields of Europe, Africa, Asia, and America, it is Sidi-Brahim which stands out in their memories, along with Rome, Sebastopol and Puebla. The best example that a combat soldier can bequeath to his comrades is the sacrifice of life for the honor of the flag without hope of winning or of being relieved. Not to give up, "potius mori" (better to die...), is the most heroic action of all. It should be honored above all others because it glorifies even defeats and exonerates the greatest mistakes. The history of this fatal day is described by a historian as follows.

SIDI-BRAHIM

"...On September 23, 1845, it was noticed that the arab posts had drawn nearer under cover of darkness. At nine in the morning, Colonel Montagnac handed over command of the camp to Commander Froment-Coste of the 8th Battalion. He started to march with the leader of the squadrons, Courby de Cognord, and his sixty cavaliers of the 2nd Hussars. They were followed by the 3rd, 6th and 7th carabinier squadrons under the command of Sergeant Bernard. The infantry was without knapsacks; the cavalry marched at a walk at the head; the colonel led the group himself.

"To guard the camp there were only the 2nd Company and the carabiniers, minus the three squadrons.

"The first column advanced to within 400 meters of the enemy and experienced initial resistance. The majority of the hussars perished in the first charge. The chasseurs retreated, at a run. A ravine appeared which they had to cross. The chasseurs had just started to cross it when masses of Kabyles attacked them from all sides. They had not expected such a strong show of

enemy force, but they managed to take a position. The square was formed with great efficiency and then a horrible scene of destruction began. Among the first to fall was Colonel de Montagnac. A few months later, those who were called to gather the precious remains of these heroic victims of duty and discipline could relate how each one died at his position 'without cartridges,' unable to counter-attack. They waited for death and fell 'like an old wall that had been breached.'

"However, the second and equally sad episode was underway. Sergeant Barbut had come crawling on his stomach to ask for help for the dying colonel. He said that everything was lost, that the emir was personally commanding enormous forces, and that there was no possibility of retreat. Commander Froment-Coste took sixty chasseurs (2nd Company) with him and rushed toward the enemy. This left Captain de Géreaux and his carabiniers to guard the camp. He arrived one quarter of a league from the field of carnage when suddenly the firing ceased. The raucous arrival of thousands

*Defense of a marabout
at Sidi-Brahim
(September 23-26,1845).*

of arabs made him realize that there was no hope for Colonel Montagnac. He quickly took up a position on his left that was more easily defended. There he formed his small troop in a square and from that point on, they were on their own. Soon they were surrounded by a mass of enemy troops who were intoxicated with their first victory. At the sight of this, a young chasseur cried out in great fright: 'We are lost, we are dead!' 'How old are you?' the commander asked him. 'Twenty-two.' 'Well, I've suffered eighteen years more than you. If we must die here, I'm going to teach you how to die with a brave heart and your head held high.' The distinguished leader of the 9th soon fell, hit in the head. The battalion adjutant Dutertre who had taken command fell soon after him as well as Captain Burgard. The adjutant Thomas rose, urging those who were left to stand up and die courageously over the bodies of their officers. Only twelve men remained, riddled with wounds.

"However, at this moment another hussar had arrived at the camp, saying that the commander and his sixty brave men were threatened or prisoners. Captain Géreaux, aide to Lieutenant Chappedelaine, rallied the men guarding the animals, the mule team drivers, the grand guard, and his carabiniers — a little more than eighty men. They rushed to the aid of the last survivors. However, he was surrounded and so decided to gain the Marabout of Sidi-Brahim located eight hundred meters away. He took it by storm. This modest victory cost the lives of five men including that of Sergeant Estayère, a brave old soldier with twenty-eight years in the service....Hoping to attract the attention of Barral's column which was moving about the area, Captain Géreaux ordered Lavayssière to pick a chasseur to fix a flag at the top of the Marabout. 'My Captain,' the brave corporal responded, 'I would rather climb up there myself because it will mean sentencing the man sent to certain death.' 'I will promise a big reward to anyone who has the courage to put up that flag,' the captain soon added.

Lavayssière took the lieutenant's red belt and knotted it over his blue trooper's tie (1), cut a branch from a fig tree, and struggled up the dome of the Marabout under a hail of shot. The bullets whistled around him, one removing the corporal's kepi without wounding him. Another hit his left shoulder. A third cut the shaft of the improvised flag he held between his hands just as he was planting it on the dome. Lavayssière was finally able to reinforce the signal flag and asked that he be thrown the captain's field glasses. He did see Barral's column but he also saw that it was being attacked and was withdrawing. All hope of salvation was lost. The captain and the wounded lieutenant rejected two demands to surrender which were sent by the arabs. A third more urgent than the first two arrived. Lavayssière received it and rushed to relay it to his leader who had gone to lie down in the Marabout beside his lieutenant. Both were suffering terribly from their wounds. The doctor, Rosaguti, could not treat them as he wanted to because

his medical equipment had been left behind in the camp. The captain did not want to respond. The corporal asked him for his pencil: 'Shit on Abdel-Kader! The Chasseurs of Orléans can be killed but they will never surrender!' He held the letter in front of his captain who still had the strength to smile and who said to him: 'You are right, Corporal. Make them take this answer.' It was in this way that the heros who are the pride of the 8th were given the task of transforming Cambronne's controversial expression into reality. Abdel-Kader then sent a dozen prisoners with their hands tied and surrounded by an escort to stand before the Marabout. He hoped that this sight would demoralize the defense and lead to a capitulation. Lavayssière, seeing some compatriots from Midi amongst these prisoners, yelled to them in the regional dialect: 'Lie down.' They immediately did so. At the corporal's command, a murderous gunfire was trained on the escort and even on the emir's entourage which had been awaiting the results of this attempt a few hundred meters away. Even Abd-el-Kader was hit in the ear. A new assault, more terrible and furious, then began. The arabs who had taken the full force of the volley pulled back. At five in the evening, combat was continued with redoubled fury.

"The battle lasted for three quarters of an hour, the men even throwing stones in defense.

"On the 24th, another assault; finally on the 25th, Captain de Géreaux resolved to attempt a break through of the enemy lines and to head for Djemaa-Ghazouat. During the night, Lavayssière went to remove his little flag, and on the morning of the 26th, the north face of the Marabout was scaled. Carbines were loaded with double charges of eight pieces of shot. The small troop still had twenty-four carabiniers, Captain Géreaux, Lieutenant Chappedelaine, Doctor Rosaguti and the interpreter Levy. Lavayssière commanded since the officers and the non-commissioned officers were weakened by their wounds. The first arab post was taken by bayonet. None of the natives survived; all had their throats cut on the spot. At first taken by surprise, the arabs rallied and closed in around the heroic phalanx. It was formed in the square and enclosed the wounded captain and the lieutenant who were supported by some chasseurs. Our brave men marched in this formation always fighting... the little column made it a distance of two leagues. Finally, they were only two kilometers from Djemaa. The captain fell; Lieutenant Chappedelaine and Doctor Rosaguti also died. Lavayssière alone remained standing with some carabiniers and the hussar Nataly.

"The little troop turned into a defile, but the enemy had gotten there ahead of them and again cut off retreat. 'Dear friends,' cried Lavayssière, 'the square is no longer possible. Advance! Bayonets!' According to Lavayssière's own words, this combat was 'madness, enraged, a massacre, an indescribable slaughter.' Finally a path was forced through and five men found themselves still standing around the heroic corporal, all unarmed. Only Lavayssière had kept his carbine. They came within 200 meters of the redoubt. Another charge: three cavaliers remained upright. A Kabyle, hidden behind a tree, wounded the hussar Nataly. Lavayssiere himself drove his bayonet into the wretch's stomach. Finally, at only 50 meters from the redoubt, Lavayssière was advancing without suspicion toward a Jew who proceeded to wound him in the left ear with a pistol shot. The Jew met the same fate as the Kabyle. Some chasseurs who had escaped the massacre rejoined the little group. Nine made it to the doors of Djemaa. The garrison made a sortie and carried back the bodies of the six unfortunate wounded. The 8th Battalion found itself reduced to fifteen survivors."

---

(1) This attempt to improvise a flag occurred again on September 8, 1855 in the battalion of the chasseurs of the Imperial Guard at the assault on Sebastopol. Commander Cornulier de Lucinière, swept along by passion and followed by only a few officers and soldiers, arrived at the Little Rodan [sic]. The cannister shot and the fussilade stopped the rest of the column. Commander Lucinière immediately wanted to take possession of the works under the eyes of the Russians. The blue belt of the sapper corporal Joubert, Lieutenant Lagranié's white handkerchief, and a red necktie were attached to the band of a carbine soon driven into the earth. Some minutes later the commander fell under the colors of France.

Officers,chasseurs à pied, undress (1853).

This kind of test can produce soldiers formed by and accustomed to danger. The chasseurs gained the admiration of the old officers of the Empire with their discipline and their indomitable courage. Some under the Empire, such as Marshal Soult, had not always been so keen on their creation. Marshal Bugeaud had been one of the most opposed. He was afraid that in recruiting them, the strength of the grenadier and voltigeur companies would be weakened. Bugeaud often used these companies in his very powerful elite battalions. He quickly lost his prejudices, however, as he was surrounded by four battalions of chasseurs (3rd, 6th, 9th, and 10th) at the Battle of Isly.

At the siege of Rome, the 1st (Commander de Maroles) and the 2nd (Commander Pursel) distinguished themselves with the accuracy and precision of their fire.

Finally, on November 22, 1853, on the eve of the Crimean War, Emperor Napoleon III doubled the number of their battalions and increased that of their companies from 80 to 200. He compared the chasseurs to a rather handy form of artillery. It was thought it would be difficult to manage this increase after the creation of two new regiments of Zouaves and the proposed formation of the Guard. However, it proved to be extremely popular in the lower ranks of the army. Here the hope of joining the service of the chasseurs who were a bit envied engendered a commendable competitive spirit.

The reorganization was quite simple. Each battalion was divided into two parts. Each part formed the nucleus of a new battalion which was quite naturally comprised of six new improvised companies. Amongst the ideas considered by the imperial government in deciding to form these ten new battalions, there was one which should be remembered today. All the corps of troops were recruited as ordinary soldiers in a similar manner, and all belonged to the same service. It was intended that each infantry division be supplied with a reserve of soldiers recruited with care and better armed who had completed their military education before entering the battalions. This provided a reserve for each brigade marching against the enemy. All the divisions of the Crimean Army, all those of the Army of Italy, received battalions of chasseurs à pied . At Bomarsund and in China, failure of the rule to include them was anathema. In Mexico, two each were given to the divisions of Douay and Castagny. In military ideas which prevailed in the past, a great deal of faith was placed in the elite corps. It was easy to come by soldiers in an army where the term of service was always from five to six years, where one re-enlisted, where the hope of obtaining a promotion and rewards was upheld by national chauvinism. Today, France resembles a little the fox in Aesop's fable. The elite corps are no longer fashionable, solely because it is no longer possible to recruit qualified people for them. All the same, the special care still taken in recruiting for the chasseurs à pied battalions and the superior effectives maintained within them is still evident.

Such was the quality of the old battalions and the strength of their new additions in 1853 that from April 1, 1854 they were all ready to enter into the campaign.

In the future there would be twenty battalions of chasseurs à pied . Twelve took a more or less active part in the siege of Sebastopol.

The 1st:	Commanders Tristan-Legros, Gambier (Alma, assault)	The 7th:	Commanders Nicolas, Maurice
The 3rd:	Commanders Duplessis, Genneau (Alma, Inkermann, Mamelon-Vert)	The 9th:	Commander Rogier (Alma, Inkermann, assault)
		The 10th:	Commander Guiomar (assault)
The 4th:	Commander Clinchant (Mamelon-Vert, assault)	The 14th:	Commander Séverin (Tractir, assault)
The 5th:	Commanders Landry-Saint-Aubin, Garnier, Thouvenin (Alma, Inkermann)	The 17th:	Commander d'Audebard de Ferussac (assault)
The 6th:	Commander Fermier de la Provotais	The 19th:	Commander Le Tourneur (Mamelon-Vert, Tractir, assault)

Chasseurs à pied. Grand maneuvers (1885).

Chasseurs à pied. Grand maneuvers (1885).

Bugler, Chasseurs à pied (1865).

The 3rd Battalion returned to France after the assault while the 16th (Commander Esmieu) arrived with the Chasseloup-Laubat Division.

During this time, the 12th had appeared at Bomarsund. A provisional 21st and a 22nd had also been formed with companies detached from the depots. They were mustered out with the peace settlement and the companies of which they were composed returned to their battalions.

The Italian campaign offered the chasseurs a new opportunity to prove their worth. As skirmishers in the open field, they were as formidable as in a siege. Ten battalions took part in this war.

Before providing the list of these battalions, it should be recalled that in 1854 and 1855 those corps destined for the Crimea were able to depart without asking for any help from the battalions remaining in France as they had just received a number of contingents. In 1859, the ten battalions attached to the Army of Italy entered the campaign as they were. In 1856, 1857 and 1858 they were given only some contingents coming from the annual graduating classes to supplement their recruitment. However, the reputation of this corps was such that soldiers were quickly found to form it. It should be noted, however, that strong, stocky recruits, especially those from the mountainous departments, were given preference in joining their ranks. The chasseur à pied is a special type of military being, a type which stands apart from the others, one who is modern and very different from the soldier of the First Empire. However, he borrows much from the latter in terms of spirit and reliablity.

During the campaign of Italy, at the same time as the chasseurs of the Guard, the chasseurs à pied won the right to hang the cross of the Legion of Honor from their flag. The 10th Battalion which captured an enemy flag at the Battle of Solferino merited this rare honor coveted by the troops of the French army.

LIST OF BATTALIONS WHICH WERE IN THE CAMPAIGN IN ITALY		
17th Battalion	Commander d' Audebard de Ferussac	1st Division,1st Corps
10th -	Commander Courrech	2nd Division,1st Corps
11th -	Commander Dumont	2nd Division,2nd Corps
8th -	Commander Merle	1st Division, 3rd Corps
19th -	Commander Le Tourneur	2nd Division, 3rd Corps
18th -	Commander Avril de Lenclos	3rd Division, 3rd Corps
5th -	Commander Thouvenin	1st Division, 4th Corps
6th -	Commander Fermier de la Provotais	2nd Division, 4th Corps
15th -	Commander Lion	3rd Division, 4th Corps
14th -	Commander Severin	2nd Division, 5th Corps

A battalion of chasseurs, the 12th, was attached to d'Hugues' division of the Army of Lyon which maneuvered on the slopes of the Alps and arrived in Milan after the Battle of Solferino. Two companies of the 13th Battalion were designated to join the small corps of the army under the command of General Wimpffen. It was responsible for operations along the shores of the Adriatic where it was to support the operations of the fleet.

The services of the chasseurs à pied were prized by generals and were gloriously and unsparingly used each time the national colors had to be deployed. However, they were not protected from the economic necessities which periodically occurred under the Second Empire on the eve of every war. On March 28, 1860, a decree ordered the disbanding of the 9th and 10th companies of each of the twenty battalions. This returned the cadres and effectives to their original state.

The 16th Battalion made an expedition to Syria in 1860.

The 2nd Battalion, commanded by Guillot de la Poterie then by Comte, made the expeditions to China and to Cochinchina.

The Mexican War laid claim to a large contingent of chasseurs. Until then, only one battalion was attached to each division for the expedition to Mexico. As already stated, each brigade had one. The organization of the expeditionary corps varied widely. However in June 1864, the four battalions of Mexico were distributed in the following manner:

7th - battalion	Commanders Cofavier d'Albici, Bréart	1st Brigade, 1st Division
20th -	Commanders Lepage des Longchamps, de Franchessin	2nd Brigade, 1st Division
1st -	Commanders Mangin, Roussel de Courey	2nd Brigade, 1st Division
18th -	Commanders Lamy, Brincourt	2nd Brigade, 2nd Division

Thus we arrive at the fatal war of 1870 where everything would be swallowed up by defeat and debacle. The twenty battalions of chasseurs à pied were all included in the first formation of the Army of the Rhine. There were hardly enough to supply the four divisions of the 6th Corps and the 3rd division of the 7th Corps.

It must have been sorely regretted that the 9th and 10th companies dissolved ten years earlier had not been reestablished. Under the influence of new ideas, the chasseurs à pied saw themselves as being a bit neglected. From this point on, they had the same service as the regiments of the line wherein elite companies had been eliminated and their soldiers reassigned to all the other companies. The introduction of the five year long military service further diminished the qualities of the elite soldiers. The chasseurs had to resign themselves to live in the glow of their past glories. When the chassepot was introduced early on, they were even forgotten although at the same time this weapon was issued to the regiments with whom they marched. It can

be recalled that, on the field of battle at Mentana, the 2nd battalion of chasseurs were seen in tight columns by half-sections on the Nomentana road with the Minie carbine on their shoulders. Meanwhile, the four battalions of the line which accompanied them were all armed with the 1866 model rifle. Below is the distribution of the Army of the Rhine.

1st Battalion	(1st Corp, 4th Division)	Commanders Bureau, Pichon
2nd -	(4th Corps, 3rd Division)	Commander Letanneur
3rd -	(2nd Corps, 1st Division)	Commanders Thoma, Petit
4th -	(5th Corps, 1st Division)	Commander Foncegrives
5th -	(4th Corps, 2nd Division)	Commanders Carré, Renaud
6th -	(7th Corps, 2nd Division)	Commander de Beaufort
7th -	(3rd Corps, 3rd Division)	Commander Costes
8th -	(1st Corps, 2nd Division)	Commanders Poyet, Viénot
9th -	(6th Corps, 1st Division)	Commander Mathelin
10th -	(2nd Corps, 3rd Division)	Commanders Schenck, Chabert
11th -	(3rd Corps, 4th Division)	Commanders de Paillot, Avril, Raynal
12th -	(2nd Corps, 4th Division)	Commanders Jouanne-Beaulieu, de Gislain, Bonnet, de Mably
13th -	(1st Corps, 1st Division)	Commanders Le Cacher de Bonneville, Potier
14th -	(5th Corps, 2nd Division)	Commander Parlier
15th -	(3rd Corps, 2nd Division)	Commander Lafouge
16th -	(1st Corps, 2nd Division)	Commanders d'Hugues, Lecer
17th -	(7th Corps, 1st Division)	Commanders Merchier, Barré
18th -	(3rd Corps, 1st Division)	Commanders Rigault, Delavault
19th -	(5th Corps, 3rd Division)	Commanders de Marque, Labrune
20th -	(4th Corps, 1st Division)	Commanders de Labarrière, Copri

Small outpost of chasseurs à pied (1871).

When the 13th Corps (Vinoy) was organized, the depot companies filled out at 250 men were attached to the 1st and 3rd Divisions. The 1st Division received two companies of the 5th and 7th Battalions. The 3rd Divison, had two companies from the 1st and 2nd Battalions. The 14th Corps (Baron Renault), like the 13th, had four companies of chasseurs à pied attached two by two to his 1st Division (companies from the 3rd and 4th Battalions) and to his 3rd Division (companies of the 6th and 9th Battalions).

The service of the chasseurs à pied — although armed like the rest of the infantry — evoked great power of prestige in the minds of the people. With its fine esprit de corps, it also inspired such confidence in the civilian and military leaders imposed on France by the Revolution of September 4th, that in Paris and the provinces the number of their *battalions de marche* (provisional battalions) were greatly increased at all costs.

Paris created three, the provinces thirty.

Having entered into the details of this gigantic effort, there should be some discussion about the remains of the service of the chasseurs à pied in the aftermath of Sedan.

The depot of the 13th Battalion had been trapped in Strasbourg and the depot of the 11th in Metz. They were subject to the same series of events as these two places. The depots of the 7th, 15th and 17th Battalions maintained garrisons at Vincennes and at Saint-Denis. They formed part of the besieged army in Paris. Thus there were fifteen depots of chasseurs à pied in the provinces of whom seven had already sent a company to Vinoy's and Renault's Corps. From the beginning of the war, each battalion had to create a 9th company. Consequently, apart from Metz and Strasbourg, the cadres of 38 companies remained in the provinces and 16 in Paris. This is without counting the depot of the battalion of the Guard. This was not very many.

Nonetheless, as the service of the chasseurs was resourceful, things were taken care of quickly and well. The young officers, who wanted to see action complained of staying at the depot while their comrades were on the brink of danger. Only the hope of going to battle pushed them to form new companies at whose heads they would march toward the enemy.

Typically, there was no lack of non-commissioned officers recalled to service nor of soldiers. The 7th, 8th, and 9th companies were very strong and demonstrated wherever they were called the same spirit as the full war battalions. However, the staffs were pressured to produce new battalions so quickly that their quality was lowered. Paris should have been less hampered than other places since it created only three battalions, that is, 24 companies with 16 staffs plus those of the Guard. Meanwhile, in the provinces, thirty battalions at four companies were produced, that is, 120 or even 137 with thirty-six companies, counting the depots. In Paris, pushed by popular feeling and after having done its duty, this troop very much belied its high reputation with regard to discipline at the end of the siege.

As noted above, everywhere officers and non-commissioned officers remaining at the depots showed an immense enthusiasm. In their efforts they did not retreat from any obstacle.

Due to problems with official documents, the means by which the provinces were able to improvise thirty new *bataillons de marche* of chasseurs à pied at four companies each cannot be revealed here. However, a book published by de Sourdeval, then battalion adjutant to the 5th Battalion, permits one to see how the depot of the Fifth did this. Evidently the other depots acted with the same zeal.

As mentioned above, this depot had detached its 7th company to the 1st Division of the 13th Corps. Soon it formed a 9th. As soon as this was ready on October 1st, it left with the 8th to converge in the formation of the 6th *bataillon de marche*. On November 8th, it created the 11th *bataillon de marche* from all these pieces. Three days later on November 11th, it formed the 12th *bataillon de marche*. On November 19th, it sent two companies to the 13th *bataillon de marche*, on the 29th one to the 21st *bataillon de marche* and finally on January 19th, two to the 27th *bataillon de marche*.

It is remarkable that it provided nothing for the creation of the 5th battalion of chasseurs *bataillon de marche* and that, on the contrary, it received wounded officers from this latter battalion. With these officers it formed the staff of a company which, with another company commanded by retired officers, completed the depot to the status of the real, former Fifth Battalion.

Thus, the depot of the Fifth produced 16 companies *de marche*, all having 250 to 300 men, uniformed, armed, and, of course, formed in haste. As for training, it is mentioned here as a matter of interest. It was as good as could be expected, given the circumstances, but better than in the line. Nevertheless, it is certain that the 5th Battalion was the most productive.

According to an official record for the location of troops at the end of January 1871, the destinations of the thirty *bataillons de marche* formed in the provinces is given below.

1st Battalion - 17th Corps	11th Battalion - 17th Corps	21st Battalion - 24th Corps
2nd Battalion - 22nd Corps	12th Battalion - 18th Corps	22nd Battalion - 19th Corps
3rd Battalion - 16th Corps	13th Battalion - 21st Corps	23rd Battalion - 16th Corps
4th Battalion - 15th Corps	14th Battalion - 18th Corps	24th Battalion - 22nd Corps
5th Battalion - 15th Corps	15th Battalion - 24th Corps	25th Battalion - 20th Corps
6th Battalion - 15th Corps	16th Battalion - 16th Corps	26th Battalion - 22nd Corps
then the Grenoble Division	17th Battalion - 22nd Corps	27th Battalion - 26th Corps
7th Battalion - 25th Corps	18th Battalion - 22nd Corps	28th Battalion - 26th Corps
8th Battalion - 16th Corps	19th Battalion - 22nd Corps	29th Battalion - Antibes
9th Battalion - 18th Corps	20th Battalion - 22nd Corps	30th Battalion - Rochefort
10th Battalion - 17th Corps		

In Paris, there were formed in succession a new 21st and a new 22nd on November 20, 1870, and on December 17 a new 23rd. For a while, it was thought that the companies of chasseurs should be made to enter into the regiments of the line. However, this idea was soon dropped. Since many artillerymen and non-commissioned officers were required in the Paris battalions, these battalions found themselves at the end of the war to be comprised almost exclusively of very young Parisian recruits. From that point on, they were inadequately commanded if one takes into consideration that their effectives on the day of the capitulation, including officers were: for the 21st Battalion - 2,006 men; for the 22nd Battalion - 1,311 men; and for the 23rd Battalion - 1,086 men. After being disarmed, they were sent to Algeria. This was all for the better. The authorities then charged with the destiny of the capital, did not know how to shield them from the worst intentions of the criminals who would soon after form the Commune.

On the other hand, many *bataillons de marche* coming from the provinces served well in the Army of Versailles. Significant amongst them were the 2nd, 10th, 17th, 18th, 19th, 23rd, 24th, 26th, and 30th.

The esprit de corps, meaning that of the chasseurs, had immediately taken hold of these young battalions. They showed themselves to be equal to the best reputations of the old battalions everywhere they went.

After the war, the *bataillons de marche* were assigned to the corresponding old battalions as was done with the regiments of the line. These old battalions filled out their ranks. This reorganization was done, as always, with an admirable efficiency. Tradition in the chasseurs was so strong that anything could be demanded of its officer corps. It was this service which the new organization of the French army so profoundly affected. Its battalions were reduced from eight companies to five, of which one was a depot company. This happened just when there was no longer any visible difference between the new and the old battalions. The amputation was made, not without deep regrets on the part of some, but with an exemplary speed.

Since 1871, the service of the chasseurs has sent some of its battalions to Algeria and to Tunisia. As in the past, it has remained an example for the regiments amongst whom it serves. Eighteen of its battalions were specially attached to the first division of each army corps. They have since been placed unattached outside the division, according to the German method, under the direct command of the corps commander. In addition, the twelve battalions left out of the great mobilization have maintained their very considerable effectives of approximately 640 men. They are garrisoned in the passes or the forts of the southeast and of the east which they will be called upon to defend in the event of war. This arrangement, which no one dreams of disputing, appears to class the chasseurs à pied as an elite force in the young army of compulsory service. This contradiction between theory and reality leads one to the eternal controversy over the usefulness of the elite corps in war time and the advantage of using veteran troops as an advance guard when great effort is required. This debate extends to the formation

Color sergeant, chasseurs à pied (1870).

Buglers, chasseurs à pied, undress (1873).

of the rear guard in the case of a difficult retreat who should inspire confidence in the engaged troops during combat.

In a work devoted to the history of the various organizations of the French army it is inappropriate to discuss the usefulness or lack thereof of the chasseurs service. Nonetheless, this question can hardly be neglected. It is quite evident that a chasseur no longer differs in appearance from an ordinary foot soldier except in the colors of his epaulette and pants. On the other hand, a battalion of chasseurs is often more flexible and potent than a battalion of ordinary infantry. This difference in pants and epaulette which is too often belittled actually indicates not only a difference in recruitment but also in voluntary enlistment. In addition, the renown of these soldiers attracts ardent officers. Then there is the tradition, the past history of the chasseurs. Whatever one says or does, a moment always arrives in a war when the soldier's memory must be jogged by the great feats of his predecessors. It is even possible that some day France will again be forced to press those old buttons of esprit de corps — the colors, the pins, the names, the legends — which prove so useful in peacetime as well as in times of war. Is it insignificant that soldiers marching into combat will sing with their buglers:

"The Fifth Battalion, stomach to the earth,
Commanded by a certain Canrobert...."?

When little things become major issues, they need to be respected. The green epaulette of the chasseur à pied is one of those little things.

The green epaulette of chasseurs à pied.

Cavalry kit (1885).

HISTORY OF THE CAVALRY

Trumpeter of the King's Guards, constitutional guard (1791).

The cavalry suffered less than the infantry from the shocks of the Revolution. This aristocratic service, however, inspired more mistrust. The difficulty, even the impossiblity, of rapidly throwing together mounted troops checked the suspicions of the most inflexible members of the Convention. In fact, to maintain a cavalry in good condition, not only does one need trained horses, but also horsemen used to riding them while wielding weapons. These men must care for and provide for the needs of their animals, love them and, to a certain extent, identify with their existences. Finally, a cavalry requires leaders who possess the highest levels of experience and a love for the details of their profession.

The Revolution did not dare to undertake a mustering out and complete remodeling of the French cavalry as did the Restoration in 1815.

It is true that in 1792, France had to repel the enemy which threatened its borders. On the other hand, in 1815, France was a defeated nation, politically protected by the conqueror. The government of Louis XVIII therefore could spend time on the transformation of the imperial army into the royal army.

The sequence of numbering was only broken once in the mounted troops. The legends of their flags are more faithful to historical fact than are those of the infantry. The subdivisons of the service were never very difficult for the cavalry. They were logical even when they had no other reason than the differences in size or breeds of horses produced in the country. However, before the invention of the rapid fire rifle and of long-range cannons, the regiments charged with breaking through infantry squares and taking batteries had to be differently armed than those assigned to the scouts service, the foragers, or to raiding parties. This is why the terms of *cavalerie légère* (light cavalry), *cavalerie de ligne* (cavalry of the line), and *cavalerie de reserve* (reserve cavalry) are rooted in the past yet have endured until the present.

Actually, a fourth category may be added: the *cavalerie de remonte* (remount cavalry) which served in the purchase, preparation, and training of the horses before they were delivered to the regiments. However, this category is not tactical. It is administrative and technical.

In the early years of French military organization, the cavalry, properly speaking, only comprised the *gendarmerie de France,* a last vestige of chivalry which appeared in the King's Household. All mounted troops or regiments, armored or not, were called light cavalry, even the carabiniers. The light cavalry gave rise to the hussars which at first marched immediately after them. The dragoons, a separate development, were cavalry who generally fought both on foot and on horseback. They appeared in the rolls after the hussars. The chasseurs, an offshoot of the dragoons, brought up the rear of the march.

In the various reorganizations of the service these subdivisions have often been mixed up as they were on the field of battle.

Dragoons have become cuirassiers. Cuirassiers, on the other hand, have been turned into dragoons. Then, from one day to the next, chasseurs have been transformed into lancers and lancers have once again become hussars. These changes occurred rapidly under the magic wand of the Minister of War. Cavalry officers were only too right in claiming that, in practice, it was impossible to respect the theoretical definitions of the various categories of cavalry. So many times in war, chasseur and hussar units have been seen filled with masses of infantry. Cuirassiers have been burdened with foragers. A regiment is forced to be able to perform any task. It has to be ready to do anything which the vagaries of war bring its way without refusing, whether it be light, line or reserve cavalry. It must confront the enemy in the order which has been determined by its leaders and by circumstances.

Now that everyone is a soldier, it is pointless to fan the warlike passions of young men with a variety and wealth of uniforms. These have been transformed with the changing role of the cavalry and the development of firearms. No one wants to be a dragoon anymore. But aren't today's cuirassiers with their reduced armor really heavy dragoons? Couldn't the chasseurs and the hussars armed with rifles be called light dragoons?

Ultimately, nothing will come of such reasoning. If the requirements for unification and simplification persist, in ten years the cavalry will all have the same uniform and name, whether lightly or heavily equipped. In twenty years, the entire army will have the same jacket, the same helmet and the same pants.

While awaiting this moment of Spartan perfection, it is still interesting to examine the history of the regiments with handsome uniforms. Their deeds and their glory have not been completely forgotten and their brillance can still be detected in their descendants.

STATE OF THE CAVALRY IN 1789

In addition to his household military which was already much more reduced than that of his ancestors, Louis XVI maintained sixty-two cavalry regiments of four squadrons: twenty-six (of which two were carabiniers); six of hussars; eighteen of dragoons; and twelve of chasseurs.

Colonel of dragoons (1789).

Only one year earlier, their leaders had exchanged the title of *mestre de camp* of the cavalry for that of colonel. The general staff included four high-ranking officers: the first colonel, a second colonel, a lieutenant-colonel, and a major. In addition there were a quartermaster, two color bearers, an adjutant, a chaplain, a surgeon and three master workmen.

The squadron was commanded by six officers: two captains, two lieutenants, two second lieutenants, plus a gentleman cadet. By regulation, it was composed in the following manner: a *marechal-des-logis chef* (sergeant-major); a *marechal-des-logis* (sergeant), a quartermaster corporal, eight *brigadiers* (corporals), 132 to 152 horsemen, depending on the service, two trumpeters, a barber, and a blacksmith. The total was 154 to 174 men. This resulted in 629 to 729 men per regiment and approximately 40,000 for the entire cavalry. These figures were never actually attained and the squadrons only had 80 to 100 horses. Although it was not large, this cavalry was magnificently equipped, mounted and trained. Its non-commissioned officers and its corporals may be cited as models. Its officers rode admirably. If the French cavalry was not considered as the best in Europe, this was very much due to a lack of effectives. Its weapons, with the exception of a few minor improvements, were similar to those of today's regiments. They consisted of the saber, a rifle or a musket, and a pistol. A single corps remained armored: the 7th Cavalry, Cuirassiers of the King.

As for the uniform it comprised the following.

For the cavalry: blue jacket with lapels in distinguishing colors, a hat modeled after the infantry's, a vest and breeches in leather; tall boots, belt and cartridge case in white buffalo skin. The horse's equipment was of dark cloth trimmed with the colonel's colors.

For the hussars: a dolman jacket, a pelisse, and a high shako.

The dragoons and the chasseurs were dressed in green. The dragoons wore a helmet without visor and with a flowing horsehair plume. The chasseurs wore the typical headgear.

Enlistments were managed as in the infantry. However, the old cavalrymen received temporary leave or even reductions in their time in the service if they brought recruits into the corps.

In the eyes of the public and of authority, the cavalry was seen as being devoted to the Court. The defense of Paris and its surroundings which were infested with brigands was entrusted to the cavalry regiments in 1789. The King turned to the cavalry regiments for protection during his flight. For this act, they are commemorated in the *Marseillaise* as the accomplices of Bouillé. Although these brave cavaliers loved the King and their officers, they always proved themselves extremely devoted to the nation. The Royal-allemand never attacked unarmed people on Place Louis XV on July 12, 1789 despite lovely engravings which have depicted this subject. They were stoned, held back the curious, and its colonel, the Prince de Lambesc not only did not kill a venerable old man but in fact saved the life of a young woman with her child in hand who had been knocked over by the crowd. Although these facts have been confirmed by a judgement from Châtelet dated June 28, 1790, the crude rabble of do-nothings repeated: "the horrible crime of the Royal-allemand and of its colonel." In the same manner, it has been repeated that at the Battle of Moscow, the cuirassiers took the redoubts by assault while many squadrons of hussars only took a sail on the Zuider Zee. Let's leave romantic historians to these amusing tales and continue. The history of the French cavalry is wonderful enough that it hardly needs such inaccurate embellishments.

The law of January 1, 1791 established the numbers of the regiments of the service in the following order:

1st Carabinier Regiment	(former 22nd Cavalry Regiment: 1st Carabiniers-de-Monsieur)	6th Hussar Regiment	(former 6th Hussar Regiment: Lauzun)
2nd Carabinier Regiment	(former 22nd-*bis* Cavalry Regiment: 2nd Carabiniers-de-Monsieur)	1st Dragoon Regiment	(former 3rd Dragoon Regiment: Royal-Dragoons)
1st Cavalry Regiment	(former 1st Cavalry Regiment: Colonel-Général)	2nd Dragoon Regiment	(former 11th Dragoon Regiment: Condé-cavalerie)
2nd Cavalry Regiment	(former 4th Cavalry Regiment: Royal)	3rd Dragoon Regiment	(former 12th Dragoon Regiment: Bourbon-cavalerie)
3rd Cavalry Regiment	(former 3rd Cavalry Regiment: Commissaire Général)	4th Dragoon Regiment	(former 13th Dragoon Regiment: Conti-cavalerie)
4th Cavalry Regiment	(former 18th Cavalry Regiment: La Reine)	5th Dragoon Regiment	(former 1st Dragoon Regiment: Colonel-général-de-dragoons)
5th Cavalry Regiment	(former 12th Cavalry Regiment: Royal Pologne)	6th Dragoon Regiment	(former 5th Dragoon Regiment: La Reine-dragoons)
6th Cavalry Regiment	(former 5th Cavalry Regiment: Le Roy)	7th Dragoon Regiment	(former 6th Dragoon Regiment: Dauphin-dragoons)
7th Cavalry Regiment	(former 6th Cavalry Regiment: Royal-étranger)	8th Dragoon Regiment	(former 14th Dragoon Regiment: Penthiévre-cavalerie)
8th Cavalry Regiment	(former 7th Cavalry Regiment: Cuirassiers du Roy)	9th Dragoon Regiment	(former 15th Dragoon Regiment: Lorraine-dragoons)
9th Cavalry Regiment	(former 23rd Cavalry Regiment: Artois)	10th Dragoon Regiment	(former 2nd Dragoon Regiment: Mestre-de-camp-général-dragoons)
10th Cavalry Regiment	(former 8th Cavalry Regiment: Royal-Cravate)	11th Dragoon Regiment	(former 16th Dragoon Regiment: Angouleme-dragoons)
11th Cavalry Regiment	(former 9th Cavalry Regiment: Royal-Roussillon)	12th Dragoon Regiment	(former 8th Dragoon Regiment: Artois-dragoons)
12th Cavalry Regiment	(former 19th Cavalry Regiment: Dauphin)	13th Dragoon Regiment	(former 7th Dragoon Regiment: Monsieur-dragoons)
13th Cavalry Regiment	(former 24th Cavalry Regiment: Orléans)	14th Dragoon Regiment	(former 10th Dragoon Regiment: Chartres-cavalerie)
14th Cavalry Regiment	(former 14th Cavalry Regiment: Royal-Piémont)	15th Dragoon Regiment	(former 17th Dragoon Regiment: Noailles-cavalerie)
15th Cavalry Regiment	(former 11th Cavalry Regiment: Royal-allemand)	16th Dragoon Regiment	(former 9th Dragoon Regiment: Orléans-dragoons)
16th Cavalry Regiment	(former 13th Cavalry Regiment: Royal-Lorraine)	17th Dragoon Regiment	(former 18th Dragoon Regiment: Schomberg-cavalerie)
17th Cavalry Regiment	(former 20th Cavalry Regiment: Royal-Bourgogne)	18th Dragoon Regiment	(former 4th Dragoon Regiment: Le Roy-dragoons)
18th Cavalry Regiment	(former 21st Cavalry Regiment: Berry)	1st Chasseur Regiment	(former 1st Chasseur Regiment: Alsace)
19th Cavalry Regiment	(former 17th Cavalry Regiment: Royal-Normandie)	2nd Chasseur Regiment	(former 2nd Chasseur Regiment: Évêches)
20th Cavalry Regiment	(former 15th Cavalry Regiment: Royal-Champagne)	3rd Chasseur Regiment	(former 3rd Chasseur Regiment: Flandre)
21st Cavalry Regiment	(former 14th Cavalry Regiment: Royal-Picardie)	4th Chasseur Regiment	(former 4th Chasseur Regiment: La Franche-Comté)
22nd Cavalry Regiment	(former 16th Cavalry Regiment: Royal-Navarre)	5th Chasseur Regiment	(former 5th Chasseur Regiment: Hainault)
23rd Cavalry Regiment	(former 25th Cavalry Regiment: Royal-Guyenne)	6th Chasseur Regiment	(former 6th Chasseur Regiment: Languedoc)
24th Cavalry Regiment	(former 2nd Cavalry Regiment: Mestre-de-camp-général)	7th Chasseur Regiment	(former 7th Chasseur Regiment: Picardie)
1st Hussar Regiment	(former 2nd Hussar Regiment: Bercheny)	8th Chasseur Regiment	(former 8th Chasseur Regiment: Guyenne)
2nd Hussar Regiment	(former 3rd Hussar Regiment: Chamborant)	9th Chasseur Regiment	(former 9th Chasseur Regiment: Lorraine)
3rd Hussar Regiment	(former 4th Hussar Regiment: Esterhazy)	10th Chasseur Regiment	(former 10th Chasseur Regiment: Bretagne)
4th Hussar Regiment	(former 5th Hussar Regiment: Saxe)	11th Chasseur Regiment	(former 11th Chasseur Regiment: Normandie)
5th Hussar Regiment	(former 1st Hussar Regiment: Colonel-général)	12th Chasseur Regiment	(former 12th Chasseur Regiment: Champagne)

Officers and cavaliers of the mestre de camp général's regiment (1790).

As can be seen, the various changes introduced into the rolls of the corps of mounted troops did not modify the proportion of categories. However, it did reverse the numbering of the regiments. The princely or provincial designations disappeared throughout, thereby eliminating tradition for some of them. In practice and in popular speech, many regiments—particularly amongst the hussars—retained their names which characterized their uniforms for awhile longer. In addition, the regiments received a new organization. The carabiniers, the hussars, and the chasseurs always had four squadrons. However, the cavalry

and the dragoons had no more than three. The squadrons were divided into two companies each having a captain, a lieutenant, two second lieutenants, a sergeant-major, two sergeants, and four corporals. The rank of major was eliminated and replaced by that of second lieutenant-colonel.

The effective strength of the squadron in times of peace was fixed at 440 to 448 men. In wartime, it was expanded to 170 men. The general effective of the service was thus 30,040 men in times of peace. The cadres were always comprised of 62 regiments, but there were no more than 206 squadrons rather than 248. The number of non-commissioned officers was slightly increased. When memoirs of comtemporaries are read, one can see that this useful class of servants of the State was composed of valuable men.

Loving their horses, their profession, their uniforms, faithful to the flag and concerned about the honor of the regiment, they were the nerves and the backbone of the cavalry. This category of mounted men was again increased under the Republic and the Empire.

The officers corps of the cavalry was naturally purged through emigration which eliminated two whole regiments: the Royal-allemand (15th of cavalry), the Saxon-Hussars (4th of hussars) and part of the Hussars of Bercheny (1st). However, in 1791, a feeling of resignation had spread through the service at the same time as a feeling of obligation to take a new oath. This latter required that the name of the King no longer by associated with them. In his excellent *History of the Second Regiment of the Cuirassiers* which is the best book available on the history of the cavalry, Colonel Baron Rothviller shows the deplorable results of this oath in the table on the second regiment of cavalry (Royal) during 1791. Colonel d'Esclignac and Lieutenant Colonels de Cacqueray and de Calonne were retired. Of the two lieutenant colonels who replaced them, one, de Sarcus, abandoned it. Of seven captains, four resigned. These were de Thilorier, d'Achard Ménil-Engrain, de Spada, and de Dixmud-Montbrun. Finally, five second lieutenants folllowed their example: de Poupart, Alexandre and Frédéric de Cacqueray, de Mailliard de Villocourt, and de la Porte. From January 1 to July 10, 1791, of thirty-two officers from the 2nd of cavalry, thirteen had given their resignations. This movement must have been fairly common throughout the regiments and was intensified again in 1792.

Trumpeter of the Saxony Hussar Regiment (1789).

In the midst of these serious events which put the cavalry within a hair's breadth of extinction, a law from June 24, 1792 ordered that only the carabiniers, cavaliers, hussars and chasseurs — with the exclusion of the dragoons — would wear a mustache. The custom of wearing the hat slightly inclined over the right eyebrow dates also to this law. Such minutiae indicate that the least detail of dress held great importance in the life of the mounted soldiers. It also explains why recruitment of the cavalry never experienced a decline. The young nobles who did not want to emigrate considered the foremost duty of a Frenchmen to be the defense of the Motherland. By choice, they enlisted in the mounted regiments. In this manner, a future *officier d'ordonnance* of Napoleon the First, the Count de Turenne, began his career. At sixteen, he entered service in the volunteer company of the Dragoons of Toulouse. Young men of high birth were not always so welcome. In the interesting *Souvenirs* about General Colbert, the descendant of Louis XIV's great minister was forced to hide his illustrious position under the blue uniform of the Marat Battalion. Despite the fact that the oldest traditions of the French army were due to his ancestor, this young man asked in vain to be transferred into the cavalry. The representative of the people charged with organizing the troops judged, in his supreme wisdom, that a former member of the nobility could have no other goal than to desert as quickly as possible in asking for such a move. Happily, there were more intelligent men than this inflexible member of the Convention whose name unfortunately has been lost to history. The ranks of the cavalry very quickly overflowed with trained young men familiar with horses since childhood. They maintained the traditions of courage and elegance of the old French nobility in the service of their choice. While the old officers, who were tied to the King by their oath of fidelity, sadly moved to the other side of the Rhine, they were replaced by a new generation of officers of their rank and blood. This new group was free of all obligations, full of love for the country and ready to distinguish themselves with weapons in hand.

One year later, in February 1794 (Pluviôse, Year II), a ministerial order still stipulated that the old nobles and priests who could be found within the ranks of the army should be sought out and marked. It is fair to add that a few days earlier a decree

Dragoons, in the field (1885).

Hussars, in the field (1885).

had indicated that no citizen could be promoted into the postion which had just been vacated in the armies of the Republic — from the ranks of corporal up to that of general in chief — if he didn't know how to read and write. The history of the great French Revolution is full of such contradictory details. Nonetheless, in the camps and on the battlefield, the Revolution always raised the officers and the soldiers to the highest levels of dedication and of honor.

The numbering system, modified by the law of January 1, 1791, was again disrupted by the emigration of Regiment No. 15 of the cavalry and No. 4 of the hussars. All the regiments of the cavalry subdivision moved up one level, beginning with No. 16 but with No. 24 remaining vacant. In the same manner, Nos. 5 and 6 took the numbers 4 and 5, leaving No. 6 vacant in the hussars. But this reduction in strength did not last long. The various powers which followed one another beginning in 1792 made a point of absorbing all the corps of volunteer cavalry as soon as they were assembled by some enterprising and willing man. Since it was necessary the provide one's own horses, which only the State was authorized to do—and with justifiable sparingness—those who wanted to raise a corps of cavalry began by soliciting a commission. Weapons were easily enough procured from the municipalities. Next, some volunteers dressed in whimsical uniforms were organized more or less in temporary barracks. Then began the debate with the military authorities who gave them horses only under the condition that they leave immediately for the army. From that point on, absorption did not take long, generally being a matter of only a few weeks.

Chasseur à cheval (1789).

It should be noted that the need for cavalry led to the mobilization of the military personnel from the police force and to forming them into mounted divisions. This action was formalized with the laws of April 12, 16 and 28, 1792 and has since been replicated. There were eight divisions at 940 men each. The policemen who formed them were replaced in their hometowns by auxiliaries. They were completely independent of the public forces in the armies. After providing excellent service as reserve cavalry to the existing eight armies, these divisions returned to the interior under the terms of the law of April 17, 1795.

Prior to entering into the details of the history of the cavalry under the Convention, the Directorate, and the Consulate, a table showing the absorptions and transformations of the regiments from this service created in 1791 on 1 Vendémiaire, Year XII (September 24, 1803) should be given.

CREATIONS AND ALTERATIONS FROM JANUARY 1, 1791 TO VENDÉMIAIRE OF THE YEAR XII (SEPTEMBER 24, 1803)

Date of creation	Regimental number	Troops used to create them
January 28, 1791	24th Cav.	Various deserters and detachments gathered at the military school in Paris. (In the year X [1801], incorporated into the 1st and 8th Cavalry Regiments.)
	25th Cav.	Various deserters and detachments gathered at the military school in Paris. (In the year X [1801], incorporated into the 2nd, 3rd and 4th Cavalry Regiments.)
November 23, 1792	6th Hus.	Bover Hussars.
	7th Hus.	Lamotte Hussars and the remainder of the Royal-allemand and Saxe Hussars.
1792	20th Cav.	Formed with three divisions of national volunteers. (Mustered out in 1795.)
	27th Cav.	Formed with three divisions of national volunteers. (Mustered out in 1795.)
February 24, 1793	19th Drag.	Former Angers Volunteers and a part of the Nord and Francs Cavalry Legions.
	20th Drag.	Jemmapes Dragoons.
1793	7th *bis* Hus.	1st corps of the Liberty Hussars, created in 1792. (Became the 28th Dragoons in the year XII [1803].)
February 26, 1793	8th Hus.	Former Fabrefond Mounted Hussars.
March 25, 1793	9th Hus.	2nd corps of the Liberty Hussars, created Sept. 1792.
	10th Hus.	Jemmapes Hussars and the former Black Hussars of the North.
March 1793	13th Chass.	Saint-George American Legion, created December 6, 1792; Midi Hussars; a company of the national cavalry organized at the camp in Paris. Also received the 13th Chasseurs bis, organized from diverse elements.
	14th Chass.	Égalité Hussars, Alps Legion and the Death Hussars.
	15th Chass.	Besser and Côte-d'Or Chasseurs.
	16th Chass.	Breteche Chasseurs.
May 9, 1793	17th Chass.	West-Flandre Belgian Chasseurs. (Mustered out April 6, 1794.)
	18th Chass.	Belgian Chasseurs and Brussels Dragoons. (Mustered out July 18, 1794.)
June 9, 1793	19th Chass.	Former Rosenthal Legion, created 1792. (Mustered out July 18, 1794.)
1793	20th Chass.	Cavalry of the Moselle Legion.
	21st Chass.	Braconniers Hussars.
	22nd Chass.	Cavalry of the Pyrénées-Orientales Legion.
	23rd Chass.	Hussars of the Ardennes Legion.
	24th Chass.	Bayonne Volunteer Chasseurs.
June 26, 1793	11th Hus.	Revolutionary cavalry of the Germanic Legion. (Became the 30th Dragoons in the year XII [1803].)
March 20, 1794	12th Hus.	Former Pyrénées Volunteers. (Became the 30th Dragoons in the year XII [1803].)
June 13, 1795	25th Chass.	Former Montagne Chasseurs.
1796 (5 Floréal of the Year IV [1795])	21st Drag.	La Manche Dragoons and the Police of Paris Legion. (Mustered out on 22 Frimaire of the Year VI [1797] and incorporated into the 1st, 2nd, 7th, 11th, 12th and 16th Dragoons.)
August 26, 1801	21st Drag. (new)	Formed from a regiment of Piémontese dragoons.
May 1802	26th Chass.	Piémontese Hussars in the pay of the Republic from August 26, 1801. (Had to take the number 17 which was vacant.)
1st Vendémiaire of the Year XII (Sept. 24, 1803)	22nd Drag.	Former 13th Cavalry.
	23rd Drag.	Former 14th Cavalry.
	24th Drag.	Former 15th Cavalry.
	25th Drag.	Former 16th Cavalry.
	26th Drag.	Former 17th Cavalry.
	27th Drag.	Former 18th Cavalry.
	28th Drag.	Former 7th bis Hussars.
	29th Drag.	Former 11th Hussars.
	30th Drag.	Former 12th Hussars.

Cavalier of the 7th regiment (1789).

Dress of cavalry regiments (1793).

Attacked on all borders, France was—or at least felt—torn between the need to form a large cavalry and the difficulty of obtaining horses. In Paris in May 1793, the requisition really had the unsettling appearance of plundering. Carriages and horsemen were stopped in the street and their horses were branded with a Liberty cap. However, things were not confiscated just for the army. Abuses became so frequent and numerous that the war administration prohibited the municipalities from demanding peoples' mounts. The administration reserved these horses exclusively for the needs of the cavalry and the artillery. Through a decree from January 13, 1794, the price of horses was fixed at 1000 pounds for the cavalry, 900 for the dragoons, and 800 for the chasseurs and hussars. These two latter groups had definitely become light cavalry and consequently were mounted. The decree did not say whether the price was in cash or in *assignats*. However, these prices do not differ substantially from today's. Therefore, they were notably superior. The Committee of Public Safety had the wherewithal to know what it wanted and to want it very much.

In the preceding table, the origin of these different organizations is easily recognized. Sometimes it is the volunteer corps (*corps francs*), at others it is the foreign corps which the French army annexed. The light cavalry component always dominates. Although the formation of four regiments of heavy cavalry and three regiments of dragoons was achieved only with a great deal of effort, fourteen regiments of chasseurs and eight of hussars could be gathered. The heavy cavalry was mustered out almost immediately and was incorporated into the old regiments of the service. The elegant uniform of the hussars and the chasseurs evidently tickled the Revolutionary fancy. In fact hussars in sky blue, light green, scarlet red, lemon yellow, white and even pink were seen. It is also true that there were black uniforms no less in vogue. These were for the "Hussars of Death" who had a short-lived existence and remained popular, and for the "Black Hussars", famous for the defense of Lille. These latter have been confused with their melodramatic rivals, the "Hussars of Death". As for foreign elements, they were numerous. However, all the foreign corps who served France did not directly enter into the regulation organizations. It is therefore useful to offer a complete list of them by nationality.

Belgians. *Chevau-legers of West Flanders*, became the 17th Chasseurs on March 25, 1793 and were mustered out on April 6, 1794, being commanded by Colonel de Rens. *Regiment of Dragoons of Brussels*, created on October 15, 1792; became the 14th then the 18th Chasseurs on May 9, 1793. Assigned to the Army of the Moselle, July 18, 1794, being commanded by Colonel de Bonne-d'Abonval.

Dutch. Eight companies of cavalry (496 men) were attached to the *Volunteer Foreign Legion* from this country, incorporated into the 13th Chasseurs in November 1793.

Germans. *Revolutionary Cavalry of the Germanic Legion*, created at the request of the Prussian Baron Anacharsis Clootz, a humanist orator; it was composed of four squadrons of light cuirassiers, four squadrons of *piquier* dragoons, and was commanded by Colonel Dambach – became the 11th Hussars on June 27, 1793 – Augereau served there as an officer and is apparently not the only Frenchman who found himself in this situation. *1st and 2nd Legions of the Franks of the North*, recruited especially in the border departments and countries - each one had four squadrons of chasseurs à cheval at two companies.

Italians. *The Volunteer Legion Allobroge*, created on August 13, 1792, had squadrons of light dragoons who were almost immediately turned into the 15th Dragoons. *The Regiment of Brempt* (German, in the service of Sardinia), – Colonel Kornfeld – in 1798 took refuge in the ranks of the French army, served in the Italian army; mustered out in November 1800. *The Italic Legion*, created on September 8, 1799, had four squadrons of chasseurs. *The 1st Regiment of Hussars of Naples* and the *1st Regiment of Roman Dragoons* – in 1799 and 1800 passed into the service of France. *Piemontese Dragoons* passed into the service of France on August 26, 1801 and became the 21st Dragoons – Colonels: 1802 – Dumas, 1809 – Ruat, 1813 – Saviot. *Piemontese Hussars* passed into the service of France on August 26, 1801, became the 17th Chasseurs, then the 26th Chasseurs in May 1802. Colonels: Armand Gros, 1802 – Dijeon, 1807 – Vial, 1813 – Muller, killed at Saint-Dizier on January 26, 1814 – 1814, Robert.

Irish. *Irish Chasseurs à Cheval of Lamoureux*, organized in 1793 for the expedition to England and mustered out in 1799. Later at the camp of Boulogne on October 5, 1803, this troop is remembered. Its remains were gathered, joined to some men who had lived in England and spoke English and formed the *Interpreter Guides of the Army of England*. On June 30, 1807, this squadron (Commander Cuvelier) was no longer useful and became the *Guides of the Prince of Neufchatel*. The expedition of Ireland, which has not yet been discussed, provides an example of the regrettable break-up of the cavalry regiments which was almost the rule in 1793. Six squadrons were affected: two of the 6th Hussars, one of the 10th and two of the 12th of the same service; finally, one of the 7th Chasseurs plus the company of guides which included 30 horsemen.

This method of dispersing the regiments had a purpose: to make the effective strength seem greater than it was in reality.

The rank of colonel had been eliminated in 1792 and replaced by that of *chef de brigade*. However the cavalry regiment was always indicated by this designation. The number of senior officers was reduced to three. From the rank of captain, the hierarchy suddenly leaped to the rank of second lieutenant colonel . Then the rank of lieutenant colonel disappeared in turn, and there were no more than two *chef d'escadrons* (majors) per regiment in the cavalry and three in the light cavalry. For the remainder of this period, promotion was very rapid for men of action. There was only the distance of a campaign or some stroke of luck separating an officer from the command of a company and that of a cavalry brigade. Young column leaders were needed in an army which trampled over past traditions and unveiled new tactics.

On May 13, 1793 five out of sixty-two regiments from the old formation were used by the three armies: the Ardennes, the North, and the Rhine. Only twelve old regiments — the 5th, 6th, 7th, 11th, 17th, 20th, 21st, 22nd cavalry and the 8th, 9th, 15th, and 16th Dragoons were available. It was also in 1793 that the greatest number of cavalry was produced. Both time and the enemy were pressing. However, there was a lack of horses. On December 6, 1793, a decree eliminated allowances for mounts which were unduly taken by the subordinate officers of the mounted infantry. In this way, 3,000 light horses were made available to the war administration.

STATE OF THE CAVALRY
MAY 13, 1793

Army of the Rhine—1st and 2nd Carabiniers; 2nd, 4th , 9th, 12th, 14th, 19th Cavalry; 1st and 11th Dragoons; 2nd, 4th, 7th, 8th, 10th Chasseurs; 4th Hussars.

Army of the Arndennes—7th, 15th, 16th, 18th, 23rd Cavalry; 2nd, 4th, 7th, 10th, 12th, 15th, 23rd Dragoons; 3rd, 9th, 11th, 12th Chasseurs; 1st, 2nd, 5th, 6th Hussars.

Army of the North—1st, 3rd, 8th , 10th, 13th Cavalry; 3rd, 5th, 6th, 14th, 17th Dragoons; 1st, 5th, 6th Chasseurs; 3rd Hussars.

In a report on the Army of the Eastern Pyrenees for September 1793, there were signs of detachments whose number indicates an unfortunate distribution. They accompanied the 14th Chasseurs who were created in March, along with the Hussars of Death, the Hussars of Justice, and the cavalry of the Legion of the Alps, Thus, part of the 15th Cavalry whose full squadrons were with the Army of the Ardennes was formed into brigades with the Cavalry of Beziers, the Uhlan Flankers and the Dragoons of Tarn.

The following year, this same army for whom the 19th and 20th Chasseurs à cheval had just been created, still counted in its ranks some detachments of the 18th Dragoons and the 18th of cavalry. Had they been brought there as escorts for the general staffs? This is likely, however, it is certain that in the border armies, the cavalry melted away like snow. The reasons for its disappearance cannot always be determined. The military government itself lent a hand in the dangerous dispersal of one of France's most precious resources. Thus, on February 13, 1794, the four regiments of cavalry bearing the numbers 2, 9, 12, and 18 received orders to supply some detachments for the Army of the West. It may be concluded from the correspondence of the leaders of the Army of the Rhine that this system of detachment had been extended to the entire cavalry. At first they speak of 1,100 then of 3,500 old cavaliers who have been taken away from them, " who were used to scorning and conquering the enemy." These leaders attributed their momentary defeats to the loss of these cavaliers.

In fact at this time, the French cavalryman's saber worked the same magic as the foot soldier's bayonet. However, horsemen and foot soldiers had to be trained and disciplined. Those recruits who did not ride well or who did not know how to wield their sabers were left to flounder like mere National Guardsmen newly drafted. These reasons for failure were not always acknowledged by the citizens representing the people, but the generals in chief tried hard to make them understand at the risk of being dismissed or even guillotined. Of course these inflexible patriots should be praised for their tenacity. Their mission was not to give up hope which they did not do when it came to the safety of the country.

Chasseurs à cheval (1796).

However, it must be added that their bloody brutality did not make victory come any sooner. The men who were cool and calm in their work in the gathering, training and outfitting of the French troops, who didn't scream futilely, who didn't threaten with death, did more for the liberation of the land than did those with bloody hands. Although the Revolution nonchalantly guillotined Saint-Just, the respect which it had for the life of Carnot and for Dubois Cranée is proof that even contemporaries of those times recognized a major difference between those who organized victory and the murderer of generals.

Meanwhile, a decree from the Convention dating from the 1st of Pluviôse, Year II (January 20, 1793) had reorganized the entire cavalry and fixed its cadres at: 29 cavalry regiments (2 of carabiniers and 27 of cavalry) at four squadrons of two companies (740 men), and 54 light cavalry regiments (20 dragoons, 23 chasseurs, and 11 hussars) at six squadrons of two companies (1,410 men).

The Convention provided the French army with a total of 97,600 horsemen. However, the decree which eliminated corps of troops raised by popular societies in the past and for the future was never fully executed, especially with respect to the effectives.

Hussars of the Army of the Rhine (1793).

The report of the Army of Sambre-et-Meuse proves that it had seventeen cavalry regiments divided amongst its various divisions in the following manner:

Lefebvre Division: 1st, 6th, and 9th Chasseurs – Grenier Division: 19th Chasseurs and 4th Hussars – Tilly Division: 12th Chasseurs – Poncet Division: 7th Dragoons – Harville Cavalry Division: 6th, 8th, 10th and 13th Cavalry (16 squadrons, 1,593 men) – Championnet Division: 1st and 12th Dragoons – Bernadotte Division: 3rd Chasseurs – Marceau Division: 11th Chasseurs – Collaud Division: 2nd and 14th Dragoons.

Of these seventeen regiments, four had about 400 horses each. The other thirteen barely had 300 which were always reduced to 250 by the escorts service, always very large. The generals had taken up the habit of trailing along behind them platoons of cavalry on the battlefield. This was hardly an unusual practice. These platoons served as the need arose in routing or charging a small enemy party. Some, indeed almost all of these generals, permitted themselves the luxury of uniforming these soldiers after their own tastes. They even took these men from their regiments to form companies of guides for the generals in chief, usually commanded by the favorite *officier d'ordonnance*. The history of the wars of the Revolution is full of organizations of this type. Wearing whimsical hussars' costumes, these small, privileged corps gave a grand appearance to the Republican general staffs. A report from the Army of the Alps on Lyon on September 28, 1793 reveals the make-up of the general in chief's company of guides as 30 cavaliers, of whom 13 were present, 1 was in the hospital and 16 were detached. Obviously this was a system which broke all the rules. It required all of Napoleon's strength to return the detached cavaliers to the ranks later on. When he took command of the Army of Italy in 1796, he recalled all the regiments and pieces of regiments available and placed them in compact groups. This was with the exception of the 20th Dragoons which he left below Mantua and the 22nd Chasseurs which remained in the Valley of the Chiuse.

CAVALRY OF THE ARMY OF ITALY IN 1796

Division attached to Masséna
1st Brigade, General PIGEON
23rd Chasseurs, 286 men. 7th Hussars, 260 men
2nd Brigade, General LECLERC
5th Dragoons, 150 men. 15th Dragoons, 184 men

Cavalry Reserve
General of division DUMAS
1st Brigade, General BEAUREVOIR
1st Hussars, 22nd, 24th, 25th Cavalry, 8th Dragoons
2nd Brigade, General BEAUMONT
18th Dragoons, 3rd, 5th, 20th Cavalry,
in total 1,000 men

Nothing better illustrates the denuding of the cavalry at this point in time than the effectives of Bonaparte's cavalry. No less than seven regiments were required to form a reserve of 1,600 horses. When he complained to the Directorate and asked that some regiments placed at the rear be rallied to his army, he received evasive answers. He had to sort out the rebuilding of his cavalry on his own, depending only on himself for remounts and their equipment.

On January 8, 1796, the Directorate tried to re-establish a bit of order and regularity in the finances of the administration. Particularly keen on economizing, it wanted to decrease the number of cavalry regiments. There were then eighty-three of them: twenty-five of cavalry of which two were carabiniers, twenty-one of dragoons, twenty-four of chasseurs, and thirteen

of hussars making up the 7th *bis* The decree of January 8th reduced them to fifty-one (twenty of battle cavalry, twelve of dragoons, eleven of chasseurs, and eight of hussars). However, the army knew about this reform before it was officially announced. The decree provoked so many valid dissensions amongst the generals in chief that on January 17th the decree of the 8th was revoked and there was no more discussion about it. At this time, the three big armies of Sambre-et-Meuse (General in Chief Jourdan), of the Rhine-and- Moselle (General in Chief Moreau), and of Italy (General in Chief Bonaparte) only took in fifty-five regiments. The poverty of Bonaparte's thirteen regiments will soon be shown. Jourdan's twenty-one regiments, although not much better in terms of quality, were in better condition. Below is a report on their effective strengths at the beginning of the German campaign.

4th Cavalry:	183 horses	7th Dragoons:	585 horses
5th Cavalry:	331	11th Dragoons:	156
7th Cavalry:	230	12th Dragoons:	577
8th Cavalry:	326	1st Chasseurs:	521
10th Cavalry:	374	3rd Chasseurs:	543
13th Cavalry:	626	7th Chasseurs:	509
17th Cavalry:	223	12th Chasseurs:	636
19th Cavalry:	426	16th Chasseurs:	116
1st Dragoons:	548	19th Chasseurs:	98
2nd Dragoons:	482	2nd Hussars:	533
		4th Hussars:	342

Some of these corps had only one squadron present, e.g.,the 16th and the 19th Chasseurs.

Moreau's Cavalry, twenty-three regiments strong, seemed the most well-organized. The Bourcier Division which formed the reserve corps had General of Brigade Forest as second in command. It included seven regiments and 3,465 horsemen in its ranks: the 1st and 2nd Carabiniers who would continue to be together (4 squadrons each); the 2nd, 3rd, 9th, 14th, and 15th Battle Cavalry (3 squadrons each). The other regiments of the Army of the Rhine-and-Moselle were the 11th, 12th, 16th, and 21st Battle Cavalry; the 4th, 6th, 10th, 16th, and 17th Dragoons; the 2nd, 4th and 20th Chasseurs; and the 8th, 9th, and 11th Hussars. During the campaign of 1799, the majority of regiments from the magnificent Bourcier Division were turned over to the command of General of Division d'Hautpoul with Compere

Camel squadron, Dragoons regiment, Army of Egypt (1798).

and Oswald for generals of brigade. This division was the first example of the masses of cavalry which Napoleon I used so effectively on the battlefield of the Empire.

With the fall of the Directorate, the cavalry was extremely neglected. It was too expensive for this outrageous government which intended to transform the French armies into instruments of oppression and their generals into instructors of tax collecting in occupied countries. The remount regiments had been almost completely abandoned leaving the armies with a dearth of mounted troops. The Army of Naples (General in Chief Macdonald) had only 300 horses for a force of 36,728 men. The horses were supplied by nine regiments (1st Cavalry; 12th, 16th, and 19th Dragoons; 7th, 15th, 19th and 25th Chausseurs; 11th Hussars) along with 600 Italian and Polish horsemen. The Army of Batavia (General in Chief Brune) had only one regiment of cavalry, the 16th Chasseurs in its entirety and the depots of the 5th and 11th. By contrast, the Army of Italy, turned over to the command of Masséna, received many cavalry reinforcements. In the future, it would have sixteen regiments: the 22nd Cavalry; the 1st, 2nd, 11th, and 17th Dragoons; the 5th, 8th, 10th, 11th, 12th, 13th, and 23rd Chasseurs; and the 4th, 5th, 7th, 8th, and 9th Hussars. This gave a total of 7,035 horsemen for an effective strength of more than 91,000 men. It was time for a firm hand to take control of military affairs.

When Bonaparte departed for Egypt in 1798, he brought nineteen unmounted squadrons with him. The men carried their arms, their saddles and their harnesses. Of these nineteen squadrons, there were only six of light cavalry. The rest belonged to a dragoons service. The latter continued to wear their helmets until the end of the campaign. These squadrons fought first on foot until they could be mounted on horses taken from the Mamelukes or bought in that country. The 7th *bis* Hussars distinguished itself particularly in the Battle of the Pyramids where it won its remounts. It is most likely these circumstances which decided Napoleon to mount the troops, especially the dragoons, even though they fought as well on foot as when mounted. The guides came from the Army of Italy. The Mamelukes and the Syrians were gathered in Egypt. They took a number of French officers and non-commissioned officers into their organization especially after the departure of Bonaparte.

CAVALRY OF THE ARMY OF EGYPT

CORPS	EFFECTIVES		
	Upon Departure June 30, 1798	On 10 Ventôse IX (February 28, 1800)	
		Men	Horses
7th *bis* Hussars: Colonel Destrée, 3 sqdns.	500	270	249
22nd Chasseurs: Colonel Lasalle, 3 sqdns.	450	279	230
3rd Dragoons: Colonel Bron, 2 sqdns.	300	255	225
14th Dragoons:Colonel Duvivier, 3 sqdns.	400	312	245
15th Dragoons:Colonel Pinon, 2 sqdns.	300	181	129
18th Dragoons:Colonel Lefèvre, 4 sqdns.	400	190	115
20th Dragoons:Colonel Boussard, 2 sqdns.	350	293	233
Guides: Colonel Bessières.	120	80	72
Mamelukes and Syrians.	—	278	163

The cavalry of Egypt may be admired for its dedication. At first commanded by General of Division Dumas, then by Generals of Brigade Roize, Bron, and Boussard, it distinguished itself on all battlefields. In 1798 it comprised two thousand seven hundred horsemen. Four years later only sixteen hundred remained. Their remnants returned to the corps depots to which they belonged. The Camel Corps was never included in the cavalry. It was entirely recruited from the infantry and upon its return was assigned to the *gendarmerie à pied*. The mounted guides, the Syrians and the Mamelukes joined the organization of the regiments of chasseurs à cheval of the Consular Guard. They later became the legendary regiment of the chasseurs a cheval of the Imperial Guard.

CONSULATE

On the 25th of Fructidor, Year VII (September 12, 1798) the Directorate again tried to carry out a reduction of the cavalry. This reductin limited the number of regiments of this service to 76: 2 of carabiniers, 25 of battle cavalry, 15 of dragoons, 22 of chasseurs, and 12 of hussars. At the same time, the regulation effective strength fell to 704 horsemen for the carabiniers, to 531 for the battle cavalry, and to 942 for the dragoons, chasseurs and hussars. Total general strength: 60,841 non-commissioned officers and horsemen. This was already quite a bit less than the 97,000 horsemen decreed by the National Convention. However, it would have been very fine indeed if the orders of the Directors were achieved. The First Consul found this order unexecuted. Once he became absolute ruler, he maintained the cavalry at an effective level of 85 regiments (2 of carabiniers, 25 of cavalry, 20 of dragoons, 25 of chasseurs, and 12 of hussars, including the 7th *bis*.)

On March 8, 1800, he ordered the gathering of a reserve army at Dijon which was actually organized on the border. Regiments were sent there in secret while on the Côte-d'Or, a large obstacle army was made with veterans and battalions of conscripts. This army would be directly commanded by Napoleon with Berthier as his second-in-command. Murat, who was already known as the best cavlary officer of the century, was placed at the head of five brigades which formed the cavalry of the future Army of Italy. On the day of the Battle of Marengo these brigades were comprised of the present effectives listed at left.

1st Brigade General KELLERMANN		2nd Brigade General CHAMPEAUX		3rd Brigade	
2nd Cavalry	120 horses	1st Dragoons	450 horses	6th Dragoons	345 horses
20th Cavalry	300 —	8th Dragoons	328 —	12th Chasseurs	340 —
21st Cavalry	100 —	9th Dragoons	428 —	5th Cavalry	110 —
	520 horses		1,206 horses		795 horses

4th Brigade General RIVAUD		5th Brigade General DUVIGNAUD	
21st Chasseurs	359 horses	3rd Cavalry	120 horses
12th Hussars	300 —	1st Hussars	120 —
	659 horses		240 horses

By adding the 369 grenadiers and chasseurs of the new Consular Guard, a total of 3720 horsemen is obtained. In thinking of the wonders Kellermann accomplished at the head of 520 men very quickly reduced to 150, one can only marvel at these brave men. In the official account of the battle, the 6th of Cavalry is named in place of the 21st which appeared in the preceding order. However, Kellermann indicates the 2nd and the 20th as being the most prominent. The 2nd had seven officers killed or wounded out of the eleven present; the 20th had six. It can thus be concluded that neither the 6th nor the 21st Cavalry played a major role in the memorable charges executed on June 14, 1800 on the Plain of Marengo.

What was the cause of the paucity of effectives in the regiments of the battle cavalries? Above all it was the difficulty of procuring tall horses. Meanwhile, the dragoons remounted themselves like the hussars and the chasseurs and did not use up all the average horses which consequently could be assigned to the as-yet unarmored cavalry regiments. In addition, the needs of the artillery and of the wagon teams for strong horses were also not met. Thus, immediately after Marengo, the future Emperor ordered that a new structuring of the cavalry be studied. While waiting to make war, he continued to requisition a third of the horses in France. This was a lot, but even so, it was still not enough. As was seen in the history of the infantry, Bonaparte created a number of elegant corps such as the hussars a pied in order to attract the young, chic set to active service. With the same goal, he organized the regiment of volunteer hussars in the cavalry, called the

Hussars, review by the First Consul (1800).

Hussars, campaign dress (1885).

Chasseurs à cheval, campaign dress (1885).

"Volunteers of Bonaparte." Created on the 1st of Germinal, Year VIII (March 22, 1799), they were mustered out on April 15, 1801. They were involved in the campaign of the Year VIII (1799) in the reserve army (Italy) and in the campaign of the Year IX (1800) with the Army of the Rhine.

While the reserve army waged the astonishing campaign of 1800 in Italy, Moreau had command of the Army of the Rhine. The First Consul had at his disposition five divisions divided into four army corps. These formed an overall total of 128,642 men of whom 16,336 were cavalrymen.

These 16,336 cavalrymen belonged to 42 regiments. The following table indicates their allocation to each division and each corps. Certain divisions only had one cavalry regiment, others a brigade. Only the Montrichard Division of Lecourbe's Corps had no cavalry at all.

Dragoons, Campaign of Italy (1800).

Corps	Divisions and Brigades	Regiments	Horses
Right Wing LECOURBE	Division VANDAMME	8th Hussars	540
	Division LORGES	9th Hussars	467
	Division MONTRICHARD	—	—
	Brigade NANSOUTY (Reserve)	11th and 12th Dragoons, 25th Chasseurs	1,280
Reserve Corps MOREAU Commander in chief	Division DELMAS. Brigade BOYER	4th Hussars, 11th Chasseurs, 12th Cavalry	1,031
	Division LECLERC. Brigade WATHIER	10th and 23rd Chasseurs	963
	Division RICHEPANCE. Brigade DURUTTE	5th Hussars, 17th Dragoons, 3th Cavalry	1,187
	Division D'HAUTPOUL. Brigade ESPAGNE	1st and 2nd Carabiniers	
	Brigade DEVRIGNY	2nd and 9th Cavalry	1,504
Center GOUVION ST-CYR	Division BARAGUAY D'HILLIERS	2nd Hussars	542
	Division THARREAU. Bde. BEAUREGARD	16th Chasseurs, 23rd Dragoons	601
	Division NEY. Brigade BONAMY	8th Chasseurs	569
	Division SARUC. Brigade SALIGNY	5th Chasseurs, 2nd Dragoons	
	Brigade DELIGNY	12th and 17th Cavalry	1,616
Left Wing STE-SUZANNE	Division COLLAUD	20th Chasseurs, 10th and 16th Cavalry	981
	Division SOUHAM. Brigade PUTHOD	1st Chasseurs, 6th Dragoons, 7th Cavalry	1,394
	Division LEGRAND. Brigade DROUET	5th Chasseurs, 13th Dragoons	1,094
	Division DELABORDE. Brigade THURING	4th Cavalry, 10th Dragoons	286
		Total	**14,055**

The 6th Cavalry is found within this offical list of names. As noted above, they mistakenly appear in certain offical reports on Marengo. The Army of Moreau included still more regiments beyond those indicated above to fill out its figure of 16,336 horsemen. The 14th and 22nd regiments of cavalry, totaling 519 men, were attached to the Montchoisy Division in Switzerland. In Mayence and Alsace, the 3rd and 6th Hussars, the 1st Dragoons and some detachments of the 15th, 16th, and 24th Cavalry comprising a total of 1,752 horses provided services in the rear of the army and along the border.

The seven regiments which Bonaparte had taken to Egypt but which had not yet returned to France should be added to the 57 regiments on campaign. Together, they represented no more than 25 to 26 thousand horsemen. There were at most fifteen thousand in Upper Italy and in France at the depots. Yet, according to the last organic rules of the service, the force was sixty thousand!

ORGANIZATION OF THE 1ST OF VENDÉMIAIRE, YEAR XII (SEPTEMBER 24, 1803).

As of Year X (1801), the First Consul perceived the absolute impossibility of recruiting tall horses. He mustered out the 23rd, 24th, and 25th Regiments of battle cavalry and assigned their cadres and effectives to the first eight regiments of the service. The 5th, 6th and 7th received the men and horses of the 23rd. The 1st and 8th received those of the 24th. The 2nd, 3rd, and 4th received those of the 25th. However, this still did not produce satisfactory results. Napoleon ordered that the 13th, 14th, 15th, 16th, 17th, and 18th battle cavalry become the 22nd, 23rd, 24th, 25th, 26th, and 27th Dragoons.

Finally, the 19th, 20th, 21st and 22nd Cavalry were dissolved and assigned as follows, according to the height of the men and horses:

The 19th Regiment into the 1st Carabiniers and the 9th, 10th and 11th Cavalry;
The 20th Regiment into the 2nd Carabiniers, the 12th Cavalry and the new 22nd and 23rd Dragoons;
The 21st Regiment into the 1st Carabiniers and the new 24th, 25th, and 26th Dragoons;
The 22nd Regiment into the 2nd Carabiniers, the 12th Cavalry and the new 24th and 27th Dragoons.

The twelve regiments of battle cavalry produced from this combination became regiments of cuirassiers. Four were already armored: the 8th (former 7th Cavalry, Regiment of the King) since before the Revolution; the 5th, 6th, and 7th, since only a few months earlier. The 7th *bis,* 11th, and 12th Hussars became the 27th, 28th, and 29th Dragoons.

This new balancing of the French cavalry was almost an accomplished fact when the decree of the 1st of Vendémiaire, Year

Officers, chasseurs à cheval and hussars (1805).

XII (September 24, 1803) appeared. It set the allocation of the 80 regiments of cavalry in the following manner: two carabiniers, thirty dragoons, twenty-six chasseurs, and ten hussars.

Another decree from September 24, 1803 established the cavalry uniforms. The cuirassiers had a breastplate and a helmet in steel with a flowing black horsehair plume and a short blue jacket. They were divided by distinguishing colors into four series of three regiments. The first was scarlet, the second *aurore* (gold), the third jonquil yellow, the last rose pink. The 13th and 14th Cuirassiers who were created later wore wine-colored uniforms. The dragoons who were at the same time horsemen and foot soldiers had a long green coat whose lapels allowed the vest to be seen. Their helmet was in copper with a flowing horsehair plume. Their distinguishing colors were, from 1 to 6, lapels and facings in scarlet; from 7 to 12, crimson; from 13 to 18, deep rose; from 19 to 24, jonquil yellow; from 25 to 30, aurore. The chasseurs had a green coat with green breeches tucked into boots *a coeur* (with heart-shaped tops), and the infantry shako with a plume.

As for the hussars, the colors of the 10 regiments from 1803 are indicated in the facing table.

These brilliant uniforms were not subject to change during the imperial period. They were somewhat legendary in the army. The cavalry generals sometimes took it into their heads to fight in the uniform of the regiments which they commanded. D'Hautpoul fell in armor at Eylau at the head of the cuirassiers who were to immortalize their glory in a heroic charge. Lasalle wore the dolman jacket of the light cavalry and

Number	Dolman	Pelisse	Braids	Waistcoat	Breeches
1	Sky blue	Sky blue	White	Scarlet	Sky blue
2	Chestnut brown	Chestnut brown	White	Sky blue	Sky blue
3	Silver grey	Silver grey	White	Silver grey	Silver grey
4	Royal blue	Scarlet	Yellow	White	Royal blue
5	Scarlet	White	Lemon Yellow	Sky blue	Sky blue
6	Scarlet	Blue	Yellow	Scarlet	Scarlet
7	Dark green	Dark green	Jonquil yellow	Scarlet	Scarlet
8	Dark green	Dark green	White	Scarlet	Scarlet
9	Scarlet	Sky Blue	Yellow	Sky blue	Sky blue
10	Sky blue	Sky blue	White	Scarlet	Sky blue

loose fitting trousers with foot straps until the day he died. He lent his name to the latter. General Pajol, commanding a division of light cavalry, wore the blue dolman of the hussars and three stars on his sleeves as a distinguishing mark of his rank during the entire campaign of 1812. In retirement, he completed this costume with a royal blue cutaway jacket with gold braid and a curved Damascus saber, a present from Princess Pauline. Murat's example was followed fairly closely by the epic hussars of the army of Napoleon the First.

The new Emperor had re-established the titles of colonel in the regiments. A third major who was soon after given the functions of lieutenant colonel with the title of major, relieved the commanding officers from part of their administrative duties. The effectives had been determined in the following manner for the regiments indicated:

Carabiniers,	4 squadrons: 820 men for 2 regiments:	164	men
Cuirassiers,	4 squadrons: 830 men for 12 regiments:	9,840	men
Dragoons,	4 squadrons: 880 men for 30 regiments:	26,400	men
Chasseurs,	4 squadrons: 1,055 men for 26 regiments:	27,430	men
Hussars,	4 squadrons: 1,055 men for 10 regiments:	10,550	men
	Total	75,860	men

Without counting the elite corps of the Imperial Guard, there were 75,860 horsemen! Such were the integral beginnings of the cavalry of the First Empire. However, in addition to the lack of horses, there were many other reasons for setbacks. The 17th and 18th numbers in the series of chasseurs à cheval were vacant. Before going further, a list of the regiments which were created between the organization of Year XII (1803) and the mustering out which followed the fall of the Empire is given below.

DATE of CREATION	NAME AND REGIMENTAL No.	ELEMENTS USED TO FORM IT
1808	27th Chasseurs	Formed from the Belgian chevau-légers of Prince Aremberg in the service of France since 1806.
May 28, 1806	28th Chasseurs	Formed from the Tuscan dragoons in the service of France since January 7, 1806.
August 22, 1810	29th Chasseurs	Former 3rd Provisional Chasseur à cheval Regiment.
December 24, 1809	13th Cuirassiers	Former 1st and 2nd Provisional Heavy Cavalry Regiments.
December 24, 1810	13th Cuirassiers	Former 2nd Dutch Curiassier Regiment.
December 24, 1810	11th Hussars	Formed at Arras from the 2nd Dutch Hussar Regiment (dolman, pelisse and Hungarian breeches – blue, waistcoat – scarlet, braids – yellow, fur – white).
August 29, 1810	30th Chasseurs	Formed in the Army of Spain from various light cavalry detachments.
June 11, 1811	1st Chevau-légers Lancers	Former 1st Dragoons. Helmet with chenille, green coat with facings of distinguishing colors, green Hungarian breeches.
	2nd Chevau-légers Lancers	Former 3rd Dragoons. "
	3rd Chevau-légers Lancers	Former 8th Dragoons. "
	4th Chevau-légers Lancers	Former 9th Dragoons. "
	5th Chevau-légers Lancers	Former 10th Dragoons. "
	6th Chevau-légers Lancers	Former 20th Dragoons. "
	7th Chevau-légers Lancers	Former 1st Vistula Chevau-légers Lancers. Retained their dress.
	8th Chevau-légers Lancers	Former 2nd Vistula Chevau-legers Lancers. Retained their dress.
	9th Chevau-légers Lancers	Former 30th Chasseurs – same dress as the first six.
June 11, 1811	New 17th Chasseurs	Formed at Lille from various elements. Without a permanent organization.
June 11, 1811	New 18th Chasseurs	Formed at Metz from various elements. Without a permanent organization.
September 7, 1811	31st Chasseurs	Formed from the 1st and 2nd Provisional Light Cavalry.
January 17, 1813	12th Hussars	Former 9th bis Hussars, organized January 10, 1812, dolman -scarlet, pelisse, collar and breeches – light blue, braids -white.
January 1, 1814	13th Hussars	Former Westphalian and Italian hussars (dress of the 2nd Regiment).
January 28, 1814	14th Hussars	Italian hussars and detachments from Spain (dress of the 8th Regiment).

Note – Thus from 1804 to 1814 only 22 permanent new numbers were created: two of cuirassiers, 13th and 14th; five of chasseurs, 27th, 28th, 29th,30th and 31st; four of hussars, 11th, 12th, 13th and 14th; and nine of chevau-légers lanciers. Two vacant numbers, the 17th and 18th Chasseurs, were filled again. However, the creation of the chevau-légers led to the elimination of six numbers in the old dragoons and of one in the new chasseurs. This reduced the creation of permanent regiments to fifteen: thirteen new and two old reformed.

Carabiniers (1806).

Napoleon could not apply procedures to the cavalry which were as simple as those he used on the infantry. More patience was required as were permanent supplies of officers and non-commissioned officers. Under the Consulate, he had sent all the infantry corps and the officers of all the most unruly services to Santo Domingo. However, at the same time, he had recalled into active service retired officers who could still prove useful. The cavalry was the service which received the greatest number of these old officers in proportion to its size. In addition, Napoleon inundated those great heros who were responsible for the glory of the French cavalry under his reign with special treatment and favors. Meanwhile, he did not forget the simple soldiers, those heros of the frontlines. For them he created elite companies in all the regiments—dragoons, chasseurs, and hussars—on September 24, 1803. These companies wore the red epaulette of the grenadiers in the dragoons and the chasseurs and the kolback in the chasseurs and the hussars. They were always identified with the No. 1 in the 1st squadron of their regiments. The honor of the color guard was bestowed upon them.

The creation of new regiments under the Empire may be divided into four very distinct categories:

1. annexations of foreign corps which will be addressed immediately;

2. gathering of provisional corps strong in number which were the Emperor's best resource as of the first Spanish campaign;

3. infrequent transformations of foreign and provisional regiments into permanent regiments;

4. creation of new corps from a number of parts, most rare.

The preceding table lists the two latter categories. The two former will now be examined in more detail.

The annexations of foreign corps began in 1807 with the introduction of the cavalry regiment El Rey into the French army.

It was commanded successively by d'Algarde and Villaviciosa. In the same year on November 27, a squadron of Ionian chasseurs was created under the command of Lastour. More chasseurs from the 25th Regiment were included in its composition than inhabitants from the seven islands, and the squadron wore its uniform. The Polish, who merit a special chapter in the history of the French army, had served France for a long time. On January 20, 1808, Napoleon created the regiment of the Lancers of Vistula: Colonels Konopka, killed in 1812, then Slokowski. This corps was turned over to the Legion of Vistula, which succeeded the Polish-Italian Legion. This last legion was itself the offspring of the 1st and 2nd Legions of the North, divided into 2 divisions and provided with artillery and cavalry. It took the Number 1. On February 7, 1811, a second regiment of Lancers of Vistula were assembled under the command of Colonel Lubienski. These two regiments figured in the creation of the *chevau-légers lanciers* (June 18, 1811). In addition to these two regiments classified in the line, there was a regiment of Polish lancers in the Guard which also included a squadron of Tartars as of August 24, 1812. The remains of this squadron were incorporated into the 3rd Regiment of Scouts, a special corps having its incorporation in the Young Guard. Finally on February 23, 1811, some lancers had been created for the 32nd Military Division at Hamburg. After having momentarily worn the number 30 in the service of the chasseurs, the lancers took the number 9 in the chevau-légers under the command of Colonel Gobrecht. This regiment had only Polish troops and a variety of foreign nationals in its ranks. It also received some light cavalry detachments taken from the Army of Spain. In 1814, it became almost entirely French.

Cuirassiers (1806).

On May 18, 1802, two regiments of Portugese chasseurs à cheval were admitted into the French service. The first was commanded by Colonel d'Aguiar and the second by the Marquis de Loule. In November 1813 they suffered the same fate as all foreigners who had served the conqueror of the world.

On April 13, 1804, the Hanoverian Legion had been organized and counted in its ranks some squadrons of chasseurs à cheval. They were turned over to the 1st Regiment of hussars on August 9, 1811. The Belgian chevau-légers—called the chevau-légers of the Prince of Arenberg—had been in the service of France since September 30, 1806. On May 29, 1808, as noted above, they became the 27th Chasseurs. In February 1813, they were commanded by Colonel Strub and in December of the same year by Colonel Saint-Georges. The Tuscan Dragoons formed on January 7, 1808 and became the 28th Chasseurs on May 28, 1808.

They had Laroche then Courtier for colonels. Finally a 13th Hussars, which had been created beyond the Alps with various Italian detachments, joined the newly organized 14th of the same service in January 1814. Colonel Saint-Sauveur had created it; after the merger, Colonel Caravaque took command of the 14th which was the permanent result of this combination.

As a note of interest, foreigners who were part of the later regiments of light cavalry were more easily assimilated than were foot soldiers into the infantry regiments. At first, this was due to the fact that there were not too many and that they were very heavily supported by the French horsemen. Then too, it was also because they almost always belonged to the wealthy classes.

On August 18, 1810, following the union of the Dutch crown with that of the French Empire, Colonel Trip's Dutch Cuirassiers became the 14th of the service. The Dutch Hussars (Colonels Gérard de Collaërt - 1812, Liégeard) took Number 11 of the hussars. The last act of military annexation by Napoleon was the formation of the Croatian Hussars on February 23, 1813, commanded by Colonel Prués.

In the cavalry there were also six Croatian regiments: 1st Regiment of Lika, Colonel Sliwarich; 2nd Regiment of Ottockats, Colonel Winther; 3rd Regiment of Ogulin, Colonel Holevocz; 4th Regiment of Sluin, Colonel Choisy; 5th Regiment of the 1st *banal*, Colonel Joly; and 6th Regiment of the 2nd *banal*, Colonel Tromelin. To complete the tally, the Regiment of Illyria, Colonel Schmitz and the Spanish Regiment Joseph-Napoleon, Colonel Tschudy, must be added. These eight regiments appear in the almanac of 1813 following the French cavalry and are outside the line.

Chasseurs à cheval, Prussian Campaign, Berlin, (1806).

The corps mentioned above were an integral part of the French army, however, they were not the only foreigners who served in the ranks of the French cavalry.

The assembly of provisional corps must be examined separately. They comprise one of the most curious components of this vast military organization which was involved in three quarters of Europe. Spain was the first attempt. The patriotism of a people who waited more than half a century to take their revenge has recently been overly praised. The Spain and Russia where invading French legions were swallowed up whole have been forgotten. Spain especially merits due justice after a long peace. Even without the English who made her pay heavily for their alliance which was motivated by self-interest, Spain would have come to the end of French troops. This was thanks to the guerilla warfare which it continuously carried out against France everywhere, and also to her ferocious autonomy which caused the French to smell warm, young flesh like the ogre in Perrault's tales. Spain attacked France at a time when the Emperor was in Germany. He had no army available, nor an army corps, nor even a regiment. Spain attacked the French flank at an opportune moment. It took all the administrative and organizational talent of the Emperor to come up with the necessary resources for a terrible war, worse even than those of the Vendée, Egypt or Germany.

It can be said that the end of 1806 and the beginning of 1807 saw the imperial cavalry at its zenith of glory and strength. The Imperial Guard, which would be expanded even more, served as the reserve for this cavalry. All the armored regiments of the line (two carabiniers and twelve cuirassiers) had four squadrons and formed their fifth. All of them had their first three squadrons in the Grande Armée. Twenty-four regiments of dragoons out of thirty had the same destination. Except for the 4th, 6th, 8th, 14th, and 15th Chasseurs and the 6th Hussars, all the light cavalry, that is, thirty-four regiments, were in the same situation. The Battle of Jena and the surrender of Magdebourg brought nine thousand horses in good condition and with new harnesses into French hands. The Emperor emptied all the depots of France, called up all the unmounted horsemen, and filled out his war regiments at 800 horses. Moreover, he had five regiments of unmounted chasseurs come to Italy carrying their saddles, their boots, and their arms. He even momentarily stopped the annual purchases of horses for the army throughout French territory. From the great cavalry depot of Potsdam, he dispatched horses to the remount depots of the interior. On January 5, 1807, all his orders were sorted out and sent, but the organization of the fifth squadrons had pushed the staffs of

lieutenants, second lieutenants and non-commissioned officers to their limits. They resorted to extraordinary means to fill in the voids, once more dipping into that great can of worms of reform and retirement and asking for officers anywhere they could find them.

The recruitment of cavalry officers grew difficult from this point on. The Emperor tried to attact young men of nobility through all kinds of incentives. On December 24, 1806, he created two squadrons of *gendarmes d'ordonnance* only to flatter the egos of rich young men and the great noble families. He was able to assemble approximately two hundred gentlemen who, after a year's campaigning in Germany, under the command of Count de Montmorency-Laval, provided, ten months later, 132 excellent lieutenants and second lieutenants in the regiments of the line.

In 1809, Napoleon took a more direct approach. He sent commissions for second lieutenant of the cavalry to a number of young nobles who still remained aloof from his government. The names of de Castelbajac, de Castries, de Chabannes, de Crillon, de l'Espinay, de la Rochejaquelein, de Rohan-Chabot, etc. were seen in this promotion. It is obvious that any means available which would enhance the glamor of the cavalry corps seemed appropriate to him.

The School of Saint-Germain, founded in 1809, only provided 315 second lieutenants up until 1814. It is totally impossible to determine the number of cavalry officers who graduated from Fontainebleau or Saint-Cyr. These schools did not provide a steady flow of cavalry officers like they did for the infantry. More energetic procedures were required. The Emperor possessed a fledgling group of excellent and active officers through the creation of elite squadrons attached to regiments of the Imperial Guard. These officers were much superior to the young men whom he culled from the masses through the methods described above. In addition, the non-commissioned officers of the Guard passed into the regiments of the line as second lieutenants. After the campaign of 1812, he requested about one hundred second lieutenants from the cuirassiers and the dragoons for the staff of non-commissioned officers of the gendarmerie. Also, any time a well-educated son of a family with money was brought to his attention, he had no problem in immediately granting him the rank of second lieutenant. In this way, he granted one to de Gonneville in order to please his cousin who was himself a distinguished colonel. In 1806, he made de Grouchy, who was a student of 17 at Fontainebleau, an officer to compensate his father for some sizeable expenses. By these means he could confront the enormous consumption of manpower which weakened his cadres.

Kit of a cavalier of the 7th Hussars

Fine fighting on the part of mere soldiers and of non-commissioned officers was also rewarded with very good promotions. On October 10, 1806, Gaindé, Guindé or Guindet (his name is written in various ways by the historians of the Grande Armée) a sergeant in the 9th Hussars, instantly killed Prince Louis of Prussia, the principal instigator of the war. He did this while fighting in the advance guard at Saelfeld with an energetic saber thrust. Seven years later, Gaindé, now an officer in the Legion of Honor, was a captain in the Grenadiers à cheval of the Guard with the rank of major. If he had not died gloriously on October 30, 1813, he would have been promoted to colonel in the line the following year.

The Emperor knew that cavalry officers were rare and that few generals could be found to lead a charge well at a critical moment. He said that with Murat at the head of the cavalry, its value was twofold. As of 1804, he provided the four services of the cavalry with colonels holding the rank of general at the same time that he created the marshals. Gouvion Saint-Cyr had the cuirassiers, Junot the hussars, Marmont the chasseurs and Baraguey d'Hilliers the dragoons. Although these titles were more ceremonial than real, they served to confer Napoleon's desire of strengthening competition amongst the generals. The titles were only awarded after distinguished service. Napoleon prepared his chosen officers for such special distinctions. Sometimes, he entrusted very important commands to his youngest division leaders when he recognized them at a glance as being deserving. Thus it was in 1807 that he temporarily formed a magnificent division for the very young division leader Lasalle. At the time, the division included thirteen regiments and more than 7,500 horsemen.

1st Brigade	2nd Brigade	3rd Brigade	4th Brigade
General LATOUR-MAUBOURG, later PAJOL	General WATHIER	General BRUYÈRES	General DUROSNEL
5th Hussars, Colonel d'Héry	11th Chasseurs, Colonel Jacquinot	1st Hussars, Colonel Rouvillois	7th Chasseurs, Colonel Depire
7th Hussars, Colonel Colbert	Bavarian Chevau-légers	13th Chasseurs, Colonel Demangeot	20th Chasseurs, Colonel Castex
3rd Chasseurs, Colonel Charpentier		14th Chasseurs, Colonel Sachs	22nd Chasseurs, Colonel Desfossés
19th Chasseurs, Colonel Leduc		Italian Royal Chasseurs	

The Emperor had splendid cavalry officers. In addition to Lasalle, there were Pajol, Montbrun, Colbert, and Exelmans. Perhaps the best known was Kellermann who was responsible for the success of Marengo. The least well-known was General of Brigade Curely who was an example of the best officers of the light cavalry. Beginning as a simple hussar in 1794, Curely slowly made his way through the lower ranks of the hierarchy. He was major of the 20th Chasseurs in 1809, colonel of the 10th Hussars in 1811, general of brigade in 1813, and he commanded a brigade at Waterloo. General de Brack speaks of his prowess as an officer of the advance guard who left the Uhlans of 1870 in the dust. The famous nickname "lunette" [spyglass] of the general in chief" was not new. Kleber used it in August 1794 when he covered a front of five leagues with a detachment of hussars commanded by Ney. To bring his cavalry to such a state of perfection and to maintain it thus, Napoleon hesitated at nothing. Brave men were always generously rewarded and were not kept waiting long for fame and fortune. "In the first battle, a cannonball or the stars," said Napoleon to Colonel Davenay of the 6th Cuirassiers. If the cannonball came sooner than the stars, the family received the *prix du sang* and a monument commemorating the hero in a manner worthy of his fame. On

January 1, 1810, the Emperor issued a decree ordering that statues of the generals Saint-Hilaire, Espagne, Lasalle, Lapisse, Cervoni, Colbert, Lacour, and Hervo—who had all died in battle—be placed on the Concorde Bridge. It is useful to relate the story of these statues to the disgrace of those who followed Napoleon. The statues were to be made in marble and of fourteen feet in height. They were completed, but the returning Bourbons relegated them to a rear courtyard of the Invalides in 1814. They were replaced by statues of the legendary heros of the old monarchy which stood on the empty pedestals awaiting Napoleon's generals. However, after 1830, it was felt that this celebration of an extremist, old branch of the monarchy was in poor taste. Thus, the Royalist stone men were sent to the Court of Honor at Versailles where they still stand. Since these statues from the bridge were few in number, given the size of the court at Versailles, an ingenious and economical curator remembered the generals of the Empire abandoned in a warehouse of outdated marbles. Unfortunately, giving one's blood for the country no longer suffices to merit the attention of the administration of the Beaux-Arts. One must have been a Marshal of France. Thus, the heads of Lasalle, de Saint-Hilaire and Colbert were cut off and replaced with those of Lannes, Masséna and Mortier. By the time Louis-Philippe learned of this crime against glory, it had already been completed. Nothing more could be done. As for the Second Empire, it was involved in other things and did not remember the decree of Napoleon the First.

This thriving status of the cavalry did not last long. With the prolongation of the campaign, the Emperor asked for horses from his depots on March 15, 1807. Four cavalry *régiments de marche* were gathered at various points across the Empire. They were formed of men from all the corps and had to be dissolved upon their arrival at the Grande Armée. There they handed over their troops to the regiments to which they had been assigned. On route, discipline and the service took their toll since it was accepted that the *régiment de marche* was able to fight until the moment its soldiers reached their destination. This method of resupplying the troops was the one most often used. Meanwhile, at times a regiment of three squadrons in the Grande Armée, upon finding itself too weakened, turned its remaining men into a squadron or two. It then sent one or two cadres to its depot who brought back new squadrons. As the Emperor was bringing reinforcements from France, General Roget, commander of the large depot of the cavalry corps at Culm, was charged with sending three officers to gather all small detachments. A number of these had taken up positions in posts which were convenient, useless, or subject to little danger. The Emperor estimated the number of these isolated cases to be 3,000. This was not much for a cavalry of 60 to 65 thousand men. However, the Emperor insisted that not a single carabinier or cuirassier be left behind. The best of armies always includes in its ranks a number of dubious troops who take cover from all danger and who entrench themselves behind an earlier order or an article in the rules to avoid facing gunfire. "The officers of this sort have as their mission the replacement of the numerous brave men ready for anything at any time," said Murat.

From 1807 to 1812, the Emperor increasingly put pressure on the groups of horses which had grown more and more compact. As soon as the quality of the infantryman decreased, his morale was raised by the obvious presence of the more numerous cavalry. Napoleon needed more artillery and more cavalry to encourage the young soldiers to march forward.

It was at this point he took recourse in the formation of the provisional regiments. This double arrangement was often awkward but nonetheless necessary for troops which had to supply detachments to many armies while facing enemies coming from all sides.

Polish Lancers (1807).

Provisional Regiments. As noted above, new creations of cavalry regiments did not enter into the views held by Napoleon I. His military politics were such that he liked to avoid the publicity which accompanied a decree increasing the lists of regiments in his army. He preferred to infinitely extend the number of squadrons of the regular corps. From three, he rapidly expanded them to four, five and even six and seven at two companies each. Then, when he was in need, he took two companies or two squadrons from one side and two others from another, named a field officer in charge of administration (major), detached two majors (chef d'escadron) and one or two adjutant-majors, and thereby formed a provisional regiment. This regiment should not be confused with the *régiment de marche*. It had a more or less continuous existence. After a month it went off to an army. Rarely did it return the companies or squadrons which it had borrowed

Hussars as skirmishers (1805-1815).

to the regiments from which they came. The latter had to replace these borrowed elements with new squadrons. (1) When a provisional regiment was dissolved, if its components were still valuable, they were turned over to the closest corps nearby. That is all that can be said about these ephemeral organizations which were nonetheless of enormous importance.

The first of these organizations appeared to be the one established on October 16, 1807. Sensing that he was going to be forced to extend his operations into Spain, the Emperor ordered the gathering of eight provisional cavalry regiments (two per army). At the same time, he ordered the creation of reserve legions for the infantry. This first organization served as a model to those which followed. It is interesting to look at it in detail since its seems later to have inspired the Minister of War in 1870-1871 at Tours and at Bordeaux.

HEAVY CAVALRY BRIGADE FORMED AT TOURS	DRAGOON BRIGADE FORMED AT ORLÉANS	CHASSEUR BRIGADE FORMED AT CHARTRES	HUSSAR BRIGADE FORMED AT COMPIEGNE
1st Regiment - 660 men 120 men each from the 1st and 2nd Carabiniers 140 men each from the 1st, 2nd and 3rd Cuirassiers **2nd Regiment - 640 men** 140 men each from the 5th and 12th Cuirassiers 120 men each from the 9th, 10th and 11th Cuirassiers	**1st Regiment - 480 men** 120 men each from the 11th, 14th, 18th and 19th Dragoons **2nd Regiment - 500 men** 140 men from the 20th Dragoons 120 men each from the 21st, 25th and 26th Dragoons	**1st Regiment - 600 men** 120 men each from the 1st, 2nd, 5th, 7th and 11th Chasseurs **2nd Regiment - 660 men** 140 men each from the 12th, 13th and 20th Chasseurs 120 men each from the 16th and 21st Chasseurs	**1st Regiment - 480 men** 120 men each from the 2nd, 3rd, 4th and 5th Hussars **2nd Regiment - 480 men** 120 men each from the 7th, 8th, 9th and 10th Hussars

Napoleon himself gave his minister of war the orders for assembling the troops since he had the conditions of his effectives at his fingertips. If he was deceived, it was only because the truth had been hidden from him. It was a sad day for the functionary who had supplied him with erroneous information, whether by negligence or for any other reason. Napoleon liked the truth when he needed it. Since he always needed it, he eventually discovered the truth. One day Marshal Jourdan sought to impress him with the results of a combat (Talavera). The Marshal was given a lesson in public which removed any desire on the part of the others to deceive the master. Thereafter and particularly with respect to the formations of corps, the Emperor usually assumed that one more error could have crept into the report or else that some event or other had affected its accuracy.

The first organization to be discussed was intended to supply cavalry to two army corps. These two corps had to follow the corps that was sent to Portugal under the command of Junot, Duke of Abrantès, into Spain.

The first corps left with seven squadrons detached from the 1st, 3rd, 4th, 5th, 9th, and 15th Dragoons and from the 26th Chasseurs. Filled out to 240 men, these squadrons were commanded by General of Division Kellermann, Count of Valmy, and represented 1,680 horses. It was a fine division of cavalry. However, as soon as they found themselves separated by the events of war, no ties bound the squadrons to each other. They did not perform as was expected. Evidently the sorry situation of the squadrons detached to Junot's Corps led Napoleon to form provisional cavalry regiments. As will be seen, this organization became the rule for all new assemblages of armies which themselves could be considered as provisional armies when compared to the Grande Armée. The future of Junot's corps is known. Its general would receive the Marshal's baton in Portugal where he would encounter only setbacks. He lost the favor of his master there and was never able to regain it.

(1) As an exception to this rule, what happened to the 4th and 5th Provisional Regiments of Dragoons in February 1810 may be cited. These regiments were formed in 1808 with the third and fourth squadrons of the 3rd, 6th, 10th and 11th Dragoons. Upon meeting up with Kellermann's Division from Ney's corps in Spain, itself formed from the four regiments just named, they were integrated. These regiments, which had fallen very low in terms of effective strength, found themselves momentarily at a full war complement. As seen in the historical records of one of them (the 6th), three months later Montbrun's reserve corps (General of Division Treillard, Generals of Brigade Cavois, Millet and Gardanne) counted not less than five thousand amongst them and were composed of the 15th, 25th, 3rd, 6th, 10th, and 11th Dragoons. However, the situation as given by another historical record from the regiment of the 15th Dragoons reduces this number somewhat, listing only 3,822 horses in September 1810 which was still not too bad. It is true that, in the interim, an order by the Emperor had made the cadres of the 4th and 5th squadrons fall back on Bayonne. These squadrons had to compete for new provisional formations. This was one of Napoleon's most frequently employed procedures.

Junot's corps was named the Observation Corps of the Gironde before it moved to the peninsula. As soon as it crossed the border, it was replaced by a second corps with the same name and about the same strength, under the command of Dupont. The heavy cavalry brigade organized at Tours and the chasseurs brigade organized at Chartres were attached to the corps and formed a division commanded by Boussart. Dupont's misfortunes are well-known. The best part of his mounted troops did not capitulate with him, however, as he had kept only a few squadrons. According to the reports on the catastrophe of Baylen and the accounts of prisoners from the island of Cabrera, it even seems that he only had a brigade of cavalry with him. This was the brigade of General Pryvé which for the most part was composed of dragoons. He had undoubtedly taken them from another army corps. On December 24, 1809, a 13th Cuirassiers was created with the remains of his heavy cavalry brigade. This regiment served with merit in Spain where it remained until 1813 bearing the nickname "the intrepid." It was one of the finest regiments of heavy cavalry until the end of the Empire.

After Dupont's departure for Spain, a 3rd corps was organized by Marshal Moncey. It had the same destination and was named the Observation Corps of the Ocean Coasts. The dragoon brigade formed at Orléans and that of the hussars formed at Compiegne served as its cavalry.

On January 13, 1808, a new division of 4 provisional regiments was assembled at Poitiers. These four regiments took the names of the 3rd Provisional Cuirassiers, the 3rd Provisional Dragoons, the 3rd Provisional Chasseurs, and the 3rd Provisional Hussars.

At the same time, Numbers 4, 5 and 6 of the Provisional Dragoons were also very rapidly formed to be sent to Spain.

Finally, on March 10, Napoleon ordered the immediate assembly of the 7th and 8th provisional dragoons and of a new provisional regiment of hussars. He wanted to be prepared for any eventuality. Since he was pressed for time, he decreed that eighteen full companies taken from 18 dragoon regiments be handed over. Those of the 1st, 2nd, 3rd, 4th, 5th, 6th, 9th, 10th, and 15th at Rennes were to form the 7th Provisional. Those of the 8th, 10th, 11th, 12th, 18th, 20th, 23rd, 25th, and 26th at Pontivy were to form the 8th Provisional.

The new regiment of hussars composed of 680 men taken from the 1st, 2nd, 3rd, 4th, 7th, 8th, 9th, and 10th regiments was organized at Saint-Omer and remained attached to the camp of Boulogne. They do not seem to have moved from there until the campaign of 1812, the period when many old and new regiments would be recalled.

Meanwhile, the campaign of 1809 forced Napoleon to again increase the cadres of his cavalry. It was thought necessary to send the twenty-four splendid regiments which Baraguey d'Hilliers had commanded during the campaign of 1806-1807 to Spain. Although for the purposes of his military policies he had let it be known that everything was finished in Spain, he could not consider removing the regiments in a single stroke. Moreover, he always surrounded himself in a fog of preparations. This was easily done in a time when the press, which was enlisted, could not commit indiscretions, when the telegraph served only the State, and when the post held no secrets for the police.

He quickly resolved to form twelve provisional regiments of dragoons on the eastern border. These regiments were formed from the cadres of the 3rd and 4th squadrons of the twenty-four regiments employed in Spain.

General of Division Beaumont, aided by Generals of Brigade Lamotte and Picard, was charged with this delicate and sudden operation ordered

General LaSalle (1806).

Officers of chasseurs à cheval, (Lithuania, 1812).

COLONELS OF THE CHASSEURS AND HUSSARS DURING THE 1ST EMPIRE

Regt.	1804	1810	1813
		CHASSEURS	
1st	Montbrun, later Exelmans	Méda	Méda, later Hubert
2nd	Bousson	Mathis	Mathis
3rd	Grosjean	Charpentier	Boyer, later Saint-Mars, then Royer, then de Potier
4th	Brugière	Lapointe	Boulnois
5th	Corbineau	Bonnemains	Baillod
6th	Laffon	Ledard	Ledard, later de Talhouët
7th	Lagrange	De Piré	De Saint-Chamans
8th	Curto	Curto	De Périgord
9th	Thuillier	Delacroix	Dukermont, later Ste-Suzanne
10th	Colbert	Subervic	Houssain Saint-Laurent
11th	Bessières	Jacquinot	Désirat
12th	Senilhac, later Defrance	Guyon	Chigay
13th	Paltiere	Demangeot	Shée
14th	Boudet	Sachs	Lemoyne
15th	Lepic	Mouriez	Faverot
16th	Durosnel	Maupoint	Lhuillier
17th	—	—	—
18th	—	—	—
19th	Bruc	Leduc	Vincent
20th	Marigny	Castex	Lagrange
21st	Berruyer	Steenhault	Sopransi
22nd	Latour-Maubourg	Desfossés	Desfossés
23rd	Saint-Germain	Lambert	Lenougerede
24th	Morin	Brunet	Ameil
25th	Soult	Christophe	Christophe
26th	Digeon	Vial	Vial
27th	—	Duke d'Aremberg	Duke d'Aremberg
28th	—	—	Laroche
29th	—	—	Maucombe
30th	—	—	—
31st	—	—	Desmichels
		HUSSARS	
1st	Rouvillois	Begougnes de Juniac	Merlin
2nd	Barbier	Gérard	Vinot
3rd	Lebrun	Laferrière	Rousseau
4th	Burthe	Burthe	Christophe
5th	Schwartz	D'Héry	Meuziau
6th	Pajol	Vallin	Vallin
7th	Marx	Colbert	Eulner
8th	Franceschi	Laborde-Debau	Domont
9th	Guyot	Gautherin	Maignet
10th	Beaumont	Briche	Monnier
11th	—	—	Collaert
9th bis	—	—	Colbert

for January 1, 1809. This formation was particularly fraught with more problems than usual in the Emperor's conception. Consequently, he at first decreed that six regiments be created which were split in half at the last moment. They provided him with two superb divisions. He had been right. On March 30, 1809, the day when he revealed the general order of battle for the Army of Germany, the six regiments whose split had been foreseen had to depart as they were. Three went to the observation corps of Elba. Three others participated in the campaign with the general reserve of the cavalry. It is useful to note here that difficulties in purchasing horses began to be felt. The remount service, theoretically centralized in the hands of a few generals, was performed by means of direct and on-the-spot purchases by the regiments. The truth is they bought whatever they could find. Napoleon's correspondence bears witness to substantial orders of horses commanded by the Emperor. Orders is the only right way to describe it. However the contractors and suppliers were accustomed to receiving the best possible price on the market. They left the orders unfilled if they did not find them to their own advantage. The squadrons which were to form Beaumont's Division thus arrived unmounted at their designated assembly location. Their horses were not delivered to them at an appropriate time. Therein lies the main reason (which is not to say the only reason) that the full execution of imperial orders was opposed.

For the campaign of 1809, the special courier services and the army's general staff, a provisional regiment of chasseurs a cheval was formed. By order of the army, it took the title of 1st Provisional Regiment of Chasseurs à Cheval. In fact it was really the fourth one that had been ostensibly organized since 1807.

This regiment was 1,000 men strong and, because of its special mission, specially comprised of 4 squadrons: two taken from the 26th, one from the 10th and one from the 22nd. It was assembled at Versailles whence it departed to join the Grande Armée.

However, as of October 7, 1809, the Emperor's concerns again focused on Spain and he decided to send a reinforcement of 80,000 men there. General Beaumont's six provisional regiments of dragoons and three new regiments assembled at Tours. Together, they were filled out with 1,000 men and entered into Napoleon's plans. From this moment on, this man of genius responded to an impulse more powerful than reason. It became impossible to clearly perceive the complexity of his thoughts.

Hussar officer, full dress (1886).

Chasseurs à cheval, on maneuvers (1885).

Trumpeters of the 1st cuirassiers regiment (1812)

In hindsight, it would be easy to demonstrate that the provisional and short-lived organizations of *régiments de marche* were the early precursors of great military dissolutions. When an army feels the need to mask its weaknesses, it is lost. Even before the campaign of Russia, the military power of Napoleon's Empire had been appraised. Its strength was out of proportion to his ambition and grand ideas. The Coalition knew the status of his forces. Its network of spies which were maintained in the embassies needed only wait for the employee "Michel" to deliver a complete record of the placement of troops to the Russian Emperor's envoy. France would have had to be twofold stronger to withstand the sacrifices which Napoleon I asked of her. However, the people loved glory and their country. The greatness of the man swept along valiant hearts and patriots. All who were impassioned by the Revolution and who still believed that he was its personification followed in his wake. They would have gladly given their lives rather than renounce the tricolor, the national cockade under which French forces had imposed law on the civilized world. This feeling is again seen in 1813 when Napoleon created the Honor Guard.

No more time should be spent on the formation of these priveleged corps than on the history of the Imperial Guard (Young and Old). Starting with 1810, the organizations spoken of here can no longer be followed. On September 15, 1810, General Fournier unexpectedly received orders to dispatch a regiment of chasseurs from Tours to Spain. It was comprised of the 4th squadrons of the 11th and 12th Regiments and of the 2nd and 4th squadrons of the 24th. This was a case of a provisional regiment formed of four squadrons while permanent regiments in the army only had three squadrons. These squadrons must have been very weak. There would even come a time when the provisional regiments would no longer be made up of squadrons. They themselves carried provisional numbers which could not be adapted to the formation lists for their category. This resulted in extending the series of permanent regiments in which they were never included. During the campaign of 1813, two brand new provisional regiments of dragoons and three of cuirassiers appeared on the lists of Rapp's Corps as well as on the Duke of Danzig's. The Emperor also created a type of provisional brigade for this campaign. It had no colonel nor major and was composed of six or eight squadrons detached from regiments used in Spain. In 1814, there would be almost no permanent regiments capable of undertaking the campaign. By taking additional squadrons into the regiments in order to form provisional regiments, it was no longer possible to sustain the war squadrons. Then there was the case of Pajol, one of the enduring heros of the late imperial period, reduced to expedients which spelled the certain ruin of the army. He had 1,229

horsemen in his corps. They had been formed for the infantry of the National Guards, the customs agents, the depots of the Young Guard, and the naval artillery but were fighting as foot soldiers and as gendarmes. Moreover, his cavaliers belonged to twenty regiments and were divided into three brigades as indicated below:

1st Brigade - provisional regiments of chasseurs: 15 officers and 445 horsemen;

2nd Brigade - provisional regiments of dragoons, General Grouvel: 21 officers and 445 horsemen;

3rd Brigade - provisional regiments of hussars, General du Coetlosquet: 19 officers and 339 horsemen.

It was the same everywhere. Another example is the light cavalry division of General Merlin, also composed of provisional regiments:

1st Brigade - General Wathiez: provisional regiment of hussars (6th, 7th and 8th Regiments); provisional regiment of lancers (1st, 3rd, 5th, 7th, and 8th Regiments).

2nd Brigade - General Guyon: 1st Provisional Chasseurs (1st, 2nd, 3rd, and 6th Regiments); 2nd Provisional Chasseurs (8th, 9th, 16th and 25th Regiments).

This division had 956 horses. It will be seen again, reduced by three quarters, in Bordesoulle's Corps beneath the walls of Paris, at Prés-Saint-Gervais, at Bagnolet, and at Charonne facing the German hussars and the Cossacks. From this point on there were only remnants. Everything was brought down by the enormous disaster. All the causes of unwillingness and fatigue came together to reduce the effectives and to separate the major participants from their depots. Men and officers were used to serving

Carabiniers, Russia, (1812).

far from their colonels. The colonels had forgotten their regiments. There was no longer any supervision and hardly any administration. Some brave men no longer incorporated but in the battle still remained. The Imperial Army was no longer a single entity but an assemblage of disparate parts. From 1806 to 1814, Napoleon had asked the cavalry for more provisional regiments than he had permanent regiments. It was a very easy and convenient way of doing things which required so little effort that the Emperor allowed himself to resort to it with incredible indifference. It was he who had made the regimental eagle the venerable symbol of honor and the military religion. He was the ultimate organizer, rigid in discipline and esprit de corps. Yet he allowed his soldiers to be transformed into nameless masses. He betrayed all his doctrines. That which had only been a means to an end at the beginning of his campaigns became a system in itself. The quality of a cavalry recruited according to such principles can well be doubted. In 1813, a 15th Cuirassiers which had not been permanent, at least in the sense that no decree had confirmed its number, organized itself at Hamburg. It was composed of elements drawn from the 2nd, 3rd, and 4th Regiments of the service, of officers from everywhere and most of all recruits. When it received its horses, the troops were barely able to ride as they had only had some condemned horses to practice on. The officers and the oldest non-commissioned officers spent one night sorting out the harnessing. In the morning, as best possible, they mounted their first squadron. At noon they left. However, no one had thought about the fact that in leaving the town, they had to post the colors, draw their sabers, and sound the trumpets. The 15th Cuirassiers then witnessed the men of their first squadron sprawled on the ground while its horses galloped away along the streets and paths. This and one hundred more examples make it clear that a man and a horse together do not necessarily produce a cavalryman. First they have to be bound to one another through training and familiarity.

It is possible to reconstruct the approximate formation of about fifty provisional cavalry regiments. Certainly there were more than sixty-five, probably as many as seventy-five. Until the end of his reign, Napoleon maintained skeleton units; they cost him little and they concealed the effective strengths and the value of his troops as much from his lieutenants as from the enemy. He had no intention of revealing his plans to anyone.

To better understand what services Napoleon I expected from his cavalry, the composition of this service in the armies during the campaigns of 1805, 1812 and 1813 must be viewed as a whole. In studying them and comparing them to historic events, it can be seen that the Emperor felt the cavalry to be both the thundering power of the battlefield before and after the campaign and a means of moral intimidation over foreign powers.

The three tables which follow are characteristic of the philosophy of the cavalry throughout its history under the First Empire. In 1805, the service was nationwide. The Imperial Guard had nothing to boast of. Each army corps of infantry had a good, solid light cavalry division except one (the 7th) which had one regiment of cavalry (the 7th Chasseurs, 530 horses).

Chasseur à cheval, the Imperial Guard, undress (1805-1815).

The general reserve had a very solid cavalry division. These 27,000 horsemen were worth more than might be imagined. However, as of September 7, 1808, the 1st, 2nd, 3rd, 4th, 5th, and 6th Corps left for Spain, only to return between 1809 and 1811 in pieces and notably weakened. The Grande Armée stationed in Germany in 1809, although still splendid, was no longer as valuable as the army of 1805, especially the cavalry.

What was covered in the chapter on infantry concerning the misfortunes of 1812 will not be repeated here. It was even more difficult to build up the cavalry than the infantry. This is obvious in looking at the cavalry of 1813. From the regiments of unrivaled importance there was little or hardly any light cavalry for the army's infantry corps. However, what truly exposes the Emperor's destitute state was the organization of his reserve. It was to have been tremendous. He wanted five corps, but after having put together two, the regiments which were left were mere shadows. They appeared only on paper and disappeared as soon as they were called upon to enter into a campaign. Moreover, many of them could not even get themselves on the road. In the meantime, he had to surmount incredible obstacles to reorganize this final cavalry! Even before the crossing of the Berezina, the French cavalry was swallowed up. The decree of Smolensk dated November 9th ordered the creation of an army corps of 6,000 horsemen under the command of General Bruyere. It consisted of a division of light cavalry and one of cuirassiers and dragoons. They formed picket regiments and were charged with guarding the army's cantonments during winter. The magnificent division of Murat's Corps will be seen torn apart, scattered and destroyed. It is doubtful that this order was executed. Ségur, though truthfully a bit of a pessimist, said that only eight hundred horses remained. Napoleon, who had returned to Paris as of December 24, 1812, occupied himself with the purchase of horses. He acknowledged that the entire artillery of the cavalry and that of the 1st, 2nd, 3rd, 4th and 6th Corps were lost. However, the artillery was only lost because it had no more cavalry and infantry to defend it. It had followed in the unfortunate steps of the rest of the army. In a letter addressed on February 26, 1813, Napoleon revealed the organization of his new cavalry. He had intended that it be reconstructed along the lines of the preceding campaign. His summary is interesting in that it demonstrates his illusions.

Cuirassiers and carabiniers—sixteen regiments, 80 squadrons: 46 to the Army of Germany, 30 in France, 4 in Spain.

Dragoons—twenty-four regiments, 120 squadrons: 57 to the Army of Germany, 16 in France, 47 in Spain. In his mind, these squadrons had 200 mounted men.

Chevau-légers—nine regiments, 45 squadrons: 25 to the Army of Germany, 20 remaining in France.

Hussars—fourteen regiments, 71 squadrons: 44 to the Army of Germany, 14 in France, 13 in Spain.

Chasseurs à cheval—twenty-eight regiments, 144 squadrons: 83 to the Army of Germany, 36 in France, 26 in Spain.

Naturally, as for the heavy cavalry, Napoleon accorded a large effective to all his light cavalry squadrons: 250 mounted men. He found horses and men in his head. For the former he would take them by requisition or by incredible purchases. As for the men, they would be provided by the remnants and by an advance of conscription. If only what he dreamed could have been executed, the soil of France would never have been trampled by foreign feet. Unfortunately, following the errors of his imagination, the reality of the glorious defeats of 1813 and 1814 reduced the French regiments to effective strengths below those of 1812. Some cavalry divisions had 250 mounted men but they fought as if they had 2,000 cavaliers in their ranks. Nonetheless, he entered the campaign with a very strong facade. Thanks to the continual activity of his lieutenants, he still had an army which could have looked and performed well on a less extended campaign front. Unfortunately it was not large enough to satisfy the plans for the campaign, nor solid enough to resist long-term hardship. Thus, in October 1813, when Pajol took command of the 5th Corps of cavalry, it counted 6,129 horsemen for its 46 squadrons and its 6 horse batteries. This was 120 men per squadron of two companies. It was good but far from 250 and from the 200 horsemen of the organization's decree. How these 6,000 men were crushed is difficult to explain other than by misery and desertion. The army of 1813 was much younger than the army of 1812. In addition, there was deep discouragement amongst the oldest participants in Napoleon's glory.

Meanwhile, the Emperor did not despair until the last day. His great depots of cavalry, under the command of General Preval, retreated as soon as the enemy advanced and always mounted the cavaliers on horses. As for him, he managed to

GRANDE ARMÉE OF RUSSIA
CROSSING OF THE NIEMEN, JUNE 30, 1812

1st Corps - Marshal PRINCE D'ECKMÜHL

Division	Brigade	Regiment	French	Foreigners
GIRARDIN	1st Brigade, PAJOL	2nd Chasseurs, 9th Polish Lancers	1,902	—
	2nd Brigade, BORDESOULLE	1st and 3rd Chasseurs	1,885	—

2nd Corps - Marshal DUKE OF REGGIO

Division	Brigade	Regiment	French	Foreigners
1st Division	1st Brigade, CASTEX	7th, 23rd and 24th Chasseurs	1,242	—
	2nd Brigade, CORBINEAU	20th Chasseurs, 8th Chevau-légers	751	—
2nd Division DOUMERC	1st Brigade, BERCKHEIM	4th Cuirassiers	980	—
	2nd Brigade, L'HÉRITIER	7th Cuirassiers	973	—
	3rd Bde, DOULLEMBOURG	14th Cuirassiers and 8th Chevau-légers (1st Sqdn.)	970	—

3rd Corps - Marshal DUKE OF ELCHINGEN

Division	Brigade	Regiment	French	Foreigners
WOELWARTH	1st Brigade, MOURIEZ	6th Chevau-légers, 28th Chasseurs	937	—
	2nd Brigade —	11th Hussars, 4th Chasseurs	1,729	—
	Wurtemburg Troops			1,748

4th Corps - PRINCE EUGENE
Second in command: General DUKE D'ABRANTES

Division	Brigade	Regiment	French	Foreigners
GUYON	1st Brigade, FERRIERE	9th and 19th Chasseurs,	1,372	—
	2nd Brigade, VILLATA	2nd and 3rd Italian Chasseurs	—	1,451
	Italian Guard, LECCHI	Dragoons, Honor Guards	—	1,429

5th Corps - PRINCE PONIATOWSKI

Division	Brigade	Regiment	French	Foreigners
KAMINSKI	1st Brigade, NIEMOIENSKI	8th Polish Lancers, 13th Hussars	1,626	—
	2nd Brigade —	7th and 11th Polish Lancers	1,849	—
	3rd Brigade, SULKOWSKI	5th and 14th Chasseurs	1,229	—

6th Corps - General GOUVION-SAINT-CYR

Division	Brigade	Regiment	French	Foreigners
	1st Bde, Count SEYDEWITZ	3rd and 6th Bavarian Chevau-légers	—	1,063
	2nd Bde, Count PREYSING	4th and 5th Bavarian Chevau-légers	—	1,016

7th Corps - General REYNIER

Division	Brigade	Regiment	French	Foreigners
	Saxon Brigade, DE FUNCK	Chevau-légers and Hussars	—	2,186

8th Corps - KING OF WESTPHALIA
Second in command: General VANDAMME

Division	Brigade	Regiment	French	Foreigners
CHABERT	1st Westphalian Bde, WOLFF	Guards, Chevau-légers	—	753
	2nd Westphalian Brigade, De LAMMERSTEIN	1st and 2nd Hussars	—	1,205

9th Corps - Marshal DUKE OF BELLUNE

Division	Brigade	Regiment	French	Foreigners
		Lancers of Berg, Hessian Chevau-légers, and Baden Hussars	—	1,333

10th Corps - Marshal DUKE OF TARENTE

Division	Brigade	Regiment	French	Foreigners
MASSEMBACH	DE HUMERBEIN (Prussian)	1st, 2nd Dragoons, and 1st, 2nd Hussars	—	2,705

CAVALRY RESERVE
THE KING OF NAPLES

1st Corps - General NANSOUTY
Chief of staff: Col. MARTIAL THOMAS
Artillery: Major CHOPIN

Division	Brigade	Regiment	French	Foreigners
BRUYERE	JACQUINOT	7th Hussars	1,147	—
	ROUSSEL D' HURBAL	9th Chevau-légers	769	—
	PIRE	16th Chasseurs, 8th Hussars	2,109	—
	NIENVIEWSKI	6th Polish Lancers, 10th Hussars, and 1st Prussian Uhlans	1,361	674
ST-GERMAIN	BESSIERES	2nd Cuirassiers	1,015	—
	BRUNO	3rd Cuirassiers	1,099	—
	QUEUNOT	9th Cuirassiers, Chevau-légers	1,124	—
VALENCE	REYNAUD	6th Cuirassiers	950	—
	DEJEAN	11th Cuirassiers	730	—
	DE LA GRANGE	12th Cuirassiers and 5th Chevau-légers (1st sqdn.)	1,214	—

2nd Corps - General MONTBRUN
Chief of staff: Colonel WATHIEZ
Artillery: Colonel SERRURIER

Division	Brigade	Regiment	French	Foreigners
WATHIER	SAINT-GENIEZ	11th and 12th Chasseurs	1,314	—
	BURTHE	5th and 9th Hussars	1,676	—
	ORNANO	1st Polish Chasseurs, 3rd Wurtemburg Chasseurs, and 3rd Prussian Hussars	973	1,273
SEBASTIANI	BEAUMONT	5th Cuirassiers	788	—
	RICHTER	8th Cuirassiers	754	—
	DORNEZ	10th Cuirassiers and 2nd Chevau-légers (1st sqdn.)	821	—
DEFRANCE	CHOUARD	1st Carabiniers	850	—
	PAULTRE	2nd Carabiniers	871	—
	BOURIER DES ECLATS	1st Cuirassiers and 4th Chevau-légers (1st sqdn.)	855	—

3rd Corps - General COUNT GROUCHY

Division	Brigade	Regiment	French	Foreigners
CHASTEL	GÉRARD	6th and 25th Chasseurs	1,253	—
	GAUTHRIN	6th and 8th Hussars	1,222	—
	DOMMANGET (Bavarian)	1st and 2nd Chevau-légers	—	1,042
LA HOUSSAYE	THIRY	7th and 23rd Dragoons	1,177	—
	SERON	28th and 30th Dragoons	1,213	—

4th Corps - General LATOUR-MAUBOURG

Division	Brigade	Regiment	French	Foreigners
ROZNIECKI	DZIENOWOSKI	2nd, 3rd and 4th Polish Lancers	2,836	—
	TURNO	12th, 15th and 16th Polish Lancers	2,671	—
LORGE	THIELMAN	Saxon Guards, Saxon Cuirassiers	—	1,344
	DE LEPELL	1st and 2nd Westphalian Cuirassiers	—	1,272
		TOTAL	48,333	20,494

Note—If to the total of the French cavalry one adds:
1. For the Imperial Guard 5,861
2. The dragoons detached from the 2nd, 5th, 12th, 13th, 14th, 17th, 19th and 20th Regiments to the Reserve Corps commanded by Marshal, the Duke of Castiglione 937 —
3. Cavalry awaited from France 7,062
If, on the other hand, one adds to the foreign cavalry:
1. Cavalry from the Austrian Corps of Prince Schwartzemberg .... — 4,000
2. For the Danish division .... — 1,304

One arrives at these frightening totals 59,219 24,778

GENERAL TOTAL 83,997

To be complete, let us give the figure for BOURCIER's division composed of French unmounted cavalry, which, under the command of brigade commanders Guiton and Duverger, offered ready replacements to the corps of the Grande Armée. 6,638
These figures have been taken from a report which recognizes detached and sick men, It is therefore a report on the men present.

GRANDE ARMÉE
1806

1st Corps

Division	Brigade	Regiment	French	Foreigners
KELLERMANN	DUMOULIN, VAN MARIZY	2nd, 4th and 5th Hussars, 5th Chasseurs	2,898	—

2nd Corps

Division	Brigade	Regiment	French	Foreigners
LACOSTE	GUÉRIN, D'ELOQUIANCY	6th Hussars, 8th Chasseurs,	1,195	—
		Batavian Dragoons and Hussars	580	—

3rd Corps

Division	Brigade	Regiment	French	Foreigners
	VIALANN	1st, 2nd and 12th Chasseurs, 7th Hussars	2,000	—

4th Corps

Division	Brigade	Regiment	French	Foreigners
	MARGARON	8th Hussars, 11th, 16th and 26th Chasseurs	2,119	—

5th Corps

Division	Brigade	Regiment	French	Foreigners
	TREILLARD	9th and 10th Hussars, 13th and 21st Chasseurs	1,984	—

6th Corps

Division	Brigade	Regiment	French	Foreigners
TILLY	DUPRÉ	Hussars, 10th and 22nd Chasseurs	2,080	—

CAVALRY RESERVE
Marshal PRINCE MURAT
Chief of staff: BELLIARD
Artillery: HANIQUE

Division	Brigade	Regiment	French	Foreigners
NANSOUTY	PISTON, LAHOUSSAYE and SAINT-GERMAIN	1st and 2nd Carabiniers, 2nd, 3rd, 9th and 12th Cuirassiers	2,724	—
D'HAUTPOUL	SAINT-SULPICE and FAUCONNET	1st, 5th, 10th, and 11th Cuirassiers	1,987	—
KLEIN	FENEROLLE, LASALLE, and MILLET	1st, 2nd, 4th, 14th, 20th and 26th Dragoons	2,373	—
WALTHER	SÉBASTIANI, ROGET, and BOUSSARD	3rd, 6th, 10th, 11th, 13th and 22nd Dragoons	2,132	—
BEAUMONT	CHARLES BOUÉ, SCALFORT and MILHAUT	5th, 8th, 9th, 12th, 16th and 21st Dragoons	2,021	—
	LAPLANCHE, SARUC and VERDIERE	15th, 17th, 18th, 19th, 25th and 29th Dragoons	2,176	—
Imperial Guard			1,210	
		TOTAL	26,899	580

GRANDE ARMÉE OF GERMANY

1813 - SITUATION AS OF AUGUST 10

Division	Brigade	Regiment	French	Foreigners
1st Corps - VANDAMME				
	KRUSTOWECKI	2nd Polish Cavalry, Col. Kossechi and 4th Polish Cavalry, Col. Kostancki	1,465	—
	GOBRECHT	9th French Chevau-légers and Hanhalt Chasseurs	380	495
2nd Corps - BELLUNE				
	HAMMERSTEIN	1st Westphalian Hussars, Col. Hammestein and 2nd Westphalian Hussars, Major Peutz	—	417
3rd Corps - PRINCE OF MOSCOW				
	BEURMANN	10th Hussars, Colonel Monnier	1,488	—
	HEIMRAD	Baden Dragoons, Cmdr. Hilpert	—	432
4th Corps - General BERTRAND				
BRICHE	DE JELT	1st Wurttemburg Chevau-léger, Col. Bismark and 3rd Wurttemburg Chevau-léger, Col. de Gaisberg	—	1,053
5th Corps - General LAURISTON - without cavalry				
6th Corps - Marshal DUKE OF REGGIO - without cavalry				
7th Corps - REYNIER				
	LINDENAU	Saxon Hussars and Saxon Lancers	—	1,645
8th Corps - PRINCE PONIATOWSKI				
		14th Polish Cuirassiers	598	—
11th Corps - Marshal DUKE OF TARENTE				
	MONTBRUN	4th Italian Chasseurs, Wurtzburg Chevau-légers, and 2nd Neapolitan Chasseurs	—	1,536
12th Corps - Marshal DUKE OF REGGIO				
BEAUMONT	WOLFF	Westphalian, Bavarian andHessian Chevau-légers	—	1,669
14th Corps - Marshal GOUVION SAINT-CYR				
	PAJOL	14th Hussars, 2nd Italian Chasseurs, and 7th Chevau-légers	1,474	759

CAVALRY RESERVE

THE KING OF NAPLES

1st Corps - LATOUR MAUBOURG
Chief of staff: Adj. cmdr. DE JUMILHAC
Artillery: Colonel LAVOY (6 horse batteries)

Division	Brigade	Regiment	French	Foreigners
CORBINEAU	PIRÉ	6th Hussars, Col. Carignan, 7th Hussars, Col. Eulner and 8th Hussars, Col du Coetlosquet	1,846	—
	MONTMARIC	16th Chasseurs, Col. Latour, 1st Chevau-léger, Col. Hatry and 5th Chevau-léger, Col. Chabert	2,054	—
	BIQUET	8th Chevau-léger, Col. Lubienski and 1st Italian, Chas., Col. Gasparinetti	1,199	955
CHASTEL	VALLIN	8th Chasseurs, Col. de Périgord, 9th Chasseurs, Col. Dukermont and 25th Chasseurs, Col. de Faudoas	1,561	—
	VANMERLEN	1st Chasseurs, Col. Hubert and 19th Chasseurs, Col. Vincent	1,733	—
	DARMONCOURT	2nd Chasseurs, Col. Mathis, 3rd Chasseurs, Col. Royer and 6th Chasseurs,Major Talharet	1,603	—
BORDESOULLE	BERCKEIM	2nd Cuirassier, Col. Rolland, 3rd Cuirassier, Col. Lacroix and 6th Cuirassier, Col. Martin	1,321	—
	BESSIERES	9th Cuirassier, Col. Murat, 11th Cuirassier, Col. Duclos and 12th Cuirassier, Col. Dandiés	1,792	—
	LESSING	1st Saxon Cuirassier, Col. de Berg and 2nd Saxon Cuir., Col. de Ziegler	—	1,329
DOUMERC	D'AUDENARDE	4th Curiassier, Col. Dugon, 7th Cuirassier, Col. Richardon, 14th Cuirassier, Col. Tripp and Neapolitan Dragoons, Col. Gualdi	1,486	761
	REISET	7th Dragoons, Col. Sapranzi, 23rd Dragoons, Col. Martigne 28th Dragoons, Commander Caroges 30th Dragoons, Col. Ordener	1,574	—

2nd Corps - General SÉBASTIANI
Chief of staff: Adj. Cmdr. DE LASCOURS
Artillery: Colonel COLLIN

Division	Brigade	Regiment	French	Foreigners
ROUSSEL D'HURBAL	GÉRARD	11th Chasseurs, Col. Nicolas, 12th Chasseurs, Col. Ghigny and 5th Hussars, Col. Fournier	1,923	—
	DOMMANGET	9th Hussars, Col. Maignet, 2nd Hussars, Col. Berruyer and 4th Chevau-léger, Col. Deschamps	2,463	—
EXELMANS	MAURIN	6th Chevau-léger, Col. Perquis, 4th Chasseurs, Col. Devence and 7th Chasseurs, Col. Saint-Chamans	1,807	—
	WATHIEZ	20th Chasseurs, Col. Lagrange, 23rd Chasseurs, Col. Marbot, 24th Chasseurs, Col. Schneidt and 11th Hussars, Col. Liégeard	2,085	—
ST. GERMAIN	D'AUGERANVILLE	1st Carabinier, Col. Laroche, 2nd Carabinier, Col. Blancard and 3rd Cuirassier, Col. Clerc		
	THERY	5th Cuirassier, Col. Christophe, 8th Cuirassier, Col. Lefaivre and 10th Cuirassier, Col. Lahubardière	1,361	—

3rd Corps - ARRIGHI, DUKE of Padua
Chief of staff: Adj. Cmdr. SOREL
Artillery: Colonel CHAUVEAU

Division	Brigade	Regiment	French	Foreigners
LORGE	JACQUINOT	5th Chasseurs, Col. Beugnat 10th Chasseurs, Commandant Duhamel 13th Chasseurs, Col. Shee	1,666	—
	MERLIN	15th Chasseurs, Major Rougiot, 21st Chasseurs, Commandant Barbier and 22nd Chasseurs, Major de Bourbel	1378	—
FOURNIER	MOURIEZ	29th Chasseurs,Commandant Montaillard 31st Chasseurs and 1st Hussars, Col. Clary	971	—
	AMEIL	2nd Hussars, Col. Rousseau, 4th Hussars and 12th Hussars	1,194	—
DEFRANCE	AVICE	4th, 5th, 12th, 14th and 24th Dragoons (one squadron each)	1,350	—
	QUINETTE	16th, 17th, 21st, 26th and 27th Dragoons, 13th Cuirassiers (one squadron each)	1,360	—

4th Corps - KELLERMAN, COUNT OF VALMY
Chief of staff: Adj. Cmdr. TANCARVILLE

Composed solely of ten Polish cavalry regiments of which two were detached to the 1st Corps; the 4th Corps of cavalry had only two divisions .... 4,236 —

A fifth corps (General MILHAUT) including 3 divisions was formed from incomplete regiments, being doubled by a fifth *bis* corps, which brought its complements from France. .... 5,417 —

It is necessary to add to these forces:

1. The cavalry of the 10th Corps (RAPP) at Danzig 1,378 414
2. The cavalry of the 13th Corps (PRINCE OF ECKMÜHL) at Hamburg, almost exclusively composed of foreigners, approximately .... — 2,000
3. The Westphalian cavalry .... — 1,910
4. The cavalry quartered in the government of Hamburg (three provisional cuirassier regiments) and the 28th Chasseurs .... 2,800 —
5. The large unmounted depots which waited for an assignment at Hamburg, Magdeburg and Frankfurt, under the command of General BOURCIER 10,034

Finally, the Imperial Guard (44 squadrons) and the four regiments of the Honor Guard presenting a magnificent effective strength of 14,245 .... —

TOTALS 79,682 15,375

GENERAL TOTAL 95,057

Dragoon, Imperial Guard, in greatcoat (1805-1815).

correspond with all his lieutenants while passing days on the battlefield or traveling the highways. He organized and recruited everything while fighting. A veteran of the First Empire told me that while the last supreme battle took place under the walls of Paris, at the military school's barracks a remount commission examined and accepted horses brought from Normandy for the Imperial Guard depots.

In his memoirs, Marmont gives the overall order of the army which defended Paris on March 30. It included three cavalry corps:

The cavalry of the provisional corps of General Compans, having under his command General of Division Chastel and General of Brigade Vincent: 1,600 men.

The 1st cavalry corps: Generals of Division Bordesoulle and Merlin, Generals of Brigade Hubert, de Foissac-Latour, Thiery and Laville: 1,745 men.

The cavalry corps of General Belliard: Division Leader Roussel d'Hurbal, Generals of Brigade: Rigaud, Sparre, Ghigny, Christophe and Leclèrc: 1,900 men.

Finally, the depots of the Guard under the command of General of Division d'Ornano and of General of Brigade Dautencourt; 320 men.

This total of 5,565 horses represented more than 30 regiments without counting the Guard. In the provinces, barely seventy thousand men carried on the campaign of whom ten thousand were with the cavalry. However, France still had considerable resources along its borders and abroad. The Restoration would put them to better use when it proceeded with the reorganization of the army.

Divisions	Brigades	Regiments	Colonels	Squadrons
SUBERVIC	Klicky	3rd Hussars	Ronsseau	3
		27th Chasseurs	Strub	4
		14th Chasseurs	Lemoine	3
	Vial	26th Chasseurs	—	3
		13th Hussars	—	4
LH'ERITIER	Quénot	2nd Dragoons	Hoffmayer	3
		6th Dragoons	Mugnier	4
		11th Dragoons	Thevenez	4
	Colbert	13th Dragoons	Mouginot	2
		15th Dragoons	Bouduchon	3
MILHAUT	Lamotte	18th Dragoons	Dard	2
	Montélégier	19th Dragoons	Mermet	2
		20th Dragoons	Desargues	3
		22nd Dragoons	—	3
		25th Dragoons	Montigny	3

6 Horse artillery batteries: Colonel COHON.

The Emperor in the field (1812).

THE DRAGOONS UNDER THE EMPIRE

The dragoons experienced their greatest moments of glory under the Empire. The decree of September 24, 1803 recognized them as having thirty regiments. The Emperor did not increase this number. In fact, he took Numbers 1, 3, 8, 9, 10, and 29 to make six regiments of lancers (Numbers 1 through 6) which he created on June 18, 1811 as noted above. These numbers remained vacant and there was no time to replace them. However, from the beginning of the Spanish War, many dragoon regiments formed extra squadrons. These squadrons sometimes took, by authority of the major, the number of their regiment, adding the qualification of provisional. This qualification was often not exact and proved misleading, as much in reviews as in the general orders.

Were the dragoons considered to be cavalry? General Bonaparte thought so. He had brought thirteen squadrons of dragoons to Egypt with him versus six of chasseurs and hussars. However, when he organized the cavalry school of Saint-Germain in 1809 to which he gave the dress, harnesses and weapons of the dragoons, he decided that the school would specialize in providing heavy and light cavalry officers.

Be that as it may, as of 1805, Napoleon organized a mixed corps of dragoons under the command of Baraguey d'Hilliers (Napoleon's correspondence from June 9 and August 24, 1805). It was composed of twenty-four regiments forming four mounted divisions and one infantry division.

Each regiment in this mixed organization was to have three mounted squadrons forming a minimum effective strength of 400 horses.

In addition, the regiment provided one infantry squadron divided into two companies each having 3 officers, 5 non-commissioned officers, 8 corporals, 2 drummers or trumpeters and 130 dragoons. The six companies assembled from one brigade formed a battalion. Battalions of the divison formed a regiment. These regiments numbered four and constituted an infantry division of 7,200 men, supplied with 10 artillery pieces.

1st DIVISION
General KLEIN
1st Brigade: 1st, 2nd, 20th Regiments
2nd Brigade: 4th, 14th, 26th Regiments
2nd DIVISION
General BEAUMONT
1st Brigade: 10th, 13th, 22nd Regiments
2nd Brigade: 3rd, 6th, 4th Regiments
3rd DIVISION
General WALTHER
1st Brigade: 5th, 8th, 12th Regiments
2nd Brigade: 9th, 16th, 21st Regiments
4th DIVISION
General BOURCIER
1st Brigade: 15th, 17th, 27th Regiments
2nd Brigade: 18th, 19th, 25th Regiments

The first evidence of this formation dates from the Camp of the North where the dismounted dragoons were taught maneuvers for embarking and disembarking. The organization of Boulogne for the campaign of 1805 was confused in the formation of the corps assembled at Kehl and at Strasbourg which were assigned to the defense of the Rhine crossing. Its organization was not well taken by the dragoons. The colonels naturally tried to keep in hand the best officers and cavaliers, designating the lesser ones for infantry service. Discouragment slowly settled into the ranks of men who missed their horses and who sometimes suffered the jeers of their mounted comrades. In order to revive them and return them to their former status, the Emperor accorded them the immediate honor of marching with the Guard. However, nothing could console them for the loss of their horses which would have to be taken from the enemy in order to obtain some.

After the Battle of Austerlitz, sixteen dragoon colonels appeared on the list of promotions for the rank of commander of a legion. These were: Arrighi of the 1st, Pryve of the 2nd, Fiteau of the 3rd, La Cour of the 5th, Maupetit of the 9th, Cavaignac of the 10th, Broc of the 13th, Lafond-Blaniac of the 14th, Clément of the 16th, Lefebvre of th 18th, Caulaincourt of the 19th, Reynaud of the 20th, Carié of the 22nd, Rigau of the 25th, Delorme of the 26th, and Tereyre of the 27th. In addition, Wathier of the 4th and Pagès of the 12th were named generals of brigade. These many rewards say a lot about the services rendered by the cavalry during the campaign of 1805.

On January 5, 1807, Napoleon wrote to General Dejean from Varsovia: "Of the thirty dragoon regiments that we have, twenty-four are with the Grande Armée, six are in Italy." The situation of the service had not been modified.

Wishing to assuage the resentment that the dragoons held for their transformation into foot soldiers, the Emperor gave each regiment eight sappers in a decree of February 25, 1808. They wore grenadier epaulettes as an elite company and the bearskin with a white band but with no plaque.

Little by little the dragoons of the Grande Armée made their way toward Spain. In 1809 during the Austrian campaign, the twenty-four magnificent regiments which formed the four mounted divisions of Baraguey d'Hilliers' Corps were all there. The service was represented in the Grande Armée by the 7th, 23rd, 24th, 28th, 29th, and 30th which were in Italy two years before. There, under the command of Generals of Division Grouchy and Prelly, they belonged to the Viceroy's corps. In reading the pages dedicated to the provisional regiments, the sacrifices which these organizations exacted from the dragoons service is evident. The 1st, 3rd, 8th, 9th, 10th, and 29th Regiments had been transformed into lancers for the campaign of 1812. During the Russian campaign, only a single division of dragoons was to be found in the army which crossed the Niémen: the 2nd (General Lahoussaye) of the 3rd Cavalry Corps (Grouchy), and the 7th, 23rd, 28th, and 30th Dragoons, commanded by Generals of Brigade Thiry and Séron. At the time of the campaign of 1813 in Germany, this same division had become the 2nd Brigade (General Reiset) of Doumerc's Division from the 1st Cavalry Corps (Latour-Maubourg) of the cavalry reserve under the command of the King of Naples. Squadrons, one per regiment, of the 4th, 5th, 12th, 14th, 24th, 16th, 17th, 21st, 26th, and 27th formed the 3rd Division (Defrance), Generals of Brigade Avice and Quinette, of the 3rd Corps (de Padoue). Two squadrons per regiment (2nd, 6th, 11th, 15th, and 25th) and a squadron of the 13th, 18th, 19th, 20th and 22nd were assembled into the 5th Corps (Milhaut) under Generals of Brigade Collaert and Lamotte. These various detachments were taken from the depots of the dragoon regiments maintained

Foot dragoons (1806).

COLONELS OF DRAGOONS
DURING THE REIGN OF NAPOLEON I

Regimental Number	Year 1803	Year 1804	Year 1810	Year 1813
1st	Viallanes	Arrighi	Dermoncourt	—
2nd	Fénerols	Pryvé	Ismert	Ismert
3rd	Fiteau	Fiteau	Grézart	—
4th	Wathier	Wathier	Delamothe	Farine
5th	L. Bonaparte	L. Bonaparte, later Lacour	Sparre	Sparre
6th	Lebaron	Lebaron	Piquet	Piquet
7th	Laveran	Laveran	Seron	Veziers
8th	Beckler	Beckler	Girardin	—
9th	Sébastiani	Maupetit	Quénot	—
10th	Cavaignac	Cavaignac	Dommanget	—
11th	Debille	Passingues	Dejean	Thevenez
12th	Pagès	Pagès	Martigny	Merlhès
13th	Levasseur	Levasseur	Laroche	Reiset
14th	Lafond-Blaniac	Lafond-Blaniac	Bouvier	Ludot
15th	Barthélemy	Barthélemy	Beaulieu	Boudinhon
16th	Clément	Clément	Vial	Grouvel
17th	Saint-Dizier	Saint-Dizier	Beurmann	Larcher
18th	Lédée	Lefebvre-Desnouettes	Lafitte	Lafitte
19th	Caulaincourt	Caulaincourt	Saint-Geniès	Mormet
20th	Raynaud	Raynaud	Corbineau	Desargues
21st	Dumas	Dumas	—	Ruat
22nd	—	Carié	Frossard	Rozat
23rd	—	Briant	Briant	Briant
24th	—	Troublé	Delort	Dubessy
25th	—	Rigau	Ornano	Leclèrc
26th	—	Delorme	Chamorin	Montelégier
27th	—	Tereyre	Lallemand	Prévost
28th	—	Destrée	Montmarie	Montmarie
29th	—	Avice	Avice	—
30th	—	Dupré	Renaut	Pinteville

Dragoons, elite company (1805-1815).

in Spain. In 1814, all the major components which had remained on the peninsula were returned to France. With the return of the veterans, the army was dazzled by the sight of their fine uniforms and venerable mustaches which contrasted sharply with the youthfulness of the recruits from 1813. It was said that the legions of forgotten veterans from distant wars had returned to help their children deliver their country from the desecration of foreigners. They were seen everywhere, standing out in the foremost ranks of soldiers.

Under the First Empire the thirty dragoon regiments were subdivided by five sets of uniforms, each set itself divided into two subsets.

The first six regiments were distinguished by the scarlet color of their coat lapels and facings. The next six had crimson ones while the 13th through 18th had deep rose. The 19th through the 24th had jonquil yellow and the last six wore *aurore*.

In each set, the first three regiments had wide pockets while the last three had long ones.

In 1812, the long coat was completely abandoned for the short one with a scooped neckline in front and copper buttons. For full dress, they wore white riding breeches and vests (for undress, grey) and always tall boots. A turban-like helmet made of tiger skin and the black horsehair plume were retained. However, grey cloth pants with leather trim were gradually introduced.

At the same time that the dragoons took up the long coat, they were permitted to grow their mustaches. In Spain they had even worn full beards like their sappers. The history of the 18th Dragoons reveals an interesting detail regarding this subject. There were problems with the cloth and the uniforms, which were often intercepted when sent by the depots. (For further information on this topic, read the military works of Marshal Bugeaud.) Due to these problems, many of the regiments were dressed in the brown cloth of the Capucines found in convents. In this color, they finished out the campaign of 1813 and that of 1814. The difficulty in obtaining epaulettes, plaques and chin straps from France explains the variety of models which have been handed down in military bric-a-brac. In Spain, the dragoons, with the generals' acquiescence, had abandoned the regulation sword for the old Toledo-type sword with three edges. This was a terrible weapon in the hands of soldiers courageous to the point of recklessness and superbly mounted on fast, agile horses.

The epaulette in the form of a claw and was of a dark color edged with a distinguishing color.

The facing table indicates the distribution of the dragoons after the mustering out of 1814 and the numbers which they again took up during the One Hundred Days.

NUMBER in 1814	COMPOSITION OF THE REGIMENTS OF THE FIRST RESTORATION		Number during the HUNDRED DAYS
1st	Former 2nd Dragoons		2nd
2nd	Former 4th Dragoons	4th squadron of the 26th, 3rd squadron of the 30th, elite company of the general headquarters.	4th
3rd	Former 5th Dragoons	3rd, 4th and 5th squadrons of the 22nd Dragoons; 1st squadron of the 24th Dragoons.	5th
4th	Former 6th Dragoons	1st and 2nd squadrons of the 21st Dragoons; 5th squadron of the 27th Dragoons.	6th
5th	Former 7th Dragoons	2nd, 3rd, 4th and 5th squadrons of the 28th Dragoons.	7th
6th	Former 11th Dragoons	1st squadron of the 28th Dragoons; 3rd and 4th squadrons of the 21st Dragoons.	11th
7th	Former 12th Dragoons	5th squadron of the 26th Dragoons; 2nd squadron of the 24th Dragoons.	12th
8th	Former 13th Dragoons	1st and 2nd squadron of the 23rd Dragoons.	13th
9th	Former 14th Dragoons	5th squadron of the 21st Dragoons; 3rd squadron of the 24th Dragoons.	14th
10th	Former 15th Dragoons	3rd, 4th and 5th squadrons of the 27th Dragoons; 2nd squadron of the 30th Dragoons.	15th
11th	Former 16th Dragoons	1st, 2nd, 3rd and 4th squadrons of the 27th Dragoons; 4th squadron of the 24th Dragoons.	16th
12th	Former 17th Dragoons	1st and 2nd squadrons of the 26th Dragoons; 5th squadron of the 24th Dragoons; 1st company of the Young Guard Dragoons.	17th
13th	Former 18th Dragoons	3rd squadron of the the 26th Dragoons; 1st and 2nd squadrons of the the 22nd Dragoons.	18th
14th	Former 19th Dragoons	1st and 2nd squadrons of the the 25th Dragoons; 4th and 5th squadrons of the 30th Dragoons.	19th
15th	Former 20th Dragoons	3rd, 4th and 5th squadrons of the 25th Dragoons; 1st squadron of the 30th Dragoons; 2nd company of the Young Guard Dragoons.	20th

Chasseurs à cheval, in the field (1886).

Dragoon trumpeter, campaign dress (1885).

1st Lancers' Regiment, Imperial Guard (1807).

THE LANCERS UNDER THE EMPIRE

There were never any lancers in the French Army. Napoleon I marvelled over the way that the Polish handled their lances. He had read in an anonymous book of some renown, *De l'Esprit militaire* by de Lessac, that the true weapon of the cavalryman was the lance. A hand-picked group of Polish lancers gave him the opportunity to form a regiment of Polish lancers which served in the Guard from 1807 under the name of chevau-légers lanciers. The regiment was dressed in blue and crimson with white epaulettes and aiguillettes. In 1810 a second regiment was created in the Guard under the name of the 2nd chevau-légers lanciers or the "red lancers."

A short time before the Russian campaign, Napoleon wanted to oppose the Cossack cavaliers who were nimble, tough and well- disciplined. With the decree of June 18, 1811, he ordered the transformation of a number of regiments of dragoons and chasseurs into lancers. The decree also provided for the admission into the rolls of the old regiments of two Polish cavalry regiments armed with lances. These regiments took the name of chevau-léger lanciers, formed the service of the lancers, and were numbered in the following manner.

The 1st Dragoons became the 1st Chevau-légers Lanciers; their distinguishing color was scarlet. The 3rd Dragoons became the 2nd Chevau-légers Lanciers (aurore). The 8th Dragoons became the 3rd Chevau-légers Lanciers (rose). The 9th Dragoons became the 4th Chevau-légers Lanciers (crimson). The 10th Dragoons became the 5th Chevau-légers Lanciers (sky blue). The 20th Dragoons became the 6th Chevau-légers Lanciers (madder).

The 1st and 2nd Polish Lancers became the 7th and 8th Chevau-legers Lanciers and kept their uniform.

Finally, the 30th Chasseurs took Number 9 in the list with buff as their distinguishing color.

The uniform of the seven French regiments was comprised of green jacket and pants. The straps of the epaulettes were also green with piping in distinguishing colors like their collars and their cuff facings. They wore a copper helmet modeled after the dragoons' but with a black crest. They had elite companies.

During the campaign of 1812, all the cuirassier divisions were compeleted with a squadron of chevau-legers lanciers. At the end of the war, as quickly as the cavalry was reduced, the cuirassiers picked up the lances of the unmounted chevau-legers and formed platoons which fought remarkably well in retreat.

In 1813, the lancers were commanded as follows: the 1st by Dermoncourt, the 2nd by Berruyer, the 3rd by Lebrun, the 4th by Deschamps, the 5th by Chabert, the 6th by Marboeuf, the 7th by Slokouski, the 8th by Lubrewski and the 9th by Gobrecht.

Big, robust men are required to handle a lance on horseback. Colonel de Brack, in his wonderful book on *The Outposts of the Light Cavalry (Les Avant-postes de la cavalerie légere)*, gave precise details about the power of the lance. When it is in the hands of experienced horsemen, it is a most formidable and murderous weapon. Of course it requires that the user knows well how to wield it. Under the Empire, when firearms often misfired, the old lancers caught a tirailleur like a fisherman reels in a carp. Moreover, the reputation of the French and Polish lancers caused all the enemy horsemen and foot soldiers to tremble in their boots. The lancers were covered in glory at Waterloo.

On June 2, 1811, fifteen days before creating the service of the chevau-légers, the Emperor put out a decree in which the formation of thirty regiments of French *chasseurs lanciers* were indicated. Not having at my disposal the archives of the Ministry of War, I find it impossible to determine what the intention of this decree was, whether it was merged with the decree of June

18, 1811, or even whether it had provided the preliminary steps for forming the regiments. For a while the cavalry regiments of the Guard had chasseur flankers thereafter transformed into scouts (eight squadrons) which carried lances. However, in an official document which gives the mustering out of all troops existing in 1814 and which indicates the destination of all these corps, one can only trace, as with the French lancers, the 6 regiments formed with the dragoons and the 9th Regiment formed with the 29th Chasseurs. Military historians seem to have improperly classified this last group with the Polish lancers.

The six regiments maintained in 1814 were formed in the following manner:

1st - Old 1st and Old 9th of the service; 4th and 5th squadrons of the 29th Chasseurs.

2nd - Old 2nd of the service and Old 29th Chasseurs; 6th squadron of the 2nd Lancers of the Guard.

3rd - Old 3rd of the service and Old 22nd Chasseurs; 7th squadron of the 2nd Lancers of the Guard.

4th - Old 4th of the service; 8th and 9th squadrons of the 2nd Lancers of the Guard.

5th - Old 5th of the service and Old 13th Hussars (formed at Cassel); 10th squadron of the 2nd Lancers of the Guard.

6th - Old 6th of the service and Old 12th Hussars.

A 7th Lancers (Polish) which was reorganized during the One Hundred Days passed into Russian service with the coming of peace.

FIRST RESTORATION

The arrival of the Bourbons was the signal for the dismissal of a sizeable portion of the army. It could not be otherwise. However, the animosity which General Dupont de l'Étang displayed toward the old army resulted not only in its dissolution but also in the complete annihilation of France's military forces. The general had capitulated at Baylen and was Minister of War from April 3 until December 3, 1814. It seems that the policies of this minister consisted primarily of dissolving the effectives and of discouraging good officers. Everything went slowly, from the hodgepodge mixing up of corps to the changes in uniform. Only one thing moved quickly and that was the ambition of schemers. Many profited from the change in power in getting themselves quietly promoted two ranks higher. There were also the voltigeurs of the Army of Conde and the Talpacks Hussars of Mirabeau's Legion. Not the least greedy of all were the unscrupulous men who fought against France wearing the Russian, English or Austrian cockade. The reduction of the cadres and the demands of emigrants, which were particularly felt by the cavalry, left few places for the old officers. The installation of the King's Household with its luxuriousness beyond the norm of the times hardly seemed to gratify the demands of those returning. Meanwhile, the King sought to attract officers of the usurper into his ranks. Napoleon especially desired that Berthier be allowed to become captain

of the Life Guardsmen. Berthier payed a terrible price in 1815 for his lack of a decision on this matter. He wished to be neither for the King nor for the Emperor and to hold back without compromising himself. Despite this prudent approach, he met with a mysterious death for which no biographer has been able to give an explanation.

An excellent measure grafted onto a necessary one had filled up the numbers created in each reduced service to a number of regiments conforming with the new status of the country.

The two regiments of carabiniers which were retained formed a brigade under the name of Monsieur's Carabiniers.

Twelve regiments of cuirassiers out of the fourteen numbered ones were retained. Naturally, these were the first twelve. The 13th Regiment was turned over to the 4th and the 9th. The 14th merged into the 10th and the 12th.

There were no longer more than fifteen regiments of dragoons, their formation having been given above.

The first six regiments of chevau-légers lanciers—all French—were retained with their numbers. The composition of the six new regiments has also been given already. The formation of the fifteen chasseurs and the seven new hussars is indicated in the table next page.

There was no question in this mixture of including the numerous provisional regiments whose subsequent organizations have been listed above. These corps were considered as having never existed. The officers, non-commissioned officers and soldiers who had been part of them had to rejoin the regiments from which they were detached. They were thus subject to the destinies of these regiments. In addition, to simplify the reorganization of the cavalry, it was assumed that all the old regiments would have five squadrons

Gardes du corps (1814).

except the 10th Hussars who actually counted six. As for the rest, desertion was such at this time and methods of escaping from police supervision were so simple for those living in the country or in smaller towns that everyone did as they pleased. Moreover, the regiments consolidated in this fashion presented only a mediocre force. The release of soldiers belonging to the classes previous to 1812 had already reduced the regiments of the old army to inferior proportions. For these reasons plus still others resulting from the social troubles of the times, the full execution of ministerial orders was hampered.

THE ONE HUNDRED DAYS

◆

Marshal Soult who had succeeded General Dupont and was better prepared than his predecessor, found himself confronting a double-sided state of affairs. The old army, driven by a powerful spirit of conservatism, saw with pain the daily progress made by the emigrated officers in its ranks. On the other hand, the political atmosphere leaned toward conspiracy with daily encouragement for revolt brought into the barracks by

1st Chasseurs	Old 1st Chasseurs.
2nd Chasseurs	Old 2nd Chasseurs: 1st, 2nd 4th, and 5th squadrons of the 19th Chasseurs; 2nd and 4th squadrons of the 26th Chasseurs; 11th, 12th 15th companies of the Young Guard Chasseurs à cheval; 7th squadron of the Scouts of the Guard.
3rd Chasseurs	Old 3rd Chasseurs: 23rd Chasseurs; 13th, 16th, 17th companies of the Young Guard Chasseurs à cheval; 8th squadron of the Scouts of the Guard.
4th Chasseurs	Old 4th Chasseurs: 1st squadron of the 26th Chasseurs; 2nd, 4th, 5th squadrons of the 27th Chasseurs; 1st squardron of the Scouts of the Guard.
5th Chasseurs	Old 5th Chasseurs: 1st, 2nd, 5th squadrons of the 21st Chasseurs.
6th Chasseurs	Old 6th Chasseurs: 2nd squadron of the Scouts of the Guard.
7th Chasseurs	Old 7th Chasseurs: 1st and 2nd squadrons of the 27th Chasseurs; 14th and 18th companies of the Young Guard Chasseurs à cheval; Mamelukes of the Young Guard.
8th Chasseurs	Old 8th Chasseurs: 25th Chasseurs; 3rd squadron of the Scouts of the Guard.
9th Chasseurs	Old 9th Chasseurs: 4th and 5th squadrons of the 24th Chasseurs; 19th and 20th companies of the Young Guard Chasseurs à cheval.
10th Chasseurs	Old 10th and 19th Chasseurs.
11th Chasseurs	Old 11th and 28th Chasseurs.
12th Chasseurs	Old 12th Chasseurs; 3rd squadron of the 16th Chasseurs; 3rd and 5th squadrons of the 26th Chasseurs; 4th squadrons of the 21st Chasseurs; 4th squadron of the Scouts of the Guard.
13th Chasseurs	Old 13th Chasseurs: 1st, 2nd and 3rd squadrons of the 24th Chasseurs.
14th Chasseurs	Old 14th and 31st Chasseurs.
15th Chasseurs	Old 15th Chasseurs: 1st, 2nd and 3rd squadrons of the 20th Chasseurs; 3rd squadron of the 21st Chasseurs.
1st Hussars	Old 1st Hussars.
2nd Hussars	Old 2nd Hussars: 1st, 2nd, 3rd and 4th squadrons of the 10th Hussars; 5th squadron of the Scouts of the Guard.
3rd Hussars	Old 3rd Hussars: 5th and 6th squadron of the 10th Hussars; 1st and 2nd squadrons of the 8th Hussars.
4th Hussars	Old 4th, 13th and 14th Hussars.
5th Hussars	Old 5th and 11th Hussars: 3rd, 4th and 5th squadrons of the 8th Hussars; 6th squadron of the Scouts of the Guard.
6th Hussars	Old 6th and 9th Hussars.
7th Hussars	Old 7th Hussars.

unknown persons. The return of the Emperor was predicted fifteen days before being officially announced. These troops whose loyalty was uncertain had to be mobilized and thrown against the usurper for whom they retained cherished memories. Regiments were suddenly found on the Emperor's side with their eagles, cockades, and even the pennons and ribbons of their trumpets. This was happening at the very moment that a reorganization was supposed to be taking place! Although Napoleon found the cavalry very weak, it was ready to receive a boost from him.

Time was especially short. The Coalition pressed Napoleon, understanding that it must not leave the great improviser any time to organize himself. The Emperor himself even believed that he would be attacked fifteen days earlier. "We must assume," he said in his instructions, "that we will have the enemy before us on June 1st." Therefore, he had to work quickly, taking no false steps, not losing a single second.

The memoirs of Pajol show that the cavalry regiments under his command counted approximately 310 horsemen at the beginning of April 1815. General Pajol, who was as good an administrator as a man of action, must have had the best maintained regiments of the army. At first the effectives had to be raised and then horses bought. The order was given to acquire 10,000 and 6,000 were requested from the gendarmerie. All the horses from the King's Household were taken. However, despite very strict instructions from the Emperor on how to find them by all sort of coercive means, they were concealed by those in whose care the State had entrusted them. Only about 500 were obtained although 2,000 should have been found. As for the men, they returned very quickly. Soldiers on six months' furlough or on leave happily returned to their corps. For the soldier raised in the religion of the glory of the country, the return of Napoleon and the tricolor was the Revolution once again. This time, however, it was with a known leader, loved by the army and favored in victory. It was said that in 1814, he had not been beaten but rather betrayed. The absence of some of his old favorites who had retired to their estates or who had gone abroad after the departure of the King proved that these people did not have a clear conscience. The Emperor knew the soul of the nation and of the army well enough to know that they would give him credit in his

Colonel, Lancers (1814).

Lancers guiding a regiment of cuirassiers (1815).

moment of bad luck. He also knew that he was playing his last card. Already the Allies had taken his wife and his son from him. To remove his name from the list of royal families, they needed only to take away his prestige as a general, the single vestige he retained of that long career begun twenty years earlier before Toulon. The orders for the assembly of the armies in 1815 are masterpieces of clarity and drive. Those who agree with Lieutenant Colonel Charras that Napoleon proved to be below himself are mistaken.

Muskets were lacking as were even uniforms. His instructions were not always understood and were rarely executed to the letter. Although the army and the people had greeted Napoleon's return with their cheers, the bourgeoisie, the bankers and major businessmen did not want him to succeed. They were not Bourbons. They would have preferred the Duke of Orléans to Louis XVIII. What they really wanted was an end to war and especially to useless sacrifices. Their dedication to freedom did not extend to the Republic nor their love of order to legitimacy. They abhorred the Empire and the Emperor. All the obstacles which Napoleon confronted in his final effort are summed up in a fact which is revealed in the history of the 2nd Cuirassiers. "At the end of April 1815, the regiment included 21 officers, 214 men under arms, 31 officers' horses and 216 men in the ranks, divided into three squadrons. The depot was in Joinville (Haute-Marne) from which 205 men could be taken. However, they had neither uniforms nor equipment. These conditions had been reported, but the supply contractor wrote to the regiment that he would not honor their contract." Thus, on May 26, the 2nd Cuirassiers could set out with only 282 cavaliers.

Meanwhile, thanks to the efforts of all the patriots and despite the resistance that they encountered from malicious people, the Army of the North was amply supplied with cavalry. This army which had been victorious at Ligny and at Fleurus was defeated at Waterloo. The regiments were not very strong but their number made up for their weakness. After having supplied the army corps of infantry with cavalry, the Emperor had formed a powerful reserve composed of four corps of two divisions each. These corps assembled at first under the superior command of Grouchy with General of Brigade Le Sénécal as head of the general staff. They were subsequently commanded by Pajol, Exelmans, the Count of Valmy, and Milhaut who were at the time the boldest cavalry generals.

In addition, corps of cavalry were attached to the various armies charged with defending the borders. Below is a summary of the effectives in June 1815. They are slightly different for the Army of the North than those which were given in detail for the composition of this army. This is due to the fact that the latter instance is from the eve of the start of the campaign when all the forces had come together. The former instance is from the early days of the same month.

Before giving the status of the twelve cavalry divisions which were part of the Army of the North and for whom Napoleon made the greatest sacrifices, a quick glance at the possibilities which he left to his lieutenants is in order. They were not great. Rapp was in the best shape. (1) Using the 5th Corps, he had to resist the Austrian Army which was appearing along the Eastern border. He had with him the 6th Cavalry

ARMY OF THE NORTH			
Imperial Guard	Light cavalry, Lefebvre-Desnouettes	14 squadrons	4,100
	Reserve cavalry, Guyot	13 squadrons	
1st Corps (D'Erlon)	Division Jacquinot	11 squadrons	1,500
2nd Corps (Reille)	Division Piré	14 squadrons	1,500
3rd Corps (Vandamme)	Division Domont	19 squadrons	1,500
4th Corps (Gérard)	Divison Morin	12 squadrons	1,500
6th Corps (Mouton)	Without cavalry		
The four corps of reserve cavalry (Grouchy)		86 squadrons	10,500
	TOTAL	169 squadrons	20,600
ARMY OF THE RHINE			
5th Corps (Rapp)	Divison Merlin	12 squadrons	1,800
ARMY OF THE ALPS			
7th Corps (Suchet)	Divison Jannet	12 squadrons	1,600
Jura Corps (Lecourbe)	Divison Castex	9 squadrons	1,600
Var Corps (Brune)		4 squadrons	500
Toulouse Corps (Decaen)		4 squadrons	500
Bordeaux Corps (Clausel)		4 squadrons	500
ARMY OF THE VENDEE			
General Lamarque		20 squadrons	3,300
	TOTAL	74 squadrons	9,800

(1) As one knows, Rapp recognized the defeat of Waterloo before being attacked by the Coalition. He would only turn over Strasbourg and let Alsace be occupied by an order of the King Louis XVIII. It was both honorable and military, but the Coalition had no intention of listening. They wanted to take Strasbourg by brute force, perhaps with the intention of keeping it after the war. Rapp brushed them away as a serious threat although he had inferior forces. In revenge, the enemy fomented a mutiny of French soldiers after having agreed to an armistice. The soldiers, foreseeing their mustering out, demanded their pay in arrears. The officers, from the general in chief to the last second lieutenant, were confined to quarters and kept under full guard. During this time, the soldiers under the command of General Garnison (Sergeant Dalouzi of the 7th Light) governed. They negotiated a loan with the bourgeoisie to pay them. However, some disaffected troops, pushed by the Austrians, tried to assassinate Rapp. The cavalry was outside the place and had a lesser part in this revolt than the infantry. Infantrymen remembered that under the Directorate they had to submit to the generals in chief of the Army of Italy. Dalouzi, meanwhile, was pardoned and was included in the reorganization of the Legion of Cher which became in 1820 the 9th of the line.

CAVALRY OF THE ARMY OF THE NORTH (JUNE 1815)

DIVISIONS ATTACHED TO THE INFANTRY CORPS

1st CORPS Count D'ERLON	2nd CORPS Baron REILLE	3rd CORPS VANDAMME	4th CORPS Count GERARD
1st DIVISION OF LIGHT CAVALRY Lieut. Gen. JACQUINOT *Chief of staff:* Adj. Gen. LEJEANS (1,706 horse)	2nd DIVISION OF LIGHT CAVALRY Lieut. Gen. PIRÉ *Chief of staff:* Adj. Gen. RIPPERT (2,064 horse)	3rd DIVISION OF LIGHT CAVALRY Lieut. Gen. DOMON *Chief of staff:* Adj. Gen. CH. MAURIN (1,017 horse)	7th DIVISION OF LIGHT CAVALRY Lieut. Gen. MAURIN *Chief of staff:* Adj. Gen. MAURIN
1st BRIGADE, General of Brigade BRUNO 7th Hussars, Colonel Marbot 3rd Chasseurs, Colonel Lawoestine	1st BRIGADE, General of Brigade HUBER 1st Chasseurs, Colonel Simonneau 6th Chasseurs, Colonel Faudoas	1st BRIGADE, General of Brigade DOMMANGET 4th Chasseurs, Colonel Desmichels 9th Chasseurs, Colonel Dukermont	1st BRIGADE, General of Brigade VALLIN 6th Hussars, Colonel Prince of Savoy Carignan
2nd BRIGADE, General of Brigade GOBRECHT 3rd Lancers, Colonel Martigue 4th Lancers, Colonel Bro	2nd BRIGADE, General of Brigade WATHIEZ 5th Lancers, Colonel Jacquinot 6th Lancers, Colonel Galbois	2nd BRIGADE, General of Brigade VINOT 12th Chassuers, Colonel Grouchy	2nd BRIGADE, General of Brigade BERRUYER 8th Chasseurs, Colonel Schneit

GRAND CAVALRY RESERVE
Marshal GROUCHY

1st CORPS Lieut. Gen. Count PAJOL *Chief of staff:* Gen. adj. cmdr. PICARD (2,536 horse)	2nd CORPS Lieut. Gen. Count EXELMANS *Chief of staff:* Gen. adj. cmdr. FEROUSSAT (3,116 horse)	3rd CORPS Lieut. Gen. KELLERMANN, Count of Valmy *Chief of staff:* Gen adj. cmdr. TANCARVILLE (3,400 horse)	4th CORPS Lieut. Gen. Count MILHAUT *Chief of staff:* Gen adj. cmdr. CHASSERIAU
4th DIVISION OF LIGHT CAVALRY Lieut. Gen. SOULT	9th DIVISION OF CAVALRY Lieut. Gen. STROLZ	11th DIVISION OF CAVALRY Lieut. Gen. LHÉRITIER *Chief of staff:* Gen adj. cmdr. SOUBEYRAN	13th DIVISION OF CAVALRY Lieut. Gen. WATHIER-SAINT-ALPHONSE
1st BRIGADE, General of Brigade CLARY 1st Hussars 4th Hussars, Colonel Blot	1st BRIGADE, General of Brigade BURTHE 5th Dragoons, Colonel Canevas de Saint-Amand 13th Dragoons, Colonel Saviot	1st BRIGADE, General of Brigade PICQUET 2nd Dragoons, Colonel Planzeaux 7th Dragoons, Colonel Léopold	1st BRIGADE, General of Brigade DUBOIS 1st Cuirassiers, Colonel Ordener 4th Cuirassiers, Colonel Habert
2nd BRIGADE, General of Brigade AMEIL 5th Hussars, Colonel Liegeard	2nd BRIGADE, General of Brigade VINCENT 15th Dragoons, Colonel Chaillot 20th Dragoons, Colonel Bricqueville	2nd BRIGADE, General of Brigade GUITON 8th Cuirassiers, Colonel Garavaque 11th Cuirassiers, Colonel Courtier	2nd BRIGADE, General of Brigade TRAVERS 7th Cuirassiers, Colonel Richardot 12th Cuirassiers, Colonel Thurot
5th DIVISION OF LIGHT CAVALRY Lieut. Gen. SUBERVIC	10th DIVISION OF CAVALRY Lieut. Gen. CHASTEL	12th DIVISION OF CAVALRY Lieut. Gen. ROUSSEL D'HURBAL	14th DIVISION OF CAVALRY Lieut. Gen. DELORT *Chief of staff:* Gen adj. cmdr. LEGAY D'ARCY (2,797 horse)
1st BRIGADE, General of Brigade COLBERT 1st Lancers, Colonel Jacquinot 2nd Lancers, Colonel Sourd	1st BRIGADE, General of Brigade BONNEMAINS 4th Dragoons, Col. Bonquerot des Essarts 12th Dragoons, Colonel Bureaux de Puzy	1st BRIGADE, General of Brigade BLANCHARD 1st Carabiniers, Colonel Rogé 2nd Carabiniers, Colonel Beugnat	1st BRIGADE, General of Brigade FARINE 5th Cuirassiers, Colonel Gobert 10th Cuirassiers, Colonel Lahubardière
2nd BRIGADE, General of Brigade MERLIN 11th Chasseurs, Colonel Nicolas	2nd BRIGADE, General of Brigade BERTON 14th Dragoons, Colonel Séguier 17th Dragoons, Colonel Labitte	2nd BRIGADE, General of Brigade DONOP 2nd Cuirassiers, Colonel Grandjean 3rd Cuirassiers, Colonel Lacroix	2nd BRIGADE, General of Brigade VIAL 6th Cuirassiers, Colonel Martin 9th Cuirassiers, Colonel Bigarne

---

Division commanded by Lieutenant General, the Count Merlin. Rapp, in his excellent but too brief *Mémoires* barely had a full disposition remaining in his troops. However, his forces can be reconstructed. Merlin's Division, not including the depot of the 19th Dragoons, included five regiments: the 11th Dragoons, the 2nd, 7th, and 13th Chasseurs, and the 2nd Hussars. Divided into two brigades, these regiments only had very weak effectives, judging from the situation of the 1st Brigade under the command of General of Brigade Grouvel (2nd and 8th Chasseurs). The 1st Brigade included 732 horses.

General Lamarque, authorized by the preceding report to have 19 squadrons, seems only to have assembled half that number. They had been organized by Pajol before his departure for Waterloo and were only comprised of hastily filled out depots. At first these were the 4th squadrons of the 4th and 17th Dragoons drawn from Moulins and from Nevers, of the 2nd Hussars taken from Fontenay, and of the 4th and 5th squadrons of the 12th and 16th Dragoons taken from Amiens and from Saintes, and of the 13th Chasseurs from Niort. These nine squadrons presented a total of 1,200 horses. Beyond this, the 4th and 5th squadrons of the 5th and 14th Dragoons from Poitiers and from Rennes had been placed at Nantes under the command of General Bigarre. Accounts from that time attribute 800 horses to them. Who supplied the 1,300 others indicated in the preceding report? In addition to the 46 regiments attributed to the Army of the North and the five at Rapp's disposal, only six entire regiments remained available. The 10th Chasseurs were with Suchet and the Army of the Alps; the 15th (Colonel Favrot) were with Clausel; the 14th Dragoons had to remain on the Spanish border. The destination of the other regiments is unknown. However, it may be assumed that the majority of the squadrons which Napoleon assigned to the leaders of the armies which were returned to the borders were almost all from the 4th and 5th squadrons waiting powerlessly for their cavaliers and their horses. On the other hand, the cavalry of the Army of the North presented a superb sight. The best officers, the most passionate soldiers, and the best horses had been called to it. Although legend indicates examples of weakness and even of treason amongst the leaders, Waterloo remains an epic page in the history of the French cavalry. Two months later, its example extracted an admission from its conqueror, the Duke of Wellington. This is as worthwhile to set down in print as was King William's admission before the charge of the Chasseurs d'Afrique at the martyrdom of Illy (September 1, 1870). "Gentlemen," said Wellington to his officers, "perhaps you are unaware of who is Europe's best cavalry today?... Well then, I must confess that it is the one which is the worst mounted of all... that is the French cavalry. Since I have personally had to withstand the efforts of its daring and perseverance, I know no other capable of surpassing it."

According to the list above, the regiments of the cavalry took back their old numbers just as the infantry did. This explains the presence of a 17th and a 20th Dragoons. New regiments were not formed although there is a 7th Lancers (Polish) discussed previously and a 16th Chasseurs composed of Belgians. These corps did not seem to have time to organize themselves and to get underway. From June 15 to 19, the Army of the North had 18,500 disabled men. Ten generals lay dead on the battlefield or died of their wounds: Lieutenants General Devaux de Saint-Maurice, Duhesme, Lefort, Michel, Girard and Generals of Brigade Baudoin,

Bonas, Aulard, Mallet, and Jamin. Among the wounded generals can be cited Gérard, Cambronne, Bonaparte (Gérôme), *Foy, Morin, Lallemand, Guyot*, Barrois, *Lhéritier, Blancard*, Durieu, Delort, Friant, and Petit. The number of colonels and field officers are not included. This was the epic battle. Although it is not inscribed on French standards, it is irrevocably engraved in the memory of those conquered by them. The names of the generals killed or wounded who belonged to the service of the cavalry are highlighted above. General Lefort was killed near the Emperor while plunging into the Prussian squares at Fleurus at the head of the service squadrons. Complete, official accounts of the series of battles waged in Belgium during the six days of the campaign of 1815 have never been published. The official brochures and books—as numerous as those which already exist on the War of 1870-1871—have all been written with the goal of justifying or blaming the early players in that great drama, including of course the Emperor. Conversely, they have been written to tell the great deeds of his soldiers. A historian (Captain Mauduit) who participated in the events at a lower rank and who gathered the testimony of his contemporaries, like many others explained the fatal impetus leading to the charge of Lhéritier's Division and of the brigade of carabiniers, despite orders from the Count of Valmy. This charge was followed by that of the Lancers and the Dragoons of the Guard. It seemed certain that all those fine troops who had been set on edge by many days of inaction and tormented by the need to confront the enemy with saber in hand were prepared to obey Ney's suggestions. They were heavily punished for this excess of energy, having been destroyed. The unfortunate General Berton, who later paid for his faithfulness to the Empire, the Emperor and the Imperial Army with his head, seems to have best summarized the situation described above. He said, "The premature use of the French cavalry in the Battle of Waterloo, which is rightfully regarded as a mistake, seemed to have been made in response to a charge of the English cavalry and not by a general order. It could have been withdrawn instead of made to press forward with such a courageous enterprise which became disastrous although its shocks had shaken and even broken open many enemy squares. It is true that too often the rapid movements of this service have been abused, tiring the horses before the end of the battle when they are so necessary, regardless of the outcome." Finally, conforming to the legend, which this time seems to be true, General Berton thinks that, despite the untimely charges, if Grouchy had debouched on the battlefield with his fresh troops, the Battle of Waterloo would have been named the "Battle of Mont-Saint-Jean" instead of the name it was logically given, the "Belle Alliance." The French had given it the former name and it was so designated for some years by the liberals.

The English could not pursue the French army. They no longer had a battalion, a squadron or a battery in any condition to make a day's march. The Prussians were charged with giving chase to the French. Thanks are due to Grouchy's well maintained troops and to Pajol's and Exelmans' cavalry which even received reinforcements during their retreat in good order. Thanks are especially reserved for the admirable discipline of the French regiments of the line who maintained their ranks. This was in contrast to some troops of the Guard who evidenced brief but immediate and inexorable discouragement. Because of these stalwart troops, the Army of the North was still able to inflict heavy losses on the enemy around Paris.

The army withdrew behind the Loire where it was dissolved, disarmed, unmounted and mustered out by French hands. Sad pages in the history of the French military! The manner in which these measures were executed by the favorites of the new regime who united with the foreigners lent a particularly odious nature to the events. The soldiers of 1815 were spared no humiliation. It was not admitted that the King had retreated before the Emperor who was returning from the island of Elba. The soldiers and officers had to obey their superiors while the latter had to obey circumstances. The army of the past was deleted from the pages of history. Its generals were dealt with outside the law and it soldiers received no justice. This was the first and last time that heros, still covered with the blood they had spilled for France, were treated like criminals. In my youth, I knew officers and soldiers from the First Empire who had suffered ostracism from 1816 on. The memory of this had left sad traces in their souls and affected their manner of being with a particular melancholy. The privates of the engravings, of the melodramas and of the light comedies from this period bore witness to it. The soldier laborer, the refugee camp, the brigands of the Loire, the return of the exile, all the legends which grew up around the officers on half-pay and the old soldiers dispossessed of their pensions and their benefits have been exacerbated by impolitic and cruel capital punishments, even those motivated by conspiracies less dangerous than general discontent. During the days of July 1830, there were more old soldiers of Napoleon I's Old Guard and more soldiers from the end of the Empire than republicans and constitutionals. It was still Napoleon's old cockade which appeared at the head of France. It was the last seed of vengeance of those generous generations who came together in their love for glory, for the victories of the First Republic and for those of Napoleon I.

Famous names of the cavalry (1800-1815).

Carabiniers of Monsieur (1820).

SECOND RESTORATION

◆

Upon their second return, the Bourbons erased the tradition of the Republic and the Empire from the cavalry just as they had done in the infantry. Evidently, the obstacles which they encountered were serious. They could not completely destroy the depots to which the horses had to be delivered after disarming the troops. However, the orders were worked out well enough so that the officers' corps could never again come together. It is true that to some extent the regiments created in 1815 could be united with the regiments of the Empire through the relationships of the depots. However, there was little interest in doing this since the tradition of the flags followed the tradition of the numbers.

The decrees of July 16 and August 19, 1815 fixed the number of cavalry regiments of the line at forty-seven, not counting the cavalry of the Guard (eight magnificent regiments.) They were not officially numbered but they took the following names: in the heavy cavalry, those of princes; in the cavalry of the line and the light cavalry, the names of the departments. In the heavy cavalry, the regiments were classified according to the rank of their leaders. In the cavalry of the line and the light cavalry, it was according to alphabetical order. The uniforms indicated their names and their classifications as described below.

HEAVY CAVALRY

Carabiniers: 1 regiment. "Monsieur" (white coat with crimson collar and cuff facings; equerry breeches and boots; copper helmet and cuirasse).

Cuirassiers: 6 regiments. (The cuirassiers have the blue coat with collar and cuff linings of distinguishing colors. Long, grey pants with piping, crested helmet.) The distinguishing color of La Reine was scarlet; Dauphin, crimson; Angoulême, aurore; Berry, deep rose; Orléans, jonquil yellow; Condé, buff.

LINE CAVALRY

Dragoons: 10 regiments. (The dragoons retain the green coat of the Empire; they take up the crested helmet and grey pants over boots with piping. They are divided into five series through distinguishing colors. The 2nd regiment of each series has green cuff facings.) Calvados and Doubs, scarlet; Garonne and Gironde, jonquil yellow; Hérault and "Loire", aurore; Manche and Rhone, deep rose; Saône and Seine, crimson.

LIGHT CAVALRY

Chasseurs: 24 regiments. The chasseurs kept the short coat buttoned right and were divided into eight series through distinguishing colors. In the 1st regiment of each series, the collars and the cuff facings; in the second, the cuff facings; in the third, the collars; and in all of them, the turn-backs, the linings, the epaulettes, and the piping were of the distinguishing colors. Green pants like the jacket, and grey in undress.

1st Series	2nd Series	3rd Series	4th Series	5th Series	6th Series	7th Series	8th Series
scarlet	jonquil yellow	aurore	deep rose	crimson	sky blue	wine-colored	black
Allier	Ariège	Corrèze	Gard	Meuse	Orne	Somme	Vendée
Alpes	Cantal	Côte-d'Or	Isere	Morbihan	Pyrénées	Var	Vienne
Ardennes	Charente	Dordogne	Marne	Oise	Sarthe	Vaucluse	Vosges

Hussars: 6 regiments. Jura, sky blue pelisse and dolman jacket, scarlet pants.
Meurthe, chestnut pelisse and dolman jacket, sky blue pants.
Moselle, grey pelisse and dolman jacket, crimson pants.
Nord, light green uniform and dolman jacket, scarlet pants.
Bas-Rhin, royal blue uniform and dolman jacket, scarlet pants.
Haut-Rhin, dark green uniform and dolman jacket, sky blue pants.

All the hussars' uniforms had braids of contrasting color mixed with the base color of the uniform.

CADRE OF THE CAVALRY AS PER THE DECREE OF AUGUST 30, 1815
(REGIMENTS AT 4 SQUADRONS)

STAFF	Per regiment	Total of the service	SQUADRON	Per regiment	Total of the service
Colonels	1	47	Captains	8	376
Lieutenant colonels	1	47	Lieutenants	8	376
Majors as squadron leaders	2	94	Second lieutenants	16	752
Majors as field administrators	1	47	Sergeant majors	4	194
Battalion adjutant majors	2	94	Sergeants	32	1,504
Paymasters	1	47	Brigade quartermasters	4	188
Officiers d'habillement*	1	47	Mounted cavalrymen	388	18,236
Color bearers	1	47	Dismounted cavalrymen	48	2,256
Surgeons	2	94	Trumpeters	8	376
Non-commissioned officers	10	470			
			TOTAL	580	27,266
TOTAL	22	1,034	Carried over: Staff		1,034
* Officer in charge of all the materiel of the troops.			GRAND TOTAL		28,300

It was thought that these modifications in the uniform colors and in the methods of designating a regiment would eliminate all memories of the past. The soldiers who were grouped by department were given many emigre officers returning from foreign armies. The elimination of the lancers service, henceforth represented solely by the Royal Guard regiment, was as painful to the army as was the loss of its glorious numbers. It is true that the fifth squadron of each of the twenty-four chasseur regiments effectively replaced the six regiments of lancers now gone. These squadrons were "comprised of the most agile men and the fastest and most easily handled horses." However an insolent public wanted only to see the humilating dispersal of the service which Colonel Bro had rendered famous on the battlefield of Waterloo. These people claimed that the treaties of 1815 forbade France to maintain more than one regiment of these formidable cavaliers. There were very few people who read the text of these treaties, however, and who therefore had anything to say about it.

Under the new organization, the division of a squadron into two companies was eliminated and the elite company of the 1st squadron disappeared. The squadron once again became both a tactical unit and an administrative unit. This was requested by all the generals of the service from 1813 on.

This cavalry was allocated 26,978 horses. However the men and horses required to fill it out were not very quickly found as evidenced by two ministerial circulars. One from April 20, 1819 fixed the provisional complement for the regiments at 240 men for the cuirassiers and the carabiniers, 300 for the dragoons, and 360 for the chasseurs and hussars. The other from October 9, 1819 raised the effective strength for the three subdivisions to 300, 400, and 480 men, respectively. A strong military spirit meanwhile sustained these regiments whose officers' corps came from rather diverse origins. A lot of work was done. In 1821, the service of the cavalry was well below its regulation effective strength, especially in terms of horses. This was with the exception of the chasseur a cheval regiments which the Spanish War had expanded for the most part to six squadrons. For lack of money, tall mounts were not bought. However the Life Guardsmen and the cavalry of the Guard, on the other hand, were buying them in great quantities. All the inspectors general of that time pointed with sadness to the poverty of the heavy cavalry regiments. They complained of difficulties encountered in training officers and the troops, and they requested horses. However, if the budgetary frugality of the times is considered, it is difficult to see how the ministers of war under the Restoration could make ends meet. For the year 1819, the Chamber of Deputies voted 168,494,000 francs for the active service. This amount was not completely spent so it was reduced to 168,198,150 francs for the 1820 fiscal period. For the latter year, the general effective strength was set at 197,742 men of whom the cavalry accounted for 20,294 men including 2682 officers. Note that the Royal Guard was included in these figures since only the companies of the Life Guardsmen were paid from the reserve funds of the civil list.

Thus it is pointless to speak of the effectives of the French cavalry before the campaign of 1823. It will be seen that this campaign took the French army by surprise. As was just explained, however, it could not be otherwise. A quarter of what is spent today on five hundred thousand or more men was spent then on approximately two hundred thousand men. French military history is almost always told without enough recognition of financial history which dominates the army with its imperious authority.

In 1821, the general effective strength went even lower. In September it was 140,661 without counting the gendarmerie, the King's Household and the general staffs. Also, the expenses of the war were always kept at a number which today would seem incredible. In 1822, expenses rose; they would reach 200 million above and beyond the extraordinary expenses. The year 1823 cost 343,364,822 francs, however, the budget of 1825 reduced it to 190 million. It is understood that military pensions were not paid from these funds, but, despite this distinction, all the details of this enormous military destitution can be seen at a glance.

The Royal Guard and the King's Household were

Officer, chasseurs à cheval (1818).

Hussar officers, chasseurs à cheval, dragoons and cuirassiers, full dress (1824).

better off. The Guard was magnificent. It was separated into two divisions of eight regiments with six squadrons (2 of grenadiers, 2 of cuirassiers, 1 of dragoons, 1 of lancers, 1 of chasseurs, and 1 of hussars). It included in its ranks 6,416 men and 5,808 horses. The tactics of the Restoration were to break up tradition at any cost and to destroy the prestige of the army of the line. At first all was sacrificed to the Guard and to the squadrons of Life Guardsmen. However, despite these deplorable circumstances to which the cavalry was subjected, it very quickly reassumed a rather good appearance. Nonetheless, it was never allowed the honor of the garrison in Paris or in the surroundings which were completely reserved for the Royal Guard.

As noted above, companies of horse guides were attached to legions of infantry, keeping in mind old memories. This arrangement which removed 600 horses from the light cavalry, was executed for the most part only on paper. Only the Morbihan Legion had its company of scouts and its company of artillery. The horses allocated to the infantry legions were returned to the cavalry regiments. The slowness with which the appropriate effective strengths were restored has been discussed above. The wars of the Empire had exhausted equine production. During the One Hundred Days, the gendarmerie was required to give up everything it could do without in order to obtain trained mounts. Meanwhile, batteries were hitched up to post horses. The remount depots were reorganized—or rather organized—on a new basis. The resurrection of the French mounted troops is due to the excellent and devoted work of the officers who directed the cavalry. It was the Restoration that was the first to permanently attach cavalry to the active army. A decision from July 13, 1827 fixed its effective strength at 192 men.

The decree of August 30, 1815 had determined that when all the regiments were formed, they would draw by subdivision the order of their numbers in a lottery. This procedure never took place. From 1815 to 1822, there were various modifications in the uniform. This was specifically intended to reduce the complications of the distinguishing colors, to give more uniformity to the dress, and also to give more substance to the training. The first regulations for maneuvers were prepared.

The Spanish War (1823) would provide this new cavalry with a very appropriate opportunity to distinguish itself. Both old and new officers awaited the war with equal impatience. They wanted to erase the differences of their pasts and mix their blood on the field of battle.

Regiments of four squadrons could not be easily mobilized as a unit. The cuirassiers designated as part of the cavalry of the Army of Spain formed themselves into three full war squadrons containing a minimum of 325 horsemen. The dragoons and twenty other chasseur regiments were ordered to create 5th and 6th squadrons. The four chasseur regiments which did not benefit from this measure were Oise, Orne, Vaucluse, and Vosges. The mobilized chasseur regiments all had from 425 to 450 horses and four squadrons. As for the hussars and the cuirassiers, they barely had 300 in each since they could only put together three squadrons.

It was seen in the order of battle for the Army of Spain (Chapter Two—History of the Infantry) that a set number of brigades and cavalry regiments were mixed into infantry divisions. All the regiments formed into brigades in this manner belonged to the light cavalry. The brigading given below was not exactly maintained during the entire campaign.

CAMPAIGN IN SPAIN (APRIL 1823)			
1st CORPS Marshal OUDINOT, DUKE OF REGGIO	**2nd CORPS** General of division, MOLITOR	**3rd CORPS** PRINCE DE HOHENLOHE	**4th CORPS** Marshal MONCEY
1st DIVISION General of division, COUNT D'AUTICHAMP	**4th DIVISION** General of division, LOVERDO	**6th DIVISION** General of division, DE CONCHY	**8th DIVISION** General of division, VENCE [Sic - Curial]
1st Brigade, General Valin 13th Chasseurs, Col. Baron Chatry de la Fosse 24th Chassuers, Col. Count de Vennevelles, later Baron Dejean (9th Light)	1st Brigade, General Pottier 10th Chasseurs à cheval, Col. Count de Serran 19th Chasseurs à cheval, Col. Count de Fournas (4th Light)	Light cavalry brigade, General Bonnemains 12th Chasseurs, Col. Bony, later Rouillé d'Orfeuille 1st Chasseurs, Col. Delamalle	1st Brigade, General Vence 18th Chasseurs, Col. de la Bonninière de Beaumont 23rd Chasseurs, Col. Baron Nicolas, later Marquis de Dreux-Nancré
2nd DIVISION General of division, DE BOURCK	**5th DIVISION** General of division, JUCHEREAU DE SAINT-DENIS	**7th DIVISION** General of division, CANUEL	**9th DIVISION** General of division, DAMAS
1st Brigade, General Larochejacquelin 7th Chasseurs, Col. Baron de Wimpffen 1st Hussars, Col Baron Colin de Verdière, later Baron Simoneau (7th Light)	1st Brigade, General Saint-Chamans 4th Chasseurs à cheval, Col. Marquis de Castries, later Count de Chateaubriand 20th Chasseurs à cheval, Col. Tessier de Marouze	Light cavalry brigade, General Hubert 17th Chasseurs, Col. Baron de Lespinay 4th Hussars, Col. Baron de Merssemann	Light cavalry brigade 22nd Chasseurs, Col. Baron Letermellier 6th Chasseurs, Col. Courtier, later Callory
3rd DIVISION General of division, OBERT	**2nd DIVISION OF DRAGOONS** General of division, DOMONT		**10th DIVISION** General of division, DONNADIEU
1st Brigade, General Vitré 5th Hussars, Col. de Muller 9th Chasseurs, Col. Count d'Hautpoul (2nd Light)	1st Brigade, General Vincent 3rd Dragoons, Col. Bergeret 4th Dragoons, Col. Güsler		Light cavalry brigade 5th Chasseurs, Col. Lenoury 6th Hussars, Col. d'Astorg, later Count Dupont de Compiègne
1st DIVISION OF DRAGOONS General of division, CASTEX	1st Brigade, General Faverot 5th Dragoons, Col. Marquis d'Hanache 10th Dragoons, Col. Baron Villatte	**RESERVE** General of division, BORDESOULLE.	
1st Brigade, General de Carignan 2nd Dragoons, Col. Rapatel, later Count de Chateaubodeau 8th Dragoons, Col. Baron de St-Geniès		Royal Guard cavalry brigade 2nd Cuirassiers, Col. de Lauriston Dragoon Regiment, Col. de Castelbajac Chasseurs Regiment, Col. d'Argout	**CURIASSIER DIVISION** General of division, ROUSSEL D'HUBAL
2nd Brigade, General Saint-Marc 7th Dragoons, Col. Count de Mornay 9th Dragoons, Col. Chevalier Jolly			3rd Brigade, General de Kermont 2nd Cuirassiers, Col. Salomon de Feldeck 4th Cuirassiers, Col. de Burggraff
			2nd Brigade 6th Cuirassiers, Col. Patarm 5th Cuirassiers, Col. de Montcalm-Gozon

A fifth army corps under the command of Marquis de Lauriston was added to the Army of Spain on June 11, 1820. It had a strength of 11,500 infantrymen and of 750 horsemen. This cavalry, attached to Ricard's mixed division was formed into a brigade under the command of General of Brigade de Chastelux and was composed of the 3rd Hussars (Colonel Viscount de Chambrun) and of the 3rd Chasseurs (Colonel Desmichels, then Marquis de Faudoas).

The return of the regiments to their numbers was a great event. It partly erased the separation which the Bourbons wanted to make between the past and the present. The soldier was happy with it and the public welcomed it. In the general report on the Spanish campaign, each of the regiments which took part in the campaign have been designated under their numbers since in practice it was in this war that they at first received the numbers from their leaders. In fact, they are frequently cited without their princely or departmental titles in the general orders of the Army of Spain. A royal decree from February 27, 1825 officially sanctioned this use with the exception of the first six regiments of cuirassiers. These latter simply added their numbers to their princely names and did not lose them until the July Revolution of 1830.

The Spanish War proved very beneficial for the French cavalry even though it was only used in operations which were very mundane for the officers and soldiers. Many of these men had seen huge deployments of cavalry from the Grande Armee in Germany. However, the cavalry did regain what it had lost; it went back to valuing its men for their actual worth. The kind of fellow from *Morveux d'officier* who slashes the old corporal de Béranger entirely disappeared in this campaign. The style then was to imitate the proper dress of the veterans, to honor them, and to recognize the services which they had performed. War is not only an art and a science, it is also a special moral test. It transforms men who engage in it intelligently.

The rapid creation of sixty squadrons, the mobilization of 164 squadrons out of 220 old ones— and of 33 out of 55 regiments although this occurred without too much of a lottery—showed the numerical weakness of the French cavalry. One managed, but everyone agreed that the French no longer had sufficient means for a serious campaign. Although the light cavalry's work had been more damaged than that of the reserve cavalry, a variety of political reasons pushed the government to revise the total organization of the service in favor of the latter. Moreover, as of the Peace of 1815, large horses five or six years old had been produced. These were the only ones with which it would be possible to remount the cuirassiers. A decree from February 27, 1825 set the distribution of the three subdivisions of the service as follows:

Reserve Cavalry—12 regiments: 2 of carabiniers and 10 of cuirassiers
Cavalry of the Line—12 regiments of dragoons
Light Cavalry—18 of chasseurs and 6 of hussars

These forty-eight regiments were to be completed at six squadrons as quickly as budgetary resources allowed. On the surface, this increased the service by only one regiment. However, in reality, if the 60 squadrons of dragoons and of chasseurs organized at the beginning of the war are included, the cavalry of the line received an actual increase of 100 squadrons. If these are added to the 188 squadrons of the organization of 1815, a total of 288 is given. Of course there were also the 32 squadrons of the Guard.

Cuirassiers, field uniform, farrier(1885).

Hussars, full dress, cavalry quarters (1886).

Officers, chasseurs à cheval, undress, and hussar officers (1822).

The doubling of the carabiniers and the transformation of the dragoons into cuirassiers was easily accomplished. The 2nd Regiment of Carabiniers was formed from detachments coming from all the heavy cavalry corps. Thus it wore blue jackets with white buttons like the 1st Regiment. The distinguishing color of the service was always crimson. The first regiment had crimson collars, facings, and piping on the cuff facings and decorating the pockets. The second regiment only had crimson piping on the collar, the cuff facings, the pockets and the turnbacks.

The 7th, 8th, 9th and 10th Dragoons became the 7th, 8th, 9th and 10th Cuirassiers. The 19th, 20th, 21st, 22nd, 23rd, and 24th Chasseurs became the 7th, 8th, 9th, 10th, 11th, and 12th Dragoons. In addition there was an exchange of horses and men between the dragoons, who became cuirassiers, and the chasseurs, who became dragoons. This was done to equalize their sizes. The procedure was more time-consuming than difficult. In 1827 at the camp of Saint-Omer, the cavalry division of General de Bourbon-Busset was exclusivly comprised of regiments which the organization of 1825 had not touched. Their numbers were as follows: 1st Brigade: 6th Hussars (Colonel de Compiègne); 2nd Chasseurs (Colonel de Bonneval); 2nd Brigade: 5th Dragoons (Colonel d'Hanache); 3rd Cuirassiers (Colonel de Saint-Belin Mâlain).

In 1830 the cavalry regiments of all the subdivisions still were not up to six squadrons. The first six regiments of cuirassiers and the six regiments of hussars still only had four. However, the last four regiments of cuirassiers, all the dragoons, and all the chasseurs were at full regulation complements.

In 1828, Colonel Marquis de Faudoas had been sent to Greece with his regiment, the 3rd Chasseurs à cheval. The entire cavalry of General Marquis de Lauriston, commander in chief of the expeditionary corps to Morocco, was there. The events of a war where politics played a more important role than strategy did not allow the 3rd Chasseurs to distinguish themselves in the classical land of Themistocles and Leonidas. However, the celebrated Ibrahim Pasha, a connoisseur of cavalry matters, marveled over this regiment's elegance of dress and the skillfulness of its maneuvers. This famous warrior had already created many fine regiments in Egypt with the help of French instructors. As a memento of October 1, 1828 when he reviewed the 3rd Chasseurs and had them perform maneuvers, he asked the Marquis de Faudoas for a uniform, a set of harnesses and a lance. He promised to use them to create in his country a corps modeled after the Marquis' regiment which he found worth imitating. The history of the former 3rd Chasseurs, who later became the 3rd Lancers then the 15th Dragoons, gives precise information about the effective strength of the regiment at Navarin on October 1,1828: 36 officers, 496 men, 58 officers' horses, and 396 horses for the troops. Thus there were one hundred horsemen detached to a cavalry regiment which had entered Spain five years earlier with 445 mounted horsemen. This demonstrates that more and more of the cavalry was maintained with strict economy. Perhaps it was hoped that the 3rd Chasseurs who had remained with the occupation corps in Spain and who had been joined there by one of their two depot squadrons with 110 horses would find excellent remounts in Greece in the local horses. This was an illusion which the ministerial general staffs too often harbored in order to avoid paying for the costly and uncomfortable expense of overseas expeditions. Experience almost always destroys this illusion.

The cavalry attached to the expeditionary corps to Algiers in 1830 and placed under the command of Colonel Bontemps-Dubarry of the 17th Chasseurs included only three squadrons: one of the 13th and two of the 17th Chasseurs. These squadrons left unmounted and their components entered for the most part into the creation of the Algerian Chasseurs, the nucleus of the Chasseurs d'Afrique and of the indigenous cavalry.

During the Restoration, the cavalry changed uniform many times. At the very beginning, it was desired, as noted above, to provide a welcome change in the appearance of the cavalrymen to the eyes of the people. This was achieved particularly by modifiying the headgear. The helmet with the horsehair plume was banished from the cuirassiers and the dragoons and

replaced by the helmet with a strap. This totally altered their riding dress and gave them a German appearance. In 1825, the helmet with strap was abandoned in the dragoons and the cuirassiers and was replaced by a helmet with a horsehair plume whose crest was surmounted by horsehair trim in the form of a stiff brush. This helmet—in iron for the cuirassiers, in copper for the dragoons—lasted until the middle of Louis-Philippe's reign.

It was said too glibly that the adoption of grey pants for the line and the reserve cavalry was borrowed from foreign armies and from the Allies, as was the helmet with strap. The madder or wine-color, which the light cavalry had very quickly adopted for the pants, was put into widespread use throughout the entire infantry by a royal decision from January 1829. A decision from February 17, 1830 ordered that the reserve and the line cavalry no longer use the grey pants as of January 1, 1831. Consequently, only red pants would be produced for the corps.

There is more evidence of impressiveness than of taste in the other uniforms from this period. The model uniforms sent by the minister of war to the administration's councils were so ugly that many colonels took it upon themselves to have them recut by their master tailors and to give them more elegance. At the end of the Restoration, Baron Létang commanded the 6th Regiment of Chasseurs. He had been one of the most brillant officers of the Imperial Guard Chasseurs and was very concerned about his dress and that of his men. The high collars and the pointed skirts of the braided uniforms which imprisoned his chasseurs as if though they were in a vice worried him greatly. He took it into his head to have all the official models altered while religiously respecting the styles of rue Saint-Dominque in order that they all conform to his own ideas. At the general inspection the inspector congratulated him on the fine dress of his squadrons. The cavaliers had presence but something bothered the general. The regiment of chasseurs which he had just reviewed before inspecting that of Baron Létang seemed totally different to him. He asked to compare the uniform to the ministerial model and found them completely identical. With the following regiment, the mystery was solved. Baron Létang was rebuked by a ministerial letter and had to re-outfit his regiment according to the decree at his own expense.

Lancer, Royal Guard (1828).

The carabiniers officially retained the right to dress their trumpeters in green with the livery trim of the Count d'Artois.(1)

These distinctions were completely abolished by the July Revolution. The livery trim which decorated the collar, the sleeves and the waists of the uniforms of the musicians, trumpeters and drummers of the first six cuirassiers regiments and in some infantry regiments disappeared. In the latter two categories, these were replaced by the tricolored trim which was likewise the livery of the new King.

LOUIS-PHILLIPE

The Second Restoration had eliminated the Imperial Guard and had replaced it with the Royal Guard. The July Government quite simply eliminated the privileged corps: the King's Guard and Household. This was a political necessity. All the elite corps cost a lot of money and trouble for those who recruited them and wanted to maintain them in good condition. They generally only had a brief existence as did the governments which had set them up. They were particularly reproached for weakening the other regiments and for serving as a constant object of jealousy for these others. Meanwhile, there was a need for a Grande Armée of solid reserves, of old soldiers who served as examples to the young ones, and of troops capable of any sacrifice. A reduced period of service excluded these types of troops. The actual military state of countries where military service is obligatory also does not permit recruiting of sovereign guards of the type such as France has had.

(1) The carabiniers left behind the title of "Carabiniers of Monsieur" before the Count d'Artois' arrival on the throne. As soon as their brigade was reformed, the two regiments were simply designated by their numbers. However, on September 21, 1824, the Cuirassiers of Angoulême (Number 3) had taken the title "Cuirassiers of Bordeaux", and the Hussars of the Jura (Number 1) had taken the name of "Hussars of Chartres." On November 17, 1826, Charles X also granted the 1st Chasseurs the title of "Chasseurs of Nemours." Under the reign of Louis-Philippe, the 1st Hussars retained its title of "Hussars of Chartres," the 1st Chasseurs became the 1st Lancers, taking the title "Lancers of Nemours." The 6th Lancers (a new creation) took that of the "Lancers of Orléans." In 1848, these latter titles disappeared. In 1857, under the final reign, the dragoons regiment of the Guard was called the "Dragoons of the Empress."

In 1830 the elimination of the Royal Guard equaled at first the sudden abolition of eight regiments which figured in the military economy of the country. From one day to the next, forty-eight squadrons were missing at roll call. To fill in this enormous gap, a regiment of lancers—the Lancers of Orléans—were created on August 25, 1830. Its command was given to Baron Sourd, one of the heros of Waterloo. Its uniform was a green *kurtka* (short jacket) with piping, jonquil yellow lapels and borders, jonquil yellow epaulettes and cords, and wine colored *chapska* (lancer's helmet) and pants. This was a compromise between the dress of the Polish Lancers of the Imperial Guard and that of the lancers of the former Royal Guard. The officers wore distinctive gold insignia.

The disbanding of the Guard was not unique within the cavalry during the July Revolution. In this aristocratic service where the officers required a certain affluence to honorably maintain their rank, the greatest names of the old French nobility had appeared beside those of the old soldiers of the Empire before 1830. The return of the tricolor satisfied the latter. However the declaration of oath required to " the King of the French" removed more than three hundred fifty officers from the ranks of the cavalry. With the Life Guard and the officers of the Guard thrown out, the service lost very close to two thousand officers. Many returned from 1831 to 1838, especially amongst the lower ranking officers. The embarrassment to the new government caused by this huge military population so violently removed by the Revolution of 1830 was apparently one of the reasons leading to the formulation of the law on the status of officers. It seemed necessary to create a neutral status for the soldier who defended his country. This would allow him to remain a servant of France, regardless of which government was in power.

During the second half of the Restoration, the Palais Royal had been a hospital residence where Napoleon's generals and officers were welcomed with favor and distinction. With the debut of the new government, all the high military positions were overrun by the celebrated military men of the First Empire. At first their influence on the army was excellent. As will soon been seen, the French cavalry regiments very quickly reached the height of their dexterity in maneuvers and of correctness in their dress. They produced students even more enamored than themselves with the precision of the wheeling drill and the imposing appearance of serried ranks. The French cavalry was not aware that the fire of the infantry and of the artillery was going further and was increasing. It was always prepared to provide heroic charges like those at Eylau and at Waterloo. These were performed with an indomitable willingness and admirable precision. However, the cavalry forgot that in modern tactics it must above all be the advance guard of the army and be constantly in front of the general in chief's field glasses.

On March 12, 1831, a royal decree reorganized the cavalry on the basis of fifty regiments:

12 of reserve cavalry—2 of carabiniers and 10 of cuirassiers
18 of cavalry of the line—12 of dragoons and 6 of lancers
20 of light cavalry—14 of chasseurs and 6 of hussars

Cuirassiers, full dress (1831).

All these regiments are at 6 squadrons but their effective strengths, be it in peacetime or during war, differ depending on the subdivision of the service.

The major innovations of this skillful and well executed organization are:

1. The separation of peacetime footing from wartime, a fairly useless separation since, during peace, the regiments never attain their regulation effective strength. During wartime, its only effect is to jam the depot with reservists and recruits.
2. The creation of the captain instructor (*capitaine instructeur*);
3. The creation of first class horsemen, a useful measure which cleverly righted the necessary injustice committed in 1815 by the disbanding of the elite companies.

An unusual step and one which was quickly erased from this fine organization, left the lance to the 5th and 6th squadrons of the chasseur regiments while removing it from the 5th and 6th squadrons of the six lancers regiments which were given muskets to replace them.

CADRE FIXED FOR ALL REGIMENTS	Peace footing	War footing
Colonel	1	1
Lieutenant colonel	1	1
Majors as field administrators	1	1
Majors as squadron leaders	2	3
Captain trésoriers*	1	1
Captain adjutant majors** 2	3	
Captain instructors	1	1
Assistant trésoriers	1	1
Officiers d'habillement*** 1	1	
Surgeon majors	1	1
Assistant surgeons	1	2
Non-commissioned officers	2	3
Adjutant baggage masters 1	1	
Primary veterinarians	1	1
Secondary veterinarians	1	2
Trumpet major	1	1
Corporal trumpeters	1	2
Staff trumpeters	—	2
Sergeant farriers	—	3
TOTAL of the staff	20	31
Platoons outside the ranks	60	67
TOTAL each regiment	80	98

* Officer of accounts and records
** Captains as battalion adjutants
*** Officers in charge of all materiel for the troops

Thus, in times of peace, the French cavalry was kept at 50,200 officers, non-commissioned officers and soldiers. Its wartime status, without counting the special cavalry already formed in Africa, was 69,080. This was a respectable figure.

In order to execute the new distribution, the 1st, 2nd, 3rd, 4th and 5th Regiments of Chasseurs à cheval became the 1st, 2nd, 3rd, 4th and 5th Lancers. The Lancers of Orléans be-

COMPOSITION OF A SQUADRON	Peace footing for all regiments	War footing		
		Reserve	Line	Light
Captains	2	2	2	2
Lieutenants	2	2	2	2
Second lieutenants	2	4	4	4
Sergeant majors	1	1	1	1
Sergeants	6	8	8	8
Sergeant quartermasters	1	1	1	1
Corporal quartermasters	1	1	1	1
Corporals	12	16	16	16
1st class cavalrymen	32	32	32	32
2nd class mounted cavalrymen	69	88	98	108
2nd class unmounted cavalrymen	20	6	16	16
Farriers	3	3	3	3
Trumpeters	3	3	3	3
TOTAL	154	177	187	197

came the 6th of the service. Following the transfer of the first five regiments of chasseurs into the lancers service, the 6th to the 18th Regiments received the numbers of the 1st through the 13th. A 14th Chasseurs was created with detachments taken from various regiments. The Revolution of 1830 returned to Paris the cavalry regiments of the line which the Restoration had scrupulously banished from the city. According to the army annual of 1831, the first corps which profited from this advantage were the 6th Dragoons (Colonel Lacour), the 1st Hussars (Colonel Pozac) and the 6th Hussars (Colonel de Lauthonnet). (1) At the same time, the carabiniers brigade took possession of the quarters at Versailles which were previously assigned to the reserve cavalry of the Royal Guard.

On November 22, 1832, an army corps which had been assembled for a year crossed the northern border to help the Belgian people affirm their independence. This corps was composed of four divisions of infantry, a mixed advance guard brigade, two brigades of light cavalry, and two divisions of cavalry. This campaign was limited by diplomacy to the siege of Anvers and, with its tightly defined conditions, provided the cavalry no opportunity to distinguish itself. However, it is possible to cite here the names of the regiments which participated in the campaign. These regiments were formed into four very fine and complete squadrons. The officers of this period whom I was able to question affirmed that their regiments were comparable to the best cavalry corps of the First Empire.

Advance guard brigade, Lancers (Belgium, 1832).

ADVANCE GUARD MIXED BRIGADE	LIGHT CAVALRY BRIGADES	DEJEAN DIVISION	GENTIL SAINT-ALPHONSE DIVISION
His Royal Majesty, the Duke of Orléans and His Royal Majesty, the Duke of Nemours	1st Brigade, Marquis de Lawoestine 7th Chasseurs, Colonel Jourdan 8th Chasseurs, Colonel Hupais de Salienne	*Chief of General Staff:* Lieutenant Colonel de Brea	*Chief of General Staff:* Colonel de Maussion
20th Light Infantry Regiment 1st Hussars, Colonel Pozac 1st Lancers, Colonel Regnault de Saint-Jean-d'Angely 4th Lancers, Colonel Couliboeuf de Blocqueville, its adjutant	2nd Brigade, Baron Simonneau 4th Chasseurs, Colonel Ybry 5th Hussars, Colonel Klein de Kleinenberg	1st Brigade, Viscount de Rigny 2nd Hussars, Colonel Ducroc, Count of Chabannes 1st Chasseurs, Colonel Prevost 2nd Brigade, Viscount Latour-Maubourg 5th Dragoons, Colonel Baron de Laffitte 10th Dragoons, Colonel de Galz Malvirade	1st Brigade, General Villatte 1st Cuirassiers, Colonel Fauvart-Bastoul 4th Cuirassiers, Colonel de la Bachelerie 3rd Brigade, General Güsler 9th Cuirassiers, Colonel Urwoy de Closmadeuc 10th Cuirassiers, Colonel Baron Bache

(1) Everyone who could honor the memory of the cavalry service cannot be kept silent. Thus it is possible to relate here the numbers of the regiments which formed a cortege around the remains of the Great Soldier which His Royal Highness, the Prince of Joinville, had gone to find at Sainte-Heléné and which he brought back to Paris. These regiments were the 5th Cuirassiers (Colonel de Chalendar), the 1st Dragoons (Colonel d'Y de Résigny) and the 7th Lancers (Colonel de Golstein). In addition, 87 non-commissioned officers from various cavalry corps participated in the procession carrying the same number of banners in the names of the 86 departments and of Algeria. The great funeral of Napoleon I was a solemn occasion, for France as well as for the army, where all hearts beat as one.

On March 9, 1834, the entire cavalry was returned to a status of five squadrons. On the eve of the July Revolution it had been expanded to six squadrons.

To complete the history of the creation of new cavalry regiments under the reign of Louis-Philippe, it should be immediately pointed out that the light cavalry had no more than eighteen regiments. The 13th and the 14th Chasseurs had been converted into regiments of lancers (Numbers 7 and 8) through a decree from November 27, 1836. At the first rumor of war on September 27, 1840, this proportion seemed too streamlined. General Despans-Cubières presented the King with a decree including the creation of six cavalry regiments: three of chasseurs (Numbers 13, 14, and 15) and three of hussars, (Numbers 7, 8 and 9). If this decree had been fully executed, the number of cavalry regiments would have been 56 at the end of the July Government. That is, it would have been equal to the number of regiments retained under the Restoration. However, with the creation of the 13th Chasseurs and the 7th, 8th and 9th Hussars, everything stopped. At the end of Louis-Philippe's reign, 54 cavalry regiments could be counted plus seven for the Army of Africa. At the same time that the decree of November 27, 1836 had increased the number of lancers regiments, it had also removed the lance from the 5th squadrons of chasseurs à cheval. However, by giving them the name of "scouts," they could retain muskets in the 5th squadrons of lancer regiments. Under the Empire, for a while muskets had even been given to the cuirassiers!

The magnificent maneuvers and the handsome uniforms of the French cavalry from 1830 to 1848 have already been mentioned. As noted, this was the work of the old division leaders of the Empire. It has also been pointed out that their students surpassed them in these areas. Under the Second Empire, the taste for handsome uniforms and a love for formal maneuvers was carried quite far. Yet those men were never better dressed than the cavalry regiments under Louis-Philippe. The fine art of detail was pushed beyond all limits. A colonel became General of Division through the science of "packaging" by which means he made both his career and his fame. However, in addition to this expense of wasted energy, there were also intelligent efforts. In the aftermath of the Revolution of 1830, an officer from the light cavalry of the First Empire had been recalled to the service. He was quite amusing and very active, and in his veins ran the blood of the Lasalles, the Montbruns, the Colberts and the Pajols. Very quickly placed at the head of the 4th Hussars, this Colonel de Bracke tried to revive within his regiment the traditions of daring from the Republic and the Empire. He was one of the first advocates of individual initiative which gives the horseman more solidity and consequently more self-confidence. He has left behind a book on the topic which is as useful as it is enjoyable: *Outposts of the Light Cavalry—Memories (Avant-postes de cavalerie légère—Souvenirs)* which is an army classic. Unfortunately this old leader of the red lancers squadrons was true to his name. He was a hothead; he wasn't taken too seriously. Attention was paid only to the kettledrummers he led one day to the Champ-de-Mars, resulting in his arrest. The influence of the heavy cavalry at this time of peace was not thwarted without reason. It is true that the light cavalry had Africa for itself. The important role that it played there alongside the special cavalry of the colony will be related further on. However, the heavy cavalry had for its part the annual camps so appropriate for training the infantry but much less useful for the training regiments. This enabled them to learn how to maneuver side by side. However, the permanent formation of the entire cavalry

Chasseurs à cheval (1835).

Officers of the 4th Hussars (1840)

into divisions would have been preferable. Twenty generals requested this change under Louis-Philippe. However, under the Monarchy of 1830, except for the camps, only the cavalry brigades of Paris, Versailles, Lunéville and Lille were other than ordinary.(1) There were also many partial mobilizations along the borders. These were very useful for the cavalry which was kept in shape by these movements. However, the mobilizations also constituted the constant thinning out of the effectives and the horses from the cavalry. This was so prevalent that in 1840, the regiments of cuirassiers and of dragoons could only put together three squadrons in the line at the first call. The influence of the heavy cavalry was such from 1830 to 1848 that all the regiments—the hussars as well as the cuirassiers—executed the same maneuvers. The shadow of Milhaut's and of Kellermann`s cuirassiers and the shadows of the immortal cuirassiers of Waterloo so foolishly sacrificed by Ney hung over the cavalry.

An important warning at the same time showed the cavalry that outside of Africa, its role was going to be remarkably modified. The flintlock, which sometimes failed in normal weather but which never worked when it rained, had been succeeded by the percussion cap which always fired. The rapid fire rifle and the magazine rifle were anticipated. The chasseurs a pied in Algeria had already been able to stop charges of countless horsemen by unhorsing their leaders at five hundred meters. The good old days when masses of cavalry swept over a corps of army infantry as if though it were a field of wheat were over. On the battlefield, the cavalryman was no more than a warrior offering much more exposed surface than an infantryman. He was no longer a thunderbolt; the thunder had passed into the hands of the man on foot. The entire value and usefulness of the mounted soldier from this point on rested in his speed. It seemed that no one immediately understood this fact. This was true even within the armies of Europe which had proved themselves more avid than the French in following the progress of military ballistics. The proportion of heavy cavalry was not decreased. It was seen to

have fallen at the beginning of the Restoration to eleven regiments, including the four regiments of grenadiers and cuirassiers of the Guard. Then it rose to sixteen and fell again to twelve with the Revolution of 1830. In the future, this figure remained fairly well fixed. However, the lancers and the dragoons did not try to make themselves lighter. Under Louis-Philippe, the dragoons staked their honor on not differing noticably from the cuirassiers. Throughout Europe these latter always laid claim to and were famous for being the elite of the cavalry. We have heard an old general recount that, while undergoing his training as an officer of the general staff in a regiment of dragoons, he was the only officer who knew how to form the regiment into battalion and how to make it perform foot maneuvers. These circumstances caused him to be picked out of the crowd by a famous inspector general. The general, marvelling at this unusual science, made him his aide-de-camp, thereby leading him to good fortune.

The light cavalry should have regained the prominence which it had had during the campaigns of the Republic and of the Empire when it had fulfilled its special mission so brilliantly. However, although the Princes of Orléans liked the officers of the light cavalry, their influence was always exerted more favorably towards the heavy cavalry regiments. The Duke of Orléans, the most African of the four brothers, never had publicly displayed his preferences. However, when the Duke of Nemours had to occupy himself more particularly and almost exclusively with the cavalry, he hid his preferences neither at court nor in the training camps, nor even in questions of promotion. The cuirassiers thus became the favorites. The practice of entrusting regiments of this service to brilliant field officers from the Chasseurs d'Afrique dates from this period.

Under the First Empire, the entire military machine had been contained in the head of a great man. If a new idea was brought to him, if he found it good, he charged a general in his confidence with making a study of it which he called an applied study. There wasn't time to consider all the very new ideas whose immediate application would have broken up his military organism. The study provided a solution, an appropriation, or a justified refusal, and he decided. He decided and had it executed. Under the Restoration, the princes returned with two types of viewpoints: on the one hand foreign and on the other reactionary. However, since they were after all intelligent, well-educated men, they very quickly understood that the military

---

(1) The composition of the camp at Compiegne for the years 1834 and 1839 gives an example of what the camps offered for the training of the cavalry. Three regiments return after a period of two years to revive themselves at the direct source of favors under the command of the Prince Royal.

It would be a strange history which wrote only of the camps under the monarchies. The same officers and the same corps were seen to be perpetuated there throughout a reign. However, it has been the same under all the regimes. Thus, the reign of Louis-Philippe should not be considered as receiving special criticism here.

THE YEAR 1834	THE YEAR 1836	
1st BRIGADE, General GROUCHY 2nd Dragoons, Colonel Imbert Saint-Armand 3rd Dragoons, Colonel de Brémont d'Ars	1st BRIGADE, General Count SOULT DE MORNAY 4th Chasseurs, Colonel Corréard 8th Chasseurs, Colonel Hupais de Salienne 5th Hussars, Col. Klein de Kleinenberg	2nd BRIGADE, His Royal Highness the DUC DE NEMOURS 1st Dragoons, Colonel Y de Résigny 2nd Dragoons, Colonel Imbert Saint-Armand 3rd Lancers, Colonel Voisin
2nd BRIGADE, General MARBOT 1st Carabiniers, Colonel Blanquefort 2nd Carabiniers, Colonel Bertaux	3rd BRIGADE, General MARBOT 1st Carabiniers, Colonel Davesiès de Pontés 2nd Carabiniers, Colonel Bertaux 5th Cuirassiers, Colonel de Chalendar	

methods of Napoleon's companions were superior to those which they had been able to learn through their hatred and their memories. They sincerely loved the army and France; they did their best. It is from their high level that the committees of the services have risen, incapable of quickly doing what is good and always prepared to let the bad go on. Under Louis-Philippe the committees took on an epic proportion. Parliamentarianism and its discussions of miniutiae were introduced into the customs of the high level general staff. In this period, he who hasn't seen a dozen generals in civilian clothes in the courtyard of the Minister of War, followed gravely by a colonel of the general staff who is armed with a notebook and a pencil and is making a horse gallop in front of them with a new bridle, knows nothing about the military practices of this period. When it was a question of considering a new pack for Lieutenant General Bougenel or a uniform from the celebrated General Hecquet, it was a holiday. All the offices were at the windows to watch the cavalry committee operate. It should be immediately added that in the other services and the other committees, things were just as solemn and equally as impractical. They never thought of having the soldiers and the non-commissioned officers come to put to the test the form of a saddle or the cut of a pair of trousers. Theory vastly overshot practicality and things reached the point where the minister rejected responsibility for everything that had to do with the committee. The committee complained of the influence of the court and the court, moved by kind feelings but obliged to defend itself, accused both the minister and the committee. Everything was beyond the law. The reason, the motive and the cause for the abundance of administrative documents, rules for training, dress, and administration under the reign of Louis-Philippe was peace. This peace was too long for a nation which spent three hundred and some odd million per year for its army. It was too long for an army which felt itself brave, strong and unified. This peace carried with it and quite heavily— especially in the cavalry—a costly inactivity for the country.

Often one wanted to compare and assimilate the French army to foreign armies. From their assimilations as from these comparisons, bastardized and hybridized systems emerged from false assumptions. An army is made for war and does not improve, does not become perfect, except through war or the hope of war. Its training in peacetime, before a long peace, under a government of peace, has no practical goal and remains in the theoretical domain. It is superb and yet one feels that there is nothing beneath the surface. In their youth, all the fifty year old men were able to see the Life Guards maneuver which the lesser German princes maintained at great expense in their little capitals. Splendid weapons, superb men, magnificent horses, olympian uniforms. However, the sixty or eighty horsemen who formed the army of one of these principalities could not have made a march of forty leagues. The services had been outfitted with a view to ceremony and recalled historic memories. The men, used to the comfort of a sedentary, bourgeois lifestyle, would not have known how to feed their horses oats. Beyond the ceremonial guards, the animals only went out with a saddle blanket. Both water and sun spoiled the sparkling colors of the embroidered uniforms of the Grand Duke's knights. Of course the French cavalry had not reached this point in 1847, but it was no longer what it had been at the beginning of the reign, and it said so itself. The old officers of the Empire who had commanded the regiment from 1830 to 1840 were gone. Their heirs did not have a glimpse of the next opportunity to imitate them on the battle field. When the Revolution of 1848 broke out, the army began to lose its affection for a regime which it had welcomed with joy, which it had saluted with its cheers, which it had served with honor and faithfulness, which it felt was in favor of its material interests, but which it meanwhile saw leave without regrets. The ease with which the enormous Army of Paris submitted in February to a change performed or tolerated by the National Guard is characteristic. On the strength of having been put in contact with the National Guard of Paris and of having given way to the Guard on their regiments, the real officers had come to believe that they actually had to obey the

Officers of carabiniers, cuirassiers, dragoons, chasseurs à cheval, lancers and hussars, full dress (1845).

Guard to the letter as well as in the spirit of the Constitution. When a resistance was to be organized at the call of a general devoted to Louis-Philippe, the following phrase was said by a colonel and was approved by many of his colleagues:

"We will not have the National Guard on our side."

Thus for the second time the National Guard overturned a monarchy. In 1830, its mustering out performed three years before had become the take-off point for an obstinate opposition by the Parisian bourgeoisie. In 1848, its intervention between the army—charged with supressing the movement —and the populace—excited more than irritated by the banning of a banquet in the 12th Arrondissement—paralyzed the final efforts of the rattled monarchy.

Meanwhile, responsibility for the duty and honor of escorting the King and the Queen to Saint-Cloud along this first stage toward an unmerited exile was incumbent upon the cavalry. The two fallen sovereigns left the capital on February 24 through the barrier of the Etoile. They were surrounded by 200 horsemen of the 2nd Regiment of Cuirassiers, having on their left General Regnault de Saint-Jean-d'Angely, commander of the Cavalry of Paris and on their right Colonel Reybell. The following day, the four squadrons of this fine regiment returned to their garrison at Rambouillet with their colonel at the head.

Under the reign of Louis-Philippe, the uniforms of the line and the reserve cavalry underwent modifications more in terms of their cut than in their color. General Hecquet—"the grand master tailor" as he was then called —flattered the pronounced tastes of the Duke of Nemours for close-fitting coats and dolmans, pants without visible pockets and the unchanging panels with false, rectilinear pockets. In parades, reviews, and ceremonies, this gave the officers a very good appearance. However, it was impossible to conduct a campaign with the clothes he had designed. The cavalry, the service reputed to be more wealthy than the others, had almost as many uniforms as it had hours in the morning.

The officers of the cuirassiers and of the dragoons had three hats: the helmet, with or without plume, according to the service; the cocked hat for the city; and the police hat for home service. They had four uniforms: the short coat for full-dress, the long coat for the city, the greatcoat, and the cloak. They wore a sword with the coat and the greatcoat.

Retreat, trumpeters of dragoons and hussars (1839).

The officers of the lancers had one coat less and the cocked hat. Generally their undress kurtka was buttoned right over the chest and was without lapels. Although this uniform was not official, it was tolerated. After having been dressed entirely in red from May 8, 1831 to February 28, 1837, they were dressed at this later date in blue and divided by distinguishing colors into two series: the first four regiments jonquil yellow, the last four regiments in madder. They lost the belt, and their blue *chapska* was decorated with a falling plume in black horsehair which became red in 1839. With the reform in dress of 1845, the *chapska*, already made lighter, was further hollowed out and the officers had cartridge box cross belts and sashes of silver fabric and distinguishing colors.

The officers of the chasseurs alone had only a *kurtka* for all their uniforms and, naturally, as for all the mounted troops, the greatcoat and the cloak.

Cuirassier, undress (1885).

Cuirassier, undress (1885).

A s for the hussars, in addition to their pelisse and their dolman laced with silver, they had an elegant dolman for undress made of material similar to that used in the full dress dolman. The undress dolman had frogs and braids in black silk. At one time, all the hussar officers, regardless of which regiment they belonged to, were to have been given a dolman in green material with trim and braid of black goat's hair for their undress uniform. The high ranking administration met with successful opposition from the officers, especially from the colonels. The hussars had seen their uniforms modified in terms of colors: the 2nd had taken blue shako and pants with white braid which called to mind the *chamboran* of the Republic. The 1st and 4th had also adopted white braid. The others had kept the mixed braids of madder and a base color. When the last three regiments were organized in 1840, they were given copper buttons with gold ones for officers due to princely caprice. The 7th seemed destined to recall the guides of popular memory while the 9th reminded one of the Hussars of Death. As for the 8th, it at first had a white dolman, like its pelisse, with golden yellow braids, a sky blue shako and blue pants with an amaranth or purplish red stripe. The 8th brought back to life the memory of the Lauzun Hussars and made quite a splash in the army where the words "Eighth Hussars" immediately were identified with the utmost in elegance. These fine uniforms had the unfortunate aspect of upsetting the finances of many an officer. However, they had the advantage of raising the public opinion of the troops and often even their own self-esteem. There are political, miltary, and social differences between one army which is too well dressed and another which, from general to soldier, walks about from morning till night in a stable jacket and a cap. These differences need to be studied before making fun of the former or overly admiring the latter. Our weakness for good looking uniforms, sufficiently lavish and worn with dignity, are not hidden here. We do think that the comfort and interest of those who wear and must pay for them should certainly be taken into greater consideration. However, without becoming stuffy over this to the point of lofty philosophy, it seems to us that outward appearances count a great deal in the respectful consideration that a wise and honest nation should give in clothing its army.

In all periods, the chasseurs had been the cavalry corps over whom the uniform manufacturers' imagination labored the most. Intended to perform exactly the same service as the hussars, one wonders at first why the chasseurs are not hussars or the hussars not chasseurs. This enormous problem of the military system has not been resolved even though the two series of regiments wear the same blue uniform, with white braid for one and black for the other. It is not astonishing that this had subsequently troubled the Republic, the Empire, and the Restoration after having upset the Ancien Regime, only to again stir up the July Government and the governments which had followed it.

1830 saw the chasseurs à cheval of the Restoration with a jacket of mixed frogs and shakos at 45 centimeters (17.5 inches) in height. This dress was very expensive for the officers since along with the braids and trim in silver, they wore epaulettes and helmet cords of the same metal. It was decided to reduce these expenses and the chasseurs received the green *habit-veste* (coat-jacket) buttoned right across the chest. Their shako was retained but it became red with less grandiose proportions and was trimmed with a falling plume in black horsehair. Meanwhile, the hussars had become so elegant that in 1840 the creation of the 7th, 8th and 9th regiments of this service with their gorgeous uniforms redirected attention to those poor chasseurs, so

abandoned and poorly equipped. Thus it was that the most handsome dress ever given them was invented. This was a green *kurtka* with a row of buttons and a narrow skirt in the Polish fashion, very nicely designed, and a busby without a bag but with a high plume. The officers had the shoulder belt carrying the cartridge box and a sash of silver and green silk.

The wine-colored pants worn by all the cavalry with the exception of the 4th, 8th and 9th Hussars, was subsequently reinforced with leather. This was either in front or behind and at the bottom in a manner which let only a narrow band of cloth on the sides be seen, or with simple spatterdashes in leather. The horseman of the reserve and of the line seemed as heavy with this trim as the "great fathers" of 1791 to 1799. The light cavalry, reinforced with leather in the same manner, was no longer very jaunty in its riding dress. However, the triumph of the entire cavalry was the street dress. In a cavalry garrison city on a Sunday, it was always a pleasure to see all these active men, healthy and well dressed, walking and mixing with the local inhabitants.

AFRICA

Until 1840, the regiments of Chasseurs of Africa and the indigenous cavalry had amply met the needs of the colonial war. However, at this time under pressing circumstances, two squadrons of 5th Hussars had to be sent to Algiers under the command of Charbonnel. They played an outstanding role in the expeditions of the Mitidja, Cherchell, Medeah and Milianah. In 1846, the four active squadrons of this regiment were in Algeria and stayed there until June 1848, at which time they were brought back to France by the Colonel, Viscount d'Allonville.

Cuirassier and mounted militia (1848).

Five other regiments of light cavalry were sent into the French Algerian colony under Louis-Philippe.

The 2nd Hussars of 1844 to 1847 - Colonel Gagnon. Sixty hussars of this regiment, under the command of Major Courby de Cognord, accompanied the column of Lieutenant Colonel Montagnac. Montagnac with the 8th Battalion of Chasseurs, delivered the glorious combats of Djemaa-Ghazaouat and Sidi-Brahim. They shared the fate of the brave men of this illustrious battalion (September 23, 24 and 25, 1845). The 2nd Hussars also played a useful role in the Battle of Isly.

The 9th Chasseurs - Colonel Dubern - 1844 to 1846;

The 2nd Chasseurs, from 1845 to 1848 - Colonels Grand and de Cotte. This regiment formed the final escort of Abd-el-Kader, taken at the end of 1847;

The 5th Chasseurs - Colonels Duport de Saint-Victor and Durringer;

The 1st Chasseurs - Colonel de Noue.

In addition to all the organizations of Chasseurs d'Afrique and *Spahis* (Algerian cavalry), eager cavalry officers, non-commissioned officers and horsemen were requested.

REPUBLIC OF 1848

Under the Second Republic, the provisional government, that of the executive commission and the two presidencies, politics was so important that no one could be seriously involved in cavalry details. At the same time, it is necessary to do justice to the governments of 1848. They did not harm the troops. Without a doubt they retired Colonel Foulque d'Oraison of the 9th Hussars in an abrupt and calculated manner. The 9th Hussars, dressed in black, owed the nickname "d'Oraison funèbre" or (of funerary Orison) to its colonel who had organized it. However, this was the only act that the presidency for its part quickly put to rights. A minor mutiny by some lieutenants and second lieutenants of the 5th Cuirassiers against their colonel led to placing the two oldest officers from these two ranks on the unemployment list with a bit of ceremony (April 2, 1848). These were the two sole events which can be turned up from that tormented period.

On April 22, 1848, the desire to create some popularity amongst the non-commissioned officers along with the possible necessity of mobilization gave the provisional government an opportunity to create a third use for the second lieutenant in cavalry regiments. In fact, an army called the Army of the Alps had been assembled in the southeast of France. It had only one division of cavalry but this was a splendid one. Its general, the Marquis Oudinot, acted simultaneously as commander in chief of the entire army until December 10.

DIVISION OF THE ARMY OF THE ALPS

1st Brigade
3rd Hussars, Colonel Genestet de Planhol
7th Hussars, Colonel Grenier
8th Hussars, Colonel Rivet

2nd Brigade
2nd Lancers, Colonel Delarue-Beaumarchais
3rd Dragoons, Colonel Hanus de Maisonneuve
9th Dragoons, Colonel de Poilloué de Saint-Mars

3rd Brigade
7th Cuirassiers, Colonel Salmon
10th Cuirassiers, Colonel Gado

Lancer, Imperial Guard, (1859).

On December 20, 1849, the Army of the Alps, of which a sizeable portion had been sent to Rome, was dissolved. Meanwhile, as it was not suitable to leave the second city of France (which had just been violently shaken by riots) without immediate help, the Army of Lyon was put together under the command of General of Divison Gémeau. It had a division of cavalry composed in the following manner:

ARMY OF LYON

1st Brigade
General of Brigade Lebon Desmottes
9th Dragoons, Colonel du Poilloué de Saint-Mars
7th Cuirassiers, Colonel Salmon
10th Cuirassiers, Colonal Gado

2nd Brigade
General of Brigade Gagnon
3rd Hussars, Colonel Genestet de Planho
8th Hussars, Colonel Rivet
12th Dragoons, Coloner Garnier de Labareyre

Since then, the Army of Lyon has always had its division of cavalry but it was reduced to four regiments.

On April 4, 1848, in expectation of a war whose threat must have weighed more on public opinion than on events, the creation of eight squadrons of general staff guides had been stopped. Each squadron commanded by a captain was to have 160 men of whom 5 were officers. At first only three squadrons were organized. A presidential decree dating from November 23, 1850 reduced it to two. Numbers 1 and 2, mixed together, formed the new Number 1 while Number 3 took the number 2.

This was the single creation of the Republic of 1848. However, there was in addition to the Army of the Alps, a large, potential gathering of cavalry. For a century now, political revolutions always take place in Paris. They are always followed by a counter coup which becomes more and more violent since changes in government are more easily made. The events of June 1848 temporarily brought together nine regiments of cavalry in Paris: the 1st and 2nd Carabiniers; the 1st, 2nd, 6th, and 7th Cuirassiers; the 2nd and 4th Dragoons; and the 5th Lancers, a total of 36 squadrons. At the time of the events in February, almost as many squadrons had been made to come but upon their arrival, had been almost immediately sent back. The manner in which the cavalry had been used with the army had left the Parisians dissatisfied with it.(1) Conversely, after June 1848, praise was lavished on the cavalry. This gathering of cavalry was not disbanded until about a month later. Paris could see the hotels of the Place Vendôme transformed into cavalry quarters, horses picketed on the Champs-Élysées, on Boulevard du Temple and in front of the *Gymnase*. This need for rapidly gathering cavalry regiments to maintain peace in Paris was the starting point for the organization of the permanent cavalry division at Versailles.

General Cavaignac had left to the presidency of Prince Napoleon the example and the obligation to protect the Holy See. It had been driven out of Rome by a revolutionary and unified young Italy. The cavalry was attached to the small corps which was charged with returning the papacy to possession of its wordly holdings. At first comprised of 300 horses from the 1st Regiment of Chasseurs under the command of Colonel de Noue, it was quickly expanded to the effective strength of a brigade under the command of General Morris (1st Chasseurs, Colonel de Noue; 11th Dragoons, Colonel de la Chaize.) Until the end of the siege of Rome, this brigade wore the Number 2 of the 1st Division commanded by General Regnault de Saint-Jean-d'Angély.

All the light cavalry regiments sent to Africa had been recalled to France after the taking of Abd-el-Kader. No more were sent until 1855.

On the domestic side, the regiments kept themselves completed. The remount service, created anew under the Restoration and which had flourished under the reign of Louis-Philippe, received all the attention of Louis-Napoleon's government. Since the Head of State liked horses, it was a given that the cavalry would be superbly mounted. Since he was an expert on horses and rode them well with elegance and confidence, the regiments quickly became magnificent. Moreover, the Emperor's nephew needed to exhibit serious military inclinations in order to achieve his political schemes. His name and his coming to power were a guarantee for the army

Cuirassiers, Imperial Guard (1859).

to whom he promised not only the rebuilding of its prestige but also possibly a European war. It cannot be too often repeated: an enormous, well organized army which does not want war loses a bit of its value every year. As soon as the officers and the soldiers allow themselves to fall into bourgeois habits, military spirit is lost little by little and cannot be easily regained. The enthusiasm which had welcomed the hope of war in 1841 and the zealousness put into prepartions which ended in nothing were an indication for the president of the Republic.

Thus he encouraged rumors which spread through the army with regard to his warlike nature. The cavalry was perhaps the service that was the most receptive.

(1) On March 12 and 14, 1849, the 6th Regiment of Chasseurs à cheval had been mandated to Paris to provide administrative orders and mounted orderlies to the numerous public administrations residing there. On March 17, the provisional government, responding to the objections of some Club members and some popularity-seeking newspapers, made the regiment leave quickly for fear that its presence would provoke disturbances.

SECOND EMPIRE

◆

Under the Second Empire, the cavalry, like the rest of the army, experienced two phases: a rising period from 1852 to 1861 and a falling off from 1861 to 1870. It hardly showed dedication under all circumstances and did not always present a good appearance. However, at the end of the first half of the first Imperial period, a certain satisfaction took over in the large general staffs. In the second half, budgetary considerations led to the elimination of the sixth squadrons in the regiments of reserve cavalry, dragoons and lancers; of two regiments of heavy cavalry; and finally, to a decrease in effectives of those corps and squadrons which were retained.

Under the presidency, as was just noted, the cavalry had been very pampered. Even though his best *officiers d'ordonnance* and later his most influential aides-de-camp—Edgard, Ney and Fleury—belonged to the light cavalry, Napoleon III had, like all the princes, a marked preference for armored cavalry and for large horsemen and horses.

Apparently, he always had in mind the German and English regiments, the Horse Guards and the *chevaliers-gardes* that he had long ago seen on the drill-grounds of the Northern courts. The uniforms which he gave to certain privileged corps are obvious evidence of this. However, the light cavalry had attracted defenders amongst the generals of Africa. By an unusual twist of fate, all the wars of the Second Empire, the Crimean, Italian, and Mexican, provided only the light cavalry with the opportunity of developing some squadrons. In addition, since they often lacked appropriate circumstances, the generals in chief of the Second Empire no longer knew how to handle or use the cavalry. They were always burdened by it, especially in the last war.

In the early months of 1852, the desire to form an Imperial Guard arose in the new Emperor. This had been heavily pressed for by his entourage. However, the cavalry committee, composed of general officers who had always served in the regiments, considered that the seven year service (actually five years and ten months) was not leaving enough elite horsemen in the ranks. It was thus not possible to suddenly remove a sizeable number. As cavalry replacements were simple soldiers (otherwise they were sent to the Chasseurs d'Afrique) the regiments offered few resources for an Imperial Guard. Its formation was thus studied by the Minister of War—Marshal Saint-Arnaud—apart from and almost without the knowledge of the committees of the services. Colonel Fleury was impatient to command an elite regiment for the cavalry. Two guides squadrons were gathered into a single corps by the decision of January 21, 1852 and re-outfitted in a uniform recalling the First Empire. It became the nucleus of a regiment of guides which took into the regiment the set of regiments of the line (October 23, 1852.) At the same time, the 13th Regiment of Chasseurs was disbanded.

The new regiment was formed at six squadrons although all the other regiments had only five. The credit of its colonel, the choice of officers assigned there, and the excellent remount service which was awarded him suffice to indicate the role which was reserved for the colonel. However, although this formation did not seem to be the result of obvious special favors for those who were included therein, it annoyed the army. It was discovered that nothing motivated it and that the reestablishment of an Imperial Guard had to have a more serious basis for being than the whim of the friends of the Head of State. Planned projects were placed on hold until the moment to take them up again was supplied by the War of the Orient.

Carabinier trumpeter, Imperial Guard (1870).

On April 20, 1854, an imperial decree had expanded all the regiments of the line cavalry to six squadrons. Promotion in the lower ranks received such a boost that everywhere the lists of proposed candidates had been renewed and depleted once again. The other services had obtained similar favors. There was a general headiness, and this time the project of reestablishing the Guard, which was to further increase the satisfaction of the army, was well received. Naturally, the guides regiment obtained an official rank which it already held in the eyes of the public.

A regiment of cuirassiers was created from a number of troops (May 1, 1854). Thus, the cavalry was going to count for something, thanks to these increases.

Imperial Guard: 2 regiments .... 12 squadrons (Cuirassiers and Guides)
Army of the Line: 52 regiments .... 312 squadrons (72 of reserve cavalry, 120 of line cavalry, 120 of light cavalry)
Army of Africa: 7 regiments .... 56 squadrons (regiments of Chasseurs d'Afrique were expanded to 8 squadrons on June 27, 1855)
Total .... 380 squadrons (18 of reserve cavalry, 126 of line cavalry, 176 of light cavalry)

Crimean Campaign. The early composition of the Army of the Orient included only two cavalry brigades: the First Chasseurs d'Afrique, 1st Regiment (Colonel de Ferrabouc), 2nd Regiment (Colonel Coste de Champéron), under the command of General d'Allonville. The second, commanded by General Cassaignolles, was attached to the reserve: 6th Cuirassiers (Colonel Salle), 6th Dragoons (Colonel de Plas).

However, it was quickly realized that this first organization was much too elementary. Little by little, ten regiments of cavalry whose distribution has just been given, made their way to the Army of the Orient. Previously, there was an attempt to assemble some corps of *bachi-bouzoucks*, a type of light cavalryman, under the name of "Spahis of the Orient." General Yusuf, arriving from Algeria, took command of this corps. However, although many energetic officers were put at his disposal, he could never get anything out of this oriental riffraff. It was a true collection of the dregs of all the neighboring peoples. They were noteworthy only for the assassination of some officers and the pillaging of some magazines. They were mustered out a short time after they were gathered.

In the Crimea, Marshal de Saint-Arnaud, due to lack of space on the transport ships, brought only some Chasseurs d'Afrique; a squadron from the 1st Regiment and some Spahis. The Battle of Alma could not be finished because of this lack of cavalry.

The primary concern of Saint-Arnaud's successor was to very quickly form the Allonville Brigade (1st and 4th Chasseurs d'Afrique) and to have Feray's Brigade arrive (4th Hussars and 6th Dragoons). They formed a division under the command of General Morris.

The Allonville Brigade participated in the Battle of Balaclava. The 4th Chasseurs d'Afrique lost 10 men there, including 2 officers. They also had 28 wounded while relieving the cavalry (which was rather compromised by Lord Cardigan) in an opportune and deftly led charge.

On November 5, 1854 (Battle of Inkermann) almost the entire Morris Division had arrived in the Crimea. It was barely engaged during this day.

On May 20, 1855 the entire cavalry which would be part of the Army of the Orient until the end of the war had arrived in the Crimea. It was composed as shown at right:

> DIVISION attached to the 1st Corps (DE SALLES)
> General of division MORRIS
>
> 1st Brigade: General CASSAIGNOLES
> 1st Chasseurs d'Afrique Regiment, Col. de Ferrabouc
> 3rd Chasseurs d'Afrique Regiment, Col. de Mézange de Saint-André
>
> 2nd Brigade: General FERAY
> 2nd Chasseurs d'Afrique Regiment, Col. de Jourdan
> 3rd Chasseurs d'Afrique Regiment, Col. de Cavigny
>
> DIVISION attached to the 2nd Corps (BOSQUET)
> General of division D'ALLONVILLE
>
> 1st Brigade, General VALSIN-ESTERHAZY
> 1st Hussar Regiment, Colonel Lion
> 4th Hussar Regiment, Colonel Simon de la Mortière
>
> 2nd Brigade, General COSTE DE CHAMPERON
> 6th Dragoon Regiment, Colonel Ressayre
> 7th Dragoon Regiment, Colonel Duhesme
>
> BRIGADE attached to the Reserve Corps
> (REGNAULT DE SAINT JEAN D'ANGÉLY)
> General of brigade DE FORTON
> 6th Cuirassier Regiment, Colonel Crespin
> 9th Cuirassier Regiment, Colonel de La Martinière

Famous names of the cavalry (1830-1859).

Hussars of the 8th regiment, full dress (1859).

The role of this cavalry, always maintained at regulation effective strength of 550 to 600 horses, was confined during the entire campaign to reconnaissance around the siege corps and to service as scouts and as an escort. It did not even have the chance to engage in battle at Tchernaia (August 14, 1855). On the days the cavalry was under arms or on the assault it had ridden, but it had never fought in any battle. On September 20, a few days after the taking of Malakoff, General d'Allonville was sent with three regiments from his division (4th Hussars, 6th and 7th Dragoons) to Eupatoria which was occupied by Ottoman troops under the command of Ahmed Pasha. On the 29th, the general left this city with a Turkish contingent, his division and the 3rd Battery of the 15th Mounted Artillery. He attacked General Korff's division of cavalry at Kanghil. The 4th Hussars took two cannon from the enemy. In the pursuit, the 6th Dragoons, supported by the 7th, took four other cannon. This combat, energetically conducted, brought the greatest of honor to the French regiments.

The War of the Orient was the occasion for a minor shift of cavalry largely ignored by the public. On January 18, 1856, half of the 1st Squadron of the 2nd Dragoons left for Greece.

There it was used for a year under the command of Captain de Moucheron to keep bandits under control.

The Peace of Paris signaled a partial decrease in the line corps and a considerable increase in the cavalry of the Imperial Guard. On December 20, 1855 it had been decided that the Guard would be expanded to 6 regiments at 6 squadrons each (2 of cuirassiers, 1 of dragoons, 1 of lancers, 1 of chasseurs and 1 of guides). However, the organization of four new regiments was only to proceed when the minister of war judged it appropriate. A major role in these new formations was to be given to the officers, non-commissioned officers, and horsemen of the Crimean regiments. At the same time, it was thought this could not be done without destroying their strength to some extent. On April 5, 1856, the 4th Chasseurs d'Afrique, who were intended to provide the foundation of the Chasseurs of the Guard, were mustered out. On the following May 23rd, the 7th and 8th Squadrons formed the previous year in the three other regiments met with the same fate. On May 4, the 9th Hussars had also been disbanded. The increase of the 24 squadrons of the Imperial Guard was thus in part compensated for by the elimination of 14 squadrons of Chasseurs d'Afrique and 6 of hussars. The French cavalry found itself with 384 squadrons, four more than at the beginning of the war.

It is astonishing that while the infantry had only a little less than a sixteenth of its cadres in the Guard, the proportion of cavalry came to more than a tenth in the same corps. It is hardly worthwhile investigating the cause of this disproportion, be it in memories of the First Empire or in the influence of a favorite aide-de-camp. The government especially wanted to encourage the cavalry officers to stay in the service. The habit of returning to civilian life as soon as the captain's epaulettes were won had already taken root in this branch of the service and was emptying its ranks. In order to try to overcome this fashion, an entire cavalry division was maintained at Versailles. Thus there were twelve cavalry regiments in the capital and its surroundings, including the Guard. This was approximately a fifth of the service. For the cavalry officers, to be in Paris or on campaign had become a type of necessity. Thus, most of the time, three regiments of light cavalry were sent to Algeria which allowed for detaching some squadrons of Chasseurs d'Afrique to Syria and Mexico. This brought the number of cavalry regiments on a wartime footing to ten (four Chasseurs d'Afrique—the 4th Regiment mustered out in 1856 was reestablished in 1865—three of Spahis and three of hussars and chasseurs), that is ten out of 65. As can be seen, a third of the service had very desirable garrisons and in some ways privileged ones. A fine cavalry would never be possible without these conditions. The basic principles of good recruiting for superior officers were only maintained by taking the most meticulous measures. It is worth mentioning that despite the formation of the Guards, the cavalry which counted 61 regiments at the time of the February Revolution had only four more in 1870: sixty-five. However it was increased to 78 squadrons.

Dragoon officer, maneuver dress (1885).

Lancers of the line (1858).

After the Crimean campaign, thanks to energetic efforts during three years of work in the Guards and in the line, all the regiments were magnificent and all the horses in good condition. Although the formation of 36 elite squadrons would deplete the corps of the line, it received a major compensation in the form of the old soldiers which the law of exoneration kept in their ranks.

The year 1859 found the French cavalry in excellent condition. This could be be seen in the report of January 1st which announced, for the line alone, 53,489 horsemen present in the ranks and 18,688 belonging to the classes of 1852, 1853, and 1854 at home on renewable leave. So wealthy in terms of manpower was the cavalry that it could relinquish a number of men to the artillery. Only horses had to be bought, but those who were in the regiments suffered initially. The assembling of mounted troops for the five corps of the Army of Italy consequently did not encounter any serious difficulties. The regiments designated to participate in a campaign and those that stayed in France could very easily mobilize their four full war squadrons at 550 to 600 horses without having to resort to those borrowings from corps to corps which are so harmful to the discipline and the solidarity of the troops. Below is the list of regiments which were attached to the Army of Italy:

Army Corps	Divisions	Brigade number	Name of the general of brigade	Regimental number and name of the colonel
Imperial Guard	MORRIS	1st	MARION	1st Cuirassier Regiment, Colonel Ameil; 2nd Cuirassier Regiment, Colonel de la Martiniére.
		2nd	CHAMPERON	Dragoon Regiment, Colonel Crespin; Lancer Regiment, Colonel Lichtlin.
		3rd	CASSAIGNOLES	Chasseur Regiment, Colonel de Cauvigny; Guides Regiment, Colonel de Mirandol.
1st	DESVAUX	1st	GENESTET DE PLANHOL	5th Hussars, Colonel Montaigu; 1st Chasseurs of Africa, Colonel de Salignac-Fénelon.
		2nd	DE FORTON	2nd Chasseurs of Africa, Colonel de Brémond d'Ars; 3rd Chasseurs of Africa, Colonel de Mézange.
2nd	—	—	GAUDIN DE VILLAINE	4th Chasseur Regiment, Colonel de Montfort; 7th Chasseur Regiment, Colonel Savaresse.
3rd	PARTOUNEAUX	1st	DE CLÉREMBAULT	2nd Hussar Regiment, Colonel Lhuilliers; 7th Hussar Regiment, Colonel de Lacombe.
		2nd	DE LABAREYRE	1st Lancer Regiment, Colonel Martin de Boulancy, 4th Lancer Regiment, Colonel de Piquet de Vignolles de Juillac.
4th	—	—	RICHEPANCE	2nd Chasseur Regiment, Colonel Lepic; 10th Chasseur Regiment, Colonel Arbellot.
5th	—	—	DE LA PÉROUSE	6th Hussar Regiment, Colonel Valabrègue; 8th Hussar Regiment, Colonel de Fontenoy.

The corps with 3 divisions of infantry commanded by the marshals had one division of cavalry. The others had only a brigade. Labareyre's Brigade (1st and 4th Lancers) had at first been attached to the 5th Corps. However, as it was late in arriving and as Prince Napoleon—who was charged with a separate mission more political than military —needed its cavalry, a transfer was ordered between this brigade and that commanded by General de la Pérouse. General de Richepance had been named General of division and was replaced by General de Rochefort in the 4th Corps.

Six of these regiments came from Africa: the three Chasseurs d'Afrique, the 4th and 7th Chasseurs, and the 5th Hussars. Together with these, the ten others of the line and the six of the Guard formed a total of twenty-two regiments or eighty-eight squadrons perfectly suited to the various needs of the campaign. A number never even saw the enemy and many arrived at the army to participate only in the Battle of Solferino . There Desvaux's Division and the majority of Partouneaux's Division distinguished themselves with glorious and useful charges. At Magenta, only the Gaudin de Villaine Brigade had taken part in the operations. It was especially during this campaign that one can note how the generals in chief neglected to make use of their cavalry.

After the conclusion of the preliminaries of the Peace of Villafranca, a cavalry division was left in Lombardy with the occupation corps. It was composed of General de Rochefort's brigade of chasseurs (2nd and 10th) and of General de La Perouse's brigade of hussars (6th and 8th). They remained without a division leader under the command of their respective generals.

As in the infantry, a complete organization into divisions was ordered for the cavalry regiments. It was much less strict than for the infantry. The problem of quartering in barracks confronted the actual assembly of more than four divisions. Of the four divisions attached to the Observation Army of the East (Marshal Pélissier), the first two were formed from regiments of heavy cavalry scattered through the garrisons of Alsace and Lorraine. The 3rd Division of Cavalry of the Line was at Lunéville and the 4th of Light Cavalry was in the camp of Châlons. The Army of Paris (Marshal Magnan) also had four divisions, but only the first was assembled. It was comprised of three brigades and six regiments from garrisons in Paris and from Versailles. The other regiments used in the first great military command had been assigned to the three other divisions. Finally, at Lyon in the camp of Sathonay and in the surroundings, a division of dragoons formed the cavalry of the army of Marshal Castellane. These thirty-eight regiments, the eleven attached to the various army corps of the Army of Italy and three recently sent to Africa, gave the total of the service. The depots, overflowing with men and horses, occupied the garrisons usually assigned to the cavalry. This left free the mobilization of the army operating in the plains of Lombardy. It bears repeating: this organization was not solid, but it was better than the dispersal ordered immediately after peace.

Perhaps the French cavalry, which will be seen to decline little by little, was supported by keeping this formation into divisions. However, this was more of an outward display than a reality. The problems created within the French mounted troops by a long peace in the second part of Louis-Philippe's reign have already been stated. The need to economize on a tool which seemed useless along with the need for budgetary equilibrium little by little wore down and destroyed the most solid military organizations. Thus it is appropriate to mark the high point of the French cavalry under the Second Empire in the years 1855 to 1859: that is to say, the period which extends from the War of the Orient to the Italian campaign. If the regiments took too much time to rejoin their army corps in 1859, they should not be taken to task. The fault lay rather with the means of communication which were not what they are today. When one considers that all the designated cavalry regiments contained a sufficient number of trained horsemen, well mounted on excellent horses, all having at least five years in the service, that

they could easily put together four fine line squadrons wihout asking for help from neighboring regiments or for a hasty remount, one is forced to recognize that Minister Randon who followed Minister Vaillant brought the death blow to the French military system. The service was certainly directed by strong and distinguished general officers and colonels. However it was overly subject to rules and instructions which had not been drawn up by the most pratical military cavalrymen. It seemed that two careers with the same advantages were open to great leaders: the committee of the service or active command. These two careers, absolutely opposed to the interests and goals which they pursued, had perpetrated an antagonism which was met with everywhere, at all levels of the hierarchy: in the regiments, in the offices, and even in the court. The Emperor, full of good intentions, very open, very desirous of doing the right thing, unfortunately was under the influence of persons for whom a military career was only a means for political ends. It was possible to achieve one's goal outside the rules and to make one's way based on appearances alone. The sovereign had personally commanded a sort of march to the front which, though glorious, was fairly easy. He succumbed to private illusions after the campaign of Italy and was overly encouraged in this. He returned from a war whose proposed objective he had not achieved because he had met insurmountable obstacles. At first he did not conceal the importance of this. He admitted it in the speech which he made at Saint-Cloud in responding to the congratulations of the great corps of the State. However, he did nothing to mitigate the problems, and was surprised by the thunderbolt of Sadowa. The failures of 1870 had deep roots which went back almost ten years. It had been necessary to prepare against the Russians for eighteen months before wielding a decisive blow against them. The Italian campaign, where much less lengthy preparations had been rapidly made with the time and means available, had been clearly cut off by a fledgling coalition more diplomatic than military. This was due to lack of numerous and solid reserves. Therein lay a double warning to which it was convenient to submit.

Under the Empire, the cavalry did not always have full rest periods. Every year, from 1858 on, four, five and even up to seven regiments formed into two or three brigades and went for training at the camp of Châlons. In 1868 and 1869 there were even two sets. Thus, in the thirteen final years of the Empire, after deducting the years when the camp was reserved for the Imperial Guard, seventy regiments passed through the plains of Châlons. This means that many regiments must have returned once or twice. The cavalry was kept sufficiently busy with Africa and the war campaigns, with Lunéville, Sathonay and Versailles. It never lost the habit of forming groups. It found itself on numerous occasions in contact with the infantry and the artillery and knew how it must and could assist them, once given the chance. However, I have heard it said twenty times: the cavalry colonels regretted that the marshals or the generals of division, who usually presided over the military events of Châlons, very often forgot that they had a division of mounted troops under their command on days when a great battle was simulated. Generally they only remembered this at the time of the defile. Then an aide-de-camp left at a gallop to order the cavalry to move into action. The military newspapers or the press—that nuisance of publicity—praised in unison the cavalry's fine dress. The habit of joining the three combat services together as one was not held in much esteem. The great leaders had rushed down a disgraceful path. Despite the best infantrymen in the world who were lacking only in number, despite cavalrymen full of eagerness and courage who asked only to do their best, France ended up in an unprecedented defeat. The French heavy cavalry regiments had been sacrificed in charges without any possible gain. The light cavalry was not required to perform the services which it was capable of executing. This was due to the leadership imparted to them. How could it have been otherwise? A general of brigade could become general of division, commander in chief, or marshal without having left his own branch of the service or having handled the other services. The commanders in chief of Châlons were generally infantrymen dating back to the sieges of Sebastopol and Italy. In those cases, the cavalry had had no role; the officers of the special arms and forces had

Cuirassiers, dragoons and chasseurs à cheval (1859).

kept to their own specialties. At last it has been understood that a general in chief must know everything, but this understanding has come too late. It is certain that the major causes of the French disappointments in 1870 were caused more by the French generals in chief than by the inadequacy of the means put at their disposal. The cavalry of Formach, Reichshoffen, Sedan and Metz could have been put to better use.

From 1860 to 1866, the expeditions of Syria, China and Mexico had caused deterioration in the cavalry's status through the organizational tendencies that were introduced there. A *régiment de marche* commanded by Lieutenant Colonel Du Preuil from the 1st Regiment of Chasseurs d'Afrique and composed of two squadrons from this regiment (4th and 5th), of a squadron from the 2nd Spahi, and of one from the 1st Hussars (the 1st) took part in the Syrian expedition.(1) For the China expedition, only a few brilliant cavalry officers joined the headquarters(2). Their mission was to assemble—if they needed them —auxiliary cavalrymen in place, using local resources and men from the expeditionary corps. For Mexico, the hope was to manage as in China. However, the extent of the theater and of the battle quickly forced a change in this plan of action. At first the expedition began with a platoon of Chasseurs d'Afrique commanded by Second Lieutenant Paploré. It subsequently required many more squadrons, then a brigade of two *régiments de marche*, then one of three regiments. One wonders today how the Empire—which had not been hampered by a preconceived plan for mobilization—took recourse in the disgraceful system of *régiments de marche*. It was free to detach entire regiments of Chasseurs d'Afrique and to stop replacing them in the French colony with regiments of hussars or French chasseurs. Evidently one thought guided the Empire. That was the weakness of the effective

Sergeants of the guides, and chasseurs à cheval, Imperial Guard (1859).

strengths and the remounts, which became more and more meager. This situation did not permit mobilization of four squadrons from a regiment counting six hundred sabers.

It was only in 1854 that regiments of light cavalry were again sent to Algeria. The 7th Hussars—Colonel Grenier—left first and did not return to France until 1858. With the four regiments of Chasseurs d'Afrique having been sent in succession to the Crimea, the 4th Chasseurs—Colonel de Montfort, the 5th Hussars—Colonels de Brancion then de Montaigu, and the 7th Chasseurs—Colonel Savaresse, were charged with replacing them. In 1859, these three latter regiments had been included in the Army of Italy. Three other regiments were called upon to replace them: 1st Chasseurs—Colonel de Bernis, 8th Chasseurs—Colonels de Vignolle then Rigau, and the 12th Chasseurs—Colonel de Bonnemains. From this time on, replacement was made methodically in a manner which established a rotation in the service of the chasseurs and the hussars. The regiments left, complete with their depots, the horsemen being unmounted. They were remounted in Algeria and returned to France bringing with them Arabian horses.

In 1861, the 1st and the 8th Chasseurs returned to France and the 12th left for Mexico. They were replaced by the 3rd Chasseurs—Colonels d'Espinassy de Venel then Hainglaise, the 11th Chasseurs—Colonels Grandvalet then Nérat, and the 3rd Husasars—Colonel Tilliard.

From 1864 and 1865 to 1867, 1868, and 1869, they were succeeded by the 4th Chasseurs—Colonels de Francq then Bachelier, the 1st Hussars—Colonel de Lajaille, and the 6th

(1) Below is the composition of the expeditionary corps of Syria which was barely touched upon in the preceding discussion.

Commander in Chief: General of Division de Beaufort d'Hautpoul; *Aide-de-Camp:* Captain Marquerie; *Officier d'Ordonnance:* Le Mintier d; Saint-Andre, lieutenant of the 8th Hussars; *Chief of General Staff:* Colonel Osmont; *Adjutants:* Major Boyer, Captains Gélis, Seigland and de Champlouis; *Commander of Artillery:* Major Rayne; *Adjutant:* Captain Bornéque; *Commander of Engineers:* Captain Servel; *Director of the Artillery Park and of Engineering:* Captian Clerc; *Political Department Head:* Lieutenant Colonel Chanzy (from the 71st of the line); *Adjutants:* Major Cerez (1st Battalion of Algerian Tirailleurs); Moch, Captain in the 69th; *Provost Marshal:* Lieutenant of the Gendarmerie Raymond; *Interpreters:* Goert and Chidiat; *Treasury and Post:* Louet; *Administrative Services:* Chief Intendant Mony; *Adjutants:* Audemard and Chassigner;; *Administrative Officers:* Guerard (*hospitals*), Boursier (*provisions*), Villereal (*encampment*).

INFANTRY	CAVALRY	ARTILLERY	ENGINEERS
General of Brigade Ducrot	Lieutenant Colonel du Preuil,	5th Battery of the 1st Regiment: Captain Farcy	6th Company of the 2nd Battalion of the 2nd
16th Battalion of Chasseurs à pied: Commander Ardant du Pic	(1st Chasseurs of Africa)	1st Battery of the 10th Regiment: Captain Guyot	Regiment: Captain Dupuy
5th of the line (1st and 2nd Battalions): Commander	1st Hussars (1st Squadron): Major Stockly	1st Company *bis* of the 1st Squadron of the Train:	
de Laguigneraye	2nd Spahis (1st Squadron): Major Tascher	Captain Bourgeois	
13th of the line (1st and 2nd Battalions): Commander Darricau	de la Pagerie		
1st Zouaves (1st Battalion): Major Lian	1st Chasseurs of Africa: (5th Squadron,		
	Captain de Nattes); (6th Squadron,		
	Captain de Montarby).		

PARKS AND ADMINISTRATIVE TROOPS

Detachment of the 6th Company of administrative workers: Lieutenant Panon; 3rd Company *bis* of the 3rd Squadron of the Train: Captain Fontaine; detachment of the 1st Company *bis* of the 2nd Squadron. Detachment of the 4th, 11th, and 15th Sections of administrative workers (commanded by Adjutant Goichot).

(2) Reboul, inactive major; Cousin de Montauban, Captain of the 2nd Lancers; Mocquard, Captain of the 2nd Spahis; De Damas, Lieutenant of the 2nd Chasseurs of Africa; De Neverlée, Second Lieutenant of the 1st Regiment of Cuirassiers; Mohamed-Ould-Caid-Osman, Second Lieutenant of the 2nd Spahis. Commander Rebout, who spoke English quite well, was attached to the general headquarters of the English Army. Captain Cousin de Montauban remained attached to his father as *officier d'ordonnance*. With a lot of trouble but a great deal of intelligence, Captain Mocquard, remaining as head of the cavalry, organized a squadron which performed useful services. It was composed of volunteer cavalrymen taken from numerous regiments along with infantrymen and artillerymen from the expeditionary corps

Officer, Empress' Dragoons Regiment, campaign dress (1859).

Chasseurs—Colonels de Maubranche then Bonvoust.

Finally, when the War of 1870 broke out, the 1st Chasseurs—Colonel Gérard, the 9th Chasseurs—Colonel Cousin, and the 8th Hussars—Colonel Charlemagne, were deployed in the French possessions in Africa. Let us return to the campaign of Mexico.

In June 1864, the status of the cavalry of the expeditionary corps gives 2,449 men of whom 2,206 were present in the ranks. They were distributed in the following manner:

Commander: Colonel De Lascours, having his general headquarters in Mexico, replacing General Du Barail who returned to France.

1st *régiment de marche* (1st and 3rd regiments of Chasseurs d'Afrique): Colonel de Lascours, 2 squadrons at San Luis Potosi; 1 squadron at Puebla, 2 squadrons at Queretaro (detachments to the counter-guerillas, partisans, remount, etc.)

2nd *régiment de marche* (2nd Chasseurs d'Afrique and 5th Hussars): Colonel Petit, 4 squadrons at Mexico and detachments in the neighboring cantonments.

12th Regiment of Chasseurs: Colonel du Preuil, 3 squadrons at Guadalajara and environs; 1 squadron at Lacatecas.

In addition, a number of French officers and non-commissioned officers were detached to the counter-guerillas of Tampico and of Tamaulipas whom Colonel Dupin of the general staff commanded.

The expedition of Mexico found the French cavalrymen as capable as ever at all tasks set before them. There the cavalry from Africa could put to good use their reputed qualities of speed and helpfulness. Although they waged war with more glory than results, the cavalry service had suffered a terrible cutback. Despite events which took place along the coast of Denmark and whose outcome was not difficult to foresee, the financial situation required economizing. In September 1865, major deletions were decreed for the cavalry.(1)

The two regiments of carabiniers were merged into a single one and replaced the 2nd Cuirassiers of the Imperial Guard which had been disbanded.

The six squadrons of cuirassiers, dragoons and lancers of the line were mustered out.

Total: elimination of 42 cavalry squadrons.

It was almost a crime, given the condition in which Europe found itself, but this did not overly concern the financiers. This elimination of 42 squadrons out of 386 was equal to a seventh of the acting effective strength of the cavlary. The cut-backs in the remounts were such that the five remaining squadrons in each of the thirty reserve and line regiments did not become more compact. They were determined not to spend money, and the Emperor was unhappily surprised when they were forced to tell him the truth. There was, however, no time to react. The reign of authority was over, succeeded by parliamentarianism. Marshal Niel, despite his ardent wish, could not obtain an increase in the cavalry cadres. The law of recruitment which was voted to him unwillingly gave him fewer immediately available men than there had been in 1859 for the campaign of Italy. As was said then, it was a future law which would reach its full effect in 1878. The marshal also tried unsuccessfully to make the general staff of the cavalry understand that, with the Dreyse rifle and the chassepot, the huge charges of Montbrun and Murat could no longer be made. They would lead to disaster for those requested to make them by ignorant leaders. Instead, the theories of Lasale, Curely, and de Brack should to be taken up again. Marshal Niel had neither the time nor the authority to return the French cavalry to good condition in terms of both

(1) The occupation of Rome and of the Pontifical States had necessitated some transfers in the cavalry, but they were of limited importance. After the departure of the 1st Chasseurs and the 41st Dragoons, the occupation corps had fallen little by little to the status of a brigade of infantry. The events which followed the Italian campaign revived the Roman question. The French troops in the Pontifical States had to be increased. In 1862, there were two divisions of infantry in Rome and its surroundings. Two squadrons of 4th Hussars (the 1st and 2nd) were assigned there and comprised the entire cavalry of the corps. Then the occupation was once again reduced. It ceased altogether when Victor-Emmanuel guaranteed the security of the Papal States—now reduced to the enclave of Saint Peter's—with the agreement of September 15. However, in November 1867, the King of Italy declared himself incapable of protecting the Pope against the attempts of Garibaldi. The responsibility of seeing that the agreement was respected fell upon France. A French army corps embarked in great haste from Toulon. It was followed by a brigade of chasseurs à cheval: General of Brigade de France: 3rd Chasseurs, Colonel Sanson de Sansal; 7th Chasseurs, Colonel Thornton. When the Roman region had been cleared of the bands which plagued it—and this was done quickly—the 3rd Chasseurs returned and only the 2 squadrons of the 7th remained. They were recalled in July 1870. The rest is well-known: the Holy See, who survived only with French support, had to submit to the Italian monarchy.

Lancer officer, Imperial Guard, undress (1859).

training and effective strength. This is not to say that some distinguished generals did not quarrel openly with their colleagues of the committee. However, their influence was offset by the defenders of formal maneuvers, of predominating marches, and of brigade charges by division or even by army corps.

The French cavalry thus found itself reduced to 330 squadrons (excluding Spahis) at the moment when possibilities of war were feared. This was a war which the foresight of Rouher and Lavalette had avoided at the time of the Luxembourg and Saint-Gothard affairs. A good quarter of the cavalry could not be mounted, at least not immediately. The budget did not allow for anything better. The cavalry music sections had been eliminated in 1867 in order to return some horses to the squadrons. Finally, there were such drastic cutbacks and such a strong desire to completely bind the hands of those in power so that they could not respond to the threatening and almost inevitable war, that Thiers asked for and obtained from Émile Ollivier a reduction of 10,000 men in the annual contingent His exact words were: "While his opinions were established on the ministers' benches ..." These are the facts which cannot be passed over in silence in the history of a service where regiments are not instantaneously improvised.

When the War of 1870 broke out, France was less ready militarily than in 1859, However, she already possessed the rolling stock of the railroad. This allowed for rapid transport of available French forces along the borders while waiting for reserves.(1)

The first act of the government was to reform the sixth squadrons in the thirty regiments which had only five (August 26, 1870). This hasty formation at the moment of entry into a campaign was yet one more obstacle to the solidity of the regiments. The promotions which it required, made by choice and seniority throughout the service, obstructed the routes of majors, captains, lieutenants and second lieutenants on their way to their new posts. It is difficult to get an idea of such disorganization at a moment when the officers should have had no other concern than making their regiments more homogenous and solid.

From the beginning of the war, thanks to the negligence and imprudence at the highest levels, thanks to budgetary cut-backs for which all political parties should bear responsibility, the war administration had to resort to three measures which indicate the complete weakness of an army: hurried purchases of horses too young and untrained; transfer of all the gendarmerie's mounts suitable for war service; creation of *régiments de marche* and changes in the personnel of permanent regiments.

It is proper to say that France was defeated before it had collected itself.

Hussar, color sergeant (1870-1871).

(1) In addition, the strength of the regiments was quite uneven. In the rare regimental histories printed and made available to the public, complete and exact information has been found for the 2nd Cuirassiers: 543 men and 503 horses; the 7th Cuirassiers: 553 men and 500 horses; the 3rd Lancers: 482 men and 429 horses. The light cavalry seemed to have been better distributed; the 3rd Chasseurs à cheval left with 687 men and was joined by its 5th squadron.

Régiments de marche, mixed, cavalry (1870-1871).

WAR OF 1870

With the declaration of war, the cavalry was distributed in the following manner:

Army Corps	Divisions	Brigade number	Name of the general of brigade	Regimental number and name of the colonel
Imperial Guard	DESVAUX	1st	HALNA DU FRETAY	Guides, Colonel Percin-Northumberlan; Chasseurs Colonel de Montarby.
		2nd	DE FRANCE	Lancers, Colonel de Lalheulade; Dragoons, Colonel Sautereau-Dupart.
		3rd	DU PREUIL	Cuirassiers, Colonel Petit; Carabiniers, Colonel Dupressoir.
1st	DUHESME	1st	DE SEPTEUIL	3rd Hussars, Colonel de Viel d'Espeuilles; 11th Chasseurs, Colonel Dastugue.
		2nd	DE NANSOUTY	10th Dragoons, Colonel Perrot; 2nd Lancers, Colonel Poissonnier, later Maillart de Landreville; 6th Lancers, Colonel Tipart
3rd		3rd	MICHEL	8th Cuirassiers, Colonel Guyot de la Rochère; 9th Cuirassiers, Colonel Waternau, later de Vouges de Chanteclair.
2nd	LICHTLIN	1st	DE VALABBEGUE	4th Chasseurs, Colonel du Ferron; 5th Chasseurs, Colonel Gombaud de Séréville.
		2nd	BACHELIER	7th Dragoons, Colonel de Gressot; 12th Dragoons, Colonel de Tucé.
3rd	CLÉREMBAULT	1st	DE BRUCHARD	2nd Chasseurs, Colonel Pelletier; 3rd Chasseurs, Colonel Sanson de Sansal; 10th Chasseurs, Colonel Nérin.
		2nd	DE MAUBRANCHES	2nd Dragoons, Colonel Mercier du Paty de Clam; 4th Dragoons, Colonel Cornat.
		3rd	DE JUNIAC	5th Dragoons, Colonel Euchène; 8th Dragoons, Colonel de Boyer de Fonscolombe.
4th	LEGRAND	1st	DE MONTAIGU	2nd Hussars, Colonel Carrelet, 7th Hussars, Colonel Chausée.
		2nd	DE GONDRECOURT	3rd Dragoons, Colonel Bilhau; 11th Dragoons, Colonel Huyn de Verneville.
5th	BRAHAULT	1st	DE BERNIS	5th Hussars, Colonel Flogny (1); 12th Chasseurs, Colonel de Tucé, later de la Porte.
		2nd	DE LA MORTIERE	3rd Lancers, Colonel Torel; 5th Lancers, Colonel Boerio, later Gayraud.
6th	DE SALIGNAC-FÉNELON	1st	TILLIARD	1st Hussars, Colonel de Beauffremont; 6th Chasseurs, Colonel Bonvoust.
		2nd	SAVARESSE	1st Lancers, Colonel Oudinot; 7th Lancers, Colonel Perier.
		3rd	DE BEVILLE	5th Cuirassiers, Colonel du Bessy de Contenson; 6th Cuirassiers, Colonel Martin.
7th	AMEIL	1st	CAMBRIEL	4th Hussars, Colonel Choury de la Vigerie, later Cousin-Montauban; 4th Lancers, Colonel Féline; 8th Lancers, Colonel Duval de Dampierre.
		2nd	JOLIF-DUCOULOMBIER	6th Hussars, Colonel Guillon, later de Ligniéres; 6th Dragoons, Colonel Tillion, later Fombert de Villers.
CAVALRY RESERVE	1st Division, DU BARAIL	1st	MARGUERITTE	1st Chasseurs of Africa, Colonel Clicquot; 3rd Chasseurs of Africa, Colonel de Galliffet.
		2nd	DE LAJAILLE	2nd Chasseurs of Africa, Colonel de la Martinière; 4th Chasseurs of Africa, Colonel de Quelen.
	2nd Division, BONNEMAINS	1st	GIRARD	1st Cuirassiers, Colonel Leforestier de Vendoeuvre; 4th Cuirassiers, Colonel Billet.
		2nd	DE BRAUER	2nd Cuirassiers, Colonel Rossetti: 3rd Cuirassiers, Colonel Lafutsun de Lacarre.
	3rd Division, DE FORTON	1st	PRINCE MURAT	1st Dragoons, Colonel de Forceville; 9th Dragoons, Colonel Reboul.
		2nd	DE GRAMONT	7th Cuirassiers, Colonel Nitot; 10th Cuirassiers, Colonel Juncker.

(1) The 5th Hussars was garrisoned at Paris at the time war was declared. Its four first squadrons met the same fate as the 5th Corps. Its fifth squadron had been directed afterwards to Metz, became the escort of the commander in chief, and made itself famous during the Battle of Gravelotte by executing a brilliant charge. This example explains how certain light cavalry regiments only had four squadrons in the armies early on, while others had five squadrons.

This distribution left free, apart from the Spahis, five regiments of light cavalry: three in Africa, the 1st Chasseurs (Colonel Gérard), the 9th Chasseurs (Colonel Charreyron), and the 8th Hussars (Colonel Charlemagne). The 7th Chasseurs (Colonel Thornton, then Mieulet de Ricaumont) whose two squadrons detached to the Pontifical States were recalled, and the 8th of the same service (Colonel Jamin du Fresnay) were added to the infantry division formed at Toulouse and charged with observing the Spanish border.

The regiments organic to the divisions had not been kept together, with the exception of the de Lunéville Division and the division from the camp of Châlons. This was not the only mistake made. Many regiments lost precious time in getting underway. Instead of rapidly throwing a thick screen of cavalry along the border which would cut communications and frighten the numerous spies who for a long time had been operating boldly and impudently in the eastern provinces, the territorial general staffs were awaited with more or less patient anxiousness. France had lost three battles. The Army of Metz was completely cut off from MacMahon's army to which all the cavalry had not yet returned.

Thus, the 11th Chasseurs, shown on the above list as belonging to the Septeuil Brigade, were still in Lyon on September 4. The 5th and 6th Cuirassiers intended for the 6th Corps (Canrobert) only rejoined MacMahon's army on August 23 and had to be placed in the 12th Corps. The Jolif-Ducoulombier Brigade (6th Dragoons and 6th Hussars) did not arrive at all in the 7th Corps. The 4th Chasseurs d'Afrique also arrived late.

In the end, all the regiments which arrived on time did not meet the fate which had been assigned to them.

In the concentrated movement of the 2nd, 3rd, 4th and 6th Corps on Metz, the 6th Corps left behind its first two brigades. As was just noted, the 3rd had not yet arrived. Meanwhile, the 3rd Lancers belonging to the 5th Corps were driven back on Metz. Finally the 1st and 3rd Chasseurs d'Afrique, while escorting the Emperor from Metz to Verdun, had been pushed back from the side of the army which formed around the camp of Châlons. These various circumstances determined the revisions in the organization of the brigades of the divisions:

1. First, to give a cavalry division to General du Barrail, who had only the 2nd Chasseurs d'Afrique under his command at Metz, then to the 6th Corps who had no cavalry at all, the de Bruchard Brigade (2nd, 3rd, and 10th Chasseurs) was detached from the Clérembault Division of the 3rd Corps. A new division was formed from these three regiments joined to the 2nd Chasseurs d'Afrique.

2. In the 1st Corps, the 9th Cuirassiers were replaced in the Michel Brigade by the 10th Dragoons of the Nansouty Brigade which had no more than two regiments. The 9th had been ruined at Woerth and, having turned over its men and its usable horses to the 8th, returned to Versailles to build itself up again.

In addition to the Bonnemains Division (1st, 4th - 2nd, and 3rd Cuirassiers), three divisions had been pieced together at the army of Marshal MacMahon but with a certain amount of confusion. At first there were only two of them: the 1st, former Division of the 6th Corps which had been able to follow Marshal Canrobert to Metz and to which division its 3rd brigade was retired. The 2nd (General of Division Lichtlin) was composed of the Leforestier de Vandoeuvre Brigade (7th and 8th Chasseurs) and of the Béville Brigade (5th and 6th Cuirassiers). This latter division served as cavalry to the 12th Corps (Lebrun). However on August 20, General Margueritte, who already had under his command the 1st and 3rd Chasseurs d'Afrique (returned from Metz to Sedan) and the 4th (arrived late), was promoted to leader of the division. The Tilliard Brigade and the Salignac-Fenelon Divisions were assigned to him. On the day that circumstances gave total independence to the two commanders in chief of the Armies of Metz and of Châlons, the greatest confusion entered into French military affairs.

During the Battle of Sedan, various events allowed six regiments to get away before the total investment

Hussar officers (1870-1871).

of Marshal MacMahon's army by the German troops. This event brought the number of old regiments who escaped the capitulations to thirteen. They are listed below:

9th Cuirassiers. Having turned over its men and its horses to the 8th after the Battle of Woerth where it had been ruined, it moved back to Versailles to rebuild itself. It was part of the Reyau Division and was attached to the Army of the Loire.

6th Dragoons. At first assigned to the 7th Corps, it was kept at Lyon until the beginning of August then directed to Paris to be attached to the 13th Corps. It arrived in Paris on August 26. First sent to Versailles, it was then sent to Reims on September 1. It returned to Paris on the 8th with the 13th Corps. It was reassigned to Versailles from where it left on the 14th with the 6th Hussars and the 1st Cuirassiers de marche for the Army of the Loire.

2nd Lancers. It participated in the beginnings of the Battle of Sedan. Toward eleven in the morning, the division of cavalry of the 1st Corps was thrown back by projectiles that it tried to avoid in a wood to the north of the Illy Plateau. General Michel gathered a council of war which decided that, the battle having been lost, Mézières must be reached by walking along the Belgian border to avoid capitulation. It came to Charleville on September 1st at six in the evening and to Paris on September 7th. It reorganized at Pontivy and formed part of the Army of the Loire (15th Corps).

5th Lancers. It formed part of the 2nd Brigade of the cavalry division of the 5th Corps at the beginning of the Battle of Sedan. In the morning, General of Division Brabant, seeing the battle was lost, rallied his regiments in the woods to the north of Illy. On the 2nd it was at Vervins, on the 9th at Versailles, and on the 10th at Poitiers. It served in the Army of the Loire.

8th Lancers. Same as for the 2nd Lancers. It was reorganized at Samur. It formed part of the Army of the Loire (16th Corps).

1st Chasseurs. It arrived in Paris on September 10, coming from Algeria. It formed part of the army defending Paris.

7th Chasseurs. It participated in the Battle of Sedan, was separated from the army, could not rejoin it, crossed into Belgium, reentered France and arrived at Rocroy on September 2. It was at Versailles on the 7th and at Carcassonne on the 13th. It formed part of the 20th Corps, Army of the East.

9th Chasseurs. Same as for the 1st Chasseurs.

11th Chasseurs. Same as for the 2nd and the 6th Lancers. The 11th Chasseurs arrived at Versailles on September and at Avignon on the 12th, then was sent to the Army of the Loire.

12th Chausseurs. Same as for the 11th Chausseurs.

3rd Hussars. Same as for the 11th and 12th Chasseurs.

6th Hussars. Same as for the 6th Dragoons.

3rd Hussars. At first it remained entirely in Africa with its depot, then it was recalled to France at the beginning of December 1871. Leaving its 5th and 6th squadrons in Algeria, Colonel Lacombe, with his first four squadrons, participated in the Battle of Mans, then fell back on Mayenne and soon after was called to the Army of Versailles.

Regiment of cuirassiers (1874).

With these thirteen regiments, some returning quite damaged from their brief contact with the enemy, the Empire left other cavalry resources. On August 26, the formation of a 6th squadron in the 30 reserve and line regiments was ordered. General Cousin-Montauban had decided on the grouping by fours into *régiments de marche* of the depot squadrons of these corps. They would be under the command of a lieutenant colonel or a colonel, assisted by a major as a second in command. The staff of these provisional corps would be formed by two majors, two adjutant majors, a paymaster, two doctors, two veterinarians, two non-commissioned adjutants, and a corporal as trumpeter.

In the mind of General Cousin-Montauban, regiments formed in this manner had to present a relative solidity.

A first regiment of cavalry *de marche*, called the Cavalry of the Imperial Guard, was to be formed with the depots of the carabiniers, cuirassiers, dragoons and lancers of the Guard. Since this corps had to be permanantly organized, it turned over its first two squadrons to another *régiment de marche* (2nd Cuirassiers de marche) and joined its two last squadrons to the guides and the chasseurs of the Guard's depots which combined to form the 1st regiments of mixed cavalry. The day of the opening of the siege of Paris, ten *régiments de marche* of cavalry were already formed (right).

1st	Cuirassier	Régiment de marche	Lieutenant Colonel M Renusson d' Hauteville, 5th, 6th, 7th Cuirassiers
2nd	Cuirassier	Régiment de marche	Lieutenant Colonel Bonaparte, later Mariani, 1st Cuirassier, Centes-Gardes, Carabiniers and Cuirassiers of the Guard
1st	Dragoon	Régiment de marche	Colonel Lhotte, 1st, 3rd, 9th, 10th Dragoons
2nd	Dragoon	Régiment de marche	Lieutenant Colonel Bonaparte, 2nd, 4th, 5th, 8th Dragoons
3rd	Dragoon	Régiment de marche	Lieutenant Colonel Durdilly, 6th, 7th, 10th, 11th Dragoons
1st	Lancer	Régiment de marche	Colonel Cousin de Montauban, 1st, 4th, 7th, 8th Lancers
1st	Chasseur	Régiment de marche	Lieutenant Colonel Rouher, 2nd, 4th, 6th, 10th Chasseurs
1st	Hussar	Régiment de marche	Lieutenant Colonel Guyon-Vernier, 2nd, 4th, 6th, 7th Hussars
1st	Mixed	Régiment de marche	Lieutenant Colonel Lefoy de Lanauze, Lancers, Dragoons, Chasseurs and Guides of the Guard
2nd	Mixed	Régiment de marche	Lieutenant Colonel Gauvenet, called Dijon, 3rd, 8th Chassuers, 1st, 5th Hussars

The government of the National Defense, before having enclosed itself in the capital, thus had at its disposal twenty-two regiments of cavalry. This includes the thirteen regiments or rather the twelve old regiments, since the 8th Hussars remained in Africa until December. The majority of these regiments rushed to Paris which already had two magnificent corps with an effective strength of twelve hundred horses. These were the cavalry of the Parisian Guard and a regiment of gendarmerie. They were mobilized since the early days of the war to make the agitators of the riots respect the calm of the capital. Despite this important reserve, it was decided to retain six additional regiments: the 1st and 9th Chasseurs coming from Africa; the 2nd of Cuirassiers de marche, the 1st Lancers de marche, and the 1st and 2nd Dragoons de marche. General Trochu, who would later state that Paris could not free itself alone—which was true—kept the cavalrymen who would have been the most useful in the provinces close to him. Their horses, ultimately, served as food for his army.

In the provinces, the fever of organization was immense. The outcome was as follows: nine regiments of cuirassiers, seven of dragoons, five of lancers, one of chasseurs, three of hussars, and nine of mixed cavalry. Total thirty-four. These regiments were formed of four squadrons taken from four, sometimes from five and even eight regiments. The following gives a list of them and their composition:

3rd Cuirassiers de marche	2nd, 3rd, 8th, 9th Cuirassiers
4th Cuirassiers de marche	1st, 3rd, 5th, 8th Cuirassiers
5th Cuirassiers de marche	6th, 7th Cuirassiers, Carabiniers and Cuirassiers of the Guard
6th Cuirassiers de marche	2nd, 3rd, 4th, 10th Cuirassiers
7th Cuirassiers de marche	2nd, 7th, 8th Cuirassiers, Carabiniers and Cuirassiers of the Guard
8th Cuirassiers de marche	1st, 4th, 5th, 6th Cuirassiers
9th Cuirassiers de marche	5th, 8th, 10th Cuirassiers, Cuirassiers of the Guard
10th Cuirassiers de marche	3rd, 4th, 6th, 9th Cuirassiers
11th Cuirassiers de marche	5th, 8th, 10th Cuirassiers, Cuirassiers of the Guard
4th Dragoons de marche	1st, 2nd, 3rd, 4th, 7th, 8th, 10th Dragoons
5th Dragoons de marche	7th, 8th, 9th, 12th Dragoons
6th Dragoons de marche	1st, 2nd, 3rd, 4th, 5th, 7th, 8th, 10th Dragoons
7th Dragoons de marche	1st, 3rd, 6th, 10th Dragoons
8th Dragoons de marche	1st, 5th, 6th, 8th Dragoons, Dragoons of the Guard
9th Dragoons de marche	1st, 4th Dragoons 5th Lancers, Dragoons and Lancers of the Guard
10th Dragoons de marche	3rd, 5th, 9th, 10th Dragoons
2nd Lancers de marche	1st, 5th, 7th, 8th Lancers
3rd Lancers de marche	2nd, 4th, 5th, 6th Lancers
4th Lancers de marche	4th, 5th, 7th, 8th Lancers
5th Lancers de marche	3rd, 4th, 6th, 7th, 8th Lancers
6th Lancers de marche	1st, 2nd, 4th, 7th Lancers
2nd Chasseurs de marche	3rd, 4th, 6th, 10th Chasseurs
2nd Hussars de marche	4th, 5th, 6th, 7th Hussars
3rd Hussars de marche	Guides, 2nd Chasseurs, 4th, 7th Hussars
4th Hussars de marche	4th, 5th, 6th, 7th Hussars
3rd Mixed cavalry	7th, 11th, 12th Chasseurs, 3rd Hussars
4th Mixed cavalry	3rd, 8th Chasseurs, 1st, 2nd Hussars
5th Mixed cavalry	9th Dragoons, 3rd Lancers, Dragoons and Lancers of the Guard
6th Mixed cavalry	6th, 7th, 9th, 11th Chasseurs, 3rd Hussars
7th Mixed cavalry	2nd, 3rd, 8th Chasseurs, 2nd Hussars
8th Mixed cavalry	11th, 12th Chasseurs, 1st, 5th Hussars
9th Mixed cavalry	3rd, 4th, 8th Chasseurs, 2nd Hussars
10th Mixed cavalry	7th, 11th Chasseurs, 1st, 3rd Hussars
11th Mixed cavalry	7th, 10th Chasseurs, 2nd, 12th Dragoons

A mixed regiment created in Paris during the investment must be added to these creations. It took Number 16 in the Dragoons after having worn Number 4 *de marche*. It should not be forgotten that after the Battle of Woerth, 28 officers, 719 non-commissioned officers, corporals, and horsemen and 484 horses belonged almost entirely to MacMahon's Corps. This corps took refuge at Strasbourg and was formed into a regiment there under the command of Major de Serlay of the 2nd Lancers.

Finally, on November 23, 1870 in the Army of the North, a new 7th Dragoons was reformed. This was done by order of the Minister of War dating from November 23 1870.

Sub-lieutenant of dragoons, officier d'ordonnance of a general of brigade, full dress (1880).

The first four squadrons of the Dragoons of the North formed at Lille with the depots of the 4th Dragoons and with detachments from the 2nd, 5th, and 12th Dragoons were used for this unit. On February 5, 1870, its 1st and 2nd squadrons were at Valenciennes and the 3rd and 4th at Cambrai. A new 11th Dragoons was also reformed for the Army of the North at Lille with two other squadrons of Dragoons of the North and a weak detachment of 8th Dragoons. This was in accordance with the ministerial decision of December 29. On February 10, this regiment was at Aire.

Thus, the govenerment of the National Defense had at its disposal sixty regiments of cavalry in addition to the African organizations: 13 old ones subjected to capitulations, 10 *de marche* created or prepared by General Cousin-Montauban, 34 formed in the provinces, one formed at Paris, and 2 regiments reformed in the North. It is difficult to say exactly what the value of these *régiments de marche* were. It depended a lot on circumstances and especially on the horses which a hasty remount supplied haphazardly and through contractors more intent upon exploiting the situation than on showing their patriotism. It should also be stated that the commanders of the provincial armies and especially de Freycinet (Gambetta's delegate who

had written up the plans for the campaign with a remarkable group) neglected to provide numerical positions. Thus, it is not possible to know the actual effectives of the cavalry which they employed.

The *garde nationale mobile* and the *garde nationale mobilisée* did not supply the cavalry with organized corps. Some *corps francs* were recruited either at Paris or in the provinces. They did not leave a very outstanding reputation behind. In general they were ready only at the end of the war. An example was the fine *régiment de mobiles à cheval* organized in the Dordogne by de Bourgoing. Despite the eagerness and great intellect of its leader, the *mobiles* only got underway on the eve of the armistice and were soon mustered out. From fine uniforms to the best of remounts, nothing had been spared to make these troops into an elite corps. Its history proves once again that cavalry cannot be improvised. The cavalry which the Parisians called the Franchetti were more modest and more useful. They made do with an effective strength of one squadron commanded by proven military men. They were recruited from amongst wealthy youths who rode well. They served as scouts for General Ducrot and showed boldness and intelligence in this difficult task. A special decree awarded them the honor of the wine-colored pants which otherwise were seen only in the army. Skeptics will laugh at learning that the Franchetti were proud of this award. Thoughtful people will say that the general who was given this reward and the young men who rejoiced in it were patriots.

In the distribution of the cavalry during the second half of the war, certain regiments did not get back together and others were called up twice. Such disorder reigned at Bordeaux that the order given to the 2nd régiment de marche of chasseurs, Lieutenant Colonel Bobin, could never be determined nor for the 11th mixed régiment de marche, Lieutenant Colonel Renaudot. The 11th had at first been attached to the 19th Corps without being formed into brigades there. It was then sent to Le Havre where under the commander in chief, General Loysel, it formed a brigade of light cavalry with a *régiment de marche* of Chasseurs d'Afrique.

Up to this point, the greatest deeds of the cavalry have not been especially told. The French armies were victorious. It seems that the cavalry has been reproached by critics from all sides for its lack of initiative. It is only fair that its prowess which astonished even the enemy also be recalled. The Prussian cavalry, which was much better mounted and more numerous than the French, also received heavy blows. What was said about the Italian campaign will be repeated about the campaign of 1870-1871. In this campaign where the French never gave battle, where they always accepted it and most often lost, the French generals in chief never knew how to use their cavalry. They were often uncomfortable with it. However, every time they requested a service, the cavalry delivered on the battlefield without showing concern for death. It is less humiliating to sincerely recognize the relative inferiority of the French cavalry when the following facts about its active troops are cited.

DISTRIBUTION OF THE CAVALRY DURING THE SECOND PART OF THE WAR OF 1870-71

Army Corps	Divisions	Brigades	Regiments
15th, DE LA MOTTE-ROUGE, later D'AURELLES DE PALADINES	REYAU, later LONGUERUE	1st, LONGUERUE	6th Dragoons, Colonel Tillion, 6th Hussars, Colonel Guillon.
		2nd, BRÉMOND A'ARS	9th Cuirassiers, Colonel de Vouges de Chanteclair; 1st Cuirassier Régiment de marche, Colonel de Renussond d'Hauteville.
	—	1st, MICHEL(detached)	2nd Lancers, Colonel Maillart de Landreville; 5th Lancers, Colonel Gayraud; 3rd Dragoon régiment de marche, Lieutenant Colonel Durdilly.
		2nd, DASTUGUES (detached)	11th Chasseurs, Colonel Bailliencourt; 1st Chasseurs régiment de marche, Lieutenant Colonel Rouher.
16th, POURCET, later CHANZY	RESSAYRE, later MICHEL	1st, TRIPART, later DE TUÉ	1st Hussars régiment de marche, Lieutenant Colonel Guyon-Vernier, 2nd Mixed régiment de marche.
		2nd, DIGARD, later BRIAND	6th Lancers, Lieutenant Colonel Leroy de Lanauze; 2nd Mixed régiment de marche, Lieutenant Colonel Bonie.
		3rd, ABDELAL	3rd Cuirassier régiment de marche, Lieutenant Colonel Trébout; 4th Dragoon régiment de marche, Lieutenant Colonel Roze.
17th, DURRIEU, later DE SONIS, GUÉPRATTE	DE LONGUERUE, later DE SONIS, GUÉPRATTE, D'ESPEUILLES	1st, DE SONIS	4th Mixed régiment de marche, Lieutenant Colonel Joubert; 6th Mixed régiment de marche, Lieutenant Colonel Vater.
		2nd, GUEPRATTE, later D'ESPEUILLES, later BARBUT	4th régiment de marche, Lieutenant Colonel de Tinseau; 5th Mixed régiment de marche, Lieutenant Colonel Boulligny.
18th, BOURBAKI, later BILLOT	DE BRÉMOND D'ARS	1st, CHARLEMAGNE	2nd Hussar Regiment, Lieutenant Colonel Saint-Jean-de-Pointis; 3rd Lancer régiment de marche, Lieutenant Colonel Pierre.
		2nd, GUYON VERNIER, later HAINGLAISE	5th Dragoon régiment de marche, Lieutenant Colonel d'Ussel; 5th Cuirassier Regiment, Lieutenant Colonel Lenez Cotty de Trécourt.
19th, DARGENT	ABDELAL	1st, Col. CRAMAZEL DE KERHUE	3rd Hussar Regiment, Colonel Cramazel de Kerhué; 4th Hussar régiment de marche, Lieutenant Colonel Bauvieux.
		2nd, DE VOUGES DE CHANTECLAIR	8th Dragoon régiment de marche, Lieutenant Colonel Loizillon; 9th Cuirassier régiment de marche, Lieutenant Colonel Grandin.
20th, CROUZAT, later CLINCHANT	—	Unbrigaded. One regiment attached to each infantry division.	2nd Lancer régiment de marche, Lieutenant Colonel Basserie; 7th Chasseur Regiment, Colonel Mieulet de Ricaumont; 6th Cuirassier régiment de marche, Lieutenant Colonel Chevals.
21st, Admiral JAURES	GUILLON	1st—	8th Hussars, Colonel Lacombe; 1st Hussar régiment de marche, Lieutenant Colonel Bonne.
		2nd—	3rd Mixed régiment de marche, Lieutenant Colonel Bonie; 8th Cuirassier régiment de marche, Lieutenant Colonel Humblot.
		3rd—	6th Dragoon régiment de marche, Lieutenant Colonel Tillay du Villay; 8th Mixed régiment de marche, Lieutenant Colonel Palanque.
	Mobile divison attached to the 21st, Corp, General CAMO.	—	4th Lancer régiment de marche, Lieutenant Colonel de Rouot; 3rd Hussar régiment de marche, Lieutenant Colonel Noirtin; 7th Cuirassier régiment de marche, Lieutenant Colonel Bergeron; 1st Mounted Gendarmerie Regiment.

22ND, LECOINTE These two corps under the command of General FAIDHERBE, formed the Army of the North; how the 7th and 11th Dragoons had been reformed for this army has been explained above.
23rd, PAULZE D'IVOY

24th, BRESSOLLES This corps seems not to have had its cavalry brigaded although it was fairly large.			7th Mixed Cavalry Regiment, Lieutenant Colonel Droz; one squadron of the 6th Dragoons and one of the 10th; 3rd Dragoon régiment de march, Lieutenant Colonel Durdilly; 2nd Chasseurs of Africa régiment de marche; 7th Dragoon régiment de marche; Lieutenant Colonel Robert; 5th Lancer régiment de marche, Lieutenant Colonel Foussat.
25th, POURCET	TRIPART	1st, DELHORME	9th Mixed régiment de marche, Lieutenant Colonel Masson; 9th Dragoon régiment de marche, Lieutenant Colonel Castanier.
		2nd, DE BRUCHARD	10th Mixed régiment de marche, Lieutenant Colonel de Barbançois; Dordogne Mobiles Mounted Regiment, Lieutenant Colonel de Bourgoing.
26th, BILLOT (forming at Lyon during the armistice)	—	1st, POLLARD	10th Dragoon régiment de marche, Lieutenant Colonel Simard de Pitray; 6th Lancer régiment de marche, Lieutenant Colonel Pierre.
		2nd, LETUVE	10th Cuirassier régiment de marche, Lieutenant Colonel Baillod; 11th Cuirassier régiment de marche, Lieutenant Colonel Tendon.

ARMY CHARGED WITH THE DEFENSE OF PARIS (Organization of November 6th)

	CHAMPERON (attached to the First Army)	1st, MOUCHETON DE GERBOIS	13th Dragoons (former 1st de marche), Colonel Lhotte; 14th Dragoons (former 2nd de marche).
		2nd, COUSIN	1st Chasseur Regiment, Col. d'Anselme; 9th Chasseur Regiment, Col. Charreyron; 1st Mounted Gendarmerie Regiment, Col. Roussel.
	BERTIN DE VAUX (attached to the Third Army)	1st, BERNIS	Regiment (former 2nd de marche), Lieutenant Colonel Mariani; 9th Lancer Regiment (former 1st de marche).
		2nd—	10th Dragoon Regiment; 2nd Mounted Gendarmerie Regiment, Colonel Bouthier.

Battle of Woerth. At about 1:30, the charge of the 8th and 9th Cuirassiers from the Michel Brigade. This general, at the invitation of General Lartigue, bravely but uncautiously rushed headlong into the streets of Morsbronn. He was at the head of his brigade. The 2nd and 6th Lancers of the Nansouty Brigade followed him without having received orders. Met by an intense fusillade, these regiments were almost destroyed. The 8th Cuirassiers had left Captains de Najac and Lot, Lieutenant Fabre, and second lieutenants Habary and Revacly dead on the battlefield. Captains Delmas and Bourru, Lieutenants Boissaubin and Paillard, and Second Lieutenants Lerat, Germain and Gaudin de Villaine were in the hands of the enemy. In addition, Captain Ginot and Lieutenants Huckel and Gresbilin were wounded. Total: 15 officers out of action. The officers' corps of the 9th was still more terribly afflicted. Colonel Waternau and his two Majors (Pimont de Cécire de Honneville and Baillaud), his two Adjutant Majors (Trefcon and de Finance de Clerbois), six captains (Rubat, Sénepart, Chatelain, Petit, Noel and le Maitre), five lieutenants (Valotte, Thomy, Mateille, Gency and Tardieu) and six second lieutenants (Parisot, Bolnot, Riquet de Caraman, Haro, de Rougé, and Desmousseaux de Givré), that is twenty-two officers, were killed, prisoners, or wounded. The 9th Cuirassiers had meanwhile lost fewer men and horses than the 8th. However, since the heart of the regiment had completely disappeared, it turned its men over to the 8th and returned to remake itself in the interior.(1) The 2nd Lancers' colonel, Poissonnier, was killed. Major Colmé, Captains Clerc and Salmon, Lieutenant Moreau, Second Lieutenants Quérido, Grivot de la Frenaye, Harris, and Vuilquin, and the color bearer Fromengeat were killed or made prisoner.

At two thirty, the Bonnemains Division—1st and 4th, 2nd and 3rd Cuirassiers—received the order to relieve the remains of the Wolff Division which was struggling on terrain between Elssashausen and Froeschwiller swept by missiles and fusillade. The charge was ordered by demi-regiment. The 1st and 2nd squadron of the 2nd Regiment rushed out first. It was commanded by Major Corot-Laquiante who accompanied Lieutenant Colonel Boré-Verrier to whom General Wolff had indicated his orders. The losses from the 1st, 3rd and 4th Regiments who were also engaged in this action were less considerable than those of the 8th and 9th. Nonetheless they were serious, if judged by the decrees for replacements. Losses were not appreciable for the 1st Regiment. It lost its colonel, Lafutsun de Lacarre, who had his head blown off by a cannonball. The 2nd Regiment possesses an excellent historical record—as must all of the corps. It shows the disabling of 9 officers: Captains Horrie

(1) In addition, the 8th received 150 mounted cuirassiers from its depot coming from the reserve. However, by the admission of its own leaders, it was better to have it retreat like the 9th since this group of men from diverse origins could not gain ground in the marches and countermarches which followed. They were under pressure and lost their heads.

Chasseur à cheval (1873).

and Verloin, Lieutenants Humbert and Bigot, and Second Lieutenants Challiet and Divin (paymaster) killed; Adjutant Teillé, Captain Cabrié and Second Lieutenant Daniel-Lacombe, prisoners. In addition Colonel Rosetti was thrown by his horse in the retreat and soon after fell into enemy hands. The 4th Regiment saw Colonel Billet, Major Broutta, Captain d'Eggs, Lieutenant Motte, and Second Lieutenant Gauthier disappear from their ranks, either killed or taken prisoner.

All of these regiments were very roughly handled. They had been thrown into the void without worrying about the insurmountable obstacles which they had before them. To finish off the inopportuneness of their efforts, a general greeted the passing of the 8th and the 9th with these words: "Go my children, as at Waterloo." These two charges were the most murderous, but Marshal MacMahon doubtlessly exaggerates the French misfortunes in saying: "Of the Cuirassiers, there were no more." Obviously they still existed. The 2nd Regiment left with 543 cavalrymen.

It left 141 behind at Froeschwiller and lost 187 horses, counting those which it had to slaughter. At the capitulation of Sedan, they only handed over 150 men in the ranks to the enemy.

At Metz, Rezonville and Gravelotte, the French regiments were better utilized. However, they acted without the special orders of the general in chief but rather under the responsibility and according to the initiative of their own generals. They showed the Germans that the French cavalry is formidable when the action of its sabers cannot be escaped. It was in one of the charges around Metz that General Legrand was killed.

Battle of Sedan. Before coming to Sedan, the French cavalry had yet to show its energy which had been so uselessly employed. The 4th Hussars at Grandpré made a useful and brilliant reconnaissance on August 24 and 25. On the 28th at Buzancy, two squadrons of the 12th Chasseurs tackled the Saxon Dragoons with advantage and inflicted major losses on them. However, the hussars suffered terrible losses (Captains Alloué and Raimond, Lieutenant Castagnié, and Second Lieutenant de Faucher de la Ligerie, killed). As it was not assisted, the chasseurs were forced to fight while retreating. On August 30 at the Battle of Beaumont, the 5th Regiment of Cuirassiers gave the army the best example of courage and of self-sacrifice when morale was already heavily shaken. It belonged to a brigade of the 12th Corps which General Lebrun had just put at the disposal of General de Failly. It obeyed the call to honor and military solidarity under the command of its brave colonel Dubessey de Contenson who came to warn Commander Haillot. It charged the enemy with spirit and force. Colonel Dubessey died in this engagement as well as Lieutenant Colonel Assant. At the Battle of Sedan, it was not only the fine 1st and 3rd Chasseurs d'Afrique who took part in the epic and legendary charge without any military

Lieutenant of cuirassiers, officier d'ordonnance to a general commanding an army corps, full dress (1880).

consequences other than the admiration of the King and of the Press. The 1st Hussars, 6th Chasseurs and some parts of cuirassier and lancer regiments from other divisions followed—or rather imitated—their glorious *élan*. This charge, which has been much discussed, seems never to have been clearly recounted because the actors could not know what was happening around them. Each one saw only what was in front of him. Yet there, one charged for the honor of the service, perhaps just so the renowned warrior of France would not disappear entirely, swallowed up in the whirlwind of defeat. The brave general Margueritte—the one called "Father Margueritte" by his old chasseurs—fell on the field of battle while reconnoitering the place where his squadrons would pass. However, in the French army, more than anywhere else, *uno avulso non deficit alter* (one sacrifice does not lack another), the charge was made and brilliantly conducted by de Galliffet. That morning, General of Brigade Tilliard and his *officier d'ordonnance* had been killed by a shell in a countermarch which brought the

---

Commander in chief: General of division DU BARRAIL
Chief of staff: Colonel BALLAND
Commander of artillery: Major PINEL DE GRANDCHAMP

1st DIVISION
General HALNA DU FRETAY

1st BRIGADE, General CHARLEMAGNE
3rd Hussars, Colonel CRAMEZEL DE KERHUÉ
8th Hussars, Colonel DE LACOMBE.

2nd BRIGADE, General DE LAJAILLE
7th Chasseurs, Colonel MIEULET DE RICAUMONT
11th Chasseurs, Colonel DE BAILLIENCOURT, called COURCOL.

2nd DIVISION - General DU PREUIL

1st BRIGADE, General COUSIN
4th Dragoons de marche, Colonel CORNAT
3rd Cuirassiers de marche, Colonel DE LASALLE.

2nd BRIGADE General DARGENTOLLE
1st Mounted Gendarmerie, Colonel ROUSSEL
2nd Gendarmerie, Colonel BOUTHIER

3rd DIVISION - General RESSAIRE

1st BRIGADE, General DE BERNIS
7th Dragoons, Colonel DE GRESSOT, later LARDEUR
9th Lancers —

2nd BRIGADE General BACHELIER
4th Cuirassiers —
8th Cuirassiers, Colonel GUYOT DE LA ROCHERE

Student of the special military school at Saint-Cyr, cavalry section (1883).

Cuirassiers, escort platoon (1885).

Chasseurs à cheval, parade (1886).

division a little to the rear to allow it to form itself for battle. The colonel of the 8th Chasseurs à cheval, Jamin du Fresnay, also died on the deathly field of battle which witnessed the fall of three cavalry generals.

That evening two squadrons from the 1st Cuirassiers, under the command of Commander Cugnon d'Alincourt tried to go back to the Faubourg de Balan, sabers in hand. However, the circle was closed; the cuirassiers were killed or made prisoners.

During the campaign, in addition to Generals Legrand, Margueritte, Tilliard, and Girard, the cavalry service of the line lost Colonels Lafutsun de Lacarre of the 3rd Cuirassiers, Dubessey de Contenson of the 5th Cuirassiers, Poissonnier of the 2nd Lancers, and Jamin de Fresnay of the 8th Chasseurs, all before September 4. General de Salignac-Fénelon was also wounded at the Battle of Sedan where the cavalry generals and officers spared no effort.

The war was barely over when sad tasks fell to the cavalry. Like the infantry, it supplied a large contingent to the army which had to rescue the capital from the hands of the bandits of the Commune and return Paris to France. Thiers called up part of the old regiments still remaining and some new ones. They at first formed the 3rd Corps (cavalry) of the Army of Versailles. At the lower left is the roll dating from April 6, 1871.

The first corps of infantry could avail itself of the Galliffet scouts brigade (9th and 12th Chasseurs). The 6th Regiment of Lancers was attached to the 2nd Corps. The 2nd Brigade (gendarmerie) of the 2nd Division was assigned to the reserve army and commanded by General of Division Vinoy. It was replaced by a brigade of dragoons composed of the 8th Regiment (Colonel de Fonscolombe) and of the 9th Regiment (Colonel Reboul).

It was the middle of the Parisian civil war, when a wretched revolt backed by foreigners sought to oust the French from Algeria, that the reorganization of the mounted troops had to be carried out. This was a much more delicate task

Special military school of Saint-Cyr, cavalry section (1884).

DISTRIBUTION OF THE RÉGIMENTS DE MARCHE INTO THE 56 OLD REGIMENTS (DECISION OF MARCH 10, 1871)

Old Regiments	Régiments de marche that received them	Old Regiments	Régiments de marche that received them
1st Cuirassiers	1st Cuirassiers de marche	2nd Lancers	Regiment complete, nothing received
2nd Cuirassiers	2nd Cuirassiers de marche	3rd Lancers	3rd Lancers de marche
3rd Cuirassiers	3rd Cuirassiers de marche	4th Lancers	4th Lancers de marche
4th Cuirassiers	4th Cuirassiers de marche	5th Lancers	Regiment complete, nothing received
5th Cuirassiers	5th Cuirassiers de marche	6th Lancers	Regiment complete, nothing received
6th Cuirassiers	6th Cuirassiers de marche	7th Lancers	2nd Lancers de marche
7th Cuirassiers	7th Cuirassiers de marche	8th Lancers	5th Lancers de marche
8th Cuirassiers	8th Cuirassiers de marche	9th Lancers, former	
9th Cuirassiers	Regiment complete, nothing received	Lancers of the Guard	7th Lancers de marche, plus two squadrons from the 1st and 5th Mixed Cavalry régiments de marche, coming from the Lancers of the Guard
10th Cuirassiers	10th Cuirassiers de marche		
11th Cuirassiers, former Carabiniers	11th Cuirassiers de marche	1st Chasseurs	Regiment complete, nothing received
12th Cuirassiers, former		2nd Chasseurs	2nd Chasseurs de marche
Cuirassiers of the Guard	9th Cuirassiers de marche	3rd Chasseurs	3rd Mixed Light Cavalry régiment de marche
1st Dragoons	1st Dragoons de marche and half of the 16th Dragoons, created in Paris	4th Chasseurs	4th Mixed Light Cavalry régiment de marche
		5th Chasseurs	1st Chasseurs de marche
2nd Dragoons	2nd Dragoons de marche, received in addition one squadron that it had provided to the 11th Mixed Cavalry régiment de marche	6th Chasseurs	2nd Mixed Light Cavalry régiment de marche
		7th Chasseurs	Regiment complete; took back one squadron which it had provided to the 11th Mixed Cavalry de marche
3rd Dragoons	3rd Dragoons de marche and half of the 16th Dragoons, created in Paris	8th Chasseurs	7th Mixed Light Cavalry régiment de marche
		9th Chasseurs	Regiment complete, nothing received.
4th Dragoons	4th Dragoons de marche	10th Chasseurs	8th Mixed Light Cavalry régiment de marche, plus one squadron which it had provided to the 11th Mixed Light Cavalry régiment de marche
5th Dragoons	5th Dragoons de marche		
6th Dragoons	Regiment complete, nothing received		
7th Dragoons	Regiment complete, nothing received	11th Chasseurs	Regiment complete, nothing received
8th Dragoons	8th Dragoons de marche	12th Chasseurs	Regiment complete, nothing received
9th Dragoons	9th Dragoons de marche	13th Chasseurs, former	
10th Dragoons	10th Dragoons de marche	chasseurs of the Guard	10th Mixed Light Cavalry Regiment, plus the two squadrons from the 1st and 5th Mixed Line Cavalry
11th Dragoons	Regiment complete, nothing received.		
12th Dragoons	6th Dragoons de marche, plus one squadron that it had provided to the 11th Mixed Cavalry régiment de marche	1st Hussars	6th Mixed Light Cavalry Regiment
		2nd Hussars	2nd Hussars de marche
13th Dragoons, former		3rd Hussars	Regiment complete, nothing received
Dragoons of the Guard	7th Dragoons de marche, plus the two squadrons from the 1st and 5th Mixed Cavalry régiments de marche, coming from the Dragoons of the Guard	4th Hussars	4th Hussars de marche
		5th Hussars	1st Hussars de marche
		6th Hussars	Regiment complete, nothing received
1st Lancers	1st Lancers de marche	7th Hussars	3rd Hussars de marche.
		8th Hussars	Regiment complete, nothing received

ORIGIN AND DATE OF FORMATION OF THE 70 REGIMENTS COMPOSING THE CAVALRY IN 1873

1st Cuirassiers — Reine Cuirassiers on August 30, 1815. 1st Cuirassiers on August 18, 1830.

2nd Cuirassiers — Dauphin Cuirassiers on August 30, 1815. 2nd Cuirassiers on August 18, 1830.

3rd Cuirassiers — Angoûlême Cuirassiers on August 30, 1815. Bordeaux Cuirassiers on September 21, 1824. 3rd Cuirassiers on August 18, 1830.

4th Cuirassiers — Berri Cuirassiers on August 30, 1815. 4th Cuirassiers on August 18, 1830.

5th Cuirassiers — Orléans Cuirassiers on August 30, 1815. 5th Cuirassiers on August 18, 1830.

6th Cuirassiers — Condé Cuirassiers on August 30, 1815. 6th Cuirassiers on August 18, 1830.

7th Cuirassiers — Manche Dragoons on August 30, 1815. 7th Cuirassiers on February 21, 1825.

8th Cuirassiers — Rhône Dragoons on August 30, 1815. 8th Cuirassiers on February 21, 1825.

9th Cuirassiers — Saône Dragoons on August 30, 1815. 9th Cuirassiers on February 21, 1825.

10th Cuirassiers — Seine Dragoons on August 30, 1815. 10th Cuirassiers on February 21, 1825.

11th Cuirassiers — 1st Monsieur Carabiniers, created on August 30, 1815 and the 2nd Carabiniers created February 27, 1825. The two regiments both took the names of the 1st and 2nd Carabiniers. Merged into one regiment; passed into the Imperial Guard on November 15, 1865. Became the 11th Cuirassiers on February 4, 1871.

12th Cuirassiers — Cuirassiers of the Guard on May 1, 1854. Became the 1st Cuirassiers of the Guard on December 20, 1855, at the same time the 2nd Cuirassiers of the Guard were created. The two regiments became a single regiment (Guard Cuirassier Regiment) on November 15, 1865. Became the 12th Cuirassiers on February 4, 1871.

1st Dragoons — Calvados Dragoons on August 30, 1815. 1st Dragoons on February 27, 1825.

2nd Dragoons — Doubs Dragoons on August 30, 1815. 2nd Dragoons on February 27, 1825.

3rd Dragoons — Garonne Dragoons on August 30, 1815. 3rd Dragoons on February 27, 1825.

4th Dragoons — Gironde Dragoons on August 30, 1815. 4th Dragoons on February 27, 1825.

5th Dragoons — l'Hérault Dragoons on August 30, 1815. 5th Dragoons on February 27, 1825.

6th Dragoons — Loire Dragoons on August 30, 1815. 6th Dragoons on February 27, 1825.

7th Dragoons — Somme Chasseurs à cheval on August 30, 1815. Became the 7th Dragoons on February 27, 1825.

8th Dragoons — Var Chasseurs à cheval on August 30, 1815. Became the 8th Dragoons on February 27, 1825.

9th Dragoons — Vaucluse Chasseurs à cheval on August 30, 1815. Became the 9th Dragoons on February 27, 1825.

10th Dragoons — Vendée Chasseurs à cheval on August 30, 1815. Became the 10th Dragoons on February 27, 1825.

11th Dragoons — Vienne Chasseurs à cheval on August 30, 1815. Became the 11th Dragoons on February 27, 1825.

12th Dragoons — Vosges Chasseurs à cheval on August 30, 1815. Became the 12th Dragoons on February 27, 1825.

13th Dragoons — Imperial Guard Dragoons on December 20, 1855. Empress Dragoons in 1857. 13th Dragoons on February 4, 1871.

14th Dragoons — Allier Chasseurs on August 31, 1815. 1st Chasseurs on February 27, 1825. De Nemours on November 17, 1826. 1st Lancers on February 19, 1831, retained the title of Nemours Lancers until 1848. 14th Dragoons on August 8, 1871.

15th Dragoons — Ardennes Chasseurs on August 30, 1815. 3rd Chasseurs on February 27, 1825. 3rd Lancers on February 19, 1831. 15th Dragoons on August 8, 1871.

16th Dragoons — Ariège Chasseurs on August 30, 1815. 4th Chasseurs on February 27, 1825. 4th Lancers on February 19, 1831. 16th Dragoons on August 8, 1871.

17th Dragoons — Cantal Chasseurs on August 30, 1815. 5th Chasseurs on February 27, 1825. 5th Lancers on February 19, 1831. 17th Dragoons on August 8, 1871.

18th Dragoons — Orléans Lancer on August 25, 1830. 6th Lancers on February 19, 1831. 18th Dragoons on August 8, 1871.

19th Dragoons — 14th Chasseurs on February 19, 1831. 8th Lancers on November 27, 1836. 19th Dragoons on August 8, 1871.

20th Dragoons — Imperial Guard Lancers on December 20, 1855. 9th Lancers on February 19, 1871. 20th Dragoons on August 8, 1871.

21st Dragoons — Formed on October 6, 1873 from four squadrons of the 3rd, 4th, 6th and 8th Cuirassiers.

22nd Dragoons — Formed on October 6, 1873 from four squadrons of the 5th, 7th, 10th and 11th Cuirassiers.

23rd Dragoons — Formed on October 6, 1873 from four squadrons of the 1st, 2nd, 9th and 12th Cuirassiers.

24th Dragoons — Formed on October 6, 1873 from four squadrons of the 2nd, 4th, 7th and 8th Dragoons.

25th Dragoons — Formed on October 6, 1873 from four squadrons of the 3rd, 9th, 13th and 18th Dragoons.

26th Dragoons — Formed on October 6, 1873 from four squadrons of the 6th, 15th, 17th and 19th Dragoons.

1st Chasseurs — Charente Chasseurs on August 30, 1815. 6th Chasseurs on February 27, 1825. Became the 1st Chasseurs on February 19, 1831.

2nd Chasseurs — Corrèze Chasseurs on August 30, 1815. 7th Chasseurs on February 27, 1825. Became the 2nd Chasseurs on February 19, 1831.

3rd Chasseurs — Côte-d'Or Chasseurs on August 30, 1815. 8th Chasseurs on February 27, 1825. Became the 3rd Chasseurs on February 19, 1831.

4th Chasseurs — Dordogne Chasseurs on August 30, 1815. 9th Chasseurs on February 27, 1825. Became the 4th Chasseurs on February 19, 1831.

5th Chasseurs — Gard Chasseurs on August 30, 1815. 10th Chasseurs on February 27, 1825. Became the 5th Chasseurs on February 19, 1831.

6th Chasseurs — Isére Chasseurs on August 30, 1815. 11th Chasseurs on February 27, 1825. Became the 6th Chasseurs on February 19, 1831.

7th Chasseurs — Marne Chasseurs on August 30, 1815. 12th Chasseurs on February 27, 1825. Became the 7th Chasseurs on February 19, 1831.

8th Chasseurs — Meuse Chasseurs on August 30, 1815. 13th Chasseurs on February 27, 1825. Became the 8th Chasseurs on February 19, 1831.

9th Chasseurs — Morbihan Chasseurs on August 30, 1815. 14th Chasseurs on February 27, 1825. Became the 9th Chasseurs on February 19, 1831.

10th Chasseurs — l'Oise Chasseurs on August 30, 1815. 15th Chasseurs on February 27, 1825. Became the 10th Chasseurs on February 19, 1831.

11th Chasseurs — l'Orne Chasseurs on August 30, 1815. 16th Chasseurs on February 27, 1825. Became the 11th Chasseurs on February 19, 1831.

12th Chasseurs — Pyrénées Chasseurs on August 30, 1815. 17th Chasseurs on February 27, 1825. Became the 12th Chasseurs on February 19, 1831.

13th Chasseurs — A 13th Chasseurs was created on November 13, 1840 and disbanded October 23, 1852. On February 4, 1871, the Imperial Guard Chasseurs took the number 13 in the series for Chasseurs.

14th Chasseurs — Sarthe Chasseurs on August 30, 1815. 18th Chasseurs on February 21, 1825. Became the 13th Chasseurs on February 19, 1831. 7th Lancers on November 27, 1836. 14th Chasseurs on August 8, 1871.

15th Chasseurs — Formed on October 6, 1873 with four squadrons of the 7th, 9th, 11th and 13th Chasseur Regiments.

16th Chasseurs — Formed on October 6, 1873 with four squadrons of the 4th and 14th Chasseurs and the 5th and 7th Hussars.

17th Chasseurs — Formed on October 6, 1873 with four squadrons of the 2nd, 5th, 6th and 8th Chasseurs.

18th Chasseurs — Formed on October 6, 1873 with four squadrons of the 1st, 10th, 11th and 12th Dragoons.

19th Chasseurs — Formed on October 6, 1873 with four squadrons of the 4th, 5th, 16th and 20th Dragoons.

20th Chasseurs — Formed on October 6, 1873 with four squadrons of the 3rd, 10th and 12th Chasseurs and 9th Hussars.

1st Hussars — Jura Hussars on August 30, 1815. Chartres Hussars on September 21, 1824. 1st Hussars on February 27, 1825. (Kept the princely denomination until 1848.)

2nd Hussars — Meurthe Hussars on August 30, 1815. 2nd Hussars on February 27, 1825.

3rd Hussars — Moselle Hussars on August 30, 1815. 3rd Hussars on February 27, 1825.

4th Hussars — Nord Hussars on August 30, 1815. 4th Hussars on February 27, 1825.

5th Hussars — Bas-Rhin Hussars on August 30, 1815. 5th Hussars on February 27, 1825.

6th Hussars — Haut-Rhin Hussars on August 30, 1815. 6th Hussars on February 27, 1825.

7th Hussars — Created by the decree of November 13, 1840.

8th Hussars — Created by the decree of November 13, 1840.

9th Hussars — Created by the decree of November 13, 1840. Disbanded on May 4, 1856. On February 4, 1871, the Imperial Guard Guides Regiment, created on May 1, 1854 with the Guides Regiment (organized on October 23, 1852), became the 9th Hussars.

10th Hussars — Alps Chasseurs on August 30, 1815. 2nd Chasseurs on February 27, 1825. 2nd Lancers on February 19, 1831. 10th Hussars on August 8, 1871.

11th Hussars — Formed October 6, 1873 with four squadrons provided by the 1st Chasseurs, 1st, 3rd, and 8th Hussars.

12th Hussars — Formed October 6, 1873 with four squadrons provided by the 2nd, 4th, 6th and 10th Hussars.

---

in the cavalry than in the other services. None of the old horses remained, and the horses bought during the war were for the most part exhausted. On the day the National Assembly voted for peace, I saw a *régiment de marche* of lancers marching past at Bordeaux which was painful to witness: exhausted and haggard soldiers, gaunt and overworked horses. It was the best argument to put before the screaming crowds in front of the Theatre of Bordeaux who demanded the continuation of the war. Sad to say, we had lost everything, even the right to respond to patriotic spirits! These poor lancers were indeed the living image of a conquered and weary country.

The merging of the *régiments de marche* with the old regiments, of which part had returned from enemy prisons, took place at the same time that the regiments of the *Ancienne Garde* took the left side in the roll call lists of their service branch. This move had been established in a decision of February 10, 1871. The old organization of the 56 regiments from prior to September 4 were scrupulously maintained.

On August 8, 1871, a presidential decision eliminated the service of the lancers and expanded the number of dragoons regiments to 20, the chasseurs to 14, and the hussars to 10. Through a lottery, seven regiments of lancers, the 1st, 3rd, 4th, 5th, 6th, 8th and 9th (former Lancers of the Guard) became the 14th, 15th, 16th, 17th, 18th, 19th and 20th dragoons. The 7th Lancers moved into the chasseurs where it took Number 14 and the 2nd Lancers became the 10th Hussars. All these regiments had six squadrons. When the law of the cadres expanded the number of cavalry regiments to seventy, such were these regiments that they only needed to take one squadron (October 6, 1873) into each of the fifty-six old regiments in order to form the 14 new

Chasseurs à cheval, 11th Regiment (1881).

regiments at four squadrons (6 of dragoons, 6 of chasseurs, and 2 of hussars.) Since then, these new squadrons have been filled out like the old ones at five squadrons. They are to have 156 men in the ranks like all the others. Within the framework of peace, the battalion adjutants were simply eliminated. It was the only drastic reduction which the cavlary was subject to up till the present time.

These seventy regiments were all permanently organized into brigades or divisions. This is an essential point. Each one of the eighteen army corps possesses a brigade composed of a regiment of dragooons and one of light cavalry. To the extent possible, this brigade is assembled near the major part of the corps in order that it can participate in its military training. Besides these 18 mixed brigades, five divisions of independent cavalry (the 1st, 2nd, 4th, 5th, and 6th) are organized at three brigades of two regiments. They set aside a brigade of cuirassiers and a brigade of light cavalry for the 19th (Africa). In the event of war, this brigade of cuirassiers along with the Chasseurs d'Afrique form the 3rd independent division whose number is vacant. As can be seen, the influence of the conquerer was dominant in the French reorganization. This is obviously rather intelligent. However, much less intelligent is the tendency to imitate the national tastes of the Germans, notably the mania for the helmet. As has been seen, it was very unpopular in the countryside and in the nation when the helmet was tried in a squadron of the 11th Chasseurs à cheval at Saint-Germain.

Each army like each nation has customs which should not be upset. These are not changed with impunity. Have the Russians and the Austrians taken up the French red pants? Yes, of course, the conquerors should be studied, but it is less ridiculous to make an act of faith and national renewal from their parody.(1)

The remount cavalry in France is comprised of five companies of horsemen of whom the first four are attached to each of the four great military territorial subdivisions. The fifth attends to the military training establishments. In 1870 they numbered seven. Their origins do not go back further than February 20, 1852. This was well after the experiments which resulted in the formation of permanent cadres of non-commissioned officers and soldiers for the remount. Veteran cavalrymen were employed in this service for a long time to whom some men detached from the regiments were added. However, this went badly enough that it was recognized that forming special corps dedicated solely to one of the

Dragoon, full dress (1876).

most important tasks of the French technical army was necessary. The French remount institutions had been established under a natural principle which brooks no discussion. It was the territorial equine production which guided this organization. Since a law called " the horse conscription" by the farmers put all horses at the disposition of the Minister of War for mobilization, the remount depots, their branches, and their annexes possess the exact statistics of the equine population of France. The misfortunes of 1870-1871, the invasion, and the consumption of horsemeat, which became food by necessity, had notably weakened equine population density. Fifteen years of peace have restored but not increased it.

The cavalry regiments were entrusted with the miltary education of the active sections of the telegraph cavalry. They can be recognized by their national blue dolman jackets and pants with collars and bands in sky blue.

Uniforms. At the same time that the cavalry service was reorganized, its uniforms were appreciably modified. In this regard, the Empire had embarked on the path of reform. After having succumbed to the error of rather luxurious uniforms, it had understood that the more the army increased in number, the more necessary it would become to eliminate the distinguishing

(1) The following details on the war formations and war effectives of France are read in the *Almanach de Gotha* which is so guarded about the armaments of Germany. It is known that usually the information from the almanac in question is drawn from quasi-official sources. For this reason, the following data is presented as a footnote since what the Germans know many French do not.

It says there: "The actual organization of the army allows 24 full army corps (1 to 24) to be raised in the first line of which 5 would be newly formed, 8 would be cavalry divisions, and 36 would be infantry battalions for the scouts service; 24 position batteries and technical troops for the railroad and telegraph service. Each of the 24 army corps would contain 25 infantry battalions (including a battalion of chasseurs), 8 squadrons of cavalry, 18 artillery batteries, 3 companies of engineers, 1 company of pontonniers, and some train detachments and medical troops. These 24 army corps together would form 4 to 5 armies. In the second line, 8 more army corps (Numbers 25 to 32) could be formed in which would be included the *régiments de marche* of the infantry, the cavalry and the artillery from the territorial army plus some proportion of other troops."

This note which contains some factual parts, includes errors or gaps. In order to have 24 army corps and 8 independent cavalry divisions (even if they were only at 4 regiments) 320 squadrons must be available. France only had 296 counting the Chasseurs of Africa. To arrive at this splendid total, it would be appropriate to mobilize the depot squadrons and to form *régiments de marche* as the French were missing more regiments than squadrons. Twenty-four army corps brigades and 16 independent division brigades comprise 80 regiments. The French have only 74. The Spahis will never provide a good regimental service in Europe as they were not created for this purpose.

We are very reluctant to say anything negative about the 18 regional regiments of territorial cavalry (144 squadrons of dragoons and chasseurs) who would have to supply these 8 supplementary corps. Formed of very devoted officers full of zealousness and of cavalrymen who are equal to their leaders, these regiments have one sole flaw. They don't have a single horse. At the annual meetings, they display their eagerness, mounted on horses which the cavalry regiments of the standing army begrudgingly loan them. However, come war, the first thought will be of the cavalry and the artillery of the standing army before horses are given to the light squadrons and the territorial dragoons. It is said that everything is determined in advance and that everyone will go ahead. Although it is regrettable, it can be concluded— as will be done soon—that a fifth of the cadres of the standing cavalry is immoblized in the depots while in the infantry these latter take only a ninth of the cadres. In the engineers and the artillery, they are still smaller percentages. Meanwhile, the wars will be short-lived and the decisive blows will be made in the early days. Thus it is not totally immaterial that, in a service where one does not improvise, a considerable proportion of the total strength should be available.

colors and to remove the differences in dress. These differences made it difficult to transfer men taken from one corps into another. The movement began with the cuirassiers who lost their distinguishing colors in 1860. Instead of the short jacket, they all took up the tunic with the wine-colored collar and lining. The buttons still bore their number. The officers no longer had the jacket but retained the cocked hat. The carabiniers had taken up equerry boots in 1853. They had the tunic in 1860. When they were classified in the Imperial Guard, they added to their magnificent uniform the scarlet aiguillette for the ranks and the silver one for officers. In 1862, the dragoons in turn lost their distinguishing colors. The 1st series (1st to 4th regiments) had traded their distinctive orange color for white. Their short green jacket with breastplate was replaced by the blue tunic with a row of copper buttons and a blue collar. As in the cuirassiers, the number on the buttons was the only differentiaton from one regiment to another. Finally, in 1869, the elegant *kurtka* of the lancers also disappeared. The eight regiments thenceforth wore the tunic with a row of half spherical buttons of pewter and a jonquil yellow collar. The *chapska* was uniformly trimmed in yellow. The epaulettes and the cords remained of white thread as in the past. The busby had been eliminated from the chasseurs in 1848 and was replaced by a wine-colored shako in the hussar style. They received a light green dolman jacket with

Officers of the Household of the President of the Republic and aide-de-camp of the Minister of War (1883).

Trumpeter, cuirassiers, campaign dress (1885).

three rows of buttons and black woolen braids without any other distinguishing mark for the regiments than the number on the button. For headgear they had a busby in black curly sheepskin, decorated with a copper tulip. It had a plume in rooster red feathers and green at the base. As for the hussars, ose favorite sons of the military outfitters, there was a great deal of hesitation before deciding to have them move to the egalitarian level of the required uniform. After having retained their nicest dolmans, their elegant pelisses, their sparkling belts, to which a ravishing curly sheepskin busby with a scarlet bag had been added in 1862, their pelisses and belts were removed. The eight regiments all wore the red wine-colored pants and a dolman with a wine-colored collar in the same form as that of the chasseurs. The 1st and the 8th had a sky blue dolman, the 2nd a chestnut one, the 3rd and the 4th a silver grey one, the 5th a deep blue one, and the 6th and the 7th a light green dolman. The braids were white in the first six regiments and golden yellow for the two last ones. (The 9th had had jonquil yellow at the time of its mustering out after having tried a sky blue one.) In the hussars, the officers' full dress uniform was trimmed with studs in the same color metal as their buttons, (silver for the first six, gold for the two latter). In the chasseurs, the braids and trim were always of black silk, with the exception of the distinguishing marks of rank. Total simplication finally won out in the light cavalry in the two final years of the Empire. In 1869, the 1st and the 8th Hussars tried a dolman tunic of sky blue with a row of pewter buttons, decorated on the chest with six square braids in white wool. The following year, the 1st, 6th, and 9th Regiments of Chasseurs received the same dress, but with braids in black wool. The busby was retained with minor modifications in the bag for the hussars and in the plume for the hussars and the chasseurs. It seemed understood that this would be the definitive uniform—but of course, temporarily—for the entire light cavalry.

After the war, the question of the uniforms was brought up for discussion. Thiers spent precious time on it. Marshal MacMahon was not unconcerned about it, and it even occupies the leisurely hours which politics frequently leaves to the French Minister of War. The cuirassiers and the dragoons received a helmet with a flowing horsehair plume. Its form was graceful, and it weighed much less when compared to its predecessors. However, the new shako of the light cavalry was flattened, inconvenient, and very ugly. As for the jacket, the uniform makers of the time were undecided between the dolman, the fatigue jacket, and the tunic. The officers of the dragoons and the officers and soldiers of the light cavalry had a dolman trimmed with black. It was dark blue for the former and sky blue for the light cavalry, the light blue showing off well against the horses. The cuirassiers (officers and troops) and the dragoons (troops) remained as they were until the end of the Empire. A useful and intelligent reform which was asked for by everyone gave white metal to the entire cavalry. There were no more regiments with gold. However, the soldiers, especially the non-commissioned officers and particularly in the regiments where the colonel did not allow whimsical clothing, complained a lot about the oversimplification of their uniforms. This applied more to the manufacture than to the cut. Before holding sufficient quantities of clothing for 1,200,000 to 1,500,000 men of the standing army and 600,000 of the territorial army in the French military magazines, the suppliers were forced to accept greatly reduced prices. As an industry never gives full value for the money paid, the suppliers' profits were made to the detriment of the French soldier. The soldier was not totally wrong in complaining of being badly dressed. As for the officers, they compensated for the regulation mediocrity of their equipment with refinements. It is always in the officers corps of the cavalry that men of proud bearing and fine dress were to be found. From then on, there was little other than a double band of gold

or silver on the pants to relieve the spartan monotony of these uniforms. This is evident when considering the officers of the military household of the President of the Republic on the day of a gala event.

The law of 1829 on the cavalry service had been completely remade. The new one raised critical numbers, but the old one lived on for half a century without ever completely satisfying anyone.

The Tunisian expedition showed the relative weakness of the new French organization since the regiments of light cavalry which had been assigned there never mounted more than three squadrons. It is true that every year the number of horses in condition to march had to increase. In this history of ninety years, it can be seen that the cavalry was, at the same time, a matter of training and a question of money. With a population as military as the French are at heart, it is not only a question of money. If the budget is generous, the cavalry is fine. If the deputies who hold the purse strings go for cutbacks, the cavalry becomes poor and, consequently, mediocre. Since numerous squadrons are required in order for training to progress, nothing is learned with drill squadrons of eighty horses. Meanwhile, come the war, after ten years of misinterpreted cutbacks which have ruined the French mounted troops, millions are spent for a mobilization which always reaches its full effect too late. Despite the "horse conscription," it will still be the same. It is much acknowledged that, in the event of war, the cavalry will leave as it is. It therefore seems that it could be immediately given a greater number of men and horses. During these last years, this has much concerned the ministers of war. The French cavalry, almost destroyed by the defeats of 1870, is in good condition. However it still errs a bit on the side of quality and especially in the number of horses. A project exists which decreases the number of field officers and of squadron officers by regiment but which increases the number of regiments. I must say that this project is not very popular in the service. This project, being linked to other reforms, probably will not soon be executed. Moreover, everything which parliamentarianism has done has been incessantly and unproductively reworked. Remember the projects of the law of recruitment and the territorial army. The revision of the law of cadres has no chance of being quickly withdrawn.

In closing, in the general reorganization of the army, the cavalry service is the one which profits the least from the terrible lessons of the last war. Although the infantry was increased by a third and the artillery by two fifths, the cavalry has barely been increased by about an eighth. In fact, before 1870, France had 348 squadrons (36 of the Guard; 150 of reserve and line cavalry; 120 of light cavalry; and 42 of African cavalry). Today, it has 392 (350 of reserve, line and light cavalry and 42 of African cavalry). However, in adding to the number of regiments of France (70 instead of 65), the number of squadrons immediately unavailable has been increased in the same proportion. By this very fact, 70 fifth squadrons instead of 56 have been immobilized from the very start as if they were depots. The actual increase in the number of available squadrons in the event of mobilization is really only thirty. This enormously reduces the value of the system initiated for the cavalry by the law of cadres and justifies study of the project.

In terms of effective strength, this glorious and hard-working service is certainly not up to the level of service which a European war would impose upon it. Unfortunately, however, it is very expensive and our political financiers always think back to what Louvois said to a colonel in the cavalry:

"Sir, your regiment costs a million per year."

However, the cavalry might well answer with the colonel hailed by the minister of the great King:

"Yes, of course, but in one hour, a good regiment pays its debt in full, be it a century old!"

Sergeant of hussars (1885).

1. L'ARMÉE FRANÇAIS: frontispiece, 1883 - 1889 deluxe edition.

2.   GENERAL OF THE FIRST EMPIRE (Detaille, 1892).
Oil on canvas (31½ × 25¾ in.), Collection of Mr. and Mrs. John D. Ellis Jr., Houston, Texas.

3. POINT OF THE ADVANCE GUARD: 9th Regiment of Hussars, 1806 (Detaille, 1893).
Gouache (32 × 23¼ in.), Musée de l'Armée, Paris.

4. INFORMATION FOR THE
GENERAL STAFF, 1805
(Detaille, 1903).
Oil on canvas (17½ × 26 in.),
Musée de l'Armée, Paris.

6. THE PRISONERS: Interrogating Austrian prisoners, 1800 (Detaille, 1893).
Oil on canvas (14 × 11¼ in.), Musée de l'Armée, Paris.

5. THE ENEMY IN SIGHT: A patrol of the 4th Regiment of Hussars, c. 1800
(Detaille, 1899). Oil on canvas (26½ × 18½ in.),
Collection of Mr. and Mrs. Don Troiani.

7. VIVA L'EMPEREUR!: Charge of the 4th Regiment of Hussars at the Battle of Friedland, June 14, 1807 (Detaille, 1891).
Detail, oil on canvas (150 × 178 in.), Art Gallery of New South Wales, Sydney.

8. THE SENTRY: Grenadier of the
Imperial Guard, First Empire (Detaille).
Oil on canvas (44 × 22 in.),
Musée de l'Armée, Paris.

9. GENERAL COUNT LASALLE AT WAGRAM, July 1809 (Detaille, 1912).
Oil on canvas (72 × 64 in.), Musée de l'Armée, Paris.

10. THE VICTORY IS OURS!: the evening of Jena, October 14, 1806 (Detaille,1894). Oil on canvas (32 × 52 in.). Musée de l'Armée, Paris.

11. THE CHECKPOINT: cuirassier and infantry of the line, c. 1875
(Detaille, 1876). Watercolor (14½ × 10½ in.),
The Forbes Magazine Collection, New York.

12. FRAGMENT FROM THE PANORAMA OF REZONVILLE:
Grenadiers of the Imperial Guard (Detaille, 1883).
Oil on canvas (85½ × 52½ in.), Musée de l'Armée, Paris.

13. FRAGMENT FROM THE PANORAMA OF CHAMPIGNY, November 30, 1870: The last of the cartridge box (Detaille and Neuville, 1882).
Oil on canvas (114 × 100 in.), Musée de l'Armée, Paris.

14. CHARGE OF THE 9TH REGIMENT
OF CUIRASSIERS, August 6, 1870
(Detaille, 1874).
Oil on canvas (55½ × 79 in.),
Collection of Albert Benamou, Paris.

15. FRAGMENT FROM THE
PANORAMA OF REZONVILLE:
Soldiers at a water pump
(Detaille, 1883).
Oil on canvas (82½ × 111 in.),
Collection of Mr. and Mrs. Mel Brooks.

16. NAPOLEON III AT THE
CAMP OF CHÂLONS,
1857 (Detaille).
Watercolor and gouache
(30 × 25½ in.),
Musée de l'Armée, Paris.

17. THE ATTACK! (Detaille).
Oil on canvas (47 × 50 in.),
The Forbes Magazine Collection,
New York.

18. PRUSSIAN CUIRASSIERS ATTACK
ON A FRENCH PROVISION TRAIN
(Detaille, 1882).
Oil on canvas (32 × 52 in.),
The Forbes Magazine Collection, New York.

19. THE DEFENSE OF CHAMPIGNY, November 30, 1870
(Detaille, 1879). Oil on canvas (48 × 86 in.),
The Forbes Magazine Collection, New York.

20. ALERT! (Detaille, 1880).
Oil on canvas (26⅜ x 22⅜ in.),
The Forbes Magazine Collection, New York.

21. THE PAUSE (Detaille, 1888).
Oil on canvas (120 × 156 in.),
Musée de l'Armée, Paris.

L'ARMÉE FRANÇAISE

2ᴱ
VOLUME

White flag. First expedition of Algiers (1830).

HISTORY OF THE TROOPS OF THE ARMY OF AFRICA

From 1831 to 1852, the French special Army of Africa was a breeding ground of valiant, active officers and, from 1852 to 1870, the reserve for the elite of the national army. It was a kind of second Imperial Guard but more flexible and more available than the actual one. Today, thanks to a law of equality which does not allow for exceptions even in troops permanently called to a tougher service, the French corps of Africa are recruited through the classes. They do not differ appreciably from the regiments of France except in uniform. Also, they possess an already enormous though recent fame—*novissima nobilita*—which makes them preferable for distant expeditions.

The special Army of Africa was permanently created under the ministry of Marshal Saint-Arnaud. This was a military man of rare wisdom and a very informed organizational genius. Previously, political fortunes, the needs of conquest, budget availability or scarceness as well as the need to advance some outstanding personalities had ruled over the organizations and the dissolutions of the corps permanently attached to the Algerian service.

On February 13, 1852, Saint-Arnaud had already been in the colony for sixteen years. He was the favorite protege of Marshal Bugeaud and also the depository of the intimate thoughts of the new French soverign. Saint-Arnaud demonstrated the usefulness of tripling the Zouaves, of bringing the recruitment of native troops into a progressive movement, and of specially compensating the military men who dedicated themselves to the prosperity of Algeria. The law instituting compulsory service unfortunately did not take enough consideration of this new, improved system which was the fruit of a half century of experience. Also, it took only a few years to show the French legislators that, in copying German military methods, they had lost sight of the fact that the Prussians did not have Algeria. It is possible that if the Prussians had had Algeria, they would have given some advantages to officers who had dedicated their lives to the problem. Today, the French have been waiting four years for the organization of an overseas army since certain fashionable political theories cannot come to an agreement on the needs of Algeria and of the colonies. An orator in France long ago pronounced these fine parliamentarian words with conviction: "Let the colonies perish rather than a principle."

THE ZOUAVES

These wonderful Zouaves have won the admiration of the enemy. Henceforth, they were succeeded by soldiers who were without a doubt full of eagerness and courage but not of the same caliber as the earlier ones. They were beneath the walls of Sebastopol, on the plains of Lombardy, and in Mexico until the final battles of that fatal war where all was lost except the honor of the French soldier. However, the old bands from Africa—those finished troopers tied to the military profession as were Napoleon the First's Old Guard—have died. There are no more and there can be no more of them.

The *Turcos* (native Tirailleurs), the *Zephirs*, or even more so the *Joyeux* (battalions of light infantry of Africa) and the Foreign Legion have retained all their originality and their primitive force along with their recruitment. The high reputation of the Zouaves is upheld only by the esprit de corps and the quality of the officers.

Naturally enough, the Zouaves and the native Tirailleurs result from the same premise as the Spahis and the Chasseurs d'Afrique. This is: the need to make use of local goodwill and to offer military hospitality to the tribes and to their chiefs. The services which were rendered to the French Occupation by the irregulars and by the allied or subjugated tribes in the early years of the conquest will not be assessed here. This is merely a history of the ten regiments of Zouaves, the Algerian Tirailleurs, the foreign

regiments, and the three battalions of Africa. This will be followed by the history of the African cavalry regiments.

On October 1, 1830 the new government which had been given to France feared European complications. It had more than half the line and light regiments of the expeditionary corps return home. Immediately, the new commander in chief, General Clausel, organized the first native corps. He was obviously haunted by his memories of Santo Domingo and Illyria. This was very rapid and daring. However, an old militia of the Dey, the *Zoudaouas*, offered its services. The opportunity was tempting for a warrior who had seen the Dalmatian and Illyrian auxiliary corps operate under Napoleon I. The Zouaves were created. French officers and non-commissioned officers were charged with training and disciplining them. The corps had two battalions which seemed to be administered separately. The command of the 1st Battalion was given to Captain Maumet of the Royal Corps General Staff. The command of the second was given to Captain Duvivier of the Engineers Corps.

The most fiery officers of the special arms and services in all the organizations of the Army of Africa asked to move into the infantry and the cavalry. They wanted to bring with them their extensive knowledge, the qualities and the high character resulting from a particularly good education. Most especially, they hoped to find advancement there in keeping with these qualities and with their ambitious activity.

As soon as they were formed, the Zouaves entered into a campaign and were baptized by fire on November 28 of the same year in the expedition against Medeah. Despite the services—or perhaps because of the services which they rendered—the two battalions did not recruit sufficiently amongst the natives. On December 6, 1832 they were mustered out and a battalion of eight French

Zouaves. Combat in the streets of Constantine (1837).

companies and two Arab ones were reorganized under the command of Commander Duvivier. He was replaced soon after by Major Kolb who was succeeded by de Lamoricière, captain in the corps since its beginnings, who was promoted to major on July 1, 1834. In the meantime, the existence of the Zouaves had been recognized by the royal decree of March 7, 1833. Until then, it had been ruled by the decrees of governors. Commander Lamoricière carried the Zouave spirit in his heart and his head. It has been said and written that the Zouaves' uniform had been established by him. It is possible that, while taking part in the first organization, he played an important role in the adoption of the new dress which has since undergone few modifications. However, the annals of 1831—*The Military Annual*, which must be considered as the best history of the army—gives the following description of the Zouaves' uniform: "Jacket with sleeves and waistcoat closed in front, without sleeves, in blue cloth. Moorish pants in wine-colored cloth. Jacket with sleeves, waistcoat, riding breeches in cotton cloth. Belt of blue cotton cloth. Greatcoat in brown cloth. Turban and red riding breeches. Shoes, legging in leather. Knapsack. Turkish cartridge box. Distinguishing marks of officers and non-commissioned officers are the same as in the Hussars service." The cadre of officers was thus composed in the following manner:

Zouaves. Drummers, Campaign dress (1886).

Native Tirailleurs, full dress (1886).

1st Battalion: Major, Maumet – Battalion Adjutant Captain, Levaillant – Captain Paymaster, Cuny - Captains Fournier, Régnault, Sanzay, Bigot, Balleiguier, Poulle - Second Lieutenants Bosc, Dufau, Martin, Raindre, Deleforty, Contrault, Lherbon de Lussats, Thiriet, Fossier, Touron, Mille, Morand.

2nd Battalion: Major Duvivier - Battalion Adjutant Lieutenant Demoyen - Lieutenant Pay–master Besoux - Captains Duval, Raphel, Duhamel, Picouleau, Juchault de Lamoricière, Abadie - Lieutenant Davière. Second Lieutenants Chaurou, Godard, Vergé, Onimus, de Gouzens, de Gardarens de Boisse, Samary, Thuilier, Tixador.

As is seen, this composition presents many irregularities. However, it offers great hope to the men who threw themselves into the unknown at the head of new troops. The high reputation quickly acquired by the Zouaves and the necessity of compensating its leader rapidly led to the reorganization of the second battalion. However, this time the two battalions formed only a single corps under Commander Lamoricière who had become the glorious personification of the Zouaves. This corps was always on campaign. It is seen at the Mouzaia Pass with General Bro (March and April 1836) and in Mitidja with Colonel Marey (September of the same year). The two majors were Cuny and Drolenvaux. The second siege of Constantine (1837) (1) was an apotheosis for the Zouaves and their young leader who was promoted to colonel and retained their command. The detailed history of the Zouaves would be that of the French Algerian colony. Therefore, we must be content in the recital of only their glorious deeds. It is nonetheless useful to measure the value of these troops as was ordered by the army by writing out the names of the Zouave

Zouaves. Combat of the Medeah Pass (1841).

officers who were involved after the Combat of Col (1841). First there is their illustrious leader whom French civil discord had so inopportunely cut off from his military career. There is Major Régnault who was more unfortunate in the aftermath of having been promoted to general. He found death in the rioters' bullets in June 1848. There was Renaud, "Renaud of the rear guard," the soldier without fear or reproach. He was killed at Champigny and died with the conviction that finally the enemy had been defeated as in the past. There are the captains Ladmirault, Bosc, Blangini, de Barral, Lieutenant le Poitevin de Lacroix, and Second Lieutenant Blaise (also killed at Paris in 1870). All those in the army who had the ambition and the fanaticism of the profession dreamed of joining the Zouaves. All dreamed of this but not everyone got there despite the fact that death harshly ravaged the chosen. When Colonel de Lamoricière was named general, Lieutenant Colonel Cavaignac replaced him. Equally courageous but less brillant than his predecessor, Eugène Cavaignac also came out of the skillful Engineers service. With his qualities as mathematician, he had understood that the shortest path from the captain's epaulettes to the general's stars lies in continuous battle, daily battle, where opportunities to show ones talents and military virtues are never lacking. The court of King Louis-Philippe took great pride in facilitating this route despite his overall character, his Republican attachments and his systematic opposition to the campaign plans of the time.

It was after their stay at Medeah (April 1841) that the Zouaves received their first flag. The Duke of Orléans had promised it to them the preceding year after the combat of the Col. "Zouaves," said the governer, "I give you this flag in the name of the King. You must be devoted to the King because he is the personification of the country. This flag will be the village bells for you, the talisman of victory. It should not stay with the reserve. You will carry it with you into the midst of battles and you will all die rather than abandon it."

At the moment of passing through la Chiffa while marching toward the Arabs, this short and ardent speech was better than a long discourse. It would produce a marvelous effect on bold soldiers and adventurers recognizing no other discipline than the call of their leaders and no other reason than that of their cartridges and their bayonets. Since all the generals wanted to have Zouaves in their column, the two battalions did not often operate together. However, they found themselves reunited for the supplying of Milianah. While the 2nd Battalion (Commander Leroy de Saint-Arnaud) distinguished itself in the combat of the Oued-Boulan, the 1st Battalion (Commander Le Flô) proved itself beyond all praise on the same day. Lieutenant Jeanningros was wounded there.

LIST OF FIELD OFFICERS OF THE OLD ZOUAVE REGIMENT

Colonels	Lieutenant Colonels	Majors	Administrative Field Officers
Caraignac, 1841 to 1844 De Ladmirault, 1845 to 1848 Canrobert, 1849 D'Aurelle de Paladines, 1850 to 1851 Bourbaki, 1851	DESPINOY, 1842 De Chasseloup-Laubat, 1843 - 1844 Bouat, 1845 Grandchamp, 1848 to 1850 Bourbaki, 1850	D'Autemarre d'Ervillé de Gardarens de Boisse de Peyraguey TARBOURIECH Espinasse Latrille de Lorences Pecqueult de Lavarande TASSIN LAURE	DE FRESNE DU KERLAN MOUROUX

(1) The first name which appears in the obituary of the 1st Regiments of Zouaves is that of Captain Bigot, killed in the expedition of Rome in 1831. The names of officers, non-commissioned officers, and Zouaves of the old corps and of the 1st Regiment are reverently mixed in this document. There were 300 Zouaves at the assault of Constantine. The losses rose to 3 officers killed or dead of their wounds, 8 wounded; 68 non-commissioned officers and soldiers killed and 68 wounded. Total: 147. Thus 153 of them remained standing. The day before, Marshal Vallee had asked Lieutenant Colonel Lamoricière: "If half of your men fell in the breach, would the others hold?" Lamoricière says, "I answered: Well, you will have command of the first column." The following day, half of the Zouaves fell in the breach but the French had Constantine.

Captains Le Flô, Le Vaillant, Martin, Gardarens de Boisse, Sanzay and Lieutenant Samary commanded the six sections at 50 men each.

The Zouaves Corps became the Zouaves Regiment in 1842 (royal decree of September 2, 1841) and was expanded from twelve to twenty-seven companies. The eighth companies of each battalion were composed solely of natives. From this point on, there were three battalions. The ninths formed the depot. Valuable officers rushed in from everywhere or were forced to choose the most meritorious from amongst the best. As many soldiers and non-commissioned officers as were needed were found. On March 20, 1842, the governor general could review these magnificent troops on the Place Bab-el-Oued in Algiers. Its general staff was as follows: Colonel, de Cavaignac; Lieutenant Colonel, Despinoy; Majors, Leroy de Saint-Arnaud, d'Autemarre de'Ervillé, Frémy; Administrative Field Officer Major, du Fresne de Kerlan.

From the early days of its organization, the regiment was dispersed into the three provinces: the 1st Battalion left for Blidah; the 2nd Battalion for Tlemcen; the 3rd Battalion for Bone. The Zouaves were recruited through voluntary enlistment and always maintained considerable effective strength of at least one hundred twenty-five men in a company. Admission into its ranks required at least two years of service. The African war also resulted in good men suddenly appearing in the regular regiments.

The names of those who became generals have been highlighted (list p.193). With Commander Leroy de Saint-Arnaud, the old regiment of Zouaves counts two Marshals of France in its active troops. De Peyraguey, a veteran of the French imperial armies, was killed in Africa as a major. Tarbouriech and Laure, who became colonels, are dead. The first died of cholera in the Crimea. The second was killed in Italy at the head of the local tirailleurs regiment.

How can one be amazed at the valor of troops with such commanders?

When the creation of three regiments of Zouaves (one per province) was permanently adopted in 1852, the question had already been tossed about at the high levels of the government. Under Louis-Philippe, this had been much desired but there were no means for making it a reality. Budgetary considerations were even against trying to talk about it in the Chambers. Marshal Bugeaud, General de Lamoricière, and the Duke of Aumale were in favor of the extension of the elite troops from which the native element had almost entirely disappeared, at least as a basic component. Under Minister d'Hautpoul, during the triennial presidency of Prince Louis,

LIST OF COLONELS OF THE FIRST THREE ZOUAVE REGIMENTS		
1st Regiment	**2nd Regiment**	**3rd Regiment**
BOURBAKI, 1851-1854	VINOY, 1852-1853	TARBOURIECH, 1852-1854
COLLINEAU, 1855-1857	CLER, 1853-1854	DE SAINT-POL, 1854-1855
PAULZE-D'IVOY, 1857-1859	SAURIN, 1854-1859	DE BONNET, MAURELHAN, POLÉS, 1855
BRINCOURT, 1860-1864	TINIER, 1859-1861	DE CHABRON, 1855-1859
CLINCHANT, 1864-1866	GAMBIER, 1861-1864	MANGIN, 1859-1864
CARTERET-TRÉCOURT, 1866-1870	LEFEBVRE, 1864-1870	TOURRE, 1864-1865
BARRACHIN, 1870-1878	DETRIE, 1870-1876	BOCHER, 1865-1870
HERVÉ, 1878-1882	GADEY, 1876-1883	CLOUX, 1871-1878
EMOND D'ESCLEVIN, 1882	THIERY, 1883	CAJARD, 1878-1881
		BERTRAND, 1881-1885
		LUCAS, 1885

a legal project for the reorganization of the army expanded the Zouave regiments to three. However, the Legislative Assembly did not have the time to be concerned with such things. It was only after the coup d'etat (February 13, 1852) that this reorganization—so much awaited and desired—was decreed. It was a question then of forming two regimental general staffs and 54 new companies. There was indescribable enthusiasm in the army as there had been in 1840 for the chasseurs à pied. The army hoped for war. It felt that these elite corps would deal serious blows to the enemy. There were a thousand requests. The Cafe Hollandais overflowed in the evening with candidates who came to Paris to further their interests, to scheme close to General Saint-Arnaud, Minister of War, and near General Peyssard and Colonel Trochu, head and second in command of personnel. The influence of the chief of state was used to lobby for the positions of mere second lieutenants. I can attest that he did not commit great injustices. Although some good officers might not have obtained the positions they sought, no second-rate officers were admitted. It was really too much and obviously dangerous for the administration of promotion to gather together so many active, intelligent and, shall we say, legitimately ambitious officers into three regiments. Nor was it in the interests of the army to do so. If the Crimean War had not come along to give them a dignified occupation, these corps of officers would certainly have badly used their military energies. This is what must have happened in the second regiment during a short absence of Colonel Vinoy. Unfortunate duals without any reason other than overly exuberant military spirit brought about severe reactions on the part of General Pèlissier.

Most of these officers became generals; four died under fire or from overwork: Paulze d'Ivoy, killed at Melegnano; Tarbouriech of the 2nd, died of cholera four days after the Battle of Alma where he was covered in glory; Gambier, of the 2nd Regiment, died in the hospital of Rochefort upon returning from Mexico; and Tourre died in Mexico from the effects of suffocation during a fire. From the reorganization to their departure for the Army of the Orient, the three Zouave regiments gave their new flags baptism by fire. All three flags which were given to them on May 10, 1852 bore the same legend: Constantine, 1837; Mouzaïa, 1840; Isly, 1844; Zaatcha, 1849; Fedj-Menazel, 1851 (1).

The three regiments were represented at the taking of Laghouat: the 1st and the 3rd each by a battalion, the 2nd Regiment by two battalions commanded by Lieutenant Colonel Cler. Major Morand (of the 2nd Regiment) was killed in the breach of Laghouat. He was the son of the celebrated general, one of the best division leaders of the Empire, and the brother of three officers who distinguished themselves in the Zouaves. In May 1853, all three regiments left for the Army of the Orient, each one at a strength of 2 battalions with 8 companies of 150 men.

The 1st Regiment was attached to the 1st Brigade (Espinasse) of the 1st Division (Canrobert).

The 2nd Regiment was attached to the 1st Brigade (de Monet) of the 3rd Division (Prince Napoleon).

The 3rd Regiment was attached to the 1st Brigade (d'Autemarre) of the 2nd Division (Bosquet).

From then on, there would be no war nor expedition, with the exception of China, where they were not necessary and where they did not lend their powerful assistance.

During the Crimean campaign, they each had their part of glory.

The 1st Regiment, after having suffered cruelly from cholera in the deplorable expedition of the Dobrutscha, embarked for the Crimea with 1,317 men. At Alma its 1st Battalion was the battalion of direction for the attack of the center. At the attack of the telegraph, the shaft of its flag carried by Second Lieutenant Payan was broken. Sergeant Major Fleury had his head taken off by a bullet while planting a tricolored flag on the tower. In the assault (September 14, 1855) under the command of General MacMahon, the 1st Zouaves had the honor of forming one of the heads of attack and of covering itself in glory. MacMahon had chosen Corporal

---

(1) Two of these flags have been decorated: that of the 2nd Regiment at Magenta for the flag taken from the Count Hartmann Regiment, and that of the 3rd Regiment for taking two Mexican flags in the battle of San Lorenzo. The flags which were given to the four Zouave regiments at the review of July 14, 1880 bear the following for the three first: 1st Regiment: Constantine, 1837; Sebastopol, 1854-1855; Melegnano, 1859; Puebla, 1863. 2nd Regiment: Laghouat, 1852; Sebastopol, 1854-1855; Magenta, 1859; Puebla, 1863. 3rd Regiment: Sebastopol, 1854-1855; Kabylie, 1857; Palestro, 1859; Puebla, 1863.

No legend has been inscribed on the flag of the 4th Regiment. This is a flagrant injustice. As the direct descendant of the Zouave Regiment of the Guard, it should bear the immortal names of Sebastopol, Magenta and of Solferino on its standard.

Lihiaut as his flag bearer. In that terrible shock, 8 officers from the regiment were killed: Major Laüer, Battalion Adjutant Rousset, Captains d'Ormoy, de Ligniville (one of the four great soldiers of Lorraine), Lieutenants de Franoux and Villeneuve, the Second Lieutenants La Fournerie and Chrétien; 18 officers wounded: Colonel Collineau (two times), Captains Bonnet, Brice de Ville, Guillemain, Ollivier, Bousson, Sée and Dupuis, Lieutenants Désandré, Blot, Sauvageot, Payan, Bordes; Ozenfant, Second Lieutenant Flag Bearer, and Second Lieutenants Jamot, Vorgère, Rousseau and Leroux, 486 men out of action. What slaughter! However, the 1st Zouaves received an officer's cross, twenty knighthoods and thirty-nine military medals by the decrees of September 27 and December 11, 1855 and of March 25 and April 16, 1856. For its part, the platoon of sappers had a chevalier's cross for sapper Corporal Leblanc and five medals for the sappers Meune, Mouton, Lafosse, Maraut, and Michel. When the Russian general in chief Luders came to visit General Pelissier after peace, it was the 1st Zouaves which supplied the guard of honor. It would be an injustice not to add to the list of the dead from the assault the names of Captain Lauréal and of Lieutenant Orliac, killed at Alma, of Major Javary, Lieutenant Romieu, and Second Lieutenant Goerdorp, killed in the trenches. On May 11, 1856, the 1st Zouaves was back at Algiers.

The 2nd Zouaves, having not taken part in the expedition of la Dobrutscha, had suffered less from cholera than the 1st and 3rd Regiments. Nonetheless, it took only 1,100 men to the Crimea. Five months before on April 23, it had shipped off 2,192 to Algiers. Its part in the Battle of Alma was difficult. It lost Second Lieutenant Esmieu. Captain Sage and Second Lieutenant de Vermondrans were wounded in a vigorous attack while applying the efforts of the Canrobert Division in the center. During the night of February 20 to 21, it did not succeed in an attack against the Russian ambush despite its spirit. This attack, begun under the worst conditions, proved fatal. It left 270 men dead, wounded or prisoner on the battlefield. Captains Dequirot, Doux, Sage and Borel, Lieutenant Bartel and Second Lieutenant Sevestre were killed, Captain Pierre and Second Lieutenant Lacaze were made prisoners; Lieutenants Lesur, Blanchet, du Mazel, Lacretelle, Second Lieutenants Guillerault, Baratchard, and Vilain were wounded. At the event of June 7, the taking of the Malakoff's white batteries, the 2nd Regiment worked marvels. However, its overly prolonged pursuit against the enemy cost it dearly: 705 men from the ranks were disabled; Captains Pruvost, Lavessiere, Perrot, Doré, de Lignerolles, Lescop and Lieutenant Michelin were killed. Captain Javary, Lieutenants de Koenigsegg, Petitbeau, Arnaud and Second Lieutenants Vincendon, Perceval and Ritter were wounded. Despite these considerable losses, it still provided a magnificent effort at the time of the fruitless attack of Mamelon-Vert on June 18. Captains Frasseto and Pouyant were killed as well as Lieutenant de Vermondrans and Second Lieutenants Gabalde and Veysser. Colonel Saurin, the two majors Lacretelle and Darbois, Lieutenants Jeanningros and Vidalenc, and Second Lieutenants Letondot, Vincent, Ritter, Escourou and Coiffé were wounded and 200 men from the ranks were disabled. In twelve days, the 2nd Regiment lost 905 Zouaves: twelve of its officers were killed, 16 wounded. Captain Lauer commanded the

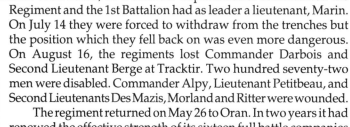

Regiment and the 1st Battalion had as leader a lieutenant, Marin. On July 14 they were forced to withdraw from the trenches but the position which they fell back on was even more dangerous. On August 16, the regiments lost Commander Darbois and Second Lieutenant Berge at Tracktir. Two hundred seventy-two men were disabled. Commander Alpy, Lieutenant Petitbeau, and Second Lieutenants Des Mazis, Morland and Ritter were wounded.

The regiment returned on May 26 to Oran. In two years it had renewed the effective strength of its sixteen full battle companies three times.

In the Battle of Alma, the 3rd Regiment took the heights at the edge of the sea. On November 5, it again distinguished itself through its spirit and lost two officers and 22 Zouaves killed, 9 officers and 141 men wounded. On March 18 and 22, 1855 in night attacks, it lost 8 officers and 53 men killed and 11 officers and 186 Zouaves wounded. Commander Banon died in the latter event and Captain Brincourt received six wounds there. At Mamelon-Vert (June 7), it lost 4 officers and 79 Zouaves killed, 11 officers, 402 men were wounded and 43 were missing. Finally at Tracktir (August 16), it stopped the first attempts of 40,000 Russians who sought to turn the army into the Valley of the Tchernaia. In this difficult campaign, the 3rd Regiment—without counting deaths from disease—lost 16 officers and 187 Zouaves killed. It had in addition 45 officers and 1,002 men wounded. Amongst the officers who appear in the history of the regiments as having most frequently distinguished themselves, Commander Dubos, Captians Japy, Dubois, Lieutenant Guerif and Second Lieutenant Taillecourt, Major Banon, killed by the enemy, and Captain Lalanne, also killed on the field of battle, must be cited. The 3rd Zouaves returned to Africa on May 30, 1856.

After having seen these long lists of killed and wounded, that statement so profoundly typical of Marshal Bugeaud comes to mind: "It is always the same ones who are killed." A lieutenant is wounded, he is named captain and compensates in another battle by being killed. It is the majors, already distinguished as captains, who always fall in the first row! General Pélissier said in the Crimea in his nasal voice: "Ah, I could be lavish with medals and crosses without fear of straining the budget! Hardly do these brave men have the ribbon, then they believe themselves obliged to show more recklessness." Now or never is the time to speak of the customs of the Zouaves and of the care they lavished

Zouaves attacking (Sebastopol, September 8, 1855).

The Theater of the Zouaves in the Crimea (1855).

on the tribe's grub and on their theater. The Zouave is at the same time Parisian and Arab, that is, he is industrious and courageous. In 1854, he was always a soldier having at least five years in the service. When he had the three long-service stripes, he was called a *marabout*, a holy man of supernatural powers. Aware of the price of everything due to the privations which civilian life had forced upon him and which he had again found in military life, he left nothing behind and collected everything. His reputation as a marauder comes from him anticipating and knowing that he will make fabric from a piece of wood or from other things which he collects, sometimes at another's expense. However others do not hold it against him since he has his ways of obtaining things or of being excused for having taken them. In this struggle with necessity, the Zouave shows himself more often amiable and philosophical than harsh and ungrateful. The tribe or the squad is always well provisioned. If the administrative officer is missing a roast or a fine bottle of liquor from a swindler, the Zouave who has them, with averted gaze, will take care that neither bone nor glass can betray the secret of his soul. The history of Lord Raglan's flock is a marvel. The English general in chief loved chops and his chief steward maintained a magnificent flock which a military shepherd took to pasture. An old Zouave, tempted by this prey, staked out the herd's path. One fine day, dressed exactly like the shepherd, he presented himself at the stable and made off with the sheep which were never to be seen again. Lord Raglan laughed till the tears ran down his face in telling this adventure to General Canrobert. The latter acknowledged very gallantly that if he had had cattle, his old soldiers would not have left them alone either. The English officers had particularly appreciated the culinary talents of the Zouaves and their unusual fashion of going to market. Lord Raglan said: "My soldiers die of hungar with triple rations; your Zouaves make a devil of a meal with nothing." "Oh well," replied General Bosquet, "your men are joined with ours and everyone eats well." What was not possible administratively was often done through camaraderie. More than once Zouaves and Highlanders have been seen mingling around an English roast beef cooked in the French manner. Courageous as well, these soldiers mixed their table pleasures as they mixed their blood on the days of battle. The Theater of the Zouaves was the product of their idleness and of their cheerfulness. At night in the encampment, a Parisian warbled a light-hearted song; another parodied the steps of a dancer from the Opera. Two set to recreating the patter of a carnival show and the following day friends and officers came to visit them. Thus the Theater of the Zouaves was created. The orchestra conductor having not yet been invented at this time, no theatrical soiree was dedicated to that famous troop of comedians who included in their repertoire the joyous Coudere of the *"Varietes"* and the Agamemnon of *"Belle Helene"* and whose dramatic exploits were readily told. At the beginning of Spring 1855, its inauguration took place. It had a superb camp almost under the fire of the battery that the Russians had established on the white peak. The soldiers, by reason of the ineffectualness of its firing, jokingly gave it the name of *"Batterie Gringalet."* We have been able to collect three programs from the Theater of the Zouaves. Their dates and the explanations which accompany them could be cause for reflection on the morals of the French soldiers when the war had not yet become what the axiom made it: Force takes precedence over law.

These programs embellished with caricatures—some on the Russians, others on the Zouaves— came from the lithographic section of the 2nd Corps. The last two were signed Woeffer. They are done with a witty and firm if somewhat inexperienced touch. During the Crimean War, the third battalions of Zouaves not only had resupplied the effectives of their war battalions which, as has just been seen, was not easy to do. They also had to wage a campaign. With the return of the war battalions, a great expedition against the Kabylie was decided upon. In 1855, a weakly conducted and badly planned expedition produced only indifferent results. In order to erase the disgraceful effects of this expedition, the government decided to give Marshal Randon the means and the auxiliaries with which it was impossible not to succeed. Peace was made, numerous troops could be made available, and an appointed division of infantry (Renault's Division) left France for Algeria. Two other divisions were formed with the old African troops and, naturally, the three regiments of Zouaves. These latter displayed a new, superb depth of character from having participated in the siege of Sebastopol.

Zouaves and Highlanders at the canteen, in Crimea (1855).

The Zouaves never rested. After the permanent submission of the Kabylie which occupied the years 1856 to 1858, European complications recalled them to the Continent. For the Italian War, the entire Army of Africa was brought together. This time the regiments left with three battalions of six companies at 150 men—that is, 2,700 men per regiment. They were placed: the 1st Regiment to the 1st Brigade (Goze) of the 3rd Division (Bazaine) of Baraguay d'Hilliers' Corps; the 2nd to the Castagny Brigade, 2nd of the 2nd Division (Espinasse) of MacMahon's Corps; the 3rd, to the 1st Brigade (Neigre) of the d'Autemarre Division, 5th Corps. They did not have the luck of participating in the Battle of Montebello which opened a new era of success for the French services. However, at the Battle of Magenta, the 1st Zouaves took the flag and 500 soldiers from the 9th Regiment's Count Hartman. The Zouave Daurière and Adjutant Savière were responsible for this glorious trophy to which the eagle of the regiment owes the signal honor of being decorated with the Chevalier's Cross. Major Fondrevaye, Captain Fayout and Second Lieutenant Levis had been killed. Commander Sainthilliers, Captains Vincendon and Marin, Lieutenants Letondot, Pianelli, Vignaud, Thiénot and Defay, and Second Lieutenants Prévaut, de Boyal and Louis were wounded. Two days later at Melegnano, Marshal Baraguay d'Hilliers, who did not want to share his success with anyone, engaged the 1st Zouaves precipitously and thoroughly. At the end of the day, they counted 13 officers killed, 20 wounded; 124 men killed, 495 wounded and 11 missing. The position had been energetically taken by storm but it would have been possible to have taken it through carefully using less men. Officers killed: Colonel Paulze d'Ivoy, Major Rousseau, Captains Brice de Ville, de la Chevardière de la Grandville, Massenat; Lieutenants Bousset, Conor, Seriot; Second Lieutenants Basset, Bertier, Lafitte. Officers wounded: Captains Colette (amputated), Désandré, Devaux, Dupuis, Fournès, Guenet, Guillemain, Jean, Payan; Lieutenants Jamot, Maréchal (amputated); Second Lieutenants Avril, Decencière, Dours, Grillon des Chapelles, Guillon, Lecarvenec, Menescal, de Saint-Hilaire, de Sparre.

The 3rd Regiment had had the worst luck of being attached to the 5th Corps whose role, as Napoleon II said, would be more political than military. It had the joy of being put at the disposal of King Victor-Emmanuel. It was able to distinguish itself at Palestro and make the enemy feel the power of its bayonets. It lost one officer—Captain Drut—and 36 Zouaves. It had 14 officers among whom Lieutenant Gouté and the second lieutenant color bearer Henry plus 225 men of the ranks were wounded.(1) At Solferino in the attack on the cemetery, the 1st Zouaves, so tested at Melegnano, lost two captains, Aubert-Armand and Castan; two Lieutenants, Cadet and Decencière; and four Second Lieutenants, des Chapelles, Guillien, Minart and Sie. In addition it had sixteen officers wounded: Colonel Brincourt, very seriously; Major Lumel; Captains Bonnet, Bordes, Devaux, Fournès, Olivier, Payan; Lieutenants Avril, de Bornschlégel, Higlin, Lafont, Minary, and Rousseau; Second Lieutenants Saleta and Galand; 73 men of the ranks killed, 411 wounded and 17 missing. The 2nd Regiment of Zouaves at the attack of Cavriana had 62 men out of action; Captain Le Gò and Lieutenants Lacaze and Des Mazis were wounded.

Only the first two battalions of the 2nd Regiment would participate in the triumphal return of the Army of Italy. They returned to Oran on August 23. There they once again found the 3rd Battalion which had landed on the 18th. The 1st Regiment, after a stay at Pavia, and the 3rd, after having been garrisoned in Milan, returned to Algeria in October.

During the campaign of Italy, the incomparable and often impatient élan of the Zouaves and their somewhat undisciplined character had raised some mild criticism. The line regiment, beneath their humble grey greatcoats, and the Guard regiments marching like walls of bronze, had shown qualities which, if not superior, were at least more useful to the goal which was pursued in the great war. This was the object of certain remarks which were drowned in a flood of justifiably merited praises. Algeria claimed them for new battles where they were uncontestably the most capable.

The expedition of Syria, in which part of the 1st Battalion of the 1st Regiment took part, presented no remarkable war actions. However, the Mexican expedition supplied the three regiments with new opportunities to show off their indomitable bravery. It was the 2nd Regiment which left first. A battalion of 500 men (Commander Cousin) arrived on January 7, 1862 at Vera-Cruz and was rejoined in April by another battalion of 1,117 men (Commander Morand). General Latrille de Lorencez led them to Puebla. In a first battle at the passage of

Eagle of the 1st Regiment of Zouaves. Return from Italy (1859).

(1) On the occasion of the Battle of Palestro, the eagle of the 3rd Regiment of Zouaves was decorated with the golden medal of the Order of Merit of Sardinia. Here is the letter which Colonel de Chabron received from King Victor-Emmanuel:

Monsieur Colonel, the Emperor, in placing under my command the 3rd Regiment of Zouaves, gave me a valuable testimony of friendship. I thought that I could not better welcome this elite troop than by immediately providing them the opportunity to add a new exploit to those which, on the battlefield of Africa and the Crimea, have rendered the Zouave name so redoubtable.

Monsieur Colonel, the irresistible élan with which the regiment marched against the enemy attack has exceeded my admiration. To throw oneself on the enemy with the bayonet, to take possession of a battery in braving the canister was a matter of seconds. You must be proud to command such soldiers and they must be happy to obey a leader such as yourself.

I appreciate the thought that your Zouaves have had of bringing pieces of artillery taken from the Austrians to my general headquarters, and I beg you to thank them on my part. I hasten to send this most wonderful trophy to His Majesty, the Emperor, to whom I have already made known the incomparable bravery with which your regiment fought today at Palestro and upheld my extreme right.

I would always be happy to see the 3rd of Zouaves fighting beside my soldiers, gathering new laurels on the fields of battle which await us.

I ask, Monsieur Colonel, that you make my sentiments known to your soldiers.

Victor-Emmanuel

Cumbres, one officer, Lieutenant Collasse, and ten Zouaves were wounded. At the unproductive assault of Puebla, the 2nd Zouaves, charged with taking the Guadalupe and Loreto forts, displayed an intrepidness and a daring which would have proved successful if success had been possible. Captains Montié, Vuibert, de Simonneau, Lieutenants Pradier, Henry, Ritter and Second Lieutenant Fourcade were killed. Captains Aubry, Vincendon, Vilain, Lieutenants Perceval, Vignaud, Second Lieutenants Jougla, Chereau, de Breuille were wounded and 289 men of the ranks were out of action. The second lieutenant color bearer was killed while breaking through into the fort. The Zouave Cavalié took up the eagle and gave it back to Colonel Gambier on the counterscarp. The check suffered before Puebla forced the imperial government to put together a solid expedition corps for Mexico. General Forey succeeded General Latrille de Lorencez. The 1st and 3rd Regiments, each with 2 battalions of 8 companies, set off and arrived at Vera-Cruz: the 1st, on August 28, the 3rd on October 19. Four companies of the 2nd Zouaves with Lieutenant Colonel Martin landed on November 6 and were to put their regiment on the same basis. From this point on, the expeditionary corps included six battalions of Zouaves as well as the line regiments and the battalions of chasseurs à pied. For five years, they were what they had been everywhere. They also left there the most solid of their officers and their soldiers. After their African combats and the Crimean, Italian, and Mexican campaigns, it is not surprising that in 1870, it again found itself daring and terribles Zouaves. They were commanded by an energetic officer elite who were always ready to sacrifice their lives for the welfare and honor of the country. The tradition was so rooted in the Zouave regiments that a recruit donning the uniform quickly took on the Zouave spirit frequently mentioned. Their officers have the sacred fire at all times and under all circumstances. In times past when there was only one regiment, a Zouave captain knew that if he lived he would surely become a general. He would brave a thousand deaths to be worthy of the stars. A simple Zouave thought himself and knew himself to be an individual. With his *chechia* set back on his head, he surveyed from the heights of his grandeur everything which was not Zouave or which did not belong to the Zouave Corps. Later, when there were three regiments, thanks to tradition, the quality did not visibly decrease. An old general who participated in the landing of three regiments at Gallipoli and who saw three corps of officers assembled in a military celebration told me that he had never seen the likes of such military youth. They were dazzling in their heart, power, robust beauty and health. Only their losses and some of their glowing actions will be noted for the Mexican campaign where the siege of Puebla was the apogee of the Zouaves' valor.

1st Regiment—Officers killed: Captains Michelon, Devaux, de Marsilly; Lieutenants de Sparre, de Bornshlégel, Estennevin, de la Haye-Saint-Hilaire, Heurteux; Second Lieutenant Boudet-Corneille. Officers wounded: Majors Carteret and Melot; Captains Guillemain (adjutant major), Renaud (adjutant major), Lalouette and Vanderbach; Lieutenants Martelli, Avègue, Duchesne, Mathieu and Duverdier; Second Lieutenants Mennetrier, Herbelin, Sonnoy, Domelly and Brochier. In this long war, the majority of the losses from the 1st Zouaves can be attributed to the siege of Puebla which recalls the battles of Saragossa. In these daily battles in the middle of a city whose square of houses were fortresses, the Zouaves delivered up battles at close range. Their adventurous bravura cost them dearly a number of times. Through deftly led counter attacks, the Mexicans took sections and entire companies from them. In the second part of the campaign which was the longest, the great mobility of the Zouaves and their passion for discovery and adventure served them well. None were more expert nor more skilled than they in the pursuit of the guerillas. The two battalions of the 1st Regiment returned to their old African terrain—their adopted country—on April 3, 1867.

2nd Regiment—Lieutenant Colonel Martin must be added to the sixteen officers named above who were killed and wounded at Cambres and in the first attack on Puebla. Martin commanded the Zouaves in the events of Ciro de Majoma although he had already been promoted to colonel in the 62nd. He was killed by a bullet there. Captains de Perthuis, de Courville and Escourron; Lieutenants

The 1st Regiment of Zouaves at Woerth (August 6, 1870).

Kermabon, Tramont, Dromzée and the Surgeon Lieutenant Mercadier, also killed; Captain Labrune; Lieutenants Caze, Laurent, Mirauchaux (Jules), Pierron and Brissaud, and Second Lieutenant Chereau, wounded. The 2nd Zouaves, who arrived first in Mexico, returned to Algeria on May 2, 1865.

3rd Regiment—The flag of the 3rd Regiment was decorated in memory of the capture of two enemy flags in the battle of San-Lorenzo during the campaign of Mexico. These flags were won by Second Lieutenant Henry and the Zouave Stum. Of the eleven officers which the regiment lost, its history cites only Captain Grateaud, killed in the Battle of Elchamal. There the 2nd Battalion distinguished itself particularly under the command of Lieutenant Colonel Roussel de Courcy. The Zouaves' aptitude for everything concerning war must be mentioned here. They were excellent cannoneers and, when required, made first rate cavalry scouts. In Mexico, the 3rd Regiment had organized a mounted company under the command of Captain Rigault which performed most useful services. Notably, on October 19, 1865, they destroyed the Ugalde band at the artillery hacienda. The two war battalions returned to Algeria in February 1867.(1)

From 1867 to 1870, the Zouaves were busily employed in small expeditions of little importance when compared to the battles of the Crimea, Italy and Mexico.(2) However, they were called to defend their country in 1870. The three regiments each formed three war battalions at six companies. They were all placed in the 1st Corps (Marshal MacMahon). The 1st Regiment was in the 2nd Brigade (du Postis du Houlbec, then Wolf) of the division (Ducrot). The 2nd Regiment was in the 1st Brigade (L'Heriller) of the 3rd Division (Raoult). The 3rd Regiment was in the 1st Brigade (Fraboulet de Kerleadec) of the 4th Division (de Lartigue).

At Woerth, the marshal fought against 130,000 with 40,000 men. The Zouaves were relentless but were almost wiped out. The famous phrase: "Cuirassiers? They are no more." could equally as well be applied to the Zouaves. They arrived with an effective strength of about 2,200 men on the eve of the Battle of Woerth with the following data given on the roll: present with the colors: 1st Regiment, 36 officers and 1,400 men; 2nd Regiment,10 officers and 820 men; 3rd Regiment: 18 officers, of whom 4 were wounded, and 415 men. The losses were not equal, however, the regiments had not been engaged in the same way. The names of the officers fallen in this massacre are listed below:

Zouaves. Campaign of France (1870-1871).

1st Regiment—officers killed: Lieutenant Colonel Gautrelet, Majors Bertrand and Marion; Captains Durand and Robert Houdin; Second Lieutenant Girard. Officers wounded: Captains Cotton, Goëpp, Guignet, Lieutenants Brunet, Boutte and de Labonne and Second Lieutenant de Méritens.

2nd Regiment—officers killed: Majors Figarol and Soye; Captains de Chevroz, Richaud, Lamothe, Million and Fonvielle; Lieutenants Chereau, Guénard, Boutin, Merlin and Lyon; Second Lieutenants de Goué, Baudin, Leclèrc, Chamerois, Grandineau and Belvèze. Officers wounded: Colonel Détrie; Lieutenant Colonel le Toullec; Major Coiffé; Captains Tulpin, Hurtel, Letandot, Luzeux, Vagnez, Watringue, Delabiche, Prudhomme, Prévault and Jouneau; Lieutenants Lascroux, Hurtel, Dessirier, Diguet, Devos, Le Monnier, Rousseau, Mailley; Second Lieutenants Soudée, Kuntz, Cheylard, de Voisins, Henaux, de La Lobbe and Dubois. As on the night of June 18, 1855, all the field officers had been hit. The 2nd was commanded by a captain. This painful honor fell upon Béhic.

3rd Regiment—Officers killed: Lieutenant Colonel Deshorties, Majors Charmes and Pariset; Captains Bruguerolle, Parson, Henry, Faval and Sorrel; Lieutenants Teissèdre, Boileau, Perret,

(1) As has been stated above, there were criticisms of the Zouaves' lack of discipline when they passed into the Army of Italy. This lack of discipline can be attributed to the high self opinion which gave to the simple Zouave the praise merited by generals and to the audiences which the military reporters lavished on them. This led to very unfortunate consequences in 1865. In October 1865, a strong detachment, assigned to the 1st and 3rd Regiments, landed at Martinique and was quartered in Fort Desaix as was customary. The governor granted only twenty-five leave passes drawn by lottery for these 800 men. Bolstered by a few troops who had returned from Mexico, the men who lost out wanted to force the orders and rushed at the gate. The guard resisted, and two Zouaves were killed. Their angered comrades rushed into the rooms of the barracks where there were rifles and cartridges. This resulted in a massacre. Obviously the governor of Martinique had acted neither with prudence nor with generousness, but the rebellion of the Zouaves was the cause of twenty deaths. The punishment was not equal to the military crime. It was almost natural and necessary, and pointed out the serious mistake of the Martinique authorities.

(2) In this monograph, which is by necessity too short for the subject it addresses, it would be unjust to remain silent about the losses of the Zouave regiments during the years which passed between their return from Mexico and the campaign of 1870. They will be given in brief. For the remainder, this time only the 2nd Zouaves have been recorded in the supplementary note: Lieutenant Guenard, wounded in the Battle of Chellala-Gueblia; Commander Soye and Lieutenant Genty were wounded in the Battle of El-Bahriat; at the attack on Ain-Chair, Lieutenant Esselin, Captains de Chevroz, Bouchard, Prevault and Second Lieutenant Domine were wounded.

Lafon, Gasc and Perotel; Second Lieutenants Saltzmann, Berthemet, Vernet and Dousselin. Officers wounded: Captains Caillard, de Mascureau, Forcioli, Jacquot, Lesueur de Givry, Gaillard de la Roche, de Rafelis de Saint-Sauveur, Gros, Ducroquet, Voisin and Corps; Lieutenants de Maussion de Candé, Blancq, Bardol, Colonna d'Istria, Dufour, Uteza; Second Lieutenants Berthelet, Bousson, Buche, Multier, Canlon, Schwoebel, Marie (color bearer).

Oh, that rank, that fine rank of major in the Zouaves, so envied in the army. This was its reward on the field of battle. The three regiments lost six out of nine commanders, and two others had been wounded. Reinforcements arrived quickly from Algeria. From August 17 to 20, the regiments received: the 1st, 400 men who brought its effective strength to 2,000 men; the 2nd, a detachment which returned its effective strength to 850 men; the 3rd Regiment, 550 men. It also had 1,100 bayonets at the time. The Zouaves appeared at Sedan on September 1 in this condition which was very shaky for the latter two regiments. There they met their ruin. The 1st had 19 officers and 600 men of the ranks out of action. (Officers killed: Commander Minary, Captains Charvilhat and Lihaut, Lieutenant Prévot, Second Lieutenants Antoine and Gombaud. Wounded: Commander Massonnaud, Captains Monnin, Noëllat and Vaillon (amputated), Lieutenat Grebus and Second Lieutenant Servière.) The 2nd Regiment which had supported the movement of the 12th Corps, left 306 men on the battlefield; Captain Champaret, Lieutenant Bihourd and Second Lieutenant Colin were killed; Commander Béhic, Lieutenants Rousseau, Le Monnier, and Abadie, Second Lieutenants Herson, Bellanger, Angéli and Franck were wounded. The 3rd Regiment had more luck. It only had to reform two battalions. One under the command of Lieutenant Colonel Méric had been charged with reoccupying the village of Daigny. It found itself cut off from the rest of the army, was able to reach Rocroy, took the railroad there, and returned to Paris under its flag which it returned to the artillery depot. The flag of the 1st Regiment was also saved thanks to César Bacot who took it upon himself to shield it from all the attempts of the Germans. It is kept in Coléa in the Garden of the Zouaves.

The battalion of the 3rd Zouaves which escaped from the capitulation of Sedan was the nucleus of a regiment which served in Paris, first under the name of Regiment of the Zouaves de marche, then of 4th Regiment of Zouaves. Detachments destined for the three regiments assembled around the Zouaves of Lieutenant Colonel Méric. There were also Zouaves not able to rejoin the three regiments who had been directed to the capital, individual Zouaves escaped from Sedan, others who had remained behind from Châlons to Beaumont, and finally, volunteers. The government of the National Defense was deceiving itself when it declared: "A regiment of Zouaves *de marche* will be formed in Paris from a battalion of each of the three regiments." The regiment filled out rapidly at Saint-Cloud and was returned to Paris on September 15. Its general staff is listed below.

Colonel Fournès; Lieutenant Colonel Méric; Assistant to the Treasurer, Condout.
1st Battalion: Commander Noëllat; Battalion Adjutant, M. Gelat.
2nd Battalion: Commander, Prévault; Battalion Adjutant, Mercier.
3rd Battalion: Commander, Jacquot; Battalion Adjutant, Colonna d'Istria.

Formed of very different components, the 4th Zouaves were not initially up to their old reputation. The Battle of Châtillon surprised them in the middle of preparations. However the regiment recovered its aplomb very quickly. Commander Jacquot was wounded there while serving as an extremely bold example to his men. In the Battle of Champigny, 22 officers and 534 men were put out of action. Officers killed: Captain de Podenas; Lieutenants Leroux and Primat; Second Lieutenants Houel, Santran and Marterer. Officers wounded: Major Noëllat; Captains Bezy, Gallangan, Gonzalès, Mercier, Mègre, Sondée; Lieutenants Bressolles, Rambaud, Lévêque, Braccini; Second Lieutenants Tavarnier, Guerne, Bertholet, Chateau and Bosseler. At Buzenval, it lost 15 more

The Zouaves of the Imperial Guard (1855-1870).

Encampment of Zouaves (1886).

Native Tirailleurs in column (1886).

officers and 153 non-commissioned officers and soldiers. The day of the capitulation, the regiment had 2,700 men. It left Paris on March 15 and landed at Marseille on the 21st. From the time of its creation, the 4th had had as colonels; 1870, Fournès; 1870-1876, Méric; 1876-1881, Gand; 1881-1884, Verrier; 1885, Faure-Biguet.

As has been seen, each of the three regiments had supplied 3 battalions of 6 companies to the First Corps. In addition, they also provided some detachments which were incorporated either into the war battalions or into the 4th Regiment. Each regiment had in addition mobilized a 4th battalion with the 7th and 8th companies of its battalions. The depots continued to be formed from three new companies. However, the volunteers flooded in. At one time, the depot of the 1st counted 8,000 men. The government of the National Defense decided through the decree of October 1st that a *régiment de marche* would be mobilized from each of the 4th battalions.

The 1st Regiment (Lieutenant Colonel Chaulan, then Parran), after having been part of the Army of the Loire, moved into the Army of the East and withdrew into Switzerland. The 2nd Regiment (Lieutenants Colonel Logerot, then Chevallier) participated in the Battle of Coulmiers. At Artenay on December 3rd, it saw Captains Audouard and Manquat fall dead. Captains Genty and Pierre; Lieutenants André, Carrignon, Hartmayer; Second Lieutenants Fanton, Roux, Calatayud, wounded. On the following day at Cercottes, another 3 of its officers were wounded: Captain Debucher, Lieutenants Halley and Dominé. However, 500 men remained on the battlefield and 800 to 900 in enemy hands. The 3rd (Lieutenant Colonel Boisson, then Bernard), fought like madmen at Beaune-la-Rolande. This regiment had 5 officers and 43 men killed; 10 officers, 264 men wounded; and 485 missing. After having participated in the failure of Villersexel and of Hericourt where it also experienced serious losses, it withdrew with the Army of the East and crossed into Switzerland. Through the decree of November 18th, the government of the National Defense ordered the creation of a 4th *régiment de marche* taken this time from the three regiments. The government wanted to use the numerous volunteers who were flocking to the Zouaves. Lieutenant Colonel Ritter was named commander. It was part of the Army of the East and after having delivered many murderous combats, it would be forced to cross into Switzerland like the rest of Clinchant's Army. There Colonel de Boisfleury succeeded Lieutenant Colonel Ritter in the 4th Zouaves. Carrying only biscuits and cartridges, they appeared through the enemy outposts, reaching Mouthe, Chapelle-sur-Bois, Bois-d'Aumont and Gex. Directed at first to Grenoble, then on to Marseille, the 4th de marche arrived at Toulon whence it sailed on April 1. In this disastrous campaign of France, the Zouaves had given lavishly of their blood and always showed they were still worthy of their reputation. They had put eight regiments in the line, without counting the Zouave regiment of the Guard. This latter also has its story. It returned to the 4th Zouaves where after the war it was merged with the 4th organized at Paris. Formed under the cannon of Sebastopol with Zouaves and chasseurs à pied, it very soon performed great services. Its colonels had been Janin, de Bonuet-Maurelbau-Polès, Guignard, Lacretelle, and Giraud. With 2 battalions at 7 companies, it formed a division with the grenadiers. It was engaged in Italy, at the Battle of Magenta. It had two officers killed, Captain Pichoud and Lieutenant Vincent. In the last war, the unfortunate commander of the Army of Metz never wanted to make use of it.

After the war, the service had to rebuild itself entirely, using resources much depleted by enemy fire. The three old regiments and the first three *régiments de marche* were merged. In addition, it took on various components which had been loaned to the 4th de marche of the provinces. This reorganization was performed in the face of a formidable insurrection. The signal for insurrection was given by Mokrani, starting in the province of Constantine. A provisional battalion had also been formed during the war for service in Algeria. It was turned over to the 1st Zouaves. The three regiments, while fighting the whole time, reformed their battalions. In 1872, the four regiments were returned to their normal bases: the 1st to Coléa, the 2nd to Oran, the 3rd to Constantine, the 4th to Algiers and Aumale. At the same time, peace was not won without costing the Zouaves new losses.

1st Regiment—Lieutenant Mézard (detached from the 80th de marche), wounded at Tizil-Mamoulu; Lieutenant Pradier, wounded at Cherchell; Second Lieutenant Jude, killed at Cherchell; Captain Cotton, wounded at Fort-National. *2nd Regiment*—Captain Buchillot, killed; Lieutenant Laporte, wounded. *3rd Regiment*—four officers wounded. *4th Regiment*—Lieutenants Larcher, Deswarte-Vandamme, wounded; Captains Hébert and Lauze de Perret, wounded.

The regiments which had retained three battalions of 9 companies were organized in February 1873 at four battalions of 6 companies. The ninths formed the depot, as throughout the Empire. The old sevenths and eighths went into the 4th battalion. On April 16, 1875, the law of the cadres reduced the battalions to four companies, and each regiment had no more than one depot company. On the following February 16th, a second depot company was created as it was recognized that this single depot company was insufficient. Four of these companies formed depots at Salon and at Arles which, in the event of mobilization, would receive reservists from France and dress and equip them.

Since then, the tasks of the Zouaves have been much less arduous. The expeditions are less numerous and the need to call them outside the Algerian territory increasingly rare. The expedition of Tunisia dislocated all of them except the 2nd. The 4th Regiment has had its headquarters at Sousse since that time. Some portions of the 2nd and 3rd Regiments have been called to the Tonkin. However, the establishment of the new method of recruiting has completely modified the customs of the Zouaves. Now recruited as regiments of the interior, they receive their military education in the corps. They even perform grand maneuvers! The method of promoting officers removes those brilliant volunteers from their ranks who endured everything to get there. However, thanks to tradition, they have somewhat retained the esprit de corps which carried them to such heights of glory. In the course of this very abridged dissertation, given the wealth of great deeds, the names of their officers who had spilled their blood on the field of battle have been given. It is right to end with as complete a list as possible of the general officers departed from their ranks since 1831.

Duvivier, de Lamoricière, Levaillant, Régnault, Renaud, Cuny, Bosc, de Ladmirault, de Gardarens de Boisse, Vergé, Bisson, Mollière, Drolenvaux, Repond, de Barral, Bourbaki, Pellé, Blangini, Maissiat, Cavaignac, Le Flô, d'Autemarre de'Ervillé, Jeanningros, Leroy de Saint-Arnaud, Le Poittevin de la Croix, de Chasseloup-Laubat, Dubos, Chapuis, Gault, Jannin, Corréard, de Saint-Pol, de Bertier, Montaudon, Chanzy, Bouat, Espinasse, de la Bastide, Grandchamp, de Lorencez, Canrobert, de Lavarande, Vinoy, Cler, Guignard, Brincourt, Picard, Collineau, Saurin, de Golberg, Lacretelle, de Chabron, Tixier, Gambier, Arnaudeau, Clinchant, Carteret-Trécourt, Detrie, Hervé, Mangin, Bocher, Bertrand, Fournès and so many others whose names are lost to memory.

Algerian Tirailleurs (1842).

ALGERIAN TIRAILLEURS

◆

As has been said: the first natives who fought for France were incorporated into the Zouaves. It was soon realized that there were difficulties—even impossibilities—in having the Arabs live side by side with the French soldiers. At first they were split into groups. Then it was necessary to completely separate them. The organizers from 1830 to 1840 never had great confidence in the Arabs. They judged it imprudent to assign them to an isolated post with arms and munitions, or to leave them to their discretion in handling the life of the French cadres, regardless of how energetic they were. In the beginning of the conquest, there were incidents which are forgotten today that fully justify the mistrust of the generals at the time. Abd-el-Kader formed and drilled his native regulars who had served a term in the French ranks. After completing their time with the French, they had gone to sell him their knowledge and their experience. Strictly from the point of view of mercenaries, there was nothing wrong with this. However, there was a massacre of French officers in the Constantine province. A number of times on the eve of an expedition, 150 tirailleurs were seen deserting all at once with arms and baggage. It is extremely difficult to find well documented and official details on the beginnings of the native infantry troops. However, in the *Campaigns of the Duke d'Orléans*, I have come across evidence that 400 foot *Koulouglis* formed part of the contingent which the Agha Mustapha led to Marshal Clauzel for his expedition of Tlemcen in 1836. This troop had nothing in common with the native troops. It is likely that the marshal took them along with him more for their effect on the morale than in the hope of using them. In the second expedition of Constantine, the Turkish infantry was organized in earnest. Might they be confused with that troop of Koulouglis and of Kabyles which *The Golden Book of the Algerian Tirailleur from the Province of Algiers* speaks? Commanded by Lieutenant Pellé, the future general of division, it was placed with the Moroccan gendarmes under the command of Captain d'Allonville of the general staff. It formed the nucleus of the Battalion of Algiers. According to the summary of the *History of the 2nd Regiment*, a similar Turkish battalion appears to have existed at Mostaganem as well. It is possible that things happened in the same manner in the province of Constantine. It was these ephemeral corps of doubtful solidity, of short-lived success, and without steady recruitment which bequeathed the name of *Turcos* to the regular corps. Nonetheless, they must have performed useful services since the generals of the three provinces insisted upon a permanent foundation for the native infantry which would be at least as solid as that of the Spahis.

On December 7, 1841, Marshal Soult proposed to the king that native miltary forces be organized separately. The first words of his report indicate that this organization "is one of the primary needs of Algeria." Nothing could be more true since it was the best means of rallying the more turbulent and the most solid peoples of the country to the French cause. The decree which gave a constitution to the native infantry formed it into three battalions with Turkish battalions for their nucleus. Naturally the officers and the non-commissioned officers who were dedicated to their education entered these battalions with promotions. The natives who were still with the Zouaves were pressured to move into the tirailleurs. There their ambitions were satisfied with the classification of the cadres under a long-term contract between the Arabs and the French. However, it was only rather later on that the native officers benefited from the privileges of the law on the status of officers.

These battalions which were the nuclei of the three first regiments at first bore the following names: Battalion of Algiers and of Tittery, Battalion of Constantine and of Bone, and Battallion of Oran, of Mostaganem and of Mascara. They had been organized by Majors Vergé, Thomas and Bosquet. The first uniform they adopted was regulation for the officers: a skirted tunic in dragoon green with golden buttons, the kepi, and wine-colored pants with green stripes. For quite a long time, the troops wore the oriental costume in dragoon green, with wine-colored, Zouave-style pants, yellow decorations and a white turban striped in blue. The sky blue uniform, which had appeared before the decree that permanently established it, must date from 1846 or 1847.

From 1841 to 1854, the native infantry did not all have the same good fortune. This was despite the fact that they were always commanded by first class majors who were all destined to climb to the highest ranks of the military hierarchy. In the Battalion of Algiers, Vergé was followed by Wimpffen, Rose, and de Maussion. In the Battalion of Constantine, Thomas was replaced by Bourbaki, Bataille and Jolivet. Finally, in the Battalion of Oran, the future Marshal Bosquet had given up his place to Pellé, Martineau-Deschenez and Butet. It is obvious that under such leaders, these troops could not remain idle. They were seen in all the important expeditions, leading their contigent with patience and courage. However, the most difficult thing was not leading these warriors under fire since they revelled in it. It was rather to maintain their numbers in active service and to break them into French discipline. This was the greatest task of the early leaders. Today, in watching a battalion of Turcos march alongside French battalions who are

Nouba. Native music of the Algerian Tirailleurs (1886).

embarking for a distant war, one does not doubt the pain and the care dedicated to the adaptation of the Arab character. The decree of December 7, 1841 allowed five thousand plus natives to be included in the three battalions. I do not believe that the regulation figure of 1,784 men per battalion has ever been reached at any point in time. Two regiments of tirailleurs, the 1st and the 2nd, have published histories which are well written. That of the 1st is in two volumes and is a veritable history book. It states therein the lack of spirit that the Arab populations at first demonstrated. The national war and the fight against the invader under well-liked leaders kindled their warlike tastes. However, manual labor scared them; they found it undignified for warriors. Instead they lived easily through open theft at the expense of all the early French agricultural, industrial and commercial ventures. According to the annals of 1845, three years after their organization (which was not completed until June 1842), the 1st Battalion (Algiers) only included six companies. The 2nd (Constantine) alone was complete. The 3rd (Oran) had only four companies. There were still only 17 native officers, of whom three were lieutenants, for the three battalions.

The native spirit was rather disinterested in the February revolution. The taking of Abd-el-Kader had cut off resistance to the French services. Native battalions had profited from the resistance without having to enlarge their regulation cadres. Hardly did the companies reach their number with very weak effectives when an event would attract the attention of all the natives. Up until this point, they had understood nothing about the political developments of their conquerors. Louis-Philippe, the Republic, the Emperor: for them, they were all the same. France—regardless of which government—was always their oppressor when one of the oldest officers of the Turcos, Colonel Wimpffen, came to Algiers to form a regiment to fight on behalf of the Sultan. The War of the Orient thus was a decisive test in favor of the native infantry troops, composed of poor men, hardened by fatigue, more ignorant than the Arabs of the great tents, whom the Spahis preferred. The native battalions were wonderfully ready to favorably receive the words of Colonel Wimpffen. This officer told of his mission with such verve that it has been recorded below.

"One evening in 1854, Colonel Wimpffen entered the salons of Marshal Saint-Arnaud whom he knew well and liked. "Ah, my dear Colonel," said the marshal to him, "I am so glad to see you because I have to speak to you. These gentlemen (and he indicated many officers) claim that the Tirailleurs can only render services in Algeria. Is this your opinion?" "No, and I even maintain, with regard to my old battalion, that one can completely depend on these brave men if he knows the commander..."

"Forty-eight hourse later, Colonel Wimpffen was summoned to the Tuileries. The Emperor informed him that to the number of opponents of the use of natives outside their country was to be added a man already having some influence although only a simple colonel. This was Trochu, attached to the Minister. "Sire," said Wimpffen, "I am very much involved with the native soldiers. I know what they are capable of doing. If their leader knows how to lead them and inspire confidence in them, my answer is that you will have an excellent troop, an elite troop, in the Arab battalions. If I were not Colonel of the 13th of the line, and if one wanted to form

a corps with the battalions of the three provinces, I would be certain to succeed if I were given command of this corps." "Alright," responded the Emperor. "If I have the Tirailleurs march, I will form a regiment of these troops of which you will be the leader." "Sire, I hope to be able to prove to you in deeds that I am not wrong, and that what I have said to Your Majesty about these courageous men is the truth." "How many do you think you could take with you?" "Two thousand. I would be happy with fifteen hundred." "You need 2,000 for a slightly longer campaign."

"A week had not passed since this conversation with the Emperor when Colonel de Wimpffen received orders to return to Africa to form a regiment of Algerian Tirailleurs who would take the name of provisional regiment. During the crossing, although he was happy and flattered by his mission, de Wimpffen wondered if his soldiers would recognize it as well. He was counting primarily on those from his battalion, thinking that the others, those of Oran and of Constantine, would have many married men not very keen on being away from their families. Deeply concerned, he landed at Algiers and presented himself to General Randon, the Governor General. Randon began by refusing the *carte blanche* given by the Emperor and granted only half of the effectives present. The colonel insisted and in the name of the Emperor ended up taking them. He soon left for Blidah, arrived at midnight and went to the Turcos barracks. The battalion, informed ahead of time, had lighted the court as if though it were daytime. It waited for its old leader who presented himself to the soldiers and in a strong voice shouted: "My sons, do you recognize me?" "Vive!" cried out a thousand voices which immediately assured de Wimpffen. "Well then! I come to find you. Do you want to come with me to defend Mohammed's flag?" "Yes, yes. All, all of us will come with you." "I warn you that you will have to endure hardships, that you will have to brave hunger, tiredness, bullets." "We will march."

The 3rd Regiment of Algerian Tirailleurs at Woerth (August 6, 1870).

"That night, the colonel had one thousand volunteers under his command. Assured of the agreement of the major of the Battalion of Oran, the colonel immediately set out for the province of Constantine. In short, eight days later, he assembled two thousand natives at Coleah. Nonetheless, only the first problems were surmounted. The battalion commanders wanted to perform the functions of corps commanders and considered themselves as acting independently from one another. To put an end to rivalries, to confront each one administering and forcing his men to live as he pleased, to merge all these personalities and to prevent the break-up of the regiment, no less than a firm hand already used to shattering obstacles was needed. This was the hand of Colonel de Wimpffen who was adored by his Arabs. As soon as the order creating a regiment with three battalions taken from all three provinces was known, a kind of revolt broke out. Thanks to the vigorous support of General Camou, commander of the province, the colonel succeeded in restoring order. However, a type of opposition on the part of some courageous officers remained, an opposition which lasted for a long time. Hardly had the regiment been formed and set off for the Orient, when Colonel de Wimpffen found himself in the presence of officers who refused all administrative functions, claiming to have come only to fight. It was with great difficulty that the personnel was rebuilt.(1)"

This fine regiment went through still more vicissitudes before going into battle. Colonel Trochu was the enemy of eccentric corps for his entire life. He wanted to include the Turcos in a measure which was to return a squadron of Spahis to Algeria who had been summoned to Turkey to serve as the nucleus of the *bachi-bouzoucks*. Fortunately, Colonel de Wimpffen was still able to avoid this direct blow. There is some inaccurate material in his account. The provisional regiment had only two battalions of nine companies. Its general staff was thus composed of only the colonel and Lieutenant Colonel Lévy, who was detached as commanding officer in the Orient and did not appear again in the corps. He was replaced on May 26th by Lieutenant Colonel Roques. The majors were de Maussion (of Algiers) and Martineau-Deschenets (of Oran). Major Vilar remained at Cherchell with the two ninth companies.

The conduct of the tirailleurs in the Crimea is known; they were admired by the three armies. Their officers' corps was severely tested.

(1) "General de Wimpffen, Response to General Ducrot", a brochure by a high ranking officer, in the 8th Arrondissement, Paris, Librairie Internationale, 1871. Pages 18 and following.

Killed—At Alma: Lieutenant Lapeyre. At Inkermann: Lieutenants Ahmed-bel-Arby and Mohammed Zersasui. At the assault of Mamelon-Vert: Captains Schweinberg, Eberlin, Pattier, de Roquefeuil, Dejoux. Lieutenants Pacaud, Hanusse, Coustère, Pelsez, Lautar, Mecaoud-ben-Mohammed; Second Lieutenants Bourgeois, Serpentini, Gérard, Loyer, Mustapha-ben-Ferkatadji, Lange de Ferrières. Assault (September 8): Lieutenant Colonel Roques, Captain Battalion Adjutant Rolland, Captain Bonnemain, Lieutenant Meynard. Total, 24 officers.

Wounded—Inkermann: Captain Schweinberg, Second Lieutenants Loyer, Véran, Saïd-ben-Ali. In the trenches: March 3, Lieutenant Kaddour Toubar; March 15, Second Lieutenant Kaddour-ben-Iza; March 22-23, Lieutenants Omar-ben-Mohammed-Tounci and Mohammed-ben-Aïssa, Second Lieutenant Loyer (second time); April 9, Major Castex (wrist lost); April 11, Second Lieutenant Gelly; April 17, Second Lieutenant Bonneval. Mamelon-Vert: Major Gibon; Captains Piétri, Conot, Pelisse; Lieutenant Véran (second time); Lieutenants Humery, Mahmoud-bel-Hadj-Mahmoud, Mohammed-ben-Amar, Chibli; Second Lieutenants Jauge, Legrand (prisoner), Masse, Raffin, Blanpied, Thierry, Mohammed-ben-Abd-el-Kader. Assault (September 8): Captains Quinemant, Dermier, Lavigue; Lieutenants Baudier, de Lammertz, Mohammed-Hamoud-ben-Ali, Mustapha-ben-Beyram; Second Lieutenants Momammed bel-Hadj, Mecaoud-ben-Ahmed. Total, 34 officers wounded of whom two twice and two whom, after having been wounded (Captain Schweinberg once and Second Lieutenant Loyer twice), were later killed by the enemy.

At Mamelon-Vert, the provisional regiment had 408 men of the ranks out of action; at the assault, there were 232 of them. When the regiment returned to Algiers on November 26, 1855 its ranks were quite depleted. In the boisterous *diffa* which was offered to the regiment by its religious brethren, although the hands of those who returned were clasped in joy, hearts shrank at the number of Tirailleurs who slept the eternal sleep in the lands of the Crimea.

At the same time that the provisional regiment had been formed, a decree (January 9, 1855) ordered the creation of and recruitment for three new battalions *bis*, one per province. At the end of that year there were, thus, in addition to the two enregimented battalions, six isolated battalions, each forming a separate corps.

ALGIERS PROVINCE	ORAN PROVINCE	CONSTANTINE PROVINCE
1st Battalion Major Péchot	1st Battalion Major Butet	1st Battalion Major Guichard
2nd Battalion Major Wolff	2nd Battalion Major Guynet	2nd Battalion Major Arnaudeau

The weakening of the provisional regiment and the uselessness, perhaps even the impossibility of recruiting determined its premature return to Algeria. The imperial governor decided to create one regiment per province. Each regiment, in addition to the two provincial battalions, received what remained of the contingent sent the preceding year to the provisional regiment. Their effective strength was raised to 4,165 men (70 French officers, 36 native, 279 men from the French cadre). It was a lot to suppose that between 15 and 16 thousand Arab infantrymen could be recruited. The general staffs of the three regiments found themselves composed in the following manner.

1st REGIMENT (Algiers Province)
Colonel Rose (of the provisional regiment)
Lieutenant Colonel Montfort (of the provisional regiment)
Major Pechot (of the 1st Battalion of Algiers)
Major Wolff (of the 2nd Battalion of Algiers)
Major Gibon (of the provisional regiment)
Major Bartel (of the provisional regiment)

2nd REGIMENT (Oran Province)
Colonel Montaudon
Lieutenant Colonel Lepoittevin de Lacroix
Major Butet (of the 1st Battalion of Oran)
Major Guynet (of the 2nd Battalion of Oran)
Two unknown majors

3rd REGIMENT (Constantine Province)
Colonel Liébert
Unknown Lieutenant Colonel
Major Guichard (of the 1st Battalion of Constantine)
Major Arnaudeau (of the 2nd Battalion of Constantine)
Two unknown majors

Color sergeant, Algerian Tirailleurs (1886).

This organization was terminated on January 1, 1856. It had not been very hard-working but then there was much to be desired with regard to the effective strength. Meanwhile, recruiting continued but it was inadequate for filling up such large cadres. However, when on March 26, 1859, the creation of a provisional regiment of three battalions at six companies for the Army of Italy was ordered, one had only to open his mouth to obtain recruits.

Colonel Laure, who had replaced Rose in the 1st Regiment, had command of this provisional regiment. His lieutenant colonel, Montfort, followed him and the three battalions were drawn up as follows: The 1st Regiment of Algiers (1,124 men), to Gibon; Battalion Adjutant, Berthe; Captains, Vanéechout, Bézard, Thomassin, Castan, Liébert, Hulot; The 2nd Regiment from the Oran Regiment, Calignon as Major; The 3rd Regiment from the Constantine Regiment, Major Van-Hoorick.

They were placed in the 1st Brigade (Lefèvre) of the 1st Division (La Motterouge) of the 2nd Corps. At Turbigo on June 3rd, at the crossing of the Tessin, they formed the head of column. At Robecchetto, Captain Vaneechout was killed; Captains Bezard and Liebert were wounded as well as Lieutenant Ben-Aouda-ben-Kaddour and Second Lieutenant Boulanger. The following day, the day of the Battle of Magenta, it lost its colonel, Laure, killed by the enemy at the head of his regiment, Captain Battionni, and Second Lieutenants Ferrat and Mohammed-ben-Mohammed-Blidi. Colonel Laure was replaced by Butet. At Solferino, the provisional regiment lost the brave commander Calignon, Lieutenants Benjamin, de Boyne, Larbi-ben-Ladgar, Ricot and Second Lieutenant de Foy

This time, the Turcos had been less severely damaged than in the Crimea, and their return to Algeria on August 14, 1859 was

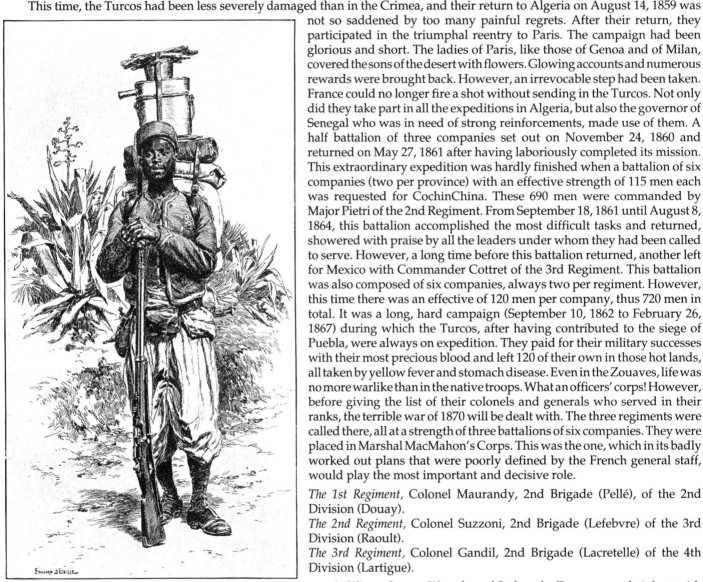

Algerian Tirailleur, campaign dress (1886).

not so saddened by too many painful regrets. After their return, they participated in the triumphal reentry to Paris. The campaign had been glorious and short. The ladies of Paris, like those of Genoa and of Milan, covered the sons of the desert with flowers. Glowing accounts and numerous rewards were brought back. However, an irrevocable step had been taken. France could no longer fire a shot without sending in the Turcos. Not only did they take part in all the expeditions in Algeria, but also the governor of Senegal who was in need of strong reinforcements, made use of them. A half battalion of three companies set out on November 24, 1860 and returned on May 27, 1861 after having laboriously completed its mission. This extraordinary expedition was hardly finished when a battalion of six companies (two per province) with an effective strength of 115 men each was requested for CochinChina. These 690 men were commanded by Major Pietri of the 2nd Regiment. From September 18, 1861 until August 8, 1864, this battalion accomplished the most difficult tasks and returned, showered with praise by all the leaders under whom they had been called to serve. However, a long time before this battalion returned, another left for Mexico with Commander Cottret of the 3rd Regiment. This battalion was also composed of six companies, always two per regiment. However, this time there was an effective of 120 men per company, thus 720 men in total. It was a long, hard campaign (September 10, 1862 to February 26, 1867) during which the Turcos, after having contributed to the siege of Puebla, were always on expedition. They paid for their military successes with their most precious blood and left 120 of their own in those hot lands, all taken by yellow fever and stomach disease. Even in the Zouaves, life was no more warlike than in the native troops. What an officers' corps! However, before giving the list of their colonels and generals who served in their ranks, the terrible war of 1870 will be dealt with. The three regiments were called there, all at a strength of three battalions of six companies. They were placed in Marshal MacMahon's Corps. This was the one, which in its badly worked out plans that were poorly defined by the French general staff, would play the most important and decisive role.

The 1st Regiment, Colonel Maurandy, 2nd Brigade (Pellé), of the 2nd Division (Douay).

The 2nd Regiment, Colonel Suzzoni, 2nd Brigade (Lefebvre) of the 3rd Division (Raoult).

The 3rd Regiment, Colonel Gandil, 2nd Brigade (Lacretelle) of the 4th Division (Lartigue).

At Wissembourg, Woerth, and Sedan, the Turcos gave their best with their characteristically generous passion. They were crushed everywhere, destroyed by that formidable German artillery which they didn't see. These intrepid children of the desert could use neither their firepower nor their bayonets against their adversaries. However, they held the ground on which they fought with heroic tenacity. At the call of their leaders, they showed themselves to be first and last in attack and in defense. However, science and mathematics thwarted their efforts and their virtues.

The 1st Regiment lost 500 men in its first engagement (Wissembourg), Nine of its officers were killed: Captains Tourangin and Kiener; Lieutenants Bellamy, Grandmont, Amar-ben-Hassen, Mouça-ben-Kouider; Second Lieutenants Cazals, Mohamed-bou-Saïd, Mohamed-ben-Ahmouda; 12 others seriously wounded on the field of battle remained in enemy hands. The following day at Woerth, the regiment was even more profoundly affected: 18 officers and 800 men fell to the earth. There, Got, Berge, Trawitz and Captain Quantin were killed. This latter said to his soldiers: "No, those are not bullets which you hear whistling above you; they are bees which buzz in your ears." At Sedan, the canister and the German bombs finished off the 1st Tirailleurs: Commander Vincelet and Ben d'Aubery died. That evening, barely 300 men gathered around the flag.

The 2nd Regiment was entirely consumed at Woerth. Its history is written out here. "The brave Colonel Suzzoni had fallen

toward three, mortally wounded in the chest by a bullet. Lieutenant Colonel Colonieu, wounded twice, had to leave the battlefield. Commander Jodosius had been killed and Commander Mathieu had been very seriously wounded. Thirteen officers and 700 men killed; 18 officers and 750 men wounded; finally, 36 officers and 780 men fallen into enemy hands." There are few examples of like disasters. That evening, three officers and 240 men rallied to the army. With 195 men and 5 officers from the depot whom they found at Châlons, this was all that was left of the 2nd Tirailleurs until the capitulation of Sedan.

The 3rd Tirailleurs lost 839 men and 27 officers of whom 12 were killed. Amongst these were Commanders Clemmer and Thienot and Captain Deschamps, a young officer with a promising future. At the moment he was hit by a German ball, his sergeant major begged him to dismount as he remained a target for enemy fire. Deschamps answered in Arabic: "The children of the desert do not obey a leader who dismounts before the enemy." Courageous men, hearts of heros. If only today, when we await intelligent generals, soldiers like you could be found. France would not weep over new defeats. The morning of Sedan, a number of Tirailleurs led by Captain Chevreul and Lieutenant Carré de Busserolles who evidently were forming a rear guard did not find themselves enclosed by the Prussian circle. They managed to escape the capitulation and rushed across the Belgian border.

In the evening which followed Woerth, the three Turcos regiments, like most of the infantry regiments of MacMahon's Corps, were shattered into thousands of pieces. Thanks to the very tentative German pursuit, these bits, these fragments of regiments were able to recognize each other and, under the shadow of night, rushed to nearby places. The Germans themselves were astonished with

Interpreters of the Army of Africa, officers of the Chasseurs d'Afrique and Spahis (1842).

Algerian Tirailleur officers (1859).

the ease of their triumph and did not understand why the marshal had not been helped in time. Turcos were found throughout the East, full of energy, resolute, carefree and always good soldiers devoted to their country of adoption. One hundred seventy-five men of the 2nd Regiment, commanded by Lieutenant Vallés, arrived at Strasbourg and formed a company. It was turned over to Colonel Blot's *régiment de marche*. Captain de Rochelambert and Lieutenant Tourret of the 3rd Regiment had also formed a company with 100 men from their regiment. Finally, about twenty men from the 2nd had, under the command of Colonel Suzzoni, brought their flag to Strasbourg. Second Lieutenant Audibert of the 1st Regiment, wounded at Woerth, was killed during the bombardment.

At Bitche, 12 Turcos of the 1st Regiment, almost all wounded at Woerth and commanded by Sergeant Abderrahman-ben-M'rabed (later named Second Lieutenant) participated in the defense. Two officers and 25 men of the 2nd Regiment were also identified in the defense of Bitche.

At Verdun, Sergeants Major Loisel and Brunet, who had succeeded in escaping with about thirty Tirailleurs of the 1st in the journey from Sedan to the border, performed useful services. Sergeant Quartermaster Monteaux of the 2nd Regiment had managed to reach this place with some comrades escaped from the disaster of Woerth.

At Paris, Captain de Toustain du Manoir, who escaped en route, also organized a company with the wounded returning by railroad after the day at Woerth. It was part of the 4th Regiment of Zouaves organized at Paris. Captain Charles Abd-el-Kader was killed at Montretout. During the siege, I saw a non-commissioned officer of the Turcos march in the 42nd of the line.

The regiment of native Tirailleurs were not content with their efforts in 1870. The defense of the territory exacted new sacrifices from them.

The cadres of the 4th Battalion and the seventh companies of the first three Battalions remained in Algeria; that is, ten cadres. For the three regiments, this was thirty. It is true they were hardly filled out since the general effective strength was far from the 14,000 men dreamed of. However, approximately half were able to be sent to France. Recruitment was under pressure and, in addition, Turcos were rediscovered just about everywhere. Various detachments of the three corps came to revitalize their war battalions. Not being able to reach them, they were sent on to Saint-Cloud. There they were swelled with men who had escaped by various means from capitulation. They were assembled into a battalion of nine companies under the command of Captain Chevreul, promoted to Major. This battalion had nine companies, the first six coming from the 1st Regiment, the 7th, 8th, and 9th belonging to the 2nd and 3rd Regiments. At the time of the investment of Paris, it was sent to Tours. On October 16th, a regiment of Tirailleurs *de marche* at two battalions of six companies was officially appointed under the command of Lieutenant Colonel Capdepont. It was part of the 2nd Brigade (Chabron), of the 1st Division (Martin des Pallieres), of the 15th Corps. A third battalion was organized. On November 26th, the *régiment de marche* had received two companies of 200 men each coming from the Province of Algiers. After a variety of mishaps, the regiment commanded by Lieutenant Colonel Lemoing was interned in Switzerland. The 1st Regiment seemed to have supplied it with eight companies, the 2nd, four and the 3rd, six. At the time of the armistice, a second regiment was formed. The sole battalion, assembled with this goal in mind, was maintained in Algeria as soon as the first symptoms of the revolt of 1871 broke out. At peace, under the fire of the revolting Arabs, the reorganization of the three regiments was hardly an easy task.

The law of March 13, 1875 eliminated nine companies per regiment and reduced them to sixteen companies plus one of depot. This offered the possibility of maintaining effectives of from 145 to 150 Tirailleurs in the ranks. This is absolutely necessary in the total absence of more solid troops than are provided by the men of four years service who make up the active battalions of the line. Now it is necessary to ask for battalions complete with Algerian Tirailleurs in the event of urgent and difficult circumstances. Generally, this measure is viewed poorly in the African military which does not wish to sacrifice the recruitment for interests totally foreign to the natives. Thus, from this point of view, it was a mistake to send them to Tonkin where the climate was particularly deadly for them. The 3rd Regiment sent its 1st and 3rd Battalions which were severely tested in the battles of Phu-Sa, Kuon-Rua, Chu, Noui-Bop, and Hao-Ha. In Phu-Sa, the 1st Battalion had 128 men put out of action. A half company was blown up in the battle of Hao-Moc while going to help relieve Tuyen-Quan. One hundred and two men of the 3rd Tirailleurs were killed or wounded there.

Below is the list of officers killed and wounded in Tonkin in the three battalions of the 1st and of the 3rd Regiments of Tirailleurs forming the *régiment de marche* of the 19th Corps.

Killed—Captain Rollandes, Lieutenants Embarck or Allia and Messaoud-ben-Allia.

Wounded—Major Comoy; Captains Noirot, Bigo, Valet, Chirouze; Lieutenants Jehenne, Mamin-ben-Turkman, Salah-ben-Ferkadadji, Lakgar-ben-el-Achi, Belli-Kassem-zid-ben-Mohamed-zid, Mahomed-ben-Mehamed, Bajol, Peiro, Guignabaudet, Berge; Second Lieutenants Peyre, Roig and Pieri.

This campaign was difficult for the poor native soldiers. As was just noted, the climate was completely unsuitable for them. It was not conceiveable that the idea of having the Algerian Tirailleurs go hither and yon had entered into the heads of the French military organizers as early as 1854. There was no need for all the resources of France, and the old troops were made available. The excuse given was that they were going to defend the standard of Mohammed. In Italy, they were sent to fight the Austrians because four years earlier they had been sent to fight the Russians. In Senegal, it was claimed that they would not leave Africa. Finally, in CochinChina and in Mexico where they sent detached battalions composed of troops taken from the three regiments, they had been selected for reasons of personal convenience. In 1870, the only time that they left Algeria for the defense of the soil of their adopted country, they faced cruel setbacks. Now they are used like colonial troops. The opinion of serious military men—in total contradiction to General Wimpffen's ideas—is that the Turcos are particularly suited to Algeria. Now that conquest is almost assured, they represent the link between the past and the future. If the French had not committed the error of giving the Jewish people notable domination at the same time that military prestige was decreased, the Arabs would better understand French politics, would not think about revolt, and would come to serve in French ranks with much less pressure. Although the organization of the tribe has a

completely social appearance, the Arab does not grasp the Republican philosophy. On a private level, he recognizes work, property and community well-being. However, in military politics, he believes only in the authority of the leader bearing the arms of command and having the right of life or death over his soldiers.

Undoubtedly, the French colonists find considerable advantages in the political emancipation of the colony. However, if a new false prophet raises his head tomorrow and succeeds in somewhat inflaming the native populations, the colonists will be the first to ask for the reestablishment of military authority. Perhaps they will even go so far as to blame the government which allowed military authority to diminish.

Thus, the question of native troops everywhere and at all times is whether the metropolitan authority in the regions where they serve is indisputable and undisputed.

Algeria has been calmed after many fairly difficult campaigns. The native Tirailleurs, on the one hand, have received an increase of a fourth regiment. This is the result of the protection of an order, as military as it is diplomatic, with which France honors Tunisia. This fine troop with its four Zouave regiments would form the four brigades of a 19th active corps, circumstances warranting.

Foreign Legion (1840).

The names of the colonels who have commanded the four regiments since their creation are listed below:

1st Regiment (Algiers Province) - Rose, Archinard, Peychaud, Morandy, Munier, Delatour d'Auvergne Lauragais, Colonna d'Istria, Mourlan.

2nd Regiment (Oran Province) - Laure, Montfort, Suzzoni, Colonieu, O'Neill, Avezard.

3rd Regiment (Constantine Province) - Liébert, Le Poittevin de Lacroix, Gandil, Barrué, Barbier, Verrier, Gerder, Jacob, and Boitard.

4th Regiment (Tunisia Province) - Vincent.

Let us add to this list the legends of the flags which they received on July 14, 1880:

1st Regiment - Laghouat, 1852 - Sebastopol, 1854-1855 - Turbigo, 1859 - San-Lorenzo, 1863.

2nd Regiment - Laghouat, 1852 - Sebastopol, 1854-1855 - Solferino, 1859 - San-Lorenzo, 1863.

3rd Regiment - Laghouat, 1852 - Sebastopol, 1854-1855 - Solferino, 1859 - San-Lorenzo, 1863.

The flag of the 3rd Regiment has been decorated with the Legion of Honor in commemoration of a flag taken from the enemy by the Tirailleur Ahmed-ben-Mijoub at the battle of San-Lorenzo.

Interpreters. In a chapter dedicated to the history of the special troops of the French Algerian colony, it is impossible to forget the valiant interpreters of the Army of Africa. Their existence, mixed with that of the expeditionary columns, was for a long time confused with that of the Algerian Chasseurs, the Moroccan gendarmes, and the Spahis. Sometimes the interpreters showed the greatest of courage, following the French generals with saber in hand. At times in Arab uniforms, they penetrated into new countries and prepared the French expeditions. Garoué, Léon Ayas, Daboussy, Huder, Gabriel Zaccar, Cohen, Cabissot, Ahmed-ben-Rouïba, and Lévy met with a brave ending, whether at the head of French troops or in important missions. The corps supplied three famous generals: Margueritte, Yousouf, and Abdelal. Many high-ranking officers, diplomats such as Léon Roches, magistrates, learned men, and men of letters came from them as well. Although a good application was not always found for it, the multiple services which it rendered must especially be taken seriously. If the interpreters of the Army of Africa had been purely and simply military men coming from an Arab Office to serve in a general staff and then passing from a general staff into a council of war, then the army would be used to viewing them as indispensible auxiliaries of the command. They would have them voluntarily classified with titles in the ranks. Did they not almost all come from the troops and particularly from the native Tirailleurs whose glorious history has just been told?

However, amongst the interpreters, many—and I believe these were not the best ones—preferred civilian careers, passing

through the corps like brilliant meteors. What attracted them was the hope of working one's way rapidly through while profiting from the changes and fluctuations of the administration in a country which had not yet been well settled despite sixty years of occupation. This mobility discredited them a bit with their comrades. That well might have been so. Although the recruitment of interpreters was not always managed with great judgement, their corps is one of the most deserving of praise.

In 1830, General Bourmont had militarized the provisional corps of interpreters for the needs of his expedition with great practicality and intuition. The following organization of the corps of interpreters attached to the expedition has been uncovered in a report from the general staff of the Army of Africa.

First class (rank of colonel): Girardin, Jacob, Habaïby, Chahin, Zaccar.
Second class (rank of major): Vincent, Muller, Eusèbe de Salle.
Third class (rank of captain): Abdelal, Boyer, Abdalha d'Asboune, Gautier, Bourcet, Dumesnil.
Interpreter guides (rank of lieutenant): Joseph Habaïby, Daboud-Habaïby, N. Lemanne, Nathan Mouty, Axaria, de Soutzos, Abdel-Malack.

Foreign Legion in front of Sebastopol (1855).

Many of these names recall the Mamelukes of the First Empire, especially those amongst them coming from the Syrian squadron. However, the list is not complete, and it was very quickly modified. It was perceived too late that the Egyptians, the Syrians, and the native youths who had been assigned to them would never be understood when they had business with the Arabs of the tribes, although they succeeded in making the Turks listen. It was absolutely necessary to recruit amongst the French and foreigners who had had commercial or other buisness with the native population. Three organizations arose in 1831, 1833, and 1838 which did not do much to strengthen personnel.

The organization of February 12, 1831 eliminated the interpreter guides and replaced them with interpreter gendarmes. However this move had no useful results. It was then that the the Duke of Rovigo had Joanny Pharaon, the son of one of Bonaparte's interpreters, come. He was the only man who knew how to speak and write Arabic as well as French. However, everything remained provisional. The real creation of the permanent corps dates to 1845. Since then, the first organization has been altered in 1846, 1849, and 1851. A decree from June 4, 1862 regulated the status of the employees who composed the corps and whose cadre was fixed in the following manner by the law of March 13, 1875.

Interpreters: Principals, 5; 1st Class, 8; 2nd Class, 12; 3rd Class, 14. Total, 39.
Assistant Interpreters: 1st Class, 15; 2nd Class, 20. Total, 35.

In addition to the names of interpreters killed by the enemy which have just been cited, a long list of their colleagues who died prematurely under the murderous influence of the African climate could also be given.

THE FOREIGN LEGION

Article 13 of the Charter of 1830 stipulates that no foreign troops can be admitted into the service of the State, except by virtue of a law. It must have given satisfaction to the victors of July whom the Swiss of the Royal Guard had not spared. The Hohenlohe Legion, then in Greece, had been transformed into the 21st Regiment of light infantry. One did not know what to do with foreign deserters and political refugees whom the Parisian Revolution attracted or which the counter coup to this event drove out of the country. On February 4, 1831, a legal project involving the creation of a foreign legion was presented to the Chamber of Deputies. It was adopted on February 21st and taken to the Chamber of Peers. The latter Chamber amended it by adding that the new corps "could not be used except outside the continental territory of the realm." This was already stated in the Charter. The Legion was thus destined (law of March 21, 1831) to be continuously on campaign, be it in Africa or elsewhere. It gloriously fulfilled this mandate. In the course of this history, some inconveniences have been recorded which arise from the unusual nature of the Legion's recruitment. At the same time, it must be stated that everywhere the Foreign Legion carried its flag, it always showed the greatest of valor and a most heroic steadfastness.

The non-naturalized soldiers of the Hohenlohe Legion and those of the Swiss regiments of the line and of the Guard who agreed to serve under the French flag formed the first recruitment. They were joined by refugees and foreign deserters.

There were great organizational difficulties. An old Swiss colonel of the first Empire, Stoffel, along with Lieutenant Colonel Komierowski, were charged with regulating the first gathering. Three segments found themseves in France in June 1831. The 1st Battalion, almost complete, under the command of Salomon de Musis was stationed at Bar-le-Duc. One company was at Auxerre, another at Agen, each forming a nucleus around which foreign deserters and political refugees would gather together. At the end of that year, the glorious Colonel Combes came to take command of the Legion and led the four first battalions to Africa. Numbers 1, 2, and 3 were assigned to the Algiers Province and Number 4 to the Oran Province. The 5th Battalion and the depots of the three first battalions remained at Pont-Saint-Esprit. A company staying in Agen continued with the recruitment work. A group of Swiss officers who had not been able to profit from the transformation of the Hohenlohe Legion into the 21st Regiment of light infantry and some second lieutenants entered the Foreign Legion as a type of spoils of war. Together with some foreign officers which the July Revolution had attracted to France, this gave a bold but fairly solid appearance to the Legion. At this time, the soldiers of the Legion were grouped by nationalities as was stipulated in the founding ordinance. The 1st and the 3rd Battalions were German, the 2nd Polish, the 4th Spanish, and the 5th Italian. The disastrous effect of this organization which was as dangerous as it was logical will soon be seen.

In this way, seven battalions came into being. These were very strong battalions which were equal in power to three ordinary

regiments. However, they were not always satisfactory with regard to discipline. They had to be dispersed. When the Legion was given to Spain on June 28, 1835, the seven battalions were composed as follows: the first three of Germans, the 4th of Spanish, the 5th of Italians, the 6th of Belgians and Dutch, and the 7th of Polish. The old Foreign Legion which had been successively commanded by Colonels Stoffel, Combes, de Mollembeck and Bernelle welcomed its change of destination with enthusiasm. Bernelle led it to Spain. After having believed in the European war, the army no longer counted on it. Few officers with French titles used the power which allowed them to return to the French regiments.

At the same time that it handed over to Spain the Legion organized under the law of 1831, the government thought of forming a new one (decree of December 16, 1835). The 1831 Legion will no longer be dealt with here. A single battalion was organized. It went to Spain (August 1, 1836) to join the seven battalions already serving there. Meanwhile, foreign deserters continued to flow into the Legion's depot. This was a great problem. A new battalion was recruited which left for Algeria under the command of Bedeau on January 11, 1837. A second battalion soon followed it and on July 18, 1837, a new Legion was reconstructed.

As has been said, the classification of soldiers by nationalities presented great inconveniences. The account of an adventure which exposes these inconveniences and shows what supervision was required with these foreign soldiers is taken from the correspondance of Marshal Saint-Arnaud. "On the night of the 19th to the 20th of March 1840, the redoubt of the Ouded-Ada was commanded by a captain and a lieutenant. Toward ten in the evening, the captain was in the hut and the lieutenant was walking around outside. Suddenly, the soldiers threw themselves on the lieutenant, felling him, striking him with bayonet blows, taking his saber from him, and wounding him seriously in the head. Upon hearing the unfortunate lieutenant's cries, the captain rushed out, saber in hand, shouting: 'To arms!' He thought that it was the Bedouins who were coming to attack. Upon his arrival and in response to his cries, the assassins abandoned the victim and ran off outside the redoubt, leaving the captain alone with ten men. The thirty miserable assassins were all Spaniards, and they deserted with arms and baggage. The captain sent two men to Kouba to warn us. I immediately mounted my horse, although I was still ill, and set off in great haste for the redoubt with sixty men. I pulled the post together again, had the wounded officer removed, and took him to Kouba where he was bandaged and sent to the hospital. The wounds were serious. I ordered numerous patrols, covered the surrounding area myself, and at two in the morning, I returned to Kouba, making my report to the colonel. It seems that amongst the one hundred twenty miserable Spaniards recruited at Pau to our misfortune, there was a plot to assassinate all the officers of the 4th Battalion, with the exception of three. An inquiry was made. Four of the thirty deserters were already in our hands. What will the consequences of this catastrophe be for us?" There were none. The culprits were shot. The Legion did not become a less solid corps under fire, but it was exceedingly difficult to control with good discipline. With a few rare exceptions, the officers of the Legion were men of the elite. Desertion recurred many times amongst the recruits due to lack of discipline. Desertions happened on a large scale most often between an enlistment on one of the French borders and arrival at the port of embarkation. This bad lot attempts to take the travel expenses allocated them upon enlistment. Since perhaps they can manage without papers, they could easily get away with it. All the nations who admit foreigners into their armies are subject to the same disappointments. In sum, it should be conceded that the French do well with the Legion since, despite reservations about its recruitment, France always ends up having two regiments. The ordinance of December 30, 1840 organized it in this proportion after the remains of the old Legion, which had been given to Spain was driven back onto French territory with Cabrera. From 1837 to November 1840, the second Legion had been commanded by Colonel de Hülsen, known as Meerscheid, of Prussian origins. He had already served France under the Empire in the Isembourg Regiment and under the Restoration in the Hohenlohe Legion.

From 1840 to 1854, the two new regiments of the Legion distinguished themselves in new expeditions and proved useful at numerous tasks. They had been at the assault of Constantine. They were at the siege of Zaatcha. Now is the time to point out those various qualities of men rejected by civilization who are in the ranks of the Legion. After having too often paid too great a price for

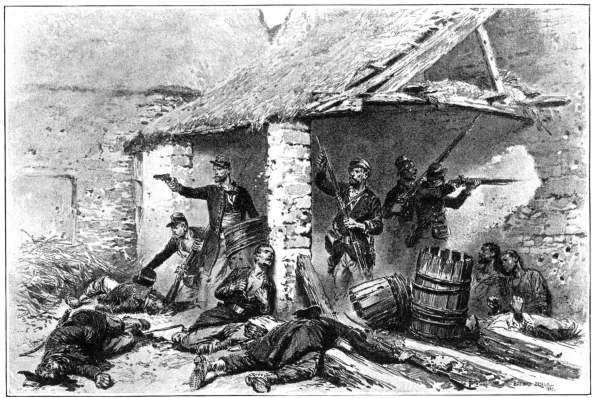

The Foreign Legion in Mexico (Camaron, April 30, 1863).

their passions, these men—some of considerable merit—wear the grey greatcoat of the Legionnaire under an assumed name to atone for the mistakes of their youth. General Carbuccia has been heard to say that he was never embarrased to have excavations carried out in the ruins of the ancient Lamboesis, ruins much admired by the Academie des Inscriptions et Belles-Lettres. "I could construct a town," said the colonel. "I had architects, engineers, and artists in my companies. When I needed a scholar, a writer or an artist, I requested him through an order and the next day the sergeants major brought me ten names instead of one. I would be able to form an institute with its assorted departments. Where do these men come from? What have they done in their country? What were their real names? They were impenetrable beyond the surface."

The colonels of the two regiments had been: for the 1st Regiment, 1840 - de Mollembeck, 1842 - Despinoy, 1843 - Mouret, 1846 - Mellinet, 1850 - Bazaine. For the 2nd Regiment, 1840 - Senilhes, March 1848 - Canrobert, September 1848 - Carbuccia, 1852 - Coeur, 1853 - de Caprez.

In June 1845, the two regiments received orders to form their war battalions and to set out for Gallipoli. During the Crimean campaign, the Foreign Legion rendered important services. At Alma, its elite battalion (4 companies of grenadiers and 4 of voltigeurs) reinforced Canrobert's Division. It was admired by the entire army for its solidity under cannonfire. Joined by the companies of the center, the two regiments permanently formed the Second Brigade (Bazaine) of the Third Division (Paté) of the First Corps (Pélissier, then de Salles) on October 17, 1854.

The elite battalion had landed at Oldfort with 23 officers and 794 non-commissioned officers or soldiers. On November 5, the 1st Regiment had still only landed 46 officers and 1,277 men of the ranks. The 2nd Regiment had 48 officers and 1,280 men. On February 10th, the 1st Regiment had 46 officers present and 1,386 men of the ranks. The 2nd had 44 officers and 1691 men. On May 20th, the 1st Regiment included 38 officers in the ranks and 1319 men. The 2nd had 50 officers and 1,189 men. On August 15th, each of the two regiments had 50 officers in the ranks. There were only 1,190 men in the First Regiment and 1,102 in the 2nd. The regiments left with 2,000 men and received rather considerable reinforcements in 1854 and 1855, but they suffered a great deal. It should be recalled that the campaign of the Orient cost France approximately 140,000 men and that the infantry regiments lost from 1,400 to 2,300 men, on average 1,800.

While the two regiments of the Legion fought in the Crimea, a Swiss lawyer whom Napoleon III had known in his youth persuaded him that it would be easy to raise a fine infantry brigade composed of Swiss. To Ochsenbein's way of thinking, it would not take too long; it would only be a matter of a few days. On January 17 and February 3, 1855, some decrees intervened which ordered the assembly of two regiments of infantry and of one battalion of tirailleurs at Besançon under the name of the 2nd Foreign Legion. The regiments were each to have two battalions of eight companies. The battalion of tirailleurs would have ten companies. For the infantry line regiments and for the battalion of tirailleurs, the uniform was similar to that of the chasseurs à pied. The only difference was the base color of the tunic which was in green cloth. Meyer received the command of the 1st Regiment. An old Swiss officer naturalized as a Frenchman, de Caprez, who was well known in Africa was put in charge of the second. Captain Lian of the chasseurs a pied was named major of the tirailleurs. The general staffs and some company cadres were improvised with some French officers who spoke German and Ochsenbein's proteges. However, the soldiers did not come. In the name of neutrality, the Swiss authorities refused to administer them the necessary papers for enlistment. The Germans did not look kindly upon this surprise recruitment along their borders. The English, with their strong subsidies, were tough competition. In the end, 350 to 400 men were assembled.

At the end of the campaign, the new Legion did not count as effective strength and its cadres were not complete. However, the two regiments of the 1st Legion had acquired new rights of recognition from France in the Crimea. They were offered naturalization which assured them more normal promotions. Then a decree from May 21, 1856 mustered out the four regiments of the two Legions and the battalions of tirailleurs. All the officers and non-commissioned officers, French or naturalized, who requested it were turned over to the line regiments. Two foreign regiments, Number 1 and Number 2, were created.

The first, formed with the Swiss from the 2nd Legion and all troops of the same nationality included in the 1st, had two battalions at eight companies and two companies of tirailleurs. It retained the green tunic and had Colonel Meyer as its leader.

The Foreign Legion at Tuyen-Quan (1886).

The second, formed from the remains of the 1st Legion, had two battalions of eight companies. It retained its old uniform and had Granet-Lacroix de Chabrière for its colonel.

They went to be organized in Africa where they maintained a garrison until the time when they were sent off to take part in the Italian War. There they formed the 2nd Brigade (Castagny) of the 2nd Division (Espinasse) of the 2nd Corps (MacMahon) with the 2nd Regiment of Zouaves. They were engaged at Magenta. However, the effective strength of the first regiment was found to be reduced to 800 men for various reasons. It did not participate in the Battle of Solferino and was detached to Milan. The colonel of this regiment, Brayer, filled the command of this place under General de Béville, aide-de-camp of the Emperor. He opened the voluntary enrollments to complete his effective strength, but the Italians did not rush to his ranks. Those who belonged to the Legion found it more profitable with the proximity of Garibaldi to go enlist in his bands.

Despite the fine conduct of the Legion during the campaign of 1859 and despite the precious blood it had spilled on the battlefield of Magenta, it underwent a new organization on October 14, 1859. At Magenta, the 2nd Regiment had lost its colonel, de Chabrière, Captains d'Astis, Alavoine and Lieutenant André. The two regiments were to have the same cadres from that point on, the same effectives, and the same uniform. The companies of tirailleurs of the 1st Regiment were eliminated. In the end, only the 1st Regiment was maintained (December 4, 1861) under the name of *Régiment etranger* (Foreign Regiment). It had three battalions of nine companies each. The Legion was in this condition when the order to leave for Mexico arrived in 1863. About 2,000 men strong, it set sail on February 2nd on the *Saint-Louis* and the *Wagram* and arrived on March 26th at Vera-Cruz. Although it did not participate in the siege of

Native officer of the Algerian Tirailleurs, campaign dress (1886).

Chasseurs d'Afrique, campaign dress (1886).

Puebla, the foreign regiment accomplished noble work in Mexico. It was in that barren land that it brought fame to its flag through the distinguished feat of arms at Camaron. This event remained the glory of the soldiers of the Legion as much as Tuyen-Quan. The Zouaves had Constantine and Sebastopol, the Turcos Alma and Inkermann, the joyous Zephirs have Mazagran, and the Legionnaires have Tuyen-Quan and before that, Camaron!

Camaron!!! It shines in golden letters on the flag of the *régiment étranger*.

This account is borrowed from the works of Commander Niox on Mexico.

"On April 30th, a company which was 62 men and 3 officers strong (Danjou, Captain; Vilain, Second Lieutenant acting as Lieutenant; and Maudet, Second Lieutenant) left the post of Chiquehuite to scout the area. After having marched part of the night, it stopped to make coffee at seven in the morning in the place called Palo-Verde. A few moments later, enemy scouts were seen on the road, on the Chiquehuite side. Captain Danjou fell back in the direction of the village of Camaron. Suddenly, he was enveloped by a cloud of cavalrymen. The company formed itself in a square and received a first charge. Taking advantage of a moment of respite, the company climbed a nearby slope and again sustained a second attack of the Mexican cavalry without being broken. Then, charging in turn, it pierced the enemy line and threw itself into the houses.

"The building in which Captain Danjou prepared himself for the resistance was composed of a square courtyard of fifty meters on a side. The side which bordered the road was closed off by a main building divided into many rooms. He occupied the court whose opening he had barricaded as well as the room located at one of the angles. At that moment, the enemy penetrated the room situated at the opposite end. It was about nine in the morning. The French detachment, enjoined to give in, energetically refused and the firing began on all sides. Captain Danjou did not hope to successfully resist, but he made his men promise to defend themselves to the end. Soon afterwards, he fell, mortally wounded. Second Lieutenant Vilain took command.

"Toward noon, the sound of drums and bugles was heard. There was a glimmer of hope amongst the defenders of Camaron who thought this was the arrival of a rescue unit. The hope was soon dashed. It was three battalions of Mexicans, each 300 to 400 men strong, which General Milan was bringing to the combat site. Meanwhile, the enemy had succeeded in making a breach on one side of the courtyard. Using this breach, they took the defenders of the other sides from behind. At two o'clock, Second Lieutenant Vilain was killed. The command passed to Second Lieutenant Maudet. The heat was overwhelming, the troops had not eaten since the day before, and no one had had water since the morning. The suffering of the wounded was atrocious. The enemy made a new summons to surrender which was again refused with the same spirit. Then one of the outside sheds was set on fire. The smoke made the torture of thirst still more unbearable. Despite everything, the soldiers kept to the loopholes and the breaches. At five thirty, the attack was suspended. General Milan, gathering his soldiers in the shelter of a house, berated them, saying that it was a disgrace that they could not finish off the few French who remained standing. These words were heard by a French soldier of Spanish origin who translated them to his comrades. Soon after, a general assault was made. The Mexicans hurled themselves all at once at all the openings. At the main door, only one man remained. He was taken. At the opposite corner, there were still four soldiers who, until that point, had succeeded in defending a breach. They were overcome by the enemy which poured into the courtyard and advanced. Second Lieutenant Maudet was barricaded in the remains of a ruined shed with four men. He defended himself there for another quarter of an hour. Then, having used the last bullet against the enemy, he ran out of the shed. All rifles were trained on him. One of his men made a shield of his body and was struck down. He himself was seriously wounded and knocked to the ground. The Mexicans rushed at the few survivors of the unfortunate company and made them prisoners.

"It was six in the evening when this handful of heroic men succumbed. They had fought more than nine hours. Two officers were killed, the third mortally wounded. Twenty non-commissioned officers and soldiers had been killed and twenty-three were wounded of whom seven died of their wounds. The others were made prisoners with the exception of a drummer left to die. This man was picked up the following day by a reconnaissance party from the *régiment étranger*. He gave them the first details of the combat. It was certain that the Mexicans had lost three hundred men of whom two hundred were dead. The energetic resistance of the company decided General Milan to let the convoys pass without attacking them. He led his troops back to Jalapa, strongly impressed by the bloody losses which the victory had cost them."

The Foreign Legion was of course involved in Emperor Maximilian's projects for military organization. This troop with its animated, fiery spirit lent itself admirably well to all types of adventures, even the most unusual. Although the Belgians and the Austrians who voluntarily joined it complained about the conditions their sovereigns imposed on them, and although the charms of Juares and of the North American recruiting offices wrought such ravages amongst the *Condottieri* of the Legion, the majority of Legionnaires were ready to devote themselves to the new monarchy. Many of them joined the battalions of *Cazadores*. The foreign regiment even saw its cadres grow. However this shifting series of dreams quickly collapsed when faced with the pacification of the United States and their willingness to intervene.

The Legion returned to Sidi-bel-Abbes. It was there at the beginning of the war and counted four battalions of eight companies. An illusion—there were many of them—led the imperial government to believe that a number of refugee Hanoverians in France, notably in the Faubourg Saint-Antoine of Paris, would voluntarily enlist for the duration of the war. To this end, a decree appointed two new companies to the Legion. The formation of a second regiment was even ordered. A fifth battalion was created only in France. The command was entrusted to Captain Arago. This battalion distinguished itself especially in the taking of and the retreat from Orléans where it was cut to pieces.

In the first fifteen days of October, the first two battalions of the *régiment étranger* left Oran under the command of Colonel Deplanque. Named General after Coulmiers, he was replaced by de Curten, lieutenant colonel of the corps. On December 10, 1870, he was succeeded as lieutenant colonel commanding the regiment by Canat. Canat kept this command in the midst of the ups and downs which so quickly brought the lieutenant colonels of the past to the heads of brigades, divisions and even to army corps. The war regiment formed from the reassembled 1st, 2nd, and 5th Battalions supplied the entire campaign of the Loire. It was called to the Army of Versailles by Thiers to work toward the retaking of Paris from the enemies of order. In the first days of June, since it was at the barracks of la Pépinière, it unexpectedly received the order to leave for Africa. The Foreign Legion thus played a major role in the Crimean, Italian and Mexican wars, against Germany, and also in the repression of the Commune. Since 1831, there has been no infantry corps with such a military record.

The formation of a sixth battalion of the Foreign Legion was ordered on January 22, 1871. Was this organization confused with an attempted gathering of Belgian volunteers at the beginning of September 1870? On a roster of troops from December 1870, it is recorded as residing in Lille, but it does not appear in any of the accounts of exploits and actions by General Faidherbe's army.

Light infantry of Africa (1840).

Moreover, the official government broadsheet of Bordeaux claims that it had nominated officers for the 2nd *régiment étranger* of whom no trace is found in any other document.

Since 1873, the Legion has been returned to the same status as an infantry regiment of the line by the law of cadres. It was seen in Tunisia, and the important services which it rendered in Tonkin caused it to be expanded to two regiments. Each one has four battalions of four companies plus a depot company. Its unusual recruitment has not lost any of its difficult aspects although many from Alsace-Lorraine join it. These are excellent, devoted, and faithful soldiers to whom no advantages are offered. Some want to reduce the five year service term to three years. Thus, the Foreign Legion is more and more needed by the French military and for French colonial policies. It is difficult, to say the least, to find men of iron in our overly young active contingents who are capable of going into battle in extreme temperatures. The eight thousand men of the foreign regiments are and will henceforth be the fundamental core of all our distant expeditions.(1) This is without a doubt not very patriotic to entrust to foreign hands a mission going to defend the French flag abroad. However, the soldiers of the Legion who, regardless of what has been said, carry and will always carry this famous name into hundreds of combats, conduct their missions with such bravery and dedication that the star that decorates their kepis and buttons has become a symbol of military glory and honor.

At Tuyen-Quan under the command of Major Domine, two companies of the Legion (8 officers and 390 men) saved the military renown of France and accomplished one of the finest feats of arms in French history. Domine was so modest and so great, yet already his name is lost to public memory. His men fought for thirty-six days against an army of 20,000 Chinese.

LIGHT INFANTRY OF AFRICA

As one knows, Algeria was a fairly heavy burden on the budget in the early years of Louis-Philippe's reign. Conquest of a white flag, excess of finances, it used up quite a few soldiers at the time when European complications were talked about. The opposition made a weapon out of this. The majority begged the government to be prudent. Thus, for King Louis-Philippe, there was certain merit in retaining this colony. He should be congratulated for having found intelligent colleagues in the early generals of the Army of Africa. The Zouaves, the Turcos, the Zephirs, the Legion, and the Spahis had been invented by these generals to keep the urban troops available.

The question of mobilization so keenly discussed today was then called the "question of availability." To solve the problem of lack of troops for the few regiments which France left at the disposition of her conquerers of Algeria, they invented new military resources. On June 13, 1832, a royal decree authorized the creation of two battalions of light infantry under the name of "First and Second Light Infantry Battalions of Africa."

These battalions had eight companies and a general staff. In total, each had 28 officers and 1,005 non-commissioned officers and soldiers. They were to be composed as follows: 1st, of military men who, upon leaving a punishment company, would have to continue their service in the army; 2nd, of those who, sentenced to correctional punishment, would have to complete the service period imposed by law after their jail term or the pardon of their crime; 3rd, of men who requested voluntary enlistment in these corps. Thus, these were not exactly disciplinary corps but rather trial corps which quickly became proven corps due to all the hardships and misery they underwent. They returned from expeditions dressed in tattered greatcoats and pants. The army, seeing them so joyous under their rags through which their skin showed, proclaimed them to be the *"zephirs a poils"* (the naked Zephyrs). To make good soldiers out of such a motley crew, the officers and non-commissioned officers called upon to take part in this all had to be willing. They were selected from amongst the most energetic and best servants, since in order to command a bunch of hotheads, it was agreed to use elite leaders. The first two commanders were Lapostol (1st Battalion) and Salomon de Musis (2nd Battalion). However, before going further, let us first list the successive commanders of the three battalions. The third was created on June 20, 1833.

1st Battalion: 1832, Lapostol. 1833, de Robillard. 1834, Secourgeon. 1836, Verberné. 1839, de Comps. 1840, de Gerandon. 1842, de Montauban. 1846, Charras. 1848, Adam. 1851, Liébert. 1852, Souville. 1855, Gérard. 1858, Roux. 1859, Amat. 1864, Duhousset. 1866, Ropper. 1871, Thomas. 1877, Carrère. 1880, Pyot. 1882, Mirauchaux. 1885, Guillet.

2nd Battalion: 1832, Salomon de Musis (killed by the enemy in 1836). 1836, Gabriac de Montredon. 1840, Cavaignac (Eugène). 1841, Blangini. 1841 Ladmirault. 1842, Damesme. 1844, Prévost. 1848, Étienney. 1850, Saurin. 1852, le Poittevin de Lacroix. 1855, Ardouin. 1858, Dulyon de Rochefort. 1864, Colonna d'Ornano. 1865, Choppin-Merey. 1866, de Briand (killed by the enemy in Mexico in 1866). 1866, Hubert de la Hayrie. 1869, Feyfant. 1870, Jamot. 1882, Dugenne. 1884, Servière.

3rd Battalion: 1833, Allouveau de Montréal. Chadeysson. Peyssard. de Liniers. Lenoir. de Golberg. 1855, Baudoin. 1855, Trompeau, Mangin. Meuziau, 1869, Roussel. 1869, Gratreaud. Gallet. 1881, Fontebride. 1885, Césari.

This list includes a good number of glorious names who later became generals. Those officers who served in the battalions as captains and who also reached the summit of the military hierarchy should also be added to this list. They are: Molliere, de Noue, Mayran, Levaillant, Plombin, Maissiat, d'Exea, de Marguenat, Clerc, Agard de Roumejoux, and O'Malley. These names prove what a sought-after honor it was to command these fallen but exalted men. They rehabilitated themselves under fire through their bravery and their dedication. Although the actual law of recruitment admitted as soldiers those whom the military service renounced in the

(1) The Foreign Legion has largely paid its dues in the Far East. It cannot be guaranteed that the following list of officers killed and wounded in Tonkin is complete. The government of the Republic has concealed French losses with extreme care. However such as it is, it suffices to show what this valiant corps lost in terms of men.

Officers killed: Captain Adjutant Major Mebl; Captains Beynet, Moulinay, Gravereau and Cotter; Lieutenant Weber; Second Lieutenant Bacqué.
Officers wounded: Captains Adjutant Major Bergoumoux and Poncet; Captains Berard, Naert, Cesari, Bouyer, Conte; Lieutenants Comignan (son of the general of this name), Durillon, Lacroix, Ruspoli, Goeury, Casanova; Second Lieutenants Vincent, de la Londe, Brore and Burel.

past, in our opinion, this was justified. The African battalions are still what they were in the past. The 200 conscripts marked by previous condemnations sometimes reach an even greater proportion than usual. This rubbish from the great cities, these vagabonds, these robbers who always have vices, even that of homosexualism, leave the penitentiaries unimproved and more corrupt than ever. They have not managed to diminish the sense of military honor in the chasseurs battalions of Africa. Usually the physical reactions of civilian ex-convicts are as low as their souls. Hospital prey, incapable of spirit, they march out of every fatigue party and become victims of the first disease. In Tonkin, it has been remarked that they all died one month after their arrival. Unworthy of wearing the noble uniform of the soldiers, they are sustained neither by esprit de corps nor by the hope of erasing their evil pasts. They die at the first hardship. It would be better to form them into work gangs of pioneers since the French legislators think that the country cannot pass up their services. There, without weapons, dressed in the helmet of infamy, they would work to win their lives. This would be both more humane and more moral since the work would be sufficient punishment for these miserables souls.

The *Joyeux*. The chasseurs of the African battalions are no longer called *Zephirs*. The *Joyeux*, the real *Joyeux*, are on the contrary most often those with their heads on backwards, the feather-brained. However, they include in their ranks many courageous men. The best proof is that everywhere they have gone—and they have been everywhere—the generals have done justice to their rash bravery and their ready willingness. The difference between a condemned civilian and a condemned military man sent to the battalions is so well understood that the latter, after one year, barring harsh punishment, can return to a regiment upon his request.

Light infantry of Africa. Taking of Couraia (1833).

The officers and the cadres are, unfortunately, not well remembered today. What is not forgotten, however, is to call them on campaign when distant expeditions demand sacrifices beyond human power. This doesn't ruffle the *Zephir*, however, and he puts his pack together and sings: "Villan, of the Battalion of Africa, *Joyeux Zephir* forward!" He leaves but he does not return. If he does return, it is to tell the tale of his misery and the death of the others, as the legend of the *Volunteer of Tonkin* says.

1st Battalion: After having participated in the expeditions of Macta, Mascara, Tlemcen and Tafna, it set sail on October 23, 1836 for the Province of Constantine where it was going to serve in the first siege. In this unfortunate expedition where it was represented by three companies, it lost five officers, thirty-three soldiers, and had 99 wounded. It is not possible to recount all the tasks and combats of this glorious battalion. Instead, the Defense of Mazagran will be addressed which is not only the culminating point of its dedication but also that of its glory. The history of the corps is as follows.

"On October 20, 1839, the 10th Company came to establish itself at Mazagran. On December 13th, it was attacked there by 300 Arabs which it victoriously repulsed. The enemy had to withdraw, leaving 120 of their men, of whom 80 were dead, behind beneath the city walls. However, this attempt was only the prelude for a more serious attack. On February 3, 1840, eight thousand Arabs rushed into the city abandoned by its inhabitants and began the siege of the redoubt in which 123 chasseurs of the 10th Company were entrenched. The entire day of the 3rd, the musketry and the cannon did not stop rumbling. When night came, the breaches had to be repaired and the wall secured to resist further attacks. On the morning of the 4th, the Arabs received reinforcements which brought them a second cannon. The attack began again with a fury which repeated the previous day's failure. Munitions were becoming scarce and the thought of being without them appeared with all its sinister consequences. Captain Lelièvre gave the order to fire only when a hit could be made with certainty.

"On the evening of the 5th, about twenty shots had crossed the walls. The mast that supported the pavilion was broken by one of them. However, the French flag still flew at the end of the day on the minaret of the mosque. On the 6th, the Arabs' fire was redoubled with intensity. When they judged the garrison of Mazagran weakened enough by this fusillade, they threw themselves into an assault. Already some were appearing on the bastion. At that critical moment, Captain Lelièvre called his chasseurs to his

side, put himself at their head, and flung himself at the enemy. Those who had had the audacity to scale the walls fell dead at the bottom. Finally discouraged by such a heroic resistance, the Arabs withdrew in disorder. A continuous fire did not even allow them to take their dead away with them. This memorable battle ended. A handful of brave, intelligent men, entrenched behind a weak wall, cut off from all communication, and having supplies and munitions for only a few days, had stopped a multitude of ferocious men, elated by fanaticism. The enemy's size alone would have shattered Mazagran if they had dared to rush its weak walls."

According to the report of General Guéhenneuc, commander of the Oran Division, the minister of war made the following general order known to the army:

> Public praises have already made the glorious defense of the Mazagran garrison known to the army. One hundred and twenty-three brave men of the 10th Company of the 1st Light Infantry Battalion of Africa were barely protected by a weak wall of dry-laid stones. The wall was chipped away by cannons, yet for five days, they pushed back the assaults of many thousands of Arabs.
>
> The King hastened to issue awards to the military men who have been identified to him as being the most remarkable in the midst of this handful of intrepid soldiers. To increase the value of these rewards, the King wished that they be celebrated in the military honors as well as under the names of the soldiers who have been cited in the report of their leaders. In the discharges which will be granted them when they leave the military service, it will be expressly mentioned that they were amongst the 123 defenders of Mazagran.
>
> Captain Lelièvre has been promoted to Major; Lieutenant Magnier to Captain. Second Lieutenant Durrand, Sergeant Major Villemot and Sergeant Giroud have been named Knights of the Legion of Honor. Quartermaster Taine, Coporal Muster, Chasseurs Leboigne, Courtès, Edit, Goepfert, Vouillon, Renaud, Dannel, Marcot, Valent and Plançon all of the 10th Company of the 1st Battalion of Light Infantry of Africa are cited in the report of General Guéhenneuc.
>
> The 10th Company is authorized to keep within its ranks the flag shot through with bullets which flew over the redoubt of Mazagran during the days of 3, 4, 5, and 6 February 1840. On every anniversary of this last day, the present general order will be read in front of the battalion.

> Paris, March 12, 1840. The Peer of France, Minister-Secretary of State for War: Cubières.

This flag is still in the hands of the commander of the 1st Battalion. He keeps it like a precious object in the orderly room and shows it to the battalion on every anniversary of Mazagran, which is still celebrated. This flag was pierced by two shots and by 120 bullets: 53 in the blue band, 35 in the white band, and 32 in the red band.

It should be added that the King had a bronze medal given to each of the heros of Mazagran, and that the Municipal Council of Paris—then very chauvinistic and patriotic—gave the name of Mazagran to a new street. A column raised on the battle site recalls it to memory.

Mascara (1841), the last struggles of Abd-el-Kader, and the taking of Laghouat (1852) provided the 1st Battalion of Africa with yet more opportunities to prove its valor. Finally, toward March 1864, 40 chasseurs from the battalion under the leadership of Sergeant Quinay were massacred by bands of *Si-Sliman* while escorting Colonel Beauprêtre.

2nd Battalion. It fired for the first time in the expedition which General Trézel directed against Bougie. He deserved the most flattering of praises for his brilliant leadership in the taking of Couraya, the key to Bougie. After some difficult tasks, it supplied a volunteer company to the first expedition of Constantine in 1836. The company was commanded by Captain Blangini who was cited after the assault of the Mansoura Bridge. It played a glorious role in all the distinguished feats of arms of the colony. In January 1864, it was sent to Mexico under the command of Major Colonna d'Ornano. It stayed there until April 1867 and proved itself ever valiant in the difficult expeditions to which it was attached.

Finally, in this latter period, it was designated to go to Tonkin where it participated in the major battles which led to the conquest of the Delta. In this last campaign, it lost more than five hundred men.

3rd Battalion. Created on September 1, 1833, this battalion traveled the most. In addition to all the campaigns of Africa, it counts those of China, CochinChina and Japan (1862 to 1864). In this single campaign it lost 7 officers and 260 men of the ranks killed or dead from disease. Recalled to the Far East on October 22, 1884, it set sail with an effective strength of 900 men and 17 officers. It had 2 officers killed in this new campaign, Captain Perrasse and Second Lieutenant Lucas, and four wounded.

From May 1836 until March 1837, a ministerial caprice had exiled the 3rd Battalion of Africa to Corsica. No troop was less appropriate to maintain its garrison in the middle of such a troubled and overexcited population. Happily, the need to assemble solid troops for the second siege of Constantine returned the 3rd Battalion to Algeria, its rightful place. It had the honor of supplying one hundred volunteers to the assault columns. They were commanded by Captains Houreaux and Caboreaux, Lieutenant Dejourdan and Second Lieutenant Adam. The conduct of these brave men was the admiration of the entire army. A chasseur named Jean was decorated with the Legion of Honor for the part he had taken in the assault. The following year, the 3rd distinguished itself especially in the defense of Setif where, deprived of water, it nonetheless inflicted considerable losses on the Arabs.

This is the beginning of a long list of daily battles, of work without end. An expedition is a good time for the *joyeux Zephir*. It is a time of rest since ordinarily he spends his life working at breaking up rocks. With a rifle in his shoulder belt and a pick or a pickaxe in hand, the Zephir marks routes and raises entrenchments

Local commanding officer and veterans (1840).

under the direction of the Engineers. In between he inflicts heavy damage on the enemy. Thanks to him, the colony enjoys its best public works and utilities. In a country where water is the main wealth (because it produces all other riches), what the chasseurs of the African battalions have done by drilling artesian wells deserves praise from the people. The Zephir's pick and pickaxe and the mule of an officer must not be forgotten in the history of the conquest of Algeria. These are the early artisans of French power and greatness! What the African battalions consumed in terms of men, only their regimental numbers know and make note of. During the siege of Sebastopol where they were not effectively commanded, they turned over approximately two thousand five hundred men to the Zouaves and to other regiments in various detachments. This is what later determined their immediate use in CochinChina and in Mexico. Today, like the soldiers of the Legion, the chasseurs of the African battalions are the missionaries of French civilization.

In October 1870, the government of Tours thought—and it was not deceived—that the African battalions could supply an excellent *bataillon de marche*. Commanded by Major Gratreaud and composed of six companies (two per province) for a total of 1,500 men, this battalion had a very strong appearance. It led to the idea of creating a regiment by adding a second battalion to these companies formed in the same manner. Gratreaud had command of the *régiment de marche* which was ultimately interned in Switzerland.

It is fairly difficult to realize what could have been done in 1870 if the authorities governing from September 4th on had known how to use the forty-five thousand soldiers of the Army of Africa in conjunction with the one hundred thousand men who were confined in Paris. There were also the two hundred fifty thousand men which the empire had already recalled in the depots and the volunteers who responded to the call of their endangered country. Unfortunately, precious time was lost through politics. The regiment of Zephirs was ready only at the end of the campaign. It could have been put on the road before September 15th.

Algeria was both a fertile land and the great refuge of military political sins. The parade commenced with the volunteers of la Charte as soon as the conquest took place. The least terrible among them had been turned over to the Zouaves and to the 67th Regiment of Line Infantry organized at Algiers. False legends exist concerning the volunteers of la Charte. We will set about to destroy them. Following the "three glorious days," a number of malicious characters took possession of various barracks in the capital. They established themselves as a regiment, asked for pay, and even threatened public security. They had to be dissolved. Then they dispersed the light infantry regiments in small groups of one hundred and fifty men. The majority persisted; they were sent to Africa. Some won the epaulette, others the rank of sergeant by virtue of a law called the law of national recompenses.

A battalion of veterans composed of six companies and bearing Number 2 received a party of privates taken from the Parisian volunteers and from the *compagnies sédentaires* of the Seine. This corps had only a brief existence and was commanded by Major Bérard (1). At the beginning of the conquest, these experiments were easily excused, but very soon the governors recognized that valid corps with staunch hearts were required for Algeria. Political shocks always determine abnormal military creations. When the history of the special corps of the city of Paris is told, it will be seen that after the Revolution of 1848, various dissolutions of the Republican Guard gave a lot of trouble to the authorities. Improvised officers and soldiers who could not be kept and who had acquired titles formed (decree of October 16, 1849) two companies of Algerian Voltigeurs. They were separately administered as auxiliaries of the gendarmes. Not being allowed to recruit, they disappeared very quickly. What remained of them was turned over to the infantry.

Disciplinary Companies. The disciplinary corps under the First Empire do not have a well defined history. The war consumed so many men that it is useless to separate the good from the bad. The regime did not have a very clear organization. As many unruly soldiers were sent to the colonies as were used on public works. The orders of December 10, 1802 and of August 8, 1804 are the only documents which exist on this topic. The Restoration at first reorganized the colonial battalions. Then, seeing the danger of very large masses of disobediant soldiers, it adopted the organization of these soldiers into companies, eliminating the three colonial battalions through the decree of April 1, 1818.

It immediately thought up the idea of subdividing them into *fusiliers* and *pioneers* according to the degree of criminality of the men who formed it. These companies were to include 180 men at most, without a very strong staff: five officers, eight non-commissioned officers, and twelve corporals. The cadres of two categories of companies wore the infantry uniform with white collar, trim, and lining edged in a deep red, a shako of standard form, pewter uniform buttons and a pewter shako plaque. The pioneers had a uniform jacket in beige cloth which buttoned right across the chest, piping, trim, and royal blue tabs. They did not have weapons; the fusiliers only kept them while on duty.

In 1830, four companies each of fusiliers and pioneers were in existence. The First Fusiliers was at Cherbourg, the Second and the Third at Besançon, and the Fourth at Arras. The First of Pioneers was at Cherbourg, the Second at Belfort, the Third on the Island of Oléron, and the Fourth at Valenciennes. The July Revolution and its outcome temporarily doubled the general effectives of the army. A fifth company of pioneers and one of fusiliers was therefore created by royal decree on November 8, 1831. On December 29, 1832, a Sixth and a Seventh Fusiliers was organized. These four last companies maintained their garrison in Africa. Some time later, the Fifth of Pioneers was converted into an Eighth of Fusiliers. Ten of these companies were divided up among the three provinces of the Army of Africa. The Third of Fusiliers was still at Besançon. The 4th Company of Pioneers had its garrison at Navarreins.

Under the Second Empire, the disciplinary companies were subsequently reduced to five of fusiliers and two of pioneers. They were all in Algeria. In 1886, there were no more than four of fusiliers and one of pioneers. They were in Africa. Compulsory service had changed

(1) The general plan of this book, which is the history of the corps of existing troops, does not permit a discussion of the veterans who were of importance in the French army. We will take advantage of this occasion to make amends for this omission. In that time when the soldier and the non-commissioned officer had to have thirty years of service in order to obtain a meager retirement pension, the veterans counted more invalids than healthy men in their ranks. It was not always this way. At the end of the wars of the Republic, many demi-brigades of veterans existed. These were old soldiers, perfectly capable and with a good war record. When the First Consul formed the camp of Dijon, the veterans were called to conceal the movement that the army was going to make in the Alps. In Year XIII (1804), the corps of veterans was composed of ten regiments commanded by Mouret (1st), Richon (2nd),– (3rd), Lasalle (4th), Okeeffe (5th), Warnesson (6th), Bedos (7th), Marchias (8th), Lamarche (9th), and Duplessis (10th). These regiments supplied active troops a number of times, but their organization was modified at the end of the Empire. In 1812, the veterans no longer counted more than twelve separate battalions. The Guard had a company of veterans which the Emperor showered with favors. It had its garrison at Versailles.

The Restoration eliminated regiments and battalions and instituted 10 companies of non-commissioned officers who were veterans. There were 45 of fusiliers and 15 of cannoneers. These latter replaced the coast guard cannoneers. The first four companies of non-commissioned officers were allocated to the Guard at Luxembourg Palace, to the Hôtel of the Minister of War, the Louvre Palace, and the Palais-Bourbon. Many of the companies of fusiliers were employed in the prison service and in the penitentiaries. The 7th was charged with the care of the Jardin des Plantes. When the Revolution of 1830 broke out, it was convenient to muster out three companies of fusiliers: the 20th, 41st, and 44th. On the other hand, the 33rd had been allocated to the military men in the gendarmes. The Revolution of 1830 awakened the appetites of all the old soldiers of the Republic and of the Empire. Seeing their old generals well received at court, they asked for pay. Some departmental companies of veterans were created to give immediate satisfaction to the old remnants of the glorious French armies. Eighty-nine were organized, one per department. The department of the Seine had four of them. This was a great expense since, in addition, twelve companies of non-commissioned officers were being maintained, 33 of fusiliers, and 13 of cannoneers. Paris began to be relieved of these non-active, insubordinate companies. They were given an offer to serve in Africa or in the 1st Battalion of Fusiliers assembled at Cherbourg. Meanwhile, 8 companies of non-commissioned officers, 10 of fusiliers, and 13 of cannoneers were being maintained, all non-active. The July Government, which was very paternalistic toward the old servants, liquidated the pensions of all those who wanted to terminate their thirty years of service in these useless, often unruly corps. In some cases, these corps gave poor examples to young soldiers of the active army. The government did even more. It gave the veterans an establishment which had not been accorded them by any government: it created special companies in each service where, despite their drunkenness and their poor manner of service, they won the right to a pension.

At the end of Louis-Philippe's reign, 8 companies of non-commissioned officers existed and 10 of fusiliers, 2 of gendarmes, 4 companies of cavalrymen attached to the remount depots of Caen, Saint-Maixent, Guéret and Auch, 13 companies of cannoneers, and one of sappers.

One by one, the Empire mustered out these corps which no longer had a reason for being with retirement at twenty-five years of age. Today, France no longer needs corps of refuge for soldiers who are worn out before their time. The word "veteran" was from that time on erased from the military vocabulary. It should be noted that this institution became spoiled by the abuses that were made within it.

the morals of the French army quite a bit. Discipline became less strict and the period of service was shorter. Thus there were fewer soldiers to be disciplined than in the past.

Some disciplinary corps which were recruited as the companies of fusiliers and pioneers in the past had inspired a justified mistrust amongst the generals. Giving them weapons was feared as was leading them into the open countryside. Meanwhile, in those terrible days from 1834 to 1835, the army was forced to entrust posts in Algeria to them where they showed steadfastness and deserved praise. Even the condemned from the bullet manufactures had to be used. Old soldiers of the Army of Africa remember still the *Chamborans* of Father Marengo. However, the honor of inscribing the numbers of their companies in the order of battle of an expedition was never granted. Military honor exacts such severity. The Fatherland had to be completely at bay before the government of Tours thought to have the fusiliers of discipline used in the defense of the territory in 1870. It was not a felicitous experiment. The men belonging to these companies who, under the eyes of their comrades in Africa would have been able to do well, were disorganized by the rigors of an unsually harsh winter. They were also unaccustomed to the liberty which wartime service gave them, a liberty for which they were not sufficiently prepared. The battalion of fusiliers of discipline commanded successively by Majors Feyfant and Segard were mustered out by the decree of December 3, 1870. This was because of their poor spirit.

CHASSEURS D'AFRIQUE

Soon after landing in Algeria, the three squadrons of the 12th and 17th Regiments of chasseurs à cheval commanded by Colonel Bontemps-Dubarry took the name of Chasseurs d'Afrique. Like the light infantry *bataillons de marche*, they depended on their regiments for administration and promotion purposes. The squadrons formed part of the Third Division (Duke Descars). A report dating from the day of their embarkation attributes an effective strength of 534 men and 505 horses to them. Contrary to what is said of the campaign of Algiers by most accounts, they left mounted. This information is taken from the journal of General Petiet, former chief of general staff for the division. The troops which composed these three squadrons were very lively. Recruited from old cavalrymen, proven officers and young volunteers including Prince Joseph Poniatowski, they immediately established the renown of the troop to which they left their name.

The first officers and soldiers of the Chasseurs d'Afrique who distinguished themselves in facing the Arabs were Captains Duez and Casin and the chasseur Goury who killed three Arabs with his own hands.

No trace of the composition of the special cavalry for the Army of Africa can be found in the military annals of 1831, the first published after the taking of Algiers. However, in the added notes, the Algerian Chasseurs' uniform is described in the following manner: "wine-colored jacket with sleeves; blue waistcoast closed in front without buttons; wide blue pants; purplish-red (amaranthe) waistband; stable cap (*calote*) in red; purplish-red turban; boots without spurs; burnoose; Turkish cartridge box; Moroccan bridle and saddle; Turkish-style stirrups." The writing and spelling are as extraordinary as the description of this strange dress. This organization of Algerian Chasseurs, without mention of the Chasseurs d'Afrique, notes that besides the two squadrons of the 17th (become the 12th) Chasseurs, there had already been an attempt

Chasseurs d'Afrique (1832).

to recruit a native mounted corps. The squadron of the 12th (become the 7th) Chasseurs returned to Sarreguemines. Feeling the need for cavalry, General Clauzel used everything at hand. For these earlier times, it is necessary to be able to consult with contemporaries since the history of the following list of short-lived corps has not been written: chasseurs, carabiniers and *chausseurs lanciers* of Africa who preceded the regular creation of the Chasseurs d'Afrique. The images retained of them are only vague memories. The buglers are seen with the wine-colored *chapskas* and *kurtkas* whereas the troops were already dressed in sky blue.

This was still the time of improvised organizations, of gatherings necessitated by an event of war, the subjugation of a tribe or the offer of assistance by some daring adventurer. It was understood that the regularization of native troops was a matter of time and experience. With this in mind, the law of March 15, 1831 had left the initiative for this process to the commanders in chief under the authorization of the king. Consequently, on April 17, 1831, a royal decree approved, rather than caused, the creation of two squadrons of Algerian Chasseurs including 21 officers and 305 men of the ranks. As many French, foreigners and natives as the needs and resources of the moment required could be included in these troops. The Algerian Chasseurs depended on the Zouaves Corps for administrative purposes. The official existence of the Zouaves had been regularized by the same decree. This hybrid organization proved to be a poor one and produced no other results than to open the way to Arabs who wished to enter into French service. Also, as of November 17, 1831—that is, seven months later—the organization of two regiments of light cavalry was decreed under the name of the 1st and 2nd Regiments of Chasseurs d'Afrique. The First, gathered at Algiers, counted no less than eight squadrons since the two squadrons of Algerian Chasseurs had been reattached to them. It also took on all the officers, cadres and cavalrymen of the 12th Chasseurs (former 17th) who wanted to join them. It was commanded by Colonel Schauenbourg. The 2nd was formed at Oran by Colonel Baron Létang, a young colonel and an old officer of the Chasseurs of the Guard who was held very much in favor. Although the regiments' name indicted that they were to stay in Algeria, many of the cavalry officers and even officers from other services— many more even than were required—requested the honor of being incorporated into its ranks. The considerable advantages for promotion—such as a high rank after a relatively short term of service—were not the only reasons which brought adventurous souls to the land of Africa. Incidentally, these advantages were to become meaningless soon after, due to the law of April 14, 1832. The political conduct of the new government already gave the army a sense of foreboding that the war of Algeria would be the major if not only military task of the reign. This was despite the breaking of the treaties of 1815 which the army had seen in the three glorious days. It will be repeated *ad infinitum*: in France, the army loves war, always believes in it, and endlessly desires it.

Today, after more than half a century, it is interesting to examine the list of officers of the two first regiments as they appear for

the first time in the *Military Annual of 1832.*

In the 1st appear the future generals Major Marey, Second Lieutenant and Assistant to the Treasurer Gastu; amongst the captains, Yusuph Mameluck, already decorated with the Legion of Honor, and de Mezange; in the middle of the lieutenants and second lieutenants, Marion, Genestet de Planhol, de Drée, Legrand, Coste de Champeron, and a future journalist, Savary, Duke of Rovigo. With Yusuph, who would much later in France wear the epaulettes of a general of division with a French title, there are only two other natives: the second lieutenants Moustapha-ben-Abdellef and Smaïn del Moulouck. The Second Regiment, in organization, still only has four squadrons available. However, it counts in its ranks, Devaux, Cassaignolles, Dubern, Tremblay and Joseph Habaiby. If the list of non-commissioned officers who gave up their stripes to come to conquer the epaulette at saber point were given, one hundred names belonging to all the aristocratic families would have to be cited. There was a frenzy to enlist in these new regiments.

Perhaps the figure of the non-commissioned officer and of the simple cavalryman of the Chasseurs d'Afrique struck a chord in the popular imagination, moreso than that of the Zouave. Imagery, literature, and theater have moreover always favored the former over the latter. In fiction, the Chasseur of Africa is always the son of a prominent family, redeeming his youthful mistakes. The Zouave, on the other hand, is most often an unruly working class youth who becomes a good soldier.

This history of the Chasseurs d'Afrique, like that of the Zouaves, follows the history of the conquest of Algeria step by step. All the famous officers of the cavalry passed through their ranks, The list of their colonels, which is given immediately below, is almost a book of nobility, of that nobility which none disputes nor contests: nobility of courage and merit.

Although the Chasseurs d'Afrique bore the lance and the chapska more in principle than in practice, they belonged to the light cavalry as far as the remount cavalry was concerned. However, they depended on the line cavalry for their

The unusual combat of Captain Morris (September 12, 1833).

1st REGIMENT (1) (Created November 17, 1831)		2nd REGIMENT (Created November 17, 1831)		3rd REGIMENT (Created November 28, 1832)		4th REGIMENT (Created August 31, 1839)	
1832	BARON DE SCHAUENBOURG (General of Brigade)	1831	LÉTANG (General of division)	1833	BOYER (General of division)	1839	MARTIN DE BOURGON (General of Brigade)
1838	THIÉRION	1833	OUDINOT (killed by the enemy)	1833	RIGAU	1842	DE TARTAS (General of division)
1839	LE PAYS DE BOURJOLLY (General of division)	1835	LEFEBVRE DE GOÜY (General of Brigade)	1835	CORRÉARD (General of Brigade)	1846	DUDUCH DE FELETZ (General of division)
1840	KORTE (General of division)	1835	SERVAT DE LAISLE	1836	LANEAU	1851	DE GOUSSENCOURT (General of brigade)
1843	MORRIS (General of division)	1839	RANDON (Marshal of France)	1840	NOEL (General of division)	1852	COSTE DE CHAMPERON (General of division)
1843	MARTIN DE BOURGON (General of Brigade)	1841	MAREY (General of division)	1846	DE MIRBECK (General of brigade)	1855	DE CAUVIGNY (General of brigade) (mustered out May 4, 1856, reorganized February 6, 1867)
1845	BARON RICHEPANSE (General of division)	1843	MARTIN DE BOURGON (General of Brigade)	1852	NEY, Prince of Moscow (General of brigade)	1865	CHAMPION DUBOIS DE NANSOUTY (General of brigade)
1851	CASSAIGNOLLES (General of division)	1843	MORRIS (General of division)	1853	DE MEZANGE DE SAINT-ANDRÉ (General of brigade)	1869	DE QUÉLEN (General of brigade)
1852	DE FERRABOUC (General of brigade)	1847	COUSIN DE MONTAUBAN (General of division)	1860	DU BARAIL (General of division)	1872	BONVOUST (General of brigade)
1855	DE SALIGNAC-FÉNELON(General of division)	1851	RAME	1863	MARGUERITTE (General of division killed by the enemy)	1875	INNOCENTI (General of brigade)
1859	DE MONTALEMBERT	1854	DE JOURDAN	1864	DE MONTARRY (General of brigade)	1882	LETENNEUR
1859	REINAUD BOULOGNE DE LASCOURS (General of division)	1855	DE BRÉMOND D'ARS (General of division)	1868	Marquis DE GALLIFFET (General of division)		
1864	MARGUERITTE (General of division killed by the enemy)	1863	PETIT (General of brigade)	1871	FLOGNY (General of brigade)		
1866	CLICQUOT DE MENTQUE (killed by the enemy)	1867	DE LAJAILLE (General of brigade)	1874	GAUME (General of brigade)		
1871	ROUHER	1874	DE PERCIN-NORTHUMBERLAND (General of brigade)	1880	DE CUGNON D'ALINCOURT		
1874	PALANQUE	1872	BIGNON	1880	DUBUQUOY		
1876	BONNAT	1875	DE SIMARD DE PITRAY				
1879	BRUNETIERE	1880	ROULLET				
1883	VUILLEMOT						
1886	BONNEFOUS						

(1) In May 1852 when the Prince President gave the eagle to the French army, the standards were inscribed with the names of five battles. Those embroidered on the eagles of the Chasseurs of Africa — regiments which had not yet once left Algeria — commemorated only the African War. In writing them down here, to some extent we are giving their status of service from 1831 to 1854.

1st REGIMENT: Constantine, 1837. - Taguin, 1843 - Isly, 1844. - Tlelat, 1844. - Zaatcha, 1849. - 2nd REGIMENT: Tamezouat, 1833. - La Sirkack, 1836. - Sidi Rached, 1843. - Sidi Joussef, 1843. - Isly, 1844. - 3rd REGIMENT: La Mafrag, 1833. - Constantine, 1837. - Tebessa, 1842. - Biskara, 1844. - Zaatcha, 1849. - 4th REGIMENT: Mered. 1842. - Milianah, 1842. - Taguin, 1843. - Isly, 1844. - Tedjenna, 1845. The standards presented to them on July 14, 1880 read: 1st REGIMENT: Isly, 1844. - Balaklava, 1854. - Solferino, 1859. - San Pablo del Monte, 1863. - 2nd REGIMENT: Isly, 1844. - Sebastopol, 1855. - Solferino, 1859. - Puebla, 1863. - 3rd REGIMENT: Constantine, 1837. - Sebastopol, 1855. - Solferino, 1859. - Puebla, 1863. - 4th REGIMENT: Milianah, 1842. - Taguin, 1843. - Balaklava, 1854.

recruitment. Never were there finer regiments, more numerous, more well maintained in every detail of dress, armaments, remounts and training. The men came there from other corps by their own request and through the process of selection. All the replacements for the cavalry were also sent there. If the volunteer enlistees who flowed into their ranks were sometimes the sons of prominent families who had played around too much, they knew how to redeem their civilian sins with some heroic strokes of the saber.

No important expedition was made without one or more squadrons of chasseurs having played an important role therein. Amongst their most extraordinary feats of arms I will cite the unusual battle of Captain Morris (since become general of division) with the chief of the Merdès tribe.

"On September 12, 1833, this warlike tribe defended the ford of the Mafrag. Captain Morris, at the head of his chasseurs, forced the passage. Admirably mounted, this officer alone had thrown himself ahead into the riverbed against a chief of the Merdes, a gigantic horseman who engaged him in hand to hand combat. A terrible battle recalling those epic duels of the Middle Ages thus ensued between the two warriors. One then the other was unseated in the shock. They abandoned their horses and set upon each other, face to face. The French and the Arabs feared hitting their champion in firing on the pair who gripped each other and who were tangled together in a fury. This left the spectators standing passively by on the two river banks. After a wonderful display of power and skill, Morris finally succeeded in killing his fearsome adversary. The chasseurs soon passed across the ford or swam the river and sabered all those still trying to resist."

On the exact spot where this battle took place a village has been created, a halting place for the troops marching from Bone on to Tunisia and who bear the name of Morris.

The first thought of Marshal Saint-Arnaud when he organized the Army of the Orient which he would command was to attach to it a brigade of Chasseurs d'Afrique. The 1st Regiment (Colonel de Ferrabouc) and the 4th Regiment (Colonel Coste de Champeron) were assigned to form it. General d'Allonville took command, attaching to it a mounted battery and a platoon of Spahis whose oriental uniform could not fail to produce an excellent effect on the imagination of the followers of Mohammed. Only this platoon and some Chasseurs d'Afrique were able to follow the general in chief to the Crimea. From the following extract from his report on the Battle of Alma, it may be seen how much this absence of cavalry proved harmful to the French. "If I had had the cavalry," said the marshal, "I would have secured major results and Menschikoff would no longer have an army... for the rest of my life I will regret having had only my two regiments of

Chasseurs d'Afrique (1842).

Chasseurs d'Afrique. The salute of the standard (1840).

Chasseurs d'Afrique." His successor's first concern was to call them up in all haste. They arrived early enough to take part in the Battle of Balaklava (October 25, 1854). Well directed by Generals Morris and d'Allonville, two squadrons of the 4th Regiment saved the remnants, who were compromised in an inopportune charge, from the English cavalry. Commander Abdelal, Captains Ollier, Burtin, and Dangla—the last one was killed—were named to the Order of the Army. The losses of the 4th Regiment on this day were 13 dead of whom 2 were officers; 7 wounded of whom 2 were amputated; 16 horses killed and 12 wounded. This was the only opportunity which the Chasseurs found in the Crimea to make the Russians feel the points of their sabers. The siege of Sebastopol could not highlight their better qualities. They were only used thereafter for reconnaissance and by squadron. The 2nd and 3rd Regiments came to rejoin them at the beginning of May 1855. The 1st and the 4th Regiments formed a separate brigade at first. Then for a while they were formed into brigades, the 1st with the 4th Hussars, the 4th with the 6th Dragoons. Finally they were assembled with the 2nd and 3rd, newly arrived, and formed a separate division attached to the 1st Army Corps.

The Chasseurs d'Afrique had everything they needed to fight with the Cossacks and to cut them down with ease, but the Cossacks were less daring than the Arabs. They were more cautious. For the Arab horseman, for the noble inhabitants of the desert, to cross swords with the Chasseurs d'Afrique was a glory which they sought. The Chasseurs supplied them the opportunity whenever they could.

As tirailleurs and as swordsmen, the chasseurs were the most formidable and the most feared adversaries of the chiefs of the Arab tribes. The great Arab chiefs were excellent horsemen, fine connoisseurs of horses, and used to living in the saddle and to handling their weapons at all gaits. They always showed the greatest admiration for the French African cavalry. They knew very well the difference between their chasseur squadrons and those of the light cavalry regiments of France newly arrived in the colony. All the regiments of chasseurs and hussars that passed through Algeria have always taken the Chausseurs d'Afrique for their models. They returned with the habits that they borrowed from the Chasseurs.

The division of Chasseurs d'Afrique sent to the Crimea was splendid. It represented the height of perfection which the French cavalry had attained. Everyone there was talented: general, commander, general staff, regiment, cadres, and cavalrymen.

Although the four first squadrons of the four regiments of Chasseurs d'Afrique manuevered as squadrons in the Crimea, the imperial government, fearing that the war would go on, ordered on June 27, 1855 that 7th and 8th squadrons be formed in these regiments. This organization did not last long. When the cavalry of the Imperial Guard was expanded from two to six regiments, not only the new 7th and 8th Squadrons of the Chasseurs d'Afrique disappeared but also the entire 4th Regiment. However, it was the Chasseurs d'Afrique (officers, non-commissioned officers, and soldiers) who formed the first recruitment of the mounted chasseurs of the Guard. This superb regiment, remounted on dappled grey Arabian horses, together with the regiment of guides, were admired by connoisseurs for their fine cavalry. It can even be affirmed that although the uniform of the mounted regiment of chasseurs was less luxurious, it was more handsome, militarily speaking.

For the campaign of Italy, the three regiments of Chasseurs d'Afrique along with the 5th Hussars formed the Desvaux Division attached to the 1st Army Corps. This division had Lieutenant Colonel Dupin as its chief of general staff. He was one of the most gifted officers of the general staff whose career was unfortunately cut short. The 1st Regiment (Colonel de Salignac-Fénélon; Lieutenant Colonel de Fénin) formed the first brigade (Genestet de Planhol) with the 5th Hussars. The second brigade (de Forton) included the 2nd Regiment (Colonel de Brémond d'Ars and Lieutenant Colonel Buraud) and the 3rd Regiment (Colonel de Mezange and Lieutenant Colonel Francq).

Some platoons of the 1st Chasseurs d'Afrique were engaged in the combat of Montebello. However, the entire division participated as a corps only when they reached Solferino. With the Partouneaux Division, it had for its mission

General of Division: Commander MORRIS
Aides-de-camp: Captains Folloppe and Gervais
Officiers d'ordonnance: Captain Thornton (outside the cadre)
and Lieutenant Bonaparte (7th Dragoons)
Chief of staff: Colonel Pajol
Adjutants: Major Hecquard and Captain De Montigny

1st BRIGADE
General CASSAIGNOLLES
Officier d'ordonnance: Captain NORMAND (7th Dragoons)
1st Chasseurs d'Afrique, Colonel de Ferrabouc
3rd Chasseurs d'Afrique, Colonel de Mezange de Saint-André

2nd BRIGADE
General FERAY
Aide-de-camp: Captain Teissier
Officier d'ordonnance: Captain Muel (1st Carabiniers)
2nd Chasseurs d'Afrique, Colonel de Jourdan
4th Chasseurs d'Afrique, Colonel de Cauvigny

The charge of the Chasseurs d'Afrique at Sedan (September 1, 1870).

linking up the 2nd and the 4th Corps. The second squadron of the 3rd Regiment executed a fortuitous charge against the Hungarian and Austrian cavalry while rallying the division. Then the entire division was called upon to charge by brigade against the enemy infantry. These charges, led with great courage, produced no major results. This was no doubt because the squares of attacked infantry had not been shaken in advance by the canister fire In these attacks, the 1st Regiment lost Captains de Roquefeuil and Guyot, Lieutenant Loeffer, and Second Lieutenant Salignac-Fénélon. The 3rd Regiment lost Captain Adjutant Major Guichon.

> General of Division DU BARAIL
> *Chief of staff:* Colonel Ferri Pisani
> *Aide-de-camp:* Captain Handerson
> *Officier d'ordonnance:* Reverony, Lieut. of the 1st Regt.
>
> 1st BRIGADE
> General MARGUERITTE
> 1st Chasseurs d'Afrique, Colonel Cliquot
> 3rd Chasseurs d'Afrique, Colonel de Galliffet
>
> 2nd BRIGADE
> General DE LAJAILLE
> 4th Chasseurs d'Afrique, —
> 2nd Chasseurs d'Afrique, Colonel de Quelén

With the peace of Villafranca, the Chasseurs d'Afrique returned to Algeria where they continued to go on expeditions until the day when they were called to Mexico. As has already been said, they had detached two squadrons for the expedition of Syria. For Mexico, seven squadrons were successively borrowed from them which were formed into *régiments de marche* with two squadrons of the 5th Hussars, their old companions from Africa and Italy. In Mexico, the Chasseurs, as tireless as ever, were dreaded by the Juarez cavalry who called them "the blue butchers." It would be impossible to recount the combats which they engaged in from the Gulf of Mexico to the Pacific coast. They were everywhere at once. One must go back to the campaigns of Germany and of Spain under the First Empire to find a cavalry which could be cited as having done more than the Chasseurs d'Afrique did in Mexico. At the battle of San Pablo del Monte below Puebla, a squadron of the 1st Regiment won the Cross of Honor which shines on the staff of its standard. It decimated the Lancers of Durango and took the flag which was offered to them by the ladies of the city.

Thus we arrive at the campaign of 1870-1871. Of course, the Chasseurs d'Afrique were called up and took part therein. Reformed at four regiments as of 1867, they were gathered in the first organization into one independent division (the 1st of the Reserve).

This magnificent division had endless problems. It was never able to be assembled as a whole. Then it was officially dispersed. The 1st, 2nd, and 3rd Regiments arrived at Metz before the investment. When the 4th Regiment rallied the army at Mouzon on August 30th, the 1st and the 3rd formed a division with the 6th Hussars and the 1st Chasseurs of France which was commanded by General Margueritte. The 1st and 3rd had left Metz to escort the emperor from Conflans to Verdun when they were formed into this division. They were joined by the 4th Regiment.

Up until this point, the poor Chasseurs d'Afrique had had no opportunity to distinguish themselves other than at Jarny. There a squadron from the 3rd Regiment destroyed and took a squadron of *Hulans* with so little trouble that only one horse—that of the trumpeter Noll—was wounded. The Chasseurs baptized this battle with the name of "Jarny without bandages."

From the night of August 31st, the Margueritte Division took its bivouac at the Calvaire d'Illy. It was on this terrain that it cooperated the following day in that charge—or rather in those heroic charges—which elicted admiration from the conqueror. The military controversy which was raised by this episode on that fatal day of Sedan seems to demonstrate that many regiments, after having wanted and believed in charging first, claimed the honor of doing so in very good faith. This is a controversy which will never die since the witnesses seem not to understand one another. All the same, the truth seems to be that on the plateau of Illy many regiments—even some which did not belong to the Margueritte Division—charged either all together or successively and alone. General Margueritte had been wounded and General of Brigade Tilliard was killed. Thus, it was de Galliffet who inherited the honor

Spahis. Escort platoon (1886).

Spahis in special festival dress (1886).

of leading the charges of the Chasseurs d'Afrique, notably of the two regiments forming the 1st brigade. With regard to this subject, we regret that an official report from the War of 1870 did not establish the roles of each. This is regrettable both for the interests of those who have done their duty as well as for keeping public opinion from going astray.

General Margueritte's end is not well known. We will borrow authentic details from a brochure entitled: *The Cavalry Division of General Margueritte at Sédan,* by an old officer of the 3rd Chasseurs d'Afrique (de Pierres) and from the *Contemporary Miltary History* by Colonel Canonge.

Says de Pierres: "At the moment that General Margueritte appeared on the ridge for the second time, he was hit by a bullet which went through both cheeks, cutting his tongue apart. He fell face down to the ground. Captain Henderson and Captain Reverony dismounted to put him on his grey horse led by one of the men from the escort. Lieutenant de Pierres also started to dismount when Reverony asked him to take the general's bay horse. This horse carried a sum of money kept in the saddlebags. They started to march on foot to go back down the slope. The general on his horse was supported on the left by the hussar telescope bearer and on the right by Lieutenant Reverony. Behind him came de Pierres leading his horse, Kergariou, Boisguéheneuc and the escort platoon. The sad cortege passed in front of the 1st Regiment of the Chasseurs d'Afrique. The chasseurs, sabers in hand and standing in their stirrups, shouted: `Forward! Let's revenge the general!' The general with head bared and tongue hanging down, his face covered with blood, had retained all his faculties. He cried out hoarsely, the sounds coming from the bottom of his throat. Trying to make himself understood, he made the signal with his hand for marching forward and charging. The sabers were not lowered in a sign of mourning as has been written in some accounts. On the contrary, there was a sublime moment of anger and of rage in this magnificent regiment. The tanned faces of those old soldiers were enlivened by virile courage. The saber blades gleamed brightly! It was at this moment that the 1st Regiment of Chasseurs d'Afrique threw themselves on the Prussian infantry without any other orders."

Lieutenant Colonel Canonge adds: "After having been wounded, General Margueritte was led to Sédan. It was there, in response to questions respectfully put to him in order to have his last thoughts that the general wrote the following note.

'We could not go into Belgium without violating its neutrality. Our hardship is great, but our glory, Chasseurs d'Afrique, remains intact, and that is something. Be considerate of your men; they deserve it in every way, and let's support the misfortune of men with heart."

Some days later, the general died in Belgium at the Château de Beauraing belonging to the Duke of Ossuna to which he had managed to be transported.

Colonel Clicquot, Lieutenant Colonel Ramond, Captain Marquier, Second Lieutenants Fugnot, Marsaguet, Le Mintier de Saint-André, Perry de Nieuil, and de Grammont of the 1st Regiment; Lieutenant Colonel de Linières, Lieutenants Renault and Leclerq, and Second Lieutenants Swember, Jardel and de Vergennes of the 3rd Regiment fell during that day on the field of battle, never to rise again.

The 2nd Regiment remained at Metz with General Du Barail commanding the 1st Division of Reserve Cavalry. It was placed in a division created with the three regiments of Chasseurs of France (2nd, 3rd, and 10th of the De Bruchard Brigade). This division, commanded by General Du Barail, was attached to the 6th Corps (Marshal Canrobert). It met the same end as the Army of Metz and went to rejoin the three other regiments of Chasseurs d'Afrique in Germany.

After September 4th, the four regiments of Chasseurs d'Afrique formed three *régiments de marche* with their two last squadrons which had not been mobilized. These were sent to France and were used in the different provincial armies.

The 1st Regiment - Lieutenant Colonel Gérard - was placed in the Cloux Brigade and reattached to the Army of Le Havre after having been part of the 19th Corps.
The 2nd Regiment - Lieutenant Colonel Gaume - was attached to the 24th Corps.
The 3rd Regiment - Lieutenant Colonel Maréchal - was part of the 16th and the 17th Corps, successively.

With peace, the squadrons of these three provisional regiments returned the squadrons which belonged to them to their permanent regiments.

Since the war, the Chasseurs d'Afrique have again taken up their traditional African functions. However, the new system of recruitment has considerably lessened the number of old cavalrymen who flock to them. The Chasseurs d'Afrique now receive recruits just like the regiments of France. The officers and non-commissioned officers teach the young soldiers. This had not yet been seen. Meanwhile, the four actual regiments are still up to their legendary reputation. They continue the tradition of the past. This was seen in Tonkin in the training and good humor of the detachment from the 1st Regiment commanded by Lieutenant Lapérine. The old type of Chasseur d'Afrique, although less notable than in the past, has not degenerated too much. A witness told us that, in Tonkin, he had seen the uniform of the Chasseurs d'Afrique everywhere and yet they were only seventy in number. They have been sorely tested. Lieutenant Lapérine, promoted to Captain, died from exhaustion upon setting foot on French soil. Second Lieutenant Linière was wounded during the retreat from Langson (June 24, 1884). This all proves that the legends of the flag, the history of the regiment, and everything which can remind the soldier of the honor of his number are all useful.

General Margueritte mortally wounded (September 1, 1870).

SPAHIS

◆

The history of the Spahis needs to be told in its entirety, but the documents published up to now are generally more incomplete than precise. At present, although they are regulated by official acts, the Spahis' organization still lacks the administrative cohesion which was given to the other French regiments through uniformed life. A historian of Algeria has written down the background of the early formation of Spahis since the conquest. That is, since the moment when their first squadrons were part of the Algerian Chasseurs until their formation into a single corps.

Mr. Behaghel says: "At first included in the cadres of the regiments of Chasseurs d'Afrique, the native cavalrymen or Spahis did not delay in forming separate corps. General Clauzel ordered the organization of the regular Spahis in 1834 under the command of two majors of the Chasseurs d'Afrique: Marey-Monge and Yusuf. Marey-Monge was at the same time named Lieutenant Colonel. Simultaneously, the irregular or auxiliary Spahis, who were paid, were put at the disposal of some military chiefs and commanders. In 1836, a third corps of regular Spahis was organized at Oran under the command of Lieutenant Colonel Leullion de Thorigny and of Major Cousin de Montauban.

"In 1838, Commander Yusuf, named Lieutenant Colonel, took command of the Spahis of Bone. Major de Mirbeck was placed at the head of the Spahis of Oran. Under the government of Marshal Valee who was a little concerned about the native troops, it was decided to eliminate the Spahis and even the Zouaves. However, this plan was stopped in the process of being carried out with the mustering out of the Spahis of Algiers who were joined to the 1st Chasseurs d'Afrique. The squadrons of Bone and of Oran were still maintained under the command of de Mirbeck and of Yusuf. The number of auxiliary Spahis was increased and, in the province of Algiers, a detachment of elite cavalrymen was organized under the name of Moorish gendarmes. One of France's general officers, Margueritte, enlisted in this corps in 1838 at the age of fourteen. He was a second lieutenant there for two years, from 1840 to 1842."

This note, although fairly vague, is the most accurate one I have come across on the beginnings of the Spahis. In the *Campaigns of the Duke d'Orléans (1835-1839)*, a book already mentioned, it can be seen that platoons or squadrons of regular and irregular Spahis were attached to all the columns then. However, the organization of the latter is often mixed up more or less with the *Goums,* the *Douaires,* and the *Smélas*. These contingents were either supplied by friendly tribes or levied through the ministrations of officers in charge of Arab affairs. Thus, the first regular organization of Spahis dates from December 7, 1841.

The corps was to have twenty squadrons commanded by a colonel or a lieutenant colonel (Yusuf); seven majors (Boyer, d'Allonville, Walzin-Estherazy, Favas, Gauthier de Rougemont, Cassaignolles, Rivet); and 7 paymasters to complete the large general staff. Each squadron had a French captain, a lieutenant and two second lieutenants and a native lieutenant and two second lieutenants.

The strength of each squadron was at 200 men of whom 24 were French. In total, with the general staff, there were 4,029 men. Amongst the captains of the period was the name of Mesmer, one of the most amazing saber wielders in the Army of Africa. Also listed are d'Arbellot and d'Allegro, the father of the current general employed by Tunisia. At the same time there was Fleury, the future aide-de-camp of Napoleon III, the only officer, I believe, who was able to put a squadron of Spahis on the same footing as a squadron of Chasseurs d'Afrique. There were also Du Barail, a future minister of war, and Curély,

The Duke of Aumale at Taguin (1843).

*Spahis. French and native officers,
full dress and undress (1840).*

one of the sons of a famous hussar from the First Empire, who appear among the lieutenants and second lieutenants. As for the native lieutenants and second lieutenants, they were the pick of the crop of Arabs from the great tents and sons of influential chiefs. Indeed, it is from this point of view that the Spahis should be considered in particular.

What has been said for the Algerian Tirailleurs, organized at the same time, will be gladly repeated by the Spahis: they were fine but the illusions of the then-organizers played too great a role in those figures which in practice could never be attained. The Spahis nonetheless did render great services, both political and military. On May 9, 1842, the recruitment and organization was going fairly well, and the need to provide Yusuf with the rank of colonel was perceived. (He was promoted 10 days later.) Therefore, a royal decree decided that the colonel commanding the Spahis residing in Algiers would have two lieutenant colonels for assistants, one at Oran and the other at Constantine. Bouscarin and Cousin-Montauban, two officers of the highest caliber, were named lieutenant colonels.

The dress of the French officers had been established by the decree of December 7, 1841. Royal blue kepi with the distinguishing marks of rank in gold braided embroidery; wine-colored spencer with black braids; royal blue pants with wine-colored stripes; tunic greatcoat in royal blue with round gold buttons and piping and collar tabs in wine; chechia for undress; as a distinguishing mark of service, a red silk waistband. For the non-commissioned officers, French and native brigade leaders, and the native officers, a wine-colored vest in the Turkish style with black braided embroidery; royal blue waistcoat and breeches; wine-colored burnoose; red waistbelt; and light boots. I was not able to find the ordinance which changes the royal blue of the previously mentioned ordinance to sky blue. It is possible that it had been restored only subsequent to the habit taken up by the Spahis' officers of wearing the stylish and charming uniform which they had made famous not only in Algeria, but also in Senegal and everywhere they were called.

On July 21, 1845, after many experiments, regimental organization was applied to the Spahis. The ordinance which established the details of the new organization gives as its main reason the necessity of putting the native corps in accord with the other French army corps. Beneath this administrative phrasing is hidden the desire to give warranted promotion to officers who had been devoted to the direction of Arab affairs. The conquest of Algeria was not just a military question. As soon as it was consolidated, the July Government felt the need to strengthen and reward this small phalanx of energetic men who had lived for forty years in the middle of the Arab peoples. The admirers of the civilian regime who had loudly proclaimed that it was appropriate to remove the colony from military domination still found people who opposed them. Commerce, industry, and agriculture could not have been set up with safety in a country where a rifle was hidden behind each bush and rock. At the same time, the desert was a threat for French establishments and a refuge for those who attacked them. The only way of pacifying the conquered country was to firmly weld together the French Arabist officers and the Arab Francophiles. The Spahis, who recruited particularly amongst the wealthy natives, the Arabs of the great tents, had been the first link through whom the French won over the intelligent Arab population. The Turcos were the plebians; the Spahis were the aristocracy. Still today, the Spahis perhaps do not render all the military services which could be rightfully required of them because of their more superficial than actual regimental assimilation. However, their influence on the tribes is great. The platoon of red burnooses which for thirty years has pranced around the French general staffs and the French Arab bureaus has done more to consolidate the French and the Arabs than all the Arabist decrees. A country with a different language, morals, and religion from that of its vanquisher is not conquered unless it gains a legal and honorable place in that language, those morals and that religion.

The ordinances of December 7, 1841 and July 21, 1845 opened the door through which many noble Arabs who had remained distanced from the French passed. Today, not only have the Spahis been in the Orient (albeit in small groups), they have also come to France in great numbers either to maintain their garrisons or to defend the soil of their adopted country. Without too much difficulty, a squadron from the 1st Regiment and one from the 3rd Regiment were brought to Tonkin to fight for a cause which must have seemed strange to them, who in the past had themselves been a conquered and subjugated people. At the time when Captain Fleury succeeded in mounting one hundred Spahis for an Algerian expedition, forcing them to leave their

Spahis (1855).

belongings and their tribe for a month, it was deemed a miracle! From that time on, the Spahis—or at least most of them—were on the French side. The Arabist politics of Louis-Philippe and of Napoleon III brought their rewards.

Since their organization of 1845, the Spahis regiments have been commanded by officers whose names are as follows:

1st Regiment (Province of Algiers). Daumas, Lauer, Law de Lauriston, Abdelal, Letuvé, Roullet, Lieutenant Colonel Fallet, Lieutenant Colonel Bechade;

2nd Regiment (Province of Oran). lieutenant colonels: Cousin-Montauban, Walsin-Estherazy, De Montrond, Durrieu, Demont de Lavalette, De Lascours, Michel, Marmier, Briand, Ramond, Brunetiere; Lieutenant Colonel Gaillard, Lieutenant Colonel Poulleau.

3rd Regiment (Province of Constantine). lieutenant colonels: Bouscarin, Desvaux, Guerin de Walderbasch, Du Paty de Clam, Digard, Thomas de Dancourt, Bruneau; Lieutenant Colonel Le Noble, Lieutenant Colonel Mohamed-ben-Daoud.

Lieutenant Colonel Mohamed-ben-Daoud came from the School of Saint-Cyr (graduated in 1856) and he passed through the Chasseurs d'Afrique. He is not the only officer of Arab nationality who would come to be educated in the French schools.

In the impossible task of recounting the detailed history of the Spahis, the successive legends of their standards and the list of general officers coming from their ranks will be given as was done for the Chasseurs d'Afrique.

1st Regiment: Flag of 1852. Mascara, 1835. Isly, 1844. Tlelat, 1844. Tedjenna, 1845. Zaatcha, 1849;
Flag of 1880. Taguin, 1843. Islay, 1844. Tenda, 1845. Zaatcha, 1849;
2nd Regiment: Flag of 1852. Sidi-Jahia, 1841. Takmarel, 1842. Isly, 1844. Les Chotts, 1844. Brézina, 1845;
Flag of 1880. Sidi-Jahia, 1841. Isly, 1844. Les Chotts, 1844. Brézina, 1845;
3rd Regiment: Flag of 1852. Constantine, 1837. Expedition of the Aracias, 1840. Biskara, 1844. L'Aures, 1845. Zaatcha, 1849;
Flag of 1880. Constantine, 1837. Biskara, 1844. L'Aurès, 1844-1845. Zaatcha, 1849.

In addition to Yusuf, the creator of the Spahis who won his epaulettes and his naturalization with his saber, here are the names of the general officers who served in this corps: Marey-Monge, Gastu, Bouscarin, Duhesme, de Ferrabouc, de Mirbeck, Cousin de Montauban, Durieu, Legrand, Lannes de Montebello, Fleury, d'Allonville, Walsin-Estherazy, de Nansouty, de Bonnemains, du Barail, Rivet, Margueritte, Daumas, Ressayre, de Salignac-Fénélon, Desvaux, de Brauer, de Bruchard, de Vernon, de Goussencourt, de Mirandol, de la Martinière, Dalmas de Lapeyrouse, Guérin de Waldersbach, Marmier, de France, Michel, de Lauriston, de Lascours, Bachelier, Briand, Abdelal, du Paty de Clam, Thomas de Dancourt, etc.

All three Spahis regiments were maintained in Algeria during the war.

Meanwhile, a decree from October 19, 1870 organized a corps which could be considered as a *régiment de marche* of Spahis. They served under the name of Algerian Scouts.

It was composed of regular Spahis and of horsemen from the Goums, commanded by a very enegetic field officer, Lieutenant Colonel Goursaud, of the general staff. It took part in the battles of Sainte-Peravy, Patay, les Ormes, Josne, Vendôme, Savigny, Vencé, le Mans, Conlie, and Sillé-le-Guillaume. It was not mustered out immediately after peace. Returned to Algeria, it was used against the insurrection and distinguished itself again in the battles of Teniet-Djaboud, Beni-Mansour, Dra-el-Mizam, and Scheridan. The troops which formed it were returned to the corps from which they came in September 1871.

The creation of a fourth regiment of Spahis was decreed recently with the intent of providing native cavalry to the fourth province, that of Tunisia. The three first squadrons have been organized through the simple assembly of platoons of mixed Tunisian companies. The others will be assembled as soon as the budget and recruitment permit.

In the event of mobilization, the Army of Africa will form the 19th Army Corps. Its numerous reservists, its territorial corps (Zouave battalions, squadrons of chasseurs, batteries of artillery) would enable the colony to defend itself during a European war. Today the colony seems to be self-sufficient in times of peace as in times of war. Meanwhile, the nervous spirit which passes through the French nation still includes the Army of Africa in its projects for reform. One wants the Army of Africa to be both an organically Algerian army for the needs of a colonial army and, if the need arises, a reserve army.

This is the threefold and glorious work which it has performed since the Crimean campaign, thanks to the organization of Marshal Saint-Arnaud.

Honors and symbols of service (Spahis and Chasseurs d'Afrique).

Soldiers of the Royal Artillery Corps and of the provincial artillery regiments (1789).

HISTORY OF THE ARTILLERY

The artillery has made immense progress since 1789. Its equipment has become formidable and its effectiveness has quintupled, even sextupled. Since the cannon was both the first and the last reckoning of war, the artillery service from 1789 on has shared the title of Queen of Battles with the infantry. It owes its development to scientific advances. However, in this history, the developments will be dealt with briefly since we must devote ourselves especially to the services which the artillery performed and to the continuous expansion of its personnel.

In 1789, although separate from the infantry, the artillery occupied Number 64 in the general rolls of the infantry regiments. Created in 1671 under the title of Fusiliers of the King (Number 51), it had become the Royal Artillery, Number 46 in 1693. In 1776, it again took Number 64 which it had exchanged for Number 63 at the time of the decree of December 2, 1790. Its organization prior to the Revolution had been very simple. The Royal Artillery itself was subdivided into seven regiments. In addition, there was a regiment for the colonies. The decree of 1790 maintained this disposition. Each regiment had twenty companies, assembled by fives in division. Two divisions formed a battalion. As with today's battery, the company had two captains and two lieutenants. Its effective strength was 55 non-commissioned officers, corporals and men of the ranks. The general staff was composed of a colonel, four lieutenant colonels, two battalion adjutants, a quartermaster, two adjutants, a surgeon major, a drum major, a corporal drummer, eight musicians, and three master workmen. These 146 companies of cannoneers were on foot and could serve 876 pieces of artillery. In addition, the service included six companies of miners assembled at Verdun, ten of workers, plus eight companies of disabled cannoneers and the companies of coast guard cannoneers. The number of schools was set at twenty. The first inspector general, a type of director of the service, was eliminated, and the school of officer cadets was re-established at Châlons-sur-Marne. It was to maintain 42 cadets (January 1, 1791). On September 8, 1791, the companies of cannoneers were increased by 15 men. Finaly on April 1, 1792, the first regulations of the artillery service appeared. On August 27, 1793, the artillery regiment and the companies of workers assigned to the service of the colonies were gathered at the land artillery which from that time on had eight regiments without counting the auxiliary companies.

The artillery entered onto the path of progress through the addition of some horse companies. This was a creation of the Revolution which was to completely modify the use of cannon on campaign. Until this time, the artillery pieces were harnessed by independent, commercial drivers who were followed on foot by their servants and their gunners. General de Gribeauval had transformed the materiel, lightened it, and made it more mobile and suitable for all speeds. However, the cannon could go everywhere. Their transport from one point to another was inevitably frustrated by the necessity of keeping them together with the cannoneers. Frederick the Great had organized companies in the Prussian army under the name of "flying artillery" whose artillerists were mounted well before the French. La Fayette, who had seen them in the camp of Silesia in 1785, extolled their virtues. On January

Foot artillery "en batterie" (1796).

11, 1792, the first two horse companies of the French army were decreed. The first (Captain Chanteclair) was attached to Luckner's Army, the second (Captain Barrois) to La Fayette's Army.

The great question of mobility in the artillery on the battlefield was resolved. Soon after a new question arose which was more administrative than technical. It concerned the combining or the separation of the three elements which constitute a complete artillery: foot artillery for defense and attack of places; field artillery for normal campaign service; and horse artillery for the services with great mobility. After ninety years of discussion which has resulted in many organizations and dissolutions, it is not yet finished. This was recently seen when General Thibaudin required the separation of foot batteries and the creation of artillery fortress battalions. Paul-Louis Courier, a man of spirit and a military eccentric, recounts that he won the displeasure of General Sorbier for having told him: "I believe, my General, that one man cannot be at the same time a cannoneer and a cavalryman, no more than a cavalryman can be an infantryman. Consequently, the horse artillery and the dragoons are bastard services formed from troops organized under false assumptions." For a liberal artilleryman, this was a little hard to swallow. However, without searching too far, you can still find officers in the service as spiritedly defending this absolutely false argument. Meanwhile, on April 17, 1792, seven new horse companies were created. After the cannonades of Jammapes and Valmy, all the generals asked for this. Soon there were thirty, then fifty. They were reattached to give status to various regiments.

The Republic and the First Empire sought especially to give substantial troops to the artillery. For the first years of the Republic, the compositions of the armies did not allow for great luxury in special general staff. The light and battle demi-brigades each had a company of foot cannoneers. The artillery service supplied only supplements to the active divisions and general reserves to the armies. The general or field officer who centralized the service of the detached companies and their provisioning with munitions disappeared along with his adjoints into the army general staff. The manufacture of materiel, munitions, the assembly of parts, recruitment and training of non-commissioned officers and officers seemed to have been the major concern of the head of the corps during the first half of the Revolutionary wars. One searches in vain in the generals' reports from this period for the constitution of the general staffs for their artillery.

After the 18th of Brumaire (November 8th) when Dubois-Crancé left the ministry, he supplied statistics for the seven armies the Directorate maintained at the time. For 653,923 men of the ranks there were 44,697 artillerists, sappers, workers, miners and pontoniers, thus, a little more than 7%. In almost all the armies, the different technical components were mixed together. However, in the armies where separation was done by specialty, the engineers, the pontoniers, the workers, and the coastal or fortress artillery comprised 4.5%.

The proportion of artillery soldiers on the field of battle could thus be estimated at 2.2%. As Dubois-Crancé does not give the number of pieces at the ready, it impossible to fix the number of cannon per thousand soldiers for 1799. This is the keystone for all military organizations and all army formations since the beginning of the century.

In his statistics which were in particular the justification for his honest financial management, Dubois-Crancé had not included the Army of Egypt. This army had been paid at first from the funds taken along by Bonaparte then by means of taxes levied on the country. Thus, the artillery organization of the Army of Egypt was the precursor to ideas which Bonaparte would put into practice in the camp of Boulogne: a kind of distribution of artillery pieces between the cavalry and infantry divisions and the reserve organization always available. General Dommartin was commander in chief of the service in Egypt. He had with him Majors Songlis, Ruty, and Dermot. Dermot was the director of the park. According to General Susane, the troops under his command were composed

Foot artillery and artillery train (1806-1812).

of the first companies of the 1st Battalion and of the entire 2nd Battalion of the 4th Regiment (1) as well as a company from the 1st Regiment. These eleven companies lost Major Delignette, Captains Nicolas, Durthubize, Martin and Lieutenants Moscal and Thierry. The 2nd Company of the 5th Mounted Regiment was also attached to the expedition. Meanwhile, this attempt of Bonaparte's which tended to give a strong make-up to the general staff of each of the skilled services does not seem to have produced excellent results at first. It is claimed that this was due more to the differences of view amongst the leaders of the engineers and the artillery than to the loss of part of the siege equipment. It is further claimed that this was due to the failure at Saint-Jean-d'Acre, a failure which so greatly affected the subsequent projects of the general in chief. It is the first argument put forth in favor of the merger of the two services every time it is discussed.

The Consular decision of October 10, 1801 again fixed the organization of the service and divided it into general staff and troops. The general staff included only general and field officers numbering 90: 8 generals of division, including one inspector general; 12 generals of brigade; 33 colonels; and 37 majors. The troops were composed of 8 foot regiments at 20 companies; 6 horse regiments at 6 companies; 2 battalions of pontoniers at 8 companies; 15 companies of workers, 8 battalions of the train, and one horse company of the Consular Guard.

The general effectives, officers and employees together climbed to 19,837 men on a peacetime basis and to 28,196 during war. It was divided into 205 companies of which 37 were horse.

On April 30, 1803, sixteen companies were added, two by two, to the eight foot regiments plus a seventh for the 6th horse regiment. The service thus had available 221 companies of which 38 were horse. However, this organization did not last long since the following year the naval artillery—which will be discussed in the chapter on the history of the naval troops—was reorganized at four regiments. A ninth foot regiment was created in 1810; the preceding year, a depot cadre had been added to all the regiments. On January 21, 1813, four companies were created in all the foot regiments. Finally, on August 1, 1814, the two companies were again expanded while the 1st, 2nd, 3rd, and 5th horse also received a new company.

At the end of the Empire, the artillery included 328 companies: 252 new foot regiments, 48 new horse regiments and 28 of the Imperial Guard (6 foot and 6 horse of the Old Guard; 1 horse and 15 foot of the Young Guard.)

Each company that was horse or foot, hauled, with the help of the artillery train, eight horse-drawn artillery pieces according to the caliber.

The artillery train included 14 principal battalions and 12 battalions *bis* of the line plus 2 Guard regiments at 12 companies each. The auxiliary troops were represented by 18 companies of workers, 6 of armorers, 3 battalions of pontoniers, and a company of Guard pontoniers. This explains how on March 30, 1814, the general report attributes an effective strength of 80,273 men to the artillery service despite the sad state of military affairs.

In his very interesting *History of the Artillery*, General Susane, himself situated at the source of information, did not give a single composition of the artillery for the armies. One has to believe that the research and collection of such documents means little in terms of their own glory in the eyes of the officers of the service, or that rather they are concealing the problems of the undertaking under an exterior of modesty and indifference.

For the armies of the Republic, the names of the generals commanding the artillery cannot be given whereas those of the chief of general staff and his assistants, the adjutant generals or commanders, can always be found. The generals of brigade of the infantry

(1) It was not exactly luck that determined the dispatch of eleven companies out of twenty from the 4th Artillery Regiment to Egypt. It was his old regiment that the general in chief called to his side. The following passage from General Susane's book establishes in an undeniable and clear manner Napoleon I's military record:

"Bonaparte entered the 4th Regiment as a first lieutenant on April 1, 1791. Arriving in Valence on June 16, he was classed in Captain de la Catonne's company of cannoneers which was the 1st of the 2nd Battalion. The regiment then included in its ranks a star-studded group of young officers which emigration and later the memory of Napoleon would carry into the foremost ranks of the artillery. These were Lieutenants Villantroys, Pernetty, d'Anthouard, Songis, Taviel, the two Delon's, Faultrier, Savournin, and Vaubois. Vaubois left the corps to become one of the famous division leaders of the Army of Italy and of Egypt.

"A short time after his arrival in Valence, Bonaparte left with his company to go to Perpignan. It was there that he received his captain's commission, dated February 6, 1792. He was then classed as captain in the 2nd of the La Pujade Company which was stationed in Grenoble and which formed part of the Army of the Alps. Captain Bonaparte, who had nothing to do at Grenoble and who was devoured by the need to act, had himself detached to Corsica to command a battalion of volunteers from his native island. After Paoli's treason which delivered Corsica to the English in 1793, Bonaparte soon joined his company which was sent to Toulon. The rest is well known. Named captain commander on July 1, 1793, major on October 19, and classed by order to the 2nd Regiment, the young conqueror of Toulon was made general of brigade on February 6, 1794 and general of division on October 14, 1795."

and the cavalry also all have their page. Must it be concluded then that the commander of artillery in the armies was more of an administrator and a supplier than a warrior? This is tempting to believe, but the services he performed even as supplier of munitions and guardian of materiel were not ones which would be relegated to a lower level officer. If a strong head were not directing the artillery, an army could see its work abruptly stopped without being able to do anything about it. The intendant and the general of artillery—those who give daily nourishment to the cannon, the rifle and the soldiers' stomachs—must be men of the highest caliber. This means that their work is not limited only to these areas. This will be seen later when discussing the pontoniers.

Under the Empire, regularity begins to hold stronger sway in the official documents, as it did in reality. The names of the artillery leaders in the principal armies can be given.

Horse artillery (1806-1812).

Campaign of 1805: 1st Corps, Éblé; 2nd Corps, Tirlet; 3rd Corps, Sorbier then Lariboisière; 4th Corps, Pernetty; 5th Corps, Foucher; 6th Corps, Séroux; 7th Corps, Dorsner; Cavalry Reserve, Hanicque.

In 1806, Hanicque moved into the 3rd Corps and Lariboisière into the 4th.

During the campaign of 1809, Lariboisière was commander in chief of the artillery, having for his second in command Lauriston in the Guard artillery. In the 2nd Corps, it was Navelet who commanded the service. In the 3rd Corps, it was Hanicque; in the 4th, de Pernetty; in the 7th, Colonel Colonge; in the 8th, Colonel Schnadows, a Wurtemburger; in the heavy cavalry reserve, Corrin; and in the Polish Corps, Lepelletier. Finally, in the Army of Italy, at the side of Prince Eugène to whom the Emperor had given Marshal Macdonald as support, this important mission was entrusted to Sorbier. In Dalmatia, it was General Tirlet at the side of Raguse. For the campaign of Russia, Napoleon had called up the elite of the service. Lariboisière still was commander in chief. In the Imperial Guard, it was Sorbier; in the 1st Corps, Pernetty; in the 2nd, Dulauloy; in the 3rd, Baron Foucher; in the 4th, d'Anthouard; in the 5th, General Pelletier had, concurrently, command of the engineers and of the artillery; in the 6th (Bavarian troops), Colonel Espinard de Cologne; in the 7th, (Saxon troops), Lieutenant Colonel de Hoyer; in the 8th Corps, it was General Allix simultaneously commanding the engineers and the artillery; and in the 10th Corps (Prussian troops), Major Von Smith. In the 1st Reserve Corps of Cavalry of the King of Naples, Major Chopin was to be found; in the 2nd, Colonel Serrurier, and in the 3rd, Grives. The chief of general staff was General Charbonnel. At Éblé's side, charged with the bridge equipment, Colonel Chapelle performed the same functions.

For the campaign of 1813, there is already a wealth of documentation. However a complete situation report on the service cannot yet be supplied. This will be done instead for the Army of the North in 1815. The Emperor had given his best efforts to this organization.

Commander in chief: General of division SORBIER *Chief of staff:* General of division RUTY *Director general of the park:* General of brigade NEIGRE *Commander of the bridge train:* General of brigade BOUCHU	Imperial Guard. General of division DULAULOY, second in command DESVAUX 1st Corps. General of brigade BALTUS 2nd Corps. General of brigade MONTGENET 3rd Corps. General of division CHARBONNEL 4th Corps. General of division TAVIEL 5th Corps. General of division CAMAS 6th Corps. General of division FOUCHER	7th Corps. Colonel VERPEAU 8th Corps. Colonel REDEL 9th Corps. General of brigade PELLEGRINI 10th Corps. General of brigade LEPIN 11th Corps. Colonel SAUTEREAU 12th Corps. General of brigade NOURRY 13th Corps. General of brigade JOUFFROY 14th Corps. General of brigade DE PERNETTY	CAVALRY RESERVE 1st Corps. Colonel LAVOY 2nd Corps. Colonel COLIN 3rd Corps. Colonel CHAUVEAU 4th Corps. Colonel N. 5th Corps. Colonel N. *Army of Italy.* General of division SAINT-LAURENT

The infantry divisions all had a battery at Austerlitz. In 1813, they had two of them. The reserve corps of the army and the army corps had followed the same development. It was necessary to vigorously support an infantry which was becoming less and less solid. In 1813, the Guard had 3,500 artillerists and twenty batteries, without counting the park train. The foot batteries were hitched to the train battalions with horses.

The artillerists of the First Empire were excellent and full of daring. They skillfully handled a very simple materiel which was adequate for the tactics of the time. The officers were all extremely good at their jobs.

Given below are the names of the generals of brigade promoted to generals of division under the Consulate and the Empire.

1800: de Sorbier, Viesse de Marmont, Andreossy, de Songis d'Escourbons. 1803: Dulauloy. 1805: Duroc, Law de Lauriston, Gassendi. 1806: de Séroux de Montbelloy. 1807: de Lariboisière, Hanicque, Foucher de Careil, de Saint-Laurent, de Pernetty. 1808: de Senarmont. 1810: d'Anthouard, Foy. 1811: de Taviel, Valée. 1812: Aubry. 1813: de Charbonnel, Tirlet, Ruty, Drouot, Desvaux de Saint-Maurice, Le Noury de la Guignardière, Neigre. 1814: Allix.

Field artillery battery. Campaign dress (1887).

Horse artillery. Run into battery. Campaign dress (1887).

Almost all of them are well-known and very famous. A list of the colonels of this period appears at right.

The First Restoration reduced the artillery troops to 12 regiments on May 12, 1814.

Eight on foot at 21 companies each - 10 officers and 18 men in the general staff - 4 officers and 62 men per company; total per regiment: 94 officers and 1,320 non-commissioned officers and soldiers.

Four horse regiments at 6 companies each - 7 officers and 8 men in the general staff - 4 officers and 62 men per company; total per regiment: 31 officers and 380 non-commissioned officers and cannoneers.

There was no more than one battalion of pontoniers at 8 companies, twelve companies of workmen, and four squadrons of the train, each having 15 officers and 256 men. The list below shows how they were combined.

According to regulation, the artillery fell from 328 companies (6 horse and 6 foot of the Old Guard; 1 horse and 15 foot of the Young Guard; 252 foot and 48 horse of the line) to 192 companies (168 foot and 24 horse). In the end, the Guard companies were eliminated. Meanwhile, the artillery service had demonstratated such flexibility under the Empire in doubling its companies, in creating companies *bis*, and companies *ter* in at least as great

1st FOOT REGIMENT:	Allix, 1800 - Law de Lauriston, 1802 - De Pernetty, 1802 - Desvaux, 1804 - Daboville, 1805 - Valée, 1807 - Gerdy, 1809 - Digeon, 1813.
2nd -	De Faultrier, 1799 - Demanelle, 1803 - Le Noury de la Guignardière, 1806 - Doguereau, 1807.
3rd -	Lobreau, 1794 - Bouchu, 1805 - Ricci, 1811.
4th -	De Niger, 1799 - Ferreur, 1800 - Buchet, 1801 - Ruty, 1802 - Desvaux, 1807 - Digeon, 1809 - De Montgenet, 1811.
5th -	Borthon, 1800 - Demarçay, 1802 - Mengin, 1805 - Gondallier de Tugny, 1806 - De Carmejane, 1810 - Hazard, 1811.
6th -	Bardenet, 1801 - De Sénarmont, 1802 - Filhol de Camas, 1806 - Laurent, 1811 - Marilhac, 1812 - Verrier, 1813.
7th -	Berthier, 1800 - Dedon, 1801 - De Bicquilley, 1803 - Lepin, 1807 - Collin, 1811 - Le Roy, 1814.
8th -	Tirlet, 1802 - Aubry, 1803 - Digeon, 1809 - Caron, 1813.
9th -	Bode, 1810 - Cottin, 1813.
1st HORSE REGIMENT	D'Anthouard, 1801 - Prost, 1806 - Baltry, 1806 - Ralfin, 1811.
2nd -	Mossel, 1799 - Forno, 1805 - Le Noury de la Guignardière, 1807 - Pellegrin-Millon, 1809 - Chopin, 1813.
3rd -	Duroc, 1797 - De Navelet, 1802 - Daboville, 1807 - Doguerau, 1808 - Marion, 1812 - Marilhac, 1813.
4th -	De Lauriston, 1800 - Taviel, 1801 - Faure de Gier, 1802 - Griors, 1811 - Lavoy, 1813.
5th -	Foy, 1800 - Berge, 1808 - Chauveau, 1813.
6th -	Desvaux, 1803 - De Charbonnel, 1804 - De Fontenay, 1810 - Marion, 1812.
Imperial Guard HORSE REGIMENT	Captain: Couin, 1799 - Major: Couin, 1802 - Colonel: Couin, 1804 - Baron Desvaux 1806, General of division: Lariboisière, commander - General of brigade: Couin, second in command.
Imperial Guard FOOT REGIMENT	Grivis.
Young Guard:	1811, Henrion.

FOOT ARTILLERY						HORSE ARTILLERY	
New number	Old corps which joined their formation	New number	Old corps which joined their formation	New number	Old corps which joined their formation		
1st REGIMENT	Former 1st Foot Regiment. - 4th, 22nd, 25th and 27th companies of the former 9th Foot Regiment. -Part of the 4th foot company of the Old Guard. - 5th, 6th, 7th and 8th foot companies of the Young Guard.	5th REGIMENT	Former 5th Foot Regiment. - 5th, 7th, 18th and 20th companies of the former 9th Foot Regiment. Part of the 4th foot company of the Old Guard. - 1st, 2nd, 3rd and 4th foot companies of the Young Guard.	1st REGIMENT	Former 1st Horse Regiment. - 1st, 2nd, 3rd and 8th companies of the former 5th Horse Regiment. - 4th, 5th horse companies of the former Old Guard.		
2nd REGIMENT	Former 2nd Foot Regiment. - 2nd, 10th, 11th, 15th, 19th, 24th and 28th companies of the former 9th Foot Regiment. - Part of the 3rd foot company of the Old Guard. 9th, 10th, 11th and 12th foot companies of the Young Guard.	6th REGIMENT	Former 6th Foot Regiment. - 16th and 23rd companies of the former 9th Foot Regiment. - 5th foot company of the Old Guard.	2nd REGIMENT	Former 2nd Horse Regiment. - 4th, 5th, 6th and 7th companies of the former 5th Horse Regiment. - 1st and 2nd horse companies of the former Old Guard.		
3rd REGIMENT	Former 3rd Foot Regiment. - 1st foot company of the Old Guard.	7th REGIMENT	Former 7th Foot Regiment. - 21st and 26th companies of the former 9th Foot Regiment. - Part of the 3rd foot company of the Old Guard. 13th, 14th and 15th foot companies of the Young Guard.	3rd REGIMENT	Former 3rd Horse Regiment. - 1st, 2nd, 3rd and 4th companies of the former 6th Horse Regiment. - 6th horse company of the former Old Guard. - Horse company of the Young Guard.		
4th REGIMENT	Former 4th Foot Regiment. - 9th, 12th, 13th and 14th companies of the former 9th Foot Regiment. - 4th foot company of the Old Guard.	8th REGIMENT	Former 8th Foot Regiment. - 1st, 3rd, 6th, 8th and 17th companies of the former 9th Foot Regiment. - 6th foot company of the Old Guard.	4th REGIMENT	Former 4th Horse Regiment. - 5th, 6th, 7th and 8th companies of the former 6th Horse Regiment. - 3rd horse company of the former Old Guard.		

The 1st, 2nd and 3rd battalions of pontoniers and the Guard pontonniers were combined into a new "pontonier battalion".
The eighteen companies of line workmen, the Guard workmen company and the five companies of workmen were paired, two by two - except for the 2nd, 4th, and 12th which remained as they were, and the 6th, 7th and 11th which received two complete companies. The 14 principal battalions of the train, the 13 battalions *bis* of the train and the 24 companies of the two regiments of train of the Old and the Young Guard were grouped much less methodically. They had to form four new squadrons each assigned to haul artillery pieces from three regiments which were divided into two groups.

numbers as the principal companies, that this decrease did not have much importance. On the other hand, the considerable reduction in the artillery train, which then carried along with it caissons and guns as well as horse artillery and foot artillery, put the artillery in the worst condition. Also, as of September 9th, the number of squadrons of the train was doubled.

Upon his return from the Isle of Elba, Napoleon concentrated on the artillery. He rebuilt the Guard artillery but he did nothing to the line. He demanded only campaign companies from the line and asked for artillery from the auxiliary troops which would serve to defend the territory. There was no lack of cannon, but cannoneers were in short supply. First, examples will be drawn from Napoleon's correspondence which is the true history of the One Hundred Days. Then, the table of artillery attached to the Army of the North will be given.

Since there were insufficient numbers of muskets, Napoleon refused to arm the working class population of Paris and Lyon. As a soldier and a good one, he thought that all stout-hearted men should place themselves resolutely in a regiment and submit to discipline rather than fight outside the rules and military authority. All of his efforts were put toward the best possible armament of the line troops and of the paid National Guard. According to his point of view, they differed solely in the length of their periods of enlistment.

On March 22, he asked the minister of war for an exact situation report on war armaments. On the 23rd, he ordered the musket factories at Tulle and

Foot artillery. Imperial Guard (1808-1815).

Horse artillery and artillery train. Imperial Guard (1804-1815).

Versailles to be rebuilt. He wanted 400,000 muskets of the 1777 model and of Model Number 1 to be fabricated in a year. On the 27th, he commanded the naval minister to have 5,900 muskets which were at Bastia returned, and the minister of war was requested to repair 66,200 other muskets stored in Montpellier, Perpignan, Toulouse and Bayonne. He discovered 61,000 muskets at Grenoble, 24,000 at Mezières, and 23,000 at Strasbourg. He gave the order to establish assembly workshops in Paris which would produce 400 muskets a day. The artillery, which was responsible for the proper execution of these orders, had to supervise the smallest details.

He paid attention to gunpowder as well as to the fabrication of projectiles. Nor did he forget the personnel of the artillery. Five generals received orders to leave on April 2nd: General de Pernetty for Toulouse; General Foucher for Douai; General Taviel for Auxonne; General Carbonnel for Rennes; and General Tirlet for Grenoble. General Evain was especially charged with coordinating their work.

At the same time, the naval artillery—from which he had fashioned a good infantry in 1813—was returned to its normal assignment. Sixty-eight companies of these excellent troops were distributed in the following manner: 20 for maritime areas; 15 for points in the North; 15 to points in the East; 10 in the Alps; and 8 in the Pyrenees. He foresaw that the enemy would want to take the offensive from the 1st to the 15th of May. He even anticipated his defeat and made arrangements so that Paris would be able to defend itself. Chateau-Thierry, Soissons, Reims, Vitry, Laon, and Langres received their armaments at the same time as all the northern locations. He also thought about the Rhône Valley since it was vulnerable at all points along the border. Although he put Rapp with the 5th Corps in Strasbourg, knowing that all of Europe were set on beating him soundly, it was because he was the only Frenchman who still represented the principles of the Revolution, of illegitimacy crowned.

ARTILLERY OF THE ARMY OF THE NORTH (JUNE 1815)

Commander in chief: General of division RUTY
Chief of staff: —
Adjutants: Captains Guillon, Lamy, Goussard, Bonnard
General direction of the parks
Director general: General of division Neigre   *Assistant director:* Colonel Tiquenot
Adjutants: Majors Lechesne, Sesilly; Captains Maurel, Taupin,
Poulin, David, Delamones, Crozet and Guyot
Director: Colonel Renaud - *Assistant director:* Major Barré
Guard general: Lieutenant Marcon - *Conductor general:* Lieutenant Erard

1st CORPS. - General of brigade DESALES. *Chief of staff:* Colonel BERNARD.
1st Division: Major Vaudrey. - 20th company of the 6th Foot Regiment, Captain Hamelin -
4 officiers, 85 men.
2nd Division: Major Poucheux. - 10th company of the 6th Foot Regiment, Captain Cantin -
3 officers, 86 men.
3rd Division: Major Garès, 19th company of the 6th Foot Regiment, Captain Emon - 4 officers, 81 men.
4th Division: 9th company of the 6th Foot Regiment, Captain Bourgeois - 3 officers, 81 men.
Cavalry Division: —. 2nd company of the 1st Horse Regiment, Captain Bourgeois - 3 officers, 70 men.
Reserve. - 11th company of the 6th Foot Regiment, Captain Charlot.   4 foot batteries, 1 horse battery
and 1 reserve battery, 46 pieces.
Artillery: 20 officers, 483 men. - Train: 10 officers, 583 men.

2nd CORPS. - General of brigade PELLETIER. *Chief of staff:* Major BOBILLIER.
5th Division. - 18th company of the 6th Foot Regiment, Captain Desault - 4 officers, 86 men.
6th Division. - 2nd company of the 2nd Foot Regiment, Captain Meunier - 4 officers, 92 men.
7th Division. - 3rd company of the 2nd Foot Regiment, Captain Barbaux - 3 officers, 74 men.
9th Division. - 1st company of the 6th Foot Regiment, Captain Tacon - 4 officers, 84 men.
Cavalry Division. - 2nd company of the 4th Horse Regiment, Captain Gronnier - 4 officers, 76 men. -
Reserve - 7th company of the 5th Foot Regiment, Captain Valnet, 4 officers, 96 men. - 1st and 4th
companies of the 4th Horse Regiment, Captains Godchereaux and Godet, 11 officers, 223 men.
4 foot batteries, 3 horse batteries and 1 reserve battery, 58 pieces.
Artillery: 30 officers, 645 men. - Train: 15 officers, 740 men.

3rd CORPS. - General of brigade DOGUEREAU. *Chief of staff:* Major LEGRIEL.
8th Division. - 7th company of the 1st Foot Regiment, Captain Chauveau - 4 officers, 83 men.
10th Division. - 18th company of the 2nd Foot Regiment, Captain Guérin - 4 officers, 81 men.
11th Division. - 17th company of the 2nd Foot Regiment, Captain Lecorbeiller - 4 officers, 96 men.
3rd Cavalry Division. - 4th company of the 2nd Horse Regiment, Captain Dumont - 3 officers, 74 men.
Reserve - 1st and 19th companies of the 2nd Foot Regiment, Captains Vollée and Labiche, 8 officers,
192 men. 3 foot batteries, 1 horse battery and 2 reserve batteries, 46 pieces.
Artillery: 30 officers, 645 men. - Train: 9 officers, 402 men.

4th CORPS. - General of brigade BALTUS. *Chief of staff:* Major RAINDRE.
12th Division. - 2nd company of the 5th Foot Regiment, Captain Fenouillat - 3 officers, 98 men.
13th Division. - 1st company of the 5th Foot Regiment, Captain Saint-Cyr - 3 officers, 97 men.
14th Division. - 3rd company of the 3rd Foot Regiment, Captain Thomas - 3 officers, 92 men.
Reserve. - 3rd, 4th, 5th and 11th companies of the 5th Foot Regiment, 13 officers, 536 men. - 4th company
of the 1st Pontonier Battalion, Captain Moutonnet, 4 officers, 65 men.
7 foot and reserve batteries, 56 pieces.
Artillery: 29 officers, 724 men. - Train: 16 officers, 648 men.

6th CORPS. - General of division Baron NOURY. *Chief of staff:* Major CHAUDON.
19th Division: Major Bron. - 1st company of the 8th Foot Regiment, Captain Parisot - 3 officers, 83 men.
20th Division: Major de Marcilly. - 2nd company of the 8th Foot Regiment, Captain Paquat -
3 officers, 88 men.
21st Division. - 3rd company of the 8th Foot Regiment, Captain Duvernay - 3 officers, 91 men.
Reserve. - 4th company of the 8th Foot Regiment, 3 officers, 92 men. 4 foot companies, 32 pieces.
Artillery: 12 officers, 354 men. - Train: 10 officers, 389 men.

CAVALRY RESERVE
1st CORPS. -   4th Division: 1st company of the 1st Horse Regiment, 2 officers, 70 men
5th Division: 3rd company of the 1st Horse Regiment, 2 officers, 74 men.
2nd CORPS. -   9th Division: 4th company of the 1st Horse Regiment, 4 officers, 55 men. Captain
Cotheraux.
10th Division: 4th company of the 4th Horse Regiment, Captain Bernard, 2 officers, 60
men.
3rd CORPS. -   11th Division: 3rd company of the 2nd Horse Regiment, 3 officers, 75 men.
12th Division: 2nd company of the 2nd Horse Regiment, Captain Lebeau, 3 officers, 75
men.
4th CORPS. -   13th Division: 5th company of the 1st Horse Regiment, 3 officers, 75 men.
14th Division: 4th company of the 3rd Horse Regiment - 3 officers, 70 men. 8 horse
batteries, 48 pieces.
Artillery: 22 officers, 554 men. - Train: 13 officers, 633 men.

IMPERIAL GUARD
Under General of division DESVAUX DE SAINT-MAURICE, the Imperial Guard formed the reserve,
as follows:

	Officers	Men
6 companies of the foot artillery regiment, General LALLEMAND	28	702
4 companies of the horse artillery regiment, Colonel DUCHAUD	19	380
5 companies of auxiliary foot artillery of the line	15	414
1 company of auxiliary horse artillery of the line	3	109
16 companies - 118 pieces.	TOTAL 65	1,605

Horse artillery and foot artillery (1816).

On June 5th, Lyon had eight pieces in battery on the Morand Bridge, four at Perrache, as many on the Bridge of the Guillotière, sixteen pieces between the Saône and the Rhône, and as many on the old walls. Paris had twenty batteries entrusted to the patriotism of all classes of society. The students from the polytechnic school, the disabled, the colleges, and the school of Alfort manned them. Tyranny which is so disparaged in a great man is at the same time useful in finding and stirring up defenders of the country. It would be a long poem as beautiful as the Iliad and as strange as the Odyssey which recounted in detail the campaign of 1815. The so-called liberals tried to tarnish it but the true patriots always retained it in memory. Napoleon was gifted with an intelligent patriotism. However, in France he had men against him whom he had raised and made wealthy and who wanted to retain their fortunes and their positions.

According to the adjacent report, which seems the most accurate of those which have been set before the eyes of the public by the debaters of the Battle of Waterloo, Napoleon had available to him 400 pieces of artillery *(bouches à feu)* served by 4,860 artillerists and 207 officers. They were hauled by 4,898 men of the train having 105 officers at their head.

For a total of 122,408 men, this gives him a little more than 3 pieces per 1,000 men. However, one needs to know if all the companies designated in the order of battle of the Army of the North got together.

Like the rest of the Imperial Army, the artillery was dissolved after the campaign of 1815. This time moreso than after their first return, the Bourbons had decided to forget nothing. The One Hundred Days had taught them that the memory of Napoleon would for a long time remain etched in the memories of the old soldiers. For the artillery—his service of choice and the one from which he had come whose soldiers he called his companions—it was decided that they would return to the traditions of a distant past as was done in the infantry and the cavalry. The new regiments formed with the remnants of the old no longer had numbers. The number seemed to the organizers of the new royal army as revolutionary and as formidable as the tricolor cockade and the flag. This was because it had made all the princely and geographic designations of the Old Monarchy subject to the egalitarian standard. Meanwhile, just as there had been numbers of seniority under Louis XV and Louis XVI, numbers of order had to be given to the regiments under Louis XVIII. The order is an inevitability to which, sooner or later, reactions—like revolutions—must submit.

After the mustering out of August 4, 1815, the twelve regiments were rebuilt on the basis of the decree of May 12, 1814. The only difference was that the eight foot regiments had no more than 16 companies and a depot cadre. This left the service with only 152

companies (128 foot and 24 horse). The effective strength was reduced to 52 men per company. This was sufficient since they were no longer able to have an army, since almost no more rolling materiel existed, and since a major portion of the French garrisons were still held by foreigners.

Until August 16, 1820, the artillery regiments bore the following names:

Foot regiments: 1st, La Fère. 2nd, Metz. 3rd, Valence. 4th, Auxonne. 5th, Strasbourg. 6th, Douai. 7th, Toulouse. 8th, Rennes.
Mounted regiments: 1st, Metz. 2nd, Rennes. 3rd, Strasbourg. 4th, Toulouse.

The Spanish War highlighted the inadequacy of the service, especially of its means of transport. Although the artillery of the Royal Guard had been formed as of 1816 and supplied with a train squadron, the service was hard pressed to provide the number of necessary companies—of either artillery or of artillery train—to put together reserves and a sufficient park in the divisions, the army corps, and the army. Recourse was sought in provisional measures. The number of non-commissioned officers, brigade leaders, and drivers in the companies put on a war footing was doubled while waiting to return the cadres and the effectives to their normal numbers

Foot artillery. Royal Guard (1824).

after the conclusion of peace. This excellent procedure is very similiar to the actual doubling in the event of mobilization, especially for the administrative corps and the transports. Less fortunate for the campaign of Trocadero than for that of Waterloo, only a very elementary and incomplete report on the artillery of the Army of Spain can be given according to a situation report from April 15, 1823.

Commander in chief: General of division Viscount TIRLET — *Aide-de-camp:* Captain TACON — *Chief of staff:* Colonel SAINT-CYR

1st Corps
Commander: Colonel RICCI

1st Division - 3rd company of the 1st Foot Regiment. - 1st company of the 2nd Foot Regiment. - 1st, 3rd and 7th companies of the 7th squadron of the train.
2nd Division - 4th company of the 8th Foot Regiment. - 3rd company of the 1st Horse Regiment. - 2nd company of the squadron of the train. - 2nd and 3rd companies of the 8th Squadron.
Reserve and park: Lieutenant Colonel Pariset - 2nd and 4th companies of the 2nd Foot Regiment. - 1st and 2nd companies of the 3rd squadron of the train. - Detachments of the 8th Squadron. - Detachments of the 2nd company of workmen.

2nd Corps
Commander: Colonel SAUTEREAU DU PART

Divisions - 1st company of the 7th Foot Regiment. - 2nd company of the 2nd Horse Regiment. - 1st and 2nd companies of the 2nd squadron of the train. - Detachment of the 3rd company of the 8th Squadron.
Reserve and park: Lieutenant Colonel Maillart - 1st and 2nd companies of the 6th Foot Regiment. - 3rd company of the 3rd squadron of the train. - Detachments of the 3rd company of the 8th squadron of the train and the 5th company of workmen.

3rd Corps
Commander:
Colonel LE FRANÇOIS

Divisions - 7th and 8th companies of the 8th Foot Regiment. - 3rd company of the 2nd squadron of the train. - 1st company of the 8th squadron of the train.
Reserve and park - Lieutenant Colonel Nacquart - 4th and 5th companies of the 8th Foot Regiment. - 4th company of the 8th squadron of the train. - Detachment of the 5th company of workmen.

Siege Park
Director: Colonel GÉRIN
Assistant director: Lieutenant Colonel MICHELIN

5th company of the 7th Foot Regiment. - 6th company of the 8th Foot Regiment. - 1st and 2nd companies of the pontonier battalion.

General Park
Director: Colonel BROUET
Assistant director: Lieutenant Colonel BOSQUETTE
Inspector general of the train: Lieutenant Colonel HUSSON

7th company of the 6th Foot Regiment. - 6th and 7th companies of the 7th Foot Regiment. - 2nd, 3rd and 5th companies of workmen. - Detachments of the 2nd and 8th squadrons of the train.
Reserve in garrison on the border - 5th company of the 6th Foot Regiment. - 8th company of the 7th Foot Regiment. - 1st, 2nd and 5th companies of the 8th Foot Regiment. - 1st and 2nd companies of the 2nd Horse Regiment. - General staff of the 2nd and 3rd squadrons. Staff of the 2nd and 3rd company of the 7th squadron.

Horse artillery and artillery train (1823-1829)

Commander in chief: Colonel Viscount de la Hitte
Chief of general staff: Major Hamart
Adjutants: Captains Roussot de Lapic, Duhamel, Pauxié
(detached to the chief of the provisional government)
Director of the siege equipment: Major Hennocque
Adjutants: Captains Trutat and Noizet-Saint-Paul

6th Company (Captain Thouvenin) and 7th Company (Captain de Broca) of the 5th Foot Regiment. 1st Company and detachment of the 6th company of the 2nd Train Squadron. Detachments of the 1st Company of the 8th Train Squadron and of the 7th Company of workmen.

Effectives present on September 1, 1828: 22 officers, 402 men. 30 officers' horses, 31 horses of the troops, and 309 draught horses. (484 men and 370 horses).

Soon after the Spanish War, there was, on February 27, 1825, a reorganization of the foot regiments to twenty companies and of the horse regiments to eight. The Guard had twelve companies: eight foot and four horse.

The campaign of Greece (1828) used the personnel above.

Under the direction of General Valée, Captains Piobert and Marcou prepared a radical revolution in the artillery. The *batterie* (thus the word entered into technical language), either field or horse, was from this time on a tactical unit. Each piece had six gunners and six drivers and all of them had to know how to maneuver cannon. In the field battery or *batterie montée*, the gunners were seated on the caissons. Of course, the artillery train disappeared, giving way to a new corps, the train of the artillery parks which hauled all the pieces and the unusual wagons serving the combat batteries.

The cadres were determined in the following manner: 1st, ten regiments of sixteen batteries each (three horse and thirteen foot of which six were always field); 2nd, a single regiment of the Guard in which the two old horse regiments and foot regiments and the train squadron were knit together (three horse batteries and five foot batteries); 3rd, five train squadrons of artillery; 4th, a general staff and workmen. This organization had thirty-three horse batteries and sixty-five foot batteries always at the ready. However, in the thoughts of the organizer of 1829, the seventy foot batteries could be quickly transformed into field batteries. Unfortunately, the number of 5,946 horses left a black hole, or rather a weak point, in this plan.

The expedition of Algiers did not affect this organization in any way. The personnel of the service for the expeditionary corps is given at left.

The troops were composed of ten foot batteries, four field batteries, one mountain battery, one company of workmen, one company of pontoniers, and a train squadron.

Commander in chief of the service:
General of brigade DUCOS, Viscount DE LA HITTE
(Aide-de-camp to the Dauphin)
Chief of staff: Colonel Count D'ESCLAIBES D'HUST
(of the 9th Regiment)
Director of the park: Lieutenant Colonel EGGERLÉ
Assistant director: Major LEGRAND

Majors: Romestin (7th Regiment) - Molin (2nd Horse Regiment) - Admirauld (3rd Regiment) - De Foucauld (9th Regiment) - Bousson (Staff) - De Julvecourt (2nd Regiment)

Captains: Ancinelle, Dieu, Mairet, Lami, Labeaume, Maléchard (aide-de-camp to the commanding general), Lelièvre, Rouvrois, Mocquard, Feraudy, Taffe, Bonet, Olry, Aubert-Vincelles, Robert, Colonet, Coteau, Lemet, Dorlodot-Depreville, Contencin, Le Denmat de Kervern, Poullain, Gaudin, Gille called Dumarchais, Veriot, Arcelin, Carnot, Gaultier, La Chèze, Marey, Gravelle, Dardart.

Lieutenants: Delamarre, Esnault, Éblé, Molard, Bardonnaut, Amoros, Marsal, Petit, Vernier, Captain, Marion, Mathieu de la Redorte, de Blois la Calande, De Préaudeau, de Livois, Romanson, Page, Descouches, Baron de Bicquilley.

Second Lieutenants: de Kergorlay, Massoule, Magnat, Leborne, Daru, Roget, Boué, Collin.

Horse artillery and artillery train. Royal Guard (1824).

ORGANIZATION IN 1829

NEW REGIMENTS

Number	Elements which entered their formation
1st	Staff and first 11 companies of the former 1st Foot Regiment; 14th and 15th companies of the former 6th Foot Regiment; 1st, 2nd, 3rd companies of the former 3rd Horse Regiment.
2nd	Staff and first 13 companies of the former 2nd Foot Regiment; 4th, 5th, 6th companies of the former 1st Horse Regiment.
3rd	Staff and first 13 companies of the former 3rd Foot Regiment; 4th, 5th, 6th companies of the former 4th Horse Regiment.
4th	Staff and first 14 companies of the former 4th Foot Regiment; 7th company of the former 1st Horse Regiment and the 7th company of the former 4th Horse Regiment.
5th	Staff and first 13 companies of the former 5th Foot Regiment; 4th, 5th, 6th companies of the former 2nd Horse Regiment.
6th	Staff and first 13 companies of the former 6th Foot Regiment; 4th, 5th, 6th companies of the former 3rd Horse Regiment.
7th	Staff and first 9 companies of the former 7th Foot Regiment; 15th, 16th and 17th companies of the former 4th Foot Regiment; 1st, 2nd and 3rd companies of the former 1st Horse Regiment.
8th	Staff and first 7 companies of the former 8th Foot Regiment; 12th, 13th, 14th, 15th, 16th and 17th companies of the 1st Foot Regiment; 2nd, 3rd and 7th companies of the former 2nd Horse Regiment.
9th	Staff the former 4th Horse Regiment; 14th, 15th, 16th and 17th companies of the former 3rd Foot Regiment; 15th, 16th and 17th of the former 2nd Foot Regiment; 10th, 11th, 12th, 13th, 14th, 15th, 16th and 17th companies of the former 7th Foot Regiment; 1st, 2nd and 4th companies of the former 4th Horse Regiment.
10th	Staff the former 3rd Horse Regiment; 8th, 9th, 10th, 11th, 12th, 13th, 14th, 15th, 16th and 17th companies of the former 8th Foot Regiment; 14th, 15th and 16th companies of the former 5th Foot Regiment; 1st company of the former 2nd Horse Regiment; 7th company of the former 3rd Horse Regiment.

The ten foot batteries were numbers 10 and 11 of the 2nd, 3rd, 4th, 7th, and 9th Artillery. The four field batteries and the mountain battery did not have numbers. At least their numbers did not appear on the report that we have seen.

The 4th Company of workmen had for officers: First Captain Grégoire, Second Captain Ditch, First Lieutenant Robilier, Second Lieutenant Robert.

The company of pontoniers was commanded by Captain Hoffet who had for lieutenants: Becquemont and Garnerin.

The 3rd Train Squadron of the Parks (new formation), commanded by Captain Anozet, formed the service of the park. Lieutenants: Feliker, Puisier, Alix, Pégurier, Pognard, and Letang. Second Lieutenants: Rey, Peyré, Geille, Bounegrau, Gaelhouste, and Roustan.

According to the departure report, the artillery included altogether: 2,327 men and 1,309 horses. They set off with thirty 24 pound pieces, twenty 16 pound pieces, 12 howitzers at eight inches, 88 mountings, 50,000 rounds of shot, 12,000 shells, 6,400 bombs and 3,846,000 cartridges.

Since the minister of war was to be commander in chief of the expedition, nothing had been forgotten. Distant operations must always have an influential commander in chief who is refused nothing or who refuses nothing.

The normal system of brigading the special troops had been abandoned this time. They were at the disposition of the general in chief who used them according to the needs of the service.

The Revolution of 1830 at first removed the artillery regiment of the Guard and did little after the creation of the 11th Regiment. The campaign of Belgium took place on this basis. On December 1, 1832, the situation report of the service in the Army of the North was as shown at left.

Major Gannal and Captains Corbin and Grandsire were killed beneath the walls of Anvers.

On September 16, 1833, Marshal Soult had the King issue a decree that reorganized the artillery to 14 regiments at twelve batteries. The first four regiments had three horse batteries; the last ten had only two.

All the foot batteries became field batteries. The first four regiments had 9 of them; the last ten had 10. Total: 168 batteries (32 horse and 136 field). This is the figure for the organization of 1829, except that, even in peacetime, the 1,008 artillery pieces were ready to fight.

The 12th Regiment was formed at Bourges with two horse batteries coming from the 6th and the 9th, two field batteries from the 2nd, two from the 3rd, one from the 6th, and one from the 9th, and four batteries from the 2nd, 3rd, 6th, and 9th transformed into field batteries.

The 13th Regiment organized at Lyon took its two horse batteries from the 8th and the 11th. Each of these two regiments also supplied it with two field batteries. The 1st Regiment provided three field batteries and one foot; the 4th, two field batteries and one foot. The two foot batteries were immediately transformed into field batteries.

Finally, a horse battery from the 7th and one from the 10th entered into the organization of the 14th Regiment. Four field batteries from

STAFF

Commander in chief: General of division NEIGRE
Aides-de-camp: Captains O'FARELL, PERIGNON, MALLET
Chief of staff: Colonel Count DE BOUTEILLER

PARK

Director: Colonel HENRAUX - *Adjutant:* Major GANNALET-MARIEZ

Advance guard brigade	2nd Horse Battery of the 1st Regiment, Captain Lecorbeiller (APM).
1st Infantry Division	4th Field Battery of the 1st Regiment, Captain Balaran.
	5th Field Battery of the 1st Regiment, Captain Truffer.
2nd Infantry Division	6th Field Battery of the 1st Regiment, Captain de Caqueray de Fontenelle.
	7th Field Battery of the 1st Regiment, Captain Lecorbeiller (MAM).
3rd Infantry Division	5th Field Battery of the 2nd Regiment, Captain Lachasse.
	7th Field Battery of the 2nd Regiment, Captain de Mosseron d'Amboise.
4th Infantry Division	6th Field Battery of the 2nd Regiment, Captain Chimiac.
	5th Field Battery of the 8th Regiment, Captain Lemarquant.
Dragoon Division	1st Horse Battery of the 1st Regiment, Captain Romagnie.
Cuirassier Division	1st Horse Battery of the 8th Regiment, Captain Jolivet de Riencourt.
General Reserve	2nd Horse Battery of the 8th Regiment, Captain Lenfumé de Lignières.
	4th Field Battery of the 8th Regiment, Captain Herbet.
	6th Field Battery of the 8th Regiment, Captain de Cayeu.
Campaign park	13th Foot Battery of the 2nd Regiment, Captain Corrard.
	10th Foot Battery of the 1st Regiment, Captain Pottier.
	11th Foot Battery of the 1st Regiment, Captain Lœwille.
Siege train	12th Foot Battery of the 1st Regiment, Captain Charles Artaud.
	13th Foot Battery of the 1st Regiment, Captain Magnier.
	10th Foot Battery of the 11th Regiment, Captain Bennet.
	11th Foot Battery of the 11th Regiment, Captain Corbin.
	12th Foot Battery of the 11th Regiment, Captain Arago.
	13th Foot Battery of the 11th Regiment, Captain François.
	14th Foot Battery of the 11th Regiment, Captain Vivier.
Bridge train	
Director: Major PAYAN	1st company of the pontonier regiment, Captain Labatie.
	2nd company of the pontonier regiment, Captain Hoffet.

5th and 6th squadrons of the park train
Part of the 6th and 12th companies of workmen

the 4th, 5th, 7th, and 10th plus six foot batteries transformed into field batteries came two by two from the 5th, 7th, and 10th Regiments.

At the same time, the eleven old regiments transformed the foot batteries which they still had into field batteries.

These changes were ended in May 1834. From that time on, France had at its disposal:

four regiments (1st, 2nd, 3rd, 4th) composed of 3 horse batteries and 12 field
six regiments (5th, 6th, 7th, 8th, 9th, 10th) having 2 horse batteries, 12 field, and 1 foot
four regiments (11th, 12th, 13th, 14th) having 2 horse batteries and 12 field batteries

This gives a total of 32 horse batteries, 168 field batteries, and 6 foot batteries for a total of 206 batteries.

As can be seen, all these organizations revolved around a thousand to twelve hundred horse-drawn pieces of artillery. However, sad to say, effectives and horses did not respond in kind to the magnificence of these figures! This situation remained fairly constant until 1848, except that the numbers for effectives—men and horses—fell quite a bit. The provisional government eliminated 14 depot cadres and created 18 foot batteries. This was a strongly criticized measure since it removed the means of hauling 56 pieces. Apparently, all the regiments had 16 batteries.

The expedition of Rome employed the personnel indicated in the table at right.

The introduction of an improved materiel brought about a radical modification in the artillery service in 1854. The system already tried of horse, field and foot regiments was substituted for the combination of horse batteries and field batteries in the regiments. This combination had allowed the various components of a regiment to help each other out in the event of partial mobilizations and gave a lot of flexibility to the service. Worse, however, was the dismounting and return to foot of a number of batteries. This deprived the army of a major portion of the forces active in the artillery. Experts placed a lot of blame on the organization of February 14, 1854. The number of regiments was increased to 16 and even to 17, including therein the regiment of pontoniers which took Number 6 again:

Commander of artillery for the expeditionary corps: General of brigade THIRY
Aide-de-camp: TOUSSAINT
Chief of staff: Major SOLEILLE
At the disposition of the general: Major BERET
Adjutant: Captain CHOPIN
Adjutant: Captain DE FAULTRIER DE SAHUQUE
Commander of artillery at Civita-Vecchia: Captain DE PISTORIS

1st DIVISION
13th battery of the 3rd Regiment, Captain Ferrand

2nd DIVISION
Major Bourdeau
Adjutant: Captain Saint-Rémy
12th battery of the 3rd Regiment, Captain Pinel
6th battery of the 7th Regiment, Captain Canu

3rd DIVISION
Major Devaux
Adjutant: Captain Fourcheut-Montrond
12th battery of the 5th Regiment, Captain Grimaudet de Rocheboüet

44 officers - 1,994 men - 1,031 horses
Officers killed:
Captain Fabar, Lieutenants Pachon and Clerc
Officers wounded:
Captains Canu, Gachot, Brissac; Lieutenants Canvière, Gouy and Tricoche.
12 non-commissioned officers and soldiers killed;
47 wounded

PARK AND RESERVE
Director: Lieutenant Colonel Larchey, commander of the reserve
Adjutant: Captain Gaudelet
Assistant director: Major Rat called Lerat
Adjutants: Captains Luxer and Grouvel

RESERVE - 7th battery of the 14th Regiment, Captain Roget.

SIEGE BATTERIES - 16th battery of the 1st Regiment, Captain Lablache-Combier; 16th battery of the 4th Regiment, Captain Gachot; 16th battery of the 8th Regiment, Captain Barbary de Langlade; 15th battery of the 11th Regiment, Captain Besençon; 16th battery of the 11th Regiment, Captain Prélat

7th company of the 15th pontoniers, Captain Blondeau - 5th company of workmen, Captain Julia - 3rd company of the 5th squadron of the park train, Second Lieutenant Lepouze

Five foot regiments (1 to 5) of twelve batteries each - total: 60 foot batteries
Seven field regiments (7 to 13) of 15 batteries each - total: 105 field batteries
Four horse regiments (14 to 17) of 8 batteries each - total: 32 horse batteries

Field artillery. Battery of four (1859).

Battery in front of Sebastopol. Opening fire (October 17, 1854).

The number of combat batteries fell from 200 to 137. The French artillery lost the horse teams for 378 artillery pieces. This mistake hung heavy over the fatal campaign of 1870. The creation of two regiments of artillery in the Guard did not compensate for it. In November 1856, when they were expanded to their greatest complement, they could only hitch up 98 artillery pieces (18 batteries of which 8 were horse). It is true that the Crimean campaign and the Italian War were engaged in with the organization of 1854. However, it should not be forgotten that these two wars were circumscribed. Moreover, the second one would be cut short due to a lack of the military means needed to face an often illusory coalition.

The artillery that took Sebastopol was slowly transported along the plateau of Chersonèse. It did not arrive all at the same time and cost the central administration a lot of effort. The poor balance in the forces ordered in the decree of February 17, 1854 came to light. Recourse was taken in the batteries *bis*. If a serious campaign along the Baltic coast had been conducted in 1856, there would have been no artillery at all in France. This was the situation on September 8th—the day of the assault—which has been selected to give the maximum table for the artillery in the Crimea (below).

Thus, the artillery sent 34 field batteries to Sebastopol, 7 horse, and 53 foot from the line (without counting the 7 batteries of the Guard), 5 companies of naval

---

Commander of artillery of the army: General of division THIRY
Aide-de-camp: Major LACROIX DE CROULTE DE SAINT-MARTIN; Captain DE VASSART—*Chief of staff:* Colonel AUGER

DIVISIONAL BATTERIES

1st CORPS, General of brigade LEBOEUF, *commanding; Aide-de-camp:* Captain Moulin; *Chief of staff:* Lieutenant Colonel Malherbe

1st INFANTRY DIVISION	2nd INFANTRY DIVISION	3rd INFANTRY DIVISION	4th INFANTRY DIVISION	CAVALRY DIVISION
Major de Tryon	Major Sibille	Major Moulard	Major Pariset	Major Liégeard
4th and 15th battery of the 8th Field Regiment.	2nd and 3rd batteries of the 13th Field Regiment	7th and 8th batteries of the 8th Field Regiment	13th and 14th batteries of the 12th Field Regiment	4th battery of the 17th Horse Regiment

2nd CORPS. General of brigade BEURET, *commanding; Aide-de-camp:* Captain Jomard; *Chief of staff:* Lieutenant Colonel de Ligondes

1st INFANTRY DIVISION	2nd INFANTRY DIVISION	3rd INFANTRY DIVISION	4th INFANTRY DIVISION	5th INFANTRY DIVISION	CAVALRY DIVISION
Major Wartelle	Major Lenglier	Major Beaudoin	Major Joly-Frigola	Major Lainsecq	—
3rd battery of the 6th Field Regiment 1st battery of the 9th Field Regiment	2nd battery of the 12th Field Regiment 4th battery of the 13th Field Regiment	6th battery of the 7th Field Regiment 6th battery of the 13th Field Regiment 2nd battery of the 14th Field Regiment	1st battery of the 7th Field Regiment 2nd battery of the 11th Field Regiment	6th and 9th batteries of the 10th Field Regiment	3rd battery of the 15th Horse Regiment

RESERVE CORPS, General of brigade SOLEILLE, *commanding; Aide-de-camp:* Captain de Narp; *Chief of staff:* Lieutenant Colonel d'Ouvrier de Villegly

IMPERIAL GUARD INFANTRY DIVISION	1st INFANTRY DIVISION	2nd INFANTRY DIVISION
Major Ferri-Pisani-Jourdan	Major Barth	Major Roche
1st and 2nd field batteries of the Imperial Guard Regiment	3rd battery of the 10th Field Regiment 3rd battery of the 12th Field Regiment	2nd battery of the 8th Field Regiment 14th battery of the 13th Field Regiment

BATTERIES OF THE GENERAL RESERVE
Commander: General of brigade FORGEOT

1st DIVISION, Lieutenant Colonel Vernhet de Laumière   **2nd DIVISION**, Lieutenant Colonel Bertrand

1st SUBDIVISION	2nd SUBDIVSION	3rd SUBDIVISION	1st SUBDIVISION	2nd SUBDIVSION	3rd SUBDIVISION
1st battery of the 8th Field Regiment (Mountain) 10th battery of the 10th Field Regiment 10th battery of the 11th Field Regiment 4th battery *bis* of the 12th Field Regiment (rocketeers) 2nd battery of the 14th Field Regiment	4th battery of the 6th Horse Regiment 1st battery of the 17th Horse Regiment	4th battery of the 15th Horse Regiment 2nd battery of the 10th Horse Regiment	5th and 13th batteries *bis* of the 1st Foot Regiment 2nd and 13th batteries *bis* of the 13th Field Regiment	9th battery of the 11th Field Regiment 12th battery of the 10th Field Regiment	3rd and 4th batteries of the Guard Horse Regiment 7th battery *bis* and 8th battery *bis* of the Guard Foot Regiment

SIEGE PARK
Director: General of brigade MAZURE

1st Foot Regiment -	1st, 3rd, 4th, 7th, 8th, 13th, 14th, 14th *bis*, 15th and 15th *bis* - Total: 10
2nd Foot Regiment -	2nd, 3rd, 4th, 9th, 10th, 12th, 13th, 13th *bis*, 14th, 17th and 17th *bis* - In addition, the 4th battery was detached to Constantinople - Total: 12
3rd Foot Regiment -	1st, 3rd, 6th, 7th, 8th, 11th, 12th, 13th, 13th *bis*, 14th, 14th *bis* and 15th - Total: 12
4th Foot Regiment -	4th, 5th, 8th, 11th, 12th, 14th, 14th *bis* and 15th *bis* - Total: 8
5th Foot Regiment -	1st, 2nd, 3rd, 6th, 7th, 10th, 12th, 13th, 13th *bis*, 14th, 15th and 15th *bis* - Total: 12
6th Regiment(pontoniers) -	3rd, 11th and 12th companies - 5th and 9th companies of workmen - Detachments of the 2nd Armorer company

COMMANDER IN CHIEF OF ARTILLERY OF THE ARMY: General of division LEBOEUF -*Aide-de-camp:* Major MOULIN
Chief of staff: General of brigade MAZURE - *Assistant chief:* Colonel D'OUVRIER DE VILLEGLY - *Adjutant:* Major ROBINOT-MARCY
Director general of the park: General of brigade BORGELLA - *Director of the grand park:* Colonel D'AUTEVILLE - *Assistant director:* Lieutenant Colonel LIÉDOT
Adjutants: Lieutenant Colonel MAIGNE; Majors PIOCT, MARION and CAMBIER
Director of the siege train: Colonel BRAMAND-BOUCHERON - *Assistant director:* Lieutenant Colonel TELLIER - *Adjutants:* Majors DUSAERT, FAULQUIER, SURVILLE and DE GIRELS

IMPERIAL GUARD , *Commander:* General of brigade DE SEVELINGES

GRENADIER DIVISION	VOLTIGEUR DIVISION	CAVALRY DIVISION	RESERVE
Major Rolland	Major Lefrançois	3rd and 4th batteries of the Horse Regiment	4th battery of the Foot Regiment
3rd and 4th batteries of the Foot Regiment	5th and 6th batteries of the Horse Regiment		2nd mixed battery

1st CORPS, *Commander:* General of brigade FORGEOT; *Chief of staff:* Lieutenant Colonel Mitrecé

1st INFANTRY DIVISION	2nd INFANTRY DIVISION	3rd INFANTRY DIVISION	CAVALRY DIVISION	RESERVE
Major Leclerc de la Herverie	Major Vautré	12th battery of the 12th Regiment	8th battery of the 16th Regiment	*Commander:* Colonel de Veulens
6th battery of the 8th Regiment	15th battery of the 10th Regiment	9th battery of the 13th Regiment		*Adjutants:* Majors Choppin and Maillot
14th battery of the 10th Regiment	7th battery of the 11th Regiment			11th battery of the 8th Regiment
				8th battery of the 9th Regiment
				17th battery of the 5th Regiment
				Park - Director: Lieutenant Colonel de Metz
				Assistant director: Major Picot de la Peyrouse

2nd CORPS, *Commander:* General of brigade AUGER, *Chief of staff:* Colonel DE SCHALLER

1st INFANTRY DIVISION	2nd INFANTRY DIVISION	RESERVE
Major Baudoin	Major Faye	*Commander:* Lieutenant Colonel Fiéret — *Adjutants:* Majors Petitpied and Narey
12th battery of the 7th Regiment	2nd battery of the 9th Regiment	11th battery of the 10th Regiment — 14th battery of the 11th Regiment
11th battery of the 11th Regiment	13th battery of the 13th Regiment	3rd and 6th batteries of the 14th Regiment — 16th battery of the 2nd Regiment
		Park - Director: Lieutenant Colonel Renaut d'Ubexe — *Assistant director:* Major Charles

3rd CORPS, *Commander:* General of brigade COURTOIS ROUSSEL D'HURBAL, *Chief of staff:* Lieutenant Colonel Ducasse

1st INFANTRY DIVISION	2nd INFANTRY DIVISION	3rd INFANTRY DIVISION	CAVALRY DIVISION	RESERVE
Major Barbary de Langlade	Major Taillesen-Laportallière	7th battery of the 9th Regiment	6th battery of the 15th	*Commander:* Colonel Bertrand
9th battery of the 8th Regiment	7th battery of the 7th Regiment	12th battery of the 11th Regiment	Regiment	*Adjutants:* Majors Saint-Rémy and Meinadier
11th battery of the 12th Regiment	10th battery of the 8th Regiment			5th and 8th batteries of the 7th Regiment
				3rd and 7th battery of the 17th Regiment
				17th battery of the 1st Regiment
				Park - Director: Lieutenant Colonel Guichou
				Assistant director: Major Chavaudres

4th CORPS, *Commander:* General of brigade SOLEILLE, *Chief of staff:* Colonel Labastie

1st INFANTRY DIVISION	2nd INFANTRY DIVISION	3rd INFANTRY DIVISION	RESERVE
Major Vassoigne	Major Verdin-Laverdit	7th battery of the 10th Regiment	15th battery of the 12th Regiment
13th battery of the 12th Regiment	12th battery of the 8th Regiment	12th battery of the 13th Regiment	10th battery of the 13th Regiment
7th battery of the 13th Regiment	9th battery of the 9th Regiment		2nd and 5th batteries of the 15th Regiment
			18th battery of the 3rd Regiment

5th CORPS, *Commander:* General of brigade FIÉRECE

1st INFANTRY DIVISION	2nd INFANTRY DIVISION	RESERVE
13th battery of the 11th Regiment.	5th and 6th batteries of the 9th Regiment	4 batteries which seemingly never completely arrived.
5th battery of the 13th Regiment		

GENERAL RESERVE
Commander: Colonel Vernhet de Laumière - *Adjutants:* Majors Liénard, Chambeyron,
Garnier-Kericault and Grimes*(mountain artillery)* - 15 artillery batteries and 6 pontonier companies.

artillery, and the disembarked marines. In the aftermath of the assault, the cadres of 13 foot batteries were brought back to France since she was beginning to lack cadres. Nevertheless, at this point, the artillery only detached 8 batteries to Algeria and one to Rome. Finally, for the Baltic expedition, it supplied only 2 batteries: the 4th and the 14th *bis* of the 1st Regiment commanded by Lieutenant Colonel Grimaudet de Rochebouët. He was assisted by the major from Metz and by Captain Vasse Saint-Ouen.

The siege of Sebastopol was, for the artillery, as much of an opportunity for considerable expenditure of power, science, dedication, and courage as it was for the engineers—not more. Although the investment army was large and the needs of the siege enormous, total order never ceased to reign over the artillery's organization and in its works, its personnel, and its materiel. This regularity, unknown until then, was remarked upon and mentioned by all the foreign military men. It was not realized at the time although it has since been seen with the Germans in 1870. Military success is only long-lasting and decisive under the express condition that the organization of an army is solid, always well maintained, and always available in all its parts. In 1859 there were some disappointments in the Army of Italy which were more painful than in the Crimea.

All the batteries did not get back together in time. This is because, if guns and carriages are always to be found in the arsenal and the men in the reserves, horses are more difficult to procure. It takes a long time to get them suitably harnessed. Official figures for the preparation of the campaign of Italy are given above. This shows how difficult it was to organize the 16 horse batteries, the 45 field batteries, and an indeterminate number of foot batteries.

On January 1, 1859, the artillery service had at its disposal 30,989 men present and 16,486 in the reserve; total: 47,475 men. However, it only had some14,000 horses. With the best intentions in the world, the line regiments would have been able to harness up at the most a fifth of their artillery pieces. It is obvious that France was far from the achievements of Marshal Soult in 1833. First, 10,500 horses were bought. Then on April 21st, 14,000 horses were requested from the remount service. Since the reserves could not be called out conspicuously, 4,000 drivers and artillerists were requested from the cavalry and the infantry. Each of

Field artillery (1856).

the five foot regiments was to have ready to march 3 foot batteries and 6 park batteries. The seven field regiments and the four horse regiments were each to have five batteries. The Imperial Guard received 1,600 new cannoneers and 800 horses from the line. Five batteries (2 field, 2 mountain, one rocket) were called up from Algeria. On April 24th, the order to march appeared.

All together there were 61 batteries; 366 guns. The 4 pound pieces were supplied with 240 rounds; the 12 pound pieces with 190 rounds. As for the siege park, since everything had of course been sacrificed to the speedy undertaking of the campaign equipment, it had been neglected a little. It began to move into Italy on June 2nd, and on July 16th that which had not been put en route was stopped from leaving.

The entire army had been split into divisions during the campaign of Italy and formed into three groups under the command of Marshals Magnan, Castellane and Pélissier. Their headquarters were, respectively, Paris, Lyon, and Nancy. Each of the eleven infantry divisions and the seven cavalry divisions which were then set up were to receive its artillery. This measure was not seriously executed. The batteries were assigned on paper and the general staffs chosen, but in practice, many divisions never saw their artillery. Or, they saw only half of it and it was still not on a war footing. However, in the army, the artillery showed itself to be at the heights which it had attained in the Crimea. It lost one of the most distinguished officers, General of Brigade Auger, the old chief of general staff at Sebastopol. He was mortally wounded at Solferino while engaging the four divisional batteries of the 2nd Corps.

The organization of 1854 was again made worse by a new reorganization which expanded the number of regiments to 20, including that of the pontoniers. It also increased the number of foot batteries, but it left almost all the battle batteries as they were. The small increase in the foot batteries was cancelled by the crime of November 15, 1865 (Minister Randon). Randon eliminated 22 foot batteries including 2 of the Guard, 12 field batteries including 2 of the Guard, and four horse batteries of the Guard. And this was during the Danish War! However, Fould imperiously demanded it and the Mexican War imposed cut-backs. In French military history and politics, in every war or financial campaign, the cadres of the French army are seen to increase or decrease according to the caprices of events and governments. The law of the cadres was thus a necessity. However, what has been done lacks flexibility and does not anticipate carefully enough the move from a peacetime situation to a wartime footing.

Ministers have had the right through a simple decree not only to modify the allotments of batteries but worse, to diminish their numbers. Because of this, France was able to harness only 986 pieces—that is 240 less than the organization of Marshal Soult had. Meanwhile, the number of general staffs for regiments has climbed from 12 to 19 and even to 21 if the Guard is counted. Regardless of what the moralists may say, the officer's spirit is more obviously affected by these major increases in the general staffs than is the soldier's spirit by the law of exoneration. In satisfying desire by giving lots of promotions, the number of batteries is decreased. The service was disrupted to advance the leaders. Who knows what the value of the 16 horse-drawn batteries (96 pieces) eliminated by Minister Randon would have been? Who knows what would have been done if, instead of being on foot, the first four batteries of the 14 field regiments (56 batteries, 366 pieces) could have been entered into the line from the beginning of the war? We would have been able to oppose the German artillery fire with 1,418 pieces instead of 986. These figures speak out clearly. This is thus more than a criticism; it is a statement for the record.

We will pass quickly on to the expeditions of China and Mexico where the service was gloriously represented. However, before giving the composition of all the general staffs and the old and new batteries which were attached to the army corps formed during th war of 1870-1871, it must be noted that never in any period of French history have 154 batteries been instantaneously at the ready.

Mountain artillery. African dress (1846).

Artillery major commanding the batteries. Cavalry division leaders.Full dress (1887).

Artillery. Non-commissioned officers of horse batteries and cannoneers of foot batteries, full dress (1886).

Commander in chief of the artillery: General of division SOLEILLE; *Aides-de-camp:* Major SERS; Captain DUBOUAYS DE LA BEGASSIERE
Chief of staff: Colonel VASSE SAINT-OUEN; *Assistant chief:* Lieutenant Colonel DE LA HITTE
Adjutant officers: Majors COUTURIER, MAIGNIEN, HURSTEL, ABRAHAM, DE MONTDÉSIR; Captains MORLIERE, DELOGE, ANFRYE

IMPERIAL GUARD

Commander: General of brigade PE DE ARROS
Aide-de-camp: Captain Saillard
Chief of staff: Colonel Melchior
Adjutants: Captains Mercier and de Geoffre de Chabrignac

GRENADIER DIVISION
Lieutenant Colonel Gerbault; Major Veilliard
1st, 2nd and 5th batteries of the Field Regiment

VOLTIGEUR DIVISION
Lieutenant Colonel Denecey de Chevilly; Major Léveillé
3rd, 4th and 6th batteries of the Field Regiment

CAVALRY DIVISION
Major Roux de Montlebert
1st and 2nd batteries of the Horse Regiment

RESERVE
Colonel Clappier
Major de Montort - 3rd and 4th batteries of the Horse Regiment
Major Dejean - 5th and 6th batteries of the Horse Regiment

1st CORPS

Commander: General of division FORGEOT
Aide-de-camp: Major Minot
Chief of staff: Colonel Schneégans
Adjutants: Major Voisin, Captains Louis, de Lahitolle, de Mecquenem
Director of the bridges: Colonel Fiévet

1st INFANTRY DIVISION
Lieutenant Colonel Lecoeuvre; Major Quellain
6th, 7th and 8th batteries of the 9th Regiment

2nd INFANTRY DIVISION
Lieutenant Colonel Cauvet; Major de Fleurey
9th, 10th and 12th batteries of the 9th Regiment

3rd INFANTRY DIVISION
Lieutenant Colonel Chéguillaume; Major de Noue
5th, 6th and 9th batteries of the 12th Regiment

4th INFANTRY DIVISION
Lieutenant Colonel Lamandé; Major de Suter
7th, 10th and 11th batteries of the 12th Regiment

RESERVE AND PARK
Commander: General of brigade JOLY FRIGOLA
Aide-de-camp: Captain Renouf-Dubreil
Chief of staff: Lieutenant Colonel Gaillard de Blairville
Commanding the reserve: Colonel de Vassart

Lieutenant Colonel de Brives
Major Venot - 11th and 12th batteries of the 6th Regiment
Major d'Haranguier de Quincerot - 5th and 11th batteries of the 9th Regiment

Lieutenant Colonel Grouvel
Major Carmejane - 1st and 2nd batteries of the 20th Regiment
Major Thouvenin - 3rd and 4th batteries of the 20th Regiment

Director of the park: Colonel Petitpie
Assistant director: Major Bial
Adjutant: Captain Bousson
8th company of the pontoniers
Detachment of the 4th company of workmen

2nd CORPS

Commander: General of brigade GAGNEUR
Aide-de-camp: Captain d'Aumale
Chief of staff: Lieutenant Colonel de Franchessin
Adjutant: Captains Gravel and Aron

1st INFANTRY DIVISION
Lieutenant Colonel Chavaudrey; Major Rey
5th, 6th and 12th batteries of the 5th Regiment

2nd INFANTRY DIVISION
Lieutenant Colonel Maintenant; Major Collangettes
7th, 8th and 9th batteries of the 5th Regiment

3rd INFANTRY DIVISION
Lieutenant Colonel Larroque; Major Bedoin
7th, 8th and 11th batteries of the 15th Regiment

RESERVE
Commander: Lieutenant Colonel Baudouin
Major Rebillot - 10th and 11th batteries of the 5th Regiment
Major de Germay - 6th and 10th batteries of the 5th Regiment
Major Gougis - 7th and 8th batteries of the 17th Regiment
Park - Director: Colonel Brady
Assistant director: Major Welter
Adjutant: Captain Schultz
2nd company of pontoniers
Detachment of the 3rd company of workmen

3rd CORPS

Commander: General of division GRIMAUDET DE ROCHEBOUET
Aide-de-camp: Major Berge
Chief of staff: Colonel de Saint-Rémy
Adjutants: Majors Dumas, Champvallier, Abrial, Jamont; Captain Namur
Director of the bridges: Colonel Marion

1st INFANTRY DIVISION
Lieutenant Colonel Fourgous; Major Leclerc
5th, 6th and 8th batteries of the 4th Regiment

2nd INFANTRY DIVISION
Lieutenant Colonel Delange; Major Teissédre
9th, 11th and 12th batteries of the 4th Regiment

3rd INFANTRY DIVISION
Lieutenant Colonel Sempé; Major Dumont
5th, 6th and 7th batteries of the 11th Regiment

4th INFANTRY DIVISION
Lieutenant Colonel Maucourant; Major de Frescheville
8th, 9th and 10th batteries of the 11th Regiment

RESERVE AND PARK
Commander: General of brigade DE BERCKHEIM
Aide-de-camp: Captain Zurlinden
Chief of staff: Lieutenant Colonel Lanty
Commander of the reserve: Colonel de Lajaille

Lieutenant Colonel Guével
Major Dauvergne - 7th and 10th batteries of the 4th Regiment
Major Jacquot - 11th and 12th batteries of the 4th Regiment

Lieutenant Colonel Delatte
Major Latouche - 1st and 2nd batteries of the 17th Regiment
Major Bobet - 3rd and 4th batteries of the 17th Regiment

Director of the park: Colonel de Bar
Assistant director: Major de Tinseau
Adjutant: Captain Joyeux
2nd company of pontoniers
Detachment of the 3rd company of workmen

4th CORPS

Commander: General of brigade LAFFAILLE
Aide-de-camp: Colonel Héricart de Thury
Chief of staff: Lieutenant Colonel Deville
Adjutants: Captains Gillet and Cazal

1st INFANTRY DIVISION
Lieutenant Colonel de Narp; Major Pulz
5th, 9th and 12th batteries of the 15th Regiment

2nd INFANTRY DIVISION
Lieutenant Colonel Larminat; Major Vigier
5th, 6th and 7th batteries of the 1st Regiment

3rd INFANTRY DIVISION
Lieutenant Colonel Legardeur; Major Legrand
8th, 9th and 10th batteries of the 1st Regiment

RESERVE
Commander: Colonel Soleille
Major Ladrange - 11th and 12th batteries of the 5th Regiment
Major Prémer - 6th and 9th batteries of the 8th Regiment
Major Poilleux - 5th and 6th batteries of the 17th Regiment
Director: Colonel Luxer; *Assistant director:* Major Voisin
Adjutant: Captain Lestandin
8th company of pontoniers
Detachment of the 5th company of workmen

5th CORPS

Commander: General of brigade LIÉDOT
Aide-de-camp: Captain Gibouin
Chief of staff: Lieutenant Colonel Fiaux
Adjutants: Captains Condren and Jouart

1st INFANTRY DIVISION
Lieutenant Colonel Rolland; Major Perot
5th, 6th and 7th batteries of the 6th Regiment.

2nd INFANTRY DIVISION
Lieutenant Colonel Bougault; Major des Prost
5th, 7th and 8th batteries of the 2nd Regiment

3rd INFANTRY DIVISION
Lieutenant Colonel Montel; Major Normand
9th, 11th and 13th batteries of the 2nd Regiment

RESERVE AND PARK
Commander: Colonel Fénelon
Major Cailloux - 6th and 10th batteries of the 2nd Regiment
Major Duchassant - 11th battery of the 10th Regiment;
11th battery of the 14th Regiment
Major Boudot - 5th and 6th batteries of the 20th Regiment
Director of the park: Colonel Gobert
Assistant director: Major Teissier
Adjutant: Captain Laurens
5th company of pontoniers
Detachment of the 1st company of workmen

6th CORPS

Commander: General of division LABASTIE
Aide-de-camp: Captain Magon de la Villehuchet
Chief of staff: Colonel de Lapeyrouse
Adjutants: Majors Tardif de Moidrey and de Novion; Captains Julliard and Demiduid

1st INFANTRY DIVISION
Lieutenant Colonel de Monthuisant; Major Vignetti
5th, 7th and 8th batteries of the 8th Regiment

2nd INFANTRY DIVISION
Lieutenant Colonel Colcomb; Major Chaumette
10th, 11th and 12th batteries of the 8th Regiment

3rd INFANTRY DIVISION
Lieutenant Colonel Jamet; Major Bernadet
5th, 6th and 7th batteries of the 14th Regiment

4th INFANTRY DIVISION
Lieutenant Colonel Noury; Major Le Bescond de Coatpont
7th, 8th and 9th batteries of the 10th Regiment

RESERVE AND PARK
Commander: General of brigade BERTRAND
Aide-de-camp: Berthier de Grandry
Chief of staff: Lieutenant Colonel Moulin
Commander of the reserve: Colonel Desprels

Lieutenant Colonel Chappe
Major de Mussy - 5th and 6th batteries of the 10th Regiment
Major Harel - 10th and 12th batteries of the 10th Regiment

Lieutenant Colonel Maldan
Major Grévy - 8th and 9th batteries of the 14th Regiment
Major de St-Aulaire - 1st and 2nd batteries of the 14th Regiment

Director of the park: Colonel Chatillon
Assistant director: Major Coccoz
Adjutant: Captain Olivier
Detachment of the 6th company of workmen

7th CORPS

Commander: General of brigade LIEGEARD
Aide-de-camp: Captain de la Valette
Chief of staff: Lieutenant Colonel Claret de la Touche
Adjutants: Captains Caro and de Tromenec

1st INFANTRY DIVISION
Lieutenant Colonel Guillemin; Major Geynet
5th, 6th and 11th batteries of the 7th Regiment

2nd INFANTRY DIVISION
Lieutenant Colonel Clouzet; Major Morand de Caluet
8th, 9th and 12th batteries of the 7th Regiment

3rd INFANTRY DIVISION
Lieutenant Colonel Bonnin; Major Medoni
8th, 9th and 10th batteries of the 10th Regiment

RESERVE AND PARK
Commander: Colonel Aubac
Major Merlin- 7th and 10th batteries of the 7th Regiment
Major Vivier - 8th and 12th batteries of the 8th Regiment
Major Malhié - 3rd and 4th batteries of the 19th Regiment
Director of the park: Colonel Hennet (AL)
Assistant director: Major Bonnefous
Adjutant: Captain Rigourd
7th company of pontoniers
8th company of workmen

RESERVE CAVALRY DIVISIONS

1st DIVISION
Major Loyer - 5th and 6th batteries of the 19th Regiment

2nd DIVISION
Major Astier - 7th and 8th batteries of the 19th Regiment

3rd DIVISION
Major Clerc - 7th and 8th batteries of the 20th Regiment

Neither has double that figure ever been improvised in eight months. It is true France was not ready for the war, but the army was ready under the conditions authorized by the budget. It must be continuously repeated to make everyone responsible for his part in the history of the French defeat. In the aftermath of the declaration of war, the direction of the artillery, having exhausted at the first blow its available horse-drawn batteries, transformed its foot batteries into field batteries. It also formed depot cadres, batteries *bis*, and batteries *ter*, and set about providing materiel and instructors to the batteries of the *garde nationale mobile*. General Susane in Paris and, in Bordeaux and Tours, General Thoumas both displayed a patriotic intelligence beyond all praise. Susane did not long survive the groundless parliamentarian calumnies of the Duke of Audiffret-Pasquier. The generals were assisted by artillery officers whose courage and devotion went as far as firing cannon forged—God knows how—by the ever infallible civilian engineers. The first formation had used up the French cadres. Officers had to be improvised but this was done with a very prudent, methodical wisdom. Far from being a burden in the future, this allowed, when it was necessary with peace, for the reorganization of the artillery on a broader foundation without modifying the habits of the service. On the adjacent page, the composition of the artillery for the Army of the Rhine is given. It is according to an official situation report dating from August 12, 1870 and signed by Colonel Vasse Saint-Ouen, chief of general staff.

Imperial Guard artillery (1855).

GENERAL RESERVE - *Commander:* General of division CANU
Aide-de-camp: Captain PERREAU
Chief of staff: Lieutenant Colonel LAFFON DE LADEBAT
*(The adjutants during this time were taken from
the second captains of the batteries of the general reserve.)*
1st DIVISION - *Commander:* Colonel SALVADOR - *Second in command:* Lieutenant Colonel PROTCHE - 5th, 6th, 7th, 8th, 9th, 10th, 11th and 12th field batteries (of 12lbers) of the 13th Regiment
2nd DIVISION - *Commander:* Colonel TOUSSAINT - *Second in command:* Lieutenant Colonel DESSAUDRAIS - 1st, 2nd, 3rd, 4th, 5th, 6th, 7th and 8th horse batteries (of 4lbers) of the 18th Regiment
PARK - *Director:* Colonel HENNET (P) - *Assistant Director:* Major CAVALIER - *Adjutant:* Captain MATHIEU (JJA)
GRAND CAMPAIGN PARK - *Director general of the park:* General of brigade DE MITRECÉ
Aide-de-camp: Captain MORVAN - *Chief of staff:* Lieutenant Colonel DE ROLLEPOT
Director of the grand park: Colonel FABRE
Assistant director: Lieutenant Colonel LUCET
Adjutants: Majors AUBERT and PORTES; Captains BOUCHARD, LEFEBVRE (SBV), GRAS and LUSSON
Reserve bridge train - 1st section of train: Major CARRE
2nd section of train: Major BERGÉRE
Inspecter of the artillery train: Major BRUYANT

For the first time, the infantry divisions had three batteries: two of 4 pound and one of *mitrailleuse*. The 154 batteries were divided up in the following manner: 22 of 12 caliber; 106 of 4 caliber; and 26 of *mitrailleuses*.

The batteries indicated below did not meet with the same fate as the corps to which they were attached. However, almost all of them were made prisoners, either at Sedan or at Metz.

The batteries of the 12th Corps met the same fate.

12th Corps. Commander; General D'Ouvrier de Villegly; Chief of General Staff: Colonel de Lapeyrouse

1st Division. Lieutenant Colonel Rollepot; Major Charron. 3rd and 4th Batteries of the 15th Regiment. 4th Battery of the 4th Regiment.

2nd Division. Lieutenant Colonel Colcomb; Major Jannisson. 4th Battery of the 7th Regiment. 3rd and 4th Batteries of the 11th Regiment.

The 3rd Division composed of naval infantry was to receive batteries from the same department. Since they did not arrive in time, it was given batteries from the 6th Corps which were not able to return to Metz. Moreover, the 12th Corps only received the 3rd and 4th Batteries of the 8th Regiment for its reserve. All the other batteries had belonged to the 6th Corps.

Those which were assigned to the 13th and 14th Corps will be seen again in the Army of Paris, particularly in the 2nd Army which was commanded by General Ducrot. They were all either old foot batteries transformed into field batteries or newly formed batteries. During the siege of Paris, the 21st and the 22nd Regiments were created. According to General Susane, there were also sixty-six batteries of personnel in Paris at the time. The naval artillery had brought along a large supporting force: sixteen batteries and a considerable number of officers of all ranks. Finally, there were fifteen batteries of the *mobile*.

General Ducrot maintained that there were ninety-three batteries of personnel just for the land forces. General Susane's figures are more believable. In any case, in addition to the campaign pieces, these batteries were to serve the 805 pieces of the perimeter wall bastions and the 1,389 pieces of the forts and the advanced posts.

For auxiliary troops, the land artillery had available to it four companies from the 1st Regiment of the artillery train and four companies from the 2nd Regiment, the 2nd Company of artificers, and the 4th, 6th, and 9th Companies of workmen. The bridge service was provided by the 5th and 10th Companies of the pontoniers regiment. In addition, the *garde nationale mobile* of the Rhône had sent two companies of pontoniers to Paris. The Navy had supplied a section of sixty elite, top-notch sailors under the command of Ensign Versnheider who was killed on November 30th at Bry-sur-Marne.

It has not been possible to reconstruct the general staff for the siege artillery of Paris. It can only be said that the commanding

Field artillery (1870-1871).

officer of the service at General Trochu's general staff was General of Division Guiod.

Thanks to the greater influence which General Ducrot had over Trochu since they had been service comrades together, Ducrot made life difficult for General Guiod. Guiod was an excellent administrator, full of dedication and ready to perform any task. He armed as many campaign batteries as he could. Ducrot made off with everything he could get his hands on. He never had enough, always wanting more. More than once, the governor had to remind him to act moderately. Meanwhile, the 2nd Army—commanded by Ducrot—was the only one which had horse-drawn cannon in Paris. The artillery defense plan for the battles of the Marne proved this artillery to be excessive. It is shown below in all its eloquence.

This well harnessed artillery formed a total of 47 batteries - sixteen of

---

Commander: General of division FRÉBAULT (Navy); *Chief of staff:* Colonel VILLIERS; *Assistant chief:* Lieutenant Colonel DE COSSIGNY

1st ARMY CORPS
Commander: General of brigade D'UBEXI
Chief of staff: Lieutenant Colonel LUCAS

1st Division: Major BRIENS - Naval artillery, 1st battery (4), Révillon; 2nd battery (4), Bernard; 12th battery (M), Chaule.
2nd Division ; Detached to the army of General Vinoy without any campaign pieces.
3rd Division: Major MAGDELAINE - 3rd of the 9th (4), Lourdel-Henaut; 4th of the 13th (4), Party; 3rd of the 13th (M), Torterue de Sasilly.
Reserve: Colonel HENNET
    1st Division: Major GUIZE - 3rd of the 6th (12), Paret; 4th of the 6th (12), Salle; 16th of the 8th (12), Jacob.
    2nd Division: Major DORAT - 4th of the 12th (12), Salin; 16th of the 9th (12), Michel; 15th, Naval (12), Caris.

2nd ARMY CORPS
Commander: General of brigade BOISSONNET
Chief of staff: Lieutenant Colonel VIGUIER

1st Division: Major MATHIEU - 7th of the 21st (4), Deschamps; 8th of the 21st (4), Jenny; 17th of the 4th (M), Perrault.
2nd Division: Major LADVOCAT - 9th of the 21st (4), Simon; 5th of the 22nd (4), Lapague; 17th of the 21st (M), Trémoulet.
3rd Division: Major DE GRANDCHAMP - 10th of the 21st (4), Nismes; 4th of the 22nd (4), Courtois; 3rd of the 21st (M), Mahieu.
Reserve: Colonel MINOT
    1st Division: Major DETHOREY - 4th of the 21st (12), Buloz; 15th of the 10th (12), Fly Sainte-Marie.
    2nd Division: Major WARNESSON - 8th of the 3rd (12), Moreau; 5th of the 21st (12), De Chalain; 16th of the 14th (12), Solier.

3rd ARMY CORPS
Commander: General of division PRINCETEAU
Chief of staff: Lieutenant Colonel GRÉVY

1st Division: Major TARDIF DE MOIDREY - 16th of the 2nd (4), Malfroy; 16th of the 10th (4), Dardenne; 15th of the 11th (M), Malar.
2nd Division: Major LEFRANÇOIS - 3rd of the 10th (4), Eon Duva; 4th of the 10th (4), Duchateau; 3rd of the 11th (M), Clavel.
Reserve: Lieutenant Colonel DELCROS
    1st Division: Major DAVID - 12th of the 3rd (12), Larquet; 18th of the 3rd (12), Lesage; 3rd of the 22nd (12), Mignon.
    2nd Division: Major FONCIN - 17th of the 10th (12), Godinot; 2nd of the 7th (12), Vaucheret; 20th of the 11th (4), Millescamps.

GENERAL RESERVE
Lieutenant Colonel LUCET

1st Division: Major LEFÉBURE - 3rd of the 14th (8), Gros; 4th of the 14th (8), Malherbe; 6th of the 22nd (8), Bajan; 7th of the 22nd (8), Froment.
2nd Division: Major BABINET - 11th Naval (12), Geoffroy; 8th of the 22nd (12), Delagréverie; 10th of the 22nd (12), Fabre.
3rd Division: - 15th of the 7th (12), Brasilier; 16th of the 15th (12), de Donato; 16th of the 7th (4), André.

4 pound, twenty of 2 pound, four of 8 pound, and seven of *mitrailleuses*: that is in total 282 pieces well supplied with munitions.

The work of the artillery's central administration in the provinces was much greater than in Paris. Cannon had to be provided to twelve army corps and to four groups of troops moving independently. The materiel remaining in the arsenals supplied 4 pound pieces and 12 pound pieces. Then the Armstrong cannon appeared along with a mass of unusual pieces bought by the State, the departments and even by the municipalities. However, it may be said that the purchases made abroad arrived late. At Bordeaux, cannon, carriages, materiel, and munitions were seen being landed every day while the National Assembly was in session there. In Paris, the artillery had a chance to try out only a few models of the 7 pound pieces manufactured by the civilian engineers before almost all of them fell into the hands of the Commune. Cast and manufactured with the contributions of the rich bourgeois of the capital, they served the radical demands of the proletariat. On the other hand, the second siege of Paris was performed with old materiel which filled the French arsenals.

The great effort of the Tours and Bordeaux administrations consisted particularly in rapidly organizing personnel and in throwing together materiel. In the lists to follow, the same name sometimes recurs in two different corps. Today's chief of general staff became tomorrow's departmental head. This was disastrous. No matter how unified or solid it may be, a corps of officers cannot be indefinitely stretched without reaching a breaking point. Worse yet, the last corps formed had been made up of the remains of the first corps which was worn out, exhausted, and broken in a disastrous campaign led by people whose least fault was to never assess the capabilities of a soldier. Their strength was to exaggerate appearances. Yet everything they did deserves the country's acknowledgement. Nobly and simply told, France's resistance to the invaders would be enough to justify the pride of those who directed it. However, although these men were capable of simplicity, it is likely that they would not have been understood by men with wild opinions whose imaginations they wanted more than anything else to inflame. If they had been more simple, it is certain that they could have better used the resources which they spent and which the country lavished on them with commendable and patriotic steadfastness.

It is rather astonishing that no military man from the artillery has yet seriously studied the artillery works during the War of 1870-71. The industriousness displayed by a beaten and conquered army which has been stripped of its regular resources by a series of rapid disasters often serves as a better learning example than the glory of an army victoriously using vast resources which it has found through the financial foresight of its country. It is all well and good to come to speak about one's patriotic fears like Jules Favre or of one's campaign plans like the engineer de Freycinet. However, fears and plans are equal in value whereas Generals Susane and Thoumas might have been able to use the cannon that they had ready for battle. This would have been better.

The various organizations of the provinces are summarized below.

15th CORPS -	*Commander:* General of brigade DE BLOIS DE LA CALANDE. *Chief of staff:* Colonel Gobert - 1st INFANTRY DIVISION: Major Massenet (1st battery of the 13th Regiment, 18th battery of the 6th Regiment, 18th battery of the 2nd Regiment) - 2nd INFANTRY DIVISION: Major Tricoche (1 battery of the 9th Regiment, 1 battery of the 12th Regiment, 14th mixed battery of the Guard field regiment) - 3rd INFANTRY DIVISION:Major Poizat (18th battery of the 14th Regiment, 18th battery of the 7th Regiment, 18th battery of the 10th Regiment) - RESERVE. *Commander:* Colonel Chappe (13th, 14th, 15th, 16th batteries of the 3rd Regiment, 19th battery of the 2nd Regiment, 11th battery of the 6th Regiment, 14th battery of the 18th Regiment, 14th battery of the 19th Regiment) - PARK. *Director:* Colonel Hugon. *Assistant director:* Major Galle.
16th CORPS -	*Commander:* Colonel Robinot-Marcy. *Chief of staff:* Lieutenant Colonel Sutter - 1st INFANTRY DIVISION: Major Rabatel (19th battery of the 7th Regiment, 18th battery of the 8th Regiment, 19th battery of the 10th Regiment) - 2nd INFANTRY DIVISION: Major de Noue (19th battery of the 9th Regiment, 5th battery of the 12th Regiment, 6th battery of the 12th Regiment) - 3rd INFANTRY DIVISION: Major Lahaye (19th battery of the 13th Regiment, 19th battery of the 14th Regiment, 20th battery of the 14th Regiment) - RESERVE. *Commander:* Lieutenant Colonel Carré - Mixed batteries: 2nd battery of the 7th Artillery and the 8th company of the 1st Regiment of the train, 14th battery of the 7th Artillery Regiment and 8th company *ter* of the 1st regiment of the train, 12th battery of the 16th Artillery Regiment and 12th company of the 1st regiment of the train, 17th battery of the 16th Artillery Regiment and 12th company *ter* of the 1st regiment of the train, 15th battery of the 18th Regiment, 6th and 7th batteries of the 20th Regiment. PARK. *Director:* Lieutenant Colonel Astruc.
17th CORPS -	*Commander:* Colonel Barbary de Langlade. *Chief of staff:* Lieutenant Colonel Gresset - 1st INFANTRY DIVISION: Major Chanel (19th battery of the 6th Regiment, 19th battery of the 8th Regiment, 19th battery of the 15th Regiment) - 2nd INFANTRY DIVISION: Major Alips (of the artillery train) - Mixed batteries: 13th battery of the 13th Regiment and the 17th company of the 2nd regiment of the artillery train, 14th battery of the 13th Regiment and the 17th company *bis* of the 2nd regiment of the artillery train, 20th battery of the 9th Regiment - 3rd INFANTRY DIVISION:Major Serron (20th battery of the 8th Regiment, 20th battery of the 10th Regiment, 21st battery of the 14th Regiment) - RESERVE. *Commander:* Lieutenant Colonel Smet (of the naval artillery) - Mixed batteries: Naval artillery and the 10th company *bis* of the 1st regiment of the train. Naval artillery and the 18th company *bis* of the 1st regiment of the train, 1st battery *bis* of the naval artillery, and a detachment of 1st regiment of the train, 15th and 16th batteries of the 18th Artillery Regiment - PARK. *Director:* Major Rabot.
18th CORPS -	*Commander:* Colonel Charles. *Chief of staff:* Lieutenant Colonel d'Artiguelongue - 1st INFANTRY DIVISION: Major Alips (of the artillery train) - Mixed batteries: 13th battery of the 13th Regiment and 17th company of the 2nd regiment of the artillery train, 14th battery of the 13th Regiment and 17th company *bis* of the 2nd regiment of the artillery train, 20th battery of the 9th Regiment - 2nd INFANTRY DIVISION: Major Blehaut (21st battery of the 9th Regiment, 22nd battery of the 13th Regiment) - 3rd INFANTRY DIVISION: Major Dolisie (1 battery of the 8th Regiment, 1 battery of the 10th Regiment, 1 battery of the 14th Regiment) - RESERVE: *Commander:* Lieutenant Colonel de Miribel (of the auxiliary arm) - Mixed batteries: Naval and the 18th company of the 2nd regiment of the artillery train, naval and the 18th company *bis* of the 2nd regiment of the artillery train, *Garde National Mobile* (Isére) and the 19th company of the 2nd regiment of the train, mobile and the 19th company of the 2nd regiment of the artillery train, *mobile* and 19th company *bis* of the 2nd Regiment of the artillery train, 16th and 17th batteries of the 19th Regiment, 21st battery of the 7th Regiment - PARK. *Director:* Major Delherbe.
19th CORPS -	*Commander:* Naval Captain Schvérer. *Chief of staff:* Lieutenant Colonel Poizat - 1st INFANTRY DIVISION: Major Faure-Durif (2 batteries of 4, 25th battery of the 2nd Regiment, 1 mountain battery) - 2nd INFANTRY DIVISION: Major Schuller (25th battery of the 10th Regiment, 23rd battery of the 13th Regiment, 1 mountain battery) - 3rd INFANTRY DIVISION: Major Wartelle (4 Armstrong cannon, 2-12lber cannon, 8 mountain cannon, 1-4lber battery) - RESERVE. *Commander:* Lieutenant Colonel Grille (3-12lber batteries, 1-4lber horse battery, 2 *mitrailleuse* batteries) - PARK. Captain Faure. Detachments of the artillery train.
20th CORPS -	*Commander:* Colonel Chatillon. *Chief of staff:* Colonel Dauvergne - 1st INFANTRY DIVISION: Major Paris (13th and 14th batteries of the 3rd Regiment (4) - 2nd INFANTRY DIVISION: Major Magalon (19th battery of the 12th Regiment (4), 21st battery of the 6th Regiment (4) - 3rd INFANTRY DIVISION: Major Crépey (23rd battery of the 2nd Regiment (4), 18th battery of the 14th Regiment (4) - RESERVE. *Commander:* Major Delahaye (14th battery of the 10th Regiment (12), 14th battery of the 8th Regiment (12), 23rd battery of the 6th Regiment (12), 21st battery of the 7th Regiment (12).
21st CORPS -	*Commander:* Colonel Suter. *Chief of staff:* Lieutenant Colonel Portes - 1st INFANTRY DIVISION: Major Chauvet (25th battery and the 25th battery *bis* of the naval artillery. 2-12lber pieces of the Maine-et-Loire *garde mobile*) - 2nd INFANTRY DIVISION: Major de Vauguyon of the *mobile* of Ille-et-Vilaine (22nd battery of the 2nd Regiment, 25th naval battery, 2-12lber. pieces from Maine-et-Loire) - 3rd INFANTRY DIVISION: Major de Magallon (21st battery of the 10th Regiment, 21st battery of the 12th Regiment, 2-12lber pieces of the Maine-et-Loire) - 4th INFANTRY DIVISION: Bretagne Corps (1 12lber battery, 14 mountain pieces, 5 American *mitrailleuses*) - RESERVE. Two batteries of 12lbers from Ille-et-Vilaine, 20th battery (*mitrailleuses*) of the 6th Regiment, foot battery of the Maine-et-Loire.

The 22nd and 23rd Corps formed the Army of the North under the command of General of Division Faidherbe who had replaced Bourbaki. Its artillery was commanded by Colonel Charon who had Major Bodin as his chief of general staff. Unfortunately, the history of the Army of the North has been very sparingly written about and always with more concern about exploiting it than about showing it precisely. It is impossible to give the distribution of the artillery in the various divisions of its two corps. All that can be said about it is that Colonel Charon demonstrated a great deal of activity and industry and raised fifteen batteries:

3rd principal Battery and 3rd Battery *bis* of the 12th Regiment - 1st Battery *bis*; 2nd principal Battery; 2nd *ter*; 3rd *bis*; 3rd *ter*; and 4th *bis* of the 15th Regiment. 1st and 2nd Mixed Naval Batteries. A battery of *mobiles* from Pas-de-Calais. Two mountain batteries of

mobiles from the Lower Seine. A battery of *mobilisés* from the Somme. A mountain battery of *mobilisés* from the Somme. Only the artillery of the 22nd Corps seemed to have been strongly organized. It was placed under the direct command of Colonel Charon, having Commander Pigouche for an adjoint. Commander Chatou was attached to the 23rd Corps.

24th CORPS	*Commander:* Colonel Wartelle, later Lieutenant Colonel Bezard - 1st INFANTRY DIVISION: Major Maillard (1st battery *bis* of the 9th Regiment (4), 3rd battery of the *Garde National Mobile* of Doubs (4) - 2nd INFANTRY DIVISION: Major Alix (10th battery of the 3rd Regiment (4), 22nd battery of the 6th Regiment(4), 3rd battery of the 3rd Regiment (4) - 3rd INFANTRY DIVISION: Major Zickel (4th and 7th batteries of the 3rd Regiment (4), 23rd battery of the 8th Regiment (4) - RESERVE. *Commander:* Major Clarinval (24th battery of the 9th Regiment (12), 25th battery of the 14th Regiment (12), 19th battery of the 19th Regiment (4), 24th battery of the 12th Regiment (12). 24th battery of the 13th Regiment (12), 2nd battery of the 13th Regiment (4).
25th CORPS	*Commander:* Colonel Chappe. *Chief of staff:* Major Zurlinden - General Pourcet, who wrote the history of the 25th Corps which he had commanded allows one to determine that although the batteries which were assigned to him arrived at their destination, the corps was never solidly organized. Majors Peyrac and Demay commanded the artillery in the first two infantry divisions. The commander of artillery of the 3rd division was not designated. The reserve was commanded by Major Vidal and the park was under the direction of Commandant Rovel. The numbers of the 16 batteries attached to the 25th Corps are given as follows: 4lber field batteries (26th battery of the 2nd Regiment, 24th battery of the 6th Regiment, 25th and 26th batteries of the 9th Regiment, 24th battery of the 10th Regiment, 26th battery of the 12th Regiment, 26th battery of the 13th Regiment, 27th battery of the 14th Regiment, 25th battery of the 15th Regiment) - 12lber batteries (26th battery of the 14th Regiment, 20th and 21st batteries of the 19th Regiment) - Horse batteries (20th battery of the 18th Regiment, 22nd battery of the 19th Regiment) - *Mitrailleuse* (1st and 2nd batteries of the *Garde Mobile* of the Basses-Pyrénèes.
26th CORPS	*Commander:* Colonel d'Artiguelongue. *Chief of staff:* Lieutenant Colonel Pion - 1st INFANTRY DIVISION: Major Wilmet (28th battery of the 14th Regiment, 27th battery of the 13th Regiment, 1 battery of the *Mobiles* of la Charente (mitrailleuse) - 2nd INFANTRY DIVISION: Major Gardot (27th battery of the 7th Regiment, 26th battery of the 15th Regiment, 1 battery of the Mobiles of the Vendée (*mitrailleuse*) - 3rd INFANTRY DIVISION: Major Lebas (29th battery of the 14th Regiment, 28th battery of the 13th Regiment, 28th battery of the 2nd Regiment (*mitrailleuse*). RESERVE. *Commander:* Lieutenant Colonel Avril (27th battery of the 9th Regiment, 27th battery of the 12th Regiment, 21st battery of the 18th Regiment, 22nd battery of the 18th Regiment (*mitrailleuse*). NOTE. The first two batteries of the three divisions had 4lber pieces and the three batteries of the reserve had 7lber pieces.
TOURS MOBILE COLUMN	*Commander:* — - 23rd battery of the 7th Regiment, 22nd battery of the 8th Regiment, 23rd battery of the 10th Regiment, 21st battery of the 15th Regiment, 17th battery of the 18th Regiment.
LE HAVRE MOBILE COLUMN	*Commander:* Lieutenant Colonel Carré - 1st INFANTRY DIVISION: Major Sauvé (2nd battery of the 10th Regiment (4), 22nd battery of the 10th Regiment (4), battery of the *Mobile* of Calvados (4), battery of volunteers (Gatling guns) - 2nd INFANTRY DIVISION: Major Romieux (31st naval artillery battery (12 and 4), 26th battery of the 8th Regiment (4), 2nd battery of the Mobiles of Basses-Pyrénées (4), 2nd battery of the Mobiles of Charente-Inférieure (*mitrailleuse*) - RESERVE. *Commander:* Captain Croizier (2nd battery *ter* of the 10th Regiment (12 and 6), 1st battery of the *Mobile* of Charente-Inférieure (*mitrailleuse*), 29th battery of the 13th Regiment (7), Rouen battery (12), Le Havre battery (7).
VOSGES ARMY CORPS	*Commander:* Ollivier, Auxiliary Lieutenant Colonel - The Garibaldi army was a revolutionary force, therefore nothing ordinary was done by it. The artillery did not seem to be regularly formed into divisions. However, it had at its disposal a considerable number of pieces. - Army batteries: 25th battery of the 2nd Regiment (12), 27th battery of the 2nd Regiment (4), 1st battery of the 9th Regiment (4), 2nd battery of the 12th Regiment (4), 1st battery of the 14th Regiment (4), 1st battery of the 1st Regiment hauled by the artillery train (4) - *Garde Mobile* batteries: Major Dyon (2nd and 3rd 4lber. batteries of the Charente-Inférieure) - Major Duban (1st and 2nd batteries of the Bouches-du-Rhône, 5th foot battery of the Bouches-du-Rhône) - *Mobiles:* 1st foot battery of the Maine-et-Loire. - Volunteers: 1st battery (*mitrailleuse*).
CREMER DIVISION	*Commander:* Camps, Auxiliary Major - 1st and 2nd mountain batteries of the 3rd Regiment, 22nd battery of the 9th Regiment, 23rd battery of the 12th Regiment, army Armstrong cannon battery.

If a historical section of the War Depot had written a complete, official history of the campaign of 1870-1871 as one minister of war had decided, then it would be possible to determine exactly the considerable effort under discussion without forgetting to praise them. It is probable that after intelligent examination of serious statistics, more praise would be in order. However, when one has been conquered, one must be modest even when honor is safe, even when the task has almost been completed. At the same time, a very useful lesson would result from the compilation of all the official details which another minister has prevented from being collected and published. It would seem to be necessary to require more men and cannon than our conquerers the Germans had to achieve such poor results.

Field artillery (1860-1870).

In the history of the infantry, an overall number was given for the armed men raised by France from the beginning of the war until peace. The harnessed batteries for the 23 army corps (including the Imperial Guard - territorial corps; 8 to 11 - removed) and for the various *mobile* groups have just been listed. By adding the batteries employed in besieged places, or rather, places not divided into brigades, it is possible to demonstrate through figures that France has tripled and probably even quadrupled its artillery forces. This is a demonstration of undeniable value. Consequently, the system of strong territorial reserves which can bring efficent help on the day of a mobilization to the standing army and permit it to raise the maximum troops for its batteries is the only reasonable system. However, the reserves must be trained. One hundred thousand artillerists cannot be improvised, and in the French artillery, as will be seen, at least one hundred thousand men are necessary.

Field artillery (1840).

Immediately after the war, the rather rapid rebuilding of the service took place on the basis of 38 regiments of artillery and 2 of pontoniers.(1)

Assembled two by two, the artillery regiments form 19 brigades assigned to the 18 army corps of the interior and to the 19th Army Corps (Algeria). The first regiment of each brigade, called the divisional regiment, supplies eight field batteries of 80 mm. for the two infantry divisions. The second regiment called the corps regiment, comprises the reserve of the corps. It is composed of eight batteries of which 6 are field at 90 mm. and two are horse at 80 mm. In addition, each regiment has four field batteries (divisional regiment) and two field and one horse (corps regiment). These batteries can satisfy the various needs of the armies. Under the ministry of General Thibaudin, the elimination of other batteries and of fifty-seven companies of the artillery train, harnessed by threes to each artillery brigade, has allowed the formation of sixteen foot artillery battalions called fortress artillery. However, a new reorganization is already being talked about which cannot be studied in this work for lack of space. What is certain about the actual state of affairs

(1) The pontoniers are a modern, even a revolutionary development. Like the horse artillery, they date from the great French Revolution. At that time, a city was taken in order to have a bridge. This took a long time. Since extremely elementary means of hauling cannon were used and the art of supply was completely unknown, a general was never advised to have a bridge train follow him. The Republican generals were quicker and more enterprising. They quickly renounced the long sieges which resulted in a crossing only after efforts sufficent to win three full-scale battles. Moreover, the crossing of rivers by ford or in boats was a delicate, uncertain operation. The Rhine—that river whose possession has been more disputed than all the empires combined—was of course the cradle of the school of pontoniers. In 1792, Biron formed the corporation of watermen into a military company on his own private initiative. The city of Strasbourg maintained them for the service of the pontoon bridges of Kehl. With three other companies raised in Alsace, they formed a battalion which elected for its leader the citizen Darbellet. After the French entered Mayence, Custine formed another battalion with the boatmen from the corporation of that city. It had Frederic Hoffel for its leader and took the name of "battalion of pontoniers and sailors of the Rhine." After the capitulation of Mayence, the two battalions found themselves in fact combined under the name of "French Revolutionary pontoniers and sailors." They petitioned for their legal union and also for a permanent organization which gave them the right to pay and to military allowances and supplies. General Susane recalls that this regularization was not easily achieved. Darbellet and Hoffel were *sans-culottes* not easy to handle. However, the commander of artillery, Dedou the elder, got them under control. He took command of the battalion on June 12, 1795. His successors were: Bouchu, October 11, 1801; Dessalles, October 16, 1805; Peyerimhoff, July 1810; Baillot, April 21, 1813; and Nacquart, August 1, 1814.

A new second battalion was formed for the Army of Sambre-et-Meuse with troops taken from private boatmen companies. It was comprised of eight companies on February 19, 1797 and was recognized by the law of September 9, 1799. For leaders it had: Tirlet, February 19, 1791; Dardenne, March 14, 1800; Ponge, October 10, 1801; and Chappuis, October 21, 1801.

These two battalions would have been enough to satisfy the needs of the armies of the Republic and the Empire. This was despite the fact that workmen from the navy, the Guard marines, and auxiliary companies had been added to them, and a train had been organized in the Guard. It can be said that these were soldiers of a special breed. In their patience, discipline and bravery, they even outshone the oldest bands of the Imperial Guard.

A third battalion was formed on April 18, 1813 at Mayence under the command of Leclerc. It only had a brief existence and was very quickly dispersed by French reverses. In 1814, the three line battalions and the pontoniers' train of the Guard were turned into one corps of ten companies under the command of Lieutenant Colonel Nacquart. The first five companies appeared at Waterloo.

After the mustering out of 1815, the corps was reorganized in 1816 at six companies. The organization of 1820 expanded the number of companies to twelve and that of 1807 to fourteen. The battalion "pontoniers artillery regiment" (No. 15 of the service in 1840, No. 6 in 1854, No. 16 in 1867) then was garrisoned at Strasbourg, except for a brief appeareance at Auxonne in 1850. It had successively for leaders: Nacquart, January 1, 1816; Préau, July 5, 1818; Etchegoyen, July 5, 1821; Leclerc, July 19, 1823; Admyrault, July 5, 1831; Drieu, November 27, 1836; Lami, June 16, 1846; Hervé, June 13, 1847; Bohn, October 13, 1849; Pradal, March 6, 1854; Mathieu, April 14, 1855; Lefrançois, July 18, 1855; Baron de Berckheim, October 14, 1859; Fiévet, January 10, 1863; Marion, April 20, 1871; and de Rollepot, July 14, 1874. The law on the reorganization of the cadres assigned two regiments to the pontoniers service. They each have fourteen companies. The first is quartered at Avignon. It has the Rhône for its training area. The second is at Angers where the Loire serves for its exercises.

The engineers are responsible for the repair of fixed bridges and for the creation of bridges, using resources taken from the countryside. The artillery is the manager, guardian and the major handler of the military pontoon bridges. The centuries-old argument between the engineers and the artillery will be solved if the reorganization presented by General Boulanger is adopted by the Chambers.

In the past, the infantry was in charge of everything which was not cavalry. The infantry had the artillery, since the artillery had a number in the foot regiments' roll. It supplied officers to the engineers. Vauban was an old *mestre de camp* of the infantry. This was simple and well understood. However, war, which is an art for the general in chief, a science for the officers, and a profession for the soldiers, has made so much progress and has increased and expanded so much in detail that the principal has become the accessory. The infantry which delivers battle and the cavalry which prepares and completes it have become in some sense secondary as branch services in the eyes of many people. Who thinks of complaining about this? It is certainly not the infantry which spills its blood in the fields of battle in ratios of 75 to 1. It is certainly not the officers of the special services who move into the infantry and the cavalry, pushed by their instinct for battle and by ambition. However, the question of rivalry between the engineers and the artillery with respect to the pontoniers is a problem of the first order subject to too much discussion. General Boulanger has not considered that, although he wanted to scatter the pontonier companies throughout the 18 army corps, he would have to keep them together for their training on the Loire, the Saône and the Rhône. It is impossible to form skilled pontoniers in the Tuileries fountain. What good does it do to separate them for administrative purposes from now on? Let us recall the flags of the two new pontonier regiments which have for their mutual inscription: Crossing of the Rhine, 1795. Crossing of the Adige, 1801. Crossing of the Danube, 1809. Crossing of the Berezina, 1812. It can be said that of all the pontoniers' feats of arms—and the crossing of the Limath on September 25, 1799 has not been inscribed on their flags—the most extraordinary one was unquestionably the construction of the bridges of the Berezina. General Éblé's pontoniers under the command of Chappuis saved the army there and acquired a renown which should save them from dispersal if the present has any respect for the great events of the past. Like the retreat of the ten thousand, the construction of the bridges of the Berezina has the principal actor in the drama for its historian. Like the *Anabase*, the story by Chappuis and his friend Chapelle is a masterpiece of style, narration, and simplicity. In 1812, Chapelle was an artillery colonel and chief of general staff for General Éblé. Chappuis was the leader of the 2nd Battalion of Pontoniers. Retired to Versailles in 1844, they have combined their memoirs and have had them printed at Dufaure, 21 rue de la Paroisse. Loredan-Larchey, son of a general of division of the artillery, found a copy of it, probably in his father's library. He republished it almost entirely in his *Library of Memoirs from the 19th Century*. General Susane took from it those excerpts which he gave in his *History of the French Artillery*. This small work deserves to be republished and to take its place amongst the army classics.

The bridge trains had been destroyed on November 20th at Orcha six days before the crossing of the Berezina. General Chasseloup-Laubat, chief of engineers of the Grande Armée, was in the impossible situation of overcoming the unforeseen and constructing a bridge with his resources and those of the countryside. General Éblé supplied everything. He had seven companies of pontoniers eight hundred men strong with him who had all kept their muskets. This was an unusual display of discipline which shows what the morale of the men was. His materiel consisted of: 1. six caissons containing the workmen's tools made of wood and iron, clamps, nails, hachets, pick axes and iron; 2. two campaign forges; 3. two wagons of coal. This indispensible and very restricted materiel had been kept and guarded by the pontoniers. Since Smolensk, each one carried a tool, fifteen big nails, and some clamps which they all faithfully deposited at the chosen place to make the preparations for the crossing. It was agreed that three trestle bridges would be built above Borisow of which two would be executed by the artillery and one by the engineers. However, General Chasseloup-Laubat could not uphold his end of the bargain. The three bridges were made by the artillery who accepted and used the work of the sappers. The price paid in pain and sacrifice is well-known. The bridges gave way and were repaired. The army passed over and the pontoniers withdrew last after having put the bridges out of service so that the Russians could not use them.

Almost all those brave men had plunged naked into the water of the Berezina which swept along ice floes. Few survived Éblé who had roused them with his example, working with them in water up to his armpits. He died on December 30th at Koenigsberg after having saved the army. The Emperor would name him first inspector general of the artillery, replacing de Lariboisière who also died from exhaustion some days earlier.

The type of pontonier from the Berezina so well portrayed by Balzac in *The Campaign Doctor* lived on in all his purity in Strasbourg until 1870. The regiment occupied this town for almost forty-five years. These robust Alsatians, sons of the Rhine which to a certain extent they considered as their domain, were succeeded by the pontoniers of Angers and Avignon. If the regimental roll is skimmed for officers of the old and new regiments, the most famous and learned names of the service are recognized as having passed through the pontoniers. At one time, officers coming out of the polytechnic school considered it a disgrace if they were sent to this corps. They soon realized their mistake. They then thought that the best way to prove the pontoon bridges belonged to the artillery was to have all the good artillerists also be good pontoniers.

is that the new French artillery pieces are perfect. In the event of war, each army corps will have sixteen batteries, that is ninety-six harnessed pieces. This leaves one hundred and twenty-three horse-drawn batteries for other purposes. Thus there is a total of 2,508 horse-drawn batteries. An army of one million soldiers would thus have approximately four cannon per thousand men. It is a proportion never before desired nor even anticipated. In addition, the territorial army possesses its own artillery.

In Algeria and Tunisia, the service is supplied by the detachment of batteries *bis*. The expedition of Tunisia required the dispatch of a number of batteries which, as in Tonkin, did not seem to have been the occasion for the formation of a command and a regular general staff. Its composition is given below right since it presents a totally new character.

The batteries no longer have a second captain, but they each have three lieutenants or second lieutenants. In the system for war mobilization, the second captains occupy the functions of *officiers d'ordonnance* and of adjoints to the army general staffs and the special general staffs. The third officer, the section leader, is provided by the cadres of reserve lieutenants and second lieutenants. On the first day of mobilization, this organization may not be perfect since an artillery officer must arrive on the battlefield complete with qualifications. However, it is impossible to hope for better than this. It is even necessary that it be decided in times of peace, organically to give only three officers to each battery. This will break with all tradition. However, the French are not at the end of the reforms agreed to be carried out if, as is dreamed, the infantry is to be given a proportionate share of artil-

EXPEDITIONARY CORPS OF TONKIN

When the naval artillery is discussed, the composition of the batteries of this corps during the first phase of the expedition will be given. The following situation report is for the land artillery at the time when General of division Roussel de Courcy took over command in chief of the expeditionary corps.

Commander in chief of the artillery: General of brigade JAMONT
Aide-de-camp: BOUCHER DE MORLAINCOURT - *Chief of staff:* Major DECHARME
Direction: Lieutenant Colonel GIBOUIN - *Park:* Lieutenant Colonel HEINTZ.
Majors: STILTZ, DU MARCHE, DE DOUVRES and PALLE.
Captains: RIVOLS, DELESTRAC, COURTADE, DE BERKHEIM, ISIDOR, RENAUT, AMOUREL (park), CARDON (park)

BATTERIES

1st Regiment	2nd battery	Commanding captain:	PERTUIS	Lieutenants:	GIRARD, LAVAL, AIZIER
12th Regiment	11th -	-	-	JOURDY	-	DOUCHEZ, THOMAS, PEYRELLE
	12th -	-	-	DE SAXCÉ	-	ELY, LARGONET, PATOUT
13th Regiment	5th -	-	-	MARIE	-	VALABRÉGUE, AUDOUIN, RÉPELIN
	6th -	-	-	DUMONT	-	LEYDET, LE GALLOIS, CASTELNAU
16th Regiment	2nd -	-	-	LELIGANT	-	LAVAIL, ANTOINE, REBAIS
23rd Regiment	6th -	-	-	POHIN	-	DE VERMEIL, STAHL, THERON
24th Regiment	6th -	-	-	ÉTIENNE	-	BOURDIER, DE COROSTARZU, DELILE
28th Regiment	2nd -	-	-	GRADOZ	-	COUROY, PICARD, MAISONORET
38th Regiment	1st -	-	-	ROUBEAU	-	DARGEOT, SEGUINAUD, BARDIN

lery. It will not be long before twenty and twenty-four division batteries and reserve batteries will be requested per army corps instead of the eight they now have. The numbers disease of men and engines haunts the spirit of modern tactics. Soon there will be no more plains big enough to hold armies. They will have to fight on fronts twenty-five to thirty leagues long. An entire border will be occupied. One nation will confront another.

Today, the artillery service is certainly the most active. Its officers corps probably contains the most organized minds of the army. The training period of their general staff and of the service is done in the other service branches with artillery officers. Thanks to the School of War, the brilliant artillerists of today are no longer inveterate cannoneers like their precursors who did not want to leave their specialty and who considered all those who did not fire cannon as their inferiors. Although General Bonaparte did not want to become an infantry general as Aubrey claims, he would never have given command of an army to an artillerist or to an officer of the engineers who had served brilliantly only in his own service branch. If Marmont did not become a marshal in 1804, it was because he had not yet given proof of his overall capabilities. In the eyes of the Great Captain, the specialization of a service did not imply its superiority. It merely affirmed its practical usefulness.

The Bange cannon (1887).

Engineer soldier's kit (1789-1870).

HISTORY OF THE ENGINEERS

The history of the Engineer Regiments will now be told.

The service of the engineers was at first mixed in with the artillery which itself was classified in the infantry. The engineers do not begin to have their own history until the Revolution. This glorious history is very difficult to sort out in the midst of the great French wars of the Republic and the Empire because the corps of troops of this service were very broken up. As has since been the case, battalions of sappers and miners served as depositories of men from which the army corps and the armies withdrew companies or sometimes simple detachments, according to their needs. Placed under the direction of general or field officers of the service, these detachments participated in sieges and in all the works of war. However, in practice, they merged so closely with the other troops that the battalion numbers and later the regiments to which they belonged disappeared in the glory which was common to all. Although the religion of duty was soldily maintained in this noble corps, it completely absorbed the religion of the number forever. Still today, although each of the nineteen French corps counts in its ranks a permanently attached battalion, the Engineers are a service which forms a whole that is infinitely divisible. Although easily manipulated, its components are tied together by a singular tradition.

In 1789, in addition to a general staff of engineers' officers, there existed six companies of sappers, as has already been seen. The artillery corps to whom the companies belonged converted them into foot cannoneers. There were also six companies of miners assembled at Verdun which the artillery absorbed for a while. However, like the Phoenix, the engineers were reborn from their ashes. Sacrificed for a time, they reappeared to shine with a more intense brilliance.

On October 23, 1793, at Carnot's proposal (who was both an engineer and a top notch organizer), the companies of miners were separated from the artillery. The separation took place on December 15th. The same day, a decree from the Convention ordered the formation of twelve battalions of sappers. This is the date of the permanent creation of the engineer troops.

There has always been a rivalry between the two services, engineers and artillery. The engineers, however, had to have their own soldiers. It seemed natural enough that for certain difficult and perilous tasks, the engineers' officers would be pleased to have at their disposal experienced state workers trained under their guidance. This was Vauban's opinion who had created the companies of sappers in 1690. As for the military bridges, it may not be immediately understandable why the engineers who were charged with the construction of trestle *(fascine)* bridges and fixed bridges did not also have the bridge trains within their safe-keeping and duties. After a little more study, however, one is forced to admit that the artillery was much better equipped than the engineers to transport pontoon bridges, especially when it still had squadrons or regiments of the train. The engineers who, moreover, presided over and worked on the construction of all the campaign works had their own special service which was well defined in all of its operations. Arguments on this subject, which have been well-worn by time, would not cease with the reversal of the order established today. The glory won in the sieges by the engineers service is so solid that gaining the pontoniers' service would not increase it. Its autonomy is universally recognized today. This is evident since the troops which it has at its disposal have been expanded since 1816 from twenty-four companies of sappers and miners to eighty-four companies of sappers and miners. This does not include its required auxiliaries, the drivers and the workmen. It has its own general staff, its employees, its regiments, its arsenals, its establishments, and its schools. As General Bardin says with bitterness, every year it reverts to taking away the most solid and intelligent soldiers from

the infantry. The best officers of the engineers and the artillery come from the polytechnic school and the school of application. Since the merger of the two special branches has been under discussion, we have heard nothing said which leads us to believe that the engineers would lose anything in its merger with the artillery, but that the artillery would have much to gain. The history of the officers of the engineers, written in detail, demonstrates that many of them—and the best—being impatient to quickly succeed, have sought more rapid means to distinguish themselves in the other services. Amongst these were Duvivier, Cavaignac, and Lamoricière. This has not prevented their names from being inscribed in golden letters on the roll of the service beside the names of Vaillant, Niel, Frossard and Guérin.(1)

The twelve battalions created on December 15, 1793 (25 Frimaire, Year II) were all to have eight companies of 200 men each. Were these battalions which were ruled by a general staff of 400 officers all organized? This can only be verified by access to the lists conserved in the archives of the ministry of war, impenetrable to the layman.

The Central Committee of Fortifications had been created in 1791 and reorganized on 14 Ventôse, Year III (April 3, 1795). The decree issued on this occasion, which at the same time expanded the organization of the entire engineers corps, deserves attention since it relates facts which, at the very least, are unusual. It says the corps of engineers is composed of 437 officers and of 6 companies of miners. The 437 officers are: 7 inspectors general of fortification (3 generals of division and 4 generals of brigade); 30 directors (colonels); 60 assistant directors (majors); 260 engineer captains of whom 12 are attached to the miners; and 80 engineer lieutenants of whom 12 are attached to the miners. The Committee was composed of inspectors general and of "officers whom the Committee of Public Safety judged appropriate to call there." Finally, Article 16 decrees that "the nine regiments of sappers attached to the engineers corps will take turns for their promotion." I have not tried to explain how Carnot's twelve battalions became nine regiments of sappers. However, it is probable that a confusion among the words regiment, battalion, and demi-brigade slipped into the official documents and that there were probably only nine battalions organized. As for the six companies of miners, they are still those from Verdun which the artillery had tried to appropriate for a while. However, it is obvious that, in 1795, the sappers and particularly their officers were only incidentally part of the engineers service. They were probably auxiliary workmen whom the engineers considered it beneath them to command while nonetheless using them. If an officer of the service had taken the trouble to delve into the mysteries of the War Depot and the Committee of Fortifications, the history of the beginnings of the engineer troops would be better established and the historical records of the regiments would not commence with the organization of 1814.

Let us briefly touch upon the ephemeral creation of the aeronaut companies. The first company, Captain Coutelle, was created on April 2, 1794 in the Army of Sambre-et-Meuse. It stayed there until 1797, passing into the Army of Egypt where it was mustered out. The second, created at Meudon on June 23, 1794 was in the campaigns of the Army of the North and the Army of the Rhine. It was mustered out on February 17, 1799. The school of military aeronauts was organized at Meudon(2) by Conte and lasted six years, from 1794 to 1800.

A decision from the Directorate in Year IV (January 24, 1798) reduced the corps of sappers to four battalions.

Under the Empire, a major change occurred in the engineer troops. The six companies of miners who had made it through the entire Revolution, first reduced to five then expanded to nine, was formed into two battalions, each with five then six companies in 1808.

The battalions of sappers were subsequently expanded to eight battalions: 5 French, 1 Dutch, 1 Italian, and 1 Spanish. After 1812, French misfortunes returned their number to five.

A battalion of the engineers train and of companies of workmen had also been created.

From 1806 on, an imperial decree had established a tool depot in the train of each of the battalions of sappers which was carried by the sapper drivers.

Portions of the corps which appeared in the midst of various armies of the Republic and of the Empire have left no trace in the divisional listings from which precise information on the infantry and the cavalry has been drawn. The engineers are always indicated there by figures wherein they are often mixed with the cannoneers and the workmen, even with the train. In Napoleon I's correspondence where the sappers and miners are often discussed, no number for battalions or for companies is recalled in a clear

Engineer Corps. Full sapping (1805-1815).

(1) Lieutenant Colonel Guérin, killed at Sebastopol on June 13, 1855, was reputed to be one of the most capable officers of the Army of Engineers.

(2) During the first Revolution, the establishment of Meudon played a mysterious role which was both military and political. Like today and at the end of the Empire, the public formed the most extraordinary conjectures on what happened there. Created on March 22, 1794, it occupied the chateaux of the Great and the Small Meudon and a palissaded area surrounded by ditches which piqued the curiosity of passersby and of spies. A company of pensioners guarded it with care, and Representative of the People Bastelier directed it. Incendiary shells, hollow shells, explosive powder, the telegraph, and hot air balloons were worked on there. The strictness which kept away the curious provided hoaxers the opportunity to claim that anti-patriotic projects with the goal of returning the tyrants to France were being plotted there. A practical joker went so far as to say that Meudon occupied the site of a camp whence Caesar left to subjugate the Gauls.

and precise manner. Finally, on the flags(1) of the three first regiments, not a single siege name from the Republic or the Empire is inscribed:

1st Regiment: Algiers, 1830. Anvers, 1832. Constantine, 1837. Sebastopol, 1854-1855.
2nd Regiment: Constantine, 1837. Zaatcha, 1849. Sebastopol, 1854-1855. Puebla, 1863.
3rd Regiment: Château de Morée, 1828. Algiers, 1830. Constantine, 1837. Sebastopol, 1854-1855.

Meanwhile, the engineers were at Saint-Jean-d'Acre and at Saragossa!

Prior to the camp of Boulogne, it is almost impossible to recognize a uniformly adopted method in the distribution of sappers and of miners. They were in the reserve as much as they were scattered throughout the divisions. This distribution was the responsibility of the acting general in chief according to circumstances. Generally, he followed the advice of his chief of engineers who himself did as he pleased. As long as the proposed goal was met, everything was fine. This is how it happened in Egypt where there were 800 miners and sappers under the command of General of Division Caffarelli-Dufalga. He had Colonel Sanson as his adjoint and for chief of general staff, Major Say. The troops were taken from the 2nd and 5th companies of Miners and from an battalion of sappers whose number is unkown. They were under the command of Colonel Crétin. Major Say, already distinguished, fell mortally wounded at Saint-Jean-d'Acre a few hours after his general died. Sanson, promoted to general after Caffarelli's death, succeeded him and retained command of the Engineers of the army under Kléber and under Menou. Another officer of the service, Major Detroye, was killed at Acre.

Colonel Chasseloup-Laubat had commanded the engineers in 1796 in Italy. It is not known what forces he had at his disposal nor which were with General Marescot during the second campaign of Italy. However, it is known that at the camp of Boulogne under Marescot, commander in chief of the service, each army corps had a general staff and each infantry division a major of the service with a company.

A general of division placed in the army general staff linked all the services and had under his direct command the general reserve and the grand park. From Napoleon on, the science of war includes an administration founded on the division of duties according to specializations. The engineers always play an influential role in sieges. However, they also open roads on campaign and teach the infantrymen temporary fortifications, the art of making trenches on a battlefield, and the protection of artillery pieces and tirailleurs with rapidly built breastworks. Napoleon I invented or renewed almost everything in military matters. Everything that is done today he did then, and better. The French have forgotten his practices while the Prussians take them up again, apply them and benefit so greatly from them that victory has deserted the French ranks to pass over under their flags. The Grande Armée of 1806 was—allowing for progress and industrial improvements—as well equipped with tools, as mobile and as compact but divisible, and as equal in all its components as the Army of the Germans of the North was in 1870. This cannot be too often repeated. This is not to console France for its defeats since she must never forget them and can only be consoled by erasing them. It is rather to pay homage to the truth.

Except for the Spanish War, history has retained the names of the leaders of the engineers during the wars of the Empire.

In the Grande Armée of 1805, the following names are found: Colonel Morio of the 1st Corps, General of Brigade de Lery of the 2nd Corps, General Andreossy of the 3rd, Colonel Poitevin of the 4th, General of Brigade Kirgener of the 5th, Colonel Cazals of the 6th, and Colonel Lagastine of the 7th. The cavalry reserve commanded by Murat also had a leader from the Engineers, General of Brigade Flayelle. This provides the opportunity to point out that in some armies, notably in the Russian Army, mounted soldiers exist in the engineers. They are not wagon drivers as in the French Army but mounted workmen. Under escort of the light cavalry, they are capable of outstripping an army corps and of preparing either a river crossing or a fortification (2).

In 1806, Colonel Touzard replaced Andreossy in the 3rd Corps and Colonel Poitevin gave up his place to Garbé in the 4th.

Engineer sappers. Imperial Guard (1810-1814).

(1) Meanwhile, on the flags distributed by Prince Louis-Napoleon to the three Engineer regiments on May 10, 1852, the relationships of the regiments descending from the battalions of the Empire are noted. On that of the 1st Regiment is written: Pampelune, 1823; Algiers, 1830; Anvers, 1832; Constantine, 1837; Zaatcha, 1849. Seen on that of the 2nd Regiment is: Huningue, 1815; Château de Morée, 1828; Constantine, 1837; Rome, 1849; Zaatcha, 1849. On that of the 3rd Regiment appears: Chambéry, 1815; Château de Morée, 1828; Algiers, 1830; Bougie, 1833; Constantine, 1837. However, these legends are mistaken at least in part. The historical records of the 3rd Regiment state that the companies it supplied for the Greek expedition did not leave France until the day that the Chîateau de Morée was taken.

(2) In France's current plans for mobilization, a captain of the Engineers is attached to the general staff of each independent cavalry division. A recent decision has just ordered the establishment, or rather the re-establishment, of skilled workmen sappers in the cavalry regiments. These workmen, armed with tools and very accustomed to and experienced in the various works relating to bridges and to the consolidation or the opening of a passage, to the repair of ramps and roads, and to temporary fortifications are under the direction of the Captain of the Engineers. They will provide great services and will take the place of the Horse Engineers.

Engineer Corps. Crowning a breach (1805-1815).

For the campaign of 1809, the Engineers service in the Grande Armée was placed under the high level direction of Bertrand, the Grand Marshal of the Palace. Chambarlbac was in the 2nd Corps; Lazowski in the 4th. General of Division Chasseloup-Laubat was with the Army of Italy and Colonel Daullé was in Dalmatia with Marmont.

The armies of the First Empire, living on enemy countryside, had extreme need of specialized men. A French division always occupied a region as if it would stay there forever. It created buildings, barracks, arsenals, and fortifications there. This explains the continuous growth in the troops of the Engineers service whose effectives often surpassed 20,000 men. If a situation report dating from June 30, 1812 can be believed, the Grande Armée of Russia did not count less than 13,932 miners, sappers and soldiers of the train from the engineers when it crossed the Niemen. General Chasseloup-Laubat was commander in chief, having for chief of general staff Colonel Liédot. In the Imperial Guard, General Kirgener with his sappers, his workmen and his auxiliaries had 2,537 men under his command. In the 1st Crops, Baron Haxo had 1,291 men; in the 2nd Baron Blein had 1,275 men; in the 3rd Corps, General Baron Dode de la Brunerie had 772 men; in the 4th General Baron Poitevin had 1,280 men; and in the 5th Corps, General Pelletier had 1,197 men. The 6th Corps (Bavarian troops), the 7th (Saxon troops), the 8th (Westphalian troops), and the 10th (Prussian troops) had neither troops nor parks from the Engineers. In the 8th Corps, General Alix commanded both the engineers and the artillery. In the 7th, Captain Damon and in the 10th Major de Markoff represented their service in the general staff of their corps. As for the 9th Corps, although composed of French troops, it had neither soldiers nor a leader from the Engineers. On the other hand, the reserve and the park were directly responsible to the commander in chief and had 4,961 men.

In addition, General of Division Count Sanson, veteran of the Army of Egypt, was chief of the Emperor's topographic bureau.

The only situation report of the Grande Armée of 1813 available to the public (August 10th) confuses the sappers, miners, artillerists, workmen, and sometimes the soldiers of the artillery train, the engineers and the baggage train in its overall figures. The engineers are placed under the high level direction of General Rogniat who has for his chief of general staff Colonel Montfort and for director of parks Major Finot. Throughout the history of the other service branches it could be seen that regularity—the strict regularity which Napoleon had so much advocated at the camp of Boulogne and which he had thereafter neglected little by little—had given way in 1813 to the most systematically organized disorder. The list of commanders of the Engineers of the Grande Armée corps from 1813 is a most convincing example of this.

Imperial Guard, General Haxo. *1st Corps*, Major Moras. *2nd Corps*, Major Bron. *3rd Corps*, Colonel Valazé. *4th Corps*, Colonle Isoard. *5th Corps*, Colonel Lamarre. *6th Corps*, Major Constantin. *7th Corps*, Colonel Verpeau (artillery and engineers). *8th Corps*, Colonel Mallet. *9th Corps*,--.*10th Corps*, General Campredon. *11th Corps*, Major Thuilier. *12th Corps*, General Baron Blein. *13th Corps*, Major Vinache. *14th Corps*, General Dode de la Brunerie. Colonel Ponchon commanded the Engineers at Hamburg and Colonel Moydier at the Army of Italy.

The Emperor had always shown a great deal of concern for the engineers. He had a great officer of the Empire in General Dejean whom he honored with a special esteem. In 1810, in addition to General Dejean, the First Inspector, the inspectors general of the engineers service were Generals Chasseloup-Laubat, Léry, Count Bertrand, and Count Sanson. In 1813, two new inspectors had been named. One replaced Bertrand whom the Emperor had called to his side and the other Count Sanson, named director of the War Depot. These two general officers were Count Rogniat and Baron Lazowski(1).

(1) In this year, 1810, the sappers of the Imperial Guard were commanded by the chevalier Major Boissonnet, having under his command Captains Emon and Guiraud. Three years later, in 1813, the Engineers of the Guard, to whom strong reserves drawn from the line had been added, had a special general staff attached to General Haxo. It was composed of General Kirgener de Planta, Major Boissonnet, Captains Guiraud and Fournier, and Lieutenant Adjutant Lebas. Captain Poulain commanded the company of sappers

Engineer captain. Full dress (1887).

Engineer sappers, campaign dress (1886).

With the mustering out of 1814, the First Restoration abandoned the distribution of companies between the special battalions of miners and sappers and adopted the regimental organization. From that time on, there were three regiments (May 12, 1814) of two battalions at six companies each (five of sappers and one of miners).

1st Regiment, at Arras. Formed with the 1st, 2nd, and 3rd companies and the depot of the 1st Battalions of Miners, Sappers of the Guard and the 1st Battalion of Sappers.
2nd Regiment, at Metz. Formed with the 4th, 5th, and 6th companies of the 1st Battalion of Miners and the 2nd and 5th Battalions of Sappers.
3rd Regiment, at Montpellier. Formed with the 2nd Battalion of Miners and the 3rd and 4th Battalions of Sappers.

A company of engineer workmen and a squadron from the engineers train were also organized at Metz with the remnants of the military workmen from the engineers and the battalion of the special train for the service.

This organization equalized the elimination of eight companies of miners and the nine companies of sappers, not counting that of the Guard. It did not seem to be executed quickly nor in the areas designated since the 3rd Engineers Regiment, which took its new troops especially from Alexandria, was still in formation in Grenoble on March 9, 1815 when Napoleon presented himself there. The entire 3rd Engineers Regiment followed the Emperor to Paris. The first battalion was then sent to the Army of the North and the second returned to Grenoble.

The Army of the North seemed to have employed at least fifteen companies of sappers from the engineers. We say at least, since the situation reports on which we have reconstructed the detachment of the service are exceedingly vague and inaccurate. They do not allow for verifying whether companies had been assigned to the eight divisions which formed it, notably for the 1st and 2nd Corps. Although all these divisions and the reserve of each corps had been provided with a company of engineers, it was the sappers of the 1st Regiment who marched. Those of the 1st Battalion went to the 1st Corps (General of Brigade Garbé commander; Colonel Baraillon, chief of general staff), and those of the 2nd Battalion went to the 2nd Corps (General of Brigade Richemont, commander; Colonel Daullé, chief of general staff). The 2nd Engineers Regiment definitely supplied six companies to the 3rd and 4th Corps and for the 1st Battlion of the 3rd, we possess the situation report of three companies assigned to the 6th Corps. Below is the distribution of these various companies.

3rd CORPS	4th CORPS	6th CORPS
Commander: General of brigade NEMPDE	*Commander:* General of brigade VALAZÉ	*Commander:* General of brigade SABATIER
	Chief of staff: Colonel MARION	*Chief of staff:* Colonel MARION
8th INFANTRY DIVISION	13th INFANTRY DIVISION	19th INFANTRY DIVISION
2nd Regiment, 2nd battalion, 2nd company, Captain Carré	2nd Regiment, 2nd battalion, 5th company, Captain Brignon	3rd Regiment, 1st battalion, 1st company, Captain Foliot
10th INFANTRY DIVISION	14th INFANTRY DIVISION	20th INFANTRY DIVISION
2nd Regiment, 2nd battalion, 1st company, Captain Lemaire	2nd Regiment, 2nd battalion, 3rd company, Captain Provence	3rd Regiment, 1st battalion, 2nd company, Captain Euzenate
11th INFANTRY DIVISION	RESERVE	21st INFANTRY DIVISION
2nd Regiment, 2nd battalion, 4th company, Captain Cotelle	2nd Regiment, 2nd battalion, miners, Captain Louis	3rd Regiment, 1st battalion, 3rd company, Captain Ferrey

All these engineers corps were placed under the command in chief of the famous General Rogniat. The topographic service was directed by Colonel Bonne. The general effective strength was at 70 officers and 1,488 non-commissioned officers and soldiers. Dissolved on October 15, 1815, the three regiments of the Engineers were reformed in 1816 at two battalions of four companies (1 of miners, 3 of sappers). The number of companies was quickly raised to five, to six, then to seven.

Below is the list of colonels who commanded the four regiments from 1816 on.

1st Regiment. Ch. Amb. Prost, Thiébault, Ressecaud, Jourjon, Le Prestre de Vauban, Prudon, Merlin, Salanson, Pleuvier, Hinstin, de Bussy, Richard, Guichard, Mensier, Lallemant.
2nd Regiment. Baron Rohault de Fleury, Vainsot, Thuillier, Cournault, Dorlodot des Essarts, Dejean, Ducasse, Teissier, Brunon, Coste, Faugeron, Riondel, Chéry.
3rd Regiment. Marquis de Foucault, Marquis de Beaufort d'Hautpoul, Olry, Baron Prelet, Romphleur, Baron de Chabaud-Latour, Dauteville, Coffinières de Nordeck, Le Baron, Danet, Durand de Villers, Bressonet, Sanglier, Gallimard, Peaucellier, Varaigne, Mengin-Lecreuix.

Under the Restoration, the engineers had their general staff composed in the following manner. The year 1825 immediately after the Spanish War is taken as an example.

The general officers of the service were Viscount Rogniat, Baron Haxo, Viscount Maureillan, Viscount Dode de la Brunerie, Viscount de Caux, and Viscount Garbé for the generals of division. For generals of brigade, there were Chevalier Nempde, Baron Valazé, Baron Déponthon, Chevalier de Montfort, Chevalier Michaux, Baron Sabatier, Chevalier Baudrand, Baron Rohault de Fleury, and Treussart.

Viscount Rogniat was inspector general of the central service, General of Brigade Sabatier commanded the Royal School of Artillery and Engineering at Metz, and General of Brigade Baudrand was head of the Office of Engineering at the ministry. All the others were inspectors attached to the Committee.

There were twenty directorships which were situated at Arras, Bayonne, Belfort, Besançon, Brest, Cambrai, Embrun, Le Havre, La Rochelle, Lille, Metz, Mezières, Nantes, Paris, Perpignan, Saint-Omer, Soissons, Strasbourg, Toulon and Verdun. The three regiments were garrisoned:

The 1st at Arras, detaching three companies to Cadix (4th and 5th Sappers of the 1st Battalion, miners from the 2nd Battalion).
The 2nd at Montpellier, detaching two companies to Barcelona (5th Sappers from the 1st Battalion and 5th Sappers from the 2nd Battalion).
The 3rd at Metz, detaching one company (4th Sappers of the 1st Battalion) to Pampelune.

There were 60 colonels and lieutenant colonels, 82 majors, and 320 captains. A number of captains had a respectable relative grade in rank (April 20, 1796) because at that time in the Engineers, the rank of field officer was given only under certain conditions of examination except when vacancies occurred in the troops. Among the second lieutenants coming from the school of application who

Sappers and miners, drummers (1824).

were waiting their four years of rank to become second lieutenant appeared the future generals Bodson de Noirfontaine, Chauchard, Lebaron, Chabaud-Latour, and Cavaignac.

The colonies of Martinique and of Guadeloupe each have a special company of sappers.

At the time of the Spanish campaign, it was deemed necessary to give the engineers more than twenty-four companies, leaving them with the organization of 1816. This campaign would entail many sieges so the engineers of the Duke of Angoulême's Army received a strong organization. The traditions of the Empire were reborn in the necessity of conducting the campaign. The Bourbons had trembled with joy at the news of the defeat at Waterloo. However, in the end, they remembered that the vanquished of this epic battle were Frenchmen who had conquered the world in the past. They felt very happy that Europe knew France had been a world power. The Army of Spain copied a bit the army which, victorious at Ligny, had succumbed at Waterloo under fatal blows. The engineers were not distributed by division there but by army corps with a strong general reserve available. General of Division Viscount Dode de la Brunerie was the head of the engineers of the Army of Spain (aides-de-camp: Major Dorlodot des Essarts and Captain Moreau). A historian was astonished by the willingness shown by the generals of the Empire to take up service again in 1823. The government of Louis XVIII would have been very unhappy if the men of swords, accustomed to making their soldiers obey, had refused to have anything to do with glory of those days. The *"rentrants a la bouillote"* (homebodies) of 1814 and 1815, as brave as they were, would have performed poorly at the head of one hundred thousand men. The prince general understood this since his second collaborator for the engineers service was a general officer from Waterloo: Bron. Bron had for his adjoints: Majors Lebeschu, Lemaire, Morvan and Foucault; Captains Véne and Larabit; and Lieutenant Crozals.

Three companies of the service marched with the grand general staff: the 1st Company of Miners from the 1st Regiment, Captain Romphleur; the 1st Company of Sappers from the 3rd Regiment, Captain Callot; and the 2nd Company of Sappers from the 3rd Regiment, Captain Giclat. A small park was joined to this group. The army corps—at least the first three—had a senior officer in their general staff commanding the engineers and a company of sappers in their ranks:

1st Corps. Commander: Lieutenant Colonel Dupau; 1st Company of Sappers from the 1st Regiment;
2nd Corps. Commander: Major Vauvillers: 2nd Company of Sappers from the 1st Regiment: Captain Brignon;
3rd Corps. Commander: Major de Merlis; 3rd Company of Sappers from the 1st Regiment.

In addition, the 3rd Company of Sappers was used in the blockade of Saint-Sébastian.

At least seven companies of the engineers service had thus crossed over the Pyrenees. The three companies of the reserve were specially attached to the Army of Cadix. As was noted above, in 1825, six companies of engineers still remained in Spain, but they were no longer the same numbers.

The companies remaining in the depots of the 1st and 3rd Regiments had to be emptied in order to establish the war companies. It was the first time since the Restoration of the monarchy that a campaign had been made. The budgeted effectives had to be used. There was the task of mobilization which was absolutely new and which made the war administration understand that the new French organization lacked both flexibility and solidity.

We have already said and will sadly repeat again that the engineers service does not have in its ranks an officer who has undertaken its history. This is not for lack of writing talent amongst the famous members of the Engineer corps. However, they all feign a certain disdain for the feats and actions of their service. It is scientific progress which interests them. With this in mind, let me make note of a charming play by Léon Gozlan: "Rain and Good Weather." In this play, a captain of the service wasted some time with a pretty woman—whom he could have much better entertained—by talking to her about the covered sap and the flying sap. If an essay were to be written here about the art of military engineering, there would be thousands of books to mention. However, we know of only one which addresses the general history of the Engineers. Is this an excess of modesty? I do not believe so. Rather there is excessive pride in this scorn for glory set down in words. For the period prior to the sieges of Rome, Bomarsund, and Sebastopol whose events have been carefully written by Marshals Vaillant and Niel, it will be possible to offer only a little on the engineers' organization in the armies. The War Depot is closed to all laymen. With regard to a contested historical quote, Victor Hugo said that it was forbidden to state the sublime in history. On the topic of historical documents which belong to the country and to all citizens being locked up, we maintain—with all due respect—that putting truth into military history is prohibited. We herein thank the generals and the colonels who have helped carry out this patriotic work with their advice, their knowledge and the documents they possess. As for the ministers who have closed the doors on the official tables of French military history, we have the consolation of being able to say that with a little intelligence and patience, one can sometimes learn more than they wish to hide.

The Spanish campaign tested the need to make the cannon of France speak. Thereafter, the Restoration sent a strong division to Greece to protect the classical land of liberty from the Turks. Two companies of engineer sappers were attached to the expeditionary corps of Morocco. They were supplied from 1828 to 1833 by the 3rd Regiment. The engineers were commanded by Lieutenant Colonel Audoy who had for chief of general staff Major Borrel-Vivier. Captains Montmasson, Lieffroy, Lebaron, Cavaignac and Garnot were adjutants. Garnot was detached to assist the president of the provisional government of Greece.

The 1st, 2nd, and 3rd companies of the 1st Battalion from the 3rd Regiment left Metz on October 31, 1828. The first two returned almost immediately. The 3rd company remained alone in Morocco and was quickly joined (October 22, 1829) by the 4th company of the 2nd Battalion. The 3rd company of the 1st Battalion returned at the beginning of 1830 and the 4th company of the 2nd Battalion returned on November 1, 1833.

Engineer sappers. Expeditionary corps of Algiers (1830).

EXPEDITION OF ALGIERS

◆

Minister of War de Bourmont had gained the upper hand over Marmont for the command in chief of the expedition, thanks to the protection of the Dauphin. He was not hampered by anyone in organizing the troops which he placed under his own command. The engineers service was well supplied. Placed under the command of General of Brigade Baron Valazé, it had a great number of miners and sappers and its general staff was particularly well chosen. As will be seen, the troops were assembled into a battalion instead of being distributed among the infantry divisions.

CAMPAIGN OF ANVERS

◆

This small campaign where diplomacy determined the voice of French cannon would be offhandedly led and terminated. The Engineers and some companies of grenadiers would play the principal role there. Again a veteran of the Empire was entrusted with the responsibility of directing the siege of Anvers. An unsual conflict between the commander in chief of the Engineers, the famous General Haxo, and the celebrated General Neigre, commander in chief of the artillery sprang up at this siege. While Neigre wanted to reduce the Saint-Laurent lunette with cannonfire, Haxo intended to bring it down with mines. Marshal Gérard thus only had to suffer the demands of Colonel Caradoc, the English commissioner. The public still wonders why a general from the Engineers never commands a siege. The answer is simple. The general in chief, usually selected from amongst the divisional leaders of the infantry—and very rarely by a cavalry general as was very clumsily done in 1849 at Rome—is charged with getting the general of engineers and the general of artillery to agree.

At right is the organization of the engineers in Marshal Gérard's Army.

Captain Jalot and Sergeant Fabre were cited in the daily orders of December 16th as well as Lieutenant Colonel Vaillant and the Guard Négrier who went alone to reconnoiter the breach made in the Saint-Laurent lunette. Captains Jalot, Couteaux, Vanéchout, Mangin, Major Picot, and Lieutenant Colonel Lafaille were also cited.

Captain Couteaux was killed and Major Paulin was wounded.

Commander: General of brigade VALAZÉ
Aide-de-camp: Captain GAY
Chief of staff: Lieutenant Colonel DUPAU
Director of the park: Major LEMERCIER

Officers attached to the staff
Majors: Chambaud and Vaillant
Captains: Beurnier, Collas, Gallice d'Oussières, Guèze, Morin, Duvivier, Duffoure, Gaulier, de Montfort, d'Espremenil, Chabaud-Latour, Bouessel, Ribot, Fourreau and Desessart
Lieutenants: Brojat, de Béville, Bouscarin, Bigot

Troops
Major LENOIR
Adjutant: POYET
Paymaster: QUARANTE

1st REGIMENT
One company of miners of the 1st battalion, Captain Romphleur
1st, 2nd and 3rd companies of sappers of the 1st battalion,
Captains Simon, Gibon and Chefneux

2nd REGIMENT
4th and 5th companies of sappers of the 1st battalion,
Captains Vandelin and Challaye

3rd REGIMENT
One company of miners of the 1st battalion, Captain Carrier
4th company of sappers of the 2nd battalion, Captain d'Hauteville;
One half-company of the train, Captain Bigarelle

Total: 8 companies including 2 of miners. - 1,310 men and 133 horses

---

Commander in chief: General of division HAXO
Aides-de-camp: Captains MENGIN and CHAUCHARD
Chief of staff: Colonel LAFAILLE
Director of the park: Lieutenant Colonel VAILLANT

Adjutants to the staff
Majors: Morlet and Picot
Captains: Vallenet, Sertour, Vanéchout, Sorel, Belmas, Desfeux, D'Autheville, Charon, Bodson de Noirfontaine, Rouganne, Hackett and Lelièvre

Troops
Commander: Major PAULIN (Charles)

1st REGIMENT
One company of miners, Captain Jalot
Six companies of sappers, Captains Vernon, Sigaut, Berlandier, Ribot,
Couteaux and Bazin

2nd REGIMENT
One company of miners, Captain Dupré
One company of sappers, Captain Baillot
2nd company of the train, Captain Ribette

This was the only opportunity the July Government would offer the army to deploy the tricolor flag in Europe. However, there was Algeria which opened up a vast field to the engineer officers. There they demonstrated their science by constructing fortifications and their courage by undertaking sieges which were often painful and difficult, such as the siege of Constantine. In this country where everything had to be done, the conquerors have forgotten to relate their feats and actions. They have done so much that they could well be excused for this omission. However, it is deplorable that in an epoch where subjects which are not worth the effort have been so easily elaborated upon, the government has not yet written a complete, accurate, and somewhat impartial history of the Army of Africa. The engineers hold a special place in that tale. The elite from amongst the officers of this elite service passed through Africa and distinguished themselves there. The list of officers who took part in the initial expedition has been given. To this will be added the list of generals of the service who have completed their apprenticeship of glory and duty there. It is filled with renowned names. Marshals Vaillant and Niel, Generals Charon, Dalesme, Chabaud-Latour, Bizot, Frossard, Tripier, Chaubin, Urtin, Dhauteville, Bouteilloux, Danet, Véronique, Riffaut, Dubost, de Vauban, Javain, Malcor, Ducasse, Le Brettevillois, Prudon, Dejean, Faidherbe, Bodson de Noirfontaine, and Vialla are found there. From 1830 until 1869, these men occupied various positions in Algeria.

Engineer Corps. Siege of Anvers (1832).

In a work dedicated by the Duke of Orléans to the *Campaigns of the Army of Africa from 1835 to 1839,* a truly princely work, praises fall like benevolent rain on a crowd of courtiers. We have nonetheless been able to discover in it details about the two sieges of Constantine which show exactly what each new step made by the conquest cost. The first expedition was attempted with 7,270 men of whom 500 were from the Engineers. Thus there were five companies placed under the command of Colonel Lemercier. The operation ran aground. Poorly prepared by Marshal Clausel who depended too much on his luck, it was taken up again the following year by General Count Danrémont. Learning from the mistakes of his predecessor, this famous general took the greatest care in the composition of the corps of the expeditionary army. Although more than 13,000 men strong, it was still not large enough to complete the investment of the place. The Engineers, commanded by General Rohault de Fleury and Lamy, included two companies of miners, eight of sappers, and a park. As Colonel Combes said on the day of the assault: "It is necessary to take Constantine or to die beneath its walls." Thus, it was a valiant affair. General Danrémont died a glorious death there by exposing himself like a young soldier wishing to win renown. The Engineers working in the soaked earth and mud accomplished the impossible during the period of attacks. They displayed a heroic courage in guiding the assault columns to the breach. Four officers of the service died there: Major Vieux, a veteran of Waterloo, and Captains Hackett, Pottier and Leblanc. The two former were under Lamorcière in the first column; the two latter were under the command of Combes in the second column.

Under Louis-Philippe's reign, the engineers service accomplished the magnificent task of the fortifications of Paris. It is still difficult to decide whether a capital should be fortified. Is it not more dangerous for both civilization and for the nation to enclose the last hopes of the country there with the revolution, so that one can no longer resist in the open countryside? Obviously, if in 1871 Paris had been able to hold out—not seven years like Troy but merely one year like Sebastopol—Germany would have been in a very sorry state. However, even with provisions, could France have lasted one year alongside people who wanted the Commune? These political rather than military considerations do not take away any of the value of the defensive works of Paris. Built in a period when artillery did not yet anticipate the distances which it would later be able to attain, the defenses stopped the German engineers for more than four months. This is the best praise they could receive.

SIEGE OF ROME

◆

The engineers had a new opportunity to particularly distinguish themselves at Rome. The city could not be invested by the small expeditionary corps which was completing itself even during the operations. Moreover, the two service branches, artillery and engineers, had to combine their efforts so that the siege moved along as rapidly as possible. At the same time, the monuments of the Eternal City—masterpieces of conservation which the French would be held accountable for by the entire world—could not be damaged by French cannon. Beginning with the siege of Rome, the Engineers' history becomes clear. Documentation abounds. Thanks to the works of Marshals Vaillant and Niel which were published with the authorization of the ministers of war, we are able to offer complete information on the personnel. First, there is the table of the Engineer troops at Rome (1859).

Two officers were killed: Commander Galbaud-Dufort and Captain de Jouslard; six were wounded: Major Frossard, Captains Boissonnet, Regnault, Puiggari, Dumont, and Lieutenant Brière. At the head of the assault columns were Galbaud-Dufort and de Jouslard who died there.

Seven non-commissioned officers or soldiers were killed and twenty wounded.

From 1859 until the first evacuation of the Pontifical States, the engineers always maintained a general staff and some companies in Rome. It is the French engineers who built the fortifications of Civita-Vecchia. Major Farre commanded them still in 1862. It was no doubt due to the good relations he had with the Holy Father that he was promoted from lieutenant colonel in 1867 to chief of the engineers of the army expeditionary corps. Under the command of General of Division de Failly, it went for the last time to protect and save the temporal power of the Pope who was attacked by Garibaldi and poorly protected by the words of King Victor-Emmanuel. Two companies were placed under his command on this occasion: the 7th company of Sappers from the 1st Regiment attached to the 1st Infantry Division (Major Gallimard) and the 10th company of Sappers from the 2nd Regiment attached to the 2nd Division (Major Vieille).

Commander in chief: General of division VAILLANT
Aide-de-camp: Major GALBAUD-DUFORT
Chief of staff: Colonel NIEL

Adjutants to the staff
Lieutenant Colonels: Ardant and Leblanc
Majors: Goury and Frossard
Captains: Regnault, Gras (André), Boissonnet, Ragon, director of the park; Bonfillon, Schoennagel (Auguste), Doutrelaine, Prévost
Guards: Urquin, Bellas, Oberlender and Toutal

Troops
1st REGIMENT
4th company of the 1st battalion, Captain Touvenaint
Company of miners of the 2nd battalion, Captain Pissis
5th company of sappers of the 2nd battalion, Captain de Jouslard

2nd REGIMENT
3rd company of sappers of the 1st battalion, Captain Puiggari
4th company of sappers of the 2nd battalion, Captain Darceau
7th company of sappers of the 2nd battalion, Captain Mayette

3rd REGIMENT
Detachment of sapper conductors

Effectives: 40 officers and functionaries, 917 men of the ranks

Engineer Corps. Workers surrendering at the trench, siege of Rome (1849).

SIEGE OF SEBASTOPOL

◆

Throughout history, there is no siege which more honors the conqueror and the vanquished. At Sebastopol, as at Constantine and at Rome, the French troops faced a place which they could not completely invest. However, although Russian communications by land were open, they were slow and difficult. If the French had owned the sea, that great route which is always open, they could have prudently come from improvised ports serving as bases of operations. In addition, the Russians have the advantage of a single, unified action over the French whereas the French general in chief must consider in perhaps too broad a manner the sensitivities of the allied nations. Finally, although France has the indomitable eagerness of Pélissier, the Russians have the industrious and knowledgeable activity of Totleben.

1st Regiment of Engineers (1854).

The siege of Sebastopol has its official history as written by Marshal Niel. It is presented with a cold technicality which does not even allow so much as a glimpse of the painful hidden side since revealed in the publication of the correspondance by the famous Marshal Vaillant with Generals Pélissier and Niel. Marshal Vaillant was an upright and honest man. He brought a unique greatness to his role as conciliator between the jealous eagerness of the general in chief and the worried sensitivity of General Niel. Niel felt he was the secret favorite of the Emperor, but he was not always right in his ideas. These struggles brought about violent outbursts between the chief and his subordinate. When the final details of the attack were being fine-tuned and Niel made a pretense of pulling an envelope from his pocket which contained orders from the Tuileries, Pélissier curtly ordered him to be silent. Then he unhooked the telegraph line so as to remain absolute master of his actions, like a captain over his ship on the open sea. The annoyed officer could only bring his complaints to his sovereign some time after the taking of Sebastopol. Marshal Niel was no less valiant and knowledgeable an officer of the engineers despite all this. His death which took place one year before the fatal war has kept his memory alive for posterity. In fact, his complacency in the Chambers when he was minister and when the law of recruitment was discussed had passed on the responsibility for defeat to his successor just as his accommodating attitude toward Napoleon III's ideas would hinder Pélissier from taking Sebastopol.

General of Division Niel had arrived at Sebastopol on January 27, 1855 on a mission as the Emperor's aide-de-camp. He was preceded by the reputation he had recently won in the taking of Bomarsund in the Baltics.

This outstanding operation, brilliantly executed, had employed only very limited forces. In addition to his two aides-de-camp, Captains Petit and Parmentier, General Niel had brought to the North Sea with him Lieutenant Colonal Jourjon, Major Cadart, and Captain Karth. A single company from the 1st Regiment (6th Sappers of the 1st Battalion, Captain Barrabé) was attached to the expeditionary corps. The dismantling and burning of the various works forming the system of islands surrounding Bomarsund were the major results of the short campaign undertaken in 1854.

When the War of the Orient began, the first shipment of troops was not exactly intended for a long-term siege. The engineers were not yet organized there in an exceptional manner. Each of the infantry divisions received its regulation company. In addition, a strong reserve and a park had been put at the disposal of the general in chief. To provide the complete picture, the status of the engineers' forces which landed in Crimea with Marshal Saint-Arnaud and which participated in the Battle of Alma are given at left.

These companies, which were already severely tested by cholera, contained an effective strength of only 767 men in the ranks. Many companies had only two or even just one officer. From the beginning of the operation until peace, fever, typhus and cholera also removed Major Toussaint, Captains Le Bescond (Joseph), Virte, Renucci, Venault, Pornain, and Lieutenant Durand.

However, soon the siege according to the rules (which required shipments of more troops) established a notable increase in the engineers and its distribution into two attack corps. Below is the complete status for the service from September 1, 1855, a few days before the assault.

Commander in chief: General of brigade BIZOT
Aide-de-camp: Captain BOISSONNET
Chief of staff: Colonel TRIPIER
Adjutant: Captain SARLAT
Director of the park: Major GUÉRIN
Adjutant: Captain MARTIN

Officers commanding the troops
Lieutenant Colonel DUBOIS-FRESNEY
Majors: Dumas, commander of the Engineers of the 2nd Division
Dubost, commander of the Engineers of the 3rd Division
de Saint-Laurent, commander of the Engineers of the 4th Division

Adjutants to the staff
Major: Rittier
Captains: Fervel, Schmith, de Préserville, Roulet, de Villenoisy, Chaper
Guards: Gross and Aldebert

Troops
1st DIVISION
7th company of sappers of the 1st battalion of the 2nd Regiment, Captain Garnier

2nd DIVISION
7th company of sappers of the 2nd battalion of the 1st Regiment, Captain Courtin

3rd DIVISION
4th company of sappers of the 2nd battalion of the 3rd Regiment, Captain Mouhat

4th DIVISION
4th company of sappers of the 1st battalion of the 3rd Regiment, Captain Hézette

RESERVE AND PARKS
5th company of sappers of the 1st battalion of the 2nd Regiment, Captain Péret
6th company of sappers of the 1st battalion of the 2nd Regiment, Captain Hudelest
Company of miners of the 2nd battalion of the 3rd Regiment, Captain Fourcade
Sapper conductors of the 3rd Regiment, Captain Pauly
Detachment of the 2nd company of workmen, Sergeant Maréchal

In front of Sebastopol. Repairs to works after a sortie (1855).

On the day of the assault, the effective strength was 2,712 men present in the ranks.

In the assault disposition, the engineers' officers who would take part directly therein were under the command of the generals of their service and of the army corps.

On the left, Lieutenant Colonel Ribot commanded the attack against the central bastion. He had under his command Captain Béziat and four brigades of sappers of 30 men, each with an officer. The officers in charge of brigades were Captain Garnier, Second Lieutenant Touzellier, Lieutenant Serval and Captain Méreau (miners). Méreau had to try to destroy the disposition of the enemy mines. For the attack of the Mat Bastion, three brigades of sappers and two brigades of miners had been given to Major Tholer.

In the attacks on the right, the column on the extreme left had as its chief of engineers Commander Ragon. He had with him Captain Bonnevay and two brigades of sappers from the Aufroy Company. The center column had Captain Schoennagel as its chief of engineers, seconded by Captain la Ruelle, and one brigade of sappers under the command of Lieutenant Pradelle. Finally in the linkage on the right, the engineers composed of two brigades of sappers from the Heydt Company were under the command of Major Renoux. He had for his adjutant Captain Salanson. In addition, Major de Marsilly directed the porters of the flying bridges. Lieutenant Joyeux with one brigade of sappers would facilitate the passage of the horse-drawn French artillery and Captain Berrier, with the miners, would be on the lookout for mines prepared by the Russians.

The losses of the engineers service during the entire siege will be listed. Lost at the assault were: Captain Schoennagel, killed and Lieutenant Joyeux, mortally wounded, 24 men of the ranks killed, and 2 missing. Major Fournier, Captains Ansous and La Ruelle, Lieutenant Pradelle and Second Lieutenant Hennequin were wounded. Some other officers had received contusions and 126 men of the ranks were wounded. Unfortunately, the engineers also left a good number of brave officers and energetic soldiers on Crimean soil. Captain Schmitz opens this list of the dead; he was killed by a shot on October 6, 1854 in a reconnaissance mission close to the Clocheton House. There followed, in order of rank: General of Brigade Bizot, who had begun the siege and who was mortally wounded on April 11th in the English trenches; Lieutenant Colonel Guérin; Majors Sarlat, Dumas, de Saint-Laurent, Masson, Lassalle de Préserville, Pingault, Abinal; Captains Fourcade, Valesque, Guilhot, Courtin, Mouhat, Duport, Hezette, Coudray, Lulé-Dejardin, Vaullegeard, Jacobé, Pillault-Delaboissière, Delaporte, Lecucq; Lieutenants Brissaud and Boyre; and Second Lieutenants Châtelain, Blaise, and Mandagout. The number of seriously wounded was as great as that of the dead. There were 31 killed and 33 seriously

wounded: Lieutenant Colonel Duboys-Fresney, Majors Rittier, Mangin, Boissonnet (twice). Captains Hézette (later killed), Lassalle de Préserville (later killed), Pornin, Ducrot, Fescourt, Deudeville, Denfert-Rochereau, Renucci, Salanson, Masselin, Lesdos, Goury, La Ruelle (twice); Lieutenants Coste, Bonnevay, Hinstin, de Lécluse de Longraye; and Second Lieutenants Dogny and Hennequin (twice). As for the contusions, they were minor things for a service which lived in the trenches in the middle of mine collapses and explosions of stone and wood. The total losses of the engineers in non-commissioned officers has not been registered by Marshal Niel. However, in the *Historical Records of the 3rd Engineers Regiment,* it can be seen that the 4th Sappers company of the 1st Battalion from this regiment lost 3 non-commissioned officers and 13 corporals or sappers killed and had 3 non-commissioned officers and 67 corporals or sappers wounded. It was truly one of the most sorely tested of all companies.

From all standpoints, the siege of Sebastopol marks the culminating point of the French military engineers. Its glory does not pale beside but is in fact equal to that of the admirable French infantry and of the incomparable artillery. Nothing better sums up the services of the engineers than the letter of congratulations written by Marshal Vaillant to the future Marshal Niel in the aftermath of the taking of Malakoff:

"I have not yet sent you my compliments," wrote the minister of war, " and yet I have quite a big one to send you! You have played a fine part in everything done of real importance since you won the epaulette: Constantine, Rome, Bomarsund... and to crown these sieges, that of Sebastopol. I was never without hope, you know; however, my hope was sometimes weak!...I do not know how to thank you enough for having known how to keep silent about some feelings of vexation which a less great man would have allowed himself to vent. You had true courage, that of duty. Thank in my name, as minister and as comrade, the officers who have so well assisted you. Tell them that I am proud to call myself one of them. I very much regret those whom we have lost. Especially Bizot who had great valor as a man and as a military being! Do not forget me to the wise Dalesme, the impetuous Frossard, Renoux, Rittier, Tholer; the others are well worthy of being named but there are too many of them. I send you my compliments for all of them. Goodbye, goodbye. My very best to you. Your friend."

The great success of the Engineers service at Sebastopol had considerable influence on the general direction of military affairs. It gave this skilled corps a dictatorial supremacy which was not to the country's advantage. For a long time confined to the specialty of their service, the ministers like Marshal Vaillant and Niel came to high level affairs with great renown but without overall or precise views. Consequently, since the siege of Sebastopol, the expeditionary corps which have been sent on distant campaigns have always been generously supplied with respect to officers and troops of the service. The officers and the sappers of the Engineers are firstly very robust soldiers who do not sulk under fire. However, in a new country where everything has to be established, they bring special qualities of work, industriousness, and science which make them particularly valuable. Thus, it could be said that they have participated in a great part of the success of our distant undertakings.

The list of ministers of war could provide an opportunity for a very interesting psychological study. France has only had truly eclectic ministers from the infantry. Before the Revolution, a minister of war could be the King's, the Court's, or a favorite's man. During the Revolution, he was always at the mercy of events. For Napoleon, the minister of war, Chief of Army General Staff Berthier, and the minister of administration, Cessac or Daru, were the absolute master's intelligent clerks. Except for Gouvion-Saint-Cyr, the Restoration did not have a minister of war. The great minister of the July Government was Marshal Soult. He left a deep imprint on France's institutions and military spirit. He was a minister of war who wanted peace at all costs and who wanted a fine, solid army corresponding to the spirit of the times. This was an army which, in its size and flexibility, did not threaten the tranquillity of Europe yet flattered national feelings. In 1840, with its excellent military laws on recruitment and on the status and the promotion of officers, France could fight in Africa. However, France could not look Europe straight in the face. In 1854 with the institutions of 1832 and 1834, when someone wanted to keep his rank, he had to rely on artificial means. In 1859, in order not to strengthen himself through help from the Revolution, Napoleon III had to stop short in front of the quadrilateral. None of the marshals Saint-Arnaud, Vaillant, nor Randon understood France's position. Saint-Arnaud, the most gifted of the three, had not had time to figure it out. Vaillant was only good for normal affairs; Randon found

Engineer company. Imperial Guard (1855).

Engineer Corps. Construction of a redoubt (1886).

Engineer Corps. Construction of a trestle bridge (1887)

himself not up to the task. When Marshal Niel came to power, the damage had already been done. Moreover, the resounding energy of the southern Frenchman became too soft in parliamentary struggles. Besides, disease was already eroding him. He saw war coming and obviously he had enough intelligence to glimpse the probable results. Marshal Leboeuf, who was so thrilled to become minister, was crushed by the bad luck of being the *deus ex machina* of a poorly prepared war foolishly undertaken, and disgracefully led.

Since 1870, France has had only one good minister, Courtot de Cissey. A bizarre series of incidents has robbed de Cissey of the glory of having remade French military institutions. It is true this remake was done according to a somewhat limited plan, but de Cissey was completely aware of the forces and needs of the nation. Since then, all the ministers of war who have passed through Rue Saint-Dominque have had to humble their military feelings in the face of the political collapse of the predominant party. There are no exceptions; none has been able to escape the necessity of being more of a parliamentary minister than an army leader, except by resigning. These are the problems which weigh too heavily on the future of the French army while a fearful Europe seems to be subjected to the yoke of Germany.

CAMPAIGN OF ITALY

———◆———

The War of the Orient had set in motion seventeen companies of sappers (counting the one which was sent to Bomarsund), one of miners, and one of sapper drivers. This was a total of nineteen, almost one third of the service and the equivalent of one regiment. The campaign of Italy needed a little more than that.

Each infantry division received one company and each army corps had one reserve. In order to be complete, the disposition of the Engineers in the Army of Italy is given below. The Engineers did little work there since peace had been concluded at the moment that the war of sieges was beginning.

General Reserve—Two companies of miners and one company of sapper drivers.

Total: 20 companies of sappers, 2 of miners, and one of sapper drivers.

A small detachment of sapper drivers and three wagons were attached to each company. With the forty wagons attached to the reserve park, this gave a total of ninety-four wagons. Today, by regulation, each army corps has seventeen wagons.

General Niel commanded the 4th Corps where he won the marshal's baton. Colonel Jourjon, who commanded the engineers of his army corps, was killed, sword in hand, at the Battle of Solferino.

Commander of the army's engineers: General of division FROSSARD
Chief of staff: Colonel LEBRETTEVILLOIS

1st CORPS
Commander: General of brigade BOUTEILLOUX

1st DIVISION, 3rd company of sappers of the 2nd battalion of the 2nd Regiment, Major Schuster
2nd DIVISION, 5th company of sappers of the 1st battalion of the 1st Regiment, Major Duval
3rd DIVISION, 6th company of sappers of the 2nd battalion of the 1st Regiment, Major Sèrè de Rivières
RESERVE, one company (never arrived)

2nd CORPS
Commander: Colonel LEBARON

1st DIVISION, 4th company of sappers of the 2nd battalion of the 2nd Regiment, Major Humbert
2nd DIVISION, 2nd company of sappers of the 2nd battalion of the 1st Regiment, Major Gras
RESERVE, 4th company of sappers of the 1st battalion of the 2nd Regiment

3rd CORPS
Commander: General of brigade CHAUCHARD

1st DIVISION, 3rd company of the 1st battalion of the 2nd Regiment, Major Jahan
2nd DIVISION, 5th company of sappers of the 1st battalion of the 3rd Regiment, Major Rémond
3rd DIVISION, 1st company of sappers of the 1st battalion of the 1st Regiment, Major Massu
RESERVE, 7th company of sappers of the 1st battalion of the 2nd Regiment

4th CORPS
Commander: Colonel JOURJON

1st DIVISION, 3rd company of sappers of the 1st battalion of the 1st Regiment, Major Worms de Romilly
2nd DIVISION , 7th company of sappers of the 2nd battalion of the 3rd Regiment, Major Coffyn
3rd DIVISION, 3rd company of sappers of the 2nd battalion of the 3rd Regiment, Major Faissolle
RESERVE, 6th company of sappers of the 1st battalion of the 2nd Regiment

5th CORPS
Commander: General of brigade COFFINIÈRE

1st DIVISION, 2nd company of the 1st battalion of the 2nd Regiment, Major Fervel
2nd DIVISION, 3rd company of the 1st battalion of the 3rd Regiment, Major de Courvil
RESERVE, 1st company of sappers of the 2nd battalion of the 3rd Regiment

The Imperial Guard had with it its two companies of sappers under the command of Captain Goury

---

CAMPAIGNS OUTSIDE OF EUROPE

———◆———

The uneasiness of France already pushed it outside of Europe, and the distant expeditions already tempted its adventurous spirit. Napoleon III wanted to show his eagles and the national tricolor beyond the seas. He yielded with too much confidence to his tastes which pushed him towards the unknown and which, despite three popular investments, would lead to his demise. These expeditions cost the country much in terms of men and money. The French brought back a little glory, however France failed to understand the formidable preparations of her traditional enemy. In these expeditions, the engineers service and its methodical, patient talents played an important role.

A single company (1860), the 6th of the 2nd Battalion from the 2nd Regiment (Captain Dupuis), was added to the small expeditionary corps of Syria. Given the small importance of the operations to be undertaken, the services of the engineers were directed by a simple captain, Servel, and the park joined that of the artillery.

For the expedition of China, Lieutenant Colonel Déroulède-Dupré, commander of the Engineers, had for adjutants Major Dussouet, Captains Alizé de Matignicourt and Béziat. Two companies of the service—the 7th company of Sappers from the 1st Battalion of the 1st Regiment and the 4th company of Sappers from the 1st Battalion of the 3rd Regiment (Captain Bovet)—linked by command to the 1st Infantry Brigade, supplied sufficent means to the expeditionary corps of General of Division Cousin-Montauban. In the campaign of CochinChina, a natural outcome of the war with China, Alizé de Matignicourt commanded the engineers. He had under his command Captains Bovet, Gallimard, Pleuvier, and Mallet, Second Lieuteannt Thénard, the Bourdillat Guard, and the 4th company of Sappers from the 1st Battalion of the 3rd Regiment. It conducted itself brilliantly at the storming of the Ki-Hoa lines and in the expeditions of Mitho, Bien-Hoa, and Baria (1861). From 1858 to 1861, the Engineers service lost the following in the Far East: Lieutenant Colonel Déroulède-Dupré, Major Alizé de Matignicourt, Captain Labbé, Lieutenant Boreau-Lajanadie, Second Lieutenant Desplanches and 51 non-commissioned officers, corporals, workmen, and sappers. In those inclement conditions, disease took more victims than enemy fire.

The siege of Puebla in the Mexican campaign offered the Engineer Corps a new opportunity to show its skills and its military virtues. The campaign, however, did not result in a major displacement in its general staff and in its troops. This campaign was

undertaken like all distant expeditions which lacked a definite goal in advance that would allow for determining the required forces. At first, it used only one single company (1862). The general staff included only one officer, First Captain Lebescond de Coatpont, who was detached from the 2nd Regiment, and the Guard Heckenbinder. The company, the 6th Sappers of the 2nd Regiment, was commanded by Barillon. However, as of 1863, the engineers of the expeditionary corps took the following proportions (at right):

For this hardworking campaign, a fifth officer ranked as second lieutenant was attached to each company.

WAR OF 1870

The bad habits inaugurated in the Crimean campaign and followed throughout the campaign of Italy were irrefutably put into practice in the first organization of the Army of the Rhine. Each infantry division had its company, each army corps its reserve and its park. The army corps had their heads of service, general officers, and all the corps were tied together by an army general staff. By means of this system, the forces were equally distributed and subjected throughout to a single direction.

As has been seen in the Army of Italy, the reserve company of the First Corps had not been able to arrive on time to participate at Solferino while other companies arrived much too late. Meanwhile, the regiment only had put on route a third of their companies! In 1870, everything was used. One had to leave as he was. Many generals complained about not having seen all their engineers companies. The fault comes especially from the fatal French organization which grouped the available companies into three garrisons. Today, they are distributed amongst four. The complete distribution for August 1, 1870 is given below for the general staffs and the companies of the service in the various corps of the Army of the Rhine.

Commander of the service: Colonel VIALLA
Chief of staff: Lieutenant Colonel DOUTRELAINE
Adjutants: Majors CORBIN, BRESSONNET; Captains HALLIER, HEYDT, ECKENDORFF, DUCY, MATHIEU, DUTILLEUX, DOMBES

Troops
Commander of the Engineers of the 1st Infantry Division: Major BOURGEOIS
Commander of the Engineers of the 2nd Infantry Division: Major LEBESCOND DE COATPONT

1st Regiment
3rd company of sappers, Captain Chrétien
4th company of sappers, Captain Michelet

2nd Regiment
6th company of sappers, Captain Barillon

3rd Regiment
13th company of sappers, Captain Groult

Sapper conductors: detachments of the 1st, 2nd and 3rd Regiments; detachments of the 2nd company of workmen

---

Commander in chief: General of division COFFINIÈRE DE NORDECK
Aides-de-camp: Major GUICHARD and Captain SERVAL
Chief of staff: Colonel BOISSONNET - Assistant chief: Lieutenant Colonel SALANSON
Adjutants: Lieutenant Colonel LACHAUD DE LOQUEYSSIE; Majors SÉGUINEAU DE PRÉVAL, CHRÉTIEN, CORD and LALLEMANT; Captains LECOISPELLIER, WAGNER, BACHARACH, MATHIEU, DE ROCHAS D'AIGLON and MOUGIN
Grand Park Director: Colonel RÉMOND. *Assistant Director:* Major ANTOINE. *Adjutant:* Captain BARDE

1st CORPS
Commander: General of brigade LEBRETTEVILLOIS
Aide-de-camp: Captain TUROT
Chief of staff: Colonel PARMENTIER
Adjutants: Major MELL, Captains LELORRAIN, PONCET, KLEIN, CARETTE and MASSU

1st DIVISION—Major Barillon, 3rd company of sappers of the 1st Regiment
2nd DIVISION—Major D'Hombres, 8th company of sappers of the 1st Regiment
3rd DIVISION—Major Lanty, 9th company of sappers of the 1st Regiment
4th DIVISION—Major Loyre, 13th company of sappers of the 1st Regiment
RESERVE—2nd company of miners of the 1st Regiment. Part of the 1st company of sappers of the 1st Regiment. Detachment of sapper conductors of the 1st Regiment

2nd CORPS
Commander: General of brigade DUBOST
Aide-de-camp: Captain CORRENSON
Chief of staff: Colonel LEMASSON
Adjutants: Captains BARBARY, POULAIN, SINN, DERENDINGER

1st DIVISION—Major Sainte-Beuve, 9th company of sappers of the 3rd Regiment
2nd DIVISION—Major Lesdos, 12th company of sappers of the 3rd Regiment
3rd DIVISION—Major Peaucelier, 13th company of sappers of the 3rd Regiment
RESERVE—2nd company of sappers of the 3rd Regiment

3rd CORPS
Commander: General of division VIALA
Aide-de-camp: Major DE PONLEVOY
Chief of staff: Colonel MONDAIN
Adjutants: Captains MENSIER, CORDAT, DUMONTIER, BOURGEOT and VOLLOT

1st DIVISION—Major Marchand, 6th company of sappers of the 1st Regiment
2nd DIVISION—Major Fulcrand, 10th company of sappers of the 1st Regiment
3rd DIVISION—Major Masselin, 11th company of sappers of the 1st Regiment
4th DIVISION—Major Fargue, 12th company of sappers of the 1st Regiment
RESERVE—Part of the 1st company of sappers of the 1st Regiment. 4th company of sappers of the 1st Regiment. Detachment of sapper conductors of the 1st Regiment.

4th CORPS
Commander: General of brigade PRUDON
Aide-de-camp: Captain FAUGERON
Chief of staff: Lieutenant Colonel GALLIMARD
Adjutants: Captains HUBERDEAU, CORDIN, BRENIER and MAINGON

1st DIVISION—Major D'Embrun, 9th company of sappers of the 2nd Regiment
2nd DIVISION—Major Mallet, 10th company of sappers of the 2nd Regiment
3rd DIVISION—Major Hinstin, 13th company of sappers of the 2nd Regiment
RESERVE—2nd company of miners of the 2nd Regiment. Detachment of sapper conductors of the 2nd Regiment.

5th CORPS
Commander: Colonel CHARRETON
Aide-de-camp: Captain DUBOIS
Chief of staff: Lieutenant Colonel DE BRÉVANS
Adjutants: Captains FESCOURT, DE SAINT-FLORENT, LAMAN and RIPERT

1st DIVISION—Major Merlin, 6th company of sappers of the 2nd Regiment
2nd DIVISION—Major Heyd, 8th company of sappers of the 2nd Regiment
3rd DIVISION—Major Hugon, 14th company of sappers of the 2nd Regiment
RESERVE—5th company of sappers of the 2nd Regiment.
Detachment of sapper conductors of the 2nd Regiment

6th CORPS
Commander: General of division DUCASSE
Aide-de-camp: Captain SEGRETAIN
Chief of staff: Colonel DUVAL
Adjutants: Captains MORELLET, VARAIGNE, RIONDEL and JOURDAN

1st DIVISION—Major Féraud, 3rd company of sappers of the 3rd Regiment
2nd DIVISION—Major Fouclaud, 4th company of sappers of the 3rd Regiment
3rd DIVISION—Major Latour, 7th company of sappers of the 3rd Regiment
4th DIVISION—Major Tanon- Péissier, 11th company of sappers of the 3rd Regiment
RESERVE—14th company of sappers of the 3rd Regiment.
Detachment of sapper conductors of the 3rd Regiment

7th CORPS
Commander: General of brigade DOUTRELAINE
Aide-de-camp: Captain BOUVIER
Chief of staff: Colonel BEZIAT
Adjutants: Captains FLEURY, BUREAU DE PUZY, COMBE and CHAIÉ-FONTAINE

1st DIVISION—Major Lesecq, 2nd company of sappers of the 2nd Regiment
2nd DIVISION—Major Dormant, 3rd company of sappers of the 2nd Regiment
3rd DIVISION—Major Helie, 4th company of sappers of the 2nd Regiment
RESERVE—12th company of sappers of the 2nd Regiment.
Detachment of sapper conductors of the 1st Regiment.

IMPERIAL GUARD
Commander: General of brigade DURAND DE VILLERS
Aide-de-camp: Captain DE LANOIX
Chief of staff: Colonel BRESSONNET
Adjutants: Major PRÉVOST, Captains DÉMOULIN, BRUNAU and PETIT

1st DIVISION—Major Hitscher, 8th and 10th companies of the 3rd Regiment
2nd DIVISION—Major Henry, 8th and 10th companies of the 3rd Regiment

GENERAL RESERVE
2nd company of sappers of the 1st Regiment (telegraphic). 1st company of miners of the 3rd Regiment. 1st company of sappers of the 3rd Regiment (railroad).
Detachments of the sappers conductors of the 3rd Regiment.

Engineer sappers (1870-1871).

This organization used 37 out of 48 companies. It left eleven of them for the supplementary needs of the standing army and for the defense of areas which defeat and the invasion would make pressing.(1) As of July 14th, the minister ordered the creation of 15th and 16th companies in each regiment and the preparation of four depot cadres of which two were converted into 17th and 18th companies. They will be seen to appear immediately in the first line.

The first defeats led quickly to that false activity which doubled French misfortunes. The Army of the Rhine found itself separated into two parts. The first, composed of the Imperial Guard and the 2nd, 3rd, 4th, and 6th Corps formed the Army of Metz. It absorbed the general staff of the former Army of the Rhine. Although he had been named governor of Metz, General Coffinière de Nordeck kept the command in chief of the Engineers. The second army under the command of Marshal MacMahon was formed of the 1st, 5th, and 7th Corps to which were joined the 12th (in new formation). For commander in chief of the engineers it had General Dejean who had just quit as interim minister of war. His general staff was formed with the one from the 1st Corps plus some officers taken from neighboring areas.

Although the honorable head of the 12th Corps General Lebrun has published the composition of his army corps in a book, we are reduced to saying that, according to him, the engineers were composed of one company from the 2nd Regiment and of five companies from the 3rd Regiment. Probably the engineers from the 12th Corps commanded by General of Division Ducasse had inherited all the companies which could not follow the 6th Corps to Metz. Ducasse had under his command Commander Bourgeois in the 1st Division and Commander Roulet in the 3rd Division. The 13th still had one entire company per division. The 14th no longer had more than one section per infantry division.

The 13th and the 14th Corps thus provided Paris with five companies of engineers. There was already one at the fortifications: the 2nd Miners of the 3rd Regiment. This was inadequate for the service of the walls, the forts and the outlying posts. Five new ones were called up: 17th, 18th, and 12th *bis* from the 2nd Regiment and 17th and 18th from the 3rd Regiment. Total: 11 companies. In addition, many civilian *corps francs* (volunteer corps) were organized for the defense:

> *The Auxiliary Corps of the Engineers*, commanded by Engineer in Chief Alphand (6 workmen companies of the staff corps and 6 sapper companies) became on November 7, 1870 the Auxiliary Engineers Legion of the National Guard.
> *The Auxiliary Battalion of the Engineers*, Commander Flachat.
> *The Auxiliary Battalions of the Engineers* (22 battalions of the National Guard to whom rifles could not be given. They were more or less employed in the interior of the capital on earthworks).
> *The Battalion of Auxiliary Miners of the Engineers*, Commander Jacquot, composed of workmen attached to the Parisian services.
> *The Auxiliary Workmen of the Engineers*, commander, Engineer in Chief Ducros.

13th CORPS
Commander: Colonel DUPOUET
Chief of staff: Lieutenant Colonel LEBESCOND DE COATPONT
Adjutants: Captains LASVIGNES, ATTELEYN, BLANCHARD, MARCILLES

1st DIVISION—Major Guyot, 1st company of sappers of the 2nd Regiment
2nd DIVISION—Major Mengin, 15th company of sappers of the 2nd Regiment
3rd DIVISION—Major de Bussey, 15th company of sappers of the 3rd Regiment

14th CORPS
Commander: Colonel CORBIN
Chief of staff: Major PERRIN
Adjutants: Captains CAFFAREL and LAFOSSE

1st DIVISION—Major Houbigant, 1st section of the 16th company of the 2nd Regiment
2nd DIVISION—Captain Bardonnant, 2nd section of the 16th company of the 2nd Regiment
3rd DIVISION—Captain Michon, 1st section of the 16th company of the 3rd Regiment
RESERVE—2nd section of the 16th company of the 3rd Regiment

---

(1) There were extraordinary lapses there which would not be believed if an official statement had not been made. At Strasbourg, a front line city, although there was no lack of high level officers in the engineers, there were only eight soldiers from this service. (Director, Colonel Sabatier; Adjutants, Lieutenants Colonel Mengin and Maritz, Major Ducrot.)

It would be unfair to say that these corps were useless. However, when one thinks of the services that they could have performed if they had been truly militarized, if they had been put into action toward one single goal, one is forced to admit that the individualism and the outrageous personalization of all these little phalanxes, especially of their leaders (whom we freely acknowledge were nonetheless eminent) greatly diminished their value. While the Germans—even their kings and princes—obeyed General von Moltke, the French obey—every one of them—their own desire to appear, to shine, and to see their names in stars.

The siege of Paris was not a remarkable page in the history of the Engineers. However, its officers and soldiers demonstrated qualities worthy of the battlefield there. Although they seemed to be very busy, they did not display that industrious activity of the Russians around Sebastopol. It is true that the German attacks did not motivate them. The Germans invested Paris and did not attack it with heavy force. General Chabaud-Latour, commander in chief of the service, shared overly in the opinions of General Trochu. He saw only heroic foolishness in the resistance of the capital still more undermined by the revolution than defended by its garrison. General Tripier of the reserve, on the other hand, was endowed with orginality and limitless eagerness. He was the soul of the romantics of the defense and of those who had maintained faith and hope. His excellent good spirits and his activity at all times whipped up devotion. His valiant spirit contrasted with the glum resignation of General Chaubaud-Latour.

The companies of engineers used in the Army of Paris were subject to frequent changes of destination. For the great sorties on November 30th and December 2nd, General Ducrot who commanded them had strongly organized the three army corps under his command. Of course, it was the brave General Tripier who, as leader of the Engineers, commanded the sortie army. None other than he

Engineer sappers. Preparing the defense of a bridgehead (1877).

was worthy of this. His entire soul and will were in the sortie. He believed in it and he perhaps wanted it even more than Ducrot.

In the 1st Corps under the high level direction of General Dupouet, the two first divisions each had one company (16th of the 2nd Regiment and 16th company of the 3rd Regiment). In the 2nd Corps, under Colonel Corbin, the two first divisions were also each provided with one company (1st and 2nd of the 2nd Regiment). As for the 3rd Corps, it had been given a chief of engineers, but companies had not been attached to it.

At that time, the service lost Major Guyot, attached to the general staff, Lieutenant Parseval, and five men of the ranks, all killed. Captain de la Taille, Second Lieutenants Azibert and Montés, and 25 men were wounded.

Like all the regiments of the other services in the provinces, those of the engineers did their best to form cadres of new companies. Their history must be very muddled if one considers that nothing remained of the regiments, the cadres, nor the officers once the new companies were sent to the armies. Thus, in the 3rd Regiment, the six new companies went to rejoin the 2nd Miners in Paris. Only one company of sappers remained (the 6th) and it was in Algeria. Meanwhile, at its two depot cadres, it could rebuild some companies *bis* in as great a number as was necessary. At one point even, the 3rd's depot combined to help the depot which had been reconstructed for the 1st Regiment taken at Metz. There was immense eagerness and considerable effort.

The list, next page, is of the general staffs and the engineer troops in the provincial armies. The list is incomplete. However, such as it is, it represents a more considerable sum of documentation than that included in the numerous works published by the general officers of the National Defense.

The 22nd and 23rd Army Corps formed, as one knows, under the command of General of the Engineers Faidherbe. He had for chief of staff Colonel (since General) of the Engineers Farre. The officers of the service flowed naturally into the general staffs. Those who can be mentioned include Commander Richard, aide-de-camp of the general in chief; Lieutenant Colonel Cosseron de la Vilenoisy, second in command of the army general staff; and Captains Peslouan and Mélard, adjutants to the general staff. They demonstrated as much *savoir-faire* in the conduct of war operations as in the manner with which they presented themselves to the public.

15th CORPS
Commander: Colonel DE MARSILLY
Chief of staff: Lieutenant Colonel BARRABÉ

1st DIVISION—Major Anfrie, 1st section of the 19th company of the 3rd Regiment
2nd DIVISION—Major Odier, 2nd section of the 19th company of the 3rd Regiment
3rd DIVISION—Major Mangin, 1st section of the 19th company of the 2nd Regiment
RESERVE—2nd section of the 19th company of the 2nd Regiment
Detachment of sapper conductors of the 3rd Regiment

16th CORPS
Commander: Colonel JAVAIN
Chief of staff: Lieutenant Colonel LAGRENÉE

1st DIVISION—Major Boitel, 1st section of the 20th company of the 3rd Regiment
2nd DIVISION—Major Coste, 2nd section of the 20th company of the 3rd Regiment
3rd DIVISION—Major de La Ruelle, 1st section of the 18th company of the 1st Regiment
RESERVE—2nd section of the 18th company of the 1st Regiment
Detachment of sapper conductors of the 3rd Regiment

17th CORPS
Commander: Colonel CHARRIER
Chief of staff: Lieutenant Colonel NOCHÉ

1st DIVISION—Major Segoing d'Augis, 1st section of the 3rd company *bis*
of the 1st Regiment, Captain Joly
2nd DIVISION—Major Guillemot, 2nd section of the 3rd company *bis*
of the 1st Regiment, Lieutenant Camus
3rd DIVISION—Major Pavillon, 1st section of the 4th company *bis*
of the 1st Regiment, Captain Marion
RESERVE—2nd section of the 4th company *bis* of the 1st Regiment, Second Lieutenant Sottas

18th CORPS
Commander: Colonel DE LA BERGE
Chief of staff: Lieutenant Colonel GOURY

1st DIVISION—Major de Vignet, 1st section of the 7th company *bis* of the 1st Regiment
2nd DIVISION—Major de Casanove, 2nd section of the 7th company *bis* of the 1st Regiment
3rd DIVISION—Major Girard, 1st section of the 5th company *bis* of the 3rd Regiment
RESERVE—2nd section of the 5th company *bis* of the 3rd Regiment
Detachment of sapper conductors of the 3rd Regiment

19th CORPS
Commander: Lieutenant Colonel BOURGEOIS
Chief of staff: Major FOLLIE

1st DIVISION—Major Gazel, 1st section of the 14th company *bis* of the 3rd Regiment
2nd DIVISION—Major Monchablon, 2nd section of the 14th company *bis* of the 3rd Regiment
3rd DIVISION—Captain Schwaab, 2nd section of the 2nd company *bis* of the 3rd Regiment
RESERVE—1st section of the 2nd company *bis* of the 3rd Regiment

20th CORPS
Commander: Colonel PICOLET (1)
Chief of staff: Major CORD

1st DIVISION—Major Coste, Company of the 3rd battalion of *Mobiles* of the Loire
2nd DIVISION—Major de Bretteville, Company of the 3rd battalion of *Mobiles* of the Loire
3rd DIVISION—Company of volunteer workmen of Tours
RESERVE—11th company *bis* of sappers of the 3rd Regiment, Captain Maillard

21st CORPS
Commander: Colonel D'ENDEVILLE
Chief of staff: Lieutenant Colonel D'ORMONT, later Major BESNIER

1st DIVISION—Major Pierre, 1st section of the 4th company *bis* of the 2nd Regiment
2nd DIVISION—Major Debons, 1st section of the 8th company *bis* of the 1st Regiment
3rdDIVISION—Major Besnier, 2nd section of the 4th company *bis* of the 2nd Regiment,
Captain Laurier
RESERVE—2nd section of the 8th company *bis* of the 1st Regiment, Captain Bertnard

(1) The 20th Corps formed the Army of the East with the 15th, 18th and 24th of which a part was forced to take refuge in Switzerland. The corps did not have a historian, like the 24th. The Army of the East had as its chief commander of Engineers General SÉRÉ DE RIVIÈRE.

General Faidherbe seemed to be the general in chief who had better understood and most flattered Gambetta's weakness for hyperbole. The Engineers of the army were placed under the command in chief of Colonel Milleroux. They were composed of four companies: the 2nd company (Captain Allard) and the 2nd company *bis* (Captain Sambuc) of the 2nd Regiment; the 2nd company of the depot, Captain Mangin, and the 1st Company *bis* of the 3rd Regiment. The engineers' park was commanded by Captain Grimaud.

When the Army of the Loire was organized, the command in chief of the Engineers fell to General Javain. He had for chief of general staff Colonel Lagrenée. General Seré de Rivière took command of the Engineers of the Army of the East.

In General Cremer's independent division which fought—and really fought—the Germans at Nuits, the engineers commanded by Captain Lemore were composed of the 22nd company of Sappers from the 2nd Regiment, Captain Lebours.

In the Vosges Corps, the situation report of February 5, 1871 states as being present the 1st company *bis* of Sappers from the 1st Regiment commanded by Captain Arrengas.

In the Le Havre Corps, on the same date, the engineers had for chief the corps leader Major Peltier. His troops were made up of the 1st company (Captain Delaporte) and the 2nd Company (Captain Oursel) of the auxiliary engineers.

At Belfort, there was a half company from the 2nd Engineers Regiment. An auxiliary was formed in the Haut-Rhin *mobile*. Under Governor Denfert-Rochereau, Major Chaplain commanded the Engineers. He had for adjutants Captains Thiers and Brunetot. Given the example of the organizers of the first armies, the Government of the National Defense would have considered it a military mistake not to give 125 men and a major from the engineers to an infantry division. Yet it only sent one half a company to Belfort! It is obviously Gambetta's and Freycinet's desire to hide errors greater than those of the Empire which has pushed the French governing bodies to oppose the publication of an official history of the French army during the War of 1870-1871.

24th CORPS
Commander: General of brigade SÉRÉ DE RIVIÈRE, later Lieutenant Colonel BARRABÉ
Chief of staff: Captain LANGLOIS

1st DIVISION—2nd section of the 3rd company *bis* of the 2nd Regiment
2nd DIVISION—Captain Thurninger, 3rd section of the 3rd company *bis* of the 2nd Regiment
3rd DIVISION—Companies of engineers of the 1st and 2nd Rhône Legions

25th CORPS
Commander: Colonel GRANIER
Chief of staff: Major AUBRY

The 25th Corps was almost organized only after the armistice. Despite the generous assertions of its commander, General of division POURCET, it seems to have had only an assortment of troops. The 8th and 11th companies *bis* of the 2nd Regiment were assigned to it as engineers.

26th CORPS
Commander: Lieutenant Colonel D'ORMONT
Chief of staff: Major GIRARDIN

1st DIVISION—Major Barisien, 1st section of the 2nd company *bis* of the 1st Regiment
2nd DIVISION—Major Giles, 2nd section of the 2nd company *bis* of the 1st Regiment
3rd DIVISION—Major Tessier, 1st section of the 3rd company *bis* of the 3rd Regiment
RESERVE—1st section of the 3rd company *bis* of the 3rd Regiment

Once the war with Germany was finished, the Engineers went through the unfortunate test of the local war. Then they rebuilt their three regiments on the basis of 16 companies, 14 of sappers and 2 of miners. On November 1, 1874, the minister of war ordered the creation in each regiment of four new sapper companies. They took the numbers 15 through 18. After January 1, 1875, the sappers and miners companies no longer distinguished between themselves, all taking the name of sappers-miners. They were numbered from 1 to 20. In addition, two companies of workmen for the railroads were created per regiment. Finally, in preparation for the permanent execution of the law of March 13, 1874, the companies of each regiment were distributed in 6 battalions of 3 companies into the three schools in the following manner:

School of Arras: 1st, 2nd, 5th, 6th, 7th, and 8th Battalions.
School of Versailles: 3rd, 4th, 9th, 10th, 11th, and 12th Battalions.
School of Montpellier: 13th, 14th, 15th, 16th, 17th, and 18th Battalions.

Two new battalions had to be organized. Then, for each of the twenty battalions, a new company cadre had to be created. This formation was very painstaking before it became permanent. In effect, it had to make each battalion number coincide with the army corps where it would serve. In this organization, four companies of workmen out of the six (2 per regiment) which had been created were maintained at first, but outside the battalions.

These companies would each be attached to a regiment. Today, after one campaign in the south of Oran, these four companies, gathered at Versailles and attached for purposes of administration to the 1st Regiment train at the railroad yard in the art of demolition and of restoring the railroads. The battalions are distributed in the regiments in the following manner:

1st Regiment (Versailles): 5th, 9th, 10th, 11th, 20th Battalions.
2nd Regiment (Montpellier)*:* 12th, 16th, 17th, 18th, 19th Battalions.
3rd Regiment (Arras): 1st, 2nd, 3rd, 4th, 6th Battalions.
4th Regiment (Grenoble): 7th, 8th, 13th, 14th, 15th Battalions.

The 20th Battalion which does not correspond to any army corps is trained, it seems, like the four companies of railroad workmen. In fact, in the event of French occupation of foreign railroads, four companies would be too few. However, the innovators too often forget that in the event of war, the mobilization would call upon the territorial engineers and the railroad specialists who are stronger in this specialty in different ways than the best trained officers of the Engineers. "To each his own," is a proverb which, although ancient, always has its applications. Everything which concerns storehousing, industry, and applied science must belong to the territorial army in the modern French system of recruitment. However, military men have great difficulty understanding the revolution which will bring limited and universal service into French war habits. Instead of using the results of this revolutionary approach by putting into action all the intellectual potential of the country in wartime, they allow the demagogues to use it in peacetime to suppress intelligence, science, art, and all the liberal professions.

The 19th Battalion is not in Algeria but in Montpellier. In Algeria and in Tunisia, there are in effect four companies of sapper-miners, but they belong to various battalions.

The eighteen army corps of the first mobilization would each have a general staff composed of: 1. one general of brigade or one colonel from the Engineers commanding; one major or lieutenant colonel as chief of general staff, and two adjutant captains; 2. two majors attached to the general staff of each infantry division and one major commanding the reserve and the park; finally, 3. two companies of engineers (one half to each division, one entire to the reserve). There still remain 46 companies for various needs. This is without counting the engineers of the territorial army whose 18 battalions could supply the fortresses with companies composed of old soldiers from the service. It can be stated for the Engineers, as was done for the artillery, that they had nothing to complain about in the reorganization of 1875. They still possess fine effectives. If their battalions are compared to the French infantry battalions and their driver companies compared to the French cavalry regiments, it is the cavalry and the infantry who must complain.

Before concluding, details on the engineer personnel at Tonkin will be given. In 1883, only one single officer remained there. The naval artillery officers performed service there. It is only in 1885 when, under the influence of unhealthy concerns, one thought to refocus France's attention on the Far East that some detachments were sent there. Major Dupommier found himself already on a mission on-site. At first, two sections were put under his command: one from the 1st Regiment (aeronauts), Captain Aron, Lieutenant Jullien, and one from the 2nd Regiment, Captain Josse, Lieutenant Borel. Then, in 1885, a complete general staff was formed: Director - Colonel Mensier; Adjutants: Lieutenant Colonel Teissandier and Majors Sorel and Dupommier; Captains Petitbon, Legaillard, Joffre, Castelin, Kreitmann, Butin, Besson, Barbin, Duval, Loustalot-Laclette, Roques, de Chappedelaine, Masselin, and Borel.

The troops put at his disposal included four detachments of one hundred twenty men each, on average:

1st Regiment: Captain Jullien, Lieutenant Clavez, Second Lieutenant Poitel. *2nd Regiment;* Captain Guyon, Lieutenant Brest. *3rd Regiment;* Captain Julien, Lieutenant Jouanne. *4th Regiment:* First Captain Pierrugues, Second Captain Josse, Lieutenant Cabaud, Second Lieutenant Bertrand.

In 1886, Colonel Mensier had been promoted general of brigade. Lieutenant Colonel Granade was named to replace him in the directorate.

In 1887, Granade still occupied the directorate; his adjutants were Major Dalstein, Captains Legaillard, Joffre, Laurette, Roques, Guyon, Masselin, Lecornu, Charpentier, Jouanne, and Lesage.

Since they have been so well endowed with troops, the Engineers have rebuilt French fortifications in the east and the surroundings of Paris. These are great, patriotic tasks in which they have displayed all their knowledge and all their zeal. However, there was only one opportunity to demonstrate these to the enemy.

By a double irony of fate, the fourth regiment—the youngest—and a humble non-commissioned officer, Sergeant Bobillot, received the honor of calling public attention to the Engineers service. Commanding eight sapper-miners and using inadequate tools, this brave lad knew how to die with dignity after having gallantly performed his service as chief of the Engineers of Tuyen-Quan.

This brave sergeant will have his statue; it will be in bronze. His name has been more repeated in six months than that of Vauban during two centuries. It is the great pride of demagogues to humiliate the superb and to glorify the humble.

Student of the Polytechnic School and student of the School of Metz (1835).

Royal gendarmerie of the departments. Royal gendarmerie of Corsica. Corsican voltigeur (1824).

HISTORY OF THE GENDARMERIE

The law of January 16, 1791 did away with the constabulary, the provost court, the provosts and everything, including the mounted constabulary, representing authorities of public order under the *Ancien Régime*. It instituted the National Gendarmerie. The former mounted constabulary was almost entirely turned over to the new corps. The law of 1791, like all those which carried the stamp and the date of the great French Revolution, was already dominant. From this day forward, the gendarmerie had the department for its organic base. The departments were grouped into twenty-eight divisions.

Division	Department	Division	Department	Division	Department
1st	Paris - Seine-et-Oise - Seine-et-Marne	10th	Ariège - Pyrénées-Orientales - Aude	19th	Aisne - Marne - Ardennes
2nd	Seine-Inférieure - Eure - Oise	11th	Hérault - Gard - Lozère	20th	Somme - Pas-de-Calais - Nord
3rd	Calvados - Orne - Manche	12th	Bouches-du-Rhône - Drôme - Ardèche	21st	Sarthe - Eure-et-Loir - Loir-et-Cher
4th	Finistère - Morbihan - Côtes-du-Nord	13th	Hautes-Alpes - Basses-Alpes - Var	22nd	Indre - Vienne - Indre-et-Loire
5th	Ille-et-Vilaine - Mayenne-et-Loire - Mayenne - Loire-Inférieure	14th	Isère - Rhône-et-Loire - Ain	23rd	Charente - Haute-Vienne - Corrèze
6th	Vendée - Deux-Sèvres - Charente-Inférieure	15th	Saône-et-Loire - Côte-d'Or - Jura	24th	Lot - Aveyron - Cantal
7th	Lot-et-Garonne - Dordogne - Gironde	16th	Doubs - Haute-Saône - Haut-Rhin	25th	Haute-Loire - Puy-de Dôme - Creuse
8th	Landes - Hautes-Pyrénées - Basses-Pyrénées	17th	Bas-Rhin - Meurthe - Moselle	26th	Loiret - Yonne - Aube
9th	Haute-Garonne - Gers - Tarn	18th	Meuse - Haute-Marne - Vosges	27th	Cher - Nièvre - Allier
				28th	Corse

Each division was commanded by a colonel and each department by a lieutenant colonel commanding two companies. The company included a captain and three lieutenants. The number of brigades per department was, on average, fifteen. At the least it was twelve, at the most, eighteen. Corsica had twenty-four brigades, mounted or on foot. Commanded by a corporal or a sergeant, the brigades were of five men, including the leader. To join the corps one had to be twenty-five years old, know how to read, have a good service record, and have not been out of active service for more than three years. Although as has been seen earlier, the gendarmerie in the capital took sides with the most violent revolutionaries, in the provinces, it generally maintained a sense of order, tact, and the prudence of the old constabulary. Its uniform differed very little from that which it wore as full dress until the adoption of the tunic. The aiguillette which decorated the constabulary uniform was eliminated from the gendarmerie's, but a white piping was added to the collar, turn-backs, and cuff facings. The uniform was tricolor like the cockade which the gendarme wore on his hat. The general effective strength was 7,455 men. The law did not fix the proportions of the horse gendarmerie nor of the foot gendarmerie.

The gendarme was as he is today: a good soldier and a good citizen. Feared by criminals and miscreants, he was respected by the working people. The sergeant of the gendarmerie was highly regarded. The military men of this rank made fine marriages and even sacrificed the hope of all promotion for the advantage of staying in their own homes. This sedentary spirit which makes good gendarmes was rather encouraged in the service in the past. The instructions sent to general inspectors recommended that they not favor transfers and changes of residence which would be authorized or stipulated by ministerial decisions unless there were urgent reasons for doing so. The gendarme is named by the minister, and his commission bears the name and the number of his brigade. The addition of new departments to the territory of the French Republic led to the creation of new brigades. The law of 25 Pluviôse, Year V (February 13, 1796) brought their number to 1,500. Then the law of 22 Brumaire, Year VI (November 12, 1797) stipulated that 453 new ones be formed. Finally, the law of 28 Germinal, Year VI (March 17, 1797) decreed that the corps of the national mounted gendarmerie be composed of twenty-five divisions. Each division was to be commanded by a colonel with two squadrons under him. Each squadron included two companies commanded by a captain and three lieutenants. The effective strength was of one hundred sergeant majors, five hundred sergeants, fifteen hundred corporals, seven thousand nine hundred gendarmes, and one hundred trumpters. Total - 10,575 men distributed into 2,000 brigades. One division of foot gendarmes was organized for the Golo and Lianome (Corsica) departments.

The pay without allowances was 7,000 francs for the colonels, 4,200 francs for the majors, 3,000 francs for the captains, 2,000 francs for the lieutenants, 1,500 francs for the sergeant majors, 1,400 francs for the sergeants, 1,300 for the corporals, and 1,080 for the simple gendarmes. They were to provide the regulation kit, food, and dress and maintain themselves with good equipment.

There were still some experiments before the gendarmerie came to the Empire perfectly organized. In 1804 it had a permanent first inspector general, Marshal Moncey. Its general staff—a type of ministry, a formidable institution of civilian and military police—was established at Paris, rue du Faubourg-Saint-Honoré, 74. It had for its head General of Brigade Bucquet. Four inspectors general, Generals of Division Gouvion and Lagrange and Generals of Brigade Wirion and Radet, split the heavy task of keeping the Head of State abreast of everything which was happening in France. At the time, the gendarmerie included 28 legions—the name was permanently adopted—including one elite legion classed in the Imperial Guard. It had 2,626 brigades of which 1,813 where mounted and 813 on foot.

Elite gendarmes. Imperial Guard (1804-1815).

This was the same geographical organization as that of 28 Germinal, Year VI (March 17, 1797) and the same principle of duplicating responsibility as soon as the hierarchy got off the ground. This was an excellent principle which was wrongly abandoned since otherwise all the high-ranking officers of the same legion could be at the departmental seat. Under the Empire, the two majors were always placed in a different city than the colonel, except at Paris. The formation of the new departmental legions and the gathering of the Army of Spain did not allow early on for more than one major in each

Number of Legion	Departments	Colonels	Majors
1st	Seine, Seine-et-Oise, Seine-et-Marne, Oise	Ponsard, at Paris	Reydy-Lagrange and Hachin-Courbeville
2nd	Seine-Inférieure, Eure, Calvados, Manche	Guérin, at Caen	Vauthier and Duhamel
3rd	Orne, Eure-et-Loir, Mayenne, Sarthe	Cavalier, at Alençon	Thomas and Germain
4th	Côtes-du-Nord, Ille-et-Vilaine, Morbihan	Mignotte, at Rennes	Gauthier-Guistière and Coroller
5th	Loire-Inférieure, Maine-et-Loire, Vendée, Deux-Sèvres	Noireau, at Angers	Huché and Jameron
6th	Loir-et-Cher, Indre-et-Loire, Indre, Vienne	Bergeron, at Tours	Chaibert and Grenier
7th	Charente, Charente-Inférieure, Gironde, Landes	Mathis, at Bordeaux	Combes and Charpentier-Laverderie
8th	Lot-et-Garonne, Dordogne, Haut-Vienne, Corrèze	Martin, at Perigueux	Fontanier and Rivaud
9th	Haute-Garonne, Gers, Hautes-Pyrénées, Basses-Pyrénées	Gérault, at Auch	Regnard and Seignan-Serres
10th	Tarn, Aude, Ariège, Pyrénées-Orientales	Barbier-Lassaut, at Carcassonne	Burette and Crosat
11th	Cantal, Lozère, Aveyron, Lot	Lecocq, at Rodez	Violette and Beteille
12th	Puy-de-Dôme, Haute-Loire, Loire, Rhône	Blanchard, at Lyon	Lecomte-Fontaine-Moreau and André
13th	Creuse, Allier, Cher, Ni0vre	Almain, at Nevers	Clément and Robquin
14th	Loiret, Yonne, Aube, Marne	Sirugue-Maret, at Troyes	Dagailler and Dubignon
15th	Nord, Pas-de-Calais, Aisne, Somme	Lafons, at Arras	Souvencourt and Thouvenot
16th	Lys, Escaut, Jemmapes, Dyle	Gauthier-Bruslon, at Brussels	Florainville and Pierre
17th	Deux-Nèthes, Meuse-Inférieure, Ourthe, Sambre-et-Meuse	Maupoint, at Liège	Angineau and Mutte
18th	Forets, Ardennes, Meuse, Moselle	Buquet, at Metz	Peytavin and Richer
19th	Vosges, Meurthe, Haut-Rhin, Bas-Rhin	Saignes, at Nancy	Lepinot and Charlot
20th	Doubs, Haute-Saône, Jura, Leyman	Pagnon-Laborie, at Besançon	Clément
21st	Côtes-d'Or, Haute-Marne, Ain, Saône-et-Loire	Bourdon, at Dijon	Moncey the elder and Bertrand
22nd	Isere, Mont-Blanc, Ardèche, Drôme	Recco, at Genoble	Coste and Talin
23rd	Hautes-Alpes, Basses-Alpes, Alpes-Maritimes, Var	Genneval, at Brignolles	Pourcher and Leclerc
24th	Bouches-du-Rhône, Vaucluse, Gard, Herault	Desbordeliers, at Avignon	Boisserolles-Boisvilliers and Gentile
25th	Rhin-et-Moselle, Roer, Sarre, Mont-Tonnerre	Lauer, at Mayence	Georgeon and Lesage
26th	Golo, Liamone	Cauro, at Bastia	Luce and Ducros-Aubert
27th	Pô, Stura, Marengo, Tanaro, Sesia, Doire	Boisard, at Turin	Pavetti, Jubé and Gayault-Maubranche
Elite	2 companies of infantry and 4 of cavalry - SAVARY, General of brigade, Colonel. Jacquin, Major.		Henry and Dautencourt

legion. In 1812, the first twenty-six legions were similar to those of 1804. However, seven new ones were created and the 27th was modified. In addition, for maritime employment, the police, the ports, and fishing, seven companies had been created and attached as follows: the 1st (Boulogne) to the 15th Legion; the 2nd (Cherbourg) to the 2nd Legion; the 3rd (Brest) to the 4th Legion; the 4th (Lorient) to the 4th Legion; the 5th (Rochefort) to the 7th Legion; the 6th (Toulon), to the 23rd Legion; and the 7th (Genoa) to the 28th Legion.

Amongst the officers cited above, many were of the greatest merit and very adept in delicate missions which the Emperor confided in his heads of the gendarmerie. Law and order was difficult in an empire as extended and as tenuously held together. However the colonels corre-

Number of Legion	Departments	Colonels	Majors
27th	Pô, Doire, Sesia, Stura	Rivaud, at Turin	Pequignot
28th	Genoa, Apennines, Marengo, Montenotte, Taro, 7th maritime arrondisement	Guillotin-Dubignon, at Genoa	Gentils
29th	Arno, Méditerranée, Ombrone	Jubé, at Florence	Le Crosnier
30th	Rome (1st), Rome (2nd), Trasiméne	Costé, at Rome	Nicolas
31st	Carniole, Carinthia, Istria, Croatia civile, Dalmatia, Raguse	Tassin, at Leybach (provost-marshal-general)	Baylin -Provosts: Rigade, Brouzet, Gallet and Favier-Dumoulin
32nd	Zuiderzée, Bouches-de-la-Meuse, Yssel supérieur	Coroller, at Amsterdam	Mahoudeau
33rd	Ems occidental, Bouches-de-l'Yssel, Frise	Cheibert, at Groningue	Boussart
34th	Bouches-de-l'Elbe, Bouches-du-Weser, Ems oriental, Ems supérieur	Charlot, at Hamburg	Ravier

sponded directly with their first inspector general and informed him better than the prefects about popular sentiment. Like the lower level tax agents but better than they, the gendarmes felt the pulse of public opinion with absolute certainty. Always in contact with the inhabitants, they were the friends of women, counselors of husbands, and often their fun-loving companions.

Whether the gendarmerie should or should not be part of the political police has always been very much under discussion. The opposition has always claimed that it should not be. However, all the governments, even those which come from the most radical opposition, have pushed the gendarmerie down this path. It can only be concluded that this is one of its necessary attributes. Besides, the gendarme has no passion for politics, and never on his own account but always under the instructions transmitted by his seniors.

As has been said in the history of the cavalry, the Republic had used mounted gendarme divisions in the armies as in the reserve cavalry. The Empire did not act exactly in the same way. Meanwhile, beyond the public forces which it joined to the provosts of the armies, it reserved a combat role for the military men of the gendarmerie through the creation of two special corps: the elite gendarmerie and the Spanish gendarmerie.

The elite legion was instituted on July 31, 1801 by a decree which regulated the gendarmerie service. At first it was not part of the Consular Guard. Quartered in the Celestins district, it served as gendarmerie corps to Paris which no longer had a police legion and which still did not have the Municipal Guard. The decision of July 3, 1803 had it join the Guard and modified its duties by entrusting it particularly with the policing of the imperial residences in peacetime and the Emperor's headquarters during war. In 1804, it was commanded by Savary who was assisted by Major Jacquin. It was composed of two infantry companies and of four cavalry companies.

The remains of the camel corps—lower-ranking officers, non-commissioned officers, and soldiers—had been turned into this corps after their return home. It followed the main army headquarters of the armies. On many occasions, its role was not limited to assuring the security of the Emperor. It was used in the police, in the Guard, and in escorting prisoners. It participated honorably on the battlefield where, as at Ostrolenka, its squadrons charged with the Guard regiments. During the retreat from Russia, its conduct was epic. Its relative orderliness is due to its steadfastness which allowed the passage of the army to be carried out on the bridges of the Bérézina.

When it left on campaign, the elite legion usually received a number of auxiliaries from the legions from the interior which would increase and even double its ranks. After the campaigns of 1813 and 1814 where it was covered in glory, it was dissolved on April 23, 1814.

During the One Hundred Days, it was hastily reorganized. The short duration of the campaign of the North did not allow it to produce great results: 104 elite gendarmes, all mounted, were attached to the main army headquarters. They were commanded by General of Brigade Dautencourt, leader of the corps, Major Dyonnet, and three other officers whose names it has been impossible to find. The grand provost of the army was General of Division Radet, and General of Brigade Baron Dentzel was charged with the prisoners service.

Gendarme lancer. Army of Spain (1813).

The Spanish gendarmerie was assembled in 1809. Napoleon gave the order at the end of this year to gather 20 squadrons of gendarmerie with 16 half mounted, half on foot and four entirely mounted. (Later there were 24 of them.) They were to scout and secure the roads from the Spanish border as far as Madrid. On January 20, 1810, Napoleon wrote to Berthier: "My cousin, inform General Bucquet as soon as the first sixteen squadrons of gendarmeries which are placed from Bordeaux to Saint-Benoit each have more than 150 men, that my intention is that they will be distributed in the following manner: the 1st at Irun, the 2nd at Hernani, the 3rd at Tolosa, the 4th between Tolosa and Vittoria, the 5th at Vittoria, the 6th at Miranda, the 7th at Briviesca, the 8th at Burgos, the 9th at Lerma, the 10th at Aranda, the 11th between Aranda and Somo-Sierra, the 12th at Somo-Sierra, the 13th at Buitrago, the 14th at Cabanillas, the 15th at Alcobendas, and the 16th at Madrid. The four other squadrons of gendarmerie will be the reserve to be used throughout wherever they are needed to reinforce the line or to stay at Madrid where I want to have six squadrons to serve as needed. As soon as the six first squadrons are ready to march, you will order General Bucquet to distribute them from Bayonne to Miranda and to push them thereafter as far as Madrid as soon as the other can replace them. You will make these dispositions known to the Duke of Dalmatia by sending him the composition of these squadrons which, at a strength of 4,000 men and 1,600 horses, are adequate to maintain complete safety along the entire line from France to Madrid. You will also make it known that my intention is that the line of communication from Bayonne and from Madrid pass through Somo-Sierra as this is the shortest and least exposed to incursions by troops which might come from Portugal... You will ask the Duke of Dalmatia for a plan to extend the inspection of the gendarmerie majors along the route ten leagues to the right and to the left so that they can secure the surrounding area."

The Spanish gendarmerie left behind the finest of military rememberances. It performed daily service. The combat of Villa-Drigo (October 1812) has often been mentioned as an example of its valor. There Colonel Beteille victoriously charged at the head of three squadrons from the 1st Mounted Legion along with the chasseurs of the 15th Regiment (Colonel Faverot). Everywhere that it had the honor of attacking the enemy, alone or beside the best regiments, the gendarmerie of the Spanish Army proved itself as formidable as at the small battle of Villa-Drigo. However, their fine defense of the Monzon Fort in Aragon is too often forgotten. The Monzon Fort was occupied by 90 foot gendarmes, 4 cannoneers, and one corporal, three officers, one surgeon, and the Guard from the Saint-Jacques Engineers. These one hundred brave men resisted 3,000 men of the Mina bands from September 27, 1813 until February 14, 1814, that is, for one hundred forty days. The enemy had indicated its intention to attack the fort with mines. The gendarmes, bowing to the demands of the service, became miners and laborers. Their wives were employed on the earthworks and in the storehouses. It was only after the taking of Lérida and of Mequinenza that this small garrison—it had 10 men killed and wounded—agreed to leave. However, it left with its arms, its baggage, forty cartridges in their cartridge boxes, the only artillery piece of the campaign which

it possessed, loaded, and fuses with a supply of sixty rounds. It had to rejoin the Army of Catalonia. However, at Lérida, the Spanish had 5,000 men and numerous cannon. They believed themselves to be strong enough to dominate the situation without danger and violated the capitulation agreement. In relating this act of heroism in his memoirs, Marshal Suchet all but says that Saint-Jacques, despite its industriousness, its heroism, and its military passion, could not have obtained as great results if it had less solid troops than the foot gendarmes with it.

The Spanish gendarmerie had the same uniform as the departmental gendarmeries except it added a plume. Little by little, the use of the white trefoil was lost, and as of 1811, the entire Spanish gendarmerie wore the red epaulette of the grenadiers, its body edged with silver. In the Army of Spain, there seems to have been one squadron of gendarme lancers. Even under the Empire, even in the gendarmeries, some generals permitted themselves some eccentricities. When the Spanish gendarmerie returned to France by squadrons, by detachments, and by platoons, it was soon used by the Empire at bay. These old soldiers were adept at everything. They had practiced all kinds of military skills in the peninsula. These brave men, either in corps or mixed with the National Guard or recruits, provided enormous services as cadres.

The history of the gendarmeries of the Empire will be completed after a word about the provosts.

The details left behind by the military historians of the Empire do not say very much about the provosts. Usually it was the provost-marshal-general, in whom the Emperor's confidence was placed, who himself composed his entire service. His proposals were usually accepted without contest. The model type of provost-marshal-general of the First Empire was General Baron Saunier. He was a very distinguished man who was brave as well as very humane. A former sergeant in the Queen's Dragoons, he joined the mounted constabulary of the Orléans on February 14, 1789 as a cavalryman. His service record states that at Auerstadt on October 14, 1806, he took a Prussian battery with 20 gendarmes and 20 chasseurs. In his capacity as provost-marshal-general, he judged the arsonists of Moscow. With regard to this topic, recall that in response to the celebrated Rostopchine brochure, General de Chambray denied—for some unknown reason—his participation in the burning of the old Russian capital. In this brochure, this general—who took it from Baron Saunier—fixed the number of arsonists arrested by the French troops at thirty-three. Twenty were absolved by the provost and thirteen were shot.

The First Restoration repatriated the gendarmes and officers who were the last to stay abroad. However, it proceeded very cautiously in the interior of the territory. During the One Hundred Days, the Emperor did not have time to concern himself with the gendarmerie other than to ask it to sacrifice its horses. It was at the end of 1815 that the reactionary spirit which was driven by emigre officers—especially those who had fought against their own country—was felt very harshly by the soldiers of the Empire. General of Brigade Count d'Olonne, head of the Eighth Division in the Ministry of War (gendarmerie and military police) was not exactly charged with the affairs of the old soldiers of the country. Like almost all those of his ilk, he called Napoleon "the ogre of Corsica"

Elite gendarmerie (1820).

and his officers "brigands." Through the decree of September 10, 1815, the gendarmerie was reduced and received a new organization. It had 24 legions, each company having one department, and all the brigades had 8 men. The general effective was 650 officers (24 colonels, 46 majors, 97 captains, and 431 lieutenants) and 17,360 non-commissioned officers and gendarmes. This wealth of gendarmerie—although the territory was diminished and the desertion and disobedience service had been virtually eliminated—did not, however, indicate a desire to retain old servants. It was the mark of a new system.

In the list below, many names of emigres and of Royalist insurgents can be seen. This was not the way to reconcile populations, but it was not very closely examined. In 1819, the corps was subjected to an amputation and was reduced to 24 legion heads, colonels or lieutenant colonels, 25 majors, 69 captains, and 476 lieutenants.

ORGANIZATION OF 1815

Number of the Legion	Headquarters	Colonels	Majors and Department	
			1st Section	2nd Section
1st	Paris	Clément	Clément: Hunt company	Le Roy: Seine
2nd	Versailles	Lemoine	Paillette-Delisle: Seine-et-Oise - Loiret	Boisson de Franqueville: Oise - Seine-et-Meuse
3rd	Caen	Baron Lefaivre	De Tonnoy: Calvados - Manche	Varin de Bretteville: Seine-Inférieure - Eure - 2nd maritime district
4th	Alençon	Baron de Charlus	De Regnier: Orne - Eure-et-Loir	De Baculard d'Arnaud: Sarthe - Mayenne
5th	Rennes	Count de Bellon	Chevalier de Jouffrey: Ille-et-Vilaine - Côtes-du-Nord	Chevalier de Sautereau: Finistère - 3rd maritime district
6th	Angers	Marquis de la Roche-Bousseau	Barnabé, Baron de La Haye: Maine-et-Loire - Loire- Inférieure	Margadel: Morbihan 4th maritime district
7th	Tours	Jameron	De Jobal: Indre-et-Loire - Loir-et-Cher	De L'Espée: Vienne - Indre
8th	Moulins	Baron de Laroque	Count d'Hoffelize: Allier - Puy-de-Dôme	De Gorgas: Nièvre - Cher
9th	Niort	Renou de Labrune	Barbier: Deux-Sèvres - Bourgon-Vendée	Trolong-Durumain: Charente-Inférieure - 5th maritime district
10th	Bordeaux	—	De Pressac: Gironde - Charente	Charlier de Vrainville: Landes - Basses-Pyrénées
11th	Limoges	Roger	Larue de Laguitardie: Haute-Vienne - Creuse	Sanzillon: Dordogne - Corrèze
12th	Cahors	Boucher de Courson	De Rouault: Lot - Lot-et-Garonne	Dardenne: Aveyron - Cantal
13th	Toulouse	Seignan de Serre	Maufort de Neuilly: Haute-Garonne - Tarn-et- Garonne	Aubriot: Gers - Hautes-Pyrénées
14th	Carcassonne	De Saint-Cricq	Chevalier de Bonfils: Aube - Tarn	De Lascous: Pyrénées-Orientales - Ariège
15th	Nimés	De Vassimon	Layre: Gard - Ardèche	Royer de Saint-Julian: Hérault - Lozère
16th	Marseille	Picard	Fitremann: Bouches-du-Rhône - Vaucluse	Count Jules Dufos de Méry: Var - Hautes-Alpes - 6th maritime district
17th	Ajaccio	—	Pascalis: Corsica (1st and 2nd companies)	—
18th	Grenoble	De Valory	Count Douhet de Sourzac: Isère	Degasq: Drôme - Hautes-Alpes
19th	Lyon	Maudet de Panhouet	Marquis de Saint-Paulet: Rhône - Saône-et-Loire	Cisternes de Vinzelle: Loire - Haute-Loire
20th	Dijon	Baron Grézard	Dagalier: Côte-d'Or - Haute-Marne	Cadoudal: Aube - Yonne
21st	Besançon	Chevalier de Bouclans	Count de Brosse: Doubs - Haute-Saône	De Beauregard: Jura - Ain
22nd	Nancy	Jourdain de Saint-Sauveur	De la Martelière: Meurthe - Vosges	De Bruges: Bas-Rhin - Haut-Rhin
23rd	Metz	Christophe de la Motte-Guery	Filleul de la Fosse: Moselle - Meuse	Count Desseoffy: Marne - Ardennes
24th	Arras	Cavalier	—: Pas-de-Calais - Somme	Moizez: Nord - Aisne - 1st maritime district

Gendarmerie. Legion of the Seine (1836).

Gendarmerie of Africa (1840).

The Restoration had not treated the legion heads of the Empire with tact. Quasi-legitimacy sacrificed the gendarmes of the Restoration on the altar of liberalism. In the following table, a comparison of the corps leaders from before and after the Three Glorious Days is given.

Out of twenty-four legion heads, seventeen voluntarily resigned, four had their residence changed, and only two were maintained at their posts. The transformations in the other ranks were no less radical. During the first six months of the July Government, there were 28 promotions of majors, 91 of captains, and 244 admissions or promotions of lieutenants and of second lieutenants in the gendarmerie. Although it had not acted with such passion as the gendarmerie of Paris, the gendarmerie of the Seine had to be disfigured to be able to continue its service. The iron sheathed hat which the friends of liberty detested was taken away. The mounted gendarmes received a bearskin with visor and the foot gendarmes had a shako with stripes in the style of the First Empire. It seemed this was enough to calm the qualms of the demagogues of the moment. The Restoration had introduced the old Royalist insurgents into the gendarmeries and the July Monarchy allowed conspirators to join it. However, these brutal or comical modifications in the appearance of authority had not been accepted without protest.

Number of the Legion	Names of the colonels In 1830	In 1831
1st	De Sanzillon	Raffé, Lt. Col.
2nd	Lebertre	Potier
3rd	Baron Christophe de La Motte-Géry	De Barthe
4th	Baron Labrune	Servatius, Lt. Col.
5th	La Pourceau de Mondoret	Jomard, Lt. Col.
6th	Cadoudal, Lt. Col.	Chousserie, Lt. Col.
7th	Baron Potier	Doutremont de Minières
8th	Clément, Lt. Col.	Rosier
9th	De la Voyrie	Brault, Lt. Col.
10th	Patarin	Lecrosnier
11th	Delmas, Lt. Col.	Delmas, Lt. Col.
12th	Maubert de Neuilly, Lt. Col.	De Bony
13th	Cournault de Fonbourgade	Gailhassou
14th	Doutremont de Minières	Thurot
15th	Barthe, Baron de la Barthe	Faye, Lt. Col.
16th	De Bellon	Canel, Lt. Col.
17th	Degare	Maziau, Lt. Col.
18th	De Valory	Degasc
19th	Baron Delaroque	Ledoux, Lt. Col.
20th	Chevalier Lebas de Bouclans	Pinel, Lt. Col.
21st	Picard	Picard
22nd	De Laleu de Sainte-Preuve, Lt. Col	Guichard
23rd	Ledoux, Lt. Col.	Blin
24th	Ravier	Ravier

To fight the Carlists who were very numerous in the departments of the West, three battalions *mobiles* of foot gendarmerie were at first organized at Angers, Rennes, and Nantes. They were under the command of Majors Nicod, Mutel, and Gauthier de la Verderie, respectively. The latter officer was condemned under the Restoration for having been involved in many military conspiracies. Soon after, these battalions were dissolved and replaced by two provisional mounted regiments assembled as follows:

The 1st at Niort. Colonel Doutremont de Minières, Major Damour, Administrative Field Officer de Bermondet de Cromières, Captain Commanders Leclerc, Longuet, Lelong de Longpré, and Destremont.

The 2nd at Montpellier. Colonel Morin, Majors Saulnier and Leforestier, Captain Cardini (with the functions of an administrative field officer), Captain Commanders Gougeon, Daugnac, Rizot, and Rebillot.

These corps disappeared with the pacification of the West.

In the meantime, the campaign of Belgium had required the assembly of a provost-marshal's troops:

Provost-Marshal-General: Colonel Delmas - Adjutants, Major François, Captain Cochet de Savigny - Divisional Provosts: Lieutenants André de Berval, Richard, Boutellier, Cécile, Ferdinand, and de Prinsac.

Before creating a gendarmerie legion for the French African colony, a provost-marshal's troop had been attached to the expeditionary troops. It was commanded at first by Lieutenant Colonel Maubert de Neuilly then after the Revolution by Major Mendiry. From 1830 to 1832, they were succeeded by Colonel Mérat who had for adjutants Majors Carrelet, Leclerc, Cardini and Captain Vergez. The Legion of Africa had been organized in 1839 at four companies. From this year until the present, it had for heads the following colonels and lieutenant colonels: Cardini, Vial, Lemaire, Fumat, Damiguet de Vornon, Parmentier, Duval, Billet, de Colonjon, Lerminier, Petitjean, and Marquet.

Minor modifications had been made in the basic plan of the gendarmerie under the Restoration. When the elite gendarmerie had been organized, the departments of Seine-et-Oise and of Seine-et-Marne had joined the 1st Legion. Thereafter, the 2nd, 3rd, and 4th had been modified. The shift of the department of the Hautes-Alpes had also taken place between the 16th and the 19th Legions. These were the only changes from 1815 to 1844. It produced an event—purely related to the elections—which was very unusual and which deserves to be told in a history of the gendarmerie. A high-ranking officer of the gendarmerie was a rich property owner in Alsace. More a voter than an influential person, he had for a long time occupied with the rank of major the command of the companies of the department where he had his properties. In June 1844, after the Haut-Rhin and the Bas-Rhin were combined into the 25th Legion of the gendarmerie, he was named its head. This still required a modification of no great interest. The Revolution of 1848 had very much wanted to tackle the gendarmeries against which it had grievances. However, the law on the status of officers opposed this. It was a good thing for civilization. The reports over five days at the time of the presidential election of December 10th demonstrated the power of the information apparatus of the service. Although the prefects and the general procurers predicted an unlikely victory for General Cavaignac, the gendarmerie announced that Prince Louis would be elected by an immense majority. There was no room for hope that the National Assembly would have to carry out the election of the first magistrate of the Republic due to lack of results in the plebiscite ballot.

At the time of the coup d'état of December 2, 1851, the gendarmes obeyed the orders of the de facto government without argument.

Gendarmes of the Guard (1855).

Throughout this time, they resisted the suggestions and the acts of the Socialist party united to the Republican party. They did not have to wait long to be rewarded for this. As of December 11th, all the company commanders became majors; many lieutenants were raised to captains. Promotion received a major boost. After the annexation of Savoy into France, their number had to be increased and the basic plan of the legions had to be reworked. Twenty-six legions were made: the three new departments were distributed between the 22nd and the 25th Legions.

At the beginning of Louis-Philippe's reign, special considerations caused the gendarmerie companies created at the end of the Empire for the special surveillance of the ports and arsenals to be turned over to the naval department. However, the public forces of the colonies remained under the war allotments. They used 22 officers and 774 non-commissioned officers and gendarmes of whom 490 were mounted. The cadre had often been modified. The gendarmerie of the colonies wore a uniform which was lighter than that of the departmental gendarmerie. It sometimes even made use of very fancy clothing. Nor should we forget the two companies of veteran gendarmes who lived at Riom for many a long year.

Gendarmerie Regiment of the Imperial Guard.
Before arriving at the campaign of 1870, it is important to discuss the regiment of the Imperial Guard and the *mobile* gendarmerie battalions from which it came. After the February Revolution, the Municipal Guard (which will be dealt with in the next chapter) was mustered out. Its lower level officers were replaced in the service from which they came. The captains were subsequently put at the end of the line and the pensions of upper level officers who had a right to them were paid off. As for the non-commissioned officers and the Guard, to shield them from popular fury—the style of the times—they were sent far from Paris. They were assembled at numerous points, relatively nearby and notably at Beaumont, in types of national work gangs. There, under the officers' leadership they had to wait for

Gendarmerie, full dress (1887).

Republican Guard and Firemen, full dress (1887).

better days. When General Cavaignac replaced the executive commission of which he was minister of war, his first concern was to have these old soldiers come to Paris. Wearing sackcloth pants, shirts, and topped by kepis which were distributed to them at the same time as rifles and kits, they were quartered in the new Ministry of Foreign Affairs building which was still under construction. Their mission was to protect the National Assembly and the military bakery. Their virile and severe attitude, their solid bearing beneath an improvised uniform, and their intact discipline totally reassured President Buchez. With the end of the events of June, as of July 4th, the grateful Assembly hurried to vote them pay and a regular organization. General Cavaignac felt that it was necessary to anticipate and to immediately suppress the disorders which could be manifested at some points in the territory of the Republic. On the following September 14th, he decreed that this battalion formed at Versailles would have an effective strength of 721 men distributed into six compnaies. As soon as they were ordered to Paris, this battalion commanded by Tisserand, former captain of the Municipal Guard, became the Guard of General Changarnier and showed a great deal of steadiness on June 13, 1849. On June 8, 1850, at the same time that it was expanded to eight companies (1,200 men), a second battalion of the same strength was formed under the command of Major Sébastien, also a former captain of the Guard. Meanwhile, Saucerotte replaced Tisserand in the 1st Battalion. In the coup d'état of December 2nd, the two battalions showed resolution and enthusiasm while the Republican Guard, much less numerous, perfectly organized, and solidly commanded by Colonel Gastu (since General) allowed itself to be paralyzed by the Prefect of Police Maupas. Maupas wanted to keep these elite troops near him to insure his own safety. Also, as of December 27, 1852, the *mobiles* battalions received the title of Elite Gendarmerie (1st Battalion: Commander d'Eggs; 2nd Battalion: Commander Joly). Then with the organization of the Imperial Guard, they moved into it with the title of Gendarmerie Regiment of the Imperial Guard (Colonel Pierre). From the moment that the Republican Guard (become the Paris Guard) became adequate for the service of the capital, the gendarmerie regiment became a useless luxury. The corps was magnificent, its music excellent, its uniform superb, and its composition very fine. Therefore, it was kept. However, when the Guard left for the Crimea, the gendarmes who had mounted guard at the Tuileries door like the grenadiers and the voltigeurs had to go with them to the Army of the Orient. The regiment at first formed in two battalions of eight companies then had three battalions at six companies. Two battalions left under the command of Colonel de Prémonville and Commander Joly. The mistake of having created a large foot gendarmerie corps was then felt. From the colonel to the youngest gendarme, they would have been better placed in the provinces to perform the gendarmerie service. On June 7, 1855 at the attack of the White Works, one of the two battalions thrown ahead conducted itself very well. It had 6 officers and 136 gendarmes killed or wounded. These losses almost all resulted in widows and orphans. Thus they were more deeply felt in Paris and at the general staff of the general in chief than those of any other regiment. The gendarmes were brought back to the rear at Kamiesch, then at Constantinople. It is not unusual that the gendarmerie can be assembled in regiments for short, defined tasks. Once these duties are finished, the corps thus formed must be dissolved under pain of seeing them decline and weaken—without it being their fault.

The gendarmerie regiment of the Imperial Guard did not participate in the campaign of Italy. It did not appear to be overly satisfied nor overly unhappy with its lot. However, its uselessness as a combat corps was unquestionable from that point on. The number of its companies was decreased. It was deliberated whether they should not be mustered out in order to turn over part of the troops to the Guard of Paris, forming a third battalion there. All these plans were aborted. The only reasonable one prevailed. On September 25, 1869, the gendarmerie regiment of the Imperial Guard died. Its two last colonels were Peytavin (1859) and Arnaud de Saint-Sanveur (1865).

At the same time that a regiment was formed with the two *mobiles* battalions (become elite gendarmeries), a gendarmerie hunt squadron (*gendarmerie de chasses*) was assembled by means of selection from the brigades of gendarmerie assigned to guard the châteaux and the forests of the Imperial domain. On April 16, 1864, this squadron ceased to be part of the Imperial Guard. It was placed under the authority of the great marshal of the palace with the title of Squadron of Elite Gendarmerie. Like the gendarmerie of the Seine, this corps wore the bearskin but with a plaque of the same model as that of the Gendarmerie Regiment of the Guard. This squadron was mustered out on October 6, 1870.

As of August 11, 1870, the need to shelter Paris—which was deprived of a garrison by the war—against a sudden strike by rioters from the Chamber and the suburbs led to the assembly of one mounted gendarmerie regiment and one foot gendarmerie regiment in the capital. The rioters sought to profit from enemy victories and to overturn the established government. The first regiment had six squadrons which, during the siege (October 17, 1871), were expanded to eight. The foot regiment at first had two battalions expanded to three on October 5th at the moment when a second mounted regiment of six squadrons was created. The first six squadrons and the first two battalions had been formed with selections from the departmental legions. The last eight squadrons and the last battalion were, as a result of the retreat to Paris, formed from gendarmes and officers belonging to the invaded departments.

The first of these three magnificent regiments was mounted. It was commanded by Colonel Martenot-Chadelas de Cordoux then by Colonel Alavène. The second, also mounted, was commanded by Colonel Potié. The third, a foot regiment, was commanded by Colonel Bouthier. However, they did not perform all the services which would be expected of them. They were not used well against the rioters, nor on September 4th, October 31st, or January 21st. The 1st Regiment at Châtillon was sent out once against the enemy. It had four officers wounded, the colonel, the lieutenant colonel and the adjutant majors Martin and Yvon, plus eight non-commissioned officers and gendarmes. In addition, for the duration of the siege, a squadron from the same regiment commanded by Captain Morel operated as scouts to the general staff of General Ducrot along with the Franchetti squadron.

The three colonels of these regiments were named generals of brigade.

Kept as foot troops by the armistice convention, the three gendarmerie regiments of the siege were more intelligently employed by Thiers against the members of the Commune. It is due to the foot regiment sent to Sèvres on the night of March 18th to 19th that French society was not overthrown with the remains of the French government. At first, the gendarmes stopped the rioters from crossing the bridge. Then on April 3rd, through their example, they swept along with them the line troops.

Thiers had such faith in the gendarmerie that not only did he keep the two mounted gendarmerie regiments under the command of General Dargenlolles throughout the period of the Commune, but afterwards, he formed a legion of gendarmerie *mobile* to insure safety for the seat of government at Versailles and to reinforce the departmental gendarmerie wherever it was in need. The beginnings of this corps should be told here since they demonstrate how troubled the people were. After having completed a confidential mission at Bordeaux, Lieutenant Colonel Lambert, former provost-marshal-general of the Army of Paris, returned to Versailles with Thiers. He was charged with organizing the Legion of Gendarmerie *Mobile*, since become a battalion. Gifted with a very spirited and flexible mind, Colonel Lambert was able in a matter of days to assemble an instantly homogenous troop possessing a most forceful and solid pride in their esprit de corps. After some minor changes in uniform, intelligent leadership quickly made of this troop of 1,200 men (eight companies and one squadron) a sort of imperial guard for the Assembly and the center of power. The representatives, who did not dare

Gendarmerie (1870-1871).

place themselves in the hands of the regiments they considered as Bonapartists (if they were formed of soldiers returning from enemy prisons) or as Republicans (if they were from the Gambetta formation) began to breathe easily again under the protection of the brave men who almost all came from former Imperial Guard regiments. In 1879, the corps was mustered out. It no longer had a reason for being and its recruitment became difficult. Majors Thyriet and Ellye succeeded Colonel Lambert.

It is now necessary to trace our steps backwards in order to explain what was done with regard to the war. Each corps of the Army of the Rhine had its provost-marshal's troops directed by a major of the service. Each infantry or cavalry division also had a captain or a lieutenant with twelve gendarmes. General Count Arnaud de Saint-Saveur was invested with the functions of the provost-marshal-general of the service. These provost-marshal's troops and the organization of the three provisional regiments assigned to the service of Paris absorbed a great number of officers and military men from the service. Then, new provost-marshal's troops had to be supplied to the twelve army corps formed by the governments of Tours and Bordeaux. Their service was harsh at all times. Without them, the war would not have lasted past the month of December. At first, the multiple needs of the service were addressed with the gendarmerie pushed back from the invaded countryside. However, these needs grew daily in formidable proportions. The military police required continuous supervision. The law was not equal for everyone. Young men called by it to the defense of the country were able to escape military service and hole themselves up in offices, even in Gambetta's. The people often resisted mobilization orders. The National Guard and even the regular troops sometimes showed discouragment in a war where they were always beaten and where no glimpse of victory was in sight. Nothing irritated them more that the pompous official bulletins which transformed their continual defeats into successes. According to Gambetta's accounts in the newspapers, the provincial armies would have killed more Germans than had ever entered into France. This obnoxious and ridiculous manner of recognizing both the enthusiasm and the efforts of a serious patriotism quickly turned against the intended purpose. A subdued inertia replaced the enthusiasm and the liveliness of the first days. Traces of this distressing state were found everywhere.

These provincial armies were troubled by lack of discipline and desertion in the middle of a country where the worst passions were being stirred up. Thus, the gendarmerie's task was not easy. The decree of October 2, 1870 invested court martials with the right of judging the guilty and of executing them within twenty-four hours. Too much pretense has been made of ignoring the fact that, in practice, they received strong approval. From October 15th on, the *Moniteur Universel* printed almost daily executions. (This newspaper replaced the *Journal officiel* at Tours and Bordeaux.) From this date until January 14, 1871—that is, three months—eighty-two executions have been uncovered of which sixteen were of civilians who served as spies or sold food to the enemy. The sixty-six others concerned military men. Many, and certainly most, executions took place. The government kept them quiet so as not to

frighten the people and to avoid giving greater confidence to the invader. Chanzy's and d'Aurelle de Paladines' works do not raise any doubt about this subject. The provost-marshal's troops were inadequate to collect the stragglers. When the stragglers were great in number, they did not mind resisting with weapons in hand and formed themselves into bands which lived by pillaging. As of October 18th, two mounted gendarmerie regiments of 500 men each and one of foot gendarmerie (1,236 men) were assembled to guard the rears of the armies. However, this did not completely meet the stated goal. On December 23rd, it was decided that the inactive gendarmerie would be mobilized to rush upon the "runaways, deserters, and disbanded troops." This decree, whose wording is signed Ad. Crémieux and countersigned Freycinet, does not show a lot of moral sense on the part of those who claimed to have raised up France with their noble beseechings. Consequently, the 2nd, 8th, 9th, 13th, 14th, 15th, 16th, 18th, 19th, 20th, 22nd, 24th, 26th, then the 25th and 17th Legions were formed into squadrons and *mobiles* regiments. There is no administrative trace left of their formation, however. The gendarmes called to the armies were replaced in their brigades by auxiliaries drawn either from the gendarme class in retirement or from the *mobilisés* of the old military National Guard. They seemed likely to perform good service in the gendarmerie. On February 27, 1871, eight days before the mustering out of the last provincial armies, the execution of the decree from the preceding December 23rd was suspended. The departmental gendarmerie again took up its basic plan of formation.

It had performed extraordinary services, having supplied four mounted regiments and two foot regiments. Many of its old officers and non-commissioned officers had rejoined the service for the duration of the war. Many general officers coming from its ranks distinguished themselves at the head of divisions and of brigades. Six of these legion heads: Gaulard, Bourdillon, Fauconnet, Deflandre, Dubois de Jancigny and Brunot du Rouvre, had been named generals with permanent titles. Four of them: Lefebvre-Desnoette, Pelletingeas, Delhorme, and de Bruchard, were named with provisional titles. They commanded either active brigades or territorial subdivisions. Its groups of *mobilisées* were very well led under fire at Orléans, Beaugency, and Vendôme. In the Army of the North, two squadrons *mobilisés* under the command of Major de Courchamp did not show themselves to be unworthy of their comrades of the Army of the Loire. At Dijon, General Fauconnet was killed while bravely leading at the head of his brigade.

The Peace of Frankfurt eliminated the 6th Legion composed of the Haut-Rhin and the Bas-Rhin. It also returned the lieutenancy of Belfort to the company of the Haute-Saône. However, immediately after the vote on the law of cadres, the gendarmerie, whose basic plan was abandoned by ministerial initiative, was expanded to thirty legions. The distribution was done in a manner such that the army corps contained entire legions. This ended in many legions being in the same corps. Thus, the 15th had three legions (22nd, 23rd, and 24th). Nine corps: the 6th, 7th, 9th, 12th, 13th, 14th, 16th, 17th, and 18th, had two of them. The eight others had only one of them. With the 1st Legion (Seine and Seine-et-Oise) created for the government of Paris, this gives a figure of thirty. Then a minister, enamored with logic, rightfully thought that this numbering system of overlapping legions did not make sense as it exceeded the numbering system of the army corps. He judged it appropriate to give the numbers *bis* and *ter* to legions which were found in doubles and triples in the corps. The former First Legion was called the Legion of Paris. The others took the numbers of their corps.

The rapid—even extraordinary—advance which these various organizations had brought about in the service drew very active officers into their ranks. Instead of being the refuge of somewhat tired although able officers, the corps appealed to the ambitions of lieutenants and captains leaving the polytechnic school and the School of Saint-Cyr who were happy to retain certain privileges of civilian life while under military harness. From that point on, all the jobs of the legion head belonged to the majors of the gendarmeries. These military men could fan the hope of achieving symbols of rank, and even stars, faster than their classmates who were faithful to the more combatant services. However, the idea of equalizing promotion predominated in the army. The gendarmerie, which had not been protected by the law of cadres, was the first victim offered to the new ideas and economic necessities imposed by the deplorable state of French finances. Meanwhile, to compensate the non-commissioned officers for what they lost in promotion to the epaulette, the minister had been forced to create a position of adjutant in each company and a position of sergeant-major in every lieutenancy so that recruitment for the gendarmerie was not stopped at the lowest levels.

Today there is only one gendarmerie legion per army corps. The governments of Paris and of Corsica—in view of their special situations—each form one of them. With Africa, this gives a total of twenty-one legions. A number of companies are only commanded by captains. All the paymasters are lieutenants. The corps finds itself reduced to the following proportions: 24 colonels and lieutenant colonels instead of 34; 32 majors instead of 82; 282 captains instead of 311; 302 lieutenants instead of 286; and, finally, 97 lieutenant paymasters instead of 33 captains and 64 lieutenants.

This reform, which subsequent increases of the service justified, was accompanied by another much more serious one. It consisted of transforming a number of mounted brigades into foot brigades. In 1885, the service counted 2,218 mounted brigades versus 1,859 foot brigades. When the reform in question is totally complete, the proportion will be reversed.

SPECIAL TROOPS OF PARIS

The history of the inactive garrison of the city of Paris is very tormented since it plays an integral part in the French political revolutions. In the aftermath of a popular victory, this garrison was always disgraced and replaced by the conquerors of the previous day. From that point on, the new troops took sides with the most advanced portion of the population. This lasted until the day when, purged, it became again a magnificent troop and succumbed after a few years to the blows of a new political revolution. For a century, there had almost always been a Guard of Paris under various names. However, it was only in 1813 after the Malet conspiracy that this Guard was permanently classed in the gendarmerie. It only ceased to be part of it for a while after the events of February 1848.

During the Revolution. In June 1789, the Guard of Paris was commanded by Lieutenant Colonel de Rulhière of the cavalry, a very close relative (the brother or the cousin of German birth) of the poet-historian. His troops did not belong to the army. They consisted of one hundred thirty-two cavalrymen and eight hundred ninety infantrymen. Composed of old, discharged military men, almost all were fairly old or married. It only took part reluctantly in the first disturbances which preceded the taking of the Bastille. It disappeared very naturally into the creation of the National Guard. Its active elements were turned over with the French Guards, the conquerers of the Bastille, and the company of la Basoche, into the companies of the paid National Guard. Its cavalry—especially its remount—was incorporated into the mounted National Guard of which Rulhière was the first commander. The infantry was given to Hulin who later became general of division. Things moved along very rapidly with organizations succeeding one another. Everything was done with no thought for the morrow. By entrusting the law and order of Paris to paid companies of the National

Guard, the new uniform of the latter was compromised. Also, a little while later, it was judged to be appropriate to entrust the supervision of the capital to the national gendarmerie who were already replacing the constabulary throughout France. Three gendarmerie divisions were specially assigned to this service.

What remained of the French Guard, the old Guard of Paris, and the paid companies was handed over to it. This produced a very nasty combination. From that time on, almost all the gendarmes of Paris were seen at the head of the rioters. Since then this has changed, fortunately, but being a true historian, what occurred I should record.

On 9 Thermidor, Year II (July 27, 1793), the gendarmerie of the Tribunals (Major Dumesnil), the squadron of gendarmerie quartered at the Luxembourg Palace which called itself the "Squadron of Men from July 14th," as a group did not seem to be for or against the Convention or for or against Robespierre. Except for the gendarme Meda or Merda—who is known to have withdrawn—the gendarmes employed in Paris demonstrated little decisiveness. Meanwhile, the following day, they maintained order on the Place de la Revolution while Samson proceeded with the execution of Robespierre and of his accomplices. This fact should be considered as very fortunate since after the insurrection of Prairial, Year III (May-June 1794), it was necessary to guillotine some gendarmes who had compromised themselves too much. The Convention ordered the mustering out of the gendarmerie of the Tribunals and of the 29th, 32nd, and 35th Divisions then employed in the capital. The service was temporarily delegated to the line troops and under Aubry's proposal, (9 Messidor [June 27th]), a Police Legion was created, composed as follows:

Legion of police (Year IV [1795]).

1. of two infantry demi-brigades, each of three battalions at eight companies of 100 men, officers included: total, 4,800 men.

2. one cavalry brigade of two dragoon squadrons and two chasseur squadrons. Each squadron had two companies of 152 men: total 1,216 cavalrymen.

These troops were to form a small army of 6,016 men. In the thoughts of the Directorate, they would replace the Army of the Interior which political necessities immobilized around Paris to the detriment of military interests. The soldiers were either the sick who sought refuge there from their very great misery or the direct heirs of the gendarmes from the Year III (1792), and even deserters. The cavalry, lacking horses, was at first reduced (10 Fructidor, Year IV [August 27, 1795]) to a single regiment of dragoons.

This militia did not inspire great confidence in those who made use of it. They always tried to separate its battalions. On 13 Vendémiaire (October 4th), a portion which was quartered at Versailles was charged by the Convention with capturing and guarding the Meudon depot and it acquitted itself well. The other part took up positions amongst the troops which defended the Hall of Deliberations of the National Representation against the Sections. However, both the legion's due compensation and the fulfilment of the promises made at the time of its formation (when it was very poorly composed) had been haggled over. Its reduced cavalry was turned over to the 21st Dragoons. Like the infantry of which a single demi-brigade had been assembled, it was vehemently suspected of having promised its support to Buanorotti for the conspiracy of equals. It was mustered out on 9 Floréal, Year IV (April 28, 1795) for having refused to obey the law. The officers were considered dismissed and the men of the ranks returned to their homes.

The uniform of the Police Legion for the cavalry and the infantry was a blue coat lined in red, white collar edged with two lines of scarlet, red turnbacks and cuff-facings with white edging, yellow buttons stamped with the words *police generale* and surrounded by a civic crown, and a hat of the standard model. The infantrymen had white waistcoats and breeches; the cavalrymen had beige. The minister of war must possess in the attics of the gendarmerie offices the rolls for the corps of which no trace can be found in the almanacs and the annuals.

Many corps which should not be forgotten thus participated in the service of the capital:

Grenadiers of the Convention and of the Legislative Corps. As of the end of September 1791, the National Assembly had taken measures to entrust the National Guard, the gendarmeries, and the army with the task of guarding its safety. However, these measures did little to protect the representatives from the crowd's vulgarities. Installed at the Tuileries, the national representation was visited almost daily by tumultuous demonstrations. On July 28, 1792, it began to forbid the public access to the Terrasse de Feuillants. The constitutional act of Year II (1793) gave the Legislative Corps the policing of law and order in its sessions. However, in September 1792, the Committee of Public Safety had deemed it appropriate to surround the site of the meetings of the Assembly with resolute and dedicated men. It ordered the creation of a Guard of the Convention. This guard which subsequently bore the names Gendarmes, Gendarme Grenadiers, Grenadiers of the Convention, and the Guard of the Legislative Corps, was organized on 4 Thermidor, Year II (July 22, 1793) at eight companies of 100 men. It was commanded by a colonel. It had not demonstrated great dedication on 9 Thermidor; however on 13 Vendémiaire (October 4th) it was better recruited and inspired by Bonaparte. It was this guard which toppled the Royalist sections in the Dauphin cul de sac. The grenadiers Brossart, Laudier, Goubert, Flackmann, and Auberger were published in the general orders. Soon thereafter, in Brumaire, Year V (October-November 1796), this guard was expanded to two battalions of 600 men. Its spirit had been modified since, on 18 Fructidor (September 4th), the adjutant general Ramel who commanded it thought he could oppose the coup d'état of the Directorate with it. However, betrayed by his second in command, Blanchard, and the officers Tortel, Ménéguin, and Viel, he had to turn over his sword to Augereau. Adjutant Commander Blanchard paid the price of his treason with the succession of Ramel. On 18 Brumaire (October 8th), the Guard of the Legislative Corps kept itself in reserve. General Lefebvre, commanding at Paris and dedicated to the movement which was going to be carried out, had to use the means available to him to paralyze the hostility of his commander.

Guard of the Directorate. This honor guard, formed by the decree of 24 Vendémiaire, Year V (October 15, 1796), was composed of some 240 men. It was commanded by General of Division Krieb and General of Brigade Jubé. It was divided into cavalry and infantry. Its infantry included two companies of grenadiers at 55 men each and its cavalry was of the same strength. It had inherited the music section from the Police Legion, directed by a distinguished clarinetist, Fairu-Guiardel. His band of twenty-five musicians performed pieces in fashion at the Luxembourg Palace to the great delight of the Parisians of the time. This music section was the same as today's music section of the Guard of Paris. There was not a single official ceremony nor a single dinner at the President's of the Directorate without Fairu-Guiardel and his musicians present.

On the morning of 19 Brumaire (November 9th), General Moulin tried to hold back the mounted grenadiers of the Guard of the Directorate: "We will go to Saint-Cloud," answered the high-ranking officer who commanded them. As for the infantry, it was already there. The grenadier Thomé who covered Bonaparte in the hall of the Five Hundred, by making a shield of his body for the emperor, belonged to the Foot Guard of the Directorate. On 20 Brumaire (November 10th), upon their arrival at the review which passed before the Consul, the four companies learned that they were to form the nucleus of the Consular Guard.

At the same time as these corps, a number of gendarmes and officers detached from their legions participated in the policing of Paris. They were gathered into a number of provisional companies. Not daring to trust these permanent corps to maintain order in the capital, the Directors addressed themselves to the gendarmes of good faith belonging to the provinces and whom they could manipulate as they intended. As for the civilian police, they were multiple, numerous, and very bad.

Bonaparte did not want this dispersal of forces. On July 31, 1801, he organized the Elite Legion with the military men from the detached gendarmerie at Paris. At first he gave a permanent name to provisional cadres. What became of the Elite Legion after its passage into the Imperial Guard has been discussed elsewhere. It continued to be part of the service of Paris.

Imperial Period. It was the First Consul who first had the idea of introducing into the budget of the city of Paris a portion of expenses for a guard charged with replacing the gendarmerie. This would also supply Paris with solid war battalions.

On 12 Vendémiaire, Year XI (October 3, 1802), a Consular decision instituted the corps which at first took the name of Municipal Guard of Paris. Composed of two regiments at two battalions of six companies each and of one dragoon squadron at two companies, it formed a total force of 2,334 men, of whom 180 were cavalrymen. The officers were named by the Consul according to the list of candidates submitted by the prefect of the Seine.

The first regiment assigned principally to the service of the ports and of the great barriers wore a green uniform lined with white, white jacket and breeches, black leggings, and red cuff facings, collar and turn-backs. It was organized by the adjutant commander Remoissenet who had already been employed in the service of Paris during the Revolution.

The second regmient would perform the interior or home service of the capital. It had a red uniform, white jacket and breeches, green cuff facings, collar, and turn-backs, and black leggings. It was organized and commanded from 1803 to 1812 by Colonel Rabbe who—unusual fate—after having been judge of the Duke of Enghien was himself condemned to death following the Malet conspiracy.

The dragoons who were still commanded by Colonel Goujet wore the iron grey uniform with red cuff facings, collar and turn-backs, and yellow buff jacket and breeches.

The infantry had copper buttons; the dragoons had pewter ones.

The decree of May 18, 1806 raised the total effective strength of the two infantry regiments to 2,660 men and stipulated that, subject to the same rules as

Guard of Paris (1806-1815).

the other troops of the Empire, the Guard of Paris—thus it took this name—would be assimilated into the line. The pay was, however, a little less substantial. In practice, the regiments alternated in the service of the ports, the gates and the interior. They changed quarters every six months to find themselves in proximity to the posts which they had to occupy. From this movement comes the popular proverb from the period of the Empire: "When the reds go away, the greens take their place." In actuality, the police of the time, more intelligent than those of today, did not look approvingly upon the soldiers charged with ensuring order in the capital combined with their prolonged stay in the same quarters. At the same time, the Guard of Paris always had one or two battalions on campaign. These battalions were formed of companies indiscriminately taken from the two regiments. In Year XIV (1805), one of these battalions was sent to the Prussian border. It returned to Paris in February 1806 without having fired a single shot. Two other battalions: one from the 1st Regiment, Major Vidal; one from the 2nd Regiment, Major David, with a strength of 47 officers and 1,076 men of the ranks, left on December 24, 1806 under Rabbe's command. They went from Hesse into Pomerania. They participated the following year at the siege of Danzig where they particularly distinguished themselves. At Friedland, they were part of the Dupas Division which was listed in the general orders. They returned to Paris on October 28, 1807. From November 15th, while their comrades returning from the Grande Armée took up the service of the capital, the two other battalions left for Bayonne and were incorporated into Dupont's army corps. With a strength of 1,058 men, the *régiment de marche* of the city of Paris was commanded by Major Esteve and Major Parsis. Soon a reinforcement of 297 men was led to it by Major Bernelle. However, it was included in the capitulation of Baylen.(1) Some months later, a new battalion of 665 men and 21 officers left for Bayonne under the command of Major Daviet. It was placed in Bessières' Corps. It remained in Spain until the middle of 1812. The decree of February 12, 1812 which recalled it to France returned the infantry of the Guard of Paris to the basis of a single regiment at two battalions with Rabbe receiving the command.

(1) An officer of the Guard of Paris, C. de Mery, left one of the most interesting accounts of his detention on the Isle of Cabrera.

Before their combination, the two regiments were organized in the following manner: administratively and militarily, they obeyed the governor of Paris or rather his deputy, General Hulin. They formed one brigade having a special general staff: commander, General de Bazancourt; aides-de-camp, Captain Blanchard and Lieutenant Reissenbach; commissioner-*ordonnateur*, Barnier.

FIRST INFANTRY REGIMENT
Colonel: Devaugrigneuse; Administrative Field Officer: De Querelles; Majors: Allard and Davanture; Quartermaster: Vandevoorde Adjutant Major: Descubes-Delascau;

1st battalion -	Grenadiers:	Viotti, Captain; Dardé, Lieutenant; Probal, Second Lieutenant
	1st company:	Dandré, Captain ; Beaumont, Lieutenant ; Forqueray, Second Lieutenant
	2nd company:	Bordérieux, Captain ; Hayot, Lieutenant
	3rd company:	Malot, Lieutenant
	4th company:	Thomas, Captain ; Richard, Lieutenant ; Chauvin, Second Lieutenant
	Voltigeurs:	Devillers, Captain ; Didier, Lieutenant ; André, Second Lieutenant
2nd battalion -	Grenadiers:	Philippe, Captain ; Lacroix, Second Lieutenant
	1st company:	Leblanc, Captain ; Saint-Paul, Lieutenant
	2nd company:	Martin, Captain ; Thory, Lieutenant
	3rd company:	Lamare, Captain ; Caillat, Lieutenant ; Alquier, Second Lieutenant
	4th company:	Watrin, Captain ; Herbin, Lieutenant ; Buer, Second Lieutenant
	Voltigeurs:	Félix, Captain ; Puech, Lieutenant ; Robin, Second Lieutenant

SECOND INFANTRY REGIMENT
Colonel: Rabbe; Administrative Field Officer: —; Major: Daviet and Thibault; Quartermaster: Pegard; Adjutant Majors: Godard and Pepe

1st battalion -	Grenadiers:	Rouff, Captain ; Palma, Lieutenant ; Leroy, Second Lieutenant
	1st company:	Grimaud, Captain ; Fauchisson, Lieutenant ; Mougey, Second Lieutenant
	2nd company:	Saint-Aubin, Captain ; Bourdillat, Lieutenant ; Maillot, Second Lieutenant
	3rd company:	Blancheron, Captain ; Carey, Second Lieutenant
	4th company:	Bérard, Captain; Canon, Lieutenant ; Choisy, Second Lieutenant
	Voltigeurs:	Lavard, Captain; Husson, Lieutenant ; Viot, Second Lieutenant
2nd battalion -	Grenadiers:	Labour, Captain ; Lemonnier, Lieutenant ; Frérot, Second Lieutenant
	1st company:	Dupré, Captain ; Bernez, Lieutenant ; Damour, Second Lieutenant
	2nd company:	Bazancourt, Captain ; Montelle, Lieutenant ; Gadolle, Second Lieutenant
	3rd company:	Bardou, Second Lieutenant
	4th company:	Lafond, Captain ; Remouss*, Second Lieutenant
	Voltigeurs:	Vidal, Captain ; Bezy, Second Lieutenant

DRAGOON SQUADRON
Colonel: Gouget; Quartermaster: Sallez

1st COMAPNY	2nd COMPANY
Captain: —	Captain: Giost
Lieutenant: Lafargue	Lieutenant: Diaion
Second Lieutenant: Cugnet	Second Lieutenant: Gourel

As for the Malet conspiracy, it was completely in this general's mind. The books, the memoirs and the writings of the time are all in agreement in demonstrating that Malet, very much influenced by the Greek and Latin classics, had no direct accomplices in the army. He counted on Imperial centralization to make a *fait accompli*. He also counted on the bloody memory of the sacrifices which Napoleon had imposed on France such that this *fait accompli*—false as it was—would allow a revolution to be installed. If the Bourbons bribed him, they kept the secret very close since today all historical documents converge to prove that Malet worked either for the Republicans or for the son of Philippe-Équalité. Following Charles Nodier, a likable literary hack who had been with all the parties, some Republican writers have adopted the legend of the "*Philadelphes*" and the "*frères bleus*", conspirators to whom Malet and the very problematical Colonel Oudet have been given as leaders. These writers would have it that Malet had relations with some officers and non-commissioned officers of the Guard of Paris. This is all pure invention and, moreover, a partisan one. Rabbe—a judge of the Duke of Enghien—was not a conspirator.(1) Captain Bordérieux and Lieutenant Beaumont, condemned to death and their comrades Godard and Rouff, acquitted, were very brave men who had obeyed military orders. Cambacérès, Rovigo, and Clarke were the most culpable amongst them since as, guardians of authority, they had let themselves be surprised. They did not dare have Rabbe shot. However, the mystery which still surrounds the affair of October 23, 1812 evidently lies in the great haste of the trial and in the rapid execution of the victims able to be exonerated who were sacrificed to the anger of the master. What is certain is that the National Guard of the cohorts and the soldiers of the Regiment of Paris were not surprised that a general whom they did not know came to wake them at night and announce to them the death of the Emperor and—what should not be forgotten—peace. The Regiment of Paris was the name of the Guard battalions of the capital, men who were old enough to have seen the incredible days of the First Revolution. Napoleon himself was not amazed at the obedience of the petty officers and the soldiers, but the stupidity of certain high-ranking officers and of the civil servants strongly irritated him. As of October 24th, one battalion of the Guard of Paris had been sent to Meaux and the other to Versailles. The Emperor ordered the dissolution of the corps (December 30, 1812) and used its cadres in the formation of the 134th Line Regiment (January 6, 1813). The dragoons which Malet had not had time to requisiton had to be turned over to the 2nd Chevau-légers lanciers Regiment of the Imperial Guard.

After having thought about re-establishing the watch, Napoleon wisely judged that he must break with custom by entrusting the law and order of Paris to simple soldiers. He felt it was appropriate to give this job to the gendarmerie. He thus created an Imperial Gendarmerie Legion of Paris for the capital. It was composed of four companies forming an effective strength of 853 men, partly on foot and partly mounted. He gave the command to Colonel Bourgeois with the title of Colonel of Services of the City of Paris.

The Restoration appropriated this organization. The Police Guard of Paris, under the name of Royal Guard of Paris and under the command of Baron Tassin, had the same composition. On January 10, 1816, it was expanded to an effective strength of 1,021 men and took the designation of Royal Gendarmerie of Paris. It kept this name until July 1830. However, under Colonel Viscount Foucault de Malembert, it very quickly became the object of all the liberals' curses and insults. A lieutenant of this corps—the brave and excellent Denest(2)—under the command of Colonel Foucault, dragged Manuel from the Tribunal after Sergeant Mercier from the National Guard refused to do it. After this time, there was no longer a gathering or a riot where the prefect of police did not throw his fine gendarmes at gawking bystanders. Also, before

---

(1) General Malet was poorly informed of what was going on in the Guard of Paris although he had a corporal of the Guard (named Ratteau) for secretary. In his marching orders for the Paris garrison, he designated the 2nd Regiment of the Guard which had not been in existence for eight months. There is a double mystery in the situation report of this Corporal Ratteau, nephew of a high-ranking magistrate, who in addition to the surveillance of his leaders, became the secretary of a suspect general who was prisoner. Ratteau delivered the order and rally call words to this general, taking an active part in the attempt to overthrow the government, and was pardoned from the death penalty with his colonel, Rabbe.

2) Lieutenant Denest, named captain for this deed, was exiled by the July Monarchy to the African gendarmerie, then to Corsica. He became major by seniority on December 12, 1833 and was retired in 1840 without having been able to obtain the epaulettes of lieutenant colonel for which he had been proposed six years earlier.

Republican Guard (1848).

crying out: "Vive la Charte!" on the night of July 26th, the rioters began by warming up with the cry: "Down with Foucault!" while throwing stones at his soldiers. Mustered out in 1813 for having not adequately defended the Empire, the special troops at Paris were dissolved after the July days for having too well defended the royal power.

The Restoration, with its police-like customs pushed to extremes, had put all the posts under surveillance. Up to a certain point, even the barracks were under surveillance by the Colonel of the City of Paris, as he was called by the decree of January 16, 1816. The adjutants of the city of Paris, charged with this routine garrison service went in order every morning to the aforementioned colonel and formed a corps of captains, lieutenants, and second lieutenants. They were as detested by the garrison as by the population of the capital. After the Revolution of 1830, this service returned to the garrisons. However, the officers who were charged with it inherited the nickname "verdigris" which their predecessors had borne. It was impossible to rediscover the origin of this gibe which bears simple testimony to the hate which the city of Paris bore for those adjutants.

The Municipal Guard of Paris (August 16, 1830), the direct heir of the Royal Gendarmerie of Paris, again took up a Republican name. At the same time, it adopted a uniform which recalled the Imperial Guard. It totally exaggerated new ideas and had the blades of its sabers engraved with the date of July 29, 1830. The corps, organized by Colonel Girard, made remarkable efforts to take on a respectable appearance as quickly as possible. At the same time as it was set on conciliating the various oppositions of the past therein, the new monarchy, as quickly as possible, removed all the troops from the past which did not fit into its organization. It then was decided that the corps would be made part of the gendarmerie.

At right is the first actual organization of the Municipal Guard of Paris (1831). There were two battalions of four companies each and two cavalry divisions of two squadrons each. The two groups were each commanded by a lieutenant colonel. Above them ruled the colonel as a general of brigade. (1)

The July Government had difficult beginnings. Before becoming quasi-legitimate, it had to absorb or destroy all ambitions and hopes that had been born in the Three Glorious Days. There were frequent riots, conspiracies, and attacks. The Municipal Guard had to frequently take up the saber on whose blade shone an important riot date in the midst of everyone. It never hesitated to give its all. In the events of June 1832 in a charge near the Panthéon, Lieutenant Colonel Dulac was wounded, Captain Turpin killed, and many non-commissioned officers and guards met the same fate. The insurrection was not put down until the Municipal Guard paid with yet more blood for its laudable efforts. Louis-Philippe, while totally cherishing his fine National Guard, did not forget his faithful Municipal Guard. He always put distinguished officers at its head. After Baron Feisthamel, it was Baron Carrelet, then Colonel Lardenois. The riot of May 12, 1839 and the ease with which it had been put down must have reassured the King. It demonstrated to him the poverty of the Republican party and the inaneness of the secret societies. However, the events had uncovered a black mark: the National Guard had not

Colonel commanding: Baron Feisthamel
INFANTRY Lieutenant Colonel Vesco
1st BATTALION: Commander Lardenois 1st company: Mason - 2nd company: Gobert 3rd company: Carbon - 4th company: Bailly
2nd BATTALION: Commander Charton 1st company: Lemaire - 2nd company: Turpin 3rd company: Rollin - 4th company: Langloy
CAVALRY Lieutenant Colonel Roize
1st DIVISION: Commander Dulac 1st Squadron: Moniot - 2nd Squadron: Wolbert
2nd DIVISION: Commader Fly de Millordin 3rd Squadron: Louapt - 4th Squadron: d'Hébrard (ant)

responded eagerly to the call and the army had witnessed it with little emotion. This was minor but for a government born of a popular movement, it was a warning. On the other hand, the Municipal Guard had applied itself unstintingly and without hesitation. It had four killed and 23 wounded of whom 3 were officers, Lieutenants Post, Tisserand, and Leblond. An ordinance from July 24, 1839 expanded the Municipal Guard from 1,444 to 2,996 men. It always had four cavalry squadrons but from this time on, it had 16 infantry companies. The following year (July 1, 1841) it was increased by one squadron and its strength was expanded to 3,189 men of whom 645 were cavalrymen. From that day on, the Municipal Guard of Paris was considered by the opposition as a political guard. It remained henceforth the prototype for the special garrison of Paris in dress, recruitment, and reputation. Popular for its splendid uniform which recalled the legions of the Empire, it was secretly hated by the workers and the good people whose pleasures it watched over daily and whose deviations from the rules it quelled. When the February Revolution came about, the Prefect of Police, Delessert, an honest man but an inept policeman, did not get it under control. He left the Guard dispersed in its quarters at Minimes, Tournon, and Faubourg Saint-Martin where it waited uselessly for orders. In 1813, on the advice of the Duke of Rovigo, Minister of Police, Napoleon had maintained the separation between the civilian and military authorities who commanded the special troops at Paris. Rovigo was in a rivalry with the Duke of Feltre, Minister of War. Feltre's dedication, which was both dubious and loud, inspired only partial confidence. In 1830, this did not result in any inconvenience because events had immediately taken a turn which put all civilian and military power into the hands of the Duke of Raguse. In 1848, on the other hand, this separation proved to be equally undecided by the three parties involved: the prefect of police, General Sébastiani, commanding the 1st military division, and General Jacqueminot, commanding the National Guard. The Municipal Guard did not perform the services which could be expected of it and was

Municipal Guard (1830-1848).

(1) The colonel commander of the Guard, which is called the "Municipal Guard", the "Guard of Paris", or the "Republican Guard," holds the post of general of brigade. He has under his command a mixed brigade. He is also both the head of the cavalry corps as well as the infantry. This situation brought forth a problem under Louis-Philippe's reign which was resolved in three different ways. What should the head of a corps wear for headgear when the helmeted cavalry and the infantry with shako are equally important in a corps? Baron Feisthamel, an old infantryman, adopted the shako. When Baron Carrelet succeeded him, he recalled that upon leaving the School of Fontainebleau, he had served in the cavalry; he took up the helmet. However, Colonel Lardenois was already an old gendarme when he came to the command of the Guard. He thought it possible to wear the cocked hat in battle. This was badly taken by the two factions of the corps who assembled to accuse him of wanting to set himself apart from the general of brigade. Since 1851, the colonels of the Guard have always appeared in a shako in all the public ceremonies and reviews.

Municipal Guard (1835).

disarmed and mustered out. Its leaders had to hide themselves and its soldiers had to leave Paris. Some were massacred at their posts on the Place du Palais-Royal and at the Place de la Concorde. The author of this book was a grenadier of the National Guard in 1848. He saw the four companies and the squadron from the Saint-Martin barracks at 3:30 p.m. on February 23rd return a flag (the one placed above the door of the barracks) to 300 National Guards. When he mentioned his surprise to Commander P., head of that fine troop, the latter replied: "We are abandoned since this morning. We don't know what happened in Paris, nor if the government still exists. The National Guard has taken charge; we must obey it."

With the unarmed Municipal Guard scattered and hunted, Paris no longer had law and order. The new governors entrusted themselves to the National Guard and to its patriotism as the sailor swears his soul to God in the middle of a storm. However, at all times and under all circumstances, the National Guard shows more good faith than patience. It consents to guard its quarters. However, if it is a question of sending it to cover the positions of the Hôtel de Ville or elsewhere, it shows little concern. Besides, last night's rioters are always today's gendarmes. The conquerors of the Bastille in 1789 had formed the first paid companies of the National Guard. In 1848, the secret societies were the first guards of the Hôtel de Ville and of the Prefecture of the Police. The citizen Chenu has written a history of these bands which had nothing in common with the regular troops except an esprit de corps pushed to extremes. This spirit violently removed from its ranks everyone who could not call himself a long-time Republican. Some spies always managed to slip in.

For these bands, there were two major places of assembly: the Hôtel de Ville where Rey commanded who was a friend of the *National*, and the Prefecture of Police which Mercier controlled who was Caussidière's brother-in-law. In the barracks of the Municipal Guard, some guards dressed in shirts and some citizens of good faith had taken care of the horses. Few were stolen. Their blankets and their large size quickly brought them to the attention of the people charged with finding them. Thus, there was an excellent remount. An unusual point is that it was Caussidière who put his hand on almost everything belong to the cavalry. Marrast, at the Hôtel de Ville, could only gather some dispatch riders. He took his revenge on April 26, 1848 by having the provisional government give an official existence to his special battalion, named the "Republican Guard of the Hôtel de Ville," which was composed of 600 men. Caussidière, who had taken the Montagnards, the conquerors of the Tuileries, and the Lyonnais with him, knew that he could obtain such a sanction. He contented himself with amazing the Parisians and making order with disorder by means of shirted men on foot or mounted who wore sashes and neckties of red serge. A few days after the events of May 15 (May 27, 1848), Caussidière's troops were mustered out by a decree of the Assembly. If they had not engaged in politics nor wanted to weigh on the future of the country and the deliberations of its representatives, one would have readily believed that they were composed of old Municipal Guards disguised. They showed so much zealousness and severity in their patrols and in the execution of orders.

The same day, May 27th, a decree organized a Parisian Republican Guard composed of 2,000 infantrymen and 600 cavalrymen. This reorganization would be implemented in the battalion of the Hôtel de Ville. At first, it was poorly done. On the 14th and the 22nd of June, some decisions appeared to deal with it, regulate it, and give it 2,200 infantrymen and 400 cavalrymen as effectives.

The serious events of June thus found the Police Guard of Paris in full reorganization.

Composed of odd elements, with disparate uniforms, coming from Caussidière's bands, the battalions of the Hôtel de Ville, and new organizations with overly simplified enlistments, the Republican Guard had representatives on both sides of the barricades. A sizeable portion directed by some officers, who were for the most part detached from the army, conducted themselves well. They showed praiseworthy dedication in spilling their blood for the defense of society. Major Lebris and Lieutenant Oubert were killed. Lieutenant Colonel Vernon, Commander Baillemont, and Captain Lisbonne were wounded. The other part, reinforced by former officers and mustered out Republican Guards who had retained their uniforms, openly took the part of the revolters and did not demonstrate any less courage. When the events of June were ended, they tried to continue with the decreed organization. However, it was impossible to form a mixed corps composed of officers owing their positions to politics, wearing insignias above their true rank, not considering themselves as totally committed to the service, and commanding non-commissioned officers and soldiers who were even more eccentric than themselves. To cut short all these attempts, it was decided on February 16, 1849 that the Republican Guard would form an integral part of the gendarmerie. On April 21st, its organization was fixed at 16 companies of infantry and 3 squadrons of cavalry (2,400 men and provisionally 2,130). The corps was seriously purged. Only a very few instigators of the Revolution were left. The Municipal Guard component returned to its dominant role. It was under these excellent conditions and under the command of a top-notch officer, Colonel Gastu, that the Republican Guard came to the coup d'état. The faintheartedness of the prefect of police on the day that the Guard was shut up in the

Guard of Paris (1852-1870).

prefecture with him reduced it to a totally negative role. This was perhaps the sole Parisian upheaval where it had not taken any part.

Under the Second Empire, the Guard, now the Guard of Paris, was content to be a maginificent corps which performed its service well and commendably in all aspects. On September 4th, it was still left to itself. The authorities of the day having been modestly withdrawn before the insurrection, it conducted itself with a lot of skill. It fell back in the face of all demonstrations of popular anger, which allowed it to be conserved and used during the defense of Paris. It is true that to save it from the jeers of the Parisian street urchin, its yellow buttons were removed and its trefoils and its orange aiguillettes were replaced with those of the gendarmerie. Although composed of old soldiers, it was not often used. Meanwhile, in all instances, it proved itself zealous as much in the foreign service as in the suppression of problems at home. The Government of the National Defense lacked industriousness and patriotism in Paris. The Republican Guard, former Guard of Paris, and the gendarmerie foot regiment were able to supply some second lieutenants and sergeants to all the new corps. Since its services were looked down upon which nonetheless could make a corps of the foot gendarmes enclosed in Paris, it was appropriate to ask their cadres for young soldiers. The gendarmerie never refused any sacrifice when it was a question of defending the country. On the day of capitulation, the Republican Guard counted 2,685 men present (cavalry, 25 officers and 581 men of the ranks; infantry, 60 officers and 2,104 men of the ranks.) It retained its arms and was charged with the Faron Division to maintain order during the armistice. On March 18th, companies or demi-companies of the Guard were added to all the columns charged with ensuring order or with taking back cannon from the insurgents who were obeying the Central Committee. The arrest of sixty foot Guards by the members of the Commune of Montmartre was due to this situation. Included in the Guards taken into custody were thirty-nine who were amongst the hostages abandoned to the savages of the Commune by Thiers' presumptuous blunder.

During the civil war, the Republican Guard attached to Vinoy's Corps was particularly employed as a prisoners' guard at Versailles and in their evacuation at the depots and the ports.

Governor Thiers never looked at expenses. His customary extravagance inspired in him the desire to endow the city of Paris with one brigade of the Republican Guard composed of two legions of 16 companies at 4 squadrons each (June 23, 1871).

The mustering out of the Imperial Guard had brought back from enemy prisons a crowd of old military men who still owed many years of service and who were happy to finish their time with good pay in the garrison of Paris. Many gendarmes who had been called

to Paris into the provisional regiments assembled in July and August 1870 asked for the same assignment. When at the end of 1871, General de Cissey reviewed the new Guard on the Champs-Elysées, it presented a superb aspect. Even a battery of six mountain artillery pieces drawn by mules had been added to each legion. This gave these police troops an undoubtedly formidable appearance in the eyes of disorderly people, but it did little to reassure calm men. This uncommon deployment (it may even be called impolitic) of the special gendarmerie of the city of Paris and of their engines of war lasted only a short while. On October 4, 1873, the Republican Guard was returned to a single legion of 21 foot companies and to 6 cavalry squadrons: 4,020 men (3,192 infantrymen, 726 cavalrymen, and 122 with the general staff). This considerable force, which is justified by the development of Paris, is very difficult to maintain with an army like the French one composed of very young soldiers. The size was lowered and the number of supernumerary Guards who were not more than twenty-five years old was increased. Nonetheless, the regulation complement can never be attained. The Republican Guard is not any less an unusual corps in Europe. The traditions of the old Municipal Guard are carefully observed there as much in discipline as in the colors of its very bright uniform. Until the present, like the gendarmerie, the Republican Guard has avoided the dolman jacket. Its infantry has retained a military form of headgear. It is said that this is going to stop. Nor should its remarkable music section be forgotten, a creation of the Empire, and one which, under Paulus and Sellenick, has preserved the reputation of the leading musical military band in the entire world. Their successor, the adept Wettge, continues their traditions.

This book was completed when there appeared on July 5, 1887 a decree returning the Republican Guard to less generous proportions. From this point on, its three battalions will each have no more than four infantry companies of 175 men, in total 2,208 men. Its cavalry will have only four squadrons comprising 688 men. Reasons of economy have been invoked for this measure. There are others which will next require new modifications. The only just reproach which may be addressed to the Republican Guard is that, in its organization, it overly resembles an ordinary regiment and it does not do enough of the gendarmerie service. The new organization still accentuates the accuracy of this reproach. One major, fifteen captains including one adjutant major, and thirty lieutenants are eliminated. Certainly in spite of the promotion which it received from 1851 to 1880, the gendarmerie has been made to atone much too harshly for its love of order and its hatred for rioters. This time will pass, however.

The cost-cutting organization of July 5th maintains a music section of forty-five musicians (conductor and second conductor included) and sixty-eight drummers and buglers. This is a bit too much noise for a police corps, but our amiable municipal council which was overly consulted in this matter, adores noise and detests the police.

The Parisians do not complain. Wettge's music is in fact the best of the military world and it would be unfortunate to change it.

Colonel Gastu had as successors: 1851, Tisserand; 1856, Texier de la Pommeraye; 1859, Faye; 1863, Letellier Blanchard; 1868, Valentin (who was Prefect of Police in 1871 and then commanded the brigade of the Republican Guard); 1871, Allavène (the 2nd Regiment was commanded from June 21, 1871 to October 15, 1873 by Grémelin); 1875, Lambert; 1877, Guillemard; 1881, Azais; and 1886, Massol.

In the event of mobilization, half of the Republican Guard marches as does half the gendarmerie. Its officers, its non-commissioned officers, and the troops most suited for war service are designated to form the provost-marshal's troops and the public forces of the various armies, army corps, and divisions.

FIREMEN

For a very long time, the firemen of the city of Paris have been workmen paid by the City. Their chiefs took officers' titles, but they had no rank in the army. Moreover, early on the corps had no arms. It appeared in the *Military Annual* only very late, after the Revolution of 1830 although a royal decree dated from October 16, 1824 conferred upon it a rank in the army. It can be seen that the firemen of Paris are very attached to their civilian and professional tasks. They have never made a special case for their military prerogatives. On July 6, 1801, a decision of the Consuls had meanwhile decided that the *gardes pompiers* (firemen's guard) of Paris was to have a military organization and a uniform. However, it was only on September 18, 1811 that the Emperor gave it the name of Battalion of Firemen of the City of Paris along with muskets. It was also subject to the obligation of contracting enlistments and of performing police service in the army branch services. Thus, the corps actually dates from 1811. It is the transformation of the firemen guard civilian workers into soldier firemen that brought about all the snags in military discipline that are uncovered in the history of this corps. On the other hand, it was so devoted to its professional work.

There are two types of men in the firemen of Paris: the worker who lives too much like a citizen to be a military man and the military man whose immobility and occupations demilitarize him.

The firemen's constitution from July 6, 1801—except for the number—was, in principle, excellent and superior to all those which have since been made. The firemen's corps, composed of 293 men, was divided into three companies. Each one had a captain, a lieutenant, two sergeants, thirty corporals, thirty first escort guards, thirty second escort guards, and two trumpeters. A head commander and a second in command, an engineer, a second engineer, and a quartermaster administered the corps which was able to serve ninety pumps. In addition, each company was to receive thirty supernumerary firemen guards and thirty student firemen guards which brought the acting effective strength of each company to 153 men.

The supernumerary guards were housed and clothed but the student guards were only housed. The time that they spent in this position counted as their military service and assured them of ending with their discharge in the corps. The recruitment was therefore good, but at the same time hostile to the military spirit, in the absolute sense. Was it this consideration or was it rather the numerical inadequacy of firemen at the great fires, notably at that of the Hôtel Schwarsemberg, which determined the Emperor to issue the decree of 1811? Today it is difficult to say. What is certain is that the militarization of the firemen's corps subjected it to a more rigorous discipline and removed from them that character of workmen which permitted admitting and maintaining within its ranks only masons, carpenters, roofers, plumbers, joiners, wheelwrights, locksmiths, saddlers, and basket makers. They all had to work for free in the manufacture of their materiel and their engines. Led by engineers who had to draw up plans of public buildings and of the various quarters, these workmen represented a considerable, intelligent force. As the service was supervised more by the police than by the military garrison, a civilian spirit which was somewhat paternalistic dominated the service. In the thirty posts of Paris where one corporal and two appointed escorts, supernumeraries or students were believed to be, there was often only one man, at most two. Instead of increasing the inadequate pay of the firemen guard, of subjecting their service to a rigorous supervision, or deciding that two breaches in the service in less than one year would lead to discharge from a very sought-after employment, the Emperor converted the corps into an infantry battalion of 576 men.

Gendarmerie, campaign dress (1887).

Lottery. Paris, Salle Saint-Jean (1887).

The battalion had 4 companies with two officers, 5 non-commissioned officers, 11 corporals, 10 salaried employees, 112 sappers, and 2 drummers. The general staff included one major, one engineer, one adjutant major, one quartermaster, and one surgeon. It was quartered with the first company at the Prefecture of Police in two houses, situated on Rue de Nazareth. The second company was at rue des Blancs-Manteaux, the third at Rue Napoléon (today Rue de la Paix), the fourth at the Jacobin's of Rue Saint-Jacques. The decree stipulated that the battalion's expenses would be supported by the City until the establishment of a fire insurance company. Evidently, the Emperor wanted to talk about a company with fixed premiums since mutual companies already existed. It should be added that these desires of the Emperor were very reasonable, but outside the military realm. Since then, over many a long year, the great companies with fixed premiums have supplied the communes of the provinces with fire pumps on the condition that their territory undertake supplying a certain amount of insurance. As for the mutual companies, their system rests on the principle of local solidarity. They generally maintain their pumps and their firemen. Therein rests the true origins of the provincial firemen's corps, all the civilian ones, and all the municipal ones, some of which are truly fine. Let us say in praise of the corps of Paris, that it always provides the departments with the best instructors and the most capable engineers.

The Emperor had also organized a company of sappers from the engineers for the imperial residences. It was at first assigned to handling the pumps in the palaces and the châteaux. However, it often served on campaign at Paris, Saint-Cloud, and at Rambouillet.

After the first organization, Colonel Ledoux commanded the corps of the *gardes pompiers* for a long time. At the end of the Empire, Commander Delalanne replaced him with Peyre for his engineer. The four companies were quartered as follows: the 1st (Captain Duperche) at the headquarters, Quai des Orfèvres; the 2nd (Captain Queru) at Rue des Guillemites in the building of the Blancs-Manteaux; the 3rd (Captain Lacon) at Rue Napoléon (today Rue de la Paix); the 4th (Captain Taissaud) at Rue Saint-Jacques.

The Revolution which brought the Bourbons back to the throne did not modify the organization of the firemen. Commander Plazanet was named major, but Engineer Peyre and the principal officers were retained. The numbering system and the location of the companies was modified. The 1st (Duperche) stayed at general headquarters, Quai des Orfèvres. The company from Rue de la Paix had Number 2. The 3rd company was placed at Rue Culture-Sainte-Catherine and the 4th at Rue du Vieux-Colombier. An excellent measure had been studied and carried out from 1812 to 1816. A depot of pumps on boats had been organized across from the Hôtel des Monnaies and thirteen post horses for the night fire barrel service had been established in each barracks and in the twelve arrondissements. At a time when water systems did not exist, when the public fountains were widely spaced, and when wells offered only a very limited resource, this was enormous progress.

In July 1830, the firemen were shut up in their barracks. The general staff let them stay there. The residents who were happy to see their firemen conduct themselves with such wisdom cried out: "Long live the firemen!" The corps doubled its chances of not being shot down like the Guard and of not laying down its arms like the Line. However, from this day on, with the encouragement of their leader and of the authorities, its military spirit deserted the battalion.

Gisquet tells about the events of June 5, 1832 in his memoirs. The firemen of Rue Culture-Sainte-Catherine who saw that they were surrounded by the riot dismantled their rifles and hid them instead of resisting. Colonel Paulin was the successor to Plazanet. He was extremely distressed and went to tell the Prefect about this. The Prefect was very angry, saying that this abstention was equal to treason. Colonel Paulin's response deserves to be related in full since it is the best defense in favor of that popular argument: the firemen, protectors and saviors of the capital's residents, legitimately retreated from the sad necessity of firing on them.

"Your displeasure is very natural, Monsieur Prefect, and I am as painfully moved as you yourself. However, would you reflect on the fact that the firemen have never been assimilated into the troops and that they are not political men. They have a special, exclusive task where they acquit themselves with zealousness. Even in the July Days, the powers did not have them fight against the people. These reflections are not mine, Monsieur Prefect. I am only the echo of that which has often been said to me. I bring it up only to mitigate the wrong about which you are complaining. However, if you authorize me to give orders to my men in another direction, you will see that we know how to rival the Municipal Guard in terms of dedication and resolution."

This was a lot to promise. All the same, the barracks of Rue Culture-Sainte-Catherine were freed by the firemen from other barracks marching with their colonel at the head. What Paulin said was and unfortunately still is right today, to a certain extent.

On September 23, 1841, the battalion was expanded to five companies. Each company had 3 officers and 160 non-commissioned officers and sappers of whom 4 were sergeants and 36 corporals.

The pay and the various expenses of the corps were entirely supported by the budget of the city of Paris. A severe order forbade the detachments called outside of their barracks by the announcement of a fire to leave the boundaries of the capital. At the time of the fire at the first Hippodrome, the firemen rushed to the Étoile boundary but could not have crossed it if the Duke of Nemours had not been working the first pump. The little newspapers, while loudly praising the prince, reported that the order in question held that no fireman could spend a night outside of Paris without permission. Verification was made. Article 48 of the ordinance from September 23, 1841 contains this order, interpreted in a strange way.

In the February revolution, the battalion went a little further than in July 1830 by purely and simply dismissing the major of artillery Vivès (Anatole) and electing in his place Lieutenant Terchou from the corps. In his memoirs, Caussidière made no allusion to this abnormal election. For him with his good revolutionary sense, the firemen were not soldiers but simple state servants charged with extinguishing fires. Most extraordinary of all was the reaction which followed the presidential election of December 10th. It let this deplorable state of affairs live on without a single officer having

Firemen of the City of Paris (1840).

Firemen of the City of Paris (1835).

protested in the name of the laws on promotion and on the status of officers which were so openly violated by the election of Terchou. Meanwhile, on May 27, 1850, the mustering out of the battalion returned things to order. The preambles of the decree of mustering out gave full and total satisfaction to the words stated above by Colonel Paulin. They noted that, in its organization and its actual composition, the corps did not satisfy the goals of its institution (firefighting no doubt) and, from the viewpoint of military discipline, it presented serious inconveniences which are important to remedy. It was believed that the decree of reorganization signed by Baroche and General d'Hautpoul was going to give ample satisfaction to the goal of the institution and demilitarization of the corps. Oh, administrative logic! It was a little more tightly militarized. Its strength was expanded to 819 men, divided into five companies of 158 men. Vivès took up its command again and, in the new battalion, a certain number of officers, non-commissioned officers and soldiers were retained.

With the seven year service, the corps recruited men having one and one-half years of service. Consequently their military education was done. They had four years to give to the firemen's service and many non-commissioned officers and corporals reenlisted. In addition, although officers obtaining promotion could be called into the infantry regiments by transfer, this was only done on rare occasions. Special training and service won out in this case since, in matters concerning fires, the officers and old firemen claimed that cold-bloodedness and experience are the two fundamental qualities of a good sapper. The others come afterwards. The best firemen are those who have maneuvered in the midst of great fires.

On February 10, 1855, a sixth company was created to put the effective strength of the battalion more in line with the needs of the capital. Ten days later, a seventh company with an effective strength of 100 men was organized under the name of expeditionary company. It was to go to Kamiesch and Gallipoli and protect French magazines from fires. They must have become very frequent to require the assembly of special personnel.

At the end of the campaign, this company which performed great services was incorporated in the battlion (October 1856). On February 7, 1859, the battalion was increased by three companies. For three years, it would be commanded indifferently by a major or a lieutenant colonel as in the past. Finally, on December 5, 1866, it became the regiment of sappers-firemen with a colonel, a lieutenant colonel, two majors and an administrative field officer. The decree of 1859 had attached it to the infantry for orders. That of 1866 made it a regiment of infantrymen. This was a misfortune, and a rather haunting one. Regardless of the effect a handsome battalion—even a regiment of sapper-firemen—produces in a review, regardless of how well they maneuver there, what makes

hearts beat at its passing is not its virile attitude. It is the thought that all those brave men are ready to risk their lives to save the city. Their dedicated actions can no longer count. It is because we esteem them above all that we relate fully and truthfully the misfortunes which have very recently caused them the defect of their organization.

During the first siege of Paris, the officers' corps requested that a war battalion be formed in the regiments and used against the enemy. It was a favorable opportunity since the capital was overflowing with firemen from the large and small suburbs. They were refugees put on subsistence in the corps for the duration of the war. This meant they were assigned to a unit other than their own for pay, food, clothing, etc. General Trochu and Colonel Willermé were ruthlessly opposed to this request. They said the firemen were not fighters and, besides, they had enough to do with putting out fires caused by the bombardment.

I will repeat again: this was an enormous misfortune. The results of this refusal to class the firemen amongst the fighters while nonetheless leaving them as military men will soon be seen. On the evening of March 18th, the colonel learned that the army was falling back on Versailles. He sent two officers including the engineer to General Vinoy to ask him for instructions. The general who was quite busy verbally responded that the corps, "not being fighters, must stay in Paris as long as their position remained tenable." Some days later, the Commune acted on its authority, as could have and should have been foreseen. It made the corps pass into the egalitarian system and ordered that the ranks in it be put up for election as in the other troops of the federation. The elections were published in orders by Colonel Willermé A single captain resisted, Captain Cluzel from the barracks on Rue Blanche. He gave his accounts to the colonel and rejoined the army at Versailles with one of his officers. The other captains in this difficult situation followed his lead soon thereafter. The colonel, whose conduct in this situation certainly lacked decisiveness, had to pay dearly for not having protested against the elections and for having in some sense supported them. He was imprisoned. As for the corps, except for some non-commissioned offcers who also made their way to Versailles, it obeyed almost to a man the revolutionary movement. What else could it have done, deprived of its officers and its protectors? The sergeant-secretary of the treasury was elected major and corps head. He performed his work well enough. The pay was administered honestly and the service insured. However, it became almost impossible to impose a punishment and to maintain some semblance of discipline in these troops revolting against military laws. Some passionate men took to the ranks amongst the combatants. However to the honor of the corps, it should be loudly announced that not a single sapper from the city of Paris was seen behind those petrol pumps. It is confirmed that these petrol pumps were not invented by the harpies of the reactionary newspapers.

Military justice's account attests to this: out of 231 sappers referred to the councils of war, only 22 were condemned, but none had been arrested for fire or pillage.

These unfortunate firemen to whom the generals of the two sieges had refused that precious status of fighters were more poorly treated than the accomplices. All the officers resulting from the election and about sixty soldiers were shot, and one hundred were sent to Africa. The corps was rebuilt, still militarily despite this terrible lesson.   There is a military historian who is a partisan for arming the firemen, especially because he envisions their status as being soldiers. (Thus, if France does not want them armed, it should have a corps of civilian firemen as in the past.) He recounts that, after the Commune and the purification, Thiers hesitated a lot in giving arms to the regiment. An employee of the minister of war who badly interpreted an order would have ordered their rearmament. The surpised authority would be resigned to ratifying the *fait accompli*. It would be better to believe that, using past lessons and trusting in the firemen's patriotism, it was not thought that the regiment could be deprived of an honor to which it had the right, just like an infantry regiment.

No doubt to instill the corps with a totally military appearance, it was given accomplished infantrymen for colonels and officers: Saint-Martin, Paris, and Couston. However, the shadow of the *gardes pompiers*—firemen because they could not be soldiers—still floats over this fine corps which Europe envies the French for its bravery, its industriousness, and its dedication. However, its distribution into twelve barracks, its special occupations, and its character recognized as non-belligerent must ensure a system of temperate lifestyle which is decidedly more civilian than military. In the event of mobilization, the firemen reservists—useless in their corps which is always kept at a peacetime complement and which does not have a war complement—are turned over to the chasseurs à pied battalions.

Since 1870, the corps has entered onto the path of technical progress. Up until then, the large and small arm pump, the knotted rope, the diving apparatus for basement fires and some other equipment formed all the materiel that the firemen possessed. Today they have steam pumps, always under pressure and ready to go, wagons for rapidly transporting the sappers, and engines of all types. However, thanks to the system of recruitment, the men are very young and pass only into the corps. Be that as it may, the traditions of the past are preciously retained. The Parisian sapper is always ready to risk his life in a fire or in a rescue operation. Lieutenant Colonel Froidevaux, crushed by a flaming girder, and the numerous sappers killed under the same circumstances whose names are inscribed on the monument raised to the glory of the regiment speak favorably of the men from this noble corps. They should not be called martyrs but rather heros of duty. In relating here its military misfortunes, we wanted to demonstrate that these misfortunes all come from the deplorable situation which its extraordinary position as a non-fighting military corps has created.

Today the regiment has twelve companies and is completely counted in the infantry service with which its officers rotate for promotion.

Firemen (1859).

The train (1805-1815).

HISTORY OF THE ADMINISTRATION

Fifteen years later, French military administration has been the object of both grandiloquent praise and the most violent criticism from the entire world but especially from France itself. A fine line exists between the most enthusiastic admiration and the least disguised contempt. Europe, which was less interested than France, should have been more calm and praised France less after the Crimean War. It should not have overwhelmed her in 1870-1871. It should be said that, although success covers up all mistakes in a successful war, the reversals caused by general circumstances in an unsuccessful war should not demand expiatory victims. In France, where public opinion reigns supreme, legends are made from hearsay although the public may be more unaware than anywhere else. Unfortunately, the people who know not only do not have the courage to state the truth but they also often exploit lies to make themselves popular. It has always been so. Therefore, time cannot be wasted on complaining about this.

Under the Ancien Régime, one had to have knowhow to administer the armies in peace as well as in wartime. The young lords offered their swords and the young bourgeois their talents. Usually the King gave his army the *intendant* of the province closest to the theater of operations as its intendant. He was a civilian intendant but perfectly prepared for the role he was going to play by nature of his functions and his knowledge of the borders. He had under his command the required number of war commissaries to ensure the service. When the sovereign did not assign a provincial intendant, the task fell to a *commissaire* (commissioner) *ordonnateur* . He then took the title "intendant of the King's armies" and kept it as an honor after his mission was completed. In 1788, the following appears on the *Military Report of France*: 2 army intendants, 23 *ordonnateurs*, 127 regular commissaries, and 20 cadets. For a long time, this administrative corps was solely recruited from civilians. Minister Saint-Germain demanded candidates who had served five years as officers. The Constituent Assembly eliminated the corps on September 20, 1791 and replaced it with 23 regular commissaries *(commissaires ordinaires)*, grand military tribunals *(grands juges militaires)*, war judge advocates *(auditeurs des guerres)*, and 134 regular war commissaries *(commissaires ordinaires des guerres)*. The law of 1791 maintained almost all the duties of the corps (1), making it quasi-independent with regard to command but its functionaries always had to strictly obey the requisitions of the command. As

(1) The duties of the corps were as follows: 1. policing and disciplining the troops; public ministry close to the war councils; 2. public displays and reviews of troops from all service branches; 3. receipt of oaths of all military personnel; 4. oversight and control of all war services in the interior; 5. direction, oversight and control of these same services in the armies; 6. policing of rations, barracks, and lodgings; 7. policing of the internal administration of the corps of troops; 8. administrative authority of all expenses concerning the ministry of war; 9. written authorization of payment for general and special expenses of each military division; 10. administrative authorization of the civilian state on campaign; exercise of all military powers attributed to the provincial or the army intendant as soon as he leaves.

The provincial intendant's powers referred to under the last number of this list were: 1. the levying, organization and mustering out of militias; the mounted police service and supervision of deserters, lodging, barracks, daily rations, hospitals, fortifications, transports, and trains; 2. control and administrative authorization of all local and interior expenses of the provinces including the expenses for fortifications, arsenals, powder and saltpeter; gathering of provisions and subsistence items.

Commissioner ordonnateurs (1796).

long as war was waged slowly, this way of doing things was adequate. However, the Revolution upset all the old methods and stamped military operations with a sudden rapidity. Then too, money was lacking and, with this lack of money, the goodwill of the contractors and munitions suppliers. At the same time, the ministers of war lowered quality. The strictest of allegiances were thus unknown in the central administration, which was handed over to intriguers and corrupt officials. That vile man, Pache, refused to ratify the treaties of subsistence passed by the generals in chief, notably by Dumouriez in Belgium. On July 10, 1793, an excessive, even brutal administration but one full of generous patriotism and formidable activity took affairs in hand. Carnot was charged with military operations and with the personnel of the armies. Prieur (from the Côte-d'Or) was in charge of the manufacture of arms, munitions, and materiel. Robert Lindet and Prieur (from the Marne) were in charge of provisions, subsistence, and finances.(1)

This division of power was already a reference point. Since then, the French have not found a more improved or more equitably balanced one. Without a doubt, it did not immediately bring well-being into the French camps. However, the talents and the noble character of those who took charge of the nation satisfied the most pressing needs and returned victory to the French flag. In September 1793, France counted 554,938 men in the various armies of the Republic. This is a bit far from the 1,800,000 men of Billaud-Varennes, reduced by instinct to 1,200,000 by Mignet. Carnot who directed them, Prieur who outfitted and armed them, and Lindet who fed them found that they were sufficiently numerous to conquer the enemies of the Republic. Moreover, if there were more of them, they would have exceeded the powers and resources of the country. The influence of the corps of war commissaries was little felt under these circumstances. The Committee seemed to have been deprived of its support. Preventive formalities in contracts regularly passed and the red-tape verifications of accountants did not satisfy the passions of public opinion. The revolutionary tribunal simply sent the conveyers, the shady dealers, and the suppliers of uniforms, subsistence, and fodder who did not fulfill their contracts to the scaffold. Although abuses were great, the means of suppressing them were terrible. Everything that was not supplied by the companies was demanded by requisition. The cities became vast workshops where all the tailors, shoemakers, and craftsmen of industries useful to the army were forced to hand over so many items every ten days at a fixed price. Assembled in haste, these items were then always conveyed to the armies by civilian firms. The "Four Wheeled Hussars" *(hussards à quatre roues)* are unaware of from where their name of "Hussars of Lanchère"comes from. These were civilian conveyers of the entrepreneur Lanchère (of Metz) whom cheeky soldiers compared to the dashing cavaliers of Chamborant and Bercheny.

In Year III (1794), the corps' personnel was replaced and it was modified in its actions. It was composed of 60 *ordonnateurs* and 540 regular commissaries of whom 240 were second class: in all, 600 functionaries. The new law defined their tasks in the most advantageous manner and with a special flavor of the period. It was stated therein: "The regular commissaries in chief of the armies are at the head of all private administrations attached to the army entrusted to their care. They are the common center from which all orders leave and where all the accounts are returned. The first duty of an *ordonnateur* in chief is to provide the subsistence of the army and all its needs. He must view himself as the Supreme Law to which all others are subordinate. The commissary *ordonnateur* in chief of an army is not the man of the general in chief. He belongs only to the Republic and it is she alone whom he must serve. However, he should seek to win the confidence of the general to whom the Republic has totally committed its own. The true way of making himself worthy is to apply himself without reserve in assisting enterprises and in providing the army with what he commands with all his power, his strength, and his actions." Fortunately, the second portion of this Republican verbiage contradicts the first. If this had not been so, the general in chief could have done nothing better than to sacrifice the feathers of his hat on the alter of his *ordonnateur*. In practice, the *ordonnateur* was always the subordinate of his general, at least when the general did not ask him to accomplish the impossible. However, the Convention had curbed its generals in chief under the yoke of those of its members who were delegated to the armies. It saw its *ordonnateurs* as civilian agents and, by virtue of *"cedant arma togoe,"*(military government must bow to the civil) it recognized in them, in principle, a right which they would never be able to exercise. Unfortunately the tyrants which the law of Year III (1794) wanted to give to the generals were recruited poorly and especially with much fickleness. A most unusual incident arose in the Army of Italy, offering General Bonaparte the opportunity to write to the Directorate. He had with him an *ordonnateur* in chief who would have no luck with the general who regarded himself as "the Supreme Law."It was essential to give the troops a few days of rest, to rally the scattered corps, and to reorganize the service of administrations which was totally put to flight. These were those gentlemen who retreated suddenly to the Gulf of Spezia. The war commissary Salva abandoned the army. His wits scattered, he saw enemies everywhere.

"He crossed the Pô and told everyone that he had encountered a fright which led him astray. He thought the Uhlans were at his heels. He ran two days and two nights by post carriage in vain; nothing reassured him. Writing from all directions: 'Save yourselves,' he arrived two leagues from Genoa. He died twenty-four hours later of a violent fever in the transports where he believed himself wounded by one hundred saber blows, always from the terrible Uhlans. This cowardliness is equaled only by the bravery of the soldiers. Many war commissaries have not been the bravest. Such is the inconvenience of the Law, Citizen Directors, which wants

(1) Carnot and Prieur (of the Côte-d'Or) were two old engineer officers. Robert Lindet and Prieur (of the Marne) had been lawyers. It is interesting to note that all four were able to save their own lives although they had been part of the terrible Committee of Public Safety. This was because, although their fearsome colleagues had heads cut off and sowed terror throughout France, these men had only worked at hunting out foreigners. Nonetheless, France could not overly recognize them. They were too compromised in the Revolution and had too much dignity to dare, like Fouché, to tie themselves to the fortunes of Napoleon Bonaparte. Since they had voted for the death of Louis XVI, they were banished by the Restoration.

Doctors and military hospital attendants (1805-1815).

the war commissaries to be only civilian agents whereas they should have more courage and military habits than the officers themselves. The courage which they need should be completely moral. (1) It is never only the product of being used to danger. I have felt, under these circumstances, how important it is to admit only men who have served many campaigns in the Line and who have given proof of their courage to fulfill the functions of war commissaries. Every man who values life more than national glory and the esteem of his comardes should not be part of the French army. It is revolting when one hears daily of individuals from the different administrations admitting to and almost vaunting of having been afraid."It is sufficent to read this letter with perception to understand that General Bonaparte profited from access to the folly of Commissioner of Wars Salva. He thereby hit upon an argument which he would hold to for his entire life: the danger of introducing a civilian element into the business of war.

Meanwhile, the corps already had its illustrious examples: Petiet, Eyssautier, Daru, and Succy whom Dubois-Crancé had remarked upon in the following manner: "an excellent commissary in all respects and made to fill a high level position to which his seniority called him."The administration of the time seems not always to have struggled very effectively to represent the Supreme Law. General staffs stole with impunity on behalf of the Directorate and for themselves. General Bonaparte was the first who took the part of the soldiers. By giving France glory, territories, art objects, and millions, the Army of Italy won its shoes, its uniforms and its pay. The day that the Directorate wanted to take everything for itself, the armies revolted.

Bonaparte was not a man to haggle over means and to give up what there was in hand of his soldiers possessions. The instincts of his ambition created in him the obligation of treating the troops well while they advised him to treat the five sovereigns haughtily who followed their own counsel. Thus, from the administrative point of view, the campaign of Egypt is one of the most unusual to be studied. The fear which he knew how to instill in the Directorate combined with their desire to see him leave allowed him to prepare his campaign with as much care as was much later put into the expedition of Algiers and the campaign of China. These were two foreign expeditions which brought great honor to the French administration.

Having *carte blanche*, Bonaparte chose the best generals and the most reputable regiments. He completed them and set sail on a fleet of fifteen vessels, fourteen frigates, two brigs and sixty other small war vessels. In addition, four hundred transport vessels were crammed with provisions and munitions. The Directorate had supplied ten million in cash, an enormous sum for the times,

(1) We have uncovered a striking example of what General Bonaparte expected in terms of moral courage. This appears in the rare brochure *H.B.* written by Merimée about his friend Henri Boyle. During the Russian campaign, Boyle was attached to the general headquarters as a judge advocate to the Council of State. Merimée says: "One morning in the Berezina area, he presented himself to Daru, shaved and dressed with great care. `You have done your beard,' he said. `Daru, you are a man with heart!' In effect, those who thought about shaving and dressing well in the Berezina surroundings had moral fiber.

which was advanced or replaced by Ouvrard. However, the strength of this army of conquest was that it brought with it the most industrious of French scholars of the times. In some senses, the genius of France was thus taken along. The following list allows one to judge what hopes were attached to Bonaparte's name.

For *mechanics:* Monge, Hassenpratz the younger, Cirot, Cassard, Adnez the elder, Conté, Dubois, Couvreur, Lenoir, the younger, Adnez the younger, and Cécile; for *astronomy:* Nouet, Quesnot and Méchain the younger; for *clock-making:* le Maître; for *chemistry:* Berthollet, Pottier, Champy the younger, Samuel Bernard, Descotils, Champy the elder, Regnaud; for *mineralogy:* Dolomieu, Cordier, Bozières, Victor Dupuy; for *botany:* Nectoux, Delille, and Coquebert; for *zoology:* Geoffroy, Savigny and Redouté; for *architecture:* Nony, Balzac, Pratain, and H. Lepère; for *drawing;* Dutertre, Denon, Rigo and Joly; for *sculpture:* Casteix; for *engraving:* Fouquet; for *printing:* Marcel, Pontis and Galland; for *geometry:* Fourrier, Costaz, Corancey and Say; for *surgery:* Dubois, Labate, Lacipière; for *pharmacy:* Pouslier and Ripault; for *music:* Villoteau and Rigel; for *literature:* Perceval and Lerouge; for *oriental languages:* Venture, Jaubert, Belletête, Magallon, Raige and Laporte.

The corps of engineers for brigdes and roads had supplied in addition two engineers in chief: Lepère the elder and Girard, and fifteen engineers: Bodart, Faye, Martin, Duval, Gratien the elder, Saint-Genis, Lancret, Fèvre, de Villiers, Jollois, Favier, Thévenot, Chabrol, Raffeneau and Arnollet. The corps of geographic engineers was also represented by the engineer in chief Jacotin and the fifteen engineers Lafeuillade, Greslis, Bestre, Lecesne, Bourgeois, Leduc, Boucher, Pottier, Dulion, Faurie, l'Évêque, Chaumont, Laroche, Jomard, and Coraboeuf. Finally four students from the polytechnic school: Viard, Alibert, Caristie and Duchanoy, completed this ensemble which no other nation except France could have removed from its heart without stopping the onward march of its intelligence.

Let us not forget the high level administrative personnel hand-picked by the master. Dubois-Crancé, who was a difficult man to satisfy and very suspicious, admired Succy's capacities who was the *ordonnateur général*. He also admired Estève, the chief paymaster; Poussielgue, general administrator of finances; Desgenettes, doctor in chief; Larrey, surgeon in chief; and Boudet, pharmacist in chief.

Thus the Army of Egypt brought along with it a generating force capable not only of making it live but vastly capable of putting to work the resources of the country it was going to conquer. Bonaparte did not just ask the scholars whom he had chosen to follow him to form an institute and to supply Vivant-Denon with memoirs for the magnificent work on Egypt since published. He also used their genius in the interests of the army: flour mills, laboratories, factories of all sorts including cannon foundries, the manufacture of arms, saddlery, and military equipment supplied the soldiers with everything they needed. The future emperor was already pressing for that imperial and authoritarian system in which all knowledge and all human power was coordinated and completed to make a nation under the powerful gaze of the master. It was a machine in which all the cogs worked together toward a single goal. This was a sublime tyranny which, luckily for the individuals involved, could not last long. It lasted for the lifetime of a man of genius who had claimed it yet still this life was fatally short. Too many people were interested in stopping it. The campaign of Egypt was a test of government whereby Napoleon left, armed from head to toe, and matured to found an administration.

Napoleon did not try to be the consul for the military that he was for civilian administration. The clear idea of decentralization of needs went back to the Commune of the arrondissement, from the arrondissement to the department, and from all the departments to the State. In the State, centralization occurred again only to descend under the command of the Government, following the same path. However, on the other hand, centralization of military matters could not be formed and distilled according to the mind of the master who wanted to be and remain the sole master of his plans.

In the history of the infantry and especially in that of the cavalry, it has been shown that Napoleon succumbed from lack of soldiers whom death and desertion took away from him. As quickly as fighting material declined in both number and quality, the master's appetites increased. One of the greatest causes of the consumption of men under the Empire was not poor military administration but the impossibility of providing a very large army spread over a considerably extended terrain and subjected to jolts of luck brought about by rapid movements. When troops formed by anticipated levies or with men who, believing themselves permanently freed, brought only discouragement with them were succeeded by the iron regiments which the Revolution had passed down to the Empire, the effectives melted away on the roads, into hospitals, and into isolated depots. Due to the negligence or complaisance shown by the officers, the detachments disappeared. The Emperor, who counted the men at the departure, was unable to understand why, after sending so many to the army, there were so few in the line. His correspondence with the marshals is full of questions of this nature. "My cousin... you should have received so many men for such a regiment. This regiment already had so many of them; it should have as many today." Yet Napoleon had the best understanding, better than that of Frederick the Great and all the generals in chief of the great wars of the 18th century and the Revolution—that the upkeep of the soldier, his food and his shoes predominated over all other questions in war. The "no bread, no rabbits" or total lack of food generally witnessed in 1792 neatly sums up a necessity well beyond that of courage, perseverance and patriotism in the great army masses. The Emperor gave all his attention to the administration of his troops. However, his efforts never attained even a relative perfection in execution even though they were very intelligent and had often anticipated all the procedures invented since, which are still used today. He did not succeed because everything was in his head. His collaborators did not have that initiative from which responsibility springs forth.

The Republic created and used the many varied talents for its armies. However, always held back by its precarious finances and still unaware of the science of credit, it could not lavish staff on its administrative services. When he reorganized the troops, the First Consul conceived of and prescribed a

Inspector of reviews (1804-1815).

system which led him to separate the war administration from the direction of military operations. This separation of duties determined the creation of a special ministerial department: the Department of War Administration. (Decree of 17 Ventôse, Year X; March 8, 1802.) This new ministry only had two titled positions under the First Empire: from March 1802 until January 3, 1810, General of Division Count Dejean; from 1810 to April 3, 1814, date of its elimination, General of Division Lacuée, Count de Cessac (1). The administration offices established at the Hôtel d'Orsay, Rue de Varennes, No. 20, was completely separate from the war offices which were already installed at Rue Saint-Dominque. The Emperor's general staff was directed by Berthier even when he became His Serene Highness, Prince of Neuchâtel and Wagram, Vice-Constable. He followed the Emperor and concerned himself exclusively with promotions and military operations. As can be seen, the Germans with their ministry of war, their major general or adjutant general, and the Emperor's military cabinet are almost literally copied from the general order invented by Napoleon I.

Since 1804, the inspectors of reviews and the commissioner *ordonnateurs* have been separated.

Six chief inspectors form the central committee of reviews and administration of the troops. In this capacity, four reside in Paris: Malus, the elder, Gualtier, Pille, and Denniée. Villemanzy is with the army of the Ocean Coasts and Servan is in Italy.

Out of thirty-one inspectors, twenty-four are attached to interior divisions. The seven others are in active service: Daru in the general staff of the camps; Monnard in the camp of Montreuil; Fririon and Arcambal in the camp of Saint-Omer; Laigle in the camp of Bruges; Aubernon in the camp of Utrecht; and Lalanne in the army of Hanover.

Fifteen first class assistant inspectors, twenty-six second class assistant inspectors and sixty third class ones are in similar assignments. Below are the names of those who, attached to the camps, engage in campaign with the Grande Armée: General Staff of the Camps: Marignier (2nd class). Saint-Omer: Lebarbier and Hugan (2nd class), Bonnet, Lehorvau, Malraison and Joinville (3rd

Train and administrative workers. Imperial Guard (1804-1815).

class). Montreuil: Dautel (2nd class); Drolenvaux and Maltus (3rd class); Bruges: Caire (1st class); Brunek, Petiet and Monet (2nd class); Berenger and Delecourt (3rd class). Utrecht: Marignier (2nd class). Army of Hanover: Gaspard (3rd class). Camp of Brest: Garrau (1st class); Berger, Bernard and Clarac (2nd class).

There are thirty-eight commissioner *ordonnateurs*. There are one hundred first class commissioners of war, one hundred second class, and fifty assistants. The career is neither closed nor exclusive. One can become a commissioner *ordonnateur* from either the civilian side or through the military ranks. Those who leave follow other career paths or even return to the troops. The officer's privileges are not yet defined nor are they declared. The Chief of State who is also general in chief chooses his colleagues as he sees fit. Carnot is a good example of this. Napoleon instituted directors and administrative councils for all the war administration branches.

There was a directorate of clothing charged with giving its opinion on contracts and examining the quality of fabric. In 1804, this directorate was presided over by Dammemme and was composed of Hambert, Dauzeret and Jouenneault. Recullé was the secretary general. In 1812, all of these members had disappeared except Recullé. They were replaced by Isambert, Salambié and an assistant inspector of reviews, Villautroys. However, the committee director seems not to have satisfied the Emperor, who remarked that the more levels of supervision that existed, the less efficient it was. It can be seen in Napoleon's correspondence that the regiments which he found the best outfitted were those which bought their cloth directly and made their uniforms themselves. The light infantry, whose

uniform was a little dull, was not appealing to the eye. However, those who proceeded in this manner obtained much better results than the battle infantry. Thus it was the great mass of the battle infantry that always found itself looking the most neglected although in reality it was the best served. This was because it found compensations in its more numerous and always supplied depots. On the other hand, the light cavalry or the hussars, for example, no longer had a completely regulation clothing service from 1812 on. In my youth, I have heard it said that General Letang along with the hussars in 1813 and 1814 engaged in campaigns in the stable waistcoat, pelisse, and wide pants. The dolman, the *hongroise* and the boots have completely disappeared. The men enlisted in the Guard during the One Hundred Days received greatcoats and pants at the magazines cut out to their size and were ordered to sew them together. As of 1813, there were no longer buttons for the greatcoats except in the Guard. The use of turned bone buttons was common. The clothing service, like the remount service, was often suspected by the Emperor, who smelled a thief in an appointed supplier. Napoleon said, that from the moment that he has a contract, the appointed supplier's interest is to serve poorly. The Emperor considered such suppliers as the enemies of the soldier. Every time that he found one at fault, he made him return his ill-gotten gains

with no other legal formality than a written order. Napoleon's theory on the execution of orders is known: "Why reissue an order? An order must be executed. When it is not, there is a crime and the culprit must be punished."Ouvrard (who was for a long time commissary general of the army) and his associates would hear about this. Napoleon not only trimmed back their benefits which were already diminished by indeterminate credit measures and tyrannical revisions, but he also compromised their credit and did away with their independence. A financier in front of his cashbox thus ran as many risks as a soldier on the battlefield. Yet he did not win the same honors.

The hospitals were always the weak point in the Imperial administration. Napoleon had the habit of saying: "With an army of five hundred thousand men, you do what you want to do." Yet he always had at least fifty thousand soldiers in his military hospitals. The people who saw war close-up knew that nothing was as ugly as the depths of a battlefield. All kinds of cowardly acts and all types of shameless actions came together there alongside all the miseries and all the suffering. The stragglers and those faking weakness, all those who fled the fight or who did not dare enter into it and who were ready to cry out: "Save yourselves" or to loot the baggage rubbed shoulders with the doctors. With lancet in hand and apron on, the doctors waited for the wounded. Two hours after the first musket shot, the ambulances were already full. In the evening, they were set up again and evacuations were begun. During a battle, the Emperor did not heed the value of a man's life. However afterwards, he wanted to have as many surgeons as the battlefield contained wounded men. Unfortunately the internal needs of a large army whose recruitment sought quantity rather than quality plus the needs of the various campaigns undertaken at a number of points simultaneously demanded too many practitioners. The regiments absorbed more than fifteen hundred surgeon-majors and surgeon-lieutenants. The hospitals of the interior, the ambulances of the armies, the depots and the various establishments ate up almost as many. It should also be recognized that victory finally consumed as many men as defeat when war was prolonged without a stop and without any limit as to its extent.

Be that as it may, the Imperial epoch had great administrators: Daru, General Mathieu Dumas, Villemanzy, Denniée and many others.

Administrative Troops Before 1815. The idea of controlling the workmen and the cart drivers used for the army's upkeep and its transports did not immediately enter into the heads of the generals in chief. For quite a long time, the commissaries carried along their materials by means of civilian convoys. The artillery itself employed the cart drivers to bring along its engines and its tools. The noble profession of arms only admitted combatants therein. It was very complicated reasoning which permitted a soldier to accept those who carried to him what was necessary for him to address the enemy to his own advantage on the day of battle. Let us add that this idea is absolutely right on the condition that it be limited. Napoleon I limited it perhaps a bit too severely, but since then, no one has shown as much scrupulousness. The famous Hussars of Lanchère have become in our days true hussars. In times of peace, they attend the squadron school although they use their sabers in wartimes. There is no need to complain about this. This is progress, yet it is useful to recount how it came about.

The hussars of the Army of Sambre-et-Meuse owe their unflattering names of "Royal Cart Grease" and "Four Wheeled Hussars" to the cart drivers of Lanchère. Under the Empire, they succeeded those of the Breidt Company. Unfortunately for the entrepreneur Breidt, Napoleon wanted to be served quickly and well. After the Battle of Eylau, the bad attitude or apathy of Breidt's agents hindered the Emperor from maneuvering as he intended. Therefore, the formation of the corps for the train was decided. Nine battalions were created on March 26, 1807. They each counted six companies commanded by a non-commissioned officer. At the head of each battalion were placed a commanding captain and a lieutenant quartermaster. Although the service of these troops was still not excellent, it was much preferable to entrepreneurship. Increasingly numerous needs brought the number of battalions to twenty-two plus one for the Imperial Guard. The headquarters of the train battalions were at Évreux under the Empire where two companies of workmen cartwrights prepared their materiel.

The First Restoration reduced the train to four battalions.

The Imperial Guard also had a battalion of administrative workmen. Many were counted in the line. However, the Imperial administration never had fine administrative troops or a well defined administrative organization. Anywhere that the

Train (1825).

Surgeon major; surgeon lieutenant; assistant veterinarian and telegrapher (1887).

Remount cavalryman. Military administrative clerks and workers. Secretaries of the general staff, military hospital attendants (1887).

Emperor could not exert direct influence, everything generally went wrong. The generals tolerated everything that the colonels did to feed their soldiers. Most of the time, the colonels looted; from the top to the bottom of the hierarchy, everyone looted. The Emperor closed his eyes to this problem. Did he not say in a victory bulletin: "Our light cavalry has tons of gold." Where would it have come from, since the pay was late, if not from the coffers of the enemy? As for the functionaries of the high level administration and their agents, they were so often taken away from their regular jobs to raise war contributions that they ended up believing that the army fed, dressed and payed only itself and least of all them. All the war memoirs of the Empire are in agreement on this point.

The ordinance of July 18, 1817 did away with the inspection of reviews and the commissariat. It founded two corps in a new organization which took the name of *intendance*. It was composed of 35 intendants; 180 assistant intendants including 15 first class, 45 second class, 60 third class, and 60 fourth class; 13 adjutants first class, 10 second class, and 10 apprentices to complete it. These functionaries were the delegates of the ministry of war for everything that concerned the army administration. They were charged with the promulgation of laws and military regulations and they exercised the functions attributed to the inspectors of reviews and the war commissioners. No one could be a military intendant before being forty years old, 30 years for an assistant intendant, and 25 years for an adjutant. To join the corps, one had to be a law graduate, speak a foreign language, and possess an income of 2,000 francs in personal funds.

Simply through eliminations, the corps immediately reached its regulation number of 250 functionaries.

On September 18, 1822, the corps was reshaped. Henceforth, it included only 235 members: 25 intendants, 175 assistant intendants (25 first class, 50 second class, 200 third class) and 35 military adjutant assistant intendants. Returning to the idea of Count de Saint-Germain and recognizing Bonaparte's sensible observations, the intendance adjutants were to be chosen exclusively from amongst the captain accountants of the army and from the general staff captains. Majors could enter the corps as assistant third class intendants. Assimilation, which until then was only a question of honor and of precedence, took on a more serious nature since it was now based on background. There was a lack of good judgment in the armies. The army imagined that the intendant cared about assimilation because of pride, whereas it was actually often necessary for him to exercise his functions, especially in times of war. War is the goal of an army. When war is declared, the administration immediately takes on such importance that the command finds itself paralyzed if the intendance does not show total dedication and perfect agreement on the proposed goal as well as complete obedience to the instructions it receives. The legislators have generally not well understood the role of the army intendance, due to lack of historical knowledge. They would have done better by creating generals, colonels, and intendant officers temporarily employed in administrative functions. These administrators would perhaps be mediocre but they would be bound to submit to the command.

In 1823 when the Restoration declared war on the Spanish Revolution, France no longer had anything left. The Allies had "borrowed" from France and took away the best of French materiel to their own countries. As has been seen with regard to the cavalry, the budgets did not allow for any future expenses. Thus war was an unforeseen right, in some ways prohibited to France by the treaties of 1815. Although the purpose of the campaign was unpopular, war soothed the inner feelings of the army. As was said at the time, the "friends of the château" burned with the desire to blacken their white cockades in the smoke of gunpowder. They wanted to show the old soldiers of Marquis de Buonaparté that they did not have any less courage for having fought in foreign ranks. However, everything had to be improvised. In January and February, three new train squadrons had to be created, four companies of ambulance soldiers, and four companies of workmen for food and forage *(subsistances)*. Finally, in April, it was decided to have Baron Denniée come to the ministry as secretary general. They could have begun by taking this step. However, this late resolve to send for a professional man had been brought about by an unusual adventure. The Duke of Angoulême was without a doubt a perfect prince and the most accomplished gentleman of his noble household. However, he had not waged war. His aides-de-camp who had magnificent names(1) had done no more than he.

In addition, the adjutant general, General of Division Guilleminot, was contradictory toward and in a permanent fight with the Ministry of War. Without the Prince's assent, he arrived at general headquarters before the entry into Spain to raise all sorts of difficulties. The Duke of Bellune was not the person to deal with this type of situation. Guilleminot thwarted a conspiracy which existed especially in the thoughts of the Court. As for the chief intendant, Sicard, there was never an administrator more tangled up than he. Assigned two days before his departure, he had not been consulted on anything. He was an excellent man who did not know where to start since he was charged with administering an army whose entrance into the campaign had not been prepared. Thus, instead of buying flour, raw wheat had been brought in bulk without concern for how to have it milled. Everything was prepared and foreseen in keeping with this approach. Transports were lacking so the army was forced to hitch oxen to the artillery park wagons. In short, the Prince General was stuck on the banks of the Bidassoa not by his great prowess, but by the incredible lack of foresight of the Duke of Bellune, while he learned that the celebrated Ouvrard was at Bayonne. There was no doubt. The Prince, like a true prince, had come to the command to gather laurels, but he found only nettles. The honor of France and of the prince was saved by taking on Ouvrard as commissary general. With ease and incomparable audacity, this devil of a man promised the peasants to pay ten times the value of their merchandise which came to him before eight in the morning on the day of his taking over. Those arriving at nine received nine times the value, eight times the value at ten, and so on, with the value reduced by one tenth per hour. With a revival of plentiful goods, the army was able to cross the Bidassoa.

Of course, the honor of a prince could not be questioned. Ouvrard did not question it since, under the signature of the Duke of Angoulême, he was willing to do his part. However, the following year, the Prince was no longer the Supreme General although it

(1) We have been able to obtain a situation report (July 1, 1823) of the general headquarters of his Royal Highness, My Lord, the Duke of Angoulême, commander in chief of the Army of Spain. We cannot resist the pleasure of publishing it.

Aides-de-camp of His Royal Highness: Generals of Brigade Duke de Guiche, Count Melchior de Polignac, Baron de Bournonville, and Colonels Count de Fontenilles and Marquis de Lur-Saluces.

Adjutant General: Count Guilleminot (with this annotation: General of Division transmitting the orders of His Royal Highness). - *Assistant Adjutant General:* Baron de Meriage (General of Brigade). - *Commander of General Headquarters:* General of Brigade Count d'Escars; *Second in Command:* Colonel Count de Roquefort. - *Baggage Master General:* Colonel de la Voierie. - *Provost Marshal General:* Lieutenant Colonel of the Gendarmerie D'André. - *Grand Chaplain:* Abbé Ducos. *Officers of the Royal Corps of the General Staff:* Colonels Lachasse de Vérigny, de Salaignac, de Noinville, de Barthillat, Le Mintier, Dubreuil de Pontbriant, de Kemar; *Colonels Commanding Services on the Line of Communications:* de Greaume at Burgos; de Maillé at Vittoria. *Head of the Topographic Bureau:* Colonel de Castres of the Geographical Engineers Corps.

In choosing Count de Guilleminot for Adjutant General (who had been given the task of military tutor for Prince Eugène by Napoleon during the Russian campaign) the Duke of Angoulême showed both courage and good sense. This obviously rubbed the instincts of his noble entourage the wrong way as they could not approve of this count from the Empire transmitting the Prince General's orders over their heads. The Spanish campaign was an excellent lesson for the Bourbons by all accounts. They returned to France with a general staff of courtiers totally alien to the progress accomplished in the country over twenty-five years. It has been said that during these twenty-five years, they learned nothing and they forgot nothing. It should be added that at the same time they contracted debts of friendship that they were generally wrong to pay too fully, to the detriment of the country and to themselves. Things did not go badly in the Peninsula because the resistance was badly led. The French performed a task which pleased the majority of the Spanish people. The prompt return of the Duke of Angoulême after the victory of Trocadero allowed for the return of all those general staffs of great lords which were brave under fire but little used to discipline. They were also unaware of administration and not very anxious to learn about it. General of Division Bourmont who took command of the occupation corps was, on the other hand, a very well trained military man and a very painstaking person. He was harshly reproached without considering that attentiveness is one of the foremost of qualities needed in commanding troops. If history did not have to criticize him for his conduct in 1815, it would have to recognize the services he rendered to the occupation Army of Spain and especially in the preparation and the first operations for the conquest of Algiers.

is true that he was still Prince. All the same, the authority of his signature was contested by the government. Ouvrard had to go to prison since the problems with the auditing of his contracts led to the suspension of their payments. The Italians were right to say: "It is not necessary to pray once you are out of danger." Apparently Ouvrard had increased his prices and made himself a lot of money. The Prince had crossed the Bidassoa due to that same money. Cost what it may, it had to be paid since no one had anticipated anything. The scandal was enormous since Generals Bordesoule and Guilleminot were accused of having favored the commissary general, for which they had to justify themselves. However, Guilleminot and Bourdesoule were not misappropriators of public funds and their reputations remained intact. Nonetheless, they had belonged to the armies of the Emperor. Despite the reconciliation cemented in Spain, they would have been willing to dishonor the old army a little bit. In any case, with the end of these events, the Restoration understood that it ought not to play with the future of the armies. It will be seen that, for the expedition of Algiers, another tack was taken and that it was found to be a good one.

The science of military administration has been discussed by people with little experience after the war of 1870-1871 such as the parliamentarians Casimir Périer, the grandson of the great minister, and the Duke of Audiffret-Pasquier. In practice, military administration requires an extremely wide range of talents. The chief intendant of an army is the administrative chief of the general staff of the commander in chief with duties of the same importance as his colleague in the active part of the service. He must know everything: the price and usefulness of everything and of all labor. Hygienist with the doctors, food producer with the merchants and the suppliers, he becomes, according to the situation, manufacturer, buyer, or seller. At any given moment, all the service branches could require his services. He must be ready for all possibilities. In addition, he is the scapegoat for all defeats without ever being recognized in the slightest way for his part in successes. Guardian of the State's money, he is accused of self-interested extravagance if he pays too dearly for scarce foods. He is held responsible for the health of the armies yet he is reproached for conforming to the letter in the rules for the distribution of goods.

The preparation for the expedition of Algiers according to the principles which have just been expounded brought the greatest of honor to Baron Denniée, chief intendant of the army. He displayed superior talents there. This preparation has remained a model. Baron Denniée's instructions are still considered as examples of science and administrative prudence.

On February 15th, he had been officially advised that a corps of 37,000 men and 4,000 horses was going to be gathered at the embarkation point and that he must prepare two months worth of provisions which the army would carry with it. These provisions had to be immediately followed by two more supplementary months worth of supplies which consequently had to be assembled

Embarking for the expedition of Algiers (June 1830).

in advance. Wanting to move quickly and to have no qualms about the quality of the goods and merchandise which would be delivered to him, he rejected the system of public adjudication which left too much room for mischief and speculation. He approached the House of Seillière. The secret mission of this house was kept under wraps while it made its purchases. As of May 1st, 78,645 sacks, casks, barrels, or parcels wrapped in two waterproof layers which contained the first two months of provisions arrived at Marseille. They were placed on commercial vessels at the same time as the dismantled caissons. Thanks to a special convention with Spain, depot hospitals were organized on the Isle of Mahon. Baron Denniée's point of departure was excellent. He thought that nothing would be found in Africa, that in the beginning the greatest difficulties would be experienced in unloading what was brought along, and finally, that it would not be easy to find one's way through 78,645 parcels. The most careful precautions were taken such that there would be no possibility for confusion. Each parcel, according to its contents, bore a large label in a special color reproduced on the ensign and the lantern of the small boat charged with carrying it to shore. Despite a terrible storm which put the convoy in danger and despite unforeseen delays, the chief intendant discharged his duty successfully. His hospitals were quickly organized and his magazines were formed in the wink of an eye. Forty-eight hours after the unloading on June 16, 1830, the improvised military storehouse with 95 sheet metal ovens and 12 brick ovens for which the materials had been brought from France provided fresh bread to the entire expeditionary corps.

An excellent division of labor between the assistant intendants, zealousness at all times, and great firmness in direction were the qualities displayed by Baron Denniée in 1830. His health was gravely affected by so much effort. However, when he retired, the French army had taken Algiers and its institutions were secured. Perhaps it is worthwhile today to also recall that the expedition which cost only 49 million francs in round figures for the entire year of 1830 was largely covered by the 53 million produced from the treasuries of the Casbah and from the resale of merchandise belonging to the Dey of Algiers. The value of money was recognized then. The Chambers were tight-fisted with the State's monies and respected the interests of the taxpayers.

A convoy in Africa (1840).

In order to insure service, Chief Intendant Denniée had at his disposal thirteen assistant intendants: de Sermet (1st class); Lambert, de Bruguière, d'Arnaud (2nd class); Evrard Saint-Jean, Ferrand de Saligny, Orville, de Fontenay, Sergent de Champigny, Behaghel, Charpentier, Frostié, de Limoge (3rd class); and some adjutants.

The health service was also very large and was directed by Roux, the head doctor, Maurichan-Baupré, head surgeon, and Charpentier, head pharmacist. The principal officer for the administration of hospitals, Michel, watched over the equipment portion with a number of adjutants. Finally, 882 men from the train under the command of Major Séguret along with four companies from the permanent workmen's battalion for administration completed this administrative ensemble for the expedition of Algiers. The companies had been recently created and were 688 men strong, all of whom laid serious claim to useful status in the life of the army. This ensemble could be surpassed in numbers but would never be surpassed in its orderliness and perfection.

The conquest of Algeria was one of the major occupations of the military administration from 1831 to 1854. It can even be said that it was the only important occupation it had. The campaign of Anvers (1832) was accomplished almost on the border. This campaign was engaged in at French expense since the Belgian Chambers refused to pay the costs. It gave rise to some unusual recriminations. The young Belgian monarchy had been founded by the French. However, during the campaign, it had not assisted the chief intendant, La Neuville, in the difficult task of winter provisioning for a corps of fifty thousand men along roads filled with potholes. The French soldiers "devastated sixteen thousand francs worth of woods."(The expression is not French but rather one from the Belgian objectors). A trial was initiated over this.

The campaign of Rome (1849) presented no administrative difficulties. However, the campaign of the Orient opened a new field to the great French administrators where their talents and ingenuity would be developed.

However, before speaking about this campaign, let us say at once that the train must be considered as one of the best agents of the Algerian conquest. Philip of Macedon had the habit of saying that he never despaired of taking a place where he could bring in a mule laden with gold. Bugeaud, France's great Bugeaud, himself said that everywhere a military man of the train could introduce a mule laden with biscuits and wine, he would be certain of introducing the Army of Africa. At all times, there were three entire train squadrons in Algeria, one per province. Today still, when the railroad, roads, and peace simplify the task a great deal, France still

maintains fourteen mixed companies *bis* in Algeria and Tunisia. She also maintains a superior officer of the train, centralizing command and the service at the main town of each province.

At the beginning of the campaign of the Orient, it was decided to send four infantry divisions to Gallipoli as a sympathetic gesture in support of the Sublime Porte. Napoleon III's government thus took upon itself the responsibility of safeguarding, by all possible means, the honor of the French services. France involved its flags in a war where the battlefield had not yet been seen nor defined. Official and private revelations have since led to the understanding that Prince Napoleon, pushed by high level Hungarian and Polish personages, had dreamed of reshaping the map of Europe. Meanwhile, the English sought only the destruction of the Russian maritime institutions. As for the Emperor, Napoleon III, beyond vengeance for unwarranted insults made against his government, he was already pursuing the realization of that foreign policy which should have brought him the support of the non-traditional parties. He wanted to oppose the Russian invasion of the Mediterranean just as, much later in the Italian war, he sought to exclude the Austrians from it. Despite the absence of a preconceived plan, there was a rush to leave. They left without having taken any precautions and without having settled anything. The beginnings of the army of the Orient denote a complete governmental and administrative lack of foresight. In the midst of divergent political and military opinions complicated by some serious political embarrassments, the administration did not know where to assemble its supplies. At first, it set up a large depot at Gallipoli. Then, when the Crimean expedition was determined, a second great depot was established at Varna. This second depot would burn to the ground in a fire set by Jewish spies in the pay of Russia. Thanks to the dedication of the generals and the soldiers, all the powder and part of the other supplies were saved. Some weeks later, a landing was made on the barren soil of the semi-island of Chersonèse. They had thirteen or fourteen days of provisions, without counting the four days that the soldiers carried with them. However, thanks to the activity of the fleet, the danger of scarcity was warded off before even being glimpsed by the army.

France no longer finds itself on Crimean soil facing a chief intendant invested with a plenary authority and gifted with a special genius like that of Baron Denniée. The chief intendant Blanchot was certainly not an ordinary man. However times have changed a lot since 1830 along with administrative procedures. The ever-finicky yet often appropriate mistrust of the parliamentary regime no longer arms public opinion with a right to control, a right which it does not always exercise with wisdom. However, the restoration of a strong central power has modified this public surveillance exercised over the functionaries without improving it. Henceforth it is the Court which judges as a last resort. Despite his goodwill and his wisdom, the sovereign's inexperience in matters pertaining to war left him at the mercy of uncertain relationships. The Court of Napoleon III abused this. Despite the mask of perpetual placidity that covered the Emperor, he was often deceived by the undignified gossip hawked even to the Empress, who was vastly wrong to judge facts about which she knew nothing. In writing the history of the engineers, it has been shown that the command in chief so solidly exercised by Pélissier was very close to succumbing to side intrigues if Marshal Vaillant, the minister of war, had not put a stop to it with much assurance and cleverness. The Imperial government, which wanted to direct military operations by telegraph, administered the Army of Crimea almost entirely from Paris.

At Kamiesch, France had found a natural military port where merchandise was unloaded at quayside. The sea belonged to France. Thus it was natural that all the merchandise that could be supplied by France be taken from there. The majority of commission contracts for the Army of the Orient passed through the Ministry of War, Rue Saint-Dominque, in the office of Intendant Darrieau, Director of Administration. The principal commissaries were the House of Seillière and Company and the House of Pastrée from Marseille. It was during the Crimean War that Alexis Godillot suddenly proved to be a first rate supplier with his improvised delivery of winter huts and warm clothing. Certainly much activity and industriousness was evidenced, but the soldier's life was not adequately protected. For many months, the administration had trouble in constantly gathering ten to fifteen days of supplies in advance. What should have been thought about first, but which was not considered, was increasing campaign rations. They were truly inadequate for men who worked so hard. In addition, it can also be asserted that although supplies were not lacking and although those that arrived were all in good condition, they were not distributed in sufficient quantity. A military hygienist, Doctor Legouest, has said: "Typhus is the disease of hunger." The French soldiers were worn out by a long campaign and were overworked to extreme fatigue. They needed to be very well fed. It was only right to double their regulation ration of meat and to increase the number of wine rations which were given to them for free. This was not done. The winter of 1855-56 weeded out all the second rate men. There were only the strongest of the strong in the surviving troops. It is true that thanks to "reimbursable provisions," the officers could save themselves from an epidemic which struck empty stomachs in particular.

Doctor surgeon lieutenant, undress (1854).

CAMPAIGN IN THE ORIENT (ADMINISTRATIVE PERSONNEL ON SEPTEMBER 8, 1855)

BLANCHOT, *Intendant General of the army*
LÉVY, *Assistant Intendant* (Head of the cabinet)
Subsistence: Assistant Intendant ROBERT
Pay: Assistant Intendant LE CREURER
Ambulances: Assistant Intendant DE SÉGANVILLE
Provisions (at Kamiesch andt Kazatch): Assistant Intendant LAGE
Transport: Assistant Intendants BAILLOD and JALLIBERT
Camps: Assistant Intendant DE LAVALETTE
Administrative service of Kamiesch: Assistant intendant DE PRÉVAL

1st CORPS
Intendant: BONDURAND
1st Division - Assistant Intendant: GEOFFROY
2nd Division - Assistant Intendant: DE MERCIER
3rd Division - Assistant Intendant: MARTIN
4th Division - Assistant Intendant: HEINA
Cavalry Division - Assistant Intendant LAPORTE

2nd CORPS
Intendant: LE CAUCHOIS FERAUD, Assistant Intendant 1st Class
1st Division - Assistant Intendant: SANSON
2nd Division - Assistant Intendant: PIRONNEAU
3rd Division - Assistant Intendant VIGUIER
4th Division - Assistant Intendant: PARMENTIER
5th Division - Assistant Intendant: ROSSY
Cavalry division - Assistant Intendant: BAGES

RESERVE CORPS
Intendant: PARIS DE BOLLARDIERE, Intendant of the Imperial Guard
Guard Division - Assistant Intendant: BOUCHÉ
1st Division - Assistant Intendant: CROISET
2nd Division - Assistant Intendant: SANTINI

The six train squadrons had been detached as follows: 15 principal companies and 12 companies *bis*. The entire 3rd company of construction workmen had left Vernon and were established in a repair workshop at Kamiesch. These troops were placed under the command and the direction of Colonel Martin and Lieutenant Colonel Charronet.

The 1st, 4th, 8th, 9th and 10th sections of administrative workmen were in the Crimea under the leadership of their administrative officers to whom a considerable number of accountants and adjutants had been added.

The well-known military doctor, Scrive, had been named head doctor of the army. A veritable army of doctors assisted him intelligently. In addition to the great general ambulances of the army, each corps and each division had its own. Great depots of convalescents cared for by the doctors, the administration officers and French orderlies had been established in Turkey and in Asia Minor. The doctors' dedication was admirable. Out of 450 who took part in the campaign, 18 died of cholera, 58 of typhus, and 6 of other diseases.

Non-commissioned officer of the train (1852).

However, at the end of the war, these provisions supplied on credit had to be liquidated by the administration. Their reimbursement caused as much trouble as complaints amongst the officers.

From the point of view of quantity, figures can make clear the poor administration of provisions to the Army of the Orient. The number of men present varied as follows: on August 1, 1854, 57,876 men were counted; on November 5, 1854 after the Dobrutscha and cholera, it had fallen to 47,917. On April 1, 1855, 77,200 men were counted in the ranks. On the day of the assault, September 8th, the situation reports give a figure of 92,161 men present and on March 30, 1856, with peace, 92,061 men. In addition to this, a good fifth—almost a quarter—of wounded, sick, and hospitalized should always be counted.

Hospital admissions for the entire war are figured at 436,144. Doctor Chenu gives the following figures for the deceased: killed or having died of their wounds, 21,019 men; dead from disease, 75,861.

In order to always have 90,000 men on average in the service, France has had to sacrifice as many as a way of administering. One can only agree that the results are deplorable. Meanwhile, France has come to the aid of its allies. The French say with fairly misplaced satisfaction that its intendance is admired by the entire world. The faultiness of the French budgetary and administrative system which consists of cutting costs with men's lives was obvious. This system could only be reformed on two conditions: that it have a strong head at the top and that public opinion—which pours out blame and praise with as much ignorance as unfairness—keeps its mouth shut. War preparation is a secret matter. Try keeping a secret with a Chamber that questions and newspapers that divulge everything! Nonetheless, the French administration still maintains its honor with its strict integrity. When calumnious voices were raised in 1862 over the regularity of expenditures for the transports of the Army of the Orient, a ceremonial inquest proved them wrong and gave full justice to the disinterestedness of the French functionaries. It should be added that Intendant Blanchot was already dead from the exhaustion of his difficult mission.

After having explained why the French political system still weighs heavily in an unfortunate manner over the French military administration, whether it be under a liberal regime or an authoritarian regime, it must be said that since the war of the Orient handed over to the English the temporary destruction of Sebastopol and Bomarsund, the French should have had advantages other than that of vanity. However, as has been repeated in the past, in face of an already considerable debt which would soon double, France was wealthy enough to pay for its glory. Emperor Napoleon I and the Germans after the war of 1870-1971 widely used the resources of the conquered countries to prepare for their new victories. These are the examples that should always be remembered. Although it is not necessary to completely approve of Clausewitz's brutal philosophy, it cannot in fact be disguised that money is still—despite superb, modern inventions—the most redoubtable engine of war. War is only the conclusion of all the military expenses made during the years preceding it. All useless military expenses constitute a criminal deed since these expenditures could have been applied to

Convoy of wounded (Italy, 1859).

some useful purpose and perhaps to a purpose which would bring about victory. A people who fear war must be thrifty and especially thrifty with regard to its army. This was the administrative system of Napoleon I, and it is the administrative system of the Germans. It is not that of the French. Rather, the French rely on improvisation or useless extravagance. If the French were reimbursed for their war expenses in 1823, 1832, 1849, and 1859 by the Spanish monarchy, the Belgian monarchy, the Papacy, Italy or Austria and if they had demanded a war indemnity from the Russians, they would have been able to have either a war treasury always available or packed arsenals. This was easy in the past when armaments lasted close to half a century without serious modifications.

It is wonderful to possess completely ready materiel. This can be judged by the preparation for the Italian campaign (1859) which was more simple than for the Crimean war. In the official work entitled *Campaign of the Emperor Napoleon III in Italy*, lofty lines are written with a kind of smugness. However, criticism is naturally kept silent and the public is kept in the dark.

Of course, the preparations for a war more extended than that of Crimea were continued until the Peace of Paris (March 1856). At the beginning of 1859, French magazines were still crammed with clothing items, camp equipment, harnessing, and hospital furnishings but there was a total lack of food provisions.

The objective was: 1. to expand a peacetime effective strength from less than 400,000 men to approximately 600,000 men; 2. to mobilize and sustain an army of 200,000 men.

It was immediately recognized that non-military companies would be powerless to manufacture the necessary items for uniforms and shoes. Therefore, the House of Godillot was charged with fabricating them. The State supplied the cloth which existed in great quantities in its magazines. This is a point to be examined since it was the Italian campaign where the system of military fabrications as an undertaking was born. This system certainly had its good points but, having provided the opportunity for a number of abuses, it is also the reason that the French army is the worst dressed in the whole world.

Thanks to accumulated reserves, France had adequate rolling stock available yet it had to resort to a civilian auxiliary train. The ambulance service was insured by 751 doctors (of which 220 were attached to the hospitals), 54 pharmacists, 146 accountant officers, and 2,186 military orderlies.

For food, France resorted to the Italian government which promised to gather—at French expense of course—fifteen days worth of food for 100,000 men and ten days of forage for 12,000 horses. This would be placed in good quantity at intervals for the date of April 23rd in the garrisons of Suze, Lanslebourg, Oulx, Turin, Alexandria, and Genoa. In addition, the merchant marine and the State

brought rations from France. The deals took place in the country and for July 1st, the army having been fed until then, 60,348,800 kilograms of food supplies of all types were available.

Distribution had been fairly regular but the troops as always complained of the small quantities of campaign rations. There were a great number of sick soldiers. For 17,054 men wounded there had been 93,166 admitted to the hospitals and the ambulances. The number of deaths from disease was approximately equal to that of soldiers killed by the enemy in a war which did not last long and which especially allowed the rapid hospitalization of the disabled.

CAMPAIGN OF 1859

Intendant General of the Army: PARIS DE BOLARDIÈRE, Intendant Inspector General. *Adjutants:* Pagès, Intendant, BROU, BLONDEAU and RAOUL, Assistant Intendants.
Administrative services: COYTIER, Commanding officer of the hospitals; TRICOU, Commanding officer of subsistence; GASTU, Accounting officer of the camp.
Medical service: Head doctor, LARREY, Doctor-Inspector; Head doctors: MÉRY, of the Imperial Guard; CHAMPOUILLON, of the 1st CORPS;
BOUDIN, of the 2nd; SALLERON, of the 3rd; FENIN, of the 4th.

Imperial Guard - Chief Intendant: Cetty, Intendant; Adjutants: Robert and Seguineau de Préval, Assistant Intendants; Division of Grenadiers: Assistant Intendant, Bouché; Division of Voltigeurs: Assistant Intendant, Viguier; Cavalry Division: Assistant Intendant, Dubut.

1st CORPS - Chief Intendant: Régnier, Intendant; Adjutants: Assistant Intendants, Lagé and Heiullet; 1st Division: Assistant Intendant, Iratzoky; 2nd Division: Assistant Intendants, Galles and Marchal.

2nd CORPS - Chief Intendant: Lebrun; Adjutant: Assistant Intendant, de Cévilly; 1st Division: Assistant Intendant, Greil; 2nd Division: Assistant Intendant, Roux.

3rd CORPS - Chief Intendant: Mallarmé, Intendant; Adjutants: Assistant Intendants de Juge and Wiriot; 1st Division: Assistant Intendants, Parmentier and Pézeril; 2nd Division: Assistant Intendants, Gayard and Baudry.

4th CORPS - Chief Intendant: Wolff, Intendant; Adjutants: Assistant Intendants, Huc de Monsegon and Puffeney; 1st Division: Assistant Intendants, de Maixant and Joba; 2nd Division: Assistant Intendants, Sanson and Liais.

5th CORPS - Chief Intendant: Moisez, Intendant.

Portable ambulance (1870).

The Italian war did not raise public criticism with regard to the administration. The sovereign had commanded in person and clothed all the personnel. Thus there were no recriminations, but neither was anyone satisfied with the manner in which the administrative services had been carried out. The army had been sluggish. Perceptive military men said that France could never profit from a victory because the following day, no one was ready to get underway. They accused the administration for this which, in turn, passed on the responsibility to general headquarters. The truth is that the French generals and intendants were not used to marching, feeding and administering 120,000 men all at once. In Africa, the columns are relatively small. In the Crimea, one fought in place. The Germans have been very attentive to French military operations since the Crimean campaign revealed to them the

Officer of the train squadron. Imperial Guard (1855-1870).

individual qualities of French soldiers. They carefully noted all the French administrative weaknesses and hurried to improve the mobility of their troops. The minor China campaign which soon followed was a marvel of precision. In the Tuileries, all the magnificent promises that had been made to General in Chief Cousin-Montauban before his departure were undoubtedly not kept. He had to take along with him a majority of the items he could not procure along his route or on-site. In addition, the expeditions the army undertakes in conjunction with the navy, sharing both costs and benefits, are always privileged. While losing a bit of their character as combatants at sea at the time of the Crimean war (which they so brilliantly rewon during the Tonkin campaign), the French marines have acquired valuable qualities. First, they have become wonderful campaign infantrymen and artillerists as well as the most ingenious transporters of men and merchandise. Their officers are good at everything: war, administration, and diplomacy. It is impossible to forget the services of all types that they have rendered for France in all the foreign expeditions. For thirty years now, they have maintained exuberant French activity yet at the same time they have brought such considerable trouble into French finances.

The Mexican campaign was commenced like the war of the Orient without any preparations and with no definite goal. It didn't do too badly with respect to administrative relations. The French intendance functionaries and their various auxiliaries were formed just about everywhere in an improvised manner. Under a regime which anticipated as little as possible and which, up to this point, had the good fortune of succeeding in wars with as little preparation as possible, the "resourceful types" were very much in fashion. Mexico was their promised land. There they displayed wonderful talent in keeping alive a small army dispersed over an enormous area of territory. They very skillfully made use of requisitions and of purchases on-site, but their success showed more spirited resourcefulness than administrative method.

Sections of Administration. The dissolving of the battalions of administrative workmen after a thirty year existence should have led to the merger of the transport troops into one vast organization if it had been logically carried out. It was to return the direction to the intendance functionaries and the use of all their means to the command and supervision of the generals. However, although the intendance wanted to keep its independence, the train wanted to remain military. The accountants for subsistence and camp equipment were only pushed into disbanding the battalion in order to have direct command of its non-commissioned officers and soldiers. Eveyone who had pleaded for his own interests found some advantage in the new organization. The train thus retained its autonomy, and its hussar-like tendencies were even encouraged.

The administrative battalion was at first broken up into companies in 1853. It was then disbanded and its officers were turned over to the infantry. Fourteen sections of military administrative workers were thus organized by the decree of August 14, 1854. Composed of artisans (wood, iron, masonry) and of commercial trade workers (bakers, butchers, bookkeepers), the effective strength of the new corps was variable. However, the report in support of the organizational decree declared that this force had to be at least 3,000 men for the moment: 700 for Algeria, 60 in Italy, 800 for the service of the Army of the Orient, and 300 for the Army of the North. Yet it still had to resort to civilian workers in Paris, Lyon, and Marseille. This division of manual labor between the civilian and the military in the administrative services will always be one of the unfortunate necessities of the French army in times of peace and times of war beyond French borders. If the introduction of universal, mandatory service manages to make it disappear more or less in times of war, it will have taken a big step forward. However, France will only succeed by imitating Germany's example where a cleverly prepared reserve supplies ample resources to the army entering into campaign at the moment of mobilization. In Germany, the administrative columns are composed only of state workers.

When the war of 1870 broke out, the administration troops were distributed in the following manner:

one section of general service clerks of the intendance : to Vincennes;
nine sections of military orderlies: the 4th, 7th, and 9th to Algeria; the six others to Paris, Versailles, Lille, Strasbourg, Lyon and Toulouse;
thirteen sections of military administration workmen: the 10th, 11th, and 12th to Algeria, the 1st to Vincennes, the 2nd and 13th to Paris, the seven others to Lille, Versailles, Marseille, Metz, Lyon, Strasbourg, and Toulouse;
four companies of military train workmen; the 1st and 3rd to the construction park of Vernon with the Direction, the 2nd to the Châteauroux construction park, the 4th to the Mustapha (Algeria) construction park;
three train regiments: the 1st to Vernon, the 2nd to Algiers, the 3rd to Châteauroux, each detaching active companies anywhere that the service demanded them.

In addition, a large number of administration officers were included for the direction of administrative services, a figure which has even increased:

1,272 principal officers, officers, and administration adjutants were distributed in the military intendance offices, the hospitals, and the subsistence, clothing, camp equipment, and military justice services. This was rather good, in fact even too good for peacetime but very inadequate when France passed over to a wartime footing. There was a desire in the general staffs to eliminate these auxiliary civilians. They were always dangerous because they were not subject to military discipline. There was little success with this movement, however. In the early days of the campaign of 1870, men were seen strolling in the courtyards of the Hôtel de l'Europe at Metz who should not have been there.   They called themselves subsistence or transports agents yet they all had the look of correspondents from the demagogue Parisian press, if they were not Prussian spies. Never had the intendance and the army general staffs been seen to be so poorly guarded. The Hôtel de l'Europe was the headquarters of the chief of staff, yet travelers were still received there. You can judge for yourselves the results.

Included in the general staff of the parks, the workmen's companies, and the train were the following: one colonel, two lieutenant colonels, 10 majors, 82 captains, 103 lieutenants, and 95 second lieutenants; 7 principal guards, 12 first class and 13 second class, in total 325 officers and functionaries.

If one considers that the 440 artillery guards, the 570 engineer's guards, the 150 inspectors of arms, and the 6 heads, assistant heads and state workmen of the engineers formed a total of 1,166 functionaries; that in each regiment there were 4 accounting officers including the administrative field officer; and that the intendance had 264 functionaries, it can be stated that, as of 1870, the French army already counted in its ranks just about 4,000 functionaries and non-combatant officers. It is appropriate to immediately add that there is not an army in Europe where a more useless accounting of manpower can be made. However, having admitted that the French administration was too large and too involved in paperwork, it should at least be said in all fairness that it is honest and hardworking.

The campaign of 1870 took France by surprise when military, political, social, and governmental conditions were rather poor. Nothing had been done in anticipation of a major war. Totally involved in the transformation which was taking place in the realm of internal politics, the Empire was astonished by the popular emotions which the police had not known about in advance, nor contained, nor even regarded coolly. It had totally neglected the threats which, since the Exposition of 1867, had arrived from the other side of the Rhine. It can be said that France was surprised. However France offers so many resources that, with a little intelligence and a lot of activity, part of the problem could have been taken care of. One wonders what fate hung over the nation. No energetic efforts were tried. With exemplary caution, the ministry which embellished itself with the name of cabinet of honest men—as though to clearly mark that it repudiated everything that had been done before it—engaged in a dead end diplomatic adventure. Although the command was scattered, the administration lost its head. We could show here one of the French chief intendants haggling over a matter of centimes with suppliers who were asked to assemble considerable provisions of fodder in the French garrisons of the East. Another quibbled over the letter of the rule with regard to railroad transports while a mass of enemy troops drove our best armies from the field. Helped by a revolution which deprived France of the right to negotiate, the enemy then advanced on the capital without meeting a single serious obstacle during sixteen days. A war must be prepared perhaps with more administrative than military care. Through strokes of genius and bravery, a General Bonaparte, followed by the soldiers of Italy and of Egypt could accomplish miracles. However, an intendant, unless he is God, cannot produce the miracle of loaves and fishes. For troops to have had everything they needed to live on while on campaign, the powers of State should have voted during peace for the required funding. One intendance functionary in those ill-fated days nonetheless showed intelligence, plenty of drive, and almost

Ambulance service (Paris, 1871).

genius. First, let us satisfy historical requirements in giving the composition of the administrative direction of the Army of the Rhine in the eight corps which formed it and in the 12th, 13th, and 14th corps assembled before September 4, 1870.

CHIEF INTENDANT: Intendant General WOLFF

Head of the cabinet: Assistant Intendant, SÉGONNE; *At the disposition of the chief intendant:* CHAPPLAIN and VUILLAUME, Assistant Intendants; *Adjutant:* POUTINGON and MARINIER.
Administration of general headquarters: Assistant Intendant, DE BOISBRUNET.
SERVICES; *Hospitals and ambulances:* Intendant, PRÉVAL; *Transport:* Assistant Intendant, GAFFIOT; *Subsistence:* Assistant Intendant, MONY; *Camps:* Assistant Intendant, RICHARD; *Funds:* Assistant Intendant, DEMONS. Artillery Reserve: Assistant Intendant, SANSON.

1st CORPS	Intendant, de Séganville; 1st Infantry Division: Assistant Intendant, Rodet; 2nd Infantry Division: Assistant Intendant, Greil; *Adjutant:* Genty; 3rd Infantry Division: Assistant Intendant, Bruyère; *Adjutant:* Robert; 4th Infantry Division: Assistant Intendant, Coulombeix; *Adjutant:* Augier; Cavalry Division: Assistant Intendant, Iratzoki.
2nd CORPS	Intendant, Bagès, Assistant Intendant: de la Granville; *Adjutants:* Bouteiller, Daussier-Romanet; 1st Infantry Division: Assistant Intendant, Saunier; 2nd Infantry Division: Assistant Intendant, de Lanoaille de Lachèze; 3rd Infantry Division: Assistant Intendant, Demartial; *Adjutant:* Marulaz (Captain of the 63rd Line); Cavalry Division: Assistant Intendant, de Grateloup; *Adjutant:* Charme (Captain of gendarmes).
3rd CORPS	Intendant, Friant, Assistant Intendant, Rossignol; *Adjutants:* Forget and Chaudruc de Crazannes; 1st Infantry Division: Assistant Intendant, Puffeney; 2nd Infantry Division: Assistant Intendant, Geoffre de Chabrignac; *Adjutant:* Retault; 3rd Infantry Dvision: Assistant Intendant, Lahaussois; 4th Infantry Division: Assistant Intendant, Pezeril; Cavalry Division: Assistant Intendant, Létang.
4th CORPS	Intendant, Gaillard; Assistant Intendant, Galles; *Adjutant:* Baratier; 1st Infantry Division: Assistant Intendant, Bouvard; 2nd Infantry Division: Assistant Intendant, Bauduin; 3rd Infantry Division: Assistant Intendant, Taisson; Cavalry Division: Assistant Intendant, Hitschler.
5th CORPS	Intendant, Lévy; 1st Infantry Division: Assistant Intendant, Bassignot; 2nd Infantry Division: Assistant Intendant, Ligneau; 3rd Infantry Division: Assistant Intendant, Galler; Cavalry Division: Assistant Intendant, Demange.
6th CORPS	Intendant, Vigo-Roussillon; *Adjutant:* Santini; 1st Infantry Division: Assistant Intendant, Gatumeau; 2nd Infantry Division: Assistant Intendant, Barry; 3rd Infantry Division: Assistant Intendant, Bonsillon; 4th Infantry Division: Assistant Intendant, Courtois; Cavalry Division: Assistant Intendant, Delannoy.
7th CORPS	Intendant, Largillier; 1st Infantry Division: Assistant Intendant, Malet (P. H. V.); 2nd Infantry Division: Assistant Intendant, Lemaître; 3rd Infantry Division: Assistant Intendant, Legros; Cavalry Division: Assistant Intendant, Bilio.
IMPERIAL GUARD	Intendant, Lebrun; *Adjutants:* Cayol and Prioul; Division of Voltigeurs: Assistant Intendant, Jallibert; Division of Grenadiers: Assistant Intendant, Brassel; Cavalry Division: Assistant Intendant, Lejeune.
RESERVE CAVALRY	1st Division: Assistant Intendant, Schmitz; 2nd Division: Assistant Intendant, Seligman-Lui; 3rd Division: Assistant Intendant, Birouste.
12th CORPS	Intendant, Rossi; *Adjutants:* Legues and Heuillet; 1st Infantry Division: Assistant Intendant, Birouste; 2nd Infantry Division: Assistant Intendant, Baratier; 3rd Infantry Division: (Naval infantry); Cavalry Division: Assistant Intendant, Bonnaventure.
13th CORPS	Intendant, Viguier; Assistant Intendant, Laurent-Chirlonchon; 1st Infantry Division: Assistant Intendant, Desbuttes; 2nd Infantry Division: Assistant Intendant, Kervenoël; 3rd Infantry Division: Assistant Intendant, Triadou.
14th CORPS	Intendant, Baillod; Assistant Intendant, Parmentier-Wuillaume; *Adjutant:* Fages; 1st Infantry Division: Assistant Intendant, Beaumetz; 2nd Infantry Division: Assistant Intendant, Dumoulin; 3rd Infantry Division: Assistant Intendant, Renaut.

The separation of the Army of the Rhine into the Army of Metz and the Army of Châlons led to a split in the personnel of the first eight corps and the upper administrative direction. This personnel seems not to have had to function regularly for a very long time. Before the disasters, it was not assembled. Immediately after, it was broken up. Thus, many of the functionaries shown on the preceding list will be seen employed either in Paris or in the new provincial armies. The administrative general staffs are given below for the latter.

15th CORPS	Intendant, Bouché; Assistant Intendant, Lamaître; 1st Division: Assistant intendant, Bassignot; 2nd Division: Assistant Intendant, Ligneau; 3rd Division: Assistant Intendant, Demange; Cavalry Division: Assistant Intendant, Lécques.
16th CORPS	Intendant, Brou; 1st Division: Assistant Intendant, Mery; 2nd Division: Assistant Intendant, Mallet; 3rd Division: Assistant Intendant, Vergnes; Cavalry Division: Assistant Intendant, Gatumeau.
17th CORPS	Intendant, Airolles; 1st Division: Assistant Intendant, de Brunier; 2nd Division: Assistant Intendant, Rétault; 3rd Division: Assistant Intendant, Thouroude; Cavalry Division: Assistant Intendant, Pernot.
18th CORPS	Intendant, Huot de Nouvier; 1st Division: Assistant Intendant, Chapel; 2nd Division: Assistant Intendant, Eranchard; 3rd Division: Assistant Intendant, Martinie; Cavalry Division: Assistant Intendant, Genty.
19th CORPS	Intendant, Rossignol (Assistant Intendant 1st Class); 1st Division: Assistant Intendant, Chaudruc de Crazannes; 2nd Division: Assistant Intendant, Séran; 3rd Division: Assistant Intendant, Dauvergne; Cavalry Division: Assistant Intendant, Perussis.
20th CORPS	Intendant, Croiset; Assistant Intendant, Legros; 1st Division: Assistant Intendant, Lecomte; 2nd Division: Assistant Intendant, Tastavon; 3rd Division:—.
21st CORPS	Intendant, Lachevardiére de Granville; 1st Division: Assistant Intendant, de Planez; 2nd Division: Assistant Intendant, Boissonnet; 3rd Division: Assistant Intendant, Baratier.
22nd and 23rd CORPS	These two corps formed the army called Army of the North. The chief intendant was Intendant Richard, who had Assistant Intendant Puffenet as his adjutant. He seems to have been occupied with the administration of the 22nd Corps. Lafosse was intendant of the 22nd Corps.
24th CORPS	Intendant, Perot.
25th CORPS	Intendant, Louet (auxiliary intendant); Assistant Intendant, Antoine; 1st Division: Assistant Intendant, Cahen; 2nd Division: Assistant Intendant, Massiot; 3rd Division: Assistant Intendant, France; Cavalry Division: Assistant Intendant, Macquin.
26th CORPS	Intendant, Millon; 1st Division: Assistant Intendant, Guillemin; 2nd Division: Assistant Intendant, d'Amade; 3rd Division: Assistant Intendant, Viroux; Cavalry Division: Assistant Intendant, Durand de Grossouvre.

When the provincial army was separated into two parts, the portion which took the name of Army of the Loire (16th, 17th, and 21st corps) had Bouché for its chief intendant. He had the assistant intendant de Prez for his adjutant.

The other part (15th, 18th, and 20th corps)(1) had the intendant General Friant for its chief intendant. He had the assistant intendants Gachet and Greil for his adjutants. The assistant intendant Lemaître had for his adjutants Bourguignon and Captain Delachaise who assumed the functions of an adjutant. Lemaître administered the general headquarters and the reserve. The intendance corps did everything possible in the midst of a civilian and military debacle where no one had a clear idea of what was going on. The revolutionary element which held the upper hand at the time made a lot of noise, did nothing, hindered almost everything, and never wanted the allow the public to be aware of the papers from 1870-1871 that the fires of the Commune spared.

In Paris, there was no difficulty finding personnel. Functionaries were in abundance. Moreover, so close to the central administration, the intendants of the active divisions and of the army corps had only to fill the functions of inspectors of reviews and were concerned only with the pay. They all belonged to the 2nd Army commanded by General Ducrot who, in the thoughts and plans of General Trochu, would pierce the Prussian armies. In order to do this, he took along with him across a ravaged country four days of provisions in his bags. Obviously it was not the intendance which had invented this sublime military scheme.

INTENDANT OF THE 2nd ARMY; *Chief Intendant:* Intendant General WOLFF; *Head of the cabinet:* Assistant Intendant SEGONNE.

1st CORPS	Intendant, Viguier; Head of the cabinet: Assistant Intendant, Laurent de Chirlonchon; 1st Division: Assistant Intendant, Debuttes; 2nd Division: Assistant Intendant, de Kervenoël; 3rd Division: Assistant Intendant, Triadou.
2nd CORPS	Intendant, Baillot; Head of the cabinet: Assistant Intendant, Vuillaume; 1st Division: Assistant Intendant, Beaumetz; 2nd Division: Assistant Intendant, Dumoulin; 3rd Division: Assistant Intendant, Renaut.
3rd CORPS	Intendant, Séguineau de Préval; 1st Division: Assistant Intendant, Richard; 2nd Division: Assistant Intendant, Leanormand; Cavalry: Assistant Intendant, Simoneau.

---

(1) In February 1871 during the armistice, Chanzy's Army remained whole. The 19th Corps at Mayenne, the 24th at Chambéry, the 25th at Bourges, and the 26th at Poitiers formed a 2nd Army whose general headquarters were at Poitiers. The 19th Corps had been used in the West, the 21st in the East; the 25th and 26th were of recent formation.

Controller of the army administration, military subintendant, and administrative officers (1887).

Officer and cavalrymen of the military train (1887).

Surgeon major and veterinarian, full dress (1855).

The general garrison service had Danlion in Paris for its chief intendant. He had for adjutants the assistant intendants Cayol and Colombani. The services were distributed in the following manner amongst the assistant intendants: Corps of Troops: Listençon. Municipal Guard: de Mallet. National Guard *Mobile*: Fages. Army General Headquarters: Moyse. Clothing: Janet. Hospitals: Blaizot. Saint-Denis Garrison: Bouvard. Pantin Garrison: Malet. Vincennes Garrison: Marchal. 1st Sector: Desbuttes. 2nd Sector: Augier. 3rd Sector: Malet. 4th Sector: Dumoulin. 5th Sector: Simoneau. 6th Sector: Fages. 7th Sector - . 8th Sector - . 9th Sector: Beaumetz. Subsistence: Perrier. Transports: de Rostang.

As can be seen, many assistant intendants accumulated two services. Others had their places reserved in the field army (*armée de sortie*) while performing garrison duty. This was of little importance since the ministry of the interior concerned itself a great deal with the *garde mobile*. The city of Paris was reserved for the National Guard while public charity was charged almost completely with the hospital service. However the subsistence service merits a special chapter. It provides an example of what a man of heart, head, and talent can do of service to his country, even if of a relatively inferior rank, when he is driven by the dual feelings of duty and patriotism.

With the declaration of war, Perrier, a 2nd class assistant intendant charged with the subsistence service at Paris, received the order to assemble the necessary provisions for resupplying the garrisons of the East which were all very much in need. As long as the railways remained free, he sent enormous quantities of food either directly to the Armies of the Rhine and Châlons or to Sedan and the garrisons of the North for their later needs. To this already enormous task there was soon added the special mission of preparing the provisions for the city of Paris and the Paris Army, in view of a prolonged siege. The first defeats had destroyed public confidence in the immense ring of perimeter forts. When the public knew that the million Germans treated as a figment of imagination by Thiers did exist, as Rouher had said, they quickly understood that the blockade of Paris was now only a matter of time and strategy. Clément Duvernois, named the emergency Minister of Commerce,

was a man of intelligence. From the first day of his short administration, he understood that the task which befell him was difficult. He consulted Rouher, the strong administrative head to whom one ran when things became difficult. A practical man, Rouher, answered that the war had to choose its most skillful commissary of provisions to be put at the head of the subsistence service. Thus it was that assistant intendant Perrier was invested with the most overwhelming mission that an administrator had ever carried out.

In twenty-four hours Perrier had assembled in Paris, placed in magazines, and classified more than three hundred fifty million francs worth of subsistences. These were all of good quality and bought at reasonable prices without fuss or commotion. This was as simply done as though the times were not particularly troubled. To those people who asked him what would be done with the quantities of wheat, flour, salted and preserved meat, rice, vegetables, salt, and salted fish that he accumulated, he merely replied:

"If I do not have enough, I will deserve to be shot; if I have too much, at most I will be blamed. I prefer to risk blame than to lose my job."

In fact, Perrier had been given *carte blanche*, and with good reason. Thanks to him, when Ferry, Arago (Étienne), Floquet, and Brisson let the food supplies of the city which should have been severely rationed from the first day of the siege go to waste through their incompetence, the army could give Paris 34,500,000 kilos of wheat and of flour. That was about 70 million rations of bread without counting the rest. The real defender of the capital, the single hero of the National Defense was thus Perrier. His industriousness, his honesty, his dedication, and his genius allowed the war to be prolonged until the end of January. However, as he was only a simple man of duty, he received the rank of intendant as compensation. If he had been a man wishing to be involved in politics, his name would be heard throughout France.

Meanwhile, after the campaign, the press helped public opinion decide that two corps must be sacrificed: the general staff, because it did not know geography, and the intendance because Bazaine, on the one hand, and Trochu on the other did not know how to use the seventy-five and the one hundred twenty-five days of provisions gathered in Metz and in Paris, respectively. Thus, as public opinion should not and cannot be deceived and since it is necessary to satisfy it because it guides the electoral current, the corps of the closed general staff was replaced by an open service. The decapitated intendance saw the *corps du contrôle* assuming what remained of it. Have these major reforms been accomplished with an even-handed intelligence? It is doubtful.

As a result, Article 17 from the law of July 23, 1873 placed the functionaries of the military intendance under the direct orders of the commander in chief in times of peace as in times of war. This was only logical since it is a question of moderation. However, for the enlightened administrative colleague—a colleague with the same title as the chief of general staff, the commander of the engineers, and that of the artillery, the new legislation wanted only to make a subordinate nothing but a subordinate. As has been noted above, the law of July 23, 1873 had forgotten to decree the right by which the intendant could accomplish the miracle of loaves and fishes with the general in chief's requisition order. To complete the dispositions of the law of 1873, the law of March 16, 1882 established the following situation for the administration: the separation of direction, management and supervision. The intendants' correspondence with the ministry was eliminated. The intendants obeyed the corps commanders and the assistant intendants obeyed the generals of division. The doctors gained control over the direction of the hospitals and ambulances without having the obligation to provide for their needs. The intendance corps continues to recruit its members from the army officers. However, the functionaries of the administrative service can compete with them.

In recent times, France has had very good intendants: the skilled Blondeau, the likeable Wolff, Friant the resourceful, and Perrier the food producer. Under difficult circumstances, they have joined a profession which they had learned slowly. In their relations with

the generals, they are seen to act only with deferential and submissive manners. The young assistant intendants acquire a heightened esprit and the sense of responsibility required to fully complete the duties of a general intendant of the army. Meanwhile, it is likely that a general in chief will always be happy to have a capable, trained, honest and hardened man for an administrative assistant. Despite the law, a general will give such an assistant complete access to all his thoughts and total freedom to act but above all, the direction of contracts. Management and supervision will thus once again be found in the hands of those who are capable of taking them on for the honor and the benefit of the army.

After the war of 1870-1871, parliamentarian foolishness and demagogical maliciousness invented the *corps du contrôle*. They had been much overexcited by the rash harangues of d'Audiffret-Pasquier and Casimir Périer, the grandson. Obviously, war finances must be supervised like those of other departments and cannot be concealed from control by the finance inspection nor from that of the revenue court. However, the creation of a corps of financial staff recruited exactly like those of the intendance is an absolute superfluity. In instituting this corps, the law of March 16, 1882 was an unfortunate one. At first it met with vigorous opposition in the intendance which felt that it was an Imperial institution of the general intendants, inspectors, and true controllers which threatened the intendance. Then, since the intendance functionaries who entered into the *contrôle* in the aftermath of its creation were the fiercest opponents from the past, the new corps was immediately discredited in the eyes of the army. The advantages that surrounded it, the uselessness of its functions, the deplorable fight which started with its original corps, and the secret services which it rendered to the civilian under-secretaries of state for war—another awful institution—completed its unpopularity. The *contrôle*, which was well provided for, was composed either of functionaries wanting to grow fat in good jobs requiring little work or of old intendants jealous of their former colleagues. Today, people openly judge it.

The *contrôle* will disappear in the very near future. It is only a matter of days. It is the fifth wheel on a vehicle which will always work well if the command and the administration are in agreement. The *contrôle* was invented by people who did not know the first thing about public administration.

Although everything seems to indicate that the administrative personnel must very soon undergo considerable modifications, its status in 1887 should be noted.

Naturally we are only including for memory's sake the *corps du contrIole* which was placed outside, even in the annual army register.

The intendance included four general intendants, 45 intendants, 255 assistant intendants third class, and 38 adjutants.

The general intendants will be allowed to peter out. The administration officers have been expanded to 1,443.

The French have one *médecin inspecteur général* (chief of the medical corps), 9 *doctor-inspectors*, 84 *médecins principaux* (surgeons) of whom 39 are first class, and 763 *médecins-majors* (surgeon-majors) of whom 255 are first class. In total, there are 1,203 practitioners, all doctors. However, in addition to them there is an entire army of old military doctors and classified civilian doctors. According to their age, they are in the active reserve or the territorial army. They ensure France the best and the largest war medical service in all of Europe.

Finally, there are 20 sections of secretaries of the general staff and recruitments, 25 sections of workmen and administration clerks, and 25 sections of military orderlies under the command of this administration.

The twenty train squadrons each have four companies which can form eight at the moment of mobilization.

Today it is the artillery's responsibility to construct the wagons for the train.

Everything is anticipated in case of mobilization.

The active intendances are assigned, the ambulances formed, and the train companies distributed amongst the various services. Every functionary knows in advance where he should go. Everything has been prepared.

It is terrible to upset such a fine organism when it has not served, when its defects have not yet been perceived and, perhaps even less so, the qualities of the system that some want to substitute in its place. However, in France immobility is torture; activity is bursting out all over. The proverb: "Make and take apart, there is alway work to do" was invented for the French governments. Yes, of course, there is always work to do but it is poor work. Upon arriving at the end of this great task, I believe we do not need to indicate the deadly tendency that makes us constantly go around in a circle. While France's traditional enemies, like all the European armies, improve their military institutions, she is changing hers. France is making something new instead of consolidating what it has.

The French army was not always well administered. However, this is not particularly the fault of the intendants. The central administration has sinned especially. It has never known how to win Parliament's confidence in a clearly intelligent and decisive manner. Let us have a ministry of war which knows how to choose well and cover its colleagues— as that is its work. Then the war administration will be as good as possible. However, if France continues to see semi-celebrities of military politics follow one after another into Rue Saint-Dominque and unload onto their subordinates the poor execution of orders badly conceived and poorly stipulated, France will participate in the perpetuation of abuses which are still more a problem of time than of people.

At any rate, the young French army is very expensive because simplicity and longevity are lacking in its administrative institutions.

The court of the Hotel des Invalides.

Headgear and arms of the naval troops (1789-1887).

HISTORY OF THE NAVAL TROOPS

◆

It has always been difficult to resolve the problem of reconciling the recruitment of cadres and of troops assigned to the colonies with the average French temperament. It has been discussed for a century and yet no one seems to have been able to find a solution. From the day that there were colonies, foreign expeditions have been presented to the adventurous spirit of French soldiers as an exceptional opportunity for advancement. Even after the American War of Independence, bands of well organized armies have been seen to leave the motherland on a number of occasions to go fight abroad.

In 1789 when the Revolution broke out, the Monarchy's roll of infantry troops counted seven colonial regiments: the Cap Français, the Port-au-Prince, the Martinique, the Guadeloupe, Isle-de-France, Ile de Bourbon, and Pondichery. There were also two battalions: one in Senegal and another in Guyana plus one company for Saint-Pierre and Miquelon. Two regiments bearing Number 11: the Marine and Number 44: Royal Vessels had no relationship to the navy, ships, or the colonies. At the time of the transformation of the King's Army into the national army, these troops passed into the war service. According to the report by Sillery made on July 11, 1791 to the National Assembly, their recruitment was almost totally done in Paris with the help of the lieutenant of police. All the bad sorts and all the sons of good families fallen into the mire were sucked up and "sent to the islands" with an enlistment. At the end of their enlistment terms, under the name of *petits blancs* (little white men), they became the scourge of the colonies they had been called upon to defend. Disbanded on September 29th, these corps entered into the composition of regiments which were later turned over to the first formation demi-brigades. For the remainder, the history of the colonial troops is totally obscure. The governors of the colonies had taken up the habit of doing what they wanted. This habit would continue for a long time since the *cipayes* of India only appeared in 1823 in the ordinances and the budgets despite the fact that companies of them had existed for some time.

On June 14, 1792 a decree from the National Assembly ordered the creation of six regiments for the naval department: two artillery and four infantry. They were not assigned to the colonies but merely to service on vessels and in the ports and arsenals. Through its severity, the First Republic dispersed the magnificent naval corps of officers which the Monarchy had formed with so much care. Its strong tendency to instantaneous improvisation kept it from seeing that the navy especially was a matter of science, experience, and tradition. It imagined that in taking old merchant sailors and in putting garrisons of artillerymen and infantrymen commanded by their officers on ships, it would win victory on the sea. This is not the place to recount how events ensured that the Republic would turn out to be deceiving itself. Besides, obstinacy was not in fashion in this epoch of spendthrifts. On June 28, 1794 a second decree intervened which eliminated the four naval infantry regiments.

Under the Republic and the Empire, military sevice in the colonies was thus most often performed by militias which the governors organized. They were trained and reinforced by detachments of line troops coming from France.

The Emperor's opinion on the specializations of the services, naval or colonial, were very fixed. He had seen close up the plague at Jaffa and yet he took no special precautions at the time of the expedition of Santo Domingo. Vaublanc who had been the *ordonnateur* there recounts in his memoirs that he spoke one night with the First Consul about this colony. The First Consul sent him to Leclerc,

Combat in the masts (1794).

his brother-in-law, who was commander of the expedition. At Vaublanc's first word about sanitary precautions to be taken in such a formidable climate, the general answered him: "All the property owners in the colonies talk like you. However, I know what I have to do." Vaublanc judged it useless to go further. He simply showed Leclerc a big officer six feet tall and said to him:

"Advise that officer, if he is going to Santo Domingo, to make his will before leaving. He will not live fifteen days in that country." Unfortunately, the prediction came true. Leclerc died of yellow fever and with him went eleven generals, 1,500 officers of all ranks, 730 doctors, 2,500 soldiers, 8,000 sailors, and 2,000 employees. In 1894, Rochambeau brought back 3,000 men, the sad remains of this immense Armada. To top off their bad luck, they were captured by an English fleet in view of Morlaix. They were taken onto English hulks and those who survived so many misfortunes left only in 1814. (1) This is a great example which has never been considered since. Barely two thousand men had succumbed under enemy fire. Napoleon thought that, with bread, shoes, and cartridges, a well commanded army should be able to go anywhere, no matter what the climate. At the same time, he did not think that the same soldiers could be required to perform equally as well on land as on sea. When he wanted to prepare soldiers from the camps of Boulogne and Montreuil for a raid on England, he ordered that they receive special training. He himself presided over it with the greatest of care.

Napoleon thus established a difference between the naval service and the colonial service.

Reports of the campaigns of the French demi-brigades and regiments drawn up carefully by Colonel Brabant and Captain Sicard prove that from 1804 until 1808, the Emperor withdrew all the cadres that had been forgotten in the colonies. The 66th Line Regiment or at least two of its battalions alone seemed to have remained on Guadeloupe until 1812. However, many regimental histories bear witness to the fact that in more than one situation, Napoleon made auxiliary battalions, as he called them. These battalions were formed of components taken from all over which he had go to the colonies when this was possible. However, unfortunately this was not usually possible. Meanwhile, after 1812 when it was necessary to improvise a replacement infantry for the one which France had left behind in the snows of Russia, the Emperor remembered that the naval department had four artillery regiments available.

On October 25, 1795, while replacing the infantry and artillery regiments eliminated or not formed, seven demi-brigades were organized which would present an effective strength of 15,975 men in times of peace and 22,023 men during war. Each brigade included three battalions. These 21 battalions, reduced to 12 on May 5, 1803, had formed 4 regiments with an effective strength of 10,800 men and 14,400 men in times of war. It was these troops that Napoleon made available for the war on January 24, 1813. They were still maintained under the authority of the Navy, which kept 500 non-commissioned officers and soldiers per regiment for the service of ports and arsenals. When he saw these troops arriving at his corps—the Sixth Corps—Marmont at first predicted nothing good would come of it. The officers were fairly poor and were stale from sedentary service and the bourgeois habits which they brought with them. Pelleport, who had the 1st Regiment in his brigade, complained a little about their relaxed discipline and their lack of skill in marching and maneuvers. In his correspondence, Marmont says that these regiments lacked everything: cartridge boxes, breeches, and surgeons. He asked for 250 cases of drums and muskets with bayonets instead of the dragoons' muskets with which they were armed. He let it be known that the Navy had kept the best cadres and the best officers in the ports. In the end, when they had been shaken up a bit, reuniformed, rearmed and especially when their cadres had been reorganized, they made an excellent service branch. The biggest mistake was to keep the recalcitrant types, old grumblers, and even old conspirators against Bonaparte's life from the Consulate period in their general staffs. Just when all the old hatreds were awakened against the Emperor, men used to the sedentary garrisons of the ports had to be put on campaign, which must have presented great difficulties at the beginning. Below is a list of their situation and their effectives on August 10, 1813.

Meanwhile, on April 17, 1813, Napoleon had already taken 8 cadres of officers, non-commissioned officers and cannoneers for 8 of Marmont's foot batteries from these naval regiments. Undoubtedly these were the thousand detached men. In addition he took 400 men for the Guard's artillery—a hard loss.

At Lutzen and Bautzen, Pelleport praised the naval artillery quite a bit; he also said the same thing in his memoirs. On the other hand, one can read in the writings of Baron Fain, the Emperor's secretary: "On our right, the army of the Duke of Raguse entered into line. The cavalry corps and the infantry corps which the enemy thought it could throw on Weissenfels were stopped short at the village of Starsidel. The Naval division received the first shock. This brave infantry, assaulted by a cloud of cavalrymen,

REGIMENTS AND THEIR COMMANDERS	TOTAL FORCE	DETACHED	SICK
1st Regiment: 5 battalions, Colonel Maréchal - Brigade PELLEPORT of the 20th Division, COMPANS	4,429	433	988
2nd Regiment: 6 battalions, Colonel Deschamps- Formed the Brigade BUQUET of the 21st Division, LAGRANGE	4,707	356	983
3rd Regiment: 3 battalions, Colonel Bormann - Brigade JOUBERT of the 20th Division, COMPANS	2,435	204	466
4th Regiment: 3 battalions, Colonel Rouvroy - Brigade JAMIN of the 21st Division, LAGRANGE	2,807	111	508

(1) Many prisoners claim that in the composition of the army corps of Santo Domingo, Bonaparte especially included officers and regiments who would be able to bar his path to the throne. Apparently there is a bit of truth in this opinion. The First Consul was happy to see certain agitators leave who asked to go everywhere that there was fighting. The following list allows one to judge the base value of the assertions of the First Consul's enemies:

General in Chief: Leclerc, then Rochambeau. Commander in Chief of Artillery: Saint-Mars; Second in Command: Clément;

Generals: Dugua, Boudet, Debelle, Pamphyle Lacroix, Jablonorski, Hardy, Watrin, Delpanque, Mayer (Swiss), Darbois, Léveillé, Rigaud;

Troops: 5th, 7th, 22nd, 31st, 74th, 79th, 86th, 89th, 110th, 113th (Polish), 114th (Polish) battle demi-brigades; 11th and 30th light demi-brigades. These 13 demi-brigades had been completed with components formed of volunteers and taken from other demi-brigades, notably from the 71st, 77th, 79th, 98th, 107th Battle, and the 19th Light. The 1st Piedmont Legion, the 3rd Helvetic demi-brigade, some German battalions, and the 19th Regiment of chasseurs à cheval were also part of the expeditionary corps. These troops, which were amply provided with artillery and with accessory services, could be estimated at 34,000 men. However, nothing had been modified in their equipment.

Marines of the Guard (1804-1815).

spread itself out in battalion squares with General Compans at its head. It held out for seven charges, giving time to the rest of the right to develop its movement." On May 9, 1813, the *Moniteur* consecrated the glory of the naval artillery. In 1814 at the time of peace, the 4 regiments went to take up their garrisons: the 1st at Brest, the 2nd at Toulon, and the 3rd and the 4th at Rochefort. On July 1st, the First Restoration reduced them to 3 regiments called "cannoneers of the navy." During the One Hundred Days, Napoleon used them to defend the coasts and the territory. They had to supply all the position batteries. Thus, they were troops of great solidity which Marmont, despite their military valor, had judged on appearance. His judgment was based especially on their superior officers who were very dissatisfied with being on campaign and leaving the good posts where they had permanently taken up positions. It is fairly useful to note that the 4 colonels who led the naval artillery onto the battlefield at Lutzen and Bautzen were not the same ones who commanded in 1812. Before tackling the colonial question and the history of the naval infantry to which it is intimately tied, it should be said that the naval artillery regiments disbanded by the Second Restoration were replaced on February 21, 1816 by 8 battalions. Each included 4 companies of cannoneers and one of bombardiers with a total effective strength of 4,144 men. These 8 battalions were dissolved on November 13, 1822. Thus, as was just seen, an artillery regiment was created and two regiments of infantry. The artillery had 117 officers and 950 soldiers, companies of workmen and apprentice cannoneers. On January 26th, when the war department was charged with supplying garrisons to the colonies, the companies that were detached there returned and the entire corps was only employed at the ports and the arsenals.

Under the First Empire, there was a corps, the Guard Marines, which avoided all assimilations. It was no longer naval since it performed so much infantry and pontonier service. However, it has left behind a renown equal to that of the foot grenadiers, the lancers, and the guides. It was created on September 17, 1803 at the moment that Napoleon was thinking of performing a raid on England. Successively commanded by Naval Captain Laugier and Vice Admiral Ganthaume, the Guard Marines participated in all the campaigns of the Grande Armée. They were mustered out on April 14, 1814. There was an attempt to reform then during the One Hundred Days.

In 1814 when it was necessary to again take possession of the colonies which were given to France, everything had to be redone. The organizations of the old governors had been destroyed by the conquest. The mother country no longer had anything—or almost nothing. Thus the responsiblity of providing the necessary troops for the Navy fell upon the ministry of war. In the early days of the First Restoration, detachments taken from the 15th and 17th Line were sent to the Antilles. On August 8th, it was decided that the 26th and the 62nd Line would each form 3 supplementary battalions into which detachments already designated in the 15th and the

70th would enter. Another supplementary battalion of the 71st left for the Island of Bourbon. Finally a battalion of the same type formed by the 5th Light was to provide for the needs of the other colonies. At the same time, in the Isles of Ré, Oleron and Hyeres, colonial battalions were organized whose existence would be confused with those of the regiments and battalions detached to France's overseas possessions. To complete the effective strength of 350 men in each of these battalions, voluntary enlistments were solicited. Eager and willing men were requested for the regiments. However, the twenty years of war just experienced had cooled the spirit of adventure to some extent. Enlistment bounties had to be used. That bad lot which is always ready to knock heads in order to make some money were offered 50, then 75 and finally 100 francs. The value of money had considerably decreased under the Empire. A bounty of five *louis* tempted no one. It was then decided to make appointments to office. The Restoration had to begin in this manner. However it produced a very poor recruitment which was suddenly interrupted by the return of the Emperor. It was not taken up again until after Waterloo. The naval ministry also awkwardly went about the recruitment of troops which the war department had lent it. In addition, officers and soldiers shied away from the necessity of leaving for the colonies, using all means imaginable. This predicament suggested to the same minds who reestablished the Swiss in the army and the Royal Guard the idea of having French foreign possessions guarded by foreigners. However, it became necessary to return to special troops belonging to the naval ministry.

Two infantry legions bearing the numbers 88 (Martinique Legion) and 89 (Guadeloupe Legion) were organized with the remains of the colonial battalions. The first was on the Isle of Ré, the second on the Isle of Oleron. Upon their arrival at their destination, they were to receive in their ranks the cadres and soldiers which had been sent previously. The supplementary battalions of the 5th Light, temporarily become the Colonial Battalion, taking the name of Battalion of the Isle of Bourbon. Finally, a battalion called the Battalion of Guyana was organized for Cayenne. It was 434 men strong including cadres. Senegal would also receive a demi-battalion. These troops left in the following order:

Naval cannoneers (1805-1815).

June 9, 1816, for Martinique: 88th Legion, 2 battalions, 2,000 men
June 19, 1816, for Senegal: 3 companies, 219 men
November 16, 1816, for Guadeloupe: 89th Legion, 2 battalions, 2,000 men
December 27, 1816, for Maurice: Bourbon Battalion, 286 men

The three companies destined for Senegal which were shipped on the *Medusa* commanded by Duroy de Chaumareix, were lost with this ship on July 7th along the Arguin Bank. Part of the force was drowned, but the disaster was remedied for the demi-battalion of Senegal by sending 120 men taken from the depot of the Isle of Ré. The depots and the recruitment battalions stayed in this last location.

Information on the colonial troops of this period lacks precision. The *Military Annual* of 1819, the first the Restoration had published, gave neither the status of the 88th nor 89th Legions, nor for any of the battalions of Senegal, Bourbon or Cayenne. Meanwhile, the ministry of war seemed not to be totally disinterested in these troops since it showed the colonial battalions appearing behind the departmental legions. It is true that the majors and the captains who were part of them were not inscribed on the general lists of seniority for officers of their service. Below is the status of these three battalions in 1819:

1st Colonial Battalion, at Belle-Ile-en-mer, Major Rousselot, 2 captains, 5 lieutenants and 5 second lieutenants;
2nd Colonial Battalion, at the Isle of Oleron, Major Amat, 3 captains, 3 lieutenants, and 3 second lieutenants;
3rd Colonial Battalion, in the Isles of Hyères, 5 captains, 5 lieutenants, 8 second lieutenants;.

This heterogeneous constitution did not present a very solid appearance. How many of the 4,600 men sent in 1819 were still there two years later? Very few actually.

The uniform of the legions and battalions was the same cut as that of the departmental legions, but blue with distinguishing colors according to the areas. The greatcoat was grey and the shako was of black felt. The officers received one and one half times the regulation pay. The troops received regulation pay plus campaign provisions. No sanitary precautions were taken. Thus, the two legions of Martinique and of Guadeloupe began to decline. The change of climate felled the effectives with a terrifying speed. The war ministry still recruited and the Navy still maintained the colonial troops. This was an awful system in a period when whims and lack of money allowed for all kinds of abuses and did not permit any serious control over responsibilities which were much too divided. The war ministry was too ready to neglect a recruitment which did not benefit it. The navy was more preoccupied with its ships and its naval personnel and only saw additional costs in the troops it received. Meanwhile, each colonial garrison was subject to special misfortunes.

In addition, the depot of the Isle of Ré was becoming a hindrance. It was dissolved only to be immediately reformed.

In Cayenne, the battalion was weakened. A company of chasseurs recruited from amongst colored men was forced to join it.

In the Antilles, at the time of the dispersal of the departmental legions in the mother country, the Martinique and the Guadeloupe legions were transformed into colonial battalions.

Finally at Senegal, where warlike tendencies were already confirmed, French troops needed to be sent. A first battalion formed at Ré, called the 1st Battalion of Africa, set sail at Rochefort for this destination at the beginning of 1819. A second battalion organized at Ré, passed through Oleron, was dissolved on May 20th, and was abruptly reconstituted under the name of Battalion of the Colonies. This is disorder raised to the level of an institution. Meanwhile, a second battalion was directed to Saint-Louis which took

Naval infantry, full dress (1887).

Honor review on board. Vice-Admiral and his aides-de-camp, chaplain, commissioner, naval doctor, full dress (1887).

the name of Battalion of Senegal while the 1st Battalion of Africa changed its name to that of Battalion of Goree. Finally in 1823, these two battalions, reduced by the rigors of the climate, were joined into a single one, the Battalion of Senegal. At the same time, the Battalion of the Colonies and the depot disappeared. In this period, the colonial battalions wore the beige coat-jacket with collar, piping and lapels in royal blue, and white buttons. The shako and the rest of the uniform were that of the light infantry. (1)

An ordinance of December 30, 1823 returned to the ministry of war only the responsibility of providing garrisons to the colonies. As of November 13, 1822, two regiments had been charged with service aboard ships and in the ports and arsenals. They remained only until August 28, 1827. This was in the midst of events which proved that the naval officer so happy to command various troops on land had none of the desired qualities for commanding on board. Thus, the 2 regiments had to be returned to the ministry of war which formed three battalions of them for the 11th, 13th, and 15th Light. In accordance with the ordinance of December 10, 1823, the 49th and the 57th Line left for Martinique and the 48th and the 51st for Guadeloupe. The 16th Light had sent a battalion of 5 companies to Senegal, one of 4 companies to Cayenne, and one of 5 companies to Bourbon. However, although it decreed that 5 regiments of line and light infantry out of the 84 that it maintained would go to the colonies, the Restoration had not decreed that they would find a favorable climate there. The 57th arrived in Martinique only in June 1826 since preparations took too long. It had to be recalled in 1827 and landed at Brest in a deplorable

Colonial battalions (1814-1823).

state. At the same time, the 45th was sent to replace it. This is the sole regular change that was made. All the corps were sent to the colonies poorly prepared, or rather, without any preparation. All would return to France disabled. In August 1827, the remains of the cadres of the 48th returned after having left their soldiers fit for service with the 51st. Meanwhile, this regrettable state of affairs troubled the minds of the ministers of the Restoration without enlightening them. They sent inspectors general and, on their advice, modified the clothing and changed everything that was normal. At last they sought to improve the life of the colonial soldier. On August 17, 1828 after thousands of experiments, permanent garrisons were accepted in principle. However, the ministry of war was still left with the task of providing for them. From that point on, three land army regiments would remain at a fixed post in the colonies: the 45th at Martinique, the 51st at Guadeloupe, and the 16th Light at Senegal, Cayenne and Bourbon. The 49th, which still found itself in Martinique, returned to France (February 1829). The officers of the regiments that stayed in the service of the colonies had the right to opt for and to request their return to France. Up until then, the two departments, war and navy, shared the costs of the troops employed in the colonies. Henceforth the naval ministry would pay for everything. Naturally this system did not please the Navy, which immediately studied ways to lighten its responsibilites. It prepared a measure to rebuild the autonomy of the troops which it used under the format of two special regiments. On May 14, 1831, this work, delayed by the July events, was finally finished. The 45th, 51st Line, and 16th Light were returned to the war department. Two naval infantry regiments (Numbers 1 and 2) were created with a common depot in France. The depot was set up at Landerneau, active companies were recruited, and the new regiment took on the uniform of the line. In this manner, the excellent advice of the inspectors from 1823 to 1827 was forgotten. It is true that their reports may have remained buried in the offices of "general correspondence," which was the most laughable of institutions perpetuated for a long time in the war ministry. It absorbed and impeded everything and performed no services whatsoever. From 1831 to 1837, parliamentarian thumb twiddling did not allow it to be involved with the colonies. All the same, in 1837, a general officer of the land army, the Count of Ligniville, was charged with inspecting the corps again coming out of the naval department in France as well as in the colonies. He was an intelligent and enlightened man. According to his observations, the general effective strength of the 2 regiments was expanded to 10,983 men. Each regiment had its separate depot; one at Brest, the other at Toulon. The revival of the colonial garrisons was done by fourths. Such was the spirit of the ordinance of November 20, 1838. It maintained the effective

(1) The *Military Annual* of 1823 gives the names of the high-ranking officers and captains whom the war department put at the diposition of the naval department for the service of the colonies:

In Martinique: two majors, Mongin and de Nogérée; seventeen captains, Bosse, Fleury, Geoffroy, Bonin, Tournier, Gabrian, de Loubières, Croquet des Hauteurs, Estourneau de Tersanne, de Roquefeuil, de Ricard, de Buce, Descarrières, Moutte, Daranjo, Claude, Forget de Bastt.

In Guadeloupe: two majors, Duperron and Caillau; nineteen captains, Alleye de Billon, Cartier, Franco, Dulyon, Bouillon, Merché, Ducré, Block de Friberg, de Marans, Chauvin, Dastugue, Rostollant, Forget, Eonnet, Béraud, Desmarets, Laffont, Gardès de Villedieu, Lormeau;

At Bourbon: a single captain, Delafosse;

In India: a battalion of cypahis commanded by Major Law de Clapernoux with four captains: Thévenin, Leprévost, de Bourcet, de l'Arches;

In Senegal: a major, Soffréon, and four captains: Borne, Daval, de Villodon, Garçon;

At Gorée, a major, Cognasse de Lage, and five captains: Chalet, Foncou, Vire, Saint-Denis, Lheureux;

Finally, at Guyana, Major de Charlemont, and three captains: Olivier, Brache and Gerbet.

In addition, two companies of engineers outside the cadres were attached in a permanent manner; the first at Martinique under the command of Captain Gibou and the second at Guadeloupe with Captain Burke O'Farrel.

As for the Recruitment Battalion of the Colonies, it was on the Isle of Oleron under the command of Major Feisthamel. His staff seemed to be more or less complete. He had a battalion adjutant, a paymaster, an officer in charge of materiel, a surgeon, seven captains, six lieutenants and five second lieutenants.

strength of the service at the same figure while expanding the number of regiments to three. Finally there was some inkling of what would make the power and strength of the naval infantry: the continual, regulation replacement by company. However, the colonial garrisons were too weak with the 90 companies, including 24 elite ones. An ordinance of August 14, 1840 increased the number from 40, that is 130 in total, and expanded the effective strength to 15,809 men.

1st Regiment. Organization of 1838 had 30 companies: 15 in France, 15 in Guadeloupe; in 1842, 21 in France, 21 in Guadeloupe.
2nd Regiment. Organization of 1838 had 30 companies: 15 in France, 15 in Martinique; in 1842, 21 in France, 21 in Martinique.
3rd Regiment. Organization of 1838 had 30 companies: 15 in France, 3 in Senegal, 6 at Cayenne, 6 at Bourbon; in 1842, 23 in France, 5 in Senegal, 6 at Cayenne, 12 at Bourbon plus the cadres for the 3 companies of *cipayes* and 4 black companies.

This ordinance of August 14, 1840 allowed the naval infantry regiments to complete themselves by borrowing officers from the land army. It remained the charter of the naval infantry. This was an accommodating charter which allowed everything, even the arbitrary. However, its flexibility sometimes permitted very major services. All the same, the naval ministry did not immediately know how to make use of it. Lacking ingenuity and clear views, the "office of the organized corps" of the time allowed the introduction into the new companies of old captains of the services, master caulkers, and officers "trying to maintain the status quo," all with epaulettes, who cast a bad light over the corps. As of December 22, 1841, a royal decision called upon the students leaving Saint-Cyr to compete for the positions of second lieutenant which were vacant in the naval infantry. For a long time, these young people felt a certain repugnance for this assignment. However, when the naval infantry inscribed the names of the five parts of the world on its flags, the top students of the school requested to serve there. Even recently, artillery and engineering officers coming from the polytechnic school have been seen requesting to move into the Tonkin Tirailleurs. In the army, merit always goes where its ambition finds satisfaction.

In the Marquesas Islands (1841), three companies from the 3rd Regiment provided France with a new conquest. Almost immediately, on June 9, 1842, a positon of general of brigade, inspector of the service, was created.

In 1843, eight companies taken from the 2nd and 3rd Regiments and turned over to the 1st Regiment were sent to Polynesia.

The occupation of Nossi-Bé and Mayotte required an increase in size of the garrison at Bourbon. A credit was requested from the Chambers, which naturally refused it. The offense caused by this refusal was able to be corrected by distributing the 130 companies in the following manner:

1st Regiment: 46 companies; 21 in France, 17 in Guadeloupe and 8 in Oceania;
2nd Regiment: 38 companies; 21 in France and 17 in Martinique;
3rd Regiment. 46 companies; 23 in France, 5 at Cayenne, 5 in Senegal, 13 at Bourbon and establishments in the vicinity.

The needs of the service restricted increasing the companies' sergeants (6 instead of 4) and corporals (12 instead of 8).

On July 1, 1845, the tunic in blue cloth with two rows of buttons and the grey-blue tinted pants with a scarlet stripe were adopted. The companies of grenadiers wore red epaulettes and the voltigeurs yellow epaulettes. The center wore the shoulder knot (*contre-épaulette*) with a blue body and scarlet rims. A colonial dress was adopted. On August 28, 1852, the 36 elite companies had been eliminated and all the companies were combined together. As in the chasseurs à pied, the soldiers, corporals, and first class non-commissioned officers were distributed into the companies and the yellow epaulettes and pompom were adopted. Meanwhile, one company per army battalion with pin carbines bore the name of carabiniers. In March 1855, this company was eliminated. All the naval infantry then received the pin carbine and the drummers were replaced by buglers. The sappers lost their hand axes, their aprons and their beards. Except for the purely administrative regimental organization, the naval voltigeurs had the same tactical make-up as the chasseurs à pied in the land army.

The July Government had been the true creator of the naval infantry. As a government which was careful in military and administrative matters, it had expressly intended to separate the troops of the war department from those of the Navy as much on military grounds as for budgetary considerations. The well-being of the service was in agreement with its tendencies on this occasion.

Service dress. Royal Navy (1828).

Landing party. Royal Navy (1840).

Although the regiments of naval infantry had not yet won that luster which surrounds them today, they were already very good troops with a solidity which increased daily. On March 21, 1847, an ordinance had permanently determined the effectives and the garrisons. Their status on December 31, 1847 is provided below.

  1st Regiment. General staff: 44 officers; non-commissioned staff: 46 men; troops, 5,526 men: at Brest, 2,282, at Guadeloupe, 2,034, in Oceania, 1,297
  2nd Regiment. General staff: 41 officers; non-commissioned staff: 47 men; troops, 4,575 men: at Rochefort, 1,435, at Cherbourg, 1,194, at Martinique, 2,034
  3rd Regiment. General staff: 41 officers; non-commissioned staff: 48 men; troops, 5,553 men: at Toulon, 2,890, at Cayenne, 602, at Senegal, 602, at Bourbon, at Sainte-Marie, Nossi-Bé, and Mayotte, 1,541, in India, 7.

For this total of 15,634 men there was in addition a special general staff of 21 officers; 2 generals of brigade of whom one was an inspector general, 3 colonels or lieutenant colonels, 7 majors, and 9 captains.

The February Revolution had no influence over the assignments of the naval infantry. During the events of June, General Cavaignac requested its help to put down the revolt. However, the means of transport had not been extended very much at this time. It was June 29th, when everything was over, that the first detachment composed of four companies arrived. The other detachments were countermanded. After having their fine dress admired by the Parisians who were not yet familiar with it, this fine battalion returned to its home port. The impression was generally good. I recall having seen them bivouac at the Panthéon and the satisfaction which they produced on amateurs of being good-looking troops. It was well known from having read the newspapers that there had been naval infantry soldiers at Tahiti, Mogador, and Vera-Cruz. However, no one knew how they were dressed, or if they maneuvered well. It could thus be said that this was their first baptism by public opinion. Their good reputation was consolidated with Senegal. This colony always had commanders haunted by a taste for battle. The war-like people who surrounded them never refused them the opportunity of making expeditions and, if necessary, they provided them. Thus it was in Senegal that the most adventurous naval infantrymen went to seek the early laurels of the corps. It was in Senegal that the the great offshoot of auxiliary corps was born (Senegalese Tirailleurs, Tonkin Tirailleurs, Annamite Tirailleurs). If the French are not careful, these companies will quickly overtake (in terms of number) the companies of naval infantry employed abroad. Senegal was not the only place to want to have a fine local battalion established within the framework of officers and of non-commissioned officers of the naval infantry. However, it required a squadron of Spahis (1) commanded by officers and non-commissioned officers taken from the 1st Regiment

(Algiers Province). This was not enough for Senegal. On two different occasions, it requested that Algeria loan it some companies of native tirailleurs for unusual expeditions. General Faidherbe, himself loaned by the war department to the navy, exported this expeditionary fever to Senegal where he won his colonel's epaulettes and his general's stars. This was a fever which in the past had excited the generals of the famous school of mutual admiration. In Senegal, military needs are excessive. It is not said whether commerical products increase considerably. Thus it is a warrior colony above all and one where officers are better formed than in Algeria or Tunisia. The Central Africans fight exceedingly well and are ferocious and swift. As great as the liberality of the navy's budget has been (it maintained a Senegalese train there), it has never put substantial means at the service of the governors. Consequently, the officers commanding the expeditions must display a great deal of energy, talent, and especially ingenuity to supplement everything they are lacking.

Until 1854, the naval infantry only carried out some colonial campaigns. For the formation of the army corps sent to the Orient, a *régiment de marche* of two battalions at eight companies taken from three regiments was attached to the 3rd Corps (Prince Napoleon). At first they were included in the 3rd Regiment for administrative purposes. The command of this *régiment de marche* was given to Colonel Bertin-Duchâteau. Then a decree from August 31, 1854 decided that a 4th naval infantry regiment would be formed. All the companies that entered into the composition of the *régiment de marche* were joined to it by a decision from January 1855. The *régiment de marche* had left without that cohesiveness which constituted the power of France's old army. There, all the components maturing together learned to be familiar with and to appreciate each other. The apprenticeship of this cohesion which French generals of the past admitted could not be done in a single day on campaign had to be done at Gallipoli and at Warna. However, men grow and develop quickly in war. As of Alma, the *regiment de marche* conducted itself energetically and deserved 8 crosses (Major Marmier, Captains Leprince, Domenech-Diego, Guillot, Gagné,

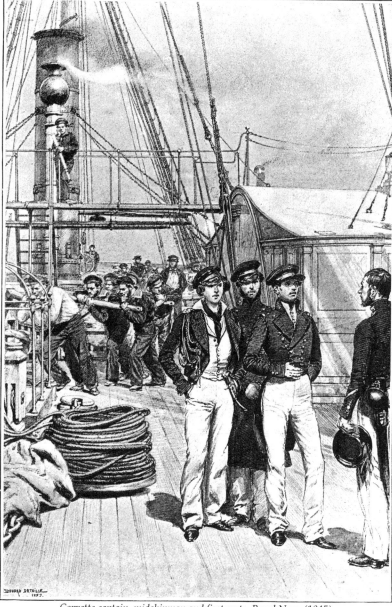

Corvette captain, midshipman and first mate, Royal Navy (1845).

Ribert, Naudot, and Martin des Pallières). However, although the *biffins* (land infantry) and the *marsouins* (naval infantry) had understood their worth in playing together with their bayonets, some officers still thought that the land army could not completely count on its brothers in the naval army. Marshal Forey, a man of spirit nevertheless, retained this bad aftertaste until Mexico. Thus in the Crimea, there were some moments of agonizing indecision. At Alma, the regiment was brilliantly led. It lost three officers, Lieutenants Poirot de Scellier and Boh and Second Lieutenant Derouet. However, on the night of February 22nd to 23rd, an attack led by Colonel Cler of the 2nd Zouaves failed. Like almost all night attacks, it failed for lack of reconnoitering and precise knowledge of the terrain. Although the colonel had to personally praise the offiers Legrand and Vagneur of the naval infantry who had snatched him from the hands of the Russians, he did not give equal praise to the two groups of troops whom he had under his command that night. Regardless, the soldiers and the officers of the 4th redoubled their zeal and their bravery. This unfortunate impression thus disappeared. Nonetheless, it seemed necessary to us to indicate the unfairness of past land generals toward the naval troops. This is an injustice which was unfortunately repeated in reverse when the expeditionary corps of Tonkin found itself temporarily placed under the command of General Brière de l'Isle.

At the assault on Mamelon Vert, the naval infantry conducted itself with so much heroism that it drew bravos even from its detractors. It lost almost half of its strength. Captain Trexon, Lieutenant Maville, and Second Lieutenants Salle and Jarry fell, never to rise again. Des Pallières, David, Valière, Vailly, Guillot and Brien were wounded. On June 18th, six more officers died: Captains Leprince and Graève, Lieutenant Eynard, and Second Lieutenants Caille, Hachon and Cerut. Ten were wounded: Reybaud, Martigny, Bazire, Dufresne, Gautret, Ribert, Noquet, Ladrière, de Barolet, and Lieutenant Colonel Bichin Cendrecourt who died of his wounds. Eight crosses, 17 medals, and 8 epaulettes were the reward for this fine conduct. In the course of the campaign, two officers had been killed in different combats: Captain Delacoux-Marivault and Second Lieutenant Barnaud. Few infantry regiments

(1) *Historical Record of the Senegalese Spahis*. The first platoon which landed under the command of Commander Petit established its reputation. In a bloody battle, 21 cavalrymen scattered 2,000 blacks. The ordinance of July 21, 1854 regularized the organization. The squadron had 170 cavalrymen of whom half were French. It was dressed like the other Spahis—the officers wore the cork helmet. It drew its remount from Algeria. In short, this was a squadron of Spahis adjusted for the service of Senegal. A recent decree has modified this simple organization. The Senegalese Spahis are very renowned in the cavalry. Although they have a special standard, the following names may be read there: Bissagos, Dalmath, Diobouldou, Les Trazras, le Oulao, Langobe, N'Diambour, Guemon, Casamance, Cayor, Golgol, Loro, Paonos, Nioro, Mecke, Coki, Sabouciré, N'dirboyan, etc. The following excerpt from their historical records gives a better idea of their efforts. "On May 1, 1881, 1,470 non-commissioned officers and soldiers had passed under the control of the squadron. Out of this number, 65 were killed by the enemy and 180 wounded. During this period, the squadron had: 6 officers' crosses of the Legion of Honor, 48 chevaliers, 117 military medals, 18 citations, and 28 non-commissioned officers named officers."

have sufferd more in the Crimea than the *régiment de marche* of the 4th Naval Infantry.

The campaign of the Orient was also the occasion for the shifting of a number of companies. When the first French troops assigned to defend Turkey crossed the waters of Greece, a portion of Forey's Division in particular was landed at Piraeus. They were to keep in check the populace which seemed to manifest too much sympathy for the Russians. Soon these troops were replaced by a brigade commanded by General Mayran. However, he was called to his tour of duty in the Crimea. A small squadron—18 naval infantry companies belonging to the 1st Regiment to which a platoon of the 2nd Dragoons was later added—came under the command of Rear-Admiral Bouet Willaumez and was established at Athens. This occupation lasted until the beginning of 1857 and was not always without its dangers. Commander Escoubet was killed there by a bullet in October 1856.

In the meantime, 220 men of the 1st, 2nd and 3rd Regiments had taken part in the expedition of Bomarsund. Lieutenants Lanchère and Caffard died there. The following year, 1855, many companies of the three first regiments were embarked on the fleet crossing the Baltic. If the war was prolonged and if it were necessary to send one or more army corps into the north of Europe, the naval department had taken its precautions to help with an entire brigade.

From this point on, it is impossible to follow each naval infantry regiment in the detachments of companies it sent to the colonies. The decree of August 31, 1854 assigned them to the following garrisons:

1st Regiment: Cherbourg and Martinique;
2nd Regiment: Brest, Guadeloupe, Oceania;
3rd Regiment: Rochefort, Cayenne;
4th Regiment: Toulon, Réunion, Senegal.

No detachment of naval infantry was called to the Army of Italy commanded by Napoleon III. However, the major role in the attack of Venice by sea was reserved for it, an attack rendered useless by the anticipated conclusion of peace. A battalion of the 4th Regiment commanded by Major Domenech-Diego landed on the Isle Lossini Grande. He was to be followed by troops which had been requested from Africa and from three other regiments.

Thus we arrive at the campaign of China, one of the most extraordinary military events of the 19th century. The whole campaign, with its restricted proportions, seems to be a marvel of science in the eyes of connoisseurs with regard to its preparation and conduct. A naval infantry *régiment de marche* of 16 companies taken from the 3rd Regiment was formed into brigades in a strong division. With considerable accessories, this formed the entire expeditionary

Service dress. Imperial Navy (1855).

corps of General Cousin-Montauban. Colonel de Vassoigne commanded this regiment and won his general of brigade's stars there. It was in this capacity that he held the direction of the troops under the command of Vice-Admiral Charner during the expedition of CochinChina, substituted for that of China. For this latter expedition, some other companies were joined to the *régiment de marche* of the 3rd.

Commander; General of Brigade, de Vassoigne. *Aide-de-camp:* de Trentinian, Major.

3rd Regiment of Naval Infantry: Lieutenant Colonels Favre and Testard; Major Derôme; Captain Gillot; Captain Battalion Adjutant, Brière de l'Isle; Paymaster, Captain Mornet; Officer in charge of materiel, Captain Bonzé; 28th Company, Captain Bouzain; 29th Company, Captain Dastuynes; 30th Company, Captain Brunet; 31st Company, Captain N.; 32nd Company, Captain Putmann; 33rd Company, Captain David; 34th Company, Captain Portalez; 35th Company, Captain Chasseriau; 36th Company, Captain Lalanne; 37th Company; 38th Company, Captain Deschamps; 39th Company; 19th Company, Captain de la Broue.

Detached companies; 4th Regiment: Major Delavau; Battalion Adjutant, Captain de Barolet; Paymaster, Lieutenant Lemerle. 5th Company, Captain Foucault; 11th Company, Captain Royer; 16th Company, Captain Genta; 19th Company, Lieutenant Gabet. Native Company, Lieutenant Wiart. 3rd Regiment: Company *de marche*, Captain Guillot. 2nd Regiment: Company *de marche*, Lieutenant Gastaldi.

These details prove that the naval infantry regiments are depositories from which one draws troops according to the needs of various components to form detachments, battalions, and companies *de marche*. They are made up of bits and pieces which the leaders see fit to dismantle as soon as they have broken them into the service for which they have been gathered. Obviously, it would be better to have a good colonial army composed of professional soldiers and especially of ones schooled in the colonies. However, the overextended military institutions do not permit this luxury to a democracy. Only the internal records of the naval infantry regiments can say how many men are consumed with the restricted service applied to the colonial garrisons. Now is the time to state that terrible phrase of a major. He said: "I can easily see those who are leaving, but I do not at all see those who will return."

This system of detachments has gone a long way. When a naval infantry regiment is provided to a colony which would not feed even one or more companies, this or that company changes regiment in following this destination. From that point on, there are no more rules or methods. Everything is taken care of by the stroke of a pen. It is not even believed that the colonels, superior officers, and company commanders give persistent and extensive attention to the military education of the men which certainly will not help them in combat. They require a great deal of virtue not to fail in their work. However, it is also very difficult for the troops to improve themselves under such conditions.

The *régiment de marche* that left with the first expeditionary corps of Mexico was twelve companies strong: nine from the 1st Regiment and three from the 2nd. Six companies came from France, three from Martinique, and three from Guadeloupe. Colonel Hennique commanded them. In the march to the front against Puebla, the regiment was formed into brigades with the battalions of naval riflemen, Allègre commanding. When one thinks that 7,300 men full of confidence went to be swallowed up in an enemy country 2,000 leagues from their homeland, and that although they suffered a check, they maintained their cohesion, it must then be recognized that the seven year service formed soldiers of a superior quality and that the officers of the time knew how to inspire great confidence in them. There was less discussion and better obedience. On the unfortunate day of May 5th, the *régiment de marche* lost five officers: Captains Léris and Lemaire, Lieutenant Courteau, Second Lieutenants Crovisier and Waïss, and thirty-six soldiers. In addition, two officers were wounded and fifty-three men of the ranks were wounded. When General Latrille de Lorencez had reestablished his communications with Vera-Cruz, the *régiment de marche* had one battlaion at Orizaba and one at Soledad. It detached one company to Vera-Cruz. These glorious and useful services should have maintained the naval infantry in the brigading of the expeditionary corps commanded by General Forey. Under the pretense to the war department of not bringing in foreign troops, this general removed the naval infantry regiment. It had been at the suffering; it should have been at the glory. The 2nd battery of the naval regiment and a moutain battery of marines remained attached to the

General of division DE VASSOIGNE - *Aide-de-camp:* BICHOT, Captain.
Officiers d'ordonnance: GOUVY, Captain; CHANU, Captain; DE GAUFRIDY DE DORDAN, Lieutenant (43rd Line).
Chief of staff: DE TRENTINIAN, Colonel - *Assistant chief:* LAMBERT, Major.
Adjutants: WENDLING, Captain; DE DOUGLAS, Lieutenant.
Commander of the artillery: GUILHERMY, Major.
Commander of the engineers: ROULET, Major.

INTENDANCE SERVICE - *Adjutant commissary:* LANGEVIN - *Assistant commissary:* RASSICOD.
Commissary aides: BONFILS DE LAFAURIE, DELACROSE, FRIOCOURT, Lieutenants.
AMBULANCE - *Principal Doctor:* GIRARD DE LA BARCERIE - *Doctors, first class:* LECONTE, CASTILLON.
Doctors, second class: BALLOT, DENOIX, CHAVANON (2nd class) - *Pharmacist:* CAZALIS.
Provost: SAUX, Captain of naval gendarmerie (21 majors, brigade leaders and gendarmes).
Naval chaplains: Abbés HAINS and LE SAOUT

1st Brigade
REBOUL, General of brigade - *Aide-de-camp:* LESSELINE, Captain - *Officier d'ordonnance:* BADENS, Lieutenant.

1st REGIMENT - *Colonel:* BRIÈRE DE L'ISLE; *Lieutenant-Colonel:* CHOMET.
Armament officer: PERRET, Lieutenant - *Paymaster:* GUICHARD, Lieutenant.
Color bearer: MERCIER, Second-Lieutenant

	CAPTAINS	LIEUTENANTS	SECOND-LIEUTENANTS
1st BATTALION	Weiler	Legendre de Fougainville	Bouguié
BOÜET, Major	Legras	Rozet (Second-Lieutenant)	Crouit-Duferrier
Montagniès de la Roque,	Vequaud	Millet (Second-Lieutenant)	Kippeurt
Captain battalion adjutant	Pressard	Remy (Second-Lieutenant)	Jacquin
Dsmoute, Surgeon major	Farcy	Lavenue (Second-Lieutenant)	Chatelain
	Maurial	Watrin	Chevalier
2nd BATTALION	Corion	Saudubray	La Madeleine
FREMIET, Major	Raison	Boillon	Le Camus
De Maussion, Captain	Campi	Bresson	Guillemard
battalion adjutant	Dorval-Alvarès	Page	Brière
Moudière, Surgeon major	Ortus	De Vanssay de Blavous (Second Lieutenant)	Cuthbert
	Jouenne	Lebouvier	Maison
3rd BATTALION	Poret	Senchet	Roulot
BONNET, Major	Astolfi	Malézieux (Second-Lieutenant)	Arnier
Yvos, Captain			
battalion adjutant	De Manceau	Lambert	Bloyard
Leclerc, Assistant surgeon major	Cornu	Pierra (Second-Lieutenant)	Recoing
	Guichard	Stanislas	Pierron
	Marchesseau	Redel	Bassand

4th REGIMENT - *Colonel:* D'ARBAUD; *Lieutenant-Colonel:* SASIAS.
Armament officer: BARTHE, Lieutenant - *Paymaster:* BOISTEL, Lieutenant.
Color bearer: NUSSBAUM, Second-Lieutenant

	CAPTAINS	LIEUTENANTS	SECOND-LIEUTENANTS
1st BATTALION	Arot	Hostalot	Jourdan
HOPPER, Major	Mathieu	Perrotte	Carré
Lebon, Captain	—	Bouvier	Lefranc
battalion adjutant	Barthélemy	Belloc	Payen
Bourgarel, Surgeon major	Vince	Signol	Pennequin
	Momet	Roustan	Taconnet
2nd BATTALION	Noyer	Garay	De Lalande-Boudan
PASQUET DE LA BROUE, Major	Troismaison	Auffray	Armoric
Anne, Captain	Audibert	Morice du Lerain	Leroi
battalion adjutant	Frémaux	Thibault	Ferry
Audibert,Assistant	Gabot	Buisson d'Armandy	Vignon
Surgeon Major	Lemerie	D'Algay	Charrier
3rd BATTALION	Beghin	De Douglas	Salicetti
CHASSERLAU, Major	Noé	Nicolini	Baule
Voyron, Captain	Bruzard	Defrance	Guimont
battalion adjutant	Frémiet	Magnin	Joubert
Chevalier, Assistant	Abribat	Desconnet	Arnault
Surgeon Major	Guillemin	Ruflat	Ginisti

1st Division. The truth is that, as was said earlier, General Forey revived old prejudices already erased in the land army. This step was, moreover, very badly viewed by the old and new regiments of the expeditionary corps. The evidence Colonel Hennique received on this occasion proved to him that the general in chief's point of view was not shared by anyone else.

In 1864, the *régiment de marche* had returned to its respective garrisons since only two companies of the colonial engineers organized specially for this expedition appeared in the report on troops borrowed from the navy.

It is likely that the legitimate complaints of an honorable corps, its pride unjustly wounded, came to the attention of the Emperor. Napoleon III had the good sense to rectify the abuses that had been indicated to him without great fanfare. He returned those who had been been withdrawn to the path of duty. In 1868 and 1869, some naval infantry *régiments de marche* were called to the camp of Châlons to participate in the training and shooting exercises of the land army regiments. They showed superior discipline there and total training. From that time on, there was not a single officer who doubted the complete equality of the *marsouins* and the *biffins*. Marshal Forey carried the last vestiges of that prejudice with him to his grave.

With the beginning of the War of 1870 on August 4th, the naval infantry had received orders to form a *régiment de marche* of 18 companies per regiment and 130 men per company. This fine division was to be the nucleus of a small army charged with operating along the Baltic coast. It was the first time that the naval department transferred an entire division. It did so with special care. The list of all the officers in this division is given above and on the next page.

Ever meticulous, the naval department had prepared depots for the four *régiment de marche*. They were soon made use of, as will be seen. The Vassoigne Division was concentrated first at Paris whence it left on August 12th for the camp of Châlons. The glory that it won in the battles around Sedan and especially in the defense of Bazeilles is known. People now say "the naval infantry at Bazeilles" as in the past they said "the cuirassiers at Waterloo." In the midst of this bloody and terrible defeat, the renown of the naval infantry emerges and gives this young service branch undying relief. It is unfortunate that custom does not permit embroidering the name

---

2nd Brigade
MARTIN DES PALLIÈRES, General of brigade
Aide-de-camp: VIGNE, Captain - *Officiers d'ordonnance:* HENNIQUE, Lieutenant; HAGRON, Second-Lieutenant.

2nd REGIMENT - *Colonel:* ALLEYRON; *Lieutenant-Colonel:* DOMANGE.
Armament officer: ADAMPIEVRAT, Lieutenant - *Paymaster:* GUYOT, Lieutenant.
Color bearer: JAY, Second-Lieutenant

	CAPTAINS	LIEUTENANTS	SECOND-LIEUTENANTS
1ST BATTALION	Brissard	Toucas	De Percin
DE STALH, Major	Delaury	Pelloux	Saint-Felix
Brunot, Captain	Oubre	Boulland	Hoerniel
battalion adjutant	Bourgey	Maimanche	Escoubet
Cosquer, Surgeon major	Escande	Testard	Renauld
	Bonzé	Duchaussoy	Caban
2nd BATTALION	Augier	De Boulet de Bonneuil	Girard
RIELH, Major	Roussel	Hugonnet	Piéton
Laprairie, Captain	Laurencin	Demaussion	Gay du Palland
battalion adjutant	Fongueuse	Bournisien de Valmot	Vincent
Batby du Berquin, Assistant	Dumesnil	Morand de la Pérelle	Hagron
Surgeon Major	Rancoulet	Danzelle	Deschard
3rd BATTALION	Portait	Collot	Briot
NICOLAZO DE BARMON, Major	Disnematin-Durat	Bermeilly	Thirion
Page, Captain	Fréchou	Dugué	Rollin
battalion adjutant	De Vougny	Wolff	Breschin
Liégard, Assistant	Bicheret	Lasalle de Lescars	Le Dentu
Surgeon Major	Aubert	Teulières	Piot

3rd REGIMENT - *Colonel:* LE CAMUS; *Lieutenant-Colonel:* DANOS.
Armament officer: SIMEON, Lieutenant - *Paymaster:* BARTET, Lieutenant.
Color bearer: DE BEAUREPAIRE, Second-Lieutenant

	CAPTAINS	LIEUTENANTS	SECOND-LIEUTENANTS
1st BATTALION	Pouilh	Meunier	Duchène
CROSNIER, Major	Benoît d'Auriac	Dehousse	Heiligenmeyer
Second, Captain	Picard	Bonnifay	Cluzel
battalion adjutant	Pommerelle	Bascans	Jean
Delassalle, Surgeon major	Bourchet	Seriot	Hayet
	Miramont	Truc	Legros
2nd BATTALION	Lanoë	Favre	Galieni
BOUYER, Major	Guillery	Poncet	Bahier
Kaindler, Captain	Dodds	Mantin	Dabat
battalion adjutant	Jolliet	Besson	Faucher
Molle, Assistant	Janelle	Brunet	Ferrette
Surgeon Major	Dujardin	Bossus	Arbod
3rd BATTALION	Arnauld-Guy	Coupé	Audirac
DAUBAS, Major	Veyne	Maine	Bouchet
Jeanne Duclos, Captain	Brullé	Berthe de Villers	Leblond
battalion adjutant	Cassaigne	Clercant	Bonnelle
De Fornel, Assistant	Cocu	Royer	Dugros de Boisseguin
Surgeon Major	Bompard	Dossat	Gabet

ARTILLERY - 11th battery, Captain Geoffroy; 12th battery, Captain Bourdiaux; 13th battery, Captain Godin.
(These batteries only arrived on August 23rd and were included in the reserve.
In the division they were replaced by batteries from the land army.)
ENGINEERS - 11th sapper company of the 2nd Regiment, Captain Haxo.

---

of a defeat in golden letters on their flag.

In the days of August 31st and September 1st, the Vassoigne Division lost 2655 men, a quarter of its effective strength.

Below are given the names of the officers who died on the battlefield or as the result of the wounds they received there:

General Staff: Captain Goury, Captain Vigne. *1st Regiment:* Major Frémiet (missing); Captains Pressard, Maurial, Poret, Vequaud; Lieutenants Legendre de Fougainville, Watrin, Boillon (missing); Second Lieutenants Groult-Duferrier, Chevalier, Maison. *2nd Regiment:* Lieutenant Colonel Domange; Captain Roussel; Lieutenants Collot and Teulières; Second Lieutenants Thirion and Piot. *3rd Regiment:* Lieutenant Colonel Danos; Major Crosnier; Captain Arnault-Guy; Second Lieutenant Bonnelle. *4th Regiment:* Majors Hopfer and Chasseriau; Captains Moinet, Beghin, Barthe, Bouvier, Clercant, de Douglas; Lieutenants Belloc, Roustan, Garay, du Lerain, d'Algay; and Second Lieutenants Carré, Leroy, Salicetti and Pillat.

For the defense of Paris, the naval infantry provided four battalions rapidly organized with the four depots.

These four battalions were formed, the 1st and the 3rd from the first two regiments and the 2nd and the 4th from the last two. They arrived in Paris with an effective strength of 3,263 men. At the end of the siege, with the voluntary enlistments and selections from the class of 1870, they numbered 4,772 men. In addition, the naval infantry was represented at Paris by two of its generals: General of Division de Barolet de Puligny and General of Brigade Faron. The latter at first commanded the 1st Sector, then the 2nd Division of the reserve army. Finally, during the armistice, he commanded the division charged with policing Paris. For aide-de-camp he had Captain

---

BATTALION NUMBER 1 (AT FORT DE ROSNY)	BATTALION NUMBER 2 (AT FORT DE ROMAINVILLE)	BATTALION NUMBER 3 (AT FORT DE BICÊTRE)	BATTALION NUMBER 4 (AT FORT DE NOISY)
Major: VESQUE	Major: BARGONE	Major: DARRÉ	Major: BOUSIGON
Captain battalion adjutant: BRAQUET	Captain battalion adjutant: LECONTE	Captain battalion adjutant: PORTAIT	Captain battalion adjutant: DULIEU
Paymaster: KELLAND, Lieutenant	Paymaster: DUPUY, Lieutenant	Paymaster: LARUE, Lieutenant	Paymaster: VILLEMAIN, Lieutenant
1st company - Lemaître, Captain	1st company - Borderel, Captain	1st company - Naudin, Captain	1st company - Chevillot, Captain
2nd company - De Rattazzi, Captain	2nd company - Kelland, Captain	2nd company - François, Captain	2nd company - Pilorge, Captain
3rd company - Lorenziti, Captain	3rd company - Bonmy, Captain	3rd company - Gillot, Captain	3rd company - Torracinta, Captain
4th company - Bertaut, Captain	4th company - Dupuy, Captain	4th company - Stanislas, Captain	4th company - Reygasse, Captain

---

Disnematin-Dorat who had escaped captivity after Sedan and made his way back to Paris. For *officier d'ordonnance*, he had Captain Cullard. He was replaced in the 1st Sector by General de Barolet de Puligny who had for aide-de-camp Captain Boutin.

During the early months of the siege, the naval infantry battalions had the same luck as the forts to which they were attached. The 3rd and the 4th were sent to the Plateau of Avron at the beginning of December. The 2nd, which had occupied the cattle station, went to join them soon thereafter. They suffered harsh conditions; close to one quarter of the force were killed by freezing. Finally, during the four last weeks of the siege, the four battalions found themselves together again in the Salmon Brigade. For the service of the provincial armies, it formed eight battalions which administratively took the numbers following the four of Paris.

These battalions had been provided as follows: the 9th and 10th by the 1st Regiment; the 5th, 8th, and 12th by the 2nd Regiment; the 6th and the 11th by the 3rd Regiment; and the 7th by the 4th Regiment. Thus, during the war, the naval infantry had brought a

---

BATTALION NUMBER 5 (5 companies)
Major: LAURENT - Captain battalion adjutant: PAGE - Paymaster: GUYOT

BATTALION NUMBER 6 (5 companies)
Major: LEMERLE - Captain battalion adjutant: GOSSE DE BILLY - Paymaster: LEBLOND

BATTALION NUMBER 7 (5 companies)
Major: KAINDLER later BARTHÉLEMY - Captain battalion adjutant: LASSOUARN later BRIONCOURT - Paymaster: BOURGES

BATTALION NUMBER 8 (— companies)
Major: PASQUET DE LA BROUE - Captain battalion adjutant: BRUNET - Paymaster: COLLARD-DESCHEVRY

BATTALION NUMBER 9 (4 companies)
Major: MEYNIER - Captain battalion adjutant: CAMPI - Paymaster: ARNAULD
(4 officers and 196 men per company)

BATTALION NUMBER 10 (4 companies)
Major: HERBILLON - Captain battalion adjutant: — - Paymaster: MERCIER

BATTALION NUMBER 11 (4 companies)
Major: AZAN - Captain battalion adjutant: — - Paymaster: LÉVÈQUE

BATTALION NUMBER 12 (— companies)
Major: FABRE - Captain battalion adjutant: PONS - Paymaster: FAUQUE

Naval infantry (Bazeilles, September 1, 1870).

relief force of 28 battalions, all the while maintaining adequate garrisons in the colonies. Sixteen of the battalions had 6 companies and the twelve others had 4 or 5. Everywhere they fought—in the Army of the Loire, the Army of the East, and the Army of the North—they proved themselves to be valiant and excellent troops, as at Bazeilles.

Battalion Number 5 deserves special mention. In December 1870, attached to the 1st Divsion of the 15th Corps, it gave a fine example of discipline after the evacuation of Orléans. With four of its companies still solidly constituted, it arrived at Vierzon which was invaded, taken by assault by 6,000 stragglers and runaways from all the services and of all ranks. Not only did they maintain themselves whole and tight like an old troop, but they militarily occupied the city and the train station. They quelled the disorder as much as they could and lost neither a single man nor a rifle. They eventually took up their position again in their division when all the other regiments were more or less suffering the ills of disorganization. It should be recalled what a rout entails to understand the fine conduct of Commander Laurent and the officers who assisted him.

Through the importance of their services during the war and their energetic conduct in the suppression of the Commune, the naval troops had deserved to participate in the advantages of the garrison of Paris. They maintained an infantry battalion *de marche* there until December 23, 1876. The companies that formed it then joined their original posts again.

THE TONKIN CAMPAIGN

Naval Captain Rivière had with him only 4 naval infantry companies of 100 men when in May 1833 he committed that heroic folly which cost him his life. It also cost France 30 million per year, not counting the 300 million spent from 1881 until the creation of the Annam-Tonkin protectorate.

Relief arrived promptly. In August 1883, Colonel Bichot had under his command Majors Chevallier, Corronnat, Lafont, Roux, Berger and Reygasse. He also had the battalion majors Blanchard, Lange and Bouchet and eighteen companies of naval infantry. Eight were from the 1st Regiment: 25th, Captain Poulnot; 26th, Captain Doucet; 27th, Captain Guérin de Fontjoyeuse; 29th, Captain Jay; 31st; 33rd, Captain Trilha; 34th, Captain Larivière; and 36th, Captain Lombard. Ten were from the 3rd Regiment: 21st, Captain Buquet; 22nd; 23rd; 24th; 25th, Captain Drouin; 26th, Captain Taccoen; 27th, Captain Larcelot; 29th, Captain Rauzier; 30th, Captain Martelière; and 31st.

On October 6, 1883, Major Bertaux-Levillain brought two new companies from the 1st Regiment. On October 25th, Rear-Admiral Courbet had been named commander in chief, Lieutenant Colonel Badens became his chief of staff, and Colonel Bichot took command of the troops. It was at this point in time that the first attempt to form the Tonkin Tirailleurs took place. At the time, they were called the *"pavillons jaunes"* (yellow section). Their first group was of approximately 400 men. However, following the pillaging they did to a friendly village, one of them had his head cut off. They showed themselves to be very dissatisfied, but their mustering out and their disarmament was done without any accidents.

Major Dulieu arrived in November with the 21st, 22nd, 23rd, and 24th companies of the 1st Regiment. Lieutenant Colonels de Maussion and Brionval took command of the *régiment de marche*. Finally, in February 1884, Brière de l'Isle took command of an infantry brigade and General Millot took command of the expeditionary corps.

During the campaign, 24 companies, that is 6 battalions *de marche*, passed through Tonkin. The companies were always maintained at an average effective strength of 200 men and consumed double that in men. The service was particularly extravagant and expensive. In the march of Lang-Son on Tuyen-Quan, an entire naval infantry company was destroyed by a buried mine. These facts are not well known by the public and will only be revealed a long time from now. For a long time, Tonkin will remain a painful event and will be concealed by the State. Howver, when this history is eventually written, the twenty-four companies of the two *régiments de marche* will find their place in the sun there.

The losses in officers were great. It was impossible for us to uncover everything in official documents, which are naturally edited before being delivered for publicity. Meanwhile, the following list has been officially communicated to us. It shows how painful and difficult was the task accomplished.

Officers killed: Lieutenant Colonel Carreau; Major Berthe de Villers, Captains Clémenceau (2nd Regiment), Jeannin (3rd); Cussy (1st); Cuny (2nd); Jacquin (3rd); Tailland (2nd); Carré (3rd); Dià (3rd); Hugot (3rd); d'Arthaud (3rd); Doucet (2nd); Bourguignon (3rd);. Lieutenants: Clavé (1st); Moissenet, de l'Estoile, Chassaigne, Aubertin (2nd); Claye (2nd); Camus (2nd); Geil (3rd); Hahner (4th); Haulon (2nd). Second Lieutenants: Bossant (general staff); Schuster (1st); Labaloure (1st); Fougères, de Goujon de Thury, Brun, Caron (1st); Vaché (4th); Lemercier de Jauville (2nd); d'Heral de Brisis (2nd).

Officers wounded: Major Blanchard (2nd); Captains Penther, Salle, Bourguinon (3rd); Bécourt (4th); Chanu (1st). Lieutenants: Adam de Villiers (4th); Pouligo (1st); Genin, Bellier, Larribe (3rd); Chenagon (4th); de Garge, Verzeaux, Lagarde (1st); Onffroy de la Rozière, Parent de Curzon, Ligier, Ozoux, Bilba (1st). Second Lieutenants: Bataille, Le Herget, Belier, Genin (3rd).

Naval fusiliers (1870-1871).

Naval infantry, full dress in the colonies (1847).

If the names of officers dead from disease is added to this long list which the naval ministry counts at thirty-two—a modest number—it can be agreed that after Bazeilles and Tonkin, there is not a corps in the French army that has done more for France in twenty years than the glorious naval infantry.

ARTILLERY

As has been stated above, the actual regiment was created on November 13, 1822. From January 26, 1825 to December 21, 1828, it was exempt from the colonial service. Many royal decrees had expanded it to 40 companies. On January 4, 1842 it was reduced to 30 companies: total force of 3,338 men including 6 companies of workmen. This force was distributed in the following manner.

Lorient, 991 men; Brest, 649; Cherbourg, 211; Rochefort, 432; Toulon, 212, Colonies, 843;

An inspector general and 36 officers employed in the direction, forges and founderies completed the corps.

As can be seen, the colonial portion was by far the weakest. However, the naval artillery has the special mission of casting cannons for war vessels and for the fortifications of ports and coasts.

In 1847 after new experiments and two reorganizations, the strength of the regiment was expanded to 3,275 men while the strength of the 6 companies of workmen was expanded to 908 men. This gave a total of 4,183 men plus 185 officers for the general staff and troops. However, military organizations are not long-lived in the naval department. On June 5, 1855, the corps—general staff and troops—was brought back to an effective strength of 3,917 men.

On January 23, 1856, the armorers of the navy were organized.

On August 22, 1860, the title of *chef de bataillon* (major) still used in the naval artillery was permanently replaced by that of *chef d'escadron* (major) and the companies became batteries as in the land artillery.

On August 14, 1861, there was a more useful reform. Three batteries, 1 company of drivers, and 1 section of rocketeers were added to the regiment, which from that point on included 28 foot batteries. The service, general staff, troops and employees presented an effective strength of 4,706 men. On December 20, 1864, a new modification increased it by 100 men. The service henceforth had 3 generals, 10 colonels, and 9 lieutenant colonels. It would follow the example of the land artillery. Finally, on March 7th, reshaping gave the artillery a general effective strength of 4,711 men, which it seems never to have attained.

The regiment supplied 5 batteries, or rather companies (3rd, 6th, 12th, 13th, and 14th) for the siege of Sebastopol. Its 1st and 2nd companies under Major Frébault, had been attached in 1854 to the small army corps that carried out the siege of Bomarsund. During the Italian campaign, it had two companies embarked on the Adriatic fleet. One of them landed in the Isles of Lossin. For the China and Mexico companies, it detached batteries which it could henceforth hitch up, thanks to its company of drivers.

As has been seen in the history of the land artillery for the campaign of 1870, it had to hitch up 3 batteries under the command of Major Guilhermy to follow the direction of Vassoigne, attached to the 12th Army Corps. In looking through the tables of batteries attached to the 12th Army Corps formed in the provinces, one can see the major role taken by the regiment in that formidable armament. The general staff and the regiments had moreover provided a large contingent to the defense of Paris.

In addition, General of Division Frébault and General of Brigade Pélissier, the defenders of Paris, counted in their ranks 6 colonels, 5 lieutenant colonels, 11 majors, 41 captains, 39 lieutenants, and 21 employees of the naval artillery. They had brought with them a number of batteries. However, many of them were classified in the land artillery batteries where they performed great services.

In Tonkin, the naval artillery had only batteries *bis*. In 1883, under the command of Lieutenant Colonel Révillon, three had already arrived: the 1st *bis*, Captain Issoir (killed on October 14, 1882); the 2nd *bis*, Captain Dupont; the 3rd *bis*, Captain Roussel. In November 1884, the 4th *bis*, Captain Roperts and the 5th *bis*, Captain Péricaud followed them. Finally, in December 1884, the 6th *bis*, Captain Dudraille arrived.

Since its creation, the naval artillery regiment has had for colonels: Falba (1822); Gobert de Neufmoulin (1830); Préaux (1839); de Gérus (1844); Zeni (1848); Favereau (1849); Dupont (1852); Tournal (1855); Olivier (1858); de Guilhermy (1871); Smet (1874); Thory (1875); Godin (1883); and Javouhey (1886). It counts in its ranks 12 colonels, as many lieutenant colonels, 31 majors, 173 captains, and 184 lieutenants. This is a great wealth of officers, especially of superior officers, for a corps whose campaign detachments are ordinarily very restricted. However, one should consider that this skilled corps has only armaments made from pieces of all calibers for the use of the French fleet and its maritime defenses. These are pieces which it would be impossible to have cast in the usual French institutions or by the French land artillery. The naval officers who all display pretentions of being excellent artillerists have never

Naval fusiliers. On expedition (1887).

Vice-Admiral, Lieutenant de Vaisseau, midshipmen, fusiliers, marines, service dress (1887).

Seaman of the Imperial Navy (1870).

been able to take this service away from the artillery—despite the great desire they might have to do so. Thus they remain the source of maritime engineers for the construction of their ships, mechanics for steam, and artillery for their cannons. This high level work of the naval artillery also explains why its general staff consists of a general of division and two generals of brigade.

List of Generals of the Naval Artillery since their creation. *Lieutenant Generals:* Thirion (1808 t0 1821); de Coisy (1840 to 1850). *Generals of Division:* de Preuilly (1858 to 1861); Pélissier (1861 to 1877); Frébault (1861 to 1880); Virgile (1876 to 1886); Dard (1880). *Maréchaux de Camp:* Brèche (1828 to 1832); Barbé (1836 to 1840). *Generals of Brigade:* Durbec (1851 to 1855); Emond d'Esclevin (1855 to 1857); Paine (1867 to 1870); Olivier (1870 to 1873); Regnaud (1873 to 1876); Lacour (1877 to 1883); Thory (1883 to 1886); Godin (1886); Borgnis-Desbordes (1886).

In the naval service, everything is specialized. The cadres of artillery generals are not to be confused ever with those of the infantry. Thus, they must be classified separately.

List of Generals of the Naval Infantry since their creation. *Generals of Division:* De Fitte de Soucy (1853); de Barolet de Puligny (1860); de Vassoigne (1868); Martin des Pallières (1870); Faron (1870); Reboul (1871); Bossant (1881); Brière de l'Isle (1885); Bégin (1887). *Generals of Brigade:* De Fitte de Soucy (1842); Rostoland (1844); de Barolet de Puligny (1855); Fiéron (1856); Brunot (1858); de Vassoigne (1860); Chaumont (1861); Hennique (1863); de Cappe (1865); Reboul (1867); Martin des Pallières (1868); Faron (1868); d'Arbaud (1871); Colomb (1873); Bossant (1876); de Trentinian (1876); Valière (1876); Alleyron (1881); Brière de l'Isle (1881); Coquet (1881); Bouet (1882); Bégin (1882) Bichot (1884); Bourgey (1887); Chanu (1887); Reste (1887); Duchemin (1887).

Let us complete this statistical information with the above list of the colonels of the four naval infantry regiments .

As can be seen, colonels change very often in the naval infantry because the regiment is considered more as a great depot than as an organic unity. The posts most envied by the colonels in the past were the military commands in the colonies. Today, the commands of the *régiments de marche* are preferred. This mutiplicity of various uses that one leaves it to take on explains why ten colonels and twenty-five lieutenant colonels are necessary to adequately ensure the service. The frequent changes which the naval infantry officers are subject to after the rank of major are much to their distaste and make many of them prematurely request their retirement.

1st REGIMENT	2nd REGIMENT	3rd REGIMENT	4th REGIMENT
De Fitte de Soucy (1838) - Despagne (1840) - Varlet (1841) - de Barolet de Puligny (1843) - Mallié (1845) - de la Faye (1847) - Pascal (1849) - Laborel (1852) - Bert (1853) - Chaumont (1855) - Bouvet (1861) - Favron (1864) - Bosssant (1868) - Brière de l'Isle (1870) - Trentinian (1870) - Colomb (1871) - Trève (1873) - de Trentinian (1874) - Azan (1876) - Trève (1877) - Outré (1880) - Bruzard (1883) - Duchemin (1884) - (Bourgey 1886) - Chaumont (1887).	Krausse (1838) - Pascal (1843) - Fiéron (1848) - Law de Clapernou (1849) - Laborel (1850) - Fiéron (1853) - Berthe (1856) - Hennique (1860) - Charvet (1863) - Martin des Pallieres (1864) - Vallière (1867) - Loubère (1869) - Alleyron (1870) - Ruillier (1872) - Bouët (1875) - Ruillier (1877) - Laurent (1879) - Bégin (1882) - Reste (1884) - Dujardin (1885).	Fournier (1838) - L'Éleu de la Ville-aux-Bois (1841) - de Barolet de Puligny (1845) - Brunot (1849) - Fiéron (1856) - de Vassoigne (1856) - Reybaud (1861) - Fabre (1861) - Charvet (1865) - Le Camus (1869) - Brossant (1873) - Alleyron (1875) - Valière (1876) - Outré (1876) - Coquet (1878) - Bourchet (1881) - Billés (1883) - Pons (1886) - Ortus (1887).	Bertin-Duchâteau (1854) - Brunot (1855) - de Cappe (1858) - Reboul (1864) - d'Arbaud (1866) - de Trentinian (1872) - Bonneau (1873) - Coquet (1874) - Loubère (1878) - Bouët (1880) - Reybaud (Paul) (1882) - Ligier (1883) - de Maussion (1886) - Dodds (1887).

The flags of the naval infantry bore the following legends in 1868:

1st Regiment: Mogador; Baltic (Bomarsund); China (Takou, Pei-Ho, Pali-Kao, Peking); Mexico (Puebla); CochinChina (Saigon, Ki-Hoa, Mitho, Winh-Long, Gocong).
2nd Regiment: Tahiti (Fatahua); Baltic (Bomarsund); CochinChina (Saigon, Ki-Hoa, Mitho, Winh-Long, Gocong); Mexico (Puebla).
3rd Regiment: Oceania (Mogador); Baltic (Bomarsund); CochinChina (Saigon, Ki-Hoa, Mitho, Winh-Long, Gocong); Mexico (Puebla).
4th Regiment: Senegal (Grand-Bassam); Alma; Sebastopol; CochinChina (Saigon, Ki-Hoa, Mitho, Winh-Long, Gocong).

These legends, a bit embellished and some of miniscule importance, have been inscribed one by one on the flags by virtue of imperial decrees. The Republic was much more sober. The flags given to the infantry on July 14, 1880 bear no more than four names:

1st Regiment: Bomarsund (1854); Forts of Pei-Ho (1860); Ki-Hoa (1861); Puebla (1863);
2nd Regiment: Fatahua (1842); Bomarsund (1854); Saigon (1859); Puebla (1863);
3rd Regiment: Mogador (1844); Alma (1854); Pali-Kao (1860); Ki-Hoa (1861);
4th Regiment: Podor (1854); Sebastopol (1854-1855); Saigon (1859); Ki-Hoa (1861).

The naval artillery carries on its standard: Lutzen (1813); Vera-Cruz (1838); Sebastopol (1854-1855); Puebla (1863).

Annamite Tirailleurs (1887).

The Tonkin expedition would enrich these lists, since the French artillery and naval infantry did not spare themselves there, as has been seen above.

Today, the naval troops actually constitute a small army. Howver, they have allowed their heart to rot. Formerly, the war department was resigned to supplying them only with some officers of war, a little cavalry in Senegal, and gendarmerie everywhere while the gendarmerie of the ports and arsenals belonged to the navy. This was after the war department had been convinced of its powerlesssness to resupply the colonies with troops in good condition. Today, it is not content to send auxiliaries or even to form an entire foreign expeditionary corps. The war department has victoriously entered into the colonial infantry. Although this is not the place for politics, we are forced to state that the various governments—descendants of our unfortunate military—have not always respected the principles learned through experience in reforming the French army. The naval infantry has become very good because the esprit de corps has imbued it with its invigorating current. Promotion there was rapid because the work was unending. At Saint-Cyr, they were spoken of as were the Zouaves and the chasseurs à pied of the past. When it was no longer a question of going to mount long guards at Pointe-à-Pitre, Saint-Louis, or Cayenne but to fight with all the adversities and the Chinese, everyone wanted to be in it. There was such a fever that the ministry of war was worried about it. As soon as promotion became more rapid in the naval infantry, the land infantry tried even harder to join it. The naval ministers allowed themselves to be infringed upon by the ministry of war. When the army for Tonkin and Annam was organized, the war department subsequently was able to form for itself two regiments of Tonkinese Tirailleurs (the last two) and four battalions of Annamite chasseurs. In addition, they were also able to introduce a number of infantry majors, captains, lieutenants, and second lieutenants with their seniority of rank into the naval infantry. However, the war department could not form the 5th Tonkinese Regiment. This was not because eager officers were lacking but because of the difficult situation facing these officers. On the one hand, they were simply detached from their regiments. On the other, there was also the very poor quality of native recruits which raised almost insoluble difficulties. No one knows what to say about the value of the last four regiments since, until now, the native soldiers have only marched buried in European platoons. These

Naval infantry (Tonkin, 1885).

regiments are commanded by a lieutenant colonel, and the primary superior officer is replaced by a captain. There is no depot. Each battalion counts 4 companies. There is no battalion adjutant to help the major. Meanwhile, the Tonkinese is still less of a good soldier than the Annamite. The 4 battalions of Annam chasseurs each have 4 companies.

On its side, the navy maintains 1 regiment of Annanites and the first three regiments of Tonkinese previously formed along the lines of the model that served the 4th. However, they are commanded by naval infantry officers.

The regiment of Senegalese Tirailleurs are already old and much more serious as troops than the Annamites and the Tonkinese. It is more solidly constituted although it includes only 2 battalions of 4 companies each and, in addition, one company for Gabon. The *cipahis* of India form a half-battalion of two companies.

Thus, in the Far East, the secondary has become the primary. However, the naval infantry officers will for a long time remember the unrealized desire their great leaders have had of passing into active service under the control of the war department. Today the winds seem to have changed a bit. It is rather a question of enlarging the superior cadres of the naval infantry than of merging it with the land army. However, ideas are quickly modified by the course of time. Nonetheless, if the three year service is adopted, it will no longer be possible to maintain soldiers and non-commissioned officers for even two years in the colonies. It will become necessary to have recourse to new methods.

The status of the infantry, which is a result of its work, energy, talent expended, and blood spilled, should rightly remain its exclusive, legitimate patrimony. Nevertheless, in this period of false equality when everyone must have his cake, those who have not suffered as well as those who have experienced total suffering have everything to fear. Not a single measure for organization of the colonial army has taken place because they all rely on false principles. They have provided an opportunity for a formidable assault on this service which for thirty-five years has been associated with

Native officer of the Senegalese Tirailleurs (1887).

everything great that the French army has done. In French defeats, it has given the most praiseworthy examples of perserverance to the Army of Châlons and to those of Paris, the Loire, the North and the East.

We have recounted what in the past became of the regiments of extended service when the ministry of war provided troops to the French colonies and when the service was ultra-pacifist. For sixteen years, it has been more military than the service in the homeland. Naturally, the war department wants to have it back. It would be unfortunate if the department succeeded.

Like the green epaulette of the chasseurs à pied, the yellow epaulette of the naval infantryman is a talisman. It is the golden bough of fairy tales. Let us not break the golden bough.

SUPPLEMENTARY NOTES
JANUARY 15, 1888

During the publication of this important work, major changes have been carried out in the French army while others are underway. In January 1888, with the conclusion of the organic history of *The French Army* since 1789, we cannot completely forget the last three years of French history.

The general staffs have remained the same. The only change is that the generals from now on must choose their *officiers d'ordonnance* from amongst the officers graduating with a certificate from the École de Guerre. The position of aide-de-camp has been eliminated. In the absence of special benefits to give them, the number of officers began to burden the regiments. Thus, it was very important to find them a position. This was their right.

A ministerial decision issued by General Farre had ordered that, in war time as during peace, the officers detached to the various general and special staffs would wear the uniform of the corps from which they came. It seemed necessary to give them a more obvious insignia than the aiguillettes to help identify them on the drill ground and on the battlefield. They were allocated large silk armbands recalling by the arrangement of their colors the pennons of the general officers to whom they were attached.

This invention which renewed old customs was not very well received. There were even very strict views about using it during the test mobilization of the 17th Army Corps. The general staffs insistently requested the old spencer which the "closed general staff corps" wore and which had the advantage of indicating to the troops the presence of representatives and aides from the high command. Moreover, the general staff's armband had the drawback of establishing an unfortunate and anti-military confusion with the armband of the non-combatants authorized by the Geneva Convention. The armband of the general staff officers had already multiplied. It was given to all the special auxiliaries taken into the regiments: stretcher bearers, mule team drivers, convoy drivers, herdsmen, telegraphists, and even bicyclists whom the Geneva Convention did not cover.

A major revolution in the officers' uniform is taking place. The Hungarian dolman which the infantry had used fanatically had also been brought into widespread use in the administration and in the medical military troops through the tolerance of the ministers of war. It had been recognized as being poor in terms of actual use and especially very costly. It has almost been decided that the epaulette will be returned to the infantry officers. They will wear it on a small overcoat whose color is still being hotly debated. Will it be dark blue or grey like the color of the soldier's greatcoat? Therein lies the question.

The French army slides into negligence. It has fallen from the uniform coat into the use of the redingote (tunic). Next, it passed through the short coat (dolman) to arrive at the *pet-en'l'air de chambre* (nightshirt). Happily for him, our collaborator and friend, Édouard Detaille, had finished his enormous task before this innovation became a reality, the result of tolerance. He, the protagonist of all our glories, did not suffer the distress of having to draw the French army in an invalid's outfit.

Five children's schools for the troops have been organized under the name of "military preparatory schools": three for the infantry at Rambouillet, Montreuil-sur-Mer, and Saint-Hippolyte-du-Fort; one for the cavalry at Autun;and one for the artillery and engineers at Billom.

The children of the troops receive a special military education there along with primary teaching. This prepares them to fulfill the functions of non-commissioned officer instructors in the service to which their school belongs. Born of the need to prepare a good recruitment of non-commissioned officers, these institutions are in flagrant contradiction of the principles of a liberal democracy. They should give the children of the soldiers entrusted to them a general education adequate for later being able to compete in the military schools of officer cadets established at Saint-Maixent, Saumur and Fontainebleau. Thus it is more than certain that they will be profondly modified when people are finally convinced that they cannot supply many good non-commissioned officers and perhaps none at all. What makes the French non-commissioned officers excellent is the path to the epaulette—the great, single hope of the man who has a taste for arms—which was open to all who were willing. The reason we have almost no non-commissioned officers is that the path is obstructed by various impediments and is often impassable.

Various alerts have been produced by different causes along the French border on the East. It seemed necessary and even indispensible to guarantee this border against quick incursions unexpectedly following unanticipated and improbable diplomatic acts. Meanwhile, things being what they are, in fact everything must be feared. All sorts of threats have been addressed to the French in words, therefore, it is necessary to put sensible precautions between the threats made and the facts feared. These precautions consist of what it has been agreed to call The Blanket. The Germans who maintain a true advance guard army almost completely on a war footing, along the Rhine, know well and even better than the French what "The Blanket" is. Compared to ours, despite the increases which the latter should have received following recent events, theirs is still superior. Be that as it may, two laws from July 25, 1887 allow the French to hope that its line of "concentration" will neither be invaded nor driven from the field before the French mobilization is completely finished. They also stipulate that the different French army corps be transported to the strategic points to which they are assigned.

At the end of the 19th century, the century of industrial and philosophical conquests, the French are reduced to seeing all the nations of Europe preoccupied above all in protecting their borders against brutal agression. Meanwhile, since it is necessary to harmonize our military worries with our national expenses which today are much more than four million, the French infantry and cavalry has been remodeled with extreme care and some slowness.

The 144 French infantry regiments of the interior and its 30 battalions of chasseurs à pied have seen their depot eliminated (two companies per regiment, one company for the battalions of chasseurs). In addition, the fourth battalions of the regiments which, in the event of war, must serve to form new army corps (either as fortress battalions or as support in the second line corps or by groupings of three) have been reduced to a staff of one major, four captains, and four lieutenants without non-commissioned officers or soldiers.

On the other hand, eighteen new regiments have been created which are commanded by a colonel or a lieutenant colonel. They have a lieutenant for *officier d'ordonnance*. These regiments were formed in the following manner by means of three old fourth battalions as the table below indicates. They are neither music sections nor sappers and bear the name of regional regiments.

These regiments already find themselves in part assembled in place. Meanwhile, in order not to impede the grand maneuvers of 1887, their organization was only completed on October 1st.

The same day, the depot companies of the thirty battalions of chasseurs à pied were dissolved and the constitution of the supplementary cadre in the fifty-four old regiments which had supplied one battalion to the new regiments proceeded. This reformation had been preceded by long studies. From the first measure which went back to 1881 came that bizarre title of regional regiments which Numbers 145 to 162 bore. This was a title that had no relationship to their nature or their goal. Their recruitment will be in fact the same as that of the other corps and they will be neither more nor less attached than those in the eighteen regions of the interior. Finally, there is not one in each region. It is true that they are placed outside the formation into divisions of the army corps.

The advantage that may be drawn from this new distribution of infantry (2,064 companies instead of 2,742) is an increase of

NUMBERS of the new REGIMENTS	GARRISONS WHERE IT IS ASSIGNED	NUMBERS of the OLD REGIMENTS that formed the battalions		
145th	MAUBEUGE & North garrisons	1st	84th	45th
146th	TOUL	51st	72nd	67th
147th	MONTMÉDY	24th	43rd	132nd
148th	VERDUN	87th	84th	82nd
149th	ÉPINAL	4th	113th	138th
150th	VERDUN	66th	85th	63rd
151st	BELFORT	131st	144th	90th
152nd	ÉPINAL	56th	134th	27th
153rd	PARIS	115th	2nd	19th
154th	COMMERCY	41st	70th	47th
155th	LAROUVILLE	64th	65th	118th
156th	TOUL	101st	125th	135th
157th	LYON	121st	105th	78th
158th	BRIANÇON	140th	96th	22nd
159th	NICE	111th	55th	40th
160th	PERPIGNAN	17th	12th	143rd
161st	LYON and Alps garrisons	133rd	139th	80th
162nd	PARIS	25th	62nd	5th

effective strength in the company on a peacetime footing. This is a major advantage for training although it has been notably weakened in practice by the method of administering discharges to the men of the ranks. There is also the free use of eighteen regiments placed outside the army corps which at first allowed reinforcing "The Blanket." They could also help Algeria in a moment of distress and, ultimately, be used for a foreign expedition. All the same, there is no longer, between the first line army and the second, a reserve of formed units from which could be drawn almost instantly an excellent portion.

Almost immediately, the hole caused by the total absence of depots was perceived.

The complete success of the test mobilization of the 17th Army Corps vis-a-vis the callup of the reservists and their merger with the men of the active service was due to the administrative power of the depot. Unfortunataly the law of the eighteen regiments had already been voted. Set en route on August 31st and arrived at their corps on the night of August 31st to September 1st, the reservists were incorporated into the men of the active service with incredible ease. The infantry regiments left their barracks on the 3rd at 10 in the morning, ready to climb onto the train. In four days, the artillery provided them the regulation number of batteries and of munitions columns. Lacking depots, would the infantry regiments have done as well? This is a good question. What is certain is that they could not have done better. And then, those 144 superior officers, those 556 captains, and those 556 lieutenants of the unoccupied staff are a very great luxury in a budget where they must be included even despite the many urgent necessities of the soldier's life. It is obvious that the accessories of the French military organization do not require the work of these 1,296 infantry officers. We would have to lose all hope in the new institutions. Thus, a new minister has requested, through a legal measure, to be authorized to make use of these officers according to the needs of the service. They would reinforce the second line corps and form one depot cadre per regiment.

The battalions of chasseurs à pied, reduced to four companies, immediately appeared very thin. Revolution operates through speed in tactical systems. The accuracy and shooting distance of firearms has naturally transformed the light troops of the past into reserve troops. In each of the French army corps, a battalion of chasseurs remains at the disposal of the commander in chief and the twelve other battalions of the service. An artillery battery and a detachment of engineers have been added to each and are charged with defending the Alpine passes, which are divided into twelve sectors.

At first, the ministry thought of expanding the number of companies to six in the twelve Alpine battlions. These would have been commanded by lieutenant colonels. However, a scheme intervened which will simply give six companies to all the battalions. They will be attached either like a reserve outside the division to an army corps or they will be used in defending the Alps.

The French infantry—Algerian troops, naval and colonial aside—thus include today 162 regiments. If one allows that the chasseurs à pied and the Army of Africa form a total equal to that of the Royal Guard and the Swiss Guard under the Restoration, one will note that the sixty infantry line regiments and the twenty light infantry regiments of 1820 would have had close to the same number of captains, lieutenants, and second lieutenants as the 162 regiments of today if they had been completed—as the fundamental ordinance decreed—at three battlions of eight companies. Only the colonels, lieutenant colonels, administrative field officers and majors have doubled.

With the repeating Lebel rifle which eats up munitions, and with a number of soldiers which exceeds 250 per company, is it very logical to have left alone the number of officers of the active service who live with the soldiers and guide them under fire? Meanwhile, the number of superior officers hovering over its leadership and directing it from a distance was doubled, and this in a time of companies of one hundred men.

The Lebel rifle is judged the best of all the American, European, French or foreign rifles. Yet many experienced officers fear that its use will be difficult to control with young service troops who are consequently a little lacking in cold-bloodness and reason. At the same time, it is generally believed that the tension of its trajectory will transform patient troops shooting little or not at all into walls of canister if they know how to wait and take advantage of a psychological moment. All the French troops will be equipped with them before the beginning of winter 1888-1889.

In completing the history of the cavalry, we will express the fear of not having seen the sixth independent division given to this service, decreed in principle by the French organization of 1875. This fear is henceforth evaporated. At the same time that they voted on the transformation of the infantry without any public discussion, the Chambers gave the ministry of war eleven new regiments of cavalry. With the 4th Regiments of Spahis recently created, this expands the number of French cavalry regiments to eighty-nine (79 for the interior: 12 cuirassiers, 30 dragoons, 21 chasseurs, and 16 hussars - 10 for Africa: 6 Chasseurs d'Afrique and 4 Spahis).

The new regiments (27th, 28th, 29th, and 30th Dragoons, 21st Chasseurs, 13th, 14th, 15th, and 16th Hussars, 5th and 6th Chasseurs d'Afrique) only have three superior officers: a colonel or lieutenant colonel and two majors of whom one fills the functions of major. Their squadrons have no more than five officers: the commanding captain, a first lieutenant, and three assisting lieutenants or second lieutenants. This is the application of the new principles of organization dreamed of by the cavalry.

It was decided that the new regiments, whose officers' staffs should be drawn from the old regiments without being replaced, would be constituted as quickly as budgetary resources permitted.

The organization of the 5th and 6th Chasseurs d'Afrique and of the 27th and 28th Dragoons was proceeded with immediately. These two latter were provisionally set at four squadrons. The two first regiments received the 6th squadrons of the four old regiments of Chasseurs d'Afrique, eliminated by the law of July 25, 1887. For the remainder, the composition of the four first regiments formed by virtue of this law are given below.

27th Dragoons at Châlons: 4th squadron from the 3rd Dragoons - 3rd squadron from the 21st - 3rd squadron from the 24th - 1st squadron from the 25th;

28th Dragoons at Châlons: 2nd squadron from the 10th dragoons - 3rd squadron from the 15th - 1st squadron from the 17th - 2nd squadron from the 19th;

5th Chasseurs d'Afrique at Algiers: 6th squadron from the 1st Chasseurs d'Afrique - 6th squadron from the 3rd Chasseurs d'Afrique - 3rd, 4th, and 5th squadrons from the 2nd Hussars; 6th Chasseurs d'Afrique at Mascara: 6th squadron from the 3rd Chasseurs d'Afrique - 6th squadron from the 4th Chasseurs d'Afrique - 3rd, 4th, and 5th squadrons from the 4th Hussars.

The second and fourth Hussars were soon reorganized into four squadrons in the following manner, by means of drawing from other regiments of light cavalry:

2nd Hussars at Châlons-sur-Marne; depot at the camp of Châlons - 1st and 2nd squadrons of the old regiment - 3rd squadron of the 11th Hussars - 1st squadron of the 12th Hussars;

4th Hussars at Sampigny: depot at Vitry-le-Français - 1st and 2nd squadrons of the old regiment - 3rd squadron of the 9th Chasseurs - 1st squadron of the 1st Hussars.

It is hoped that the eight regiments of dragoons which have come together to form the 27th and 28th Dragoons will be reorganized at five squadrons as of March 1, 1888; that the 21st Chasseurs will be formed before July 1st; and that by autumn of the same year, it will be possible to proceed with the formation of the 29th Dragoons.

The numbering of the new cavalry regiments has raised some criticism. It is known that a regiment bears on its flag or its standard the names embroidered in gold letters of four victories where its number was valiantly employed. To obtain this enormous quantity of glorious memories, it was necessary to add to the personal baggage of the French regiments, all of which were organized since 1815. The old pasts of the regiments of the Republic and of the Empire were used to this end. It is by virtue of this fiction that the number does not die and is reborn at the ministry's wish. In this manner, despite many reorganizations and groupings, the legend and the historical records of the regiments have been firmly established. Thus the new regiments usually find a great heritage. It is for this reason that the 27th Dragoons already bear on their flag the names of Austerlitz, Friedland, and Albuera, and the 28th those of Wagram and Moscow.

It is therefore somewhat astonishing that the numbers 15 and 16 of the hussars has been given to two of the new light cavalry regiments when there have never been more than fourteen regiments of hussars in the French army. Also, only one 21st Chasseurs was created and under the First Empire thirty and even thirty-one regiments of this sevice and twenty-four under the Restoration existed. Surely it would have been preferable to restore the numbers 22 and 23 to the chasseurs who had gloriously worn them than to break new ground with the numbers 15 and 16 in the hussars.

Finally, the break-up of twelve regiments of dragoons and light cavlary has been criticized. A squadron has been raised which must reconstitute it. Also criticized is the almost complete renewal of the 1st and the 4th hussars. Thus the existence of fourteen regiments has been disturbed to form four new ones. In reality it is only three since one of the two Chasseurs d'Afrique was barely created by the elimination of the four sixth regiments of the old. However, the similarity of uniforms, the short-term service, promotion in all services, and the custom used for twenty years of breaking the old regiments into pieces to create new ones has made the actual organizers forget that esprit de corps could and should still be awakened by the number. Isn't regional recruitment requested with the intention of reviving the old esprit de corps? Henceforth, to face the enemy, the reservist joins the flag under which he received his military training, where he is known to its leaders and whose officers he knows.

The new division of independent cavalry has taken Number 3 which was vacant; it occupies the following locations:

Divisional Headquarters: Châlons-sur-Marne

6th Brigade of Cuirassiers. Headquarters at Niort: 11th Regiment at Niort, 12th Regiment at Angers;

5th Brigade of Dragoons. Headquarters: 27th and 28th Regiments at the camp of Châlons;

2nd Brigade of Hussars. Headquarters at Châlons-sur-Marne: 2nd Regiment at Châlons-sur-Marne. 4th Regiment at Sampigny. Other important measures will completely change the basic structure of the special services, give the bridges to the engineers, mix the pontoniers with the sappers, and create pioneers alongside the cannoneers. This organization and many others did not seem to us sufficiently simple for us to dare anticipate already that they will be voted for without contest.

We feel that this book would not be totally complete if we did not say a word about the administrations of the railroad and of the remarkable role which they have played in the test mobilization of the 17th Corps.

The important, decisive part to be played by the railroads in a general mobilization is known. It is also known that the successful concentration of the French armies depends absolutely on them. The line of concentration has been judiciously chosen and is wisely protected. Still, the railroads can and should carry and unload within a given time materiel, horses and the personnel of the French army corps onto the platforms at border points.

When it was necessary to concentrate the entire 17th Corps between Carcassone and Castelnaudary, the companies of Midi and of Orléans found themselves in the presence of special advantages and disadvantages which should be taken into consideration.

The advantages were to have only to occupy their region and to be able to concentrate their materiel over a short distance.

The disadvantages were more serious. Traffic in travelers and merchandise which would be interrupted in the event of war had to be continued and the army corps unloaded after having embarked it. The embarkation was anticipated throughout France but unloading was anticipated and prepared for only at border points. It became necessary that a major portion of the engines be

concentrated on part of the Midi line between Castelnaudary and Carcassonne. On the various lines, they had to serve the embarkations and the unloadings of materiel on a clear track either in the stations or on the sidings when warranted. These engines are practical machines fitted with iron ramps that are firmly leaned against the merchandise wagons and the trucks at their floor levels. With a slope of 25 degrees, these allow the soldiers of various services to slide the cannons and wagons to the ground or to lead horses by hand.

These manuevers have been executed with remarkable spirit and praiseworthy precision by civilian workmen carrying and placing the ramps. It has succeeded marvelously everywhere. It would be impossible to demand more willingness and speed even if the enemy was thought to be at our doors. With pleasure and confidence, the army saw the high level personnel of the railroads put themselves and their auxiliaries at the disposal of its chiefs and work with them toward the execution of the orders given.

Although no foreign officers have been invited to this private testing of French military competence, it was felt everywhere that Europe's attention was fixed on Toulouse and its surroundings. Never before have the hotels and the restaurants of Midi had so many foreign accents. The French government seems to have worried itself about it a little more than was necessary.

Ultimately, the ministry of war and that of foreign affairs could only be delighted to show France's enemies as well as its friends regiments passing from a peace time footing to a war footing in less than three days. The railroads were also as well prepared to embark them, transport them, and especially to unload them everywhere without encumbrances, without embarrassment, and as if it were an everyday affair.

If one wants to calculate the work of the French railroads in the event of general mobilization of the army, he must first think that they will have to transport the reservists from their homes to their regiments. Then the army corps will be mobilized and they will have to carry them to the line of concentration.

The 17th Corps had an effective of 1,007 officers, 35,800 men of the ranks, 10,876 horses and mules, 108 cannon, 1844 wagons, and 21 boats and pontonier skiffs on pallets which required 109 trains.

In addition to the eighteen and even the twenty army corps, a general concentration must gather other units. Thus, in deducting the border corps, at the minimum 2,200 trains are required to perform the movement. In this way, everything is taken care of. The materiel is adequate and even beyond adequate. It is catalogued, counted, numbered, and classified. There are no other instructions to give to put it to work than this: "Upon receipt of the order for mobilization, apply such or such a graphic."

Should it be concluded that France is ready for war?

No. A nation is never ready the day before. It must be prepared constantly and without relaxation to await the morrow with confidence and resolution. If she is victorious, no one will criticize her mistakes; she will have none and she will have never had any.

If she does not win victory, she will have made every mistake. He head will be too old, her general staff will not know its geography, her intendance will be ignorant of its profession, her most valiant soldiers will be called "capitulators." Her worst soldiers will say that they were distributed ammunition that could only make noise and artillery cartridges full of ashes. The army will be betrayed and the nation will be in despair that it has not been replaced by a national guard under the orders of an intelligent non-commissioned officer. Then history will be made as merciless as legend. Thus it is necessary that we become again a victorious people so as to take up again our good, old-fashioned Gallic sense and our proverbial French generosity.

It is in fact a Gaul who said: *"Voe victis!"* It is true that he was a conqueror and that he spoke of conquered Romans. Today, we have applied these words to ourselves too often. We must have them engraved on the metal casings of the Lebel rifle. In putting them on his rifle, each soldier, each Frenchman would think of the outcome that awaits him if he does not shoot his enemy first.

GLOSSARY

aiguillette - braided shoulder cord

bataillon de marche - march, or provisional battalion
busby - fur hat with attached cloth bag (flamme)

carabiniers - light infantry grenadiers; heavy cavalry
chapska - Polish lancer helmet
chasseurs à cheval - light cavalry
chasseurs à pied - light infantry
chevau-léger - light cavalry
chevau-léger lanciers - light cavalry lancers
corps francs - volunteer corps
corps mobiles - field service militia
cuirassiers - armored heavy cavalry

demi-brigade - 1) during Revolutionary and Napoleonic periods, merger of old army and volunteer National Guard, so named to avoid royalist taint of "regiment"; 2) later, any composite infantry unit, often with one regular and two volunteer battalions
dolman - braided hussars jacket
dragoons - mounted infantry

flanquers - light infantry
Francs-tireurs - partisans of 1870-71
fusiliers - common infantrymen

garde du corps - Life Guardsmen or bodyguard
garde mobile - militia; universal reserve force of 1870
garde nationale - volunteer National Guard
garde nationale mobilise - national militia
garde nationale mobilisée - national militia mobilized in the provinces
garde nationale sedentaire - national guard for local defense
gardes pompiers - firemen guards
grand maneuvers - annual maneuvers conducted each autumn
grenadiers - elite infantry

Hulans - Uhlans, lancers
hussars - light cavalry

Imperial Guard - the elite of Napoleon's army
Invalides - military hospital in Paris

Joyeux - battalion of light infantry in North Africa, formerly called Zephirs

kurtka - lancers jacket

légère - light troops
levée en masse - mass conscription of 1793
line - regular army troops
lunette - outer fortification

mitraille - canister, grapeshot, shrapnel
mitrailleuse - early breech-loading machinegun

piquier - pikesman (Revolutionary period)
pontoniers - pontoon bridging units

régiment de marche - provisional regiment

sapper - engineer; trench digger
Spahis - Algerian cavalrymen
spencer - short jacket

tirailleurs - skirmishers, sharpshooters
trefoil - clover shaped epaulette
Turcos - native Algerian tirailleurs

Uhlan - lancer

voltigeur - light infantry, skirmishers

Zephirs - battalion of light infantry in North Africa
Zouaves - Algerian and French infantry unit first formed in 1830 in North Africa

TRANSLATIONS OF RANKS

adjoint - assistant or adjutant
adjutant major - battalion adjutant

brigadier - corporal or brigade commander

caporal - corporal
chef de bataillon - major
chef de brigade - colonel
chef d'escadron - cavalry major
chef d'état major - chief of staff
chirurgien-major - surgeon-major
commissaire ordonnateur - chief commissary

éclaireur - scout

fourrier - quartermaster corporal

intendant - administrative officer; commissary or supply officer

lieutenant general - general of division

major general - chief of staff; adjutant general
maréchal de camp - general of brigade
maréchal des logis - cavalry sergeant
maréchal des logis chef - cavalry sergeant-major
maréchal ferrant - farrier

officier d'ordonnance - staff officer; orderly; aide-de-camp
officier d'habillement - officer in charge of uniforms
officier payeur - paymaster
ordonnateur - bursar

porte-étendard - color bearer
prévôt - provost

sous-lieutenant - second lieutenant
sous-officier - non-commissioned officer

trésorier - officer of accounts and records; treasurer; paymaster
trompette - trumpeter

vaguemestre general - baggagemaster general